Promoting Income Security as a Right: Europe and North America

Edited by
GUY STANDING

Anthem Press

Anthem Press
An imprint of Wimbledon Publishing Company
75-76 Blackfriars Road, London SE1 8HA
or
PO Box 9779, London SW19 7QA
www.anthempress.com

First edition published by Anthem Press 2004
Revised edition published by Anthem Press 2005

British Library Cataloguing in Publication Data
A catalogue record for this book is available from the British Library.

Library of Congress Cataloging in Publication Data
A catalog record for this book has been requested.

1 3 5 7 9 10 8 6 4 2

ISBN 1 84331 174 7 (pbk)

Typeset by Footprint Labs Ltd, London
www.footprintlabs.com

Printed in India

CONTENTS

Section 4. Building Towards Basic Income

National and Regional Initiatives

LIST OF FIGURES

LIST OF TABLES

INTRODUCTION

Guy Standing[1]

In the view of T.H. Marshall, the eighteenth century was the century of civil rights, the nineteenth was the century of political rights, and the twentieth was the century of social rights. If this is so, there is a reasonable prospect that the twenty-first century will be dominated by advances in *economic rights*.

In the era of globalization and flexible labour relations, inequalities and insecurities can be expected to remain pervasive, which will mean that new form of redistribution and social protection will be required to rectify what many see as intolerable strains. And yet in the early years of the century, mainstream policymakers seemed resolutely determined to give as little attention to redistribution as possible. Both 'Third Wayists' and 'Compassionate Conservatives' have placed most of their emphasis on the 'duties', 'obligations' and 'responsibilities' of individuals. They have gone further, much further, in telling people how they should behave, and in seeking to use taxes and benefits to encourage behaviour of which they approve, reward those who behave in the approved way and punishing those who do not. The resultant *fiscalization* of social policy is one of the great trends of the era. It is bringing with it shades of social engineering.

In short, in the first decade of the twenty-first century, the rhetoric of rights has run ahead of the reality, often cloaking less laudable objectives. This period will surely give way to a more promising discourse about what we call *real freedom*. The orthodox way of thinking may still be dominated by the axiom 'no rights without responsibilities'. But this is a conservative way of looking at 'freedom', because it sits uncomfortably with the idea of freedom as allowing and enabling people to make choices *themselves*. Who determines what is and what is not 'responsible' behaviour? Social policy that is *moralistic* is invariably in danger of becoming coercive and freedom-damaging, rather than freedom-enhancing.

This book is about an idea that has a long and distinguished pedigree, the idea of a right to a basic income, seen by some as a right of citizenship or as a 'republican right'. It may seem a radical proposal, but in modern societies the conditions for moving in this direction are falling into place. It means having a modest income guaranteed, as a right without conditions, just as a citizen of a good society should have the right to clean water, fresh air and a decent education. Responsibilities flow from rights; rights are inalienable. And yet the early years of the new century have seen the supremacy of 'think tanks' and politicians who have preached a very paternalistic alternative vision. Having an unconditional right is opposed by 'leftist' paternalists because they fear freedom from state control; they like the 'nanny state'. It is opposed by 'rightist' libertarians because they do not like the idea of equality of outcomes. Fortunately, there are others who might come from across the political spectrum who appreciate that paternalism blends into coercion, and that both are inefficient and inequitable.

The arguments for and against the right to basic income security are considered in this book and elsewhere. In the 1980s, some of us who favoured moving social protection in that direction – strengthening universalism and social solidarity – predicted that the 1990s would be a decade in which opposite trends would predominate, resulting in increased selectivity (or 'targeting') combined with variants of 'workfare'. The past decade has indeed been one of increased state paternalism in social policy, often shielded by slogans such as 'social integration' and 'ending welfare as we know it'. It has been the period of the erosion of industrial citizenship rights; some of this might have been justified, in that labour-based entitlements had become rigid and an obstacle to the advancement of genuine rights. But the immediate effect was a terrible increase in social and economic insecurity. The next decade should be a more promising one, in which a critique of those trends should restore the claims of *universalism* and *social solidarity*. Most of the authors represented in this book hope so.

A basic income for all, as a right of citizenship, may seem fanciful. Opposition from even those who profess they wish to do away with poverty can take the form of a torrent of abuse. It is in that context that one should reflect on two pieces of wisdom expressed by two great social scientists of the twentieth century. Richard Titmuss, probably the earliest analyst of the welfare state, pointed out that state benefits that are *only* for the poor are invariably poor benefits. He understood that if social protection did not promote universalism and social solidarity, it would wither. The system of social protection that has emerged in the past two decades would have upset him.

Second, Albert Hirschman has reminded us that every great progressive idea is opposed initially on three grounds – through the claim of *futility* (it cannot be done), the claim of *jeopardy* (if done, it would endanger other goals) and the claim of *perversity* (if done, the unintended consequences would undermine the benefits). Once introduced, many reforms previously opposed on those grounds have soon been seen as normal and civilized. Many of the contributors to this book believe this situation will apply to the proposal for basic income security, which should become one pillar of a decent twenty-first century society.

The Ninth BIEN Congress

In 1986, a group of economists and other social scientists from various European countries founded BIEN – the Basic Income European Network – to extend debate and research on a basic income. It drew on a long tradition. At the time it was a small group. But among those who have given their support are Nobel Prize-winning economists such as James Meade, Jan Tinbergen, Robert Solow, James Tobin and Milton Friedman, all of whom saw that moving in the direction of a basic income would create the basis for a good society as they saw it.

Many of those in BIEN have had reservations about aspects of the idea, such as whether there should be a 'full' basic income (one on which a person could live comfortably) or a 'partial' basic income (a low-level amount, perhaps topped up by other types of transfer), whether it should be introduced gradually or as a 'big bang' reform, and whether it should take the form simply of a monthly grant or a one-off capital grant. Over the years, most of the issues have been discussed and thinking has crystallized. It could be afforded; the necessary conditions for its introduction are now established; there is no reason to presume that it would have a big negative effect on work; there is ample reason to believe it would help break down gender inequalities The chapters that follow are based on papers presented at BIEN's Ninth Congress, held in the International Labour Organization in late 2002. It followed similar Congresses, held in Louvain-la-Neuve, Antwerp, Florence, London, Paris, Amsterdam, Vienna and Berlin. The Geneva Congress brought together nearly 300 participants from 30 countries, and was organized by a group consisting of the BIEN Executive Committee and a Geneva-based committee.[2] On the inaugural day of the Congress, to promote a basic income in Switzerland, a BIEN-Suisse network was formally established, with Professor Andràs November as its President.

The themes set for this particular Congress were as follows:

i. Income security as a right. Should a universal income be included among economic rights? Is that desirable and feasible? Should income security be provided through constitutional or other guarantees or by 'targeting'?

ii. Assessing selectivity. Across the world, social security has shifted from universalism towards complex forms of selectivity, with increased reliance on means-testing, behaviour-testing and other forms of conditionality. Are such policies equitable and efficient? Do they penalize some vulnerable groups in society? What, if any, forms of selectivity in social transfers are desirable?

iii. Legitimizing basic income politically. How could the idea of a guaranteed basic income become appealing to a broad cross-section of the public in a context of more stratified societies in which notions of social solidarity are under strain if not dismissed?

iv. Citizenship credit cards. As countries move towards the integration of tax and benefit systems, and as information technology advances to make this more affordable and sensible, we are moving into an era in which electronic means of income transfer are likely to become the norm. The questions this trend prompt include: Are such transfer cards feasible? Are they desirable? What dangers do they possess? What form of card offers the best prospect of facilitating income security?

v. Income security as a development right. Most of the debate has focused on affluent industrialized societies, but increasingly there are moves to promote a trend towards basic income security as a transparent, affordable means of social protection in developing countries. The Congress wished to take stock of experiments and moves in various parts of the world.

Numerous papers were presented at the Congress and its parallel sessions on these various themes. It is as well to stress that a Congress, as we see it, is not and should not be the same as a standard technical conference. A Congress is a forum in which to exchange ideas, to open up avenues of thought, and steer thinking on some aspects in new directions. This is why some of the papers were sketchy, almost *pensées*. We have included some of those in this book, risking the wrath of some of those excluded from it.

The Congress began with a session that set out to give both a development context and a historical context. Being held in Geneva, it seemed appropriate to try to draw inspiration from the two great sages associated with the city, Calvin and Rousseau. This was harder in the case of Calvin, although he did see the grace of salvation as being given gratuitously by God to those he freely chooses; it could not be earned through one's deeds (Dommen, 2001). As for Rousseau, he could be seen as providing a more formative spirit.

Geneva, Rousseau and Basic Income

Jean-Jacques Rousseau was born and raised in Geneva in the early eighteenth century, and the city shaped his ideas of republicanism. He lived in the artisanal district of St. Gervais, was the son of an artisan watchmaker and became an artisanal music copier late in his life. The artisan is the decent worker, the person with a sense of occupational security, a niche in which to refine and apply skills, gaining status and respect as he or she does so – a model citizen.

Although I have never seen him described as such, Rousseau was in a sense an artisan's philosopher, a thinker who wanted to see a society of artisans living in small city states, similar to the ancient Greeks' notion of the Good Society, in which the general will could prevail. Anyone who has read his introduction to his 'essay' on the origins of inequality, in which he extols the virtues of the men and women of Geneva, will have a sense of what he saw as the Good Society.

Rousseau is most famous for his influence over the French Revolution, and for refining the principles of the general will and the social contract, drawing on the ancient Greeks. As G.D.H. Cole fully recognized – and Cole is important for our tradition of thinking – Rousseau presented the social contract as an assertion of democratic rights. What is most relevant for the following paper is that he gave equal emphasis to liberty and equality:

> If we ask in what precisely consists the greatest good of all, which should be the end of every system of legislation, we shall find it reduce itself to two main objects, liberty and equality – liberty, because all particular dependence means so much force taken from the body of the State, and equality, because liberty cannot exist without it (Rousseau, 1913, Book II, Ch. XI, p. 42).

He went on to define equality as moderated inequality, such that in his Good Society

> In respect of riches, no citizen shall ever be wealthy enough to buy another, and none poor enough to be forced to sell himself.

In a footnote to this statement, Rousseau made a telling aside:

> If the object is to give the State consistency, bring the two extremes as near to each other as possible; allow neither rich men nor beggars. These two estates, which are naturally inseparable, are equally fatal to the common good; from the one comes the friends of tyranny, and from the other tyrants. It is always between them that public liberty is put up to auction; the one buys, and the other sells.

Although he himself did not formulate any scheme for a basic income or a citizenship income, it is not too fanciful to suggest that Rousseau's view on the inseparability of equality and liberty played a strong role in inducing others to do so. We know he influenced Tom Paine, who advocated a form of basic income and who had his own vision of a society of artisan-citizens. And as a corollary of the idea of a general will based on individual liberty, one can claim that a social contract requires all citizens to have basic security in which to make rational decisions. Thus he argued:

> the fundamental compact substitutes, for such physical inequality as nature may have set up between men, an equality that is moral and legitimate, and that men, who may be unequal in strength or intelligence, become every one equal by convention and legal right (*Ibid.*, Book I, Ch. IX, p. 19).

For Rousseau, liberty meant both independence and security. To use the famous distinction made by Isaiah Berlin, he understood that real freedom must be based on both negative and positive liberty – an absence of oppressive controls and an existence of decent opportunities; the essence of security.

Possibly the most intriguing aspect of Rousseau's thinking for our concerns is what Stuart White (2000) has described as the idea of a republican property right, a right to private property as a claim-right of citizenship. This links his notion of equality with his two-sided notion of liberty. A *claim-right* can be said to be what each individual can hold against the community, and in this respect is a decent minimum of property (income and wealth) that, in the circumstances of time and place, is necessary to maintain economic independence. Indeed, for Rousseau the right to property is limited by the need for a universal right to subsistence – in effect, property must serve liberty. It is this sense of *claim-right* that motivated Paine and the many others who have advocated capital grants and basic income.

There is another aspect of Rousseau that is indirectly relevant. Undoubtedly, Rousseau would have been an *anti-globalizer*. His ideal was the city-state, a community small enough for meaningful democracy. While it must be acknowledged that, in principle, Rousseau was against representative democracy, he was pragmatic enough to admit 'if there are partial societies [within the State], it is best to have as many as possible and to prevent them from being unequal' (*Ibid.*, Book II, p. 23). In this, we think he had a powerful influence on Cole and those with him, who lost out through association without to the 'State socialism' of the twentieth century, but whose ideas seem so relevant to a vision of decent work and security in the twenty-first century. In modern parlance, Rousseau favoured deliberative democracy; every 'citizen' must have adequate assets.

In sum, Rousseau could be seen to belong to a line of thinking in which equality and liberty were the twin pillars of a Good Society. While two and a half centuries later, we may have our differences from him, we can still draw considerable inspiration from his legacy.

If we were able to make connections with the past, we were also pleased that in his welcoming speech, the Canton of Geneva's Minister of Social Affairs and Health, Pierre-Francois Unger, told the Congress that he was going to abolish one impediment to income security, the so-called 'assistance debt'. This has been a 'super-tax' on the usually low incomes received by former welfare recipients, through which they were supposed to repay the benefits they had received. Rousseau would have been pleased at that modest reform.

Besides looking backwards for inspiration, the opening session of the Congress also looked forward. Three speakers set the tone in this sense. First, the Congress was privileged to have an address by the Prime Minister of Mozambique, Pascoal Mocumbi, who spoke fervently of wanting his country to experiment with minimum income schemes of the type being operated in Brazil and other parts of Latin America. The ensuing debates on the appropriateness of moves towards a basic income in developing countries will be reproduced in a companion book to this one (Khan and Standing, forthcoming).

Second, the Director-General of the ILO, Juan Somavia, made a passionate appeal to imagine what could be done if the will were there. He asked what would be required to provide every person in the developing world with $1 a day. It could be done. He concluded, 'Yes, the moment may be near when your ideas will become common sense.'

Third, Sir Tony Atkinson suggested that in western Europe a basic income was likely to emerge through the back door, possibly unheralded, perhaps under another name. Others in the Congress were to follow in this spirit, and their papers are included in this book or in the companion books. The key point is that the *conditions* for a straightforward, transparent route to economic security are indeed established.

The Congress had both invited papers, some of which are included here, and submitted papers, some of which are also included here. In addition, a set of papers assessing existing minimum income schemes in European countries were commissioned and presented, and are reproduced in a separate book.

A set of studies of the basic income grant proposal for South Africa has also been published separately (Standing and Samson, 2003).

The Congress was the first of BIEN's Congresses to be organized in the new century. Around that time, all attempts at trying to peer forward were affected by the international climate. The tone of international debate was ugly, with a background of violence being met with violence. Retribution seemed to be triumphing over redistribution and justice. Human rights, freedom and democracy were words that seemed to have become toys to be tossed around. Poverty, economic insecurity and chronic inequality have always bred intolerance. But throughout history, albeit too late for some, in the end wiser heads have somehow prevailed. When statesmen reflect on the need for real freedom for all, in the coming years, the *claim-right* to income security will be there or thereabouts.

Notes

1   Director, Socio-Economic Security Programme, International Labour Office, Geneva, Switzerland.
2   The members were Bridget Dommen, Édouard Dommen, Eric Etienne, Jeanne Hrdina, Mark Hunyadi, Azfar Khan, Lena Lavinas, Tracy Murphy, Andràs November, Robert Pattaroni and Guy Standing (chair). Financial support was kindly provided by the City of Geneva and the Rockefeller Foundation.

References

Dommen, E. 2001. 'Si tout est donné, pourquoi travailler? La gratuité de la grâce, l'allocation universelle et l'éthique de travail, Textes de Jean Calvin', paper presented at 9th BIEN Congress, Geneva and reproduced in A. November and G. Standing (eds.) *Un revenu de base pour chacune* (2003).

Khan, A. and Standing, G. (eds.) *Income Security as a Development Right* (forthcoming).

Rousseau, Jean-Jacques. 1913 (1762). *The Social Contract Discourses*, Book II (London, Everyman).

Standing, G. and Samson, M. (eds). 2003. *A Basic Income Grant for South Africa* (Cape Town, University of Cape Town Press).

White. S. 2000. 'Rediscovering republican political economy', in *Imprints*, Vol. 4, No. 5, pp. 213–235.

1

ABOUT TIME: BASIC INCOME SECURITY AS A RIGHT

Guy Standing

1. A Vision: Basic Income Security and 'Decent Work'

We live in strange times, in a world of greater monetary affluence than at any time in history, yet with more people living in wretched poverty than ever before. Wars and retribution make the news every day, and the voices of peace have been reduced to a whisper. There is economic insecurity almost everywhere, which has helped fan intolerance, and the anger of relative and absolute deprivation. This in turn has been feeding extremism, 'angst', bitterness and anomic consumerism. And yet, so much of all this is so unnecessary. Politicians, their advisers and policymaking civil servants should step back and think again.

There is a desire for something better and calmer. People around the world have begun to say with increasing conviction that, unless policies and institutions can be made to reduce injustice, insecurity and inequality, we will live an existence in which more and more resources will be devoted to police, prisons and weapons, extended to protect the relatively privileged from the effects of rising anger among the poor and insecure. We surely do not wish to see a fortress world for the privileged, in which everybody feels unsafe. Finding more effective ways of providing universal basic security should be at the top of the international agenda.

In the early years of the twenty-first century, can we form a vision of the Good Society of the future? Let us start with two fundamental questions, to keep at the back of our minds. Bearing in mind that all theories of distributive justice espouse the equality of something, the first grand question is:

What is it that should be equalized in the Good Society of the twenty-first century?

We may start with an underlying premise, which is that readers are *egalitarian* in some sense of that word, believing that a Good and Just Society must rest on some principle of social justice in which something should be equalized, whether it be income, wealth, status or opportunity to work, save, invest, and live a decent life. In this respect, we may claim that society should rest on a simple principle, that everybody should have *basic security* – to be equally free, equally protected against morbidity, and have equally good opportunity to develop their competencies and capabilities. Across a broad political spectrum, this fundamental principle is surely accepted. It defines our civilization and our civility, the basis of our inter-generational, intra-generational and cross-national discourse.

So, the essence of the answer is that for real (substantive) freedom, everybody in society must have *equal basic security*. This must be *unconditional* and *individualized*, the former being critical for liberty and for combating paternalism, the latter being critical for gender-related (and many other) issues. The word 'real' is used to signify that there must be a combination of 'negative liberty' – the negation of deprivation and unchosen controls – and 'positive liberty' – the opportunity to make informed and worthwhile choices. Real freedom might be described as the opportunity and capacity to function rationally and purposefully and to develop one's capacities or capabilities.

The second, complementary grand question is:

Assuming a *veil of ignorance* (i.e. not knowing where they would be in the distribution of outcomes), what sort of society would we want to leave for our children?

The gist of my own answer is that they should be living in a society celebrating a diversity of lifestyles, constrained only by the need to avoid doing harm to others, and living in circumstances in which a growing majority of people work on their enthusiasms, and pursue their own sense of occupation – combining their competencies or 'functionings', varying their work status, and possessing the means to be responsible to their family, neighbours and wider community. People live in an environment of co-operative individualism, in which individual freedom of action and reflection is backed by collective agency. This notion of development may be called occupational security – the security in which to develop capabilities and a working life combining forms of activity, including the stillness of contemplation. This is very close to what the ILO is espousing through its 'decent work' concept. This is also a vision of the Good Society based on real freedom and on equal basic security, or what might be called complex egalitarianism.

This paper contends that a citizenship income is essential for the Good Society of the twenty-first century, and that it could promote both individual liberty and personal and communal security, without which one cannot envisage a flourishing of all the talents.[1] Before continuing, let us pause here to reflect on the key words. The concept of basic income security obviously encapsulates three concepts – 'basic', 'income' and 'security'. Each of these words begs for a definition, as do each of the couplets (basic income, basic security, income security), and even the notion of *universalism* that often accompanies each of them.[2]

A key point about 'basic' is that it must be meaningful, in that it would have to be more than a charitable gesture. It means that it would have to be sufficient for survival. A key point about 'income' is that the payment must be in a form that allows the individual to decide for him- or herself how to allocate the resources. It is non-paternalistic in this respect, unlike a food subsidy, for example. A key point about 'security' is that whatever is provided must be assured. There should be no 'moving of the goalposts', which has been a striking feature of most welfare states over the past fifty years or so.

Adequate socio-economic security is the bedrock of real freedom. However, one must allow that, both for individuals and for society, too much security holds as many dangers as too little. Without basic security, you cannot be expected to be able to make rational decisions. However, freedom does require democratically chosen restraints, to check recklessness and selfish opportunism. These restraints must presumably pass some *veil of ignorance* test – that they apply equally to all groups and individuals, and that we accept them regardless of what position we occupy in the system of distribution.

Let us assume that we accept that universal basic economic security is a fundamental principle of a Good Society. If so, two policy-decision principles seem to follow. The first, following Rawls but making security the locus of strategy, may be called the *Security Difference Principle*:

> A policy, or institutional change, is socially just only if it reduces (or does not worsen) the insecurity of the least secure groups in society.

In other words, real freedom cannot be advanced if, say, supply-side policies, such as 'structural adjustment' strategies or 'shock therapy', deliberately worsen the insecurity of those at or near the bottom of society. And this would hold regardless of claims made on behalf of political democracy, i.e., if a majority could be induced to vote for policies that would make the worst-off worse off.

This decision rule, or principle of constitutionality, provides justification for a floor, to protect and enhance freedom in moving towards universal basic security. After all, if one accepts that real freedom is the opportunity to pursue a life of dignified and dignifying work, then one must recognize that this is about *distributional* outcomes – the woman outworker, the labourer and the peasant should have the same (or equivalent) basic security as the lawyer, the economist or the shareholder.

The first policy decision rule should be complemented by one dealing with the threat of various forms of paternalism and state control, which also threaten freedom. This may be called the *Paternalism Test Principle*:

> *A policy, or institutional change, is just only if it does not impose controls on some groups that are not imposed on the most free groups in society, or if it reduces controls limiting the autonomy to pursue occupation of those facing the most controls.*

Thus, unless husbands are subject to the same controls as wives, unless the poor the same as the rich, and the unemployed the same as the employed, then policy, institutional or relational controls should be opposed as invalid. And they would remain invalid even if a political majority could be engineered to vote for them. Reducing the freedom of a minority (or a majority, in the case of women in many societies) cannot be accepted, even if the change enhances the freedom of others.

The *Paternalism Test Principle* will be crucial in the first decade of the twenty-first century, because of the dangers of ostensibly benign State paternalism. The bristling *machismo* of politicians and their 'think tanks' in recent years has condemned universalistic social protection without behavioural conditions through the use of loaded terms such as 'nanny State' and 'dependency'. The irony is that State paternalism, in the form of 'workfare', 'welfare- to-work' and other directive schemes, more deserves the epithet of nanny State – although such euphemisms should be treated with some disdain.

If the *Paternalism Test* and *Security Difference Principles* were respected, we should favour policies and institutions that move people's work away from external controls, and towards greater autonomy, security and equality. This is not just about laws and regulations. It is also about work structuring – shaping work to suit people, not merely shaping people for jobs, or to make them more 'employable', or even to give them more 'human capital' or 'human capability'.[3] Freedom cannot be equated with capabilities or entitlements, unless one defines these terms so broadly that they lack specificity. We should wish to provide basic security for all, since that is essential to facilitate the individual's *freedom to develop*. By the latter is meant a freedom to develop ourselves through a creative, multi-sided existence, in which our work and our contemplative sides are balanced and balancing. It is of course clear that the way social security and social protection systems have been evolving around the world is in no way compatible with this vision. Before considering the latter in more detail, therefore, let us highlight – very schematically – the most relevant broad characteristics of the emerging economic system and the patterns of distribution associated with it.

2. The Context

We live in a 'globalizing' world, in which social and economic insecurities seem pervasive, in which there is no prospect of 'full employment' in the Keynesian sense of the word (and arguably no good justification for making that the primary social policy objective). There are extensive, and probably growing, inequalities of income, wealth and the opportunity of making either. Corporations and governments are mostly eager to create more flexible labour markets and labour relations, and unions are too weak in most places to do much about it.

Above all, we live in a world in which traditional family and community networks of social protection are breaking down, and where extended families are becoming more rare, where household membership becomes more transient, where 'bowling alone' is becoming a more prevalent way of living. It is also a world in which employers are increasingly disinclined to provide a wide array of social benefits for ordinary workers, and in which the State is shrinking in the sense of being able and willing to provide a growing array of decent 'cradle to grave' benefits and entitlements.

One may criticize these trends or one may welcome them. The key point is that we must take them into account in thinking of feasible and desirable options for moving towards basic income security. Good policy is not based on unrealistic assumptions.

The context, then, is one of widespread and growing economic and social inequality and insecurity. We are in the midst of a great transformation, in which the economy has become disembedded from society, such that there are no adequate systems of regulation, redistribution or social protection to moderate the inequalities and insecurities being thrown up. Globalization and the spread of flexible, informal labour markets are associated with capital and labour *fragmentation*, in which *controls* over workers and citizens are becoming more complex and indirect, and in which income flows are also becoming more complex. A small minority are receiving income mainly from capital, with a small part coming from performance of highly paid labour. At the top is an elite, blessed by absurdly high incomes and windfall gains that are a spreading dark stain on global capitalism. The stain is spreading, not just because more executives are demanding that level of remuneration but because these incomes convert into huge wealth that is passed from generation to generation, producing the concentration of financial wealth that is a starting point for our deliberations.

Alongside the wealthy elite, a shrinking *core* group of workers are receiving income from a variable mix of wages, state benefits, enterprise benefits and capital (shares). Below both groups in terms of income, a heterogeneous group has mushroomed, which for present purposes may be called *outsiders* (flexi-workers, unemployed, and a lumpenized detached group of homeless or socially ill people scraping by). The outsiders instil the fear of insecurity in the stomachs of the insiders, who in turn retreat into implicit or explicit 'concession bargaining' with their firms.

One can complicate this basic labour market model, and for many purposes should do so. But for our purposes it is sufficient to depict the fragmentation in this way. The inequalities have become destabilizing, yet are unchecked. For example, in Latin America, and in other parts of the world, there have been well-documented lurches to greater income inequality in recent decades.

This has mostly occurred during periods of dictatorship or of military juntas. But the increased inequality has been maintained in subsequent periods of so-called democratization. There is compelling evidence that the top 1 per cent and top 10 per cent of income earners have gained strongly relative to the bottom 90 per cent of the population. As Gabriel Palma (2002) shows, this skewed trend is not picked up in the standard measures of income distribution (gini coefficients). In Europe and North America, there is evidence of comparable developments. No Good Society can emerge unless that gross inequality is addressed, and that can only come about through a redistribution of income and assets. Meanwhile, even in the most industrialized countries, poverty remains high, even in countries performing very well economically.[4] The bottom groups have lost in terms of secure wages, occupational welfare and state benefits.

It is the latter groups with whom this paper is most concerned. The following merely highlights a few key trends:

- Proportionately fewer workers are in labour statuses that enable them to have access to fringe benefits and 'occupational welfare' in firms or employing organizations.
- More workers are in jobs paying individualized and unstable or unpredictable earnings. Even within the countries of the European Union, nearly one in every ten employed workers has an income that puts her or him in poverty, a point brought out well in a later chapter.[5] Remarkably, half of the poor in the EU live in households in which at least one person works in a job full-time. Moreover, statistics from industrialized countries show that in recent years high employment has not been associated with poverty reduction (Cantillon, Marx and Van den Bosch, 2002).
- A majority of the unemployed in industrialized countries do not have access to unemployment benefits.[6] Conditions for entitlement have been tightened, fewer workers manage to qualify for them, the level of benefits has fallen, the duration of entitlement has been shortened, and there has been a steady

drift from *insurance* to *assistance* (means-tested) benefits. 'Unemployment traps' have been very strong, particularly for women (D'Addio, de Greef and Rosholm, 2002). One can predict that by 2010 there will scarcely be any traditional unemployment benefit system in the world.

- There has been a strong shift from *defined-benefit* pensions to *defined-contribution* schemes, which are intrinsically more insecure, in terms of level of pension and assured receipt of it; there has also been a shift from universal basic state pensions to means-tested schemes.

- Many countries have raised the minimum age of retirement pensions, thereby intensifying the income insecurity of elderly workers. The age of entitlement has been raised – for women, in one in four countries, for men, in one of every five countries.[7] During the 1990s, one country in every four that had state pension schemes raised the number of years of contribution required to obtain entitlement to a pension.

- More and more families and a growing proportion of the population of Europe and other parts of the world are dependent on *mean-tested benefits* – or '*social assistance*' – in order to avoid poverty.[8] As numerous surveys have shown, these suffer from low and erratic take-up, for behavioural and informational reasons, as well as because of bureaucratic inefficiency and arbitrary application of rules. Not only are such benefits being cut in value, but conditions for entitlement are also being made more stringent.

- Indexation of benefits has been weakened, intensifying the income insecurity of those dependent on them: in some countries, the intervals between adjustments to inflation have been lengthened, and in others the value of benefits has been linked to prices rather than to per capita income, so allowing their real value to decline relative to the income of other groups in society.

- Often, the actual value of benefits has been cut, or the period of entitlement has been reduced.

- Only just over one in three countries has provided income protection for all eight standard spheres of social security – sickness, maternity, old age, invalidity, survivors, family allowances, work injury, unemployment. Unemployment benefits only exist, in partial form, in one out of every two countries.

- On average, only about 12 per cent of GDP is spent on providing income security through social security schemes – just over 21 per cent in industrialized countries, and merely 2.2 per cent in developing countries. There is no evidence that an increasing share of GDP is correlated with lower economic growth, and indeed up to about 33 per cent there is a positive correlation – social protection is growth- enhancing, yet has been constrained.

- Above all, behavioural conditions have been applied and tightened, thereby forcing people to conform to a standard behavioural model, often in a way that many cannot do. 'Workfare'-type schemes have spread, in which limited entitlement to income transfers has been made dependent on the performance of labour.

In short, we live in an era of selectivity, conditionality and paternalistic controls that are a threat to real freedom, creating societies in which, inside the labour market, on the edges of the labour market and beyond it into old age, income insecurity is rife and shows no prospect of being reversed. Society and the economy need not be like that. There is an alternative.

3. About Time

Before coming to that, permit me an extended digression. All the great utopias depicted throughout modern history have placed importance on the qualities of gentleness, conviviality, fraternity and social solidarity.[9] Any progressive strategy should be compatible with these features. With this thought in mind, what is the biggest challenge that we face in the affluent parts of the world?

Let us be blunt. In the industrialized world, we live in an *apolitical era*, in which there is pervasive class fragmentation and a generalized lack of identity. The 'I'-word dominates over the 'We'-word. The young are cynical – and rational – about the politics on offer. In 2000, for the first time, more of those under the age of 30 who voted in the US Presidential election voted for the Republican candidate than for the Democrat – about 40 per cent for the former, 20 per cent for the latter, and 40 per cent for 'independent'. In France, in the first round of the French Presidential election held in April 2002, a majority of that age group stayed at home, leaving the extreme rightist candidate Le Pen to beat all candidates of the left. In the following weeks, chauvinistic individuals and groups in the UK and the Netherlands, among other places, attracted levels of electoral support that sent shivers of concern through the body politic.

In this context of disembedded populism, it may not seem an auspicious time to propose any Good Society. Yet surely that would be a faulty reading of the challenge. The fear should be that the voices of the Third Way that prevailed in the 1990s will continue to pander to such apathy, fostering individualism rather than trying to create the collective agencies and spaces in which a fraternal 'We' can evolve. If this continues, the young (and the not-so-young) will continue to be politically disengaged. Unless those in the public sphere who worry about the insecurities and inequalities offer a *politics of paradise*, the long-term prospects of a Good Society will remain bleak. It is not good enough for Third Wayists to say that the young should vote for them because if they do not do so a Le Pen or his equivalent will obtain power.[10] It is better for the politicians to be taught sooner rather than later that pragmatic adjustment to the dominant economic orthodoxy can *never* be part of the onward march.

One hypothesis to explain the declining turnout in national and sub-national elections in most affluent countries is that people are encouraged to be individualistic by market norms, whereas voting derives from a sense of social community and valued social relationships. The significance of the political disengagement is that a Good Society must surely be built on the energies and the anger of youth, which have always provided the backbone of progressive movements, and not on the *adaptations* that the young are obliged to make in order to adjust to current realities. It must surely appeal not to their *weakness of will*, but to their enthusiasms.

What *asset* do the young lack most? And what are the *reasons* for this? Furthermore, what makes the young *angry*?

Beyond those teenage years of 'angst', the asset the young lack most is *time*, both currently and, more importantly, in prospect as they move from 'school' to 'work'. In modern affluent societies, there is constant pressure to use every moment, with work demands competing with the need to make contact with peers, through the internet, through emails, through mobile phones and so on. Men and women in their twenties and thirties – and often in their forties and fifties – have to face 'multi-tasking', and take their work home, and their home to work. The reasons for this frenzied loss of time are that the pressures to consume and to compete are intensified in electronically connected individualistic capitalism. To pause is to risk becoming obsolescent, passed by in the latest splurge of gadgeting, or displaced by those with the capacity to perform a revised set of tasks.

It is a lifestyle that is psychologically threatening, leaving both the successful and the failures teetering on the edge of a sort of hysteria. The notion of 'bowling alone' is operating alongside the notion of 'burn out'. Even the 'right to silence' is jeopardized.[11]

While this intense pressure on time causes resentment – often turned inwards, resulting in a sense of inadequacy and stress – the young and others are also infuriated by a sense of injustice. In several respects this is unlike the sense of injustice that predominated in past ages. In a global society, it takes the shape of revulsion against the gap between the affluence in rich countries and the grinding poverty in low-income developing countries, and between the absurdly wealthy elites of the world and those detached from the mainstream of society living a precarious and lumpenized existence. It also takes the form of anger about ecological decline, a worry that the quality of the environment is deteriorating as corporate greed and technological prowess threaten the sustainability of our planet. The poor in general, the hassled workers rushing to work by bus and underground, the slum dwellers, the inner-city dwellers, and numerous other groups all live in crowded spaces, while they see the affluent living in space where they are in control of their environment. The young see the rainforests shrinking, the range of species declining, and the coral reefs disappearing. But they also crowd into cramped city spaces, on overloaded buses or trains, in small costly apartments, permanently in a rush. Time and space are crowded, and they neither own nor control their own time or space. This contributes to a pervasive sense of existential insecurity.

A progressive politics and vision must tap the most critical source of deprivation and anger in its potential supporters, and thus be about a redistribution of those assets perceived as the most scarce and most valued, and most unequally distributed. In a feudal society progressives tapped the anger of the landless; in an industrial society they tapped the anger of those lacking the physical means of production. In the twenty-first century, the key assets which youth and the median 'middle-class' worker lack are *time* and *security*.[12] Progressives should be tapping the anger created by this new lack.

The underlying malaise is not accidental. Modern capitalism has an interest in *time compression* among those who consume its products and among those who work to its rhythms. It is almost a truism that more and more people are living under a pressurized mix of inducements and incentives to 'spend time' – 'purchase, possess and display' is the law of the modern prophets.[13] In such circumstances, a subversive politics should be about wresting *control* over time for the 'dispossessed', and it should recognize that such control is the essence of real security. As in every radical moment in history, the progressive vision should be about redistributing the key scarce asset from those who possess too much of it to those with too little or none at all. No progressive agenda ever mobilized the masses unless it offered a strategy to redistribute the key scarce asset.

This is where we reach a dilemma for those wishing to create a Good Society: the demographics are in conflict with the potential politics. While the young are concerned by a lack of time and angered by a sense of ecological injustice – a sense of deprived space – the age group that is growing as a proportion of the total population is the elderly. In part because of the nature of social policy derived from industrial society, this age group does not lack time. The welfare state, even in its residual Anglo-Saxon form, was built on the presumed norm of the labouring man, the 'breadwinner', who received income transfers to compensate for 'temporary interruptions of earning power'. Old age was expected to be a short interruption between labour and death. Although never justified, this was closer to a norm in the middle decades of the twentieth century. It certainly no longer applies in the early years of the twenty-first century.

There is no intrinsic justification for the over fifty-year-olds to have a disproportionate share of society's 'free time'. Yet once having been granted it through pay-as-you-go pension systems during the second half of the twentieth century, they are scarcely likely to give it away – and in this they will be supported by those coming their way.

The demographic dilemma is compounded by the awkward fact that there is an obvious reason for the elderly having little opportunistic interest in the main source of anger motivating youth under globalized capitalism. Youth fears ecological decay, global warming, closing spaces and all the spectres that come with them. Where will 'we' go in thirty years' time, when the waves have come up round that island of peace and tranquillity, and when those frenetic years are behind us? The elderly will understand this existential insecurity, and some will be motivated by altruism to the point of protesting alongside their grandchildren. But they do not have a direct interest in those distant times, for the very simple reason that they do not expect to be around.

So, here we have the dilemma. The angry generations, the potential energisers for any utopian vision, lack time, lack security and feel the ecological pain. The growing generations – the 'wrinklies', 'grey power' – have ample free time and have only an altruistic concern for the primary source of anger among their younger citizens, a lack of 'quality time'. This is scarcely a recipe for a strong model of social solidarity. A formula for a new social solidarity has to be found – or we can kiss good-bye to any hope of a progressive vision, and come to accept a landscape of Warholian politics, of populist individuals or parties flitting before electorates for their proverbial fifteen minutes of fame and electoral fortune, catching the passing mood with a flurry of buzzwords, playing on the fears of the crowd, swayed by the turbulence of global capitalism. The crass politics of globalization and pervasive insecurity are populism and personalization. The *politics of paradise* must defeat that.

Recapturing control over time is a fundamental part of that politics. While preparing this paper, I heard that, apparently, in the 1968 US Presidential election the average 'soundbite' of the Presidential candidates lasted forty-five seconds, suggesting some substantive reasoning process, whereas in the 2000 Presidential election the average 'soundbite' had been shortened to eight seconds. A reasonable interpretation of this and other symptoms of time pressure is that the populace is suffering from a National Attention Deficit

Disorder syndrome – reproducing at societal level a pervasive modern illness among children and young adults that is now a recognized learning disorder.

Induced to flit idly between a flurry of time-filling activities, it is scarcely surprising that the young seem to lack an appreciation of history.[14] Dare one say that lacking a sense of past time is connected to the lack of a sense of future time? Do not expect a vision of a Good Society from those who lack a sense of where they have come from and where they are going.

The challenge is clear. The contours of the solution are no less clear – decommercialization of the spirit and decompression of time. Every imagined Utopia has met those challenges. An agenda for the twenty-first century Good Society should at least face them.

4. A Future Somewhere: Towards a New 'Social Contract'

The claim is that in this era of 'globalization' the economic system has been disembedded from society, to the detriment of security and stability. Embeddedness requires appropriate systems of regulation, of protection and of redistribution. Social thinkers everywhere are struggling to redefine all three in the new global (dis-)order.

Let us start with *regulation*. How can effective and equitable *regulation* be achieved? The starting point should be that regulations should become progressively less paternalistic. The use of *fiscal regulation* of individual behaviour should be reduced and be subject to the two policy-decision rules stated earlier. Regulation of individual behaviour by manipulation of taxes and income transfers is anathema. In fiscal policy, the principle of *behavioural neutrality* should be developed. In other words, fiscal policy should not be designed to be a vehicle of social engineering. And where it does impinge on individual behaviour, as far as possible it should adhere to those decision rules.

Old-style statutory regulations are of limited efficacy. Although useful in setting standards and guidelines, they veer between bureaucratic rigidity and lax gestures, depending on the administrative effort put into them. The priority should be to reinvigorate *voice regulation*, which means rethinking issues of tripartism, neo-corporatism and the new euphemisms of 'governance' and 'social capital'. Any agenda that sees the extension of rights or freedoms without collective *representation security* could mean only that the vulnerable would remain vulnerable. But in thinking about *voice*, we must avoid the danger of being tied atavistically to the twentieth century labourist agenda.

The Good Society needs as many types of representative association as there are *interests* to represent. Rousseau's concern about partial societies remains compelling, but so too does G.D.H. Cole's insistence that we need a multitude of interest representations. This means, *inter alia*, a need for independent organizations to bargain on behalf of 'flexiworkers', so-called 'informal workers', voluntary workers, care workers, the unemployed and so on. And there is a need for legitimate *occupational associations*, that is, bodies that can defend and enhance standards and practices but which must avoid the danger of being monopolistic rent-seeking devices, as has been the case of many professional bodies. We can see positive signs, as well as some negative ones, in the spread of social clubs based on ethnic background, gender, type of work, and so on. To complement group-based and occupational associations, there is also a need to strengthen *community associations*.

What then of *redistribution* in the emerging global context? Even the World Bank (2002) is recognizing the need for asset redistribution. Suffice it to assert that we need new mechanisms rather than to give up the search for redistribution on the dubious grounds that 'there is no alternative' to living in a more inegalitarian world because of globalization. The returns on capital and technological innovation have risen relative to those on labour, and the functional distribution of income may have become more skewed in favour of capital. Use of progressive direct tax has become problematical because of pressures of 'competitiveness'. So, re-embedding the economy requires policies and institutions to raise the capital market participation rate (CMPR) towards the labour force participation rate (LFPR), so that all of us have a broad portfolio of forms and sources of income. This means reviving ideas of *stakeholder capitalism* within firms and within local communities, as well as social investment-fund and community profit-sharing schemes. Social reformers will eventually grab them and make them instruments for complex egalitarianism.

So, what then of *social protection*? Surely – and this is a founding principle of the ILO's Socio-Economic Security Programme – the overall system of social protection must shift away from its almost exclusive focus on *risk compensation* to one of extending and enhancing individual and collective rights, based not on labour as in the twentieth century, but on citizenship in its broadest sense. Protection is not equivalent to a 'social safety net'; it should be a means of *liberation*. We should play on the Kennedy aphorism: ask not what social protection must protect you *against*; ask what social protection can protect you *for*. It is in this context that basic security requires an unconditional basic income – or what might be called a solidarity or security income. Real freedom requires a system of social protection that allows people of all backgrounds to be able to make decent choices. Ultimately, social protection, regulatory and distributive policies must be integrated in a way that facilitates and extends what might be called *occupational security*.

This is related to the great debate on *the right to work*. There have been numerous attempts to define this right and a right to income security. There have been contributions from philosophers, theologians, psychologists, economists, sociologists and sundry others. Thus, a Christian perspective is well illustrated by Torsten Meireis' paper for the BIEN Congress which – drawing on a modern reading of Luther – concludes with a ringing statement with which many could agree:

> Since Christian active life is to be characterized by serving one's neighbour in a spirit of love, a social order of distribution that condones only integration into gainful employment organized by the market (unless a person is independently wealthy or renounces all welfare) – denouncing other ways of life or stigmatizing those who are unable to forage for themselves – is not acceptable, not least because it effectively reduces the freedom to follow one's calling to a small elite.[15]

A related perspective, derived from Calvin, is presented by Édouard Dommen (2002) in the Congress. Many religious thinkers and practitioners have been drawn to the desirability of a right to income security without linking it to any duty to perform labour. Thus, the Archbishop of Cape Town said in a meeting on basic income in South Africa in January 2002: 'An unconditional basic income is essential for tackling poverty and inequality in South Africa.'

Others have referred to the right to dignity and the enhancement of individual freedom and autonomy, or self-respect. The *Universal Declaration of Human Rights*, Article 25, commits all countries that are members of the United Nations to the principle:

> Everyone has the right to a standard of living adequate for the health and well-being of himself [sic] and his family, including food, clothing, housing and medical care and the necessary social services...

This is a right without specified obligations. How far reality is from that vision to which governments around the world have been ostensibly committed ever since it came into effect over fifty-four years ago. And others, such as Rolf Kunnemann (2002), have linked it to the right to food.

Some have noted, often with regret, that in the sphere of human rights, economic rights have lagged behind others – a point made by Mary Robinson, the former UN High Commissioner for Human Rights. Thus, the UK's Human Rights Act of 1998 (implemented as from 2000) provides for a right to life (including basic health care) and the right to schooling, but does not provide a universal right to adequate subsistence, shelter or social care. In this connection, some observers have distinguished between universally enforceable rights and those that are not enforceable – or what one observer has called 'manifesto rights'. The right to basic income security would no doubt belong to this category, to the extent that the distinction is meaningful and desirable.

The crucial point is that a right to income security should not be linked to a right to work. The fundamental criticism of twentieth century welfare states is that for the most part entitlements to income transfers were linked to the performance of labour or the willingness to do so, or to the payment of contributions from labour income. This systematically undervalues other forms of work that are not labour.

A Good Society, in which decent work or occupational security is promoted, based on the image of an *artisanal society* that underlay Rousseau's concerns for liberty and equality, should not elevate labour above other forms of work. Moreover, in the twenty-first century it is very clear that making income security dependent on wage labour leads to widespread and growing denial of access to income transfers, which is precisely what has been happening in all types of economy.

5. The Options: Alternatives to Basic Income

Let us assume that we all accept that moving towards basic income security for all is desirable. Many different routes have been proposed, and many have been tried in various parts of the world. It is worth recalling the main alternatives, if only to contrast them with the favoured option proposed by this paper. I do not intend to discuss them in any detail, merely to list them and indicate the main concerns that have been raised in each case.[16]

Income security can be enhanced for those involved in economic activity, for those doing some other form of work, and for those not doing any form of work. Most attention over the past century has been given to policies to 'make work pay'.

A statutory minimum wage: A classic tool to give income security to those at or near the bottom of labour markets.

Main drawbacks: While a minimum wage can provide a floor for those in wage labour, it obviously does not cover those outside it, and with the growing informalization of economic activities, it is harder to apply than in the case of an economy based on regular full-time wage employment. It is hard to apply effectively or equitably in flexible labour markets, and is costly to administer.

Social insurance: Compensatory income transfers for so-called 'contingency risks', requiring workers to pay contributions or have them paid for them, typically by employers, in return for which they receive a benefit should the risk materialise. As many observers have noted, the notion of social insurance is often a fiction, albeit a convenient one that has helped legitimize it as a system.

Main drawbacks: It does not reach many workers, leads to opportunistic evasion, to moral hazards. It raises non-wage labour costs, tending to reduce employment. It leads policymakers to 'move the goalposts', contravening the principle of insurance. It focuses on labour rather than on work.

Social assistance*:* Benefits or income transfers provided to families or individuals based on means tests, often with behavioural conditions attached to them. Although long regarded as anathema for equitable and effective social protection, they have grown enormously over the past two decades.

Main drawbacks: Such benefits stigmatize and have a low take-up, tending to exclude those most in need. Usually they become embroiled in additional 'behavioural tests' that threaten liberty through constraining individual freedom of choice.

Workfare: A genre of schemes in which a person has to perform a job or take some specified training or other 'employability'-enhancing activity in order to gain or retain an entitlement to a benefit. This route to so-called 'social integration' became the vogue in the 1990s, epitomized by the 1996 welfare reform in the USA, in the UK's 'New Deal', and in comparable schemes in other countries.

Main drawbacks: This is the new paternalism, and is a threat to liberty and equality in the twenty-first century. Its avowed rationale – the so-called 'reciprocity' principle – is arbitrary, inequitable and leads towards authoritarian controls over the poor and relatively vulnerable.[17] It can also create a new form of dependency.

Employment or wage subsidies: Payments or tax credits paid to employers (usually) for employing workers, intended to enable firms to create more jobs, and workers to receive higher wages, than might be justified by the productivity of the jobs or of the workers.

Main drawbacks: These entail large 'deadweight' and 'substitution' effects, and tend to distribute income regressively, giving to 'capital' not to workers.

Public works: Classic schemes, particularly widespread in developing countries, in which the poor are paid to do something, usually labour-intensive activity.

Main drawbacks: These have deadweight and substitution effects, are stigmatizing, often do not reach the most vulnerable groups, and tend to have low productivity.

In-work benefits: Increasingly popular schemes that blur into the subsidies mentioned above and tax credits (mentioned below). Essentially, the term refers to income transfers intended to encourage workers to stay in intrinsically low-paying jobs.

Main drawbacks: They may reduce pressure on firms to raise productivity and encourage them to pay lower wages.

Tax credits: The fastest-growing measure designed to provide income security, epitomized by what has become the largest income transfer scheme in the world – the US Earned Income Tax Credit – which has been adopted in one form or another in various other countries. For many in BIEN, it is seen as a precursor to a genuine basic income scheme.

Main drawbacks: They have a limited coverage at the lower end of the income range, and are family-based. However, they are potentially a precursor to a basic income.

6. Basic Income: A Definition and Antecedents

A basic income is an income unconditionally granted to everybody on an individual basis. It is *unconditional* in the sense that it does not require any prior behaviour by or on behalf of the individual receiving it and does not require any current behaviour, or future behaviour as a commitment made on receipt of the income. It also does not require any proof of 'contribution', unlike the idealized (but not realized) model of social insurance.

A basic income, as conceived by its advocates, would be paid on an equal basis to each individual, regardless of gender, age, work status, marital status, household status or any other perceived distinguishing feature of individuals. Usually, advocates propose that a lower amount should be paid to children, up to the age of fourteen or sixteen, and propose that supplements be provided for those with special, socially defined needs, such as physical or mental impairments. Most advocates of an unconditional basic income argue strongly that it should be paid on an individual basis, and not on a family or household basis. However, there have been exceptions, including the proposal for a family-based citizen's income by Sam Brittan and Steven Webb (1990).

One aspect of the definition of a basic income is the intended level. Most advocates support a basic income as an unconditional right to an independent income sufficient to meet basic living costs, such that it would prevent poverty rather than be merely relief from poverty. Of course, this leaves open how to define poverty, what constitutes basic living costs, and so on. One way out of this impasse may be to make the level overtly a political issue, as envisaged by some proponents.

Historically, those who have advocated a basic income of some sort include some outstanding people, including Thomas More, in his *Utopia*, written in 1516, Tom Paine, in his *Agrarian Justice* of 1795 and less explicitly in *The Rights of Man*, William Morris, in his *News From Nowhere*, Bertrand Russell, in his *Roads to Freedom*, and more recently James Meade, most notably in his *Agathotopia*.[18]

Among those who have become convinced of the virtues of the basic income approach are several Nobel Prize-winning economists of surprisingly diverse political convictions: Milton Friedman[19], Herbert Simon, Robert Solow, Jan Tinbergen and James Tobin (besides, of course, James Meade, who was an advocate from his younger days). Milton Friedman said recently that 'a basic income is not an alternative to a negative income tax. It is simply another way to introduce a Negative Income Tax.' The negative income tax (NIT) is not quite the same as a basic income, because it still starts from the basis of someone earning an income, has been conceived as based on the family as the taxable unit, and is paid on an *ex post* basis whereas a citizenship income would be paid on an *ex ante* basis, as a right, to individuals. However, the NIT or the earned-income tax credit is a powerful move in the direction of the integration of tax and benefits that is an essential feature of a basic income.

7. Popular Attitudes

The Finns are much more thrilled by a basic income than are the Swedes.[20]

One of the challenges for those advocating basic income security as a right is to obtain popular support for the principle. It runs up against the much-touted *reciprocity principle* – the claim that someone should receive an income transfer only if they do some labour in return. This notion has been subjected to detailed critique by many social scientists.

How to build a coalition in favour of basic income security is something that is addressed in countries as diverse as South Africa, Brazil and Finland. What is intriguing about the survey results reported by Andersson and Kangas is that a majority of adults under the age of 30 were in favour of a basic income – 59 per cent in Sweden, 78 per cent in Finland. Not surprisingly, the affluent were least likely to favour it.

In a series of psychological experiments in deliberative democracy, a solid majority of people from a wide range of social backgrounds expressed support for the 'floor principle', and it was apparent that the process of social deliberation led to an increased tendency to support it relative to alternative principles of distributive justice.

An interesting paper for the BIEN Congress by Stefan Leibig and Steffen Mau has examined the moral intuitions of people in their attitude towards a guaranteed social minimum, concluding tentatively that while the authors could not reconstruct the justice principles underlying people's reasoning, a large majority regarded a minimum income as socially just.[21] Another paper by Rosamund Stock dealt with the psychological issues more directly.[22]

Finally, in the People's Security Surveys carried out in various countries by the ILO's Socio-Economic Security Programme, a majority of the thousands of respondents have expressed support for providing everybody in society with a guaranteed minimum income (Tables 1.1 and 1.2). Finding the way to translate such incipient support for practical action is the subject of much of the Congress.

8. Moving Towards Basic Income Security

Advocates of basic income accept that a major difficulty arises from how to introduce it. There are matters of cost, administrative challenges, political legitimation, and the difficulties of phasing out other schemes. There are some brave souls who advocate a big bang solution – introduction of a full basic income on the dawn of the morning after an election victory. Most advocates put their utopian dreams aside, and advocate some form of phased introduction.

The favoured options can be briefly summarized. Some believe that a *partial basic income* should be the first step, i.e., a low amount paid to each individual as a right. Among those who have openly advocated this is Mimi Parker (1989), long a stalwart of the UK's basic income group (under its several names).[23] The essential point of the partial basic income is that it would not be a full substitute for other minimum income and transfer schemes but would be a modest amount paid to all, providing a slowly increasing proportion of state benefits. Some advocates of a partial basic income believe that this should be the final objective, while others believe that a *full basic income* should be introduced at the highest sustainable level. Among the advocates of this position is Philippe van Parijs (1995). Many BIEN members take this position, although the network is eclectic.

Another option, again seen as a pragmatic step towards the ideal of a full basic income is a *participation income*. This is associated with Tony Atkinson (1995, 1996), among others. What is involved in this proposal is a basic

Table 1.1 Opinions on income limits (weighted %), multiple responses

	South Africa	Bangladesh**	Tanzania	Gujarat, India	Hungary	Ukraine
Upper limit on income						
Yes	39.7	21.7	20.8	52.9	47.8	33.7
No	42.7	78.3	52.0	41.3	52.2	66.3
Don't know	17.6	0.4	27.2	5.8	–	–
Lower limit on income						
Yes	56.3	55.2	45.6	98.0	84.7	71.0
No	28.1	44.5	31.2	1.6	15.3	29.0
Don't know	15.6	0.3	23.2	0.4	–	–
No limit but help poor						
Yes	64.1	80.8	69.4	n.a.	71.5	59.9
No	21.4	19.2	14.2		28.5	40.1
Don't know	14.5	0.0	16.4		–	–
Similar incomes						
Yes	26.7	4.0	18.5	n.a.	3.5	7.7
No	60.7	95.6	50.2		96.5	92.3
Don't know	12.6	0.4	31.3		–	–
Number of respondents	2099	1011	1521	1236	955-993	6111

Note: **Bangladesh results are not weighted. n.a.: not asked in Gujarat survey.
Source: People's Security Surveys, ILO Socio-Economic Security Programme.

Table 1.2 Opinions on income limits (weighted %), single response

Income limits	Argentina	Brazil	Chile
(1) Both upper and lower	26.5	24.9	26.1
(2) Upper limit only	8.2	11.6	9.4
(3) Lower limit only	24.9	10.1	24.0
(4) No limits	17.5	10.9	21.8
(5) Equal incomes	22.9	42.5	18.7
Sample size	2792	3904	1106

Source: People's Security Surveys, ILO Socio-Economic Security Programme.

income proposed on condition that the individual agrees to do some work activity, possibly for 'the community'. This has sometimes blurred into variants of 'workfare', as with the initial position of André Gorz.[24]

A variant of the participation income has been the RMI (*revenu minimum d'insertion*), first introduced by President Francois Mitterand in France. Variants of this have been considered or introduced in various parts of Europe, including the Canton of Geneva, where the RMR (*revenu minimum de reinsertion*) has been debated for some years, as discussed by Andràs November (2002).[25]

A further approach is simply to cut back on the conventional conditions and forms of selectivity, weakening them until their abolition could become a matter of formality. It would not be surprising if a majority of basic income advocates favoured this route.

Another approach is to phase in a basic income by providing it for certain social groups, and then extending it to others until the whole of society is covered. There is something of this approach in the *renda minima* and *bolsa escola* schemes in Brazil and several other parts of Latin America. In this case, women with young children are provided with a basic income, provided they send their children to school regularly; a nominal means test may help in legitimizing the policy, but the hope of many of its advocates is that, once legitimized, it could be extended to other groups in society. This is the position of Senator Eduardo Suplicy (2002), of São Paulo. It seems that many of those contributing to the debates in Brazil also hold this position, including Cristovam Buarque, former Governor of the Federal District, Brasilia.[26]

A variant of this approach has been envisaged for South Africa, where the *social pension* has been regarded as easily the most successful anti-poverty device in the country. This has been paid mainly to rural blacks, most of whom have been elderly women; nominally means-tested, it has in fact been given with minimal conditionality. The proposal is that the social pension should be extended to all groups in society.[27] A related approach is to provide 'senior citizens' with a basic income, and gradually reduce the age at which the grant is provided. This is roughly what Maria Cruz-Saco (2002) proposes for Peru.

Another approach is simply to extend tax credits, by attaching a value of non-income-earning activities. This sort of extension is taking place in some countries, an example being the caregiver credit in the USA and the introduction of such measures as care insurance in Germany.[28] Once care becomes recognized as work to be protected and remunerated, the way is open.

Citizens or Residents

One issue that comes up in discussions of basic income, and of the idea of universality in particular, is whether every individual in a given country should be provided with a basic income. With porous national borders, argue the critics, it would be a recipe for mass immigration if a generous basic income were provided to everybody, regardless of citizenship. If there is a consensus on this, it is probably that the basic income should be provided to all citizens and all who are legally resident in the country, with some advocating that the legal residence should have been for a minimum threshold period of, say, two or five years. The debate and proposals relating to migrants are complex, although many in BIEN are convinced that the issues do not represent insurmountable barriers to basic income security.[29]

---

9. Paying for a Basic Income

The challenge of finding the optimum way of paying for a basic income has exercised the minds of many basic income advocates, and many ingenious methods have been proposed. Possibly the most popular have been wealth taxes and ecological taxes, although in both cases they have been seen as supplements to the taxation used to raise income for the conventional array of social transfers, many of which would be merged wholly or in part into the basic income.[30] Thus, the UK's Basic Income Research Group's position has been that a basic income

> would phase out as many reliefs and allowances against personal income tax, and as many existing state-financed cash benefits as practicable; and would replace them with a basic income paid automatically to each and every man, woman and child.[31]

Many advocates who have tried to 'cost' a basic income have done so on the basis of an assumption of 'tax neutrality', i.e., that no new or higher tax rates would be involved, and have estimated a feasible level of basic income on that assumption. But, of course, there is no need to make that particular stringent assumption, since there is no known optimum tax rate, just as there is no known optimum level of social protection expenditure.

Philippe van Parijs (1995) has proposed that there should also be a 'tax on jobs' to help pay for a basic income, on the grounds that jobs in a market economy with involuntary unemployment are a form of scarce 'asset'.[32] Other basic income advocates have argued against this position.

Another favourite proposal to pay for all or part of a basic income is the so-called Tobin Tax (Silva, Basso and de Pinho, 2002). Disowned by James Tobin himself just before his death as a tool for fighting global poverty, the idea of a levy on foreign exchange dealings retains an appeal among many 'developmentalists', and has been seen as a potential source of funds to pay for minimum income protection.

Finally, there is the approach represented by the establishment of a *capital fund* of some sort, which would be responsible for investing and distributing the proceeds as a basic grant, the amount being determined by the size and rate of return of the fund's investments. This is epitomized by the Alaska Permanent Fund, an analysis of which was presented at the BIEN Congress.[33] In Brazil, Eduardo Suplicy has also proposed a Citizens' Brazilian Fund, made up of resources from taxes, public service concessions and property sales, to fund a guaranteed minimum income that would grow as the fund developed.

These fund-based proposals have an affinity to the *social dividend* proposals that have long featured in the basic income debates. Among advocates of economic democracy based on a social dividend has been James Meade, most notably in his *Agathotopia*. The *social dividend* has a long pedigree (van Trier, 2002).[34] The main point here is that many advocates of a basic income have seen it as one part of a redistributive strategy, intended to promote income security, equality and economic dynamism.

10. Capital Grants Versus Citizenship Income

...Create in every nation, a national fund, to pay to every person, when arrived at the age of 21 years, the sum of 15 pounds sterling, to enable him or her to begin the world. And also, 10 pounds sterling per annum during life to every person over the age of 50 years, to enable them to live in old age without wretchedness, and go decently out of the world.

Tom Paine, *Agrarian Justice*, 1795.

There has been debate in recent years around the relative merits of capital grants – one-off payments to every individual at some point in their life – versus a basic income. In some respects, there is not much difference; Tom Paine clearly saw the need for both. The capital grant idea has been considered in previous BIEN Congresses, notably by Bruce Ackerman in the Berlin Congress of 2000 and by Edwin Morley-Fletcher in his opening address to the Amsterdam Congress in 1998.[35]

The so-called stakeholding grant or capital grant idea, which should be called a Coming-of-Age Grant (COAG), has been given additional relevance by its adoption by the UK Government, in the form of what has been called a 'baby bond'. This may be described as a COAG with a coming-of-age defined as registered-date-of-birth.[36] In this paper, I want to bring out differences between it and the Citizenship Income Guarantee (CIG), but in doing so also highlight why a social dividend approach should give a place both to a CIG and to some form of capital grant. The variant of the latter that is desirable is closer to what might be called a Community Capital Grant (COG).

Capital grants and basic income have a common heritage and set of objectives, which might be summarized as a desire to enhance real freedom and a desire to promote a more egalitarian form of capitalism. A danger of the debate between advocates of CIG and COAG is that both can be depicted as contrasting panaceas, when neither side believes in that. A basic income advocate would argue that it is a necessary but not sufficient component of a package of policies to create the Good Society, whereas a COAG is neither necessary nor sufficient. A COAG advocate might argue that while neither would be sufficient, a COAG would be helpful in enhancing economic freedom, whereas a CIG would not be politically feasible.

10.1 The Arguments Over CIG

A CIG would be a basic income grant paid monthly to each individual regardless of work status, gender, marital status or age, although a smaller amount would probably be paid to those counted as 'children'. It would be an equal amount paid to every legal resident, subject to some practical rule of time lived in the country. It would replace most other benefits, although supplements would be provided to certain groups with special needs, such as those with disabilities. As such, it would not be as radical as either its critics or some of its proponents like to believe. To some extent, it would amount to a consolidation of the patchwork of existing transfers coupled with a reduction in the number of conditions and administrative layers that exist today.

The standard objections to a basic income are that it would be too expensive, it would reduce labour supply, would offend some notion of 'social reciprocity', would weaken governments' resolve to lower unemployment, and would weaken the use of a minimum wage. These objections are dealt with at length elsewhere. Here we will just deal with the main ones, while concentrating on the advantages of moving in the direction of separating basic income security from any labour obligation.

First, a CIG would be a means of integrating the tax and benefit system and consolidating much of the existing patchwork of out-of-work, in-work and out-of-labour-market income transfers and paternalistically provided social and personal services. In doing so, the gross cost would be the cost of shifting to a universal income support scheme, which would be the cost of including those currently not included. The net cost would be less because there would be a saving on the administrative costs of policing the wide range of different conditions and tests for existing benefits. There would also be a further saving that would be hard to estimate, as the removal or reduction of poverty traps, unemployment traps and savings traps would encourage more income-earning activity and more legal work activity. This is because individuals would start paying tax on any income earned above the basic income, and would not face a very high marginal tax rate going from non-employment to employment, or crossing a threshold of income. As for the alleged cost of 'churning' – paying out to everybody and taxing it back from most people – this objection is disappearing because of the integration of tax and benefit systems made possible by electronic processes.

The cost of existing systems is systematically underestimated. The systems across Europe are riddled with poverty traps, unemployment traps, savings traps and *behaviour traps* that are arbitrary, inefficient and inequitable. This is partly because of the spread of selective, means-tested and behaviour-conditioned schemes. It is also partly because of the growing flexibility of working patterns and lifestyles. The response of bureaucrats and politicians almost everywhere has been to tighten conditions for entitlement and extend paternalistic controls.

Whatever the truth about long-term trends away from 'permanent' full-time employment, it is in principle desirable that more people at all ages move in and out of the labour force, take temporary jobs, combine several income-earning activities, and in the process do not conform to the simple three-stage model of life and work made the norm of industrial society, going straight from school or college into thirty or forty years of employment and then sharply shuffling off the stage into retirement. Means-tested benefits are scarcely appropriate for such a society, and nor are those arbitrary behavioural tests that technocratic 'Third Way' policymakers and their special advisers love so much.[37]

A common criticism of basic income is that it would be a 'handout', which would offend a sense of social reciprocity and lead to a fall in labour supply, idleness, shirking, and a lack of discipline in jobs. This is a criticism from across the political spectrum. There are two ways of meeting it, one defensive and one normative. In assessing its validity either way, bear in mind that most advocates of a basic income envisage a modest amount sufficient just to cover basic subsistence needs, equivalent to the minimum income of social assistance schemes applied in many European countries.[38]

The defensive or pragmatic response to the criticism is to suggest that any adverse effect would be small or insignificant.[39] The criticism presumes a pessimistic interpretation of the human species. We work for many reasons, and numerous surveys indicate that most people want to work and would do so even if they had enough income from other sources on which to subsist. Very few people are satisfied with basic subsistence, and aspire to much more; this is rather well known. In any case, there are two types of person who could be expected to reduce their labour supply, those with a high opportunity cost of doing income-earning activity (i.e., those wanting to pursue education or training, those wishing to care for relatives, those in poor health, etc.) and those doing low-productivity and/or onerous forms of labour. In both cases, we should want to induce labour market and policy changes that would be welfare enhancing. In the case of those with more socially or personally valuable non-labour activity, surely cutting back on a labour activity would be desirable. In the case of the person who withdrew from or cut back on the amount of time spent doing a low-productivity, onerous job, there would be a tendency for wages to go up, inducing others to fill the gap, or a tendency for labour-saving technological change to be introduced, or even for people to realize that they did not want or need those jobs performed.

Another standard criticism of a basic income is that it would offend some *reciprocity principle*. This 'principle', so favoured by Third Wayists and compassionate conservatives, is dealt with elsewhere. And as antidotes to its charms, several papers for the BIEN Congress are recommended reading.[40] The 'sexist bias' implicit in the policymakers' resort to it is also nicely brought out by a quotation from Nancy Fraser:

> The free-rider worry, incidentally, is typically defined androcentrically as a worry about shirking paid employment. Little attention is paid, in contrast, to a far more widespread problem, namely, men's free riding on women's unpaid domestic labour (Fraser, 1994, p. 615).

Leaving aside all the intricacies of the reciprocity principle, the normative response to the criticism about the effect on labour supply is based on an interpretation of the emerging mainstream character of twenty-first century capitalism, and returns us to that earlier digression. We live in an era when globalization and market capitalism are eroding the social welfare and regulatory framework so painstakingly erected during the twentieth century – and so assiduously presented to the rest of the world as the model to follow. One should not be too sentimental about the erosion, since the era of welfare state capitalism had many flaws and limitations. Equally importantly, we should not be lulled into thinking that the ill-defined 'European social model' has essentially survived and is resilient enough to be sustainable with minor refinements.

While we should neither exaggerate nor belittle the changes taking place, it is reasonably clear that under the aegis of global market forces there is a widespread loss of identity – of class, community and occupation. Belonging to a fixed group is becoming harder. And yet there is a paradox – *individualization with homogenization,* or in plain language a tendency for people to be on their own, seemingly an individual, while all rushing to adopt a similar lifestyle, buying the same goods, watching the same films and TV shows, and so on. We live under incessant pressure to consume, and to labour to earn enough, which is never enough. Accordingly, at least in the middle years of life more and more people are driven into an intense frenzy of labour-related activity. The story is too well known to need elaboration here. Electronic control systems, represented by personal computers, with their imperatives of email and the internet, and by mobile phones, are only one side of this intensification, in which the borders of workplace and home, and of leisure and work, are blurred. We are losing control of time. This is not a 'middle-class' phenomenon only, because the poor everywhere have rarely had any control to lose.

Providing a basic income as a citizenship right, in providing a sense of basic security, would help in the necessary process of gaining control over the sense of time – more freedom from domination.[41] It would allow for more rational deliberation, more freedom in which to make choices about how to allocate time. Here I want to suggest a link with that earlier digression. We possess time as a collective asset, liberated by the efforts of past generations. Yet the privileged are able to enjoy a disproportionate share of liberated time. A basic income would be a means of sharing it more equally and fairly.

A related way of arguing for a basic income is by reflecting on the social struggles in the past century as capitalism has evolved. Broadly speaking, the progressive struggle in the early days of the twentieth century was to secure societal control over the means of production and to decommodify labour. This led to the policy of nationalization both of production and the welfare state. The latter was, in effect, a way of *decommodifying labour,* alongside corporate benefits and services, in which the wage became a smaller share of total compensation and of personal income, as state benefits and services grew. This strategy tended to produce rigidities and inefficiencies that became unsustainable as the era of open economies emerged, and it was also always paternalistic, giving labour-based security at the price of limited freedom of choice. Under globalization, there has been a recommodification of labour, with individualized wages, a cut in enterprise and state benefits and services (or a shift to user-paying schemes) and a weakening of protective statutory regulations. The challenge ahead is to ensure that while labour is commodified, the worker (labour power) is not. A basic income could help make that a reality.

In short, a basic income could reduce the commodification of people (commodification implying loss of control over key social assets, namely time and security) while allowing for the continued commodification of *labour*. In this, it would be compatible with a globalized economic system, while eroding the power of capital over people. It could also give rise to a twenty-first century form of Keynesianism, since it would provide a means of stabilizing aggregate demand.

10.2 The Dilemmas with COAG

Now let us consider the currently topical idea of capital grants. A COAG would be a one-off grant given to twenty-one-year-olds, or spread over several years in certain circumstances, and given to all those who had graduated from secondary school, excluding 'drop-outs' and those who have foolishly criminalized themselves before they reached that age. The UK 'baby bond' scheme would not apply such conditions, apparently.[42]

By contrast, a CIG would provide *basic* economic security, through which to avert the worst excesses of labour commodification, and it would do so in an essentially non-moralistic way. It would not make a judgment on *when* a person deserves a blast of security, and would not make any moralistic judgment about who should receive it and who should be excluded. A COAG seems to fail on both these scores. Giving a twenty-one-year-old a huge lump sum offends the idea of *basic* security. It is also arbitrary, because the age twenty-one is not necessarily ideal or optimal; people mature at widely different ages, and their capabilities develop differently. In addition, the development of a capacity to make rational choices will vary across individuals and groups and communities. And excluding those twenty-one-year-olds who have been criminalized or who have failed to complete high school seems both moralistic and arbitrary, as well as inegalitarian.[43] A COAG offers enhanced security, wealth and future income for the more secure (the middle class) relative to the least-secure groups in society. It thereby offends the Security Difference Principle.

A COAG is also not neutral in terms of what type of behaviour it encourages and rewards. It offers to benefit the commercially astute over those who have no commercial acumen. In what way is that fair? A COAG would enhance the opportunity of the already relatively talented (high-school graduates without criminal records) to become winners in a winners-take-all, losers-lose-all market society. Further, both a COAG and a CIG would be given to individuals. A danger is that schemes for individuals can be depicted as *individualistic*, i.e. encouraging and facilitating selfish and opportunistic behaviour and attitudes. Surely a Good Society could not come about if policies and institutions were to promote individualistic behaviour in the absence of policies to facilitate *social solidarity*? One of the concerns about a block grant such as a COAG is that it would indeed foster the ethos of competitive individualism, while further eroding the already weak sense of social solidarity in most industrialized societies. It is definitely not neutral in that respect.

As globalization gathered strength in the last quarter of the twentieth century, governments all over the world moved to cut back on policies that were mechanisms of social solidarity and to create more individualistic systems, limiting protective regulations, putting controls on unions, and cutting back on redistributive direct taxation. These trends accelerated the growth of more fragmented labour markets and social structures. How would a COAG affect this? It might give more meaning to *equality of opportunity*. But it would be equalizing the opportunity to become more unequal. It would not affect the societal fragmentation or resultant inequalities in a direct way. By contrast, a CIG would strengthen the income security (albeit modestly) of those we have called *outsiders*, and would increase the bargaining position of 'flexiworkers', simply because increasing basic security usually strengthens backbones. Presuming that increased bargaining capacity would result in their obtaining higher incomes, this would thereby help to reduce inter-class income differentiation.

What about the impact of a COAG and a CIG on the so-called self-employed, a poorly named group that includes a lot of people working on contract or on a piecework basis? On the face of it, both a COAG and a CIG would boost the *supply* of self-employed, including the number of petty capitalists (all those 'small-is-beautiful' enterprises), for whom a grant would help in dealing with set-up costs whereas a CIG would make risk-taking less daunting. But one cannot be so confident about the impact on *demand* for the self-employed workers' goods and services, which might be such that average net incomes would fall among this group, even widening the income differential between them and those employed in (core) wage labour. This is an empirical issue.

The COAG also seems more problematical in that, by targeting young labour force entrants, it is in effect a subsidy to the young that gives them an advantage over older workers.[44] As such, it suffers from the defects of any selective subsidy. It would enable the young to accept lower wages, and thus help them displace older, more experienced workers. This could, on certain assumptions, actually lower overall productivity, and even output, of the self-employed as a group. It might also have negative effects on the skill-repro-duction propensities of older workers, discouraging them from trying to update or enlarge their skills because they would face a double competitive disadvantage (being older, and facing a subsidized competitor group in the labour market). By contrast, a CIG does not give one group an inbuilt advan-tage, and if anything would help to reduce segregation. This is an advantage of a universal income scheme.

Finally, in thinking of a COAG on its own terms, one must allow that such a concentrated influx of money targeted on one narrowly-defined age group is almost certain to raise the price of goods and services consumed by that age group – good news for surf-board makers, bad news for thirty-year-old new surfers. And interest rates for loans to this age group will tend to rise. The out-come could be that much of the transfer would go to other groups, leaving the young little better off.

10.3 A COAG Versus a COG

A more general concern with a COAG is that it fills the space that could be occupied by another variant of a capital grant fulfilling the laudable objec-tives of the COAG's proponents and the dictates of a Good Society, without the behavioural and distributional drawbacks. What are the *ideal* properties of a utopian capital grant scheme? Before considering that, let us consider the semantics.

What attracts us to the underlying idea of a capital or stakeholding grant is that it suggests a capital *sharing* device, coupled with a *participatory* component and a *redistributive* capacity. The principal proponents of the COAG use the term Stakeholding Grant, which has these connotations. However, in fact they are liberals and are primarily concerned with what they believe are the scheme's *freedom-enhancing* characteristics, rather than its redistributive egali-tarian properties (which are not too hot). One does not doubt the laudable motives, but the term is misleading. And in using the term 'stakeholding' they tend to block consideration of genuinely more utopian capital-sharing or stakeholding ideas.

Now let us consider the big question. If what is attractive about the idea of stakeholding or a capital grant is a complex image of sharing, redistribution, participation and freedom-enhancement, then we could say that, in terms of that Good Society, the *optimum* design of a scheme is that it should (1) encour-age, or at least not discourage, investment, (2) encourage investment that is more ecologically and socially responsible, (3) redistribute income to the most insecure and disadvantaged groups in society, (4) promote participation in economic and social activities, (5) strengthen (or at least not weaken) a sense of *social solidarity*, (6) strengthen real democracy, (7) promote good 'corporate governance', and (8) limit economic opportunism.

No scheme could do well on all these counts. And neither CIG nor COAG address most of these issues directly and are not intended to do so. However, unlike a CIG, a COAG might be seen as occupying the space for a more progressive stakeholding grant.

In this respect, there is surely more to be gained by promoting moves towards *economic democracy through collective forms of profit sharing*. This brings to mind something like the early version of the Swedish *wage-earner funds*, as proposed by Rudolf Meidner, and even the Alaska Permanent Fund.[45] We may call the ideal a COG (Community Capital Grant). Its exact shape should reflect the emerging character of the productive system and the distributive system emanating from it.

A COG is close to what seemed to be at the heart of the 'stakeholder capitalism' debates that emerged in the late 1980s and early 1990s, when stakeholding was primarily seen as a quasi-Keynesian method of promoting growth and employment. The emphasis was on *profit-related pay*, but many economists also touted collective profit sharing for incentive and capital-sharing reasons. Most crucially, any desirable COG scheme must be at least partly *collective*, must go beyond the firm as a unit, and must allow for workers and their representatives to have a Voice in decisions over the use of the resultant funds. The democratic governance is crucial. The main difficulties with a purely company-oriented approach to stakeholding is that it would exclude the 'flexiworkers' (casual workers, contract workers, agency workers, etc.) on the edges of companies; and it would be a scheme that would widen inequalities between workers in high-tech, high-profit, tradable firms relative to those working in or for low-tech, non-profit-oriented and non-tradable firms and organizations, including those working in public social services.

This is why an ideal model of capital-sharing or stakeholding should have a broader *community* element, which might take the form of a *social investment fund*, by which a percentage share of profits would go into a fund that would be governed democratically, as a means of social infrastructural and skill development. Such a fund could be broken into one component for re-investment inside the firm and another that would be for the community outside the firm, which would facilitate redistribution to those other than the privileged insiders.[46]

If properly designed, a COG could limit the leakage of capital from the national and local economy, because a key point of the system should be a restructuring of corporate governance, with the social investment fund participants having voting rights on firms' investment strategies as stakeholders in their own right.[47] This contrasts with the classic so-called Anglo-American model of shareholder capitalism, because in the latter the *principals* (shareholding elites, including nominal salaried employees) are only interested in their income, which comes mainly from shares.[48]

As such, there are good reasons for thinking that a COG could combat the biggest threat to the emergence of a moderately egalitarian capitalism, by providing a capital-sharing scheme with inbuilt mechanisms to limit capital flight. Whether or not companies report that tax rates on corporate profits and capital are influential in determining their location and marginal investment decisions, the fact is that, over the past twenty years, country after country has reduced or abolished taxes on capital. A sensibly constructed COG could check capital flight and encourage high and socially responsible investment in the local economy. It would also make for a greater degree of participation in corporate and communal decision-making and so encourage economic democracy. This is what stakeholding should be all about.

The proponents of COAG have sold it as a stakeholder grant, and have claimed that it would be 'democratic'. Yet it is neither an extension of democracy nor a reflection of stakeholding in the production process. By contrast, a COG would be an extension of real democracy – economic democracy – and would be real capital-sharing.

Almost incidentally, a COG would also have the potential to improve the way people live and work (unlike the commercialized individualistic frenzy that would be opened up by a generous COAG). By giving workers and working communities a greater Voice inside firms *and* inside the surrounding communities, a COG would tend to give workers a means of altering labour relations and workplace organization, so taking the place of the weakening Voice of old-style trade unionism.

A COAG is a populist measure, in the proper sense of that emotive term. It is likely to appeal most to those who do not have a stake in the system, but it does not touch the basic *structure* of capitalism. In that sense, it is profoundly un-utopian. One could imagine TV chat shows and tabloids having endless items on 'how Jane splurged her $80,000', and another patting Jim on his broadening shoulders for having been an exemplary young adult in investing his money well.[49] There would be a splurge of sentimentality. If anything it would help legitimize the unequal society by encouraging people to adopt a casino-type set of attitudes.[50]

By contrast, a basic income is a low-key measure that could reduce the extent of frenzied commercialism, facilitating and encouraging a more gentle pace of life, and facilitating the sort of workstyle that is the essence of all

Utopias painted throughout the ages, a mix of labour force work, care work, voluntary community work and constructive leisure.[51] It would not discourage work *per se*, and would actually encourage labour compared with the current means-tested social assistance, through weakening poverty traps and unemployment traps.

11. Towards a New 'Social Contract'

The celebrated social policy thinker of the middle period of the twentieth century, T.H.Marshall, pointed out that the eighteenth century was when civil rights became established as the legitimate goal of social reform, the nineteenth century was when political rights became legitimized, and the twentieth century was when social rights became recognized. One may predict that the twenty-first century will be the century of economic rights.

In that spirit, consider again the question posed at the outset: What is it that should be equalized in the Good Society of the twenty-first century? All theories of distributive justice believe in the equality of something. Third Wayism believes in equality of merit. Those who do their duty earn, or merit, social rights, which are based on labour. We see in this the attempted resurrection of the Weberian 'Puritan ethic'. Libertarians – and compassionate conservatives (who prefer a pot pourri of Third Wayism and libertarianism) – are less squeamish. They believe in procedural and contractual justice, and the equality of due process. As long as legally sanctioned procedures are followed correctly, unequal outcomes are not just acceptable but socially just. Dealing with the losers is left to charity and philanthropy, and good neighbours (even in the global village that they envisage, with billionaires disbursing their marginal millions to the causes they consider most worthy).

In contrast to the Third Wayists and libertarians, we assert that the answer to the great question is what might be called *complex egalitarianism*. The fundamental economic right is or should be a right to *equal basic security*. This requires a basic income, achieved in some way or another. However, in order to enable the vulnerable and less well-endowed to retain basic security, there must also be equal *Voice-representation security*, at the collective and individual levels.

Finally, the policies and institutions of social protection, regulation and redistribution must be based on the legitimation of *all* forms of work, not just labour. This is essential to give meaning to the *right to work*. We must not let paternalists of any kind – Third Wayists, religious groups, Leninists, populists or whatever – to turn that right into a duty. If you focus only on labour, or paid work, other forms of work are further debased and their performers probably more oppressed, and one perpetuates an ethos of competitive individualism

rather than one of what might be called social individualism based on a recognition – and celebration – of mutual interdependencies. So, policies must
ensure that equal protection is given to those doing 'jobs' and other forms of
work – care work, voluntary work, community work, ecological work, civil society work and all our creative enthusiasms. This means separating income security from the obligation to perform, or be willing to perform, mere *labour*.

The key example is the work of care or caring, which straddles the uneasy
division between a gift-relationship and a market-exchange relationship. If we
think of development as freedom, then our emphasis on basic security and
Voice as the two pillars of the Good Society means that we should want basic
income security for care-givers, surrogates of carers, and those needing care.
There should also be equally strong Voice for both sides of the relationship.
Rethinking care work in the context of ageing and the fragmentation of
old-style norms of family and household, leads to an answer to the second
question posed at the outset of this paper.

It is a vision of diversity, based on equality. Basic security should be what is
equalized, where security is defined in terms of freedom from morbidity, freedom from controls that fail the paternalism test, and equal good opportunity
to pursue our individual sense of occupation.

Freedom and complex egalitarianism – the pillars of the Good Society –
require basic security (the prerequisite for real freedom), capital-sharing (high
inequality being freedom-constraining) and basic Voice representation security (equally strong for all representative interests in society). Basic income
security, capital-sharing and Voice regulation should be the mainstays of the
Good Society. Without those three elements, the Society on offer would not
be worth visiting.

12. An Afterword – Legitimizing, Lobbying

Globalization is not incompatible with universal social protection, contrary to the
claims of those who fear pervasive 'social dumping'. This is the first point that we
must make again and again, and is well made by Bob Deacon (2002). However,
we must understand that for some time to come it will require a firm rebuttal of
the Jeremiahs. There can be a good alternative to a residual welfare state.

Basic income belongs to an expanding set of proposals for extending liberty
in an egalitarian way and for strengthening economic rights. Capital grants of
various types will continue to figure in that scenario. So too will the idea of
income vouchers and credits.[52] In this respect, one ingenious idea has been
proposed recently by Bruce Ackerman and Ian Ayres (2002) – a citizenship
voucher for political engagement. Simon Wigley, with good reason, holds that
'the incorporation of a citizen voucher into the basic income would help to

bring about democratic citizenship rather than just economic citizenship'.[53] No doubt that will evolve in unexpected directions. The problems of disengagement and the manipulative power of business interests are real enough. If some such action is not taken, democracy will become a melodramatic sickness. However, one must remain optimistic that enough people and organizations will coalesce for greater political security – democratic citizenship – just as they will for economic citizenship.

There are grounds for fear. One is the fear of electronic systems of control, coinciding with policymakers' increasing realization that they can use – and get away with using – tax and benefit policies as *fiscal regulation* to control individual and group behaviour. This is a threat to real freedom and to the development of that Good Society based on occupation – dignified or decent work. The politics of paradise will defeat that.

When BIEN was established in 1986, most relevant observers, to the extent that they took any notice at all, were prone to dismiss the proponents of basic income as 'mad, bad and dangerous to know'. Scepticism came from the political left as well as from the right. What struck many of us was the *vehemence* of the opposition, often coming from people who stated just as vehemently that they wanted to combat poverty and inequality. The problem was that the idea of basic income security united strange bedfellows – leftist paternalists (labourists) did not like the emphasis on individual liberty, rightist paternalists did not like the emphasis on equality.

Attitudes have softened since then. There is still some way to go, but as Tony Atkinson has argued, the idea of basic income has been moving up the political ladder. Yet as Steven Shafarman points out, in recalling Franklin Roosevelt's exhortation to lobbyists for a policy that he liked, it is necessary for advocates and supporters to turn more to putting pressure on the policymakers and politicians.[54] This is the future. It starts now.

Notes

1 Some of the themes in this introductory chapter are elaborated in a recent book: Standing (2002).
2 For a fascinating discussion of the evolution of universalism in Scandinavian welfare states, see Chapter 20 by Nanna Kildal and Stein Kuhnle.
3 The terms 'employable' and 'employability' have been hugely influential in European policymaking circles. The emphasis is always on altering the characteristics of people, including their attitudes and behaviour, so as to make them more pliable, adaptable, disciplined and so on. Rarely does one see anything like as much attention being given to making jobs more workable, or whatever the equivalent term might be.
4 Even in Ireland, one of the fastest growing of all industrialized economies, the percentage of people living with incomes below the poverty line has increased substantially. See Healy and Reynolds (2002).

5 See Chapter 17 by Wolfgang Strengman-Kuhn.

6 Even in a country such as Finland, where traditionally a very high proportion did receive unemployment benefits, reforms in the 1990s have reduced the share to a minority, as brought out in a paper for this Congress by Aho and Virjo (2002).

7 Over the past decade, the average age has risen by about one year for women and half a year for men.

8 In the United Kingdom – admittedly near the extreme in this respect – it is projected that in 2003, 25 million people (43% of the entire population) will be on means-tested benefits. This will include about half of all pensioners.

9 Think of Thomas More's *Utopia*, or the idyllic crafts community on the Thames painted by William Morris in *News from Nowhere*, or the favourites from other cultures and traditions.

10 The lack of a progressive vision may have contributed to the precipitous drop in membership of political parties of the left. In 1988, the French *parti socialiste* had 200,000 members; in 2002, it had only 80,000. In the UK, membership of the Labour Party declined between 1997 and 2001 by almost 100,000, while activism by its members declined even more dramatically – most do not do any work for the Party (*The Guardian*, June 18, 2002, p. 11).

11 Is 'freedom' the freedom to be bombarded by advertisments and incessant noise – simulated nature included – in shops, in the streets, in work, and in other hitherto social spaces? People seem to be responding to the public noise by retreating into an illusion of private space, listening to 'walkmen', sending text messages endlessly to 'friends', and so on. This retreat from society is called *hikikomori* in Japan, a terrified withdrawal from the clamour and confusion of the outside world (Inoki, 2001).

12 These are also lacking for the poor almost everywhere, although some mistakenly portray the poor as having ample time. In reality, because they lack 'time-saving' devices and because they have access only to low-productivity activities, they have to spend more time to achieve any given income, and have to spend more time on sheer survival activities.

13 Over 30 years ago, Steffan Linder wrote a book called *The Harried Leisure Class* depicting the increased goods-intensity of non-working time. The problem is more general now.

14 While preparing this paper, a report was published showing that most high-school graduates in the USA did not have even a basic grasp of their country's history, let alone know much about the rest of the world's history.

15 Chapter 11 by Torsten Meireis, p. 131.

16 For development of the criticisms, see Standing (2002).

17 Among relevant contributions, see Zelleke (2002). For a critique of workfare reforms, see Chapter 34 by Joel Handler.

18 Walter van Trier (1995) has chronicled the debates in the early part of the twentieth century. Walter has extended his interest to the conversion of André Gorz in the last decade of the century, as indicated in his paper for the Congress.

19 Milton Friedman proposed a 'negative income tax' in his 1962 book, *Capitalism and Freedom*. In a recent exchange with Eduardo Suplicy, he has said that he sees basic income and a negative income tax as similar.

20 Chapter 19 by Jan Otto Andersson and Olli Kangas, p. 267.

21 See Chapter 15.

22 See Chapter 7.

23 In case anybody should think basic income is a 'leftist' proposal, it is worth adding that Mimi was a staunch member of the British Conservative Party, as was her benefactor,

Sir Brandon Rhys Williams, who in turn drew his inspiration from his mother, who had advocated it many years earlier.

24 For his later view, see Gorz (1997).

25 See also Etienne (1998). For a review of the debates that have taken place in the Canton of Fribourg, see Bertrand Oberson (2003).

26 On the developments in Brazil, see papers for the BIEN Congress by Lena Lavinas, Marcelo Silva, Leonardo Basso and Fernando de Pinho, and Eduardo Suplicy.

27 See the papers by Pieter le Roux, Michael Samson (et al), Heidi Matisonn and Jeremy Seekings, Haroon Bhorat, and Guy Standing (Standing and Samson, 2003). See also the Report of the Commission on the Comprehensive Reform of Social Security, Cape Town, 2002.

28 Chapter 24 by Theresa Funiciello and Chapter 25 by Michael Opielka. See also Daly (ed.) (2002).

29 On this subject, see Chapter 6 by Ron Dore and Chapter 5 by Roswitha Pioch.

30 *Inter alia*, Eduardo Suplicy proposes eco taxes and wealth taxes to pay for a basic income in Brazil.

31 *BIRG Bulletin*, No.7, Spring 1988, p. 1. The BIRG subsequently became the Citizen's Income Trust.

32 For an argument against this, see Standing (2002).

33 Chapter 33 by Scott Goldsmith.

34 Recent advocates have included John Roemer. See also, Standing (2002).

35 Ackerman and Alstott (1999) is the main work proposing this. See also Morley-Fletcher (1998). An antecedent in the USA was Haveman (1988).

36 Parenthood for the 'baby bond' idea is somewhat contested: Kelly and Lissauer (2000); Nissan and Le Grand (2000).

37 Across Europe and other industrialised countries there are thousands of variants. Thus, only if You, as an unemployed youth, look for a job three times a week and have written evidence to show you are prepared to travel to work 20 miles from home are you entitled to a benefit. Only if You, a disabled elderly person, have less than £2,000 (or Euros) in savings can you be entitled to a grant to pay for care services. Of course, we exaggerate. But we all have our favourites.

38 Some advocates, including Philippe van Parijs, have in mind a larger amount. Most envisage a modest amount, just enough to cover the basics in life. It is possible that a lot of confusion in the debate arises from different images of what level of basic income is envisaged.

39 This is exposed, brilliantly, in Karl Widerquist's paper for the BIEN Congress, based on a review of no less than 345 'scholarly articles' (Chapter 31). He essentially concludes that all the empirical research done was inconclusive, which did not stop ideological opponents from drawing exaggerated conclusions. Karl makes an even more telling point in his own conclusions. For a good assessment on labour supply in France, see Chapter 30 by Didier Balsan, Claude Gamel and Josiane Vero.

40 Besides papers cited earlier, see chapter 26 by Erik Christensen. Also recommended is Karl Widerquist's 'alternative paper', *Who exploits who?* (2002).

41 Chapter 16 by Daniel Raventós and David Casassas.

42 Note that an advantage of the baby bond over the Ackerman-Alstott proposal is that, presumably, no recipient would have a criminal record, so it would be more universal.

43 It also offends a basic principle of justice, that a person should not be punished twice for the same offence. One senses that the proposal to exclude those who have fallen foul of the justice system is merely a sop to gain middle-class political support for the COAG.

44 Also, of course, it would worsen the relative and absolute position of the youth who have been criminalized or who have dropped out of school. This is an inegalitarian feature of the COAG. Another distorting aspect is that it would alter inter-generational relations, notably inside families. A COAG would give teenagers or 21-year-olds financial freedom from their parents, compromising parental guidance and potentially severing inter-generational ties. One may or may not like that prospect; one should not ignore it.

45 Both emerged in the mid-1970s, the last time when a redistributive agenda was in the ascendancy.

46 Of course, deciding what is 'the community' is a political and administrative matter. Although it had earlier antecedents (Paine et al), the modern thrust to this way of thinking was Rudolf Meidner's original version of 'wage-earner funds' in Sweden in the mid-1970s. This was partly stimulated by the strains in the Swedish *solidaristic wage policy*, and in particular by the way Volvo was bypassing the wage policy by introducing individual profit-sharing pay, thereby increasing wage inequality.

47 The *agents* would become part-*principals*, just as many managers and chief executives have become largely *principals* (receiving most of their income from capital).

48 The Enron implosion is indicative of the danger of having elite *principals* divorced from the *agents*, which management is expected to be in shareholder capitalism. If corporate executives receive most of their income from share options rather than from their salary, they will not have the interest of their workforce very high on their priority list.

49 Hissing and loud clapping in the studio would be amplified, with appropriate music.

50 I recall visiting 'middle-class' families in small-town Pennsylvania who were living from State lottery to State lottery, all their hopes crystallised in the monthly set of numbers. Is this freedom?

51 A CIG would also reduce the widespread tendency, induced by flexible labour markets and the international trend to conditionality and means-tested state benefits, for much labour to drift into the grey or illegal economy, evading taxes and contributions, and thereby contributing to pervasive disentitlement. For instance, a CIG would do away with the arbitrary conditionality of unemployment insurance benefits, which have long been a misnomer.

52 For example, Morley-Fletcher (2002).

53 Chapter 32 by Simon Wigley.

54 Chapter 14 by Steven Shafarman.

References

Ackerman, B. and Alstott, A. 1999. *The stakeholder society* (New Haven, Yale University Press).

———— and Ayres, I. 2002. *Voting with dollars: A new paradigm for campaign finance* (New Haven, Yale University Press).

Aho, S. and Virjo, I. 2002. More selectivity in unemployment compensation in Finland: Has it led to activation or increased poverty?, in G. Standing (ed.), *Minimum Income Schemes in Europe* (Geneva, ILO).

Atkinson, A.B. 1995. *Public economics in action: The basic income/flat tax proposal* (Oxford, Oxford University Press).

———— 1996. 'The case for a participation income', in *The Political Quarterly*, Vol. 67, No.1, January-March 1996, pp. 67–70.

Brittan, S. and Webb, S. 1990. *Beyond the welfare state* (Aberdeen University Press).

Cantillon, B., Marx, I. and Van den Bosch, K. 2002. 'Welfare state protection, labour markets and poverty: Lessons from cross-country comparisons', in G. Standing (ed.), *Minimum Income Schemes in Europe* (Geneva, ILO).

Cruz-Saco, M. 2002. *A basic income policy for Peru: Can it work?*, paper presented at the 9th BIEN Congress, Geneva, September 2002.

D'Addio, A., De Greef, I. and Rosholm, M.2002. Assessing unemployment traps in Belgium using panel data sample selection models, in G. Standing (ed.), *Minimum Income Schemes in Europe* (Geneva, ILO).

Daly, M. (ed.). 2002. *Care work: The quest for security* (Geneva, ILO).

Deacon, B. 2002. *Tracking the global social policy discourse: From safety nets to universalism*, paper presented at the 9th BIEN Congress, Geneva, September 2002.

Dommen, E. 2002. Si tout est donné, pourquoi travailler? La gratuité de la grace, l'allocation universelle et l'éthique de travail, in A. November and G. Standing (eds.), *Un revenue de base pour chacun(e)* (Geneva, ILO).

Etienne, E. 1998 *Vers un Revenu minimum...a Genève: expériences et perspectives*, Mémoire de diplome, Lausanne, Institut de hautes études en administration pulique (IDHEAP).

Fraser, N. 'After the family wage: Gender equity and the welfare state', *Political Theory*, Vol. 22, No.4, p. 615.

Gorz, A. 1985. 'L'allocation universelle: Version de droite and version de gauche', in *Revue Nouvelle*, No. 81, pp. 419–28.

_____ 1997. *Misère du present, richesse du possible* (Paris, Galille).

Harvey, P. 2002. *Human rights and economic policy discourse: Taking economic and social rights seriously*, paper presented at the 9th BIEN Congress, Geneva, September 2002.

Haveman, R. 1988. *Starting even: An equal opportunity programme to combat the nation's new poverty* (New York, Simon and Schuster).

Healy, S. and Reynolds, B. 2002. From poverty relief to universal entitlement: Social welfare and basic income in Ireland, in G. Standing (ed.), *Minimum income schemes in Europe* (Geneva, ILO).

Inoki, L. 2001. 'Why Tokyo turns a deaf ear to nature', in the *Financial Times*, September, p. XXII.

Kelly, G. and Lissauer, R. 2000. *Ownership for all* (London, Institute for Public Policy Research).

Kunnemann, R. *Basic income: A State's obligation under the human right to food*, paper presented at the 9th BIEN Congress, Geneva, September, 2002.

Mon, J-P. 2002. *Pour une conditionnalité transitoire*, paper presented at the 9th BIEN Congress, Geneva, September 2002.

Morley-Fletcher, E. 1998. *Basic stock vs. basic income*, opening address, BIEN Congress, Amsterdam, September 10–12.

_____ 2002. *Vouchers and personal welfare accounts: New tools for socio-economic security*, paper presented at the 9th BIEN Congress, Geneva, September 2002.

Nissan, D. and Le Grand, J. 2000. *A capital idea: Start-up grants for young people* (London, Fabian Society).

November, A. 2002. 'Le revenu minimum social à Genève: douze ans de débats politiques', in A. November and G. Standing (eds.), *Un revenue de base pour chacun(e)* (Geneva, ILO).

Oberson, B. 2002. 'Les mesures d'insertion sociale dans le canton de Fribourg', in A. November and G. Standing (eds.), *Un revenue de base pour chacun(e)* (Geneva, ILO).

Palma, G. 2002. *Income polarization in Latin America* (Geneva, ILO Socio-Economic Security Programme).

Parker, H. 1989. *Instead of the dole* (London, Routledge).

Silva, M., Basso, L. and de Pinho, F. 2002. *Tobin tax, minimum income and the eradication of famine in Brazil*, paper presented at the 9th BIEN Congress, Geneva, September 2002.

Standing, G. 2002. *Beyond the new paternalism: Basic security as equality* (London, Verso).

_____ and Samson, M. (eds.) 2003. *A basic income grant for South Africa* (Capetown, University of Cape Town Press).

Suplicy, E. 2002. *Renda de cidadania. A saida e pela porta* [Citizen's Income: The Exit is Through the Door] (São Paulo, Cortez Editora e Editora Fundação Perseu Abramo).

The World Bank 2002. *World Development Report* (Washington, D.C., The World Bank).

van Parijs, P. 1995. *Real freedom for all: What (if anything) can justify capitalism?* (Oxford, Clarendon Press).

van Trier, W. 1995. *Every man a king!* (Leuven, Departement Sociologie, Katholieke Universiteit Leuven).

_____ 2002. *Who Framed Social Dividend?* (University of Antwerp), mimeo.

Widerquist, K. 2002. 'Who exploits who?', Unpublished manuscript.

Zelleke, A. 2002. 'Radical pluralism: A liberal defence of unconditionality', paper presented at the 9th BIEN Congress, Geneva, September.

2

HOW BASIC INCOME IS MOVING UP THE POLICY AGENDA: NEWS FROM THE FUTURE

Anthony Atkinson[1]

1. Introduction

One morning some years in the future you, a citizen of Europe, wake up to the sound of the radio news: 'The Government has just announced the introduction of a basic income.' You doze off back to sleep, and then suddenly re-awake, having absorbed the news. 'How ever did we get to this situation?' you ask yourself. What scenario has led to the achievement of the dream of so many people, from Tom Paine to the Basic Income European Network? Is there some crucial detail that you have missed?

As Walter van Trier (1995) has aptly described, the idea of a basic income has had a cyclical history, going through periods of enthusiastic discovery followed by sceptical evaluation, and then fading away. There were, for example, the social dividend proposals made in the United Kingdom during and immediately after the Second World War. At that time, people had in mind a new beginning. The basic income, or social dividend, would have been a clean break with the past. Social policy was a 'green field site'. Here, however, I am concerned with how the basic income idea may emerge through a natural evolution of existing policy, with how basic income may be moving up the policy agenda. In planning terms, I am concerned with a 'brown field', rather than a 'green field', development.

In the paper I describe three possible answers to the question asked by the hypothetical radio listener. Looking back from the introduction of a basic income, how did we get there? The key lessons to be learned from this exercise in fictional history are summarized in the concluding section.

2. The Inexorable Rise of In-work Benefits

Each of the scenarios begins with a policy position that is well known to us today. We start from familiar territory, and from territory not apparently directly related to the final destination of a basic income (BI).

The first is the widespread drive towards *in-work benefits*. In a sense this *is* related to BI. One of the merits consistently claimed for BI is that it is paid to all, regardless of their labour market status. The fact that it cannot be said to distort the work/leisure choice is one of the planks on which BI supporters have campaigned. An influential book on the subject by Hermione Parker (1989) is called *Instead of the Dole*. In this respect, BI is seen as superior to social transfers paid conditional on people not being in work. Social insurance forms the backbone of social protection in most European countries, and has been designed in such a way as to minimize the distortionary impact (for example, by requiring job search activity and by disqualification in the case of voluntary job leaving). By insuring people against risk of job loss, social insurance has a positive function in attracting people into the labour force and in underwriting the modern employment relationship (Atkinson, 1999). But to the extent that these transfers have been generalized, and contribution conditions weakened, via the use of social assistance rather than social insurance, the impact on employment may become negative. Fears that this is the case have been one of the reasons for proposals for in-work benefits. The first Report on the European Economy by the European Economic Advisory Group at CESifo argued that 'traditional social programmes … have concentrated on replacing the earnings which are not enjoyed by those without jobs. [We propose an alternative] in which tax credits are used to supplement the wages available to low productivity workers' (Sinn *et al.*, 2002, p. 5).

The classic in-work benefit is child benefit, paid at a uniform rate for all children of a given age irrespective of the income or labour market status of their parents. Child benefit is in essence a BI for children. There has been a wide range of agreement among social security analysts and campaigners that child benefit should be the cornerstone of anti-poverty policy. Yet there have been two main problems. The first is that the level of the benefit has been too low. Beveridge (1942) proposed that child benefit should cover the 'subsistence' needs of a child. Applying the European Union risk-of-poverty criterion, and the Organization for Economic Cooperation and Development (OECD) scale, this requires that child benefit be a quarter of mean equivalent disposable income. Most, if not all, countries fall short. The second problem is that this strategy does not provide for the needs of adults or for households with no children.

The standard response to the first problem has been to seek a 'cheaper' solution by targeting transfers for children to those in families with low incomes. Selectivity has been the watchword. This principle underlay the introduction of the Family Income Supplement in the UK in 1971, which paid a sizeable transfer to families where at least one parent was in paid work but tapered the transfer with total family income. In other countries, benefits are paid via the income declared for income tax, but the effect is the same: the benefit is scaled-down with income. If there is a minimum hours condition, and a minimum hourly wage, generating a minimum monthly level of earnings, then a government can set the payment at this 'origin' (point O in Figure 2.1) sufficient to meet its poverty objective, S, but limit the benefit to those families with an income less than T (see the solid line in Figure 2.1). This is a process that began with families with children but which the UK Government plans to extend to other family types with the Working Tax Credit due to come into operation in 2003 (Brewer, Clark, and Myck, 2001).

But targeting comes at a cost. We have now had enough experience to know that there are two major shortcomings. First, the administration of the income test means that some people do not receive the benefit to which they are entitled: 'even in the most well regulated countries, studies have shown means-tested schemes have take-up rates as low as 20%' (Standing, 2002, p. 98). Where a scheme's operation requires people to make a claim on the basis of their income, a proportion fail to do so. There is none of the automatic quality associated with paying a BI each month into a person's bank account.

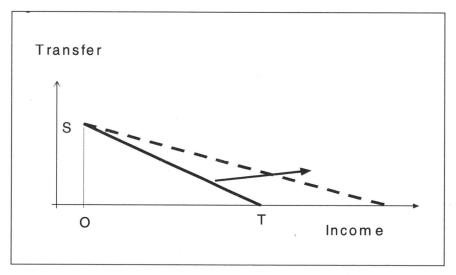

Figure 2.1 In-work income-tested benefit

Where the employer administers the scheme, some workers are deterred from claiming since they do not wish their employer to know their personal circumstances.

The second problem is the high marginal tax rate on earnings. The withdrawal of the transfer inevitably involves an increase in the total tax rate, whether the withdrawal is applied to gross earnings or to earnings net of income tax and social security contributions. The marginal tax rate with the present UK Working Families Tax Credit is, for a taxpayer, 69.4 per cent. This is substantially higher than the rate for top earners, which is 40 per cent.

The likely result of such a high marginal tax rate, combined with the positive income effect of the transfer, is that people are discouraged from working longer hours or changing to a better paid job. Of course, the conditionality provides a positive incentive, in that people may come back to work, or increase their hours to the minimum required to qualify. But once in receipt the targeting acts as a disincentive.

The effect of high marginal tax rates has been extensively analysed (Blundell, 2001), but this literature concentrates almost exclusively on the reactions of individual workers. Yet there are two other important players in the labour market: employers and trade unions. They too may react to the high marginal tax rates. Suppose that output depends on worker effort, which is continuously variable and is fully observable. Employers have a pay policy that relates wages in part to productivity. Workers determine their effort-level by taking account of the benefit to them in terms of the productivity bonus, but this is reduced by the marginal tax rate. Employers in turn take account of the workers' reaction when designing their remuneration policy. If the marginal tax rate is increased by the introduction of in-work income-related benefits, then the power of the bonus incentive is reduced, and the employer may react by reducing the productivity bonus proportion. The final effect, taking account of the employer reaction, may be a more marked reduction in effort and hence output. There are thus adverse consequences for productivity.

Consideration of the employers is important not only because they are separate actors, but also because it highlights how the effect of selective in-work benefits depends on the *proportion of the work force covered*. An employer has to devise a pay policy for the labour force as a whole. The fact that a small fraction of workers are receiving in-work benefits will not cause employers to change policy. With the extension of transfers up the income scale, it begins to have an effect. There is therefore a possibly unstable dynamic. Concerns about high marginal tax rates have led governments to amend the scheme. The point S is fixed, as it is necessary to meet the anti-poverty objective, so that the government swings the line round anti-clockwise. The new scheme is the dashed line in Figure 2.1, lowering the marginal tax rate but bringing more families into the benefit area. More employers find that their workers are affected, and more adjust their policies, generating a further reaction.

The reaction of employers to the high marginal tax rate is to reduce wages paid, and this may be seen as moderating wage pressure (see Lockwood, Sløk and Tranæs, 2000). The same applies to trade unions. It has been argued that progressive taxation reduces the marginal pay-off to a wage increase, giving unions less of an incentive to pursue wage increases at the expense of employment (Hersoug, 1984). On the other hand, the effect of the income-related transfer scheme is to raise the take-home pay of the non-unionized workers as well as the unionized, and in the simplest case these effects cancel.[1] Moreover, the union objective may be different from the utility or 'U' function (wage, employment) assumed in this literature. Unions may have a target net real wage (see Malcomson and Sartor, 1987, although it should be noted that their empirical evidence for Italy contradicts this formulation). If workers keep only a third of their net increase, this means that the union has to secure a €30 increase to get a €10 increase in take-home pay. Here again the proportion covered by the tax credit scheme is important. Unions negotiate on behalf of all their members. The fact that a few are receiving tax credits makes no difference, but once they begin to be a significant, and vocal, proportion, then the union will take account of the marginal tax rate.

It is here that we find the first possible explanation of the shock radio announcement. For we have to look at collective bargaining in the context of European monetary union (I am assuming that by this time the UK will have joined). With a common interest-rate policy, and constraints on fiscal policy, member-state governments will increasingly resort to old-fashioned measures. They are deeply worried that wage demands will make their goods uncompetitive, so that they intervene explicitly or implicitly in wage-setting. Using a tried and tested approach, they offer union leaders a deal: you moderate wage demands, and we will compensate you through the fiscal system. One consequence may well be the anti-clockwise swing in the in-work benefit schedule. This increases the net incomes of all recipients, so allowing union leaders to claim increased take-home pay. But the implied extension of coverage also means that the marginal tax rate (while lower) figures more prominently next time in wage demands. The dynamic is unstable, and the end result is likely to be a situation where virtually everyone is receiving a guaranteed payment of S and facing an increased tax rate. Which is how the BI came about.[2]

Is there a catch? Yes. The payment is conditional on working a minimum number of hours, or else qualifying for the out-of-work benefits (which means being available for work unless another condition is satisfied). In other words, the announcement was of a *participation income*, rather than an unconditional BI. The government has listened to Tony Atkinson rather than to Phillipe van Parijs. Surfers are not to be fed.

3. Crumbling Pension Pillars

The second possible starting point of our journey from the present to the hypothetical future is the well-known World Bank proposal for a three-pillar approach to pension provision. The study *Averting the Old Age Crisis* (World Bank, 1994) advocated a limited public pillar, modest in size, with the goal of alleviating poverty, combined with a second mandatory pillar based on fully-funded and privately-managed pensions, coupled with a third voluntary pillar. The move from funded to unfunded pensions has been seen as offering a solution to the problems of an ageing population via improved economic performance (Holzmann, 1999).

Again this has no direct link with BI, but we can see how a connection may emerge if we consider the design of the first pillar. The World Bank described at least three options: (a) a means-tested programme, (b) a minimum pension guarantee, and (c) a flat-rate insurance benefit. The main emphasis has been on the first. Concern with restraining public sector costs has led governments to use means-testing as a way of maximizing the contribution from other forms of support. The UK Labour Government elected in 1997 decided to give priority to the Minimum Income Guarantee (MIG), subject to both income and assets tests. This meant that the budget constraint facing people, as they consider saving for old age, has a horizontal segment, where an increase in the income from saving yields no benefit in terms of net income, as the MIG payment is reduced £1 for £1 – see the heavy line in Figure 2.2. (In fact, the implicit tax rate was over 100 per cent in view of the fact that the assumed income from capital exceeded that obtainable by the typical small saver.)

This generates a 'savings trap'. People who do not expect to save enough to clear the minimum guarantee in effect face a 100 per cent tax rate on their income. As a result, 'If people realize that they will face this position in advance, they may decide there is little point in saving or building up pension rights below a threshold' (Hills, 1993, p. 29). Again the impact depends on the numbers affected. For as long as a relatively small proportion of relatively less well-off pensioners faced the severe disincentive, then the issue received little attention. The raising of the MIG has however brought more people prospectively into the trap, and in the UK it has received extensive media coverage, making people more aware of the way in which 'if you've got your own private pensions, then you're penalized' (respondent to Financial Services Authority survey, quoted in *Citizen's Income Newsletter*, 2002, No. 2, p. 7).

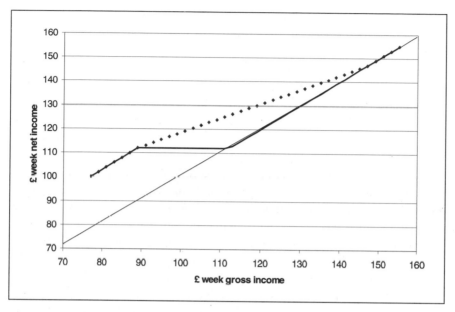

Figure 2.2 Pensioner credit in the United Kingdom

The savings trap undermines the third, voluntary pillar of pension provision. What about the second, mandatory pillar? The replacement of state pay-as-you-go pensions by a private funded scheme may appear straightforward. Suppose that the employer administers the private scheme. Assuming that the mandatory second tier offers workers terms no less favourable than private savings, at worst it displaces savings under the third pillar. But this ignores the fact that the savings trap still operates. A worker who sees no personal gain from the savings will regard the mandatory pension contributions as a reduction in the net wage, and part of the burden will be shifted to the employer. Employers will see their wage costs increased, just as they are increased by state scheme contributions.[1] Again the crucial feature is the percentage of the work force potentially affected by the savings trap. The generalization of means-tested pensions will call into question the acceptability of the second, mandatory tier.

To this one must add the declining confidence in funded pensions. The arguments for replacing pay-as-you-go pensions were in essence based on the rate of return to capital, r, exceeding the rate of growth of the wage bill, n. It is true that, in the early days of pay-as-you-go pensions, the extension of coverage allowed n to exceed its long-run value. Recognition that, in the future, n will be relatively low led to the enthusiasm for funding. But r has also been overstated in recent decades as a result of the revaluation of equities. There has been a fall in prospective returns, as competition has increased following globalization and market liberalization. It is now less evident that funding offers a panacea. In the same way, the ageing of the population has been seen as a problem for pay-as-you-go pensions, with the rise in the dependency ratio. But it also raises problems for funded pensions, as is evidenced by the increased funding requirements for defined benefit plans and by the worsening annuity rates for those with defined contribution funds.

More generally, there is increasing anxiety about pensions. This is not just a question of risk. Small savers have become accustomed to being told that 'investments can go down as well as up' or that there is a 10 per cent risk that the portfolio will not meet their target yield. Now, however, they have to come to terms with *uncertainty*, to use the phrase of Frank Knight (1921). Put crudely, uncertainty means that we cannot even list the events over which we need to form probabilities. It concerns the truly unexpected. For example, it would have been a particularly perspicacious investment adviser who warned you in the year 2000 that one ought to investigate the accounting practices of corporations. For most people, the accounting scandals came quite out of the blue.

All of this may lead us back to basic income, providing a second possible explanation for the radio announcement. The title of this Congress is 'Income Security as a Right'. How can this be assured for the elderly? For the reasons I have described, the World Bank's three pillars each look distinctly shaky, and governments may turn instead to an Old Age Basic Income (OABI). Payment of a basic income to all persons over a specified age, with no means testing, only taxation as under the income tax, would provide a secure base. It would allow people to make supplementary provision, either privately or via employer schemes or state schemes. The 'catch' is that the scheme would apply only to the elderly. Our hypothetical listener missed the first two words in the name of the new scheme. We would have child benefit for those aged under eighteen and OABI for the elderly, but nothing for those aged eighteen to sixty-four.

4. Taking Social Europe Seriously

The third point of departure is again one that is not directly linked with BI. The story begins in March 2000 at the European Summit in Lisbon, where EU Heads of State and Government decided that the Union should adopt the strategic goal for the next decade not only of becoming 'the most competitive and dynamic knowledge-based economy', but also of achieving 'greater social cohesion'. This reflected the feeling of many people that the social dimension of Europe deserved more priority. Later in 2000, at the Nice Summit, it was agreed to advance social policy on the basis of an open method of coordination, an approach that recognizes that, under the principle of subsidiarity, social policy remains the responsibility of member states (which is why the announcement of the introduction of a BI came from the national government, not Brussels). It was decided that each member state should implement a national two-year action plan for combating poverty and social exclusion, setting specific targets. The first National Action Plans on Social Inclusion were submitted in June 2001, and a further round is due in 2003.

As part of this process, the EU has developed a set of social indicators, embodying the commonly-agreed objectives (see Atkinson *et al.*, 2002). The Social Protection Committee established a Sub-Group on Social Indicators, whose report (Social Protection Committee, 2001) was accepted by the Employment and Social Affairs Council in December 2001, and now forms the basis for European Union policymaking. The indicators encompass financial poverty, income inequality, and regional variation in employment rates, long-term unemployment, joblessness, low educational qualifications, low life expectancy and poor health. A range of indicators was reported in the *Joint Report on Social Inclusion* (European Commission, 2002).

A key indicator is the number of Europe's citizens living in financial poverty. Measured in terms of the proportion living below 60 per cent of the median equivalent disposable household income, as shown for individual Member States in Figure 2.3, the overall EU income poverty rate was 18 per cent in 1997. In its Communication to the Spring European Council in

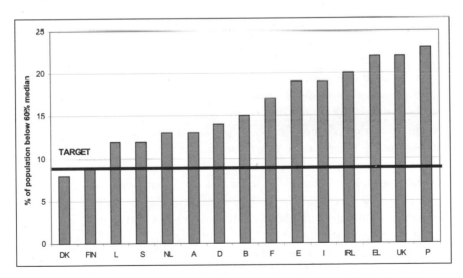

Note: DK = Denmark; FIN = Finland; L = Luxembourg; S = Sweden; NL = Netherlands; A = Austria; D = Germany; B = Belgium; F = France; E = Spain; I = Italy; IRL = Ireland; EL = Greece; UK = United Kingdom; P = Portugal.

Figure 2.3 Poverty rate in EU, 1997

Barcelona, the European Commission proposed that the European Council should set the target of halving the poverty rate to 9 per cent by 2010 (European Commission, 2002a, p. 16).[2]

Here we find a third possible explanation for the radio news announcement, and indeed for the first time an indication as to *when* it may happen. The Commission documents show the EU poverty rate as 18 per cent in 1997 and a series of blank entries until the target of 9 per cent in 2010. The aspiration is to reduce the numbers over the decade. In their National Action Plans, member states have set out a variety of policy initiatives (see Atkinson *et al.*, 2002; Ruxton and Bennett, 2002, and Atkinson, 2002). In a number of countries, these build on policies already in force. Ireland initiated its National Anti-Poverty Strategy (NAPS) in 1997, in response to the 1995 UN Social Summit in Copenhagen. In the UK in 1999, a high-profile commitment was made to eradicating child poverty in twenty years and halving it in ten (Blair, 1999).

The policies set in train by member states may well have significant effects, but many of them are long-term in their impact. Investment in human capital takes time to yield its full return. Many of the children benefiting from current policies will not enter the labour force until after 2010. Measures to activate those not currently in the labour force will require changes in social attitudes and culture that take time to bring about. Regional policies may involve investment in infrastructure. It is therefore quite possible that, as 2010 approaches, Europe's leaders will find themselves contemplating the need for more rapid action – or else have to admit that the aspiration is unattainable in the indicated timescale.

It is here that we find the third possible origin of the radio announcement. The most rapid effect can be achieved via cash transfers, and the introduction of a European BI provides for European leaders the lifeline they need. Each member state will be required to ensure a minimum basic income, related to average equivalent disposable income in their country. It is to be provided without test of means, since otherwise the impact may be undermined by incomplete take-up, but the form is to be determined, under subsidiarity, by member states. It could take the form of a minimum state payment, rolling up existing state payments. In the case of the elderly, for instance, additional payments would only be made where the existing pension income fell short of the minimum (see Atkinson *et al.*, 2002b, for an analysis of a European minimum pension). It could be household-based, reflecting the form of the poverty calculation. This would mean that a single man living with his parents would receive nothing if their existing state benefits, divided by the equivalence scale, were above the minimum.

The European BI would therefore be playing a clear political role, and this dictates its form. The 'catch' in this case is that it would be a *partial* BI. The rate would be set, not by an independent assessment of the income needed, but by a calculation of the figure required to achieve the target poverty reduction.

5. What Have we Learned?

From these three stories, I draw two main conclusions – apart from the obvious moral that campaigners should not give up. The first is that BI may be introduced in a less than ideal form. There may be a 'catch' in the government announcement, so that one has to listen to the details. But each of the incomplete BI schemes described here would be a step on the road. The second is the importance of exploiting existing trends in policy making. Politicians may not be persuaded by the pure logic of a BI but may support its introduction because it is the logical terminus of policies already in train (in-work benefits), because it resolves a policy dilemma (the pensions crisis), or because it advances the European agenda (poverty targets). One has to work with, not against, the flow, harnessing the economic and social situation to one's advantage. Otherwise, BI may remain simply a dream.

Notes

1　Nuffield College, University of Oxford, United Kingdom.
2　The key element is the elasticity of net union gain with respect to changes in the gross wage. The derivative is reduced by $(1-t)$, where t is the implicit tax rate, but with a constant taper the net gain versus the non-union wage is also reduced by the same amount.
3　After this was written, I received the *Citizen's Income Newsletter*, 2002, No. 2, reprinting Professor Patrick Minford's article from the *Daily Telegraph* (May 13, 2002), in which he argues that 'basic income could prove an escape route from the benefits trap'.
4　With the state scheme, the contributions are handed over at once; with the mandatory second tier pension, the process is less direct. The employer pays the contribution into a fund that becomes the property of the worker on retirement, who then hands it back to the Government in the form of a reduced MIG supplement.
5　The Presidency Conclusions refer to Member States 'being invited to set targets, in their National Action Plans, for significantly reducing the number of people at risk of poverty and social exclusion by 2010' (European Commission, 2002b, p. 5).

References

Atkinson, A. B. 1999. *The economic consequences of rolling-back the welfare state* (Cambridge, MIT Press).
_____ 2002. *Evaluation of the National Action Plans on Social Inclusion: The role of EUROMOD* (Cambridge, Microsimulation Unit), EUROMOD Working Paper.
Atkinson, T., Cantillon, B., Marlier, E. and Nolan, B. 2002a. *Social indicators: The EU and social inclusion* (Oxford University Press).
_____ 2002b. 'Microsimulation of social policy in the European Union: Case study of a European minimum pension', in *Economica*, Vol. 69, pp. 229–243 .
Beveridge, Sir William (later Lord) 1942. *Social insurance and allied services* (London, HMSO).

Blair, T. 1999. 'Beveridge revisited: A welfare state for the twenty-first century', in R. Walker (ed.) *Ending child poverty* (London, Policy Press).

Blundell, R. 2001. 'Welfare reform for low income workers', in *Oxford Economic Papers*, Vol. 53, pp. 189–214.

Brewer, M., Clark, T. and Myck, M. 2001. *Credit where it's due?* (London Institute for Fiscal Studies, Commentary 86).

European Commission 2002. *Joint report on social inclusion,* Directorate-General for Employment and Social Affairs (Brussels, European Commission).

———— 2002a. *The Lisbon strategy – Making change happen* Communication to the Spring European Council in Barcelona (Brussels, European Commission COM {2002} 14 final).

———— 2002b. *Presidency conclusions* (Brussels, Barcelona European Council).

Hersoug, T. 1984. 'Union wage responses to tax changes', in *Oxford Economic Papers*, Vol. 36, pp. 37–51 .

Hills, J. 1993. *The future of welfare* (York, Joseph Rowntree Foundation).

Holzmann, R. 1999. 'On economic benefits and fiscal requirements of moving from unfunded to funded pensions' in M. Buti *et al.* (eds.) *The welfare state in Europe* (Cheltenham, Edward Elgar), pp. 139–196 .

Knight, F. H. 1921. *Risk, uncertainty and profit* (Boston, Houghton Mifflin).

Lockwood, B., Sløk, T. and Tranæs, T. 2000. 'Progressive taxation and wage setting: Some evidence for Denmark', in *Scandinavian Journal of Economics*, Vol. 102, pp. 707–723.

Malcomson, J. M. and Sartor, N. 1987. 'Tax push inflation in a unionized labour market', in *European Economic Review*, Vol. 31, pp. 1581–1596 .

Parker, H. 1989. *Instead of the dole* (London, Routledge).

Ruxton, S. and Bennett, F. 2002. *Developing a coherent approach to child poverty and social exclusion across Europe* (Brussels, Euronet).

Sinn, H.-W., Vives, X. and others. 2002. *Report on the European economy 2002* (Munich, Ifo Institute for Economic Research).

Social Protection Committee 2001. *Indicators sub-group: Report from the Chairman to the SPC* (Brussels).

Standing, G. 2002. *Beyond the new paternalism* (London, Verso).

van Trier, W. 1995. *Every one a king* (Leuven, Departement Sociologie, Katholieke Universiteit Leuven).

World Bank (WB) 1994. *Averting the old age crisis* (Oxford, Oxford University Press).

3

CAN THERE BE A RIGHT TO A BASIC INCOME?

Raymond Plant[1]

1. Introduction

The aim of this paper is strictly limited. It will explore some of the characteristics of rights as they are generally conceived, features which in the view of critics entail that social and economic rights, including rights to income, cannot be regarded as genuine rights. I shall not seek to develop a general theory of rights because of limitations on space. Rather my approach will be more like an immanent critique: taking standard arguments against social and economic rights and showing either that they are not plausible or that they demonstrate too much from the point of view of their protagonists, since these arguments, if they were to be regarded as plausible, would actually undermine what these critics would regard as genuine rights, namely civil and political rights. I shall consider the arguments under the following headings:

- Rights and liberty;
- Rights, scarcity and obligations;
- Rights and needs.

2. Rights and Liberty

It is often argued that there is a close connection between rights and liberty: that rights exist and, indeed, are justified because they protect liberty. To be free is not to be coerced: not to be compelled to do something that one would not otherwise do or compelled to abstain from doing what one would otherwise do. Rights protect people from unjustified coercion and are therefore to be seen as central to the protection of liberty. On this view liberty has to be understood as negative freedom: freedom from compulsion, coercion, interference, the use of force, physical assault and so forth. Rights protect a domain of freedom and this freedom is classical negative freedom. That is to say, rights do not exist to protect so-called positive freedom – the freedom to do things and thus the associated abilities, capabilities, resources and opportunities which such freedom would entail. Rights do not protect such sorts of freedom in the view of the critic because such freedoms are essentially misconceived. There has to be a sharp distinction between on the one hand freedom as freedom from coercion and on the other ability and capability. To be free to do X is not the same thing as the ability to do X. No one is able to do all that he or she is free to do. I am free to do an indefinitely large number of things, namely, those things which I am not prevented from doing by the actions of others, and no one is able to do all the actions that a person is not prevented from doing. Thus the concepts of freedom and ability have to be seen as categorically different. It follows, therefore, that rights, which protect liberty, have to be distinguished clearly and categorically from the *soi disant* rights to resources and opportunities, which would enhance abilities and capabilities. These are not genuine freedoms and indeed are, at the most, contingent conditions for making genuine freedoms and rights (i.e. negative liberties and negative rights) effective. Rights like liberty are negative: they are forms of protection from interference and coercion. They are not positive, implying rights to resources and opportunities. A right to a basic income would, on this view, not be regarded as a genuine or basic right, but rather as a disputable contingent condition for the exercise of genuine rights.

It thus appears that a defence of the idea of a right to basic income would have to undertake one of two strategies. The first, to be considered later in the paper, would be to argue that, while rights may well be forms of protection for negative forms of liberty, they are not exclusively founded on such a set of considerations, and that there is a strong case for basing rights on, for example, needs as well as on liberty. The second alternative approach is to argue that in fact the concept of freedom used by those who argue against social rights is defective and that there is a compelling alternative view of freedom to the strictly negative view propounded by such critics. It is to this approach that I turn first.

The argument of the critic depends upon the view that freedom and ability are categorically distinct and that this categorical difference blocks any account of positive freedom in terms of ability, capability, resources and opportunities. There are reasons to doubt this.

The first thing to notice is that such an approach makes the idea of the value of freedom to human beings difficult to explain. Why should I want to be free from coercion? Surely the answer will be that if I am free from coercion then I shall be able to live a life shaped by my own intentions, goals and purposes. That is why freedom is valuable to me. However, if the value of freedom is explained in terms of what I am then able to do with it then it becomes quite difficult to maintain that freedom and ability are totally separable. This point can however be made much tighter than this. Freedom is of no value to a stone or a blade of grass. The fact that they are left alone and not interfered with does not mean that this absence of interference is of any value to these things or, indeed, that it makes sense to say that they are free. Freedom applies to human beings because they are able to make choices, entertain goals and to act as agents. If this capacity or set of capacities among humans is not just a matter of explaining why freedom is valuable to human beings, but also why the category of freedom applies to them, then it can hardly be claimed that freedom can be understood in the absence of a characterization of the capacity for choice and agency. Hence, it cannot be argued that freedom can be defined independently of some account of a basic capacity or capability amongst human beings, namely the capacity for choice and agency. Thus, it follows not only that the value of freedom has to be explained with respect to what freedom enables us to do – to live a life shaped by our own goals – but also that freedom is only meaningful as a concept if it is linked to some account of choice and agency. Obviously this argument is a long way from justifying a right to income but it does have the merit of undermining the idea that freedom and ability are two radically different things. If rights protect freedom and freedom has to be understood in terms of choice and agency then rights have to protect these capacities. It is unpacking our understanding of these capacities that will lead us towards the argument that there can indeed be genuine social rights, amongst which is a right to income.

This point can be backed up in other ways too. As another way of illustrating the centrality of human agency to an account of liberty, one can argue that a generalized ability to do X is a necessary condition of determining whether or not A is free to do X. It is only because there is a general ability to sign cheques or to fly on aircraft that it makes sense to ask whether A is or is not free to undertake these actions. Hence, not only are agency and choice conditions of the meaningfulness of freedom but particular examples of generalized human capacities are also conditions of determining whether an individual is free or not. Again it is not possible to maintain a strict distinction between freedom and ability/capacity/agency, which a strict account of negative freedom and a strict account of negative rights presupposes. If it can be shown that a right to resources such as income is a generic condition for the exercise of such agency then it could be seen as a genuine right on this view.

The point can be further reinforced by taking into account an argument from the Canadian philosopher Charles Taylor (1985). In his essay *What's Wrong With Negative Liberty?*, he argues that if the purist account of negative freedom is correct, then the answer to the question of whether country X is freer than country Y will be a purely quantitative one – turning upon the number of rules there are preventing or requiring action in these two different societies. Hence, it is quite possible then to say that Enver Hoxha's Albania was a freer society than, say, the UK if there were fewer such rules. It is quite likely that there would be fewer such rules since Albania was a very underdeveloped country under Hoxha and had little or no financial sector and very few cars. So there would be unlikely to have been as many rules preventing or requiring actions in these sectors than in the UK at the time. This would then lead to the unbelievable judgment that, given fewer rules, Hoxha's Albania was freer than the UK. The answer for the proponent of strict negative liberty has to be quantitative, because otherwise we would be weighting rules not purely in terms of their preventing/requiring characteristics but in terms of the types of things that the rules prevented or required. This would make liberty positive by linking it to abilities, goals and purposes. Given that the negativelibertarian cannot do this without self-contradiction, he or she has to be prepared for a quantitative outcome in terms of judgments about how free two societies are, which will produce results that are very difficult to believe. The appropriate point here is that what made the UK a freer country than Albania is that people were able to do things like emigrate and criticize the government which are regarded as valuable human capacities (and freedoms). What makes these freedoms valuable and more valuable than others is that there are certain basic capacities for agency, which we regard as being more valuable, and these freedoms protect these capacities. We have to have a qualitative view of human freedom and not just a quantitative one. This means that rights, which protect freedom, will have to be linked to ideas about basic and valuable human capacities. It also means that freedom cannot be understood only negatively; there are also centrally important positive aspects to liberty and thus to rights. As was stated at the end of the discussion of the previous point, if an income is regarded as a generic condition of the exercise of human agency, then it would make perfectly good sense to regard a right to such an income as a genuine right and also one that was involved in defending a fundamental freedom.

These issues can be brought to bear more directly upon the issue of income in the following way, utilizing an argument from G.A. Cohen (1995). Even if we take a wholly negative view of liberty it is still the case that the lack of money explicitly becomes a restriction on liberty. Take the following two cases. In a totalitarian country there is a law restricting travel for various groups of people. If I am in one of those groups then that is a restriction on my freedom and this restriction is in the form of a law prohibiting travel. That this sort of example constitutes a restriction on freedom seems to be completely uncontroversial. Take another society in which having a valid ticket to travel depends upon having had the resources to pay for it. If I turn up at the airport without a ticket (i.e. not having had the money to purchase it) I shall be prevented from flying and it will be the law that prevents me from flying and I will have committed an offence if I fly without the purchased ticket. Now defenders of negative liberty have argued that the lack of resources is not a restriction on liberty. Such restrictions arise out of the intentional acts of others: individuals, groups and the State. However, the example given shows that it is not possible to distinguish clearly in this sort of case between a legal restriction on my choice to travel and a resource restriction; not having the resources will in fact mean that I fall within a legal restriction which prevents people flying if they do not have a valid ticket. This point is well made by Adam Swift in a comment on Cohen's argument:

> The law restricting the freedom of those without the means to get a ticket may well be a justified law, and the restriction of freedom implied is a justified restriction. The point of the example is very specific. It is simply to bring out the fact that the kind of constraint on freedom in question is the law backed by the coercive power of the state…. Having money gives you the legal right to do things that you would not otherwise have the right to (i.e. be free) to do…. We may be right to have the laws about private property and money that we do. But we should acknowledge that such laws imply deliberate restriction by the state … of people's choices about how they live their lives. They are in that sense formal restrictions on people's freedom (Swift, 2002).

The political importance of this argument is very great. The British politician Sir Keith Joseph once claimed in his book on *Equality* (with Jonathan Sumption) that 'poverty is not unfreedom'. He had adopted a purely negative view of liberty in terms of which it was assumed that the lack of resources was not coercive. However, as the example shows, it is impossible to separate the issue of liberty from issues about resources. The question of whether people should have a specific set of resources is, of course, a different matter. But having a right to resources cannot be ruled out on *a priori* grounds in terms of a logical analysis of the concept of liberty because, as the Cohen example shows, even a pure theory of negative liberty implies a resource dimension. If rights are to be seen as ways in which liberty is protected, and if no account of liberty that neglects resources and neglects the capacity for agency is available, then rights imply resources – those resources that will facilitate the capacity for agency.

The final point that I want to discuss under the liberty heading is that of choice and the range of choice. I argued earlier that it was not possible to explain the nature of freedom without linking it to an account of choice and agency. However, it has to be said that defenders of a strict form of negative liberty do not accept one obvious consequence of this, namely that the more choice you have the freer you are. On their view the range and quality of choice have nothing to do with freedom. This is, for example Hayek's argument in *The Constitution of Liberty*:

> The range of physical possibilities from which a person can choose at a given moment has no direct relevance to freedom. The rock climber on a difficult pitch who sees only one way out to save his life is unquestionably free, though we would hardly say that he has any choice…Whether a person is free or not does not depend upon the range of choice.

It is clear why Hayek would want to defend this position as a believer in a pure form of negative liberty, because to link freedom to the exercise of choice and to the range and character of choice would make negative liberty into positive liberty – concerned with whether individuals had trivial or non-trivial choices that they could make, whether one person had a wider range of options than another, for example. This position is however is not very plausible. First of all, as Richard Norman points out in *Free and Equal*, if in the example the climber literally has no choice then the question of freedom does not arise. Also if access to a mountain range is prohibited by law (as it has been at times in the Himalayas) then that is clearly a restriction on choice and of liberty. If liberty is linked to the range of choices open to a person and if, as the Cohen argument showed, the lack of money can be seen as (a possibly justified) restriction on freedom, then a right to an income which could secure an adequate range of choice could be seen as essential to freedom and thus as a genuine right.

3. Rights, Scarcity and Obligation

I now want to turn to a second set of issues that are frequently raised by critics of the idea of positive social and economic rights, of which a right to an income would be one. These issues are concerned with the interlinking questions of scarcity and obligation. My aim is not to show that these are not real and genuine questions – indeed they are – but rather to argue that the way in which critics of social rights deploy these arguments is in danger of cutting the ground from under other sorts of rights too, namely civil and political rights.

Let me set out in a programmatic way what the critic's argument is. Genuine rights (in the critic's view), namely civil and political rights, are fundamental ways of protecting negative liberty. Negative liberty is to be free from coercion and interference. Hence the duties that correspond to negative rights are clear and categorical: they are to abstain from interference. The duties are to abstain from coercion, compulsion, assault, rape etc. Since the duties corresponding to such rights are duties to abstain and to forbear from action, it follows that they do not involve resources. Since they do not involve resources and involve not doing anything, then they are always capable of being performed. They are duties that can always be performed simultaneously in relation to right-holders. I can simultaneously perform the duty of not interfering with everyone who has the right not to be interfered with. The duties are in this sense perfect duty – they are not subject to constraints and can be performed simultaneously towards all right-holders. They are also clear and categorical as to what performing the duty means – namely to abstain from action. One has a clear sense of the nature and the limits of the duty.

Contrast this with *soi disant* positive rights (of which a right to a basic income would be one), according to the critic. Positive social rights do raise questions about scarcity and resources. Because in respect of at least some sorts of social rights, resources will be in relatively short supply, there will be a need to ration the resources which each individual is entitled to claim under the right. Thus such rights cannot be realized simultaneously nor can the duties be discharged simultaneously, as they can be in respect of negative rights. The duties and the rights cannot be clear and categorical because it is not clear what would be regarded as fulfilling a social right such as a right to health care. The duties will be subject to political negotiation rather than being completely definite as they are in respect of negative rights. Because of the indeterminacy of the right, both rights and duties will be in a constant process of dispute, negotiation and adjudication, unlike negative rights where it is clear where and when coercion, interference, assault etc. has taken place. I will use an extended quotation from Charles Fried's book *Right and Wrong* to illustrate the point. Fried, who is Professor of Jurisprudence at Harvard, argues first of all that: 'Rights are categorical moral entities such that violation of a right is always wrong.' He then goes on to make the following case:

A positive right is a claim to something – a share of a material good or to some particular good like the attention of a lawyer or a doctor, or perhaps to a result like health or enlightenment – while a negative right is a right that something not be done to one, that some particular imposition be withheld. Positive rights are always to scarce goods and consequently scarcity implies a limit to the claim. Negative rights, however, the rights not to be interfered with in forbidden ways do not appear to have such natural, such inevitable limitations. If I am let alone, the commodity I obtain does not appear of its nature to be a scarce or limited one. How can we run out of not harming each other, not lying to each other, leaving each other alone?

and:

> It is logically possible to treat negative rights as categorical entities. It is logically possible to respect any number of negative rights without necessarily landing in an impossible and contradictory situation.... Positive rights, by contrast, cannot as a logical matter be treated as categorical entities because of the scarcity limitation.

Hence there cannot be a genuine right to a basic income because positive social rights run up against scarcity constraints and are therefore not categorical moral entities like negative rights.

The critics' point about the indeterminacy of a positive right and its corresponding duties can be sharpened up a bit by looking at further conceptual and empirical implications of the recognition of positive rights, of which a right to a basic income would be one. The conceptual point is that a right to resources would inevitably bring into play issues concerned with social justice and fairness. If there are positive rights to scarce resources then there has to be a way of distributing such scarce resources according to defensible criteria of social justice. The provision of resources to meet positive rights cannot be left to the vagaries of the market within which ideas of just distribution and fairness in terms of outcomes do not operate. If rights are rights then they must involve some framework of provision for their claims, and this is going to give rise to questions about distributive justice and fairness. However, in the view of the critic, this is a further fatal defect in the whole programme of social rights because the idea of social justice is fraught with indeterminacy. If social justice is at all meaningful, and some critics such as Hayek deny that it is, then what justice requires can only be resolved through political processes and therefore the claims of right are put at risk through these processes. Hence, in the view of the critic there is a clear line to be drawn between genuine and categorical rights and *soi disant* rights to resources.

A great deal in these arguments can be doubted and, where the points that are made are valid, I shall argue that if they are fatal to positive rights to resources they are fatal to negative rights too. Although usually theories of negative liberty underpin theories of negative rights, let us put on one side my criticisms of a theory of pure negative liberty and look at the current arguments on their own merits.

The central issue, as Fried suggests, is one of scarcity because it is scarcity that must change the nature of the obligations from a clear and categorical claim to non-interference to a politically mediated set of obligations about a fair or just allocation of resources. There is a fairly obvious answer to this point and it has been made frequently, but in order to undermine the critic's claim it has to be made more sophisticated. The rather crude version of the argument is that, as a matter of fact, the protection of negative rights such as the right to be free from assault or interference involves the police, the courts, imprisonment and other things such as street-lighting and security measures in at-risk areas and so forth. So, it is argued, a negative right does imply the commitment of resources in much the same way as positive rights; this will inevitably mean that questions of distributive politics will arise as well as making the distinction between negative and positive rights seem less clear cut or perhaps even completely undermined. This is a good argument in itself but there is a potential reply from the defender of the distinction. Recall that Fried argued that it was logically possible to treat negative rights as categorical entities. It would be open therefore for the defender of this particular claim to argue that there is in fact still a logical or conceptual difference between negative and positive rights. This might involve two points.

The first would be that, while it may be true in the world as we know it that the protection of negative rights may involve the commitment of resources with the difficulties attendant on that, nevertheless logically they are distinct. It is possible to imagine a world like, for example, Kant's Kingdom of Ends – or for that matter the Kingdom of Heaven – in which all obligations of forbearance in respect of negative rights are always respected. In that possible world, negative rights would not involve anything to do with resources, whereas in such a possible world, positive rights would still of their very nature imply claims on resources. Hence, there is a logical difference and this difference of logical type would justify preserving the idea that rights are negative and that positive rights are not genuinely rights.

The second argument would be that resources are at best conditions for the protection of negative rights. They are not part of the internal nature of negative rights. In the case of positive rights, however, the resources are internally or logically connected to the nature of the claim. (This argument parallels a claim made in respect of negative liberty: that, at the most, resources are contingent conditions for the realization of negative freedom, whereas positive liberty of necessity implies resources; and that this is a reason for arguing that genuine liberty is one and not the other.) So, the critic could reply to the counterexample of resources being required for the protection of rights, that these may be conditions of rights but they are only contingently related to such rights claims and are therefore not part of their basic internal logical nature.

As far as the first argument about possible worlds is concerned there are two not very important *ad hoc* responses that might be made. The first is that if the critic of positive rights wants to posit a possible world in which there is no scarcity of motivation for forbearance (unlike in the real world) then it could equally be open to the defender of positive rights to posit a possible world in which there was an abundance of material goods, so that questions of scarcity of goods and all of the consequences which the critic argues go with that, would be dissipated.

Second, in both cases, the issue is scarcity: in the negative rights case, of the scarcity of the motivation of forbearance; in the positive rights case, the scarcity of material resources. These can be imagined away by combining Kant's Kingdom of Ends and the Garden of Eden, but this seems to show what common sense should already have shown by now, namely that if we lived in a combination of the Kingdom of Ends and the Garden of Eden there would be no need for rights of any sort. In addition, rights are about what kind of protection individuals can have in a world of scarcity both of motivation and resources.

There is, however, a deeper response that could be made to the critic's argument. It will not do to regard resources as some detachable condition to negative rights and not somehow part of their conceptual or logical nature. The reason is this. There is a conceptual connection between the idea of a right and enforceability. The reason for this is as follows. We have all sorts of desires, preferences, needs and interests, only some of which are turned into claims of right. Those that are so turned into rights have to illustrate two things. The first is that these are basic, vital human interests of one sort or another and not just passing claims or preferences. Second, that it makes sense to believe that others can be put under an enforceable obligation in respect of those rights. So while a need for love may be a basic human interest, it makes no sense to turn this into a right because there is no way of creating a corresponding enforceable obligation. Even if there were it would actually destroy what the claim is a claim to. If enforceability is an essential feature of rights, including negative rights, then this is of necessity going to involve resources, in that it is not feasible to think of enforceability as costless. If this is so, then enforceability costs are not, as it were, contingent conditions for the protection of rights but are part of the logical structure of rights claims.

If this is so, the arguments about resource allocation and its problems apply to negative rights and their enforceability as much as they do to positive rights. These will be subject to political mediation in terms of policy and practical discretion in terms of provision of resources. Policy and politics will determine the level of resources dedicated to the protection of different sorts of rights, and there is no philosopher's stone to determine outside such processes what the level of resource should be. This applies to the protection of negative and positive rights. At the level of provision there will have to be discretion, and if this is regarded as being fatal to positive rights it is difficult to see why that is not so in relation to negative rights. Take the following example. A police service is part of the enforcement aspects of negative rights in so far as it secures compliance with forbearance and non-interference; a hospital service is part of the enforcement aspects of a positive right to health care. In the latter case it is clear that managers and doctors will have to use their professional discretion in terms of their allocation of resources between patients, all of whom, it is supposed, have a right to health care. In the view of the critic, such discretion in allocation undermines and renders invalid the whole idea of a right in this context. It is certainly a very long way from Charles Fried's idea of a right as a categorical entity. However, if this point is fatal against the idea of a positive right, a similar argument in relation to the police is equally fatal against the negative rights thesis if it is accepted that enforceability is an essential feature of rights and not just a contingent condition of them. In the same way as the doctor has to use discretion to manage resources, so the police chief will have to decide on the basis of professional judgment the level of resources that should be put into the investigation of a particular crime that has involved the breach of someone's negative rights. So this argument about discretion can prove far too much for the negative rights theorist. It makes that person's position impossible to sustain if the argument about the incompatibility between rights and discretion is regarded as fatal to the idea of positive rights.

It is worth noting at this juncture, that if there can be a right to a basic income, it is a right that, given some assumptions, is less likely to involve the exercise of discretion than many other rights – whether positive or negative. Once the sum payable as a basic income has been fixed as the result of political decision, then on the assumption that the income is paid to each citizen on an individual and unconditional basis above a certain age there is no scope for discretion. If the income is made conditional on some forms of participation – for example, caring or working in the voluntary sector – there will be greater scope for discretion in terms of what is or is not an adequate level of commitment by an individual to the participatory framework, which is the gateway to the income. Even in this case, however, the inevitable role of discretion does not militate against the claim that there can be such a right since, as we have seen, the connection between rights and resources is an essential one. The problems associated with the exercise of discretion therefore apply across the board.

This completes the discussion of the relationship between rights, scarcity and obligation. There are genuine and complex problems involved in resolving the relationship between rights and social justice, but I hope that I have argued sufficiently cogently that these are problems for the generality of rights and not just rights to resources including basic income.

4. Rights and Needs

So far my argument has been rather negative and opportunistic. I have argued that if there are any rights, there is no good case for denying that positive rights to resources are genuine rights; the claims that deny that such rights embody essential logical features of genuine rights do not carry conviction. In these concluding remarks I shall sketch the basis of a moral framework within which it would make positive sense to claim that there is a right to a basic income. The argument was worked out in much more detail than is possible here in the book I wrote in 1981 with Harry Lesser and Peter Taylor-Gooby called *Political Philosophy and Social Welfare*; some aspects have been taken much further and dealt with in a much more rigorous and sophisticated manner in Ian Gough and Len Doyal's book on needs. What I want to show is the link between needs and rights, and to do this we need to go back to an argument from the first section of the paper in relation to liberty. I argued there that it is impossible to make sense of the idea of freedom without some conception of the nature of human choice and agency. If agency is essential to an account of freedom, then it seems reasonable to argue that any general or generic conditions of the exercise of agency will be of particular importance in relation to a full account of the nature of freedom. In our 1981 book we argued that indeed there are such general conditions for the exercise of agency: well-being and autonomy. Well-being in the sense that basic needs are satisfied in a reasonably predictable way; autonomy in the sense that the capacity for autonomy seems to be what the end result of the exercise of human agency and freedom would be. Let me just say a few words about autonomy first. It might well be argued that autonomy is the main site of negative freedom. Autonomy requires that individuals are free from interference and coercion so that they can live lives shaped by their own purposes. This is what makes negative freedom valuable to us and indeed intelligible. Negative freedom, and the negative rights associated with it, is not to be understood as an end in itself but is rather valuable or instrumental in achieving a broader and more basic good – that of autonomy. I have already argued that this conception of freedom and rights involves resources and in that respect both the freedom and rights have positive aspects.

However, autonomy is something that has to be developed. It is an achievement, not some kind of antecedent status, and the development of autonomy creates certain sorts of basic needs, which are essential to its realization. These are the needs connected with well-being, without which an autonomous character will not be developed. For the capacity for autonomy to exist, there has to be a degree of physical integrity and health in so far as this is achievable and alterable by human agency; there has to be an appropriate level of education;

and there has to be an appropriate level of security in terms of income and social security, in that individuals will not develop the capacity for autonomy if the whole of their lives is devoted to securing the basic means of subsistence. If this is correct (as a sketch), then autonomy, freedom and an account of the fulfilment of basic needs have to go together. Negative freedom – freedom from coercion – is a generic condition of agency and autonomy; positive freedom – access to resources and opportunities and the satisfaction of basic needs – is also a generic condition of autonomy. If this is so then there is a good case for seeing a basic income as being part of positive freedom, for two interrelated reasons.

The first is that a basic income will increase autonomy in terms of enhancing an individual's capacity for choice and for living his or her life in his or her own way. As we saw in relation to liberty, income as the possession of money can increase the choices open to you because the lack of money will mean that you will be legally proscribed from being able to undertake an action. Also as I argued, contrary to the defender of pure negative liberty, the range and quality of choice does have a central bearing on the meaning of liberty.

The second point is that a basic income increases autonomy relative to provision in kind in that in spending the income the purchases will reveal the preferences of the agent rather than that of government and its agencies. As I have already argued, it diminishes the possible role of discretion in the provision of resources.

So if autonomy and agency are central to freedom, in that both negative and positive freedom acquire their value and, as I argued earlier, their intelligibility in relation to the idea of a person as a centre of choice and agency, then the generic conditions of agency will determine the content of both negative and positive freedom. Negative freedom will define the forms of unjustified coercion and interference, which would limit autonomy; positive freedom will define those sorts of goods, which are necessary conditions for the achievement of the capacity for agency and autonomy. I have argued that a basic income could be seen as one of these conditions of agency.

There is, however, a major problem remaining, namely the specific argument for turning the general conditions of agency, including an income, into the idea of a right. I am not going back on my earlier arguments in saying this. I have argued that there is no reason for thinking that a right to a basic income cannot be thought of as a right. But the argument has been conditional: if there are any rights at all then positive rights in general, and a right to a basic income in particular, are genuine rights in the sense that they share in the general features of rights. This leaves a central problem untouched: would it not be perfectly possible for an individual to recognize in his/her own case that the capacity for agency depended on a combination of negative and positive freedom, and indeed to recognize the same situation in respect of others, that their capacity for agency depended also on such negative and positive forms of freedom, without recognising that this was the basis of a claim to a right to these negative and positive forms of freedom of which basic income would be one? I believe that there is an answer to this problem. It has been given in the remarkable writings of the Chicago philosopher Alan Gewirth over the past twenty-five years and in particular his books *Reason and Morality* and *The Community of Rights*. We have to get from recognition that there are common pre-conditions of agency to the idea that these preconditions can be conceived of as rights and thus as matters for collective and governmental concern imposing strict duties on all members of society. Gewirth's argument is complicated but crucial and it has to be repeated in full.

First of all there is the recognition, which I have already stressed, of the centrality of agency and action. So when I act I do so to attain some good for myself – not necessarily a moral good but something which I think is worthwhile. Hence the first step in the argument is:

1. I do X for end or purpose E.

The second step is:

2. E is good.

Since the generic goods of agency are necessary for me to value and to seek to attain E the next step becomes:

3. The generic goods of agency (freedom and well-being) are necessary goods.

Given this, an individual agent has to be committed to:

4. I must have freedom and well-being (i.e. the necessary goods of agency).

The next step is crucial in that Gewirth argues that on the basis of (4) the individual has to accept

5. I have rights to the basic goods of agency.

Now this is a big step and the reasons for it are as follows. Imagine that having got as far as (4), the agent rejects (5). It then follows, given the link between rights and obligations, that he gives up any claim that other people should refrain from interfering with his access to the necessary or generic goods of agency. If I do not claim them for myself as rights, then I have no reason for resisting the idea that others can interfere with these goods. It then follows logically that I regard it as permissible that I do not have access to the basic goods (i.e. because not claiming them as rights for myself means that others have no strict obligation to respect the goods that I need for agency and action).

However, this claim contradicts (4) which follows from (1)–(3). Since every agent has to accept (4) because it recognizes the necessary conditions of agency and action, any agent therefore has to reject the idea that it is permissible for other agents not to have an obligation to respect my need for the necessary goods. Since this would follow from the denial of (5), any agent must accept (5) and therefore the necessary or generic goods of agency and action have to be accepted as rights. Given that I have already argued (as does Gewirth in *The Community of Rights*) for the view that a basic income is one of these generic goods, it follows from this argument that there can be a right to a basic income, and none of the strictures against this claim from defenders of a pure theory of positive liberty and of purely negative rights count against it.

Note

1   University of London, United Kingdom.

References

Cohen, G.A. 1995. *Self ownership, freedom and equality* (Cambridge, Cambridge University Press).
Doyal, L. and Gough, I. 1991. *A theory of human need* (Basingstoke, Macmillan).
Fried, C. 1978. *Right and wrong* (Cambridge, Mass., Harvard University Press).
Gewirth, A. 1978. *Reason and morality* (Chicago, Chicago University Press).
_____ 1996. *A community of rights* (Chicago, Chicago University Press).
Joseph, K. and Sumption, J. 1979. *Equality* (London, J. Murray).
Norman, R. 1987. *Free and equal* (Oxford, Oxford University Press).
Plant, R., Lesser, H. and Taylor-Gooby, P. 1981. *Political philosophy and social welfare* (London, Routledge).
Swift, A. 2002. *Political philosophy* (Cambridge, Polity Press).
Taylor, C. 1985. *Philosophical papers Volume 2* (Cambridge, Cambridge University Press).

4

WASTEFUL WELFARE TRANSACTIONS: WHY BASIC INCOME SECURITY IS FUNDAMENTAL

Claus Offe[1]

1. Introduction

As is the case in any other policy area, so too with policies to fight poverty and exclusion: policymakers and administrators need to take decisions on what to do and what not to do, including decisions concerning the selection of a universe of options from which policy choices are to be made. Before making (rational) decisions, we must be aware of the options at hand, as well as their costs and consequences. I take it as axiomatic that decision-making, as well as the choice of the range of choices, is costly. These costs come in numerous forms, beginning with the salaries of decision-makers, search and information costs, the risk of making ineffective, counterproductive or otherwise mistaken decisions, etc. The costs to which I refer are not the amount of money to be paid out to the recipients of transfers, but those incurred in running the apparatus that eventually makes these payments and establishes the relevant rules.

The cost of decision-making falls upon the decision-makers and those who are bound by their decisions. Apart from the direct budgetary programme costs themselves, three kinds of costs (using a highly inclusive notion of the term) can be distinguished. First, the transaction costs that are involved in the decision itself, including the costs of its enforcement. Second, the costs or losses of those who have opposed the decision made and whose alternative proposal has been defeated. Third, the costs/losses of those upon whom the decision may impose burdens, obligations or constraints, and whose freedom of action it curtails. My thesis here is that many of these costs, losses and disutilities, not to speak of moral hypocrisies and irresolvable practical dilemmas involved in welfare policy ('as we know it'), can to a large extent be avoided through the introduction of an unconditional and universal basic income (BI). The argument that I am going to outline is to substantiate the claim that BI is not only a *normatively* attractive answer to issues of distributive justice in the context of the labour market crises of economically advanced societies, but is also the most *efficient* policy to fight poverty. BI is a policy that substantially economizes on the costs and various disutilities involved in traditional approaches to poor-relief and its administration.

How can a policy be 'efficient'? Efficiency is increased whenever the same (or better) overall outcome is achieved with fewer resources spent in the process. Note that even when a *marginal* loss in terms of intended effects/outcomes is the result of adopting a *substantially* less costly policy, the trade-off may be efficiency-superior. For instance, some tax laws are so complicated for the authorities to administer and to enforce (and for the taxpayer to understand and comply with) that abolishing them would involve savings which may be far greater than the resulting loss in tax revenues. (This loss, in its turn may well be diminished because taxpayers are no longer frustrated and alienated by virtually incomprehensible legal stipulations and, as a result, are now ready to comply with rules that are now reasonably transparent).

The costs involved in political programmes can be measured at three points. The most obvious is the *administration* of programmes for clients. These costs come in the form of offices, the wages of administrative officers, the costs of their training, the costs of settling complaints in court, etc. Costs come also in the less tangible form of the complaints, frustration, stigma and perceived loss of freedom experienced by clients in the course of interaction with officers. Second, before a programme can be administered, it must be decided upon at the *legislative* level, which precedes administration and usually involves a time- and manpower-consuming process of gathering information, buying the resources that experts and analysts bring to bear upon the programme design, exploring policy options, building coalitions, reconciling political conflict, etc. Third, and subsequent to the administrative stage, some programmes at least must be *implemented* over time. The rights and duties of clients as determined through administrative decision must be continuously supervised, monitored and enforced, people must be 'processed', and overall programme outcomes must be registered and evaluated as to their conformity with stated programme objectives, a process that often results in a critical assessment of policy outcomes and a feedback into policy revision and reform.

While all these different kinds of costs (transaction costs, programme costs, costs in terms of conflict, frustration and 'process disutilities') defy overall quantification, the argument that I will pursue relies on the possibility of making plausible estimates of 'more' or 'less'.

2. Micro-transactions: The Administration of Welfare

Let us start with the *micro-level* of welfare transactions, which is located at the interface of the administration and the individual claimant/client. First, if people claim to be poor and apply for transfers, the claims they make and the conditions they report are not necessarily true. They may well own property or savings by which they are able to support themselves. Hence administrators need to apply a *means test*.

Even if they turn out to be poor, they may be poor in a way that does not entitle them to social assistance because, according to welfare laws, there are others on whose resources they are entitled to rely, e.g. spouses or other family members. Hence we need a *family-support test.*

If no such family members can be found, chances are that the person is well able to support him/herself through income earned in labour or other markets. Hence proof must be provided that this is not the case (employment or employability test).

If the proof can be provided, the question as to whether or not the by now positively 'poor' person does in fact have claims against the welfare administration must be settled. This is normally not the case (or if so, to a much more limited extent) if the person is a foreigner and asylum-seeking refugee *(test of nationality and residence-status).*

After an answer to this question is found, the remaining question is what needs to be done to lift the person out of the condition of poverty, which usually involves a check of household size, dependent children, housing status, health status, etc. *(needs test).*

These five transactions concern just the *micro*-level of the on-the-spot administration of legal rules to individual claimants. Administrators act as gatekeepers checking who is admissible and who is not. These rules help to decide the two questions that are at the root of any welfare administration, namely (a) how do we tell the 'truly' poor from the non-poor, and (b) how do we tell, among the poor thus certified, the deserving from the non-deserving poor? To be sure, some of these testing procedures can be made less costly by standardization, such as when the nationality test is performed by asking clients to present a valid passport, or if an individualized needs test is substituted for by a routine assignment of need in monetary terms. Others among the above tests may involve a detailed documentation and proof of the claimant's family relations or education, health, and employment conditions, a procedure that is costly not only in terms of the internal costs of administration, but also in terms of the typically underaccounted-for 'external process disutilities' of administration, such as stigmatization, invasion of privacy, the time wasted while waiting in lines, and the sense of powerlessness experienced by the claimant.

BI is an alternative to welfare policy that radically economizes on the administrative overhead costs of fighting poverty, provided that the BI transfer is sufficiently high to afford the basic means of subsistence. By its definition of being 'unconditional', BI allows for four of the five tests to be done away with, with the only remaining one being the test of (national or European) citizenship. To be sure, and following its definition of being universal, BI would be available not just to the poor, but to all citizens, the vast non-poor majority of whom would have to pay back, through direct or indirect taxes or/and lower wages and in a distributionally neutral way, the 'undeserved' transfer payment received.

3. Macro-Transactions: Making and Revising Welfare Policy

Before this costly micro-interaction between the administration and the individual client can take place, there is a *macro-transaction* in the process by which the legal rules and strategies of welfare policy are set up and, typically, continuously revised and reformed. Let us now look at what is involved, in terms of decision-making and other transaction costs, at the stage of designing and deciding on welfare and poverty policy. In the rich democracies of the OECD – the only countries where reasonably elaborate state policies for poverty relief are likely to exist, as poor societies typically cannot afford a welfare policy and tend to leave care for the poor to families and religious communities – poverty is a matter that must be dealt with through formal mechanisms such as legislation, administration, adjudication, the professional practice of trained social workers, as well as statistical documentation and scientific analysis of poverty-related data. This apparatus of formal policies and agencies is brought into being and driven by a mix of *moral norms* of care and compassion, on the one hand, and *prudential considerations*, on the other.

There is first the 'deontological' moral and legal commitment of public policy, inspired by a sense of compassion, to the relief of the poverty of those who cannot be held responsible for caring for themselves. Before this principle can be applied, it must be transformed, typically through a contentious political process, into an operational set of rules specifying who are admissible claimants, how we define poverty, how we recognize incapacity for self-help, and what must be done, according to some moral point of view that is sometimes built into constitutional principles.

Second, a large number of 'consequentialist' and prudential considerations enter into the political process of welfare policy. The standard consequentialist assumptions add up to a dilemma. On the one hand, poverty needs to be addressed, because if we fail to do so, its persistence and potential further growth will cause negative externalities (ranging from public-health issues to crime) that affect 'all of us'. On the other hand, neither considerations of moral obligation nor those of negative externalities can commit us to (a) adopt *ineffective* policies (let alone counterproductive ones) or (b) adopt policies that involve burdens that are deemed *unacceptable*[2] by those upon whom they fall, such as local taxpayers.

Three modes of argument similar to what Albert Hirschman has described as the three *topoi* of the 'rhetoric of reaction', welfare policy is plagued (and significantly more so than any other branch of social policy where there is typically, as in pensions, a large overlap of contributors and beneficiaries). First, welfare spending does not have the desired impact on the incidence and prevalence of poverty. Second, if anything, the impact is negative. Third, even if either of the above were demonstrably untrue, voters are simply unwilling to shoulder the burden of welfare; instead, they will punish in the voting booth those who propose to impose that burden upon them, thus putting some fragile 'welfare consensus' into jeopardy. All welfare policy is thus chron ically entangled in the contradictory imperatives of what *needs to be done* (following the combined concerns of compassion and/or avoiding collective negative externalities of poverty) and what *can be done* in terms of both effectiveness (winning the 'war' on poverty) and political feasibility (maintaining the political support of the vast majority of net contributors to welfare spending). Thus welfare policy is a constant debate between those who bring forward moral and prudential reasons *for* welfare spending and those who argue *against* such spending for lacking effectiveness or feasibility. What is being tested here is not the neediness, employability etc. of welfare *recipients* (which occurs at the micro-level discussed before), but the norms and beliefs underpinning welfare *policy* itself.

Note that the parties to this debate are unequally armed. Proponents of (more generous) welfare spending must appeal to compassion and prudence, which, in the latter case, means making the (necessarily somewhat speculative) argument that unless we do X, the undesirable consequences will be more costly than the costs of X itself. Who knows whether that is right? Who can possibly know it? Opponents, by contrast, are in the much more comfortable position of relying on what passes for currently available 'facts', which provide evidence supporting any or all of the assertions that welfare is ineffective, counterproductive, or politically unsupportable. These facts do not need to be 'true'; it suffices that they are widely *believed* to be true or just *preferred* to be true, even when exposed as perfect myths.

Participants in this policy discourse bring to bear upon the production of the operational rules of welfare policy cognitive resources ranging from hard social science knowledge to more or less explicit cognitive frames including assumptions and prejudices about 'human nature' and 'facts of life'. In addition to the truth content (validation through independent empirical and analytical research) of the knowledge employed in making prudent choices, the adoption of such knowledge units (either of the kind 'p is a fact' or 'x is likely to contribute to y') is also determined by their 'popularity'.

Social scientists have even used the analogy of a 'knowledge market', suggesting that if policymakers adopt and publicly invoke some knowledge unit A, they are much more likely to be 'remunerated' in terms of attention, consent and support than if they were relying upon some less popular knowledge unit B, which it thus may be politically wise to ignore or repress. By 'knowledge market', I do not mean the familiar phenomenon of data and analysis being purchased for money from academic and commercial research organizations. The concept of a 'knowledge market' refers rather to the fact that some beliefs fare better than others in terms of the disposition of audiences to listen, to accept a belief as valid, to take it for granted that other people will be persuaded by its validity as well, and to support actors who express their commitment to this belief and propose to adopt it as a premise for action. Beliefs compete with each other for such favourable responses from mass audiences, and the currency in which preferred beliefs are rewarded is that of attention, consent, support and acceptance. Some beliefs are pleasant to particular recipients, others highly unwelcome. Independent of their demonstrable truth content, they have a popularity content or political exchange-value. This differential exchange-value of knowledge units is conceivably quite independent of their truth content, particularly so as the latter can be hard to determine by mass audiences or may be easily forgotten due to its complexity.

What determines the political exchange-value of beliefs? Preferences for belief A over belief B may result from considerations of its intrinsic or instrumental value, such as avoidance of cognitive dissonance ('if B were true, I would have to revise some other firmly held belief') or anticipated utility for the prudential foundation of a particular policy option ('if B were true, it could be used as an argument in support of policy P that I dislike because of its distributional implication'). Hence the beliefs that are promulgated in welfare policy discourses are likely to be jointly determined by their truth-value and their exchange-value. One can save money while preserving a good conscience in terms of deontological and prudential commitments, if one disseminates and adopts beliefs that suggest the ineffectiveness, counter-productivity, or fiscal unfeasibility of welfare programmes. To the extent that these beliefs can be validated either through objective measurement and analysis or through public acceptance and widely shared interpretive consensus, we can live in the best possible world of remaining faithful to our principles while having a perfect excuse for not living up to them. This is what one might call the equilibrium of hypocrisy: 'We would love to do something about poverty, but unfortunately we have reason to believe that there is no way actually to do it.'

These considerations lead us to expect a dynamic demand for impossibility, counter-productivity, and unacceptability theorems – a demand that, if supplied with appropriate beliefs and frameworks, will trump or weaken many prudential and moral policy motivations. In the field of welfare policy and welfare reform, some of the scholarly findings and widely-shared interpretive frameworks which cater to this demand, are the following:

- *Poverty trap*: If we really were to lift the deserving poor to a level high enough to take them permanently out of poverty, there would be a disincentive for them to seek and accept low-wage jobs. Generous welfare spending will create a permanent 'welfare class', while low-wage/low-productivity jobs will remain unfilled;

- *Dependency culture*: People become used to living on welfare and lose the habits and virtues that are required in labour markets – another effect inflating and perpetuating (near-) poverty outside the labour market;

- *Budgetary effects:* The burden that poverty-related welfare systems impose upon (local) budgets drains resources available for investment, local employment and job creation, which in turn swells the ranks of the unemployed and, as a consequence, welfare claimants;

- *Administrative failure:* Welfare offices are insufficiently equipped to effectively filter out fraudulent welfare claims of clever but 'unworthy' poor (or, further, are staffed by people who side with their clients out of excessive generosity or out of self-interest in perpetuating their bureaucratic role);

- *Political effects:* If welfare transfers were sufficiently generous to seriously put an end to poverty, taxpayers would resent the fiscal burden of paying for other people's 'free lunches'. It is thus in the best interest of the poor themselves, as well as of the advocates of welfare policy, to avoid provoking such a welfare backlash by not being overly serious about ending poverty;

- *Migration effects:* If poor people (such as potential asylum-seekers) 'elsewhere' learn that generous welfare is provided 'here', they will migrate to benefit from this provision, which will inflate the ranks of welfare claimants to unaffordable levels;

- *Population effects:* If single mothers can receive welfare, this incentive structure will encourage young single women to have children, and more children than they would have for 'intrinsic' reasons or that they can care for adequately. These children are likely to grow up in near-poverty and will eventually form the core of the next generation's welfare class, a segment of the population whose very existence is undesirable from the point of view of society at large;

- *Moral demonstration effects:* Providing a near-comfortable level of subsistence through welfare entitlements will generate negative 'moral externalities' by demonstrating that it is feasible to make a living without entering the labour market and/or without getting married. This will mislead morally weak persons into imitating the model.

It is probably easy to fill a bookshelf with the theoretical, empirical, and political literature on each one of these proposition and beliefs, many of which are highly priced in the knowledge market while often lacking valid and consistent empirical support. Taken together, these beliefs amount to a logical muddle of the following sort: 'If you want to fight poverty, do not do it in a serious way. For if you were to do it seriously, you would end up increasing rather than eliminating the ranks of the poor.' The management of this multidimensional dilemma absorbs the activities and energies of experts, policy makers, interest groups, academic researchers, journalists, etc., all of whom busy themselves with criticizing, designing, evaluating, financing, economizing, revising, fine-tuning, reforming, and advocating policies and programmes, building coalitions, feeding public opinion with appropriate beliefs, and attaching, in a way that is politically as well as morally often highly divisive, various kinds of evaluative labels and cognitive frames (laziness, irresponsibility, fraud, etc.) to various segments of the client population of welfare (women, the elderly, asylum-seekers, the long-term unemployed, single mothers, the unskilled). These activities make up the substance of the politics of welfare reform. One of the attractions of BI is that it would relieve us from having to ask and answer these essentially unanswerable questions.

As long as they are being asked and answered, the outcomes of these generally unappealing, often entirely futile, and essentially wasteful policy debates and decisions result in one of three approaches. One is the *market liberal* idea that 'welfare does not work, workfare does not work, only work works'. In other words, it is the virtual absence of statutory welfare provisions and social rights of the poor that forces people to earn their own means of subsistence, thus ending poverty via the dictates of the market. On the way to implementing this ideal, both entitlements to welfare and the level of welfare transfers must be cut. A second one is the conservative approach of creating a moral sanctuary for 'worthy' claimants – basically (single) mothers and their children, plus women whose performance of mothering in the past has prevented them from earning adequate pensions – while denying entitlements to all those who are (deemed to be) able to work. The third approach is that of 'Third Way' social democrats who propose to 'activate' the poor, male and female alike, so as to enable and encourage them to practice self-reliance through labour market participation.

For the remainder of this paper, I am going to discuss the merits of this latter approach, which comprises most cases of welfare reform of the 1980s and 1990s in both the USA and Europe. Its proponents base their case on two considerations, one macro-economic and one micro-moral. The macro-economic argument states that it is always preferable to subsidize productive activity (whatever its level of productivity) than to subsidize idleness. The corollary moral argument claims that if the poor claim social rights from society, they have an 'obligation' to do something useful for society in return. Social rights must be 'earned'. In order to implement this *quid pro quo*, it is not enough to transfer money to people. Instead, people must be treated, transformed, challenged, enabled etc. to earn the rights that they should no longer be given access to 'for nothing'. This notion of *processing* and *treating* people, so that they eventually, at the end of some possibly lengthy process of rehabilitation, become 'normal' members of a society of self-reliant individuals, involves a complex mix of sticks and carrots. Should they refuse to enter into a state-sponsored process of work-centred normalization and to cooperate with the authorities supervising this normalization, they must expect to be punished by the reduction of their welfare claims to a bare minimum. If, however, they are willing to cooperate, they can expect to be helped and rewarded appropriately.

The reinterpretation of welfare rights as something that must be 'earned' rather than something on which citizens can rely unconditionally and as part of their original endowment with the rights of citizenship has parallels in other fields of social policy. This reinterpretation has been criticized for blurring the line that separates the *rights* tied to citizenship from the *rewards* tied to activities valued in the market, or from status to contract.[3] Now there are two (and only two, I submit) philosophical arguments available that could be cited in defence of this transition.

One is an argument from *civic duty* – the moral imperative that 'thou shalt not rely on fellow citizens' resources unless absolutely necessary, and even then only to an extent and for a duration of time that is also absolutely necessary'. While arguably perfectly valid in principle, this moral imperative of civic duty is notoriously hard to translate into an uncontested operational meaning. How do we decide, and who has the right to decide, whether or not something is 'absolutely necessary'? Moreover, it can be questioned whether there is in fact a unidirectional flow of benefits from the vast majority of contributors/taxpayers to recipients of transfers; there is always the possible argument that people who rely on transfers without 'earning' them provide some reciprocal benefit to those having to pay for those benefits. For instance, the non-working poor serve the working non-poor in that they make the supply side of labour markets less crowded than it otherwise would be.

Also, they perform a service as they obey the rules of civilized conduct, which they would find difficult to do if they had no access to benefits. Furthermore, they provide reason for the working non-poor to entertain the satisfying belief that they live in a reasonably just society. Moreover, if a moral rule of civic austerity applies, it should apply not only to the poor, but also to all citizens with equal force – including, for instance, the recipients of agricultural subsidies.

If this argument for having to 'earn' welfare rights remains somewhat nebulous and will be essentially contested for the reasons just mentioned, proponents of the 'Contractualization of Welfare' who believe in 'Third Way' methods of 'Activating' social and labour market policies might rely on the only other argument available. This is the argument from *liberal paternalism*. 'You will see', or so the moral intuition guiding this argument can be summarized, 'that if "we" ration your rights according to the obligations you fulfil in return, this is not primarily in "our" interest (that of saving welfare expenditures), but in "your own" long-term self-interest, properly understood.' This kind of 'we-know-better-what-is-good-for-you'-argument in support of the contractarian reinterpretation of welfare rights is one that liberalism typically reserves for children who, by definition, are not yet able to make responsible judgments for themselves. Its validity is contingent on the strength of the assumption that once they *are* grown-up, they will accept paternalist practices as reasonable and thus retrospectively validate the conditions they have been exposed to. But that does not serve as an equally valid argument when applied to people who are adults already! To be sure, mandatory continuing education and life-long upgrading of skills may be a good idea (i.e. one that may be appreciated in retrospect by those having undergone training). If so, the question becomes: why limit such mandatory training to poor adults, rather than extending it to all adults? Arguably, society as a whole could benefit much more if the employability, flexibility, skills and work habits of those already in stable employment were systematically enhanced than if such programmes were selectively targeted on those whose labour market potential is limited in the first place.

In spite of the weaknesses of the moral foundations of 'activating' workfare programmes, such programmes aiming at increasing the employability of welfare recipients have become the rule through the welfare reforms that were introduced in OECD countries in the 1980s and 1990s and which are still continuing in many countries. The poor are no longer seen as being in need of transfer payments; they are case as being in need of *treatment* that will eventually help them to overcome their reliance on payments. The implementation of this philosophy involves a number of costly transactions, which could be saved by a BI.

4. The Meso-Level: The Costs of Running Workfare Programmes

The state-sponsored management of the mass exodus from welfare into work is clearly a project that is as ambitious concerning its intended outcome (i.e., integrating the poor into the labour market and gainful employment that allows them to become self-reliant) as it is costly concerning the arrangements, expenditures, and administrative measures required. As it is arguably too early to venture a general assessment of what welfare-to-work programmes can actually achieve in terms of this ambitious goal, let me dwell here mostly on those costs.

First, the poor living outside the labour market on welfare must be 'freed' for the labour market. This involves the costs of day-care services (single mothers are targeted for labour market integration) as well as transport from home to work and back. People who suffer from chronic health conditions and handicaps may need special provisions in order to make them available for employment. While there is of course nothing wrong with spending on (public) day-care and (public) transport, these facilities tend to be particularly scarce in residential areas where the poor are concentrated. As a consequence, some targeted build-up of these facilities is typically called for.

Second, welfare-to-work programmes usually start with measures designed to provide the target population not only with appropriate skills, but also with desirable work habits to make them fit for employment. While reasonably reliable social technologies (namely, formal training through schooling and courses) are available for most skills, the disposition of poor people to spend the requisite effort on skill acquisition and/or to endure the discipline of work cannot typically be taken for granted. Neither can it be easily and reliably 'taught'. Hence motivating people to learn and work, to habituate them to what it means to be a worker through counselling, case assessment, the communication of promises and threats, as well as actual administration of negative and positive sanctions, are seen to be an important ingredient of the treatment eventually leading to employability.

Third, the transition must be engineered from the employability thus created to actual employment. This step involves not only the search- and matching-activities of private and public labour exchanges and employment offices. It also involves the creation of the jobs to be filled. As far as the public sector is concerned (and depending on the budgetary situation of the respective municipality), it will be relatively easy to create low-income/low-skill jobs, such as cleaning parks. But considerable enforcement costs will be entailed in making workfare recipients perform jobs that they have not chosen freely and that they are hence unlikely to find rewarding and fulfilling.

Fourth, private sector jobs are no less costly to come by, depending on the quantity and quality of private sector demand for labour. Private employers show a consistent preference for employing new entrants into the labour market or workers who have been employed before, rather than former welfare recipients. Thus – provided there are openings for low-skill labour at all – employers must be paid for reversing this preference ordering. In order to make jobs available, welfare-to-work policies will typically have to adopt either negative income tax schemes (which allow job seekers to price themselves into the market at very low wage rates without suffering at the same time from very low incomes) or subsidies to the wage and non-wage costs of workfare workers to be paid to their employer. In either case, administrative measures will have to be taken to ensure that workfare employment will be 'additional', meaning that employers are effectively prevented from hiring cheap workfare workers and firing regular employees instead.

Fifth, subsidiary welfare programmes will still have to be provided and funded for those who either fail to achieve employability and employment or who fail to keep a job once found, whether because their skills and work habits are found to be insufficient or because of decline in the business cycle or other economic contingencies.

Finally, and due to the 'fuzzy' and uncertain social technology of transforming poor non-workers into no-longer-poor workers according to the welfare-to-work logic, policymakers and programme administrators will find it necessary to spend substantial resources on the ongoing supervision and evaluation of overall programme results, as well as the design of experiments and innovations that can be expected to improve outcomes.

Taking these costly efforts together, the question seems to be wide open whether on balance the savings on welfare payments plus the overall productive contributions made by the people who have now found a permanent job are at all equivalent to these expenses. Chances are that the answer is negative, and that the only conceivable rationale for making those costly efforts is to make a case for the doctrine that work is to be preferred to welfare, regardless of the costs of implementing that rule.

5. Conclusion

Are these three broad categories of 'costs' (including the transactions costs, costs of process and outcome disutilities, risks of programme failures, etc.) that I have discussed – the costs of running welfare programmes, reforming welfare policy, and replacing welfare by workfare – worth paying for? The answer is, of course, 'It depends.' Efficiency is a relational measure, comparing one particular pattern of employing means towards some end with a different pattern that, if it can be shown to absorb fewer means while achieving roughly the same ends, can be said to be superior in efficiency. Efficiency comparisons are quite reliable where the manufacturing of shoes is concerned. It is quite a different matter if entire institutional sectors and policy areas are under consideration. This is so for three reasons: (a) because the ends achieved by different arrangements are never quite identical if we change the means by which they are being achieved, (b) because there is no handy metric (such as money, or hours of time) by which the means can be added to a sum representing 'total costs', and (c) because some of the means employed are not just instruments to achieve ends but rather ends in themselves, representing an intrinsically valued way of getting things done, thus defying any standard of economic rationality.

This having been said, I still think that two conclusions are worth drawing from the discussion of the costs of welfare/workfare policy. One is the substantial proportion of overhead costs that are being spent on the making, reforming, administering etc. of welfare/workfare policies and programmes compared to the amount of funds that end up in the pockets of the poor. A power station that turns out to spend half its electricity output on, say, lighting its own premises would rightly be considered a scandalously wasteful economic operation. But we seem to be much more generous when it comes to evaluating public policies and the institutional apparatuses which run them.

The other conclusion is that it is worth arguing for basic income not just in terms of justice, but also in terms of efficiency. The costs involved in welfare policies in general and 'welfare-to-work' policies in particular can provide a check-list for making this argument. Most of the items and costly operations I have specified would be saved in a well-designed BI scheme. Arguing for BI in terms of efficiency seems attractive because, in a way, it allows us to reverse the argument. Many critics of BI ideas are market liberals, and as such, are committed to cutting the wasteful activities of the public sector; these activities are held to impose unnecessary burdens upon the taxpayer or unnecessary constraints upon individuals' freedom of action, or often both. If that is their honest concern, market liberals should be anxious to support BI solutions to welfare and inclusion.

Opponents of BI have routinely argued that BI is wasteful because it disburses tax money to people who either do not *need* it (i.e., the self-reliant and hard-working middle class) or who do not *deserve* it (i.e., the work-shy surfers on the beach). The first objection can be dealt with by pointing out that all serious design proposals for BI propose to compensate for such middle-class windfalls by increasing taxes. As to the second, the charge can be refuted by pointing out that the time-honoured principle of less eligibility of poor laws remains under any BI scheme. And by implication, so does the economic incentive to seek employment or self-employment, which will be greater if all the necessary facilities for training and continuing education are in place. Moreover, the work-shy surfer would be quite an exceptional character should he never feel the ambition to do something that he considers useful for others, and should he permanently escape the social expectations and pressures to engage in freely chosen kinds of activity from which social recognition and self-esteem are to be gained. Should he actually turn out to be that exceptional character, he deserves our compassion rather than coercive, as well as massively inefficient, 'workfare'.

Notes

1   Humboldt University, Berlin.
2   Claims of unacceptability of welfare burdens are ambiguous. One might assume that the claim is unlikely to be brought forward, given that the 'deserving poor' in whose favour resources must be redistributed are defined in such a way that they make up a relatively small minority. As a consequence, the burden can be shared among a large majority and therefore should not be perceived as particularly painful. However, this large majority will find it easy to bring its political weight to bear upon the issue, thus transforming minor individual pains into a powerful collective political complaint.
3   See Ch. 34 by Joel Handler.

5

MIGRATION, CITIZENSHIP AND WELFARE STATE REFORM IN EUROPE: OVERCOMING MARGINALIZATION IN SEGREGATED LABOUR MARKETS

Roswitha Pioch[1]

1. Migration and Basic Income

The idea of a guaranteed basic income for all citizens has fascinated many people for a long time. Social philosophers have devoted themselves to it in search of a balance between social justice and capitalist markets (van Parijs, Cohen and Rogers, 2001; van Parijs, 1995; van Parijs 1992). In political debates about the future of the welfare state the idea of a citizens' income guaranteeing basic security to all inhabitants has been brought up by various political parties (Pioch, 2000; Pioch, 1999). A basic income is a form of guaranteed minimum income, which differs from all existing social security schemes in Europe. First, it is paid to individuals rather than households; second, everybody is entitled to it irrespective of any other income resources; and third, it is paid without any conditions regarding work performance in the labour market or the willingness to accept a job if offered. According to recent economic predictions, full employment cannot be re-established in advanced welfare states such as Germany because of the development of technology and the evolution of international markets. In the light of this labour market prognosis, a basic income would seem to be the appropriate solution to bridge the gap between insiders and outsiders, between unemployment and full-time work (Pioch, 1996). Moreover, economists have shown the technical feasibility of a basic income in various convincing ways (Atkinson, 1995; Beer, 2000; Beer, 1995; Mitschke, 2000; van Parijs, Jacquet and Salinas, 2000).

While a guaranteed basic income would appear to answer the call for social justice in modern welfare states, the issue needs to be reconsidered at a time when the nation state is being put under increasing international constraints. The questions to be raised are how processes of globalization, internationalization and economic integration affect national welfare states and what are the consequences for the basic income proposal. In this paper I will discuss the following thesis: when national welfare states lose control over their national boundaries, citizenship as the criterion of eligibility for a basic income becomes questionable. Onlyas long as the areas of responsibility of welfare states are congruent with their national borders, can one clearly speak of a guaranteed basic income as a citizens' income. The basic income was conceived as a universal right of all citizens to receive an income, to receive a share of the commonly-produced gross national income regardless of their work performance in the labour market. Today we are facing a situation where the basic income proposal has to be reconsidered in two ways. First, in the light of international migration, can citizenship still be an adequate claiming principle for a basic income? At times of international migration and immigration a substantial number of people do not fulfil the criterion of citizenship. For reasons of social justice, these people should not be excluded at the outset from participation in a guaranteed basic income scheme. These days, national citizenship has less and less to do with place of residence and work. Simply put: who deserves a basic income at a time of international mobility? Second, in the light of international constraints, can the national welfare state still be considered the appropriate distribution unit for a basic income? Two alternatives have been discussed. One is the proposal of a global basic income. The other is a Euro stipend, a much more realistic proposal that designates Europe as the new distribution unit for a basic income (Schmitter, 2000).

In the following I will argue that the basic income discussion needs to take account of continuing and increasing trends in international mobility as one feature of national welfare states (Section 2). I will discuss how welfare states adjust to economic integration and increasing international labour mobility (Section 3). Finally I will argue that national welfare states still serve as redistribution units under international economic constraints. The comparative advantage of tax-financed welfare states is that they provide opportunities for future, possibly more radical reforms, such as the introduction of a basic income. Moreover, if they took this step, they would be best prepared for avoiding social exclusion of ethnic minorities (Section 4).

2. European Integration and International Mobility

When we examine the changing conditions of social policy within the European integration process, it is useful to start by looking at the external borders of European welfare states. Eastern enlargement will not only have to integrate new countries, it will have to bridge much larger welfare gaps than have ever existed before in the European Union. The environment of national welfare states will change when neighbouring countries such as Poland and the Czech Republic become EU members. The huge welfare gap between the new countries and countries such as Germany and Austria will be an important issue for the enlarged European Union to address (Vobruba, 1997). Table 5.1 shows the income differences between the present member states and the EU applicants today in terms of Purchasing Power Parities.

I assume that the welfare gaps shown here undermine the political viability of a basic income. Why is this so? The drastic welfare gaps in the enlarged European Union will undoubtedly lead to increasing migration flows.

Table 5.1 Selected indicators on GDP levels and factor prices, 1998

	GNP per capita as % of EU-15	PPP-GNP per capita as % of EU-15	Gross wages and salaries as % of EU-15
Bulgaria	6	21	6
Czech Republic	23	47	18
Estonia	15	28	14
Hungary	20	40	15
Latvia	11	26	10
Lithuania	12	24	13
Poland	16	33	17
Romania	7	20	9
Slovak Republic	17	42	14
Slovenia	42	64	46
CEECs-10	**15**	**32**	**15**
Austria	124	113	102
Belgium	117	116	115
Denmark	154	118	157
Finland	112	100	107
France	115	111	101
Germany	120	103	151
Greece	54	64	51
Ireland	85	91	97
Italy	94	100	75
Luxembourg	202	185	133
Netherlands	115	107	110
Portugal	49	71	39
Spain	65	80	72
Sweden	119	97	145
United Kingdom	99	102	107
EU-15	**100**	**100**	**100**

Source: Boeri and Brücker (2001).

However, various economic models show that the expected migration from eastern to western Europe has tended to be largely overestimated. The more recent the estimations, the lower the migration balance they predict (Brücker and Boeri, 2000; European Commission, 2001a, p. 34). Even so, people will fear welfare migration and hesitate to support anything like an unconditional basic income. I presume that it is the notion of a tight connection between welfare states and EU membership that makes people fear welfare migration (Dore, 2002). The crucial problem remains the following, as Bill Jordan puts it:

> The central problem for advocates of basic income who take account of boundary issues of equality and justice is therefore the paradox of mobility and membership. Equality and open borders seem to demand a global basis for distribution; justice among members, democracy and pluralism point to a national system, which has rules allowing access after a period of residence. The challenge of justification, and of technical feasibility, therefore shifts towards questions of exit, voice and loyalty, and beyond those of work obligations and feasible funding (Jordan, 2002, p. 28; Jordan, 2003).

In any case, the freedom of mobility rules within the EU-treaties will not let us restrict a basic income to citizens. It must be extended to residents. And this leads to a discussion of what residency status qualifies for a basic income and what does not.

EU member states have to take these wide welfare gaps into consideration in designing their migration policy as well as their social policy. So far, the two policy fields have been only weakly harmonized despite common European regulations. In respect to migration policy there has been harmonization of external border control through a common visa policy. On 14 June 1985, the Federal Republic of Germany, France, Belgium, Luxembourg and the Netherlands signed the Schengen Agreement (Schengen being a town in Luxembourg) on the gradual abolition of checks at their common borders. On 19 June 1990, the Convention implementing the Schengen Agreement was signed. Its key points relate to measures designed to create a common area of security and justice, once the border checks within the Schengen area have been done away with. Specifically it is concerned with harmonizing provisions relating to entry into and short stays in the Schengen area by non-EU citizens. It harmonized the visa policies of Schengen countries via a common list of third countries whose nationals require visas. Furthermore it harmonized asylum matters by determining to which member state an application for asylum may be submitted. These rules determining competence for asylum procedures have been largely replaced by similar provisions in the Dublin Convention of 15 June 1990, which came into force on 1 September 1997. It provides a mechanism for determining which Dublin Convention country is responsible for examining an application for refugee status. However, migration policy issues, like all matters of integration and naturalization, still belong to the realm of the national states.

One of the most important pillars of European social policy is based on EU rules guaranteeing the freedom of movement of persons. Regulation (EEC) No 1408/71 of the Council of 14 June 1971, on the application of social security schemes to employed persons and their families moving within the Community, aims to ensure that such persons do not suffer disadvantages in their social security rights. The Regulation does not replace national rules. What it does is establish rules and principles to coordinate the social security systems of the member states and the European Economic Area (comprising Liechtenstein, Norway and Iceland). It aims to ensure that application of the different national systems does not adversely affect persons exercising their right to freedom of movement. It enables workers to transfer their claims to social insurance benefits when they moves from one country to another. Social insurance benefit cannot be cut or denied because the worker has moved within the EU or EEA. The possibility of transferring claims to social benefits exists in all branches of social insurance that provide benefits in case of invalidity, old age or for surviving dependants, no matter whether these claims derive from universal or contribution-based social insurance systems. However, the Regulation is not applicable to social assistance. It aims to facilitate the movement of workers, and was initially formulated to cover employed and self-employed persons and members of their families, i.e. 'active' members of the population and their dependants. It aims at welfare state inclusion of those who are already productive. 'Non-active' people, who are not covered by a general insurance scheme for workers, are not covered by the Regulation. However, in case of family reunification or disability or old age of the migrant worker, the country of entry has to provide all social benefits to all legally residing persons regardless of their labour market participation.

In social policy the fundamental principle of equal treatment of EU nationals and citizens of a member state requires that all social benefits a member-state provides to its citizens have to be provided to all EU nationals residing in the country. Therefore it is argued that countries that provide generous income support have become vulnerable to welfare migration under the EU's freedom of mobility rules. The principle of equal treatment also implies that if a basic income is introduced in any one of the member states of the European Union, it cannot be offered as an exclusive citizens' income. It must also be offered to nationals of other EU member states residing legally in the country.

Whatever concrete solutions are opted for, the answer to the question of how to organize social security provisions will remain the responsibility of the national welfare states. To sum up, social security, like major parts of migration policy, will remain an issue for the national welfare state, despite the fact that in some social policy areas such as occupational safety and health and gender policy, there are examples of positive integration via common European regulations.

In social policy, employment policy and, recently, migration policy, a new instrument deserves our attention: the so-called Open Method of Co-ordination (European Commission, 2001; Hodson and Maher, 2001). Following this method each member state delivers a migration report once a year and announces a national action plan for its migration policy. Additionally, the Commission works out a synopsis of all migration reports. On this basis, it is hoped, member states can inform each other and learn from each other regarding migration, social and employment policy. The Open Method of Co-ordination serves as a tool to define common goals and achievements for the future of Europe (Vandenbroucke, 2002). At present no one can say what will emerge from this new method. Although it presents an opportunity to harmonize social and migration policy further, for the moment we have to assume that migration policy remains mainly a national policy task, and that the national welfare state is not about to transfer its regulating power to the European level. This does not mean that ongoing global processes do not have an impact on national welfare states. On the contrary, economic processes of internationalization and globalization sharpen the competition among national welfare states. Therefore, national welfare states – if they want to survive – have to adapt to the changing conditions and new constraints posed by European integration, Eastern enlargement and global economic changes (Streeck, 1998).

3. Migration and Social Policy in Europe

In social policy, two different types of welfare system are usually distinguished. In the Bismarckian system, social security is basically financed through the contributions of workers. In the Beveridge system, social security provisions are financed out of taxes. Eastern enlargement and the expected migration flows make it necessary to reconsider which mode of welfare state financing can cope better with increasing migration. It is commonly assumed that contribution-based welfare states are better equipped to deal with increased migration than tax-financed welfare systems. In a short-term perspective, this assumption seems plausible. Tax-financed systems where the claims to social security are not directly connected to prior work in the labour market will need to make bigger adjustments. To quote Leibfried and Pierson:

> Coordination requirements work best with individualized, earned social rights of the employed, and worst with collective provisions of services to all citizens. Policymakers are thus encouraged to follow the program design of Bismarck (benefits based on contribution) rather than Beveridge (universal, flat-rate benefits). [...] Some smaller member states like the Netherlands and Denmark (and now Sweden), which has a long-standing universalist tradition, will be under EU-induced pressure for more substantial reforms (Leibfried and Pierson, 1995, pp. 57–58).

Social security systems vary in their sensitivity and vulnerability to greater mobility of benefit claimants. In particular, universal pension benefits, which rely on residency rather than being tied to prior contributions, could give an incentive to welfare migration. In the following I suggest looking empirically at recent welfare reforms in Germany, the Netherlands and Sweden and asking to what extent they have reformed their basic pension in respect to European integration and Eastern enlargement. This way we have an empirically informed basis for discussing the chances of introducing a basic income in an era of migration and European integration.

Until the last pension reform in 2001, Germany – the prototype of a Bismarckian welfare state – did not have a basic pension system. The contributory pension system covers those who have worked, and entitlements depend on prior wages. The main problem resulting from this regulation was that women who had interrupted their working career or had been paid very little were insufficiently insured. Therefore a reform was passed which added a basic security provision to the contributory pension scheme. If we look at the debate before the reform was passed, we find precisely the argument that imminent Eastern enlargement would not permit introducing a tax-financed pension scheme into the contributory scheme. According to the German pension expert Franz Ruland, if a means-tested basic pension is considered part of the pension insurance, it will fall under EU Regulation 1408/71. Even if it fell under the annex, which excludes the export of special provisions, it would be necessary to offer it also to nationals from other EU countries residing legally in Germany. Because of the principle of non-discrimination it would not be possible to restrict the basic security to German citizens. Therefore it was argued that the upcoming Eastern enlargement would make it necessary to anticipate a much larger group of beneficiaries (Ruland, 1999). Meanwhile the Social Democrat/Green Government passed a law introducing a means-tested basic pension scheme. According to the new legislation, which came into force on 1 January, 2003, the basic pension is not part of the contribution-based pension scheme (Rahn, 2001). It is a tax-financed basic security with its own administration. Legally, it is intended to protect old people from the need to resort to social assistance. In practice, it is a means-tested provision.

People over sixty-five with a pension or another income below the social assistance level are eligible to claim the new basic security. In sum the benefits are slightly higher than social assistance. Up to an income level of €100.000 the general principle that adult children and their parents support each other, which still exists in German social assistance, has been abandoned for this basic security. It is hoped that this will eliminate hidden poverty. Because it is a tax-financed provision like social assistance, the export of basic security entitlements outside Germany is not possible. Only permanent residents in Germany are entitled to it. In the new legislation, asylum-seekers and all other foreigners in Germany without a permanent resident permit are explicitly excluded from entitlement. Asylum-seekers are entitled to asylum-seeker benefits, which are 20 per cent below social assistance benefit rates and are often paid as in-kind support, such as vouchers. Illegal immigrants, including those who refuse to disclose their identity, are usually only entitled to medical aid. The recent reform in Germany succeeded in introducing a basic minimum pension to retirees and disabled persons by separating the contribution-based security scheme from additional tax-financed provisions. One may interpret this as a small, but nevertheless important step towards basic security in a Bismarckian welfare state.

How did countries that already had a universal basic pension scheme react to increasing international movement of persons? In the Swedish case the basic pension was indeed adapted to requirements of European integration (Schludi, 2001a). As Schludi points out, prior to 1993, all Swedish citizens above 65 were entitled to a full basic pension. Foreigners, however, needed a minimum of five years of residence for a full basic pension and were not allowed to receive their basic pension outside the country. These rules were not compatible with EU provisions about the equal treatment of nationals and non-nationals. Moreover, the extension of the existing rules for Swedish citizens to non-nationals would have meant that everyone who had resided in Sweden at some time would have been entitled to a full pension. As a consequence, shortly before joining the EU in 1995, Sweden introduced a residence requirement, according to which forty years' residence (or thirty years' contribution to the general supplementary pension, the 'ATP') is needed for a person to be able to claim full basic pension. It is obvious from the Swedish example that universal benefit schemes are subject to special adjustment pressures that do not burden Bismarckian-type systems, where the link between contributions and benefits is relatively strong.

In the Netherlands there is also a universal basic pension scheme, which provides a basic pension to all residents over 65. An additional occupational pension scheme provides income-related pension benefits to more than 90 per cent of workers. The basic pension scheme was introduced in 1957 for all retirees over sixty-five. In the Dutch case no adjustment to increasing labour mobility due to EU integration was necessary. From the very beginning the basic pension was tied to a fifty-year residence requirement for full pension entitlement (Anderson, 2000; Anderson, 2001). All in all, confronted by European integration, tax-financed basic security schemes appear to be more vulnerable than contribution-related benefit schemes. Their eligibility principles need to be adapted to international movement of persons on one hand, and equal treatment of nationals and non-nationals on the other. In which direction they adjust, whether they restrict or open up the schemes for non-residents, asylum-seekers and foreigners with non-permanent resident status, is a question of political will and political decision-making.

4. Overcoming Segregated Labour Markets

In the following I will argue that even though tax-financed security schemes might, in the short-term, seem more vulnerable at a time of international mobility than contribution-based schemes, in a long-term perspective they could be better suited for dealing with international migration in modern societies. The advantage of tax-financed social security schemes is that they do not put the burden of financing social security upon labour relations. This is especially valuable in the low-wage segment, where we find that the contributions employers and employees have to pay for social security have a negative impact on job creation. In other words, a shift from contribution-based social security to tax-financing of social security could foster employment. A well-balanced labour market broadens opportunities for a less restrictive migration policy. Moreover, tax-financed social security schemes reinforce the idea of universal solidarity compared to the categorical structure of contribution-based welfare states. Tax-financing of social security benefits supports a liberal migration policy, not only because it is efficient, but because it promotes the idea of solidarity and social justice.

A comparative study of twelve welfare states conducted by Fritz Scharpf and Vivian Schmidt shows that there is indeed a relationship between the tax system and private employment, but this is not because high taxes in general have negative employment effects (Scharpf and Schmidt, 2000a). Rather they contend that employment effects vary greatly on both the employment and the tax side of the relationship:

Employment in internationally exposed industrial and service branches seems hardly affected at all by the size of the overall tax burden. Instead, negative effects seem to be concentrated in branches in which services are produced and consumed locally. On the tax side, in turn, it seems that private sector employment is not affected by differences in the levels of personal and corporate income taxes, whereas social security contributions and consumption taxes have strongly negative employment effects (Scharpf, 1999, p. 20).

As we can learn from Scharpf, the market-clearing wages of less productive services might be at or near the level of social assistance benefits that define the lowest net reservation wage in advanced welfare states. Therefore, the costs of taxes and social contributions levied on such jobs cannot be shifted to employees, but must be added entirely to the costs of production (Scharpf, 1999; Scharpf, 2000b; Scharpf, 2000a). The same argument explains the variation in the impact of income tax and social contributions. Social contributions are usually raised as a proportional tax on total wages, up to a limit at medium wage levels. Hence they fall heavily on low-wage jobs, while the burden on highly productive and highly paid jobs is relatively smaller. By contrast, personal income taxes usually allow for a standard tax deduction. Income taxes are only collected on the income above the standard exemption. Since income tax rates are generally progressive, the burden of income taxes on low-wage jobs tends to be minimal. Under conditions of internationalization and globalization all welfare states are under pressure to increase private sector employment, to raise the efficiency of welfare state spending, and to reduce the negative impact on employment of welfare state financing and welfare state benefits (Scharpf, 1999; Schludi, 2001b). However, from the comparative study of twelve advanced welfare states we learn that national welfare states differ greatly in their vulnerability to international economic pressures (Scharpf and Schmidt, 2000b). Private sector employment stagnates in continental welfare states such as Germany, because social contributions, consumer taxes and minimum wages cumulate to increase labour costs. Private sector employment could increase significantly in Germany, if the costs of financing welfare benefits were shifted at least partially from social contributions towards income tax, or if at least, as in the Netherlands, social contributions were collected at progressive rates (Scharpf, 2000b).

Finally, it is worth looking at the effects of different social policy solutions on migration policy. Tax-based welfare state financing improves the chances of increasing private sector employment. A high level of employment, especially in the low-wage sector, which is the most relevant job market for ethnic minorities, increases the number of immigrant political actors that could be allowed into the country. This is the efficiency argument. Contribution-based welfare state financing strengthens the idea of equivalence because of the strong relationship between the direct input of the beneficiaries and their work performance. In contrast, tax financing stands for the idea of universal solidarity. Taxes are collected to finance common welfare. It is the job of the political decision-making process to define who belongs in the inner circle of the legitimate claimants of welfare benefits. Thus, by supporting the idea of universal solidarity, tax-based welfare state financing provides the normative foundation for a less restrictive migration policy. This is where the good old liberal idea of a citizens' income comes in again.

These days, however, the idea of an unconditional citizens' income must be adjusted to a modern concept of an open multicultural society. Today, it is necessary to reconsider whether citizenship should be the fundamental claiming principle of a guaranteed basic income. In Europe, the national welfare state will remain the redistribution unit of welfare state benefits even in the future (Offe, 2001). Thus, the question is: who belongs to the inner circle of legitimate receivers of a basic income? Under what conditions do migrants and ethnic minorities belong to it? A debate about these questions will contribute to the future of advanced welfare states for efficiency reasons and for reasons of social justice. Basic income is a fascinating tool to bridge the gap between insiders and outsiders in the labour market. However, at a time of international mobility, basic income proposals must include not only citizens but also migrants who reside in national welfare states. 'Dignified work needs basic security, or real freedom is denied. Dignified work only evolves if ordinary people have the capacity to say "No"' (Standing, 2002). This must also be true for migrant workers. So far, the proponents of a basic income have scarcely touched the topic of immigration, social justice and social security. They would be well advised to take a stand on the issue. They should, at least, be aware that their political opponents have already started the debate.

Note

1   Max Planck Institute for the Study of Social Sciences, Cologne, Germany.

References

Anderson, K. M. 2000. *The impact of European integration on public pensions: Convergence or divergence?*, Paper presented at the 12th International Conference of Europeanists, Chicago, March 30–April 2, 2000.

_____ 2001. *European integration and pension policy in the Netherlands and Germany*, Paper presented at the Biennial Conference of the European Community Studies Association, Madison, Wisconsin, 31 May – 2 June 2001.

Atkinson, A. B. 1995. *Incomes and the welfare state* (New York, Cambridge University Press).

Beer, P. de. 1995. 'Sociaal-economische mythen en het draagvlak voor een basisinkomen', in R. van der Veen and D. Pels (eds.) *Het basisinkomen. Sluitstuk van de verzorgingsstaat?* (Amsterdam, Van Gennep), pp. 79–123.

_____ 2000. 'In search of the double-edged sword', in R. van der Veen and L. Groot (eds.) *Basic income on the agenda: Policy objectives and political chances* (Amsterdam, Amsterdam University Press), pp. 41–52.

Boeri, T. and Brücker, H. 2001. 'Eastern enlargement and EU-labour markets: perceptions, challenges and opportunities', *IZA Discussion Paper No. 256* (forthcoming in *World Economy*), (Bonn, Institute for the Study of Labour, Bonn University).

Brücker, H. and Boeri, T. 2000. *The impact of Eastern enlargement on employment and labour markets in the EU Member States*, paper commissioned by the Employment and Social Affairs Directorate-General of the European Commission (Berlin and Milan, European Integration Consortium).

Dore, R. 2002. 'The Liberal's dilemma: Immigration, social solidarity and basic income', paper for BIEN Congress, Geneva, September 2002.

European Commission 2001a. *The free movement of workers in the context of enlargement* (Brussels, European Commission),.

_____ 2001b. *Mitteilung der Kommission vom 11.7.2001: Offener Koordinierungsmechanismus für die Migrationspolitik der Gemeinschaft* (Brussels, European Commission).

Hodson, D. and Maher, I. 2001. 'The open method as a new mode of governance: The case of soft economic policy coordination', in *Journal of Common Market Studies*, No. 39, pp. 719–746.

Jordan, B. 2002. *Migration, mobility and membership: The boundaries of equality and justice*, unpublished manuscript, University of Exeter.

_____ and Düvell, F. 2003. *Migration: The boundaries of equality and justice* (London, Polity Press).

Leibfried, S. and Pierson, P. (eds.) 1995. *European social policy: Between fragmentation and integration* (Washington D.C., The Brookings Institution).

Mitschke, J. 2000. 'Arguing for a negative income tax in Germany', in R. van der Veen and L. Groot (eds.) *Basic income on the agenda. Policy objectives and political chances* (Amsterdam, Amsterdam University Press), pp. 107–120.

Offe, C. 2001. 'Pathways from here', in P. van Parijs, J. Cohen and J. Rogers, (2001), pp. 111–129.

Parijs, P. van (ed.) 1992. *Arguing for basic income: ethical foundations for a radical reform* (London, Verso).

_____ 1995. *Real freedom for all. What (if anything) can justify capitalism?* (Oxford, Clarendon Press).

_____, Cohen, J. and Rogers, J. (eds.) 2001. *What's wrong with a free lunch?* (Boston, Beacon Press).

_____, Jacquet, L. and Salinas, C. C. 2000. 'Basic income and its cognates: Partial basic income versus earned income tax credit and reductions of social security contributions as alternative ways of addressing the "new social question"', in R. van der Veen and L. Groot (eds.) *Basic income on the agenda: Policy objectives and political chances*. (Amsterdam, Amsterdam University Press), pp. 53–84.

Pioch, R. 1996. 'Basic income: Social policy after full employment', in A. Erskine (ed.) *Changing Europe. Some aspects of identity, conflict and social justice* (Aldershot, Avebury), pp. 148–160.

_____ 1999. 'Ideas of social justice in the welfare state in Germany and the Netherlands', in P. Littlewood *et al.* (eds.) *Social exclusion in Europe: Problems and paradigms* (Aldershot, Ashgate), pp. 124–142.

_____ 2000. *Soziale Gerechtigkeit in der Politik – Orientierungen von Politikern in Deutschland und den Niederlanden* (Frankfurt/M., Campus).

Rahn, M. 2001. 'Einführung einer bedarfsorientierten Grundischerung im Alter und bei Erwerbsminderung', in *Deutsche Rentenversicherung*, Nos. 6-7, pp. 431–437.

Ruland, F. 1999. 'Contra: Bedürftigkeitsorientierte Mindestsicherung', in *Deutsche Rentenversicherung*, Nos. 8–9, pp. 480–493.

Scharpf, F. W. 1999. 'The viability of advanced welfare states in the international economy: Vulnerabilities and options', MPIfG Working Paper 99/9 (Cologne, Max Planck Institute for the Study of Societies).

_____ 2000a. 'Basic income and social Europe', in R. van der Veen and L. Groet (eds.) *Basic Income on the agenda: Policies objectives and political chances* (Amsterdam, Amsterdam University Press).

_____ 2000b. 'Der globale Sozialstaat. Umfangreiche Sicherungssysteme schaden nicht der Wettbewerbsfähigkeit – vorausgesetzt sie werden überwiegend steuerfinanziert', in *Die Zeit*, 8 June, 2000.

Scharpf, F. W. and Schmidt, V. (eds.), 2000a. *Welfare and work in the open economy: Diverse responses to common challenges* (Oxford, Oxford University Press).

_____ 2000b. *Welfare and work in the open economy: From vulnerability to competitiveness* (Oxford, Oxford University Press).

Schludi, M. 2001a. 'Pension reform in European social insurance countries', Paper prepared for the Biennial Meeting of the European Community Studies Association, Madison, Wisconsin.

_____ 2001b. 'The politics of pensions in European social insurance countries', MPIfG Discussion Paper 01/11 (Cologne, Max Planck Institute for the Study of Societies).

Schmitter, P. C. 2000. 'How to democratize the EU ... and why bother?', in *Governance in Europe* (Lanham, Rowman and Littlefield).

Standing, G. 2002. *Beyond the new paternalism: Basic security as equality* (London, Verso).

Streeck, W. 1998. 'Einleitung: Internationale Wirtschaft, nationale Demokratie?', in W. Streeck (ed.) *Internationale Wirtschaft, nationale Demokratie. Herausforderungen für die Demokratietheorie* (Frankfurt/M., Campus), pp. 11–50.

Vandenbroucke, F. 2002. 'The EU and social protection: What should the European convention propose?', MPIfG Working Paper 02/6 (Cologne, Max Planck Institute for the Study of Societies).

Vobruba, G. 1997. *Autonomiegewinne. Sozialstaatsdynamik, Moralfreiheit, Transnationalisierung* (Vienna, Passagen Verlag).

6

THE LIBERAL'S DILEMMA: IMMIGRATION, SOCIAL SOLIDARITY AND BASIC INCOME

Ron Dore[1]

1. Introduction

Liberal? I use the word in the American sense – not the free-market liberal sense – of leftward-leaning, what the Italians call *persone per bene*. I assume that proponents of a basic income belong to that category. I also assume that one characteristic of such people is likely to be a hostile reaction to xenophobic out-cries against asylum-seekers, immigrants, health-service tourists etc. They are likely to be tolerant unchauvinistic multiculturalists, horrified by the Le Pens and Haiders of this world, in favour of internationalism and cosmopolitanism. But it is reasonable to suppose that there is a connection between cultural diversity/homogeneity, the strength of a sense of national identity, and social solidarity. Immigration and the diversity it brings weaken social solidarity. For basic income, as a sharing of income within a given, usually national community, to be politi-cally acceptable, there needs to be some sense of sharing membership in that community on the part both of the givers in the exchange and the receivers.

2. Why Social Solidarity Counts

Perhaps British exceptionalism is too pronounced to take its welfare problem as typical of European societies, but the most likely route by which the United Kingdom will arrive at a basic income system is through a combination of wage subsidies and growth in benefit fraud.

3. Why a Continuing Growth in Wage Subsidies?

The growing dispersal of the primary earned income distribution in OECD economies is a complex phenomenon, but a primary factor is a slow but

continuous shift in scarcities along the skilled/unskilled spectrum, due primarily
to the continuing cumulative growth in the body of technical knowledge
deployed in money-earning activity. Although this growth in 'things to be
learned' can be matched by a similar growth in training facilities, experience
has shown that there is a limit to the extent to which improvements in education can bring a matching upward shift in the distribution of learning abilities. Where 'work not welfare' ideologies dominate, wage subsidies seem to be
the only effective way of keeping the low-paid out of poverty. In the UK the
system which, when it began, was limited to families with children, is being
extended to all low-paid workers.

4. Why a Growth in Benefit Fraud?

The adjustment of the primary distribution towards lesser inequality and the
prevention of outright poverty increasingly takes the form of a growth in targeted, means-tested benefits, as opposed to universal benefits, especially of
those types of benefit which invite collusion in fraud between beneficiary and
landlord or beneficiary and employer. With this expansion of the potential
occasions for fraud goes the continuing decline in deference, and continuing
globalization with its tendency to erode a sense of belonging to a national
community and hence of having obligations to a national State.

5. Why should Wage Subsidies and Fraud Lead to a Basic Income?

As the wage subsidy budget grows, the extra cost of shifting to a universal
basic income at a level that makes a large part of the means-tested benefits
unnecessary would diminish. As fraud increases, its consequences (indignation
of honest tax-payers and anger at Government which does not prevent it;
hardening of fraudsters' sense of alienation from mainstream society with
possible consequences for criminality etc.) make a shift to universal benefits
more attractive.

6. A Paradox

It is a paradox that the diminution of the sense of social solidarity produced
by increasing fraud should spawn a system whose acceptability depends on a
sense of social solidarity. Can the argument 'we shall thereby cure these anti-
social tendencies, we shall help to reknit the ties which bind us together in one
national community' be effectively used politically to promote the shift? And
is it likely that the promise of that argument will be fulfilled? And does it make
a difference to the answers to both of those questions whether there is a large
proportion of immigrants in the population, or whether the immigrant ratio

is higher among benefit recipients or benefit fraudsters than in the population at large?

7. Questions for Social Scientists

How much does the literature on citizenship help one to specify the sort of 'social solidarity' that makes income redistribution via taxation and universal benefits politically acceptable? In particular, how does one explain the apparent paradox that the sort of individualism which one would imagine antithetical to that sense of community which can promote income redistribution, seems to promote rather than inhibit the sense of community, which in turn leads to aggressive patriotism. Think of Mrs Thatcher at the time of the Falklands War and the flag-waving United States after September 11, 2001.

8. Rights and Duties

My expectation has always been that a switch to universal income rights would have to be accompanied by an increased emphasis on, and some kind of institutionalized requirement for, the performance of citizen duties. (Something more than jury service, and more on the lines of the national service still preserved in most continental countries.) I would prefer that the two were not directly linked in a participation income – i.e., that failure to perform duties would not be punished by removal of that particular income right. But is the acceptance or otherwise of citizen duties one way both of discriminating between those eligible and non-eligible for a citizen's income, and also one way of politically justifying the introduction of basic income?

9. Questions for Liberals

That has implications for the multiculturism versus assimilation question. Insistence on citizen duties would imply deliberate efforts at assimilation. Are recent British moves towards assimilation a step in the right direction? .

Note

1   London School of Economics, United Kingdom.

7

THE PSYCHOLOGICAL RATIONALE FOR BASIC INCOME

Rosamund Stock[1]

1. Introduction

This paper is intended to give a short overview of those areas of social psychology which have a bearing upon the arguments for and against a basic income. What I hope to demonstrate is that the distribution of resources has real-world consequences and those consequences are the result of the psychology of distributions.

2. The Psychology of Distributions

Many people have heard of something called equity theory, and it is often presented (almost always by non-psychologists, and almost always by economists) as *the* psychological theory of justice. It was first formulated in 1963 by John Stacy Adams and says that people will perceive their rewards to be fair when those rewards are in an appropriate proportion to their inputs. However, since the early 1970s, this has been considered to be only one possible distribution rule, or principle of justice.

Work in developmental psychology, in organizational psychology and in bargaining studies all suggested that there was more than one rule of distributive justice and that these rules were not simply versions of one single all-embracing principle. Researchers noticed that people tended to choose or advocate different distribution rules in different situations. For example, children often use equality in a team situation, although they are quite capable of understanding and using equity (Lerner, 1974).

A series of experiments bringing people together to work on group tasks (Deutsch, 1985) found that when people were encouraged to get on as a team they tended to choose equality; and when they knew that their rewards, usually their group bonus, would be distributed equally, they tended to be cooperative and get on as a team. In addition, their productivity increased, even though the people themselves believed that a proportional distribution would motivate them best. When people did work under a proportional distribution, when they were paid by results, they tended to see other people as different and less cooperative. They felt less positive about them, and this form of performance-related pay did not, by and large, increase their productivity.

Another series of experiments (Frohlich and Oppenheimer, 1992) tried to investigate how Rawls' famed 'veil of ignorance' would affect the choices made by a group of people who were working together and had the chance to discuss how their rewards should be distributed (and no one chose Rawls' difference principle). They found that redistribution encouraged those who were producing least (this was a proof-reading task) to increase their contribution to the group's output, and by a bigger proportion than any of the other, better performing, participants. The move towards greater equality had motivated a significant increase in productivity.

Over the last thirty years, three general principles of justice have come to be recognized by justice researchers:

• *proportionality or equity*: members of a group should receive rewards in proportion to their contribution, input or investments.
• *equality*: all should get the same.
• *need*: resources should go to those in greatest need.

An important area of justice research has developed to deal with the way that these different rules are associated with quite different motivational orientations in the individual, with different attitudes to the group, and with quite different types of social relationship between the members of the group. A theory of distributive justice says that these three different types of distribution are qualitatively different; they are not versions of the same thing. There is an accumulation of evidence that links proportional (equity-based) distributions to competitive or individualistic orientations and relationships, equality to cooperation, and need-based distributions to caring or communal relations.

When, for example, I asked people to describe the distribution of resources in society, it was very noticeable that when they were talking about proportionality or equity they tended to describe other people as different, differentiated from each other (Stock, 2003). When they talked about equality, they tended to describe people as essentially similar. But when they talked about need, they rarely bothered to mention the characteristics of individuals at all. In the same way, when they were being asked to explain these distributions, they talked about society as a caring society with need, or a community based on equality, but when thinking in terms of proportionality they hardly bothered to mention groups at all.

Thirty years of evidence in social psychology links equality to cooperation and often to greater productivity. There is also evidence that need-based distributions foster communal, welfare-based relationships. Proportional (differential or unequal) distributions go with competitive or individualistic attitudes and do not, except under very tight constraints, improve productivity (Johnson *et al.*, 1981). The distribution of resources in society is about the kind of relationships we have with each other, and therefore about the kind of society we can have.

3. Basic Income in Relation to Equality or Need

So the first conclusion from the psychological literature is that the type of distribution in which people participate can have a profound effect on how they perceive the group around them, and that this effect can often be in spite of the beliefs they themselves have about the motivating power of those distributions.

There is a second very important psychological factor in considering basic income. The above evidence implies that a basic income, given to everyone as of right and as a form of equality will, in fact, foster co-operative attitudes in society, and motivate greater cooperation. The evidence from psychology also suggests that more egalitarian distributions tend to increase productivity, especially for tasks requiring cooperation; most tasks in our highly interconnected and interdependent society require cooperation and coordination.

However, more than one review of the justice literature has questioned whether the link between rules and types of social relationship really is anything more than cultural accident. In different social situations different rules are used, and the different situations often include different social relationships. If, on the other hand, you concentrate on how the participants actually see the situation, then there is a fairly robust association between how they see the social relationships and the rules they describe or advocate.

Again, it has long been known that people have apparently quite contradictory attitudes to distributions; Burgoyne *et al.* (1993) have pointed out that these contradictions disappear when you look in detail at what psychologists call 'framing' effects (Tversky and Kahneman, 1981). Responses will differ depending on whether someone sees an outcome as a gain or a loss; whether, for example, they are thinking about income as a social good, or as pay in the workplace, even though for most people these are pretty well the same thing. They will disapprove of private medicine when they are thinking about overall outcomes in society, but accept it when they are thinking of the individual's right to make provision for him- or herself.

So it is necessary to consider how basic income will be seen. Will it be a 'citizens' income' given to everyone as a right? Or will it be a 'basic income' intended to cover 'basic needs'? After all, someone with multiple disabilities has a far greater basic requirement than a fit and healthy adult, and it may not look very equal to them. This is a debate we need to have.

4. The National Health Service (NHS) in the United Kingdom

The central rationale in this paper is that knowing how ordinary people perceive, think about and talk about distributions is important for how basic income is seen, and thus for how we should present it and argue for it. But it is also important for the broader political arguments we make because it has the potential to have a profound impact on the sort of society we have.

When people talk about the society they live in and when they use different distribution rules, or principles of justice, they come up with a coherent set of descriptions of the society around them. These include the nature of society as a group, the nature of social relationships and descriptions of people; they also include descriptions of the distribution mechanism. Bill Morris, General Secretary of the Transport and General Workers Union in the UK, at a rally against the creeping privatization of our health service, insisted that how we provide our public services is about the kind of society we are. He is right, because how something is provided is intrinsic to what is provided: the NHS is an institution whose goal is the provision of healthcare according to clinical need.

The NHS in the UK is not only extremely popular with ordinary people, it is crucial to the kind of society we are (Taylor-Gooby, 1991). If a child is born with serious multiple defects and disabilities, that child will go to the Hospital for Sick Children in Great Ormond Street. No one will ask the parents if they can afford it. But more than that: paying, exchanging money, simply does not come into it; it is not a money-based transaction. And we take it completely for granted. When I asked people to talk about the distribution of resources other than income, I did not elicit a great deal of material concerning the distribution of healthcare, perhaps because of this attitude. Waiting lists and delays in accident and emergency treatment notwithstanding, the principle still stands: if you need treatment you are treated and you do not even have to think about paying for it.

In the 1960s, Garfinkel did a famous piece of research, which laid the foundations of much social phenomenology. In one example, he asked his students to go home and play the role of a lodger in their families: their families were outraged at what they saw as bizarre and uncooperative behaviour. The students were challenging assumptions about the situation which were completely and utterly taken for granted. The taken-for-granted is very powerful psychologically.

The ILO has undertaken a large-scale survey of socio-economic security, in which access to healthcare is seen as part of basic security. I would like to suggest that such access, as exemplified by the British NHS, and in particular its taken-for-grantedness, has a profound effect on what our world feels like, and on the kind of society we are.

Note

1   London School of Economics, United Kingdom.

References

Adams, J.S. 1963. 'Towards an undertanding of inequity', in *Journal of Abnormal and Social Psychology*, Vol. 67, pp. 422–436.

Burgoyne, C., Swift, A and Marshall, G. 1993. 'Inconsistency in beliefs about distributive justice: A cautionary note', in *Journal for the Theory of Social Behaviour*, Vol. 23, pp. 327–342.

Deutsch, M. 1985. *Distributive Justice* (Yale: Yale University Press).

Frohlich, N. and Oppenheimer, J.A, 1992. *Choosing Justice: An Experimental Approach to Ethical Theory* (Berkeley, CA, University of California Press).

Garfinkel, H. 1967. *Studies in Ethnomethodology* (Englewood Cliffs, New Jersey, Prentice-Hall).

Johnson, D.W., Maruyama, G., Johnson, R., Nelson, D. and Skon, L. 1981. 'Effects of cooperative, competitive and individualistic goal structures on achievement: a meta-analysis', in *Psychological Bulletin*, Vol. 89, pp. 47–62.

Lerner, M. 1974. 'The justice motive: Equity and parity among children', in *Journal of Personality and Social Psychology*, Vol. 29, pp. 539–550.

Stock, R.E. 2003. 'Explaining the choice of distribution rule: the role of mental representations', in *Sociological Inquirer*, 73, pp. 177–189.

Taylor-Gooby, P. 1991. 'Attachment to the welfare state', in R. Jowell, L. Brook and E. Taylor (eds.) *British Social Attitudes: the 8th Report* (Dartmouth, Aldershot).

Tversky, A. and Kahneman, D. 1981. 'The framing of decisions and the psychology of choice', in *Science*, Vol. 211, pp. 453–458.

8

THE LIMITS OF PRODUCTION: JUSTIFYING GUARANTEED BASIC INCOME

Sibyl Schwarzenbach[1]

1. Introduction

> For what is government itself but the greatest of all reflections on human nature?
>
> James Madison[2]

Surely a part of the reason it is so difficult for many to accept the idea of a guaranteed basic income has to do with prevailing assumptions regarding the nature of not just the liberal citizen, and the necessary obligations and labour he is expected to perform, but also the very nature and purpose of the modern State. I shall argue here that, in contrast to older conceptions, the modern nation State is implicitly based on a particular conception of labour: what I call the Lockean production model. Moreover, it is in comparison with this model of labour – viewed as the paradigm of all free labour – that guaranteeing a basic income for all citizens of a society, irrespective of their own capacity for work, appears a perverse incentive for laziness and a foolish handout to the unworthy at best. At worst, such a basic income is viewed as outright theft, and the direct violation of the rightful, hard-earned property of others.

If, however, we begin from a different paradigm of work – what I will call 'reproductive labour' in an extended *ethical* sense – many of the perceived difficulties in justifying basic income vanish. For, on this model of labouring activity, the goal is not the production of things but the maintenance and 'reproduction' of human relationships. In the best case, in my analysis, the aim is relations of what Aristotle called *philia* or friendship – whether personal or civic. Thus such labour has, as part of its very nature, the end or goal of sharing with others and of helping them. Moreover, this model is hardly utopian; indeed it is still performed by at least half the population, namely women. Finally, if this is the case, then we are left with the question: why should this model of labour (and aspect of our human nature) not also be reflected in government, in our conception of the citizen and as a part of their necessary obligations to others? Universal basic income might be grounded in an alternative political vision of the democratic state: one that furthers not simply the political values of freedom and equality, but the third value of a civic friendship as well.

2. The Production Model

Allow me first to delineate central characteristics of what I am calling the production model – that model of labour which ascends to prominence in the seventeenth century with the rise of the modern market. It is best conceived by recalling John Locke's famous metaphor of man in the state of nature who rightfully 'owns' that with which he has 'mixed his labour' (Locke, 1992, para. 27). Central characteristics of this 'mixing' or production model are as follows: i) labour is here conceived as essentially a technical mastery over the physical world (whether agricultural, artisan labour or even working in a factory). More importantly, ii) all such labour is a form of what the ancient Greeks called *poiēsis* (also *technē*); these are activities done primarily for the sake of a 'product'. That is, the activity is not performed for its own sake (what the Greeks called *praxis*) but for the end result – in the modern period typically some form of exclusive private property (crop, money or wage, etc.) Further, iii) it becomes clear that at least from the seventeenth century onwards our conception of the liberal citizen becomes intimately tied with the performance of such free productive labour. In addition to military service (a requirement since ancient times), the capacity for productive labour now becomes a criterion for independence and 'full' or 'active' citizenship. (In the ancient world, by contrast, such labour was performed primarily by slaves, illiterate craftsmen and foreigners – that is, by non-citizens.)

Nowhere is the early modern concern with the production of actual physical objects more visible than in a passage by Kant where he attempts to distinguish between active and passive citizen. Kant goes so far as to attribute to the wig-maker (who produces an independent physical object, namely, the wig) full-fledged active citizenry, whereas he denies full citizenship to the barber who merely 'serves' another and cuts his hair! (Kant, 1990, para. 46). But it is not only the Germans who reveal this obsession with the production of objects (and later with 'services'). Adam Smith also classifies all occupations which approach most closely to ethical reproductive activity – occupations such as those of churchmen, physicians, men of letters, dancers and even opera singers – together with that of the 'menial servant' and the 'buffoon' which Smith considers the lowest form of 'unproductive labour'.[3]

Finally, even the State now comes to be viewed on this model. That is, whereas in the ancient world the *polis* was viewed as the highest expression of man's communal nature and of *praxis* – as an expression of the best of his relationships – in the modern period the State becomes a means to other ends: to glory, acquisition, security, wealth, fame, etc. 'For by Art (*poiesis*) is created that great Leviathan called a Common-wealth or State' writes Hobbes at the beginning of *Leviathan* (1988). Not only is one of the State's central functions now the protection of property and the regulation of productive competition, but its very nature is seen as the result of production as well; it becomes purely instrumental.

If the production model of labour indeed plays such a deep and powerful role in the modern period, it is hardly surprising that guaranteeing a basic income to all citizens – independently of their role in production – causes consternation. For on this model, the incentive for people to perform the holy mandate – the production of things and services – is private or monetary reward. Granting them such a reward (namely income) *prior* to any 'mixing of their labour' puts the cart before the horse; it violates what appears to be a most self-evident and basic axiom of natural law.

3. Ethical Reproduction

Locke's mixing metaphor, however, and its concomitant rights to private use and to exclusive private property, was not always viewed as self-evident. As mentioned above, in the ancient world, the majority of labour mixing was done by slaves – precisely those who own no property. But we need not travel back so far in history to see the limits of this famous metaphor. Women, after all, have been 'mixing their labour' for centuries – with their children, their family, household, etc. – but never with the goal of private property (until perhaps recently). On the contrary, what property they did possess was typically shared with their husband and children (under Blackstone's community of persons). Rather than dismissing (as has been the tradition) such activity as non-labour in the first place – for it is surely a production of use values as well as necessary – it appears we are dealing with a different model of labouring activity, characteristics of which I will next elaborate.

First, whereas the model of craft (farm or technological) labour involves a working subject confronting a given material object, the model of what I am calling 'reproductive' labour (always in a non-biological sense) is one in which a subject essentially confronts another subject: the child (the aged, the lover, the other). Such labour is thus not merely indirectly social or other-directed, but directly so; its proper end is direct need satisfaction of the other, as well as the encouragement of his or her abilities. This is not to claim that women's traditional labour is necessarily any less greedy, self-seeking, etc.; my point here is structural not psychological. Unless the mother, or caretaker in deed looks after the child (the aged, etc.) the latter will not flourish. Moreover, at least in the case of the mother or of a good friend, such work is usually not pure self-sacrifice; the mother or friend often receives great personal satisfaction. This may be explained, I believe, by viewing the reward in such instances as the *establishment* (maintenance, furtherance) *of a relationship*. As Aristotle wrote, *philia* (a broad term covering the friendship between parents and children, siblings, lovers and even fellow citizens) is – in its genuine form – an end-in-itself. In the best case, reproductive activity emerges as a form of *praxis*, done for its own sake. Of course, where similar activity is performed for essentially other reasons – say the case of the day-care worker whose primary aim is her wage – I will continue to call this reproductive *labour*.

Finally, I wish to note various implications of this alternative model of activity for the question of ownership. Traditionally, a woman's children have typically been considered 'hers' in some sense, as have the household, its items, etc. Women's traditional labour and activity thus point to important aspects of shared, communal property maintained in the modern period. But so too, unlike the paradigm of property *qua* commodity (which may be acquired and disposed of at will), the children and home of a woman have traditionally been hers in an ascriptive and not an acquisitive sense; that is, they are primarily her responsibility. This form of 'owning' emerges as fully consistent with the traditional, legal sense of 'possession' whereby objects are considered highly 'restricted objects of the will'. Ownership emerges on this model of labour as a form of guardian or stewardship.

Now my question becomes: why should this form of activity – labour as a form of taking care and encouragement, and ownership as a form of guardian or stewardship – not also be reflected in our notion of the modern nation State? Elsewhere I have argued that I believe it actually has been so reflected to some extent, not just in Plato and Aristotle or in the thought of Karl Marx, but even in Locke (where there are strict natural and civic limits on property acquisition, as well as the recognition of individual right) and certainly in John Rawls (with his famous difference principle whereby differences should work to better the disadvantaged). The problem (as I see it) is that this second model remains submerged, only vaguely intuited as well as under-theorized, whereas the paradigm of production and private property has clearly dominated.[4] One author recently noted that liberals – even the most progressive – have a hard time accepting the idea of a guaranteed basic income (Wax,

2002). I believe we can now see why; liberalism remains wedded to a production model of labour and to its various implications. Here I believe theorising traditional women's labour – and realizing that half of us (at least) still perform such labour in the midst of advanced industrial capitalism – may help loosen up this 400-year obsession.

4. The New State

I have argued that historically the modern liberal State is wedded to a production model of labour (as is also, by the way, the socialism of Karl Marx).[5] But what would a State look like that gave, not exclusive, but let us say *equal weight* to reproductive *praxis* or at least to reproductive labour? And is such a State feasible? I believe one institutional change that such a transformation of the State would entail is the guarantee of a material baseline – some form of guaranteed basic income. Moreover, women entering the State *en masse* are poised to help bring this about. Why?

My argument here is not merely that reproductive labour is just as necessary and important as productive labour, which it clearly is; producing objects is presumably for the good of people and their relations not *vice versa*. Nor is my claim simply that women (and the nature of their traditional activities) deserve recognition in the public institutions of the democratic State. Again, I believe they do, but the persuasive force of why this *has to be* remains limited – at least for many. There is a further reason, however, why aspects of reproductive *praxis* should be reflected at the political State level. Here the argument I wish to make reaches back to Aristotle: relations of civic friendship between citizens are a necessary condition for genuine justice. How does this third argument go?

According to Aristotle, friendship whether personal or civic has three necessary ingredients. Friends must reciprocally i) *be aware* of each other as some form of moral equal, ii) they must *wish each other well* for the other's sake (and not their own), and iii) they must *practically do* things for one another (*Nicomachean Ethics*, Bk. VIII). On the civic or political level such moral awareness, wishing well and doing (as John Cooper has argued) works via the constitution, the public laws as well as the customs and habits of the citizenry; citizens may be educated to each others' situations, know what they can expect, and consider it their obligation to help (whether through taxes, civic service, in times of disaster, etc.). Surely, a guaranteeing of material basics to all citizens would be an expression of and, insofar as genuine friendship necessitates a practical doing, even a requirement for a civic friendship. But it is still not clear why such a civic friendship and its practical expression is a *necessary requirement* for justice? Why would a guaranteed basic income not just be charity or simple generosity?

Aristotle writes 'for when men are friends they have no need of justice, while when they are just they need friendship as well, and the truest form of justice is thought to be a friendly quality' (*Nicomachean Ethics*, 1155a, pp.22–28[6]). Aristotle's point here is that in a general atmosphere of distrust, ill will or indifference, true justice remains impossible. On my reading, the reason is because citizens in this case could still – and often will – perceive themselves to be unjustly treated even if some narrow notion of justice is strictly being adhered to. Again, justice by means of force (a fair distribution imposed on parties unwillingly) is an inferior sort of justice to an arrangement willingly acknowledged (the former breeds resentment in turn, is less stable, etc.) Thus, given our natural and often unreasonable propensities to favour ourselves, true justice can only result if a flexible give-and-take and friendly background (quality) exist to make us yield. Citizens must be able to recognize and to accept in practice *the burdens* of justice in any particular case.

It is for this reason, I believe, that Aristotle considers the cultivation by the legislator of a civic friendship in a population even more important than justice itself (*Nicomachean Ethics*, 1155a, p. 22[7]); it is a necessary precondition. Without a reciprocal moral awareness, goodwill and practical doing expressed in the background social institutions and system of rules, justice is revealed as nothing more than the imposition of the will of the stronger.

I personally do not think a guaranteed basic income is enough for genuine justice, even as it is not sufficient for a genuine civic friendship. That is, the cultivation of goodwill among the citizenry and the disposition to help one another must come through education, laws, custom and habit as well – in short through numerous social and political 'reproductive' institutions. But although not sufficient, I have argued that guaranteeing a basic material security is necessary, and perhaps a first step, for without this minimal practical doing, justice remains a sham.

So, what might this new State – which theorizes and acknowledges the model of reproductive activity equally with production – look like? First, it would still have the duty of protection, regulation of commerce, etc. but such functions would now take up a smaller portion of the revenues it draws and the obligations it has, for now the market – and the role of production – would be far smaller. Emphasis on the production and consumption of things and services could recede and the rewards or satisfaction of human relationships (the life of the mind, art, education, play, etc.) emphasized, at least to the extent that they are 'reproductive' of flourishing relations. And such a conception of the State implicated in civic relations would clearly affect the State's international affairs as well; a bloated military could give way to foreign aid and international programmes.

But perhaps the central difference would be that a necessary and weighty part of Government's function would now include reproductive or *affirmative obligations*: particularly a concern with the satisfaction of *basic need*, but also with *the quality of civic relations*. Guaranteed basic income (or in the form of guaranteed medical care, housing, food and education) I believe is superior to past welfare programmes, for it is superior according to all the three criteria of civic friendship noted above. A moral awareness of equality is expressed, in that benefits are universally granted with no grovelling or bureaucratic nightmare for the poorer segments. So too, the income is unconditional, an expression of minimal political friendship, for the sake of the other without thought of return; just as one would help a friend if one could, and without thinking. In fact, a hypothetical test for the duties of this new Government might now be formulated thus: would you allow this to happen to a friend? If not, then Government should not politically allow it either.

Finally, regarding the criteria of 'reciprocity', and whether citizens should 'labour' in return for a guaranteed income. We all know a one-way friendship is impossible, but friendship likewise ends when a strict 'tit-for-tat' results. That is, one of the distinguishing attributes of a true friendship is its flexibility and emphasis on quality over quantity. Thus a universal obligation to make a productive contribution to the collective enterprise cannot stand as a fundamental precept of the new State and its guaranteeing of basic income. I myself see nothing wrong in expecting or even requiring all citizens to perform *x* amount of time in civil service (which is not production); but this is not the same as saying that a guaranteed basic income should be conditional on such service. A civil service can be justified on other – actually on ethical reproductive – grounds.

Of course, Aristotle's basic argument will not appeal to those who remain enamoured of the production model. Moreover, I am sure to hear someone object somewhere: this is all well and good, but Aristotle's ideal life of leisure and *praxis* rested on the institution of slavery! At this late date I can only respond: yes, indeed. But your grand life of production and value creation has likewise rested on the unpaid reproductive labour of others – primarily women. It is time to find an entirely new solution.

Notes

1   City University of New York, USA.
2   *The Federalist Papers*, 51 (LeftJustified Publiks, 1997).
3   In all these cases, according to Adam Smith, the activity 'perishes in the very instance of its performance' and seldom leaves any trace behind it (Smith, 1981, Vol. 1, pp. 330–31).
4   See my discussion in Schwarzenbach (1987 and 1986).
5   I argue this in Chapter 5 of Schwarzenbach (forthcoming).
6   *Nichomachean Ethics*, in *The Ethics of Aristotle*, trans. J. A. K. Thomson (Penguin, 1976, repr. 1978).
7   *Nichomachean Ethics*, in *The Ethics of Aristotle*, trans. J. A. K. Thomson (Penguin, 1976, repr. 1978).

References

Hobbes, T. 1988. *Leviathan* (New York, Prometheus Books).

Kant, I. 1785. *The fundamental principles of the metaphysics of morals*, Translated by T.K. Abbot (1990) (New York, Prometheus Books).

Locke, J. 1992. *The second treatise of Government* (New York, Prometheus Books), para. 27.

Schwarzenbach, S. (forthcoming) *On civic friendship: Including women in the State* (Ann Arbor, Michigan, University of Michigan Press), forthcoming.

_____1986. 'Rawls and ownership; The forgotten category of reproductive labour', in *Science, Morality and Feminist Theory (Canadian Journal of Philosophy supplement)*, Vol. 13.

_____1987. 'Locke's Two Conceptions of Property,' in *Social Theory and Practice*, Vol. 14, pp. 14–172.

Smith, A. 1981. *Wealth of nations* (Indianopolis, Liberty).

Wax, A. 2002. '*Something for nothing: The Liberal case against work requirements*', Paper presented at the US Basic Income Guarantee Network Conference, New York, 8 March.

9

LIBERAL AND MARXIST JUSTIFICATIONS FOR BASIC INCOME[1]

Michael Howard[2]

1. Marxist Arguments for and Against Basic Income

David Schweickart, commenting on my proposal for combining a basic income (BI) with economic democracy, a model of self-managed market socialism, offers the following series of objections, to which I attach respective replies:

> A. Deontological: We do not have a moral right to a BI. We do have a moral obligation to work. When we consume, we take from society. Justice requires that we give something back in return. But if we have a moral obligation to work, since 'ought implies can', we have a moral 'right to work'. That is to say, the government has a duty to serve as an employer-of-last-resort.

Let me first note that the right and obligation claimed here do not entail rejecting BI. Pragmatic defences of BI as a more effective way of eliminating the poverty trap than means-tested and work-linked alternatives are compatible with a view that there is no fundamental moral right to BI, and that there is in principle an obligation to 'work' or at least to give back in some way. Proponents of 'participation income' explicitly recognize this obligation, or its political salience, and make the BI at least loosely contingent on giving back. And one argument for BI is that it enables people to work by pricing themselves into a job (Atkinson, 1996; Barry, 1996).

To address these two principles head on, surely it depends on the level of BI, or more generally what society gives to its members? Public schools, some health care, roads and other goods are provided by society, whether someone undertakes a work career or loafs. Even prior to BI, there is a minimal level of public sustenance that it is generally considered appropriate to give, without getting anything back. Only when consuming beyond that level are people expected to contribute: when they leave school and expect an income, society expects a contribution as a condition of the income.

Or does it? In capitalist societies, those who inherit sufficient wealth, or manage to accumulate sufficient capital in some way, are legally entitled to an unearned income without any corresponding obligation to work. For most social-ists, this legal entitlement is morally illegitimate, resting as it does on exploitation. But why not think about unearned income and wealth in another way? Consider the following thought experiment: imagine an island in which the fruits of nature are so abundant and the climate so temperate that a person can eat nutritionally and live exposed to the elements without any labour beyond that necessary to pick the fruit from the trees and gather leaves for a bed. Not everyone chooses to live at comfortable subsistence; some engage in crafts, exchanging the fruits of their labour for money, and buying commodities with the money earned. But everyone equally enjoys the free goods provided by nature, as a human right.

In advanced capitalist societies we tend to focus on wealth as the product of human labour, given the predominance of labour as a factor of production in our economies. But we then lose sight of the unearned wealth that is nature's contribution, which we all share in and which some own and control more of than others do. If we were to socialize all of nature's contribution – the land, the natural resources, etc. – and distribute the value of these equally to all citizens, this is another way to move from capitalist inequality to social-ist equality (see the Alaskan citizens' fund as an illustration). The principle of equality of unearned wealth does not negate the principle of income in accor-dance with work, for income above this social dividend could still be propor-tional to work. Now extend this idea of equality of one's share of natural resources to include socially inherited capital wealth, and one arrives at some-thing like Roemer's social dividend (Roemer, 1994).[3] More controversially, factor in the 'employment rent' enjoyed by many workers as unearned income, and the value of the dividend will rise further (van Parijs, 1995, Ch. 4). But whatever basis one settles on, the basic principle is that some wealth is inevitably unearned, not the product of labour, and if this is significant in quantity, it should be factored in alongside work as a basis for entitlement of all people who inhabit the planet. It would appear to follow that we do have a right to a BI up to a certain level, and no obligation to work, so long as our consumption does not exceed a certain minimum. Under certain natural and social conditions, this minimum will be below the level of subsistence, which would in effect impose a moral obligation to work on all able-bodied people. I return to one aspect of this deontological objection in Part II of this paper.

B. Utilitarian: Work is essential to human dignity and human happiness, so utilitarian considerations also favour a 'right to work' over a mere 'right to consume'. Many empirical studies have documented the sense of shame, degradation and embarrassment suffered by the unemployed (see Solow (1998) for a sampling).

Again, one motivation for BI is enabling people to escape the poverty trap and price themselves into a job. BI is not an alternative to work, but a complement to a full employment strategy. It is also a way of valorizing many forms of social contribution, such as child care, care of the elderly, or political activism, that are not remunerated in the wage economy, and thus helping to remove the sense of shame experienced by those who do this work when 'unemployed'.

C. Early Marxian: BI masks our basic species dependency and hence perpetuates our alienation from our species being. The fact of the matter is, we, as human beings, are dependent, 'suffering' beings. We need other people. BI, with its promise of 'real freedom' perpetrates and intensifies our illusory independence.

The obligation to work in exchange for income beyond BI, which most people will seek, should shatter any illusions about independence. The logic of this objection would lead one to put a price on every public good, giving out public education, for example, as a loan that must be paid back, rather than as a citizenship entitlement that affirms the worth of each as a person, not just as a worker.

The coercion to work is the core aspect of alienation. BI at a sustainable level is a step beyond alienation because it gives more workers the option to say no, and thus will exert some pressure on employers – whether capitalists or collectives of workers – to make the conditions of work more palatable. As work becomes more humane, the worker works more freely, and thus can become interdependent in a non-alienated way.

It is worth noting also that wage workers often depend on others for the relatively high wages they enjoy, and this dependence is masked by too tight an allocation of income in proportion to work. For example, particularly in the United States in the 1950s and 1960s, the male wage earner implicitly was being paid for his own reproduction through the labour of a wife who was not remunerated, and who was economically dependent on the male in an invidious way. A basic income enabling homemakers to stay out of the wage labour market, and to be less economically dependent upon a male wage earner, is one way to acknowledge this unpaid labour and call attention to a kind of interdependence that has been masked, without turning housework into wage labour (the household wage idea). Important here also is the dependence of the money economy and its agents on informal, household, and other economies that cannot easily survive transformation into commodity form. Becoming aware of this sort of interdependence is also a step beyond alienation. (I am a market socialist. But the only way the 'socialist' in market socialism can be sustained against the alienating forces of the market is if the sphere of the market is clearly limited. The market should not dominate the household, the media, education, health care, or politics) (Walzer, 1983).

> D. Foucauldian: We should distinguish between genuinely progressive features of social democracy – universal free education, universal health care, universal pension coverage, universal provision of child care (or payment to people who want to care for their children at home), and those institutions that have attempted to mitigate the social costs of capitalism: long-term unemployment insurance and 'humane' prisons. (Both of the latter can be understood in Foucauldian terms as mechanisms for keeping the working class divided, and for a liberal-conservative pseudo-politics to be played out in the electoral arena). BI belongs to the latter category.

First, any of the 'genuinely progressive' features of social democracy mitigate the social costs of capitalism, and can divide the working class. See Marx's comment on Adam Smith's early proposal for universal free education 'in homeopathic doses' as a response to the effects of the division of labour on the moral, intellectual, and martial virtues of workers.[4] Within capitalism, at a low (politically) sustainable level, perhaps BI would have a divisive effect – the 'basic income apartheid' that Gorz warns against – but in a socialist context, it can be an important pillar of social solidarity, one of the entitlements that a socialist society can sustain more effectively than capitalism (Gorz, 1992).

Second, most other socialist ideas can have regressive effects within a capitalist context. Workplace democracy can divide the working class between the relatively well-off workers in primary sector labour markets – e.g. airline pilots and mechanics – and the relatively worse-off workers and unemployed. What we have to address is how to put together a package of social programmes that will bring everyone together in a commonly shared social movement, despite the potential for divisions.

Third, workfare, by establishing a discipline that is socially required but economically unnecessary, would seem to be the more Foucauldian version of welfare reform, not BI.

> E. Historical materialist: It is in fact true that it would be easier and cheaper to provide everyone with a BI (or its Rawlsian equivalent – an

income floor beneath which no one would be allowed to sink) than it is to provide everyone with a decent job. It is in fact impossible to do the latter under capitalism. We have here another classic 'contradiction' of capitalism: in undermining feudal privilege, capitalism generated the ideology that everyone should work – but its institutions, in demolishing slavery, serfdom and the guilds, made it increasingly impossible for many people to find work. Moreover, since wage labour requires unemployment as a disciplinary mechanism, unemployment cannot be eliminated under capitalism. It can be done under Economic Democracy – though with difficulty. [Brief look at Solow: 1) the market does not automatically create enough jobs; 2) many people are mentally and physically unfit for those jobs that are there and those that might be created.] But it is the historical task of socialism to clean up the messes left by capitalism.

This task is furthered by empowering people to refuse degrading jobs. Most will work, because most will not be content with a minimum, but work will not be the only source of income or benefit. We also need to ask, looking down the road to the 'higher phase of communism' whether the work ethic – especially that focused on paid work – is not one of the messes of capitalism. Marx's historical materialist scheme for transition to communism suggests that the principle of distribution according to need only comes after an extended period governed by a work ethic, and only after the division of labour has been overcome, abundance has been achieved, and work has become 'life's prime want' (Marx, 1977a). But to the extent that one approaches these conditions in certain respects under capitalism, can it not be possible to begin introducing need as a standard alongside work, and over time phasing out the latter while phasing in the former? (van der Veen and van Parijs, 1986). Is this not part of the appeal of shortening the working day and the workweek? Does not a historical materialist approach to distributive justice support this over a deontological assertion of universal rights and obligations?[5]

F. Rebuttals: The claim that BI would remove the stigma of welfare is spurious. Every worker, looking at his pay stub, would see at once whether he was gaining or losing from BI. Distinction between helping those who cannot help themselves – species solidarity – and the 'duty' to provide for those who do not want to work.

It is important to take note, with respect to this point, of who would gain or lose from BI. Anthony Atkinson calculates that, with some tweaking of the tax system, in England every child could receive £12.50 a week, and every adult between £17.75 and £18.25 a week, without increasing taxes overall. 'With such a citizen's income, the number dependent on means-tested benefits would be reduced by half a million. A third of families would be worse off in cash terms; 10 per cent would be virtually unaffected; and 57 per cent would gain. Among the latter would be many women.' An increase of about 10 per cent in the tax rates would more than double the basic income to nearly £40 a week and more than quadruple the number freed from dependence on means-tested benefits (Atkinson, 1996, pp. 67–70). If the tax structure and welfare system in the United States is anything like that in Britain, it is clear that this is a not insignificant benefit, and that most workers would gain, even without any increase of taxes on the richest 4 per cent who make as much as the bottom 51 per cent.

The worker who now looks at his pay stub often resents the small percentage of his taxes that goes to those who cannot help themselves (though in many cases with a distorted image of the recipients and an inflated notion of the percentage of the budget that goes to welfare). So much for species solidarity. We would be closer to this ideal if the benefits were universal, rather than dividing society into payers and receivers, typically along race and gender lines.[6]

> G. In sum: I see no good reason for society choosing to supply each citizen with a BI instead of committing to Rawlsian welfare payments to the needy to keep them above a decent minimum – and I think there are good reasons for preferring welfare payments to BI.
>
> But even more than that, I think a genuine socialist alternative to capitalism should 'abolish welfare as we know it', and undertake the difficult task of redesigning our institutions so that every citizen can make a meaningful, productive contribution to the well-being of his or her fellow citizens. Not 'real freedom for all', but rather, 'real work for all' – 'real work' that allows us to develop our individual abilities and to contribute meaningfully to our collective being.

A genuine socialist alternative should begin by acknowledging the ambivalent moral significance of work. On the one hand it is one of the key ways we contribute to society, integrate ourselves into it, find our identity, exercise our capacities for creativity, etc. On the other hand it is necessary and, one way or another, human beings are constrained to labour in order to survive. The reality of work is that it shares in both of these aspects, some kinds of work more closely approximating the first, other kinds the second. The best summation I know of was made by Marx in *Capital*, Vol. III:

> The actual wealth of society, and the possibility of constantly expanding its reproduction process, therefore, does not depend upon the duration

of surplus labour, but upon its productivity and the more or less copious conditions of production under which it is performed. In fact, the realm of freedom actually begins only where labour which is determined by necessity and mundane considerations ceases; thus in the very nature of things it lies beyond the sphere of actual material production. Just as the savage must wrestle with Nature to satisfy his wants, to maintain and reproduce life, so must civilized man, and he must do so in all social formations and under all possible modes of production. With his development this realm of physical necessity expands as a result of his wants; but, at the same time, the forces of production, which satisfy these wants, also increase. Freedom in this field can only consist in socialized man, the associated producers, rationally regulating their interchange with Nature, bringing it under their common control, instead of being ruled by it as by the blind forces of Nature; and achieving this with the least expenditure of energy and under conditions most favourable to, and worthy of, their human nature. But it nonetheless still remains a realm of necessity. Beyond it begins that development of human energy which is an end in itself, the true realm of freedom, which, however, can blossom forth only with this realm of necessity as its basis. The shortening of the working day is its basic prerequisite (Marx, 1997b, pp. 496–97).

Economic Democracy addresses the rational regulation of our interchange with nature 'under conditions most favourable to, and worthy of' our human nature. Basic income is a step toward the realm of freedom, constrained in its extent by the realm of necessity as its basis. Real work for all and real freedom for all, those should be the long-term goals of socialism.

Fortunately, these two goals are complementary. As van Parijs argues, in comparison with employer subsidies that keep up the pressure on workers to seek employment,

UBI [universal basic income] makes it easier to take a break between two jobs, reduce working time, and make room for more training, take up self-employment, or join a cooperative. And with UBI, workers will only take a job if they find it suitably attractive, while employer subsidies make unattractive, low-productivity jobs more economically viable. If the motive in combating unemployment is not some sort of work fetishism – an obsession with keeping everyone busy – but rather a concern to give every person the possibility of taking up gainful employment in which she can find recognition and accomplishment, then the UBI is to be preferred (van Parijs, 2001, p. 9).[7]

Schweickart does not say how he proposes to redesign our institutions so that everyone will have work, and I do not mean to suggest that he covertly favours employer subsidies. But we must be careful not to be so tied to paid employment that we propose even under socialism something akin to employer subsidies – subsidies to cooperatives might have the same effect *vis-à-vis* an unemployed worker – and in the process perpetuate 'work fetishism'. Of even greater practical importance, should we oppose a reform that is feasible under capitalism, and could be continued and expanded under socialism, and thereby indirectly strengthen the movement for employer subsidies as the default option in the effort to reduce unemployment?

2. Basic Income and Liberal Neutrality

Since the second part of this paper is framed in terms of 'liberal neutrality' I should first clarify what I mean by this, and explain why it should be taken seriously. I am using the term, as does Rawls, to refer to a theory of justice that is not biased towards a particular substantive conception of the good life. Immediately one might wonder whether such a theory of justice is even possible, or if it is, whether it would be so empty as to have nothing interesting to say about justice.[8]

I think both horns of this dilemma can be avoided if we understand the 'neutrality' aimed for not to be absolute, but relative to the substantive and conflicting conceptions of the good that otherwise divide a political community. It is the standpoint one moves to, in the face of irreconcilable normative convictions, in order to achieve justice. Rawls himself conceives of it as an extension of the principle of religious tolerance. European societies came to the realization that no reasonable universal agreement could be expected among the warring religious factions, and agreed to disagree. Moreover, this mutual toleration came to be a core liberal principle in each of the main religious traditions, so that these traditions themselves supported, by an overlapping consensus, the principle of religious tolerance. So too, comprehensive metaphysical and moral doctrines about which reasonable people disagree should not be among the premises of the theory of justice; rather we should assume neutrality toward such doctrines, or in other words a principle of respect for differences (Rawls, 1993; Larmore, 1987).

That said, the theory of justice is not devoid of moral commitments – such as the priority of justice, certain notions of what constitutes a person, the primary goods, and other ideas that people can agree upon despite their conflicting ideals of the good life. Nor is the theory of justice a mere *modus vivendi*. The neutrality of the theory is not simply a truce among warring parties; rather it is the result of incorporating into conflicting traditions a principle of tolerance as central to those traditions themselves.

What this means of course is that in any contemporary society, perhaps any society at all, there will be people, and groups, who will not consent to justice. The theory will not speak for them or to them. I have in mind not merely hardened criminals but more to the point, people whose conceptions of the good life preclude respect and toleration of other reasonable conceptions. No theory of justice can be expected to persuade everyone.

3. Neutrality, Work and Leisure

In Rawls's original formulation of the theory of justice, the primary goods that are the focus of distribution – those goods that one wants, whatever else one wants – included basic liberties, opportunity, wealth, income, power and authority, and the bases of self-respect (Rawls, 1971). Absent from the list was leisure, until it was pointed out that this absence biased the theory toward the Lazy, those with a preference for leisure (Musgrave, 1974; Rawls, 1988).

To see why this is the case, consider the following. If we leave leisure off the list, and then assume further that the parties to the original position would choose the Difference Principle (DP) for the distribution of wealth, income, power and authority, the Lazy will be favoured over those with a preference for higher income available through work (following van Parijs, 1995, Ch. 4, let us call them 'the Crazy' to avoid a bias in our discussion). DP stipulates that distribution should maximize the minimum for the least advantaged group. Now suppose over time there is an increment in total wealth and income. Those who live only on the socially guaranteed minimum – including the Lazy – will get the maximum sustainable share of this increase. The Crazy can protest that the Lazy – unlike those dependent on this minimum who are unable to work or to find employment, or to meet basic needs from their wages – are favoured on account of their conception of the good life, which involves a lot of leisure and low consumption.

To avoid this bias, Rawls added leisure to the list of primary goods, defined as 'twenty-four hours less a standard working day. Those who are unwilling to work would have a standard working day of extra leisure, and this extra leisure itself would be stipulated as equivalent to the index of primary goods of the least advantaged' (Rawls, 1988, p. 257). This entails that there is no right to income or wealth that is not conditional on willingness to work or inability to work.

Van Parijs has argued that Rawls, in the way he addressed the original bias in favour of the Lazy, 'swings all the way and introduces the opposite bias' in favour of the Crazy (van Parijs, 1995, p. 90). Let us go back to the hypothetical increment in total wealth and income, and this time further stipulate that the increase is due to some external good such as plentiful rainfall, or discovery of

oil, rather than greater expenditure of labour. What happens to the least advantaged group – in particular those who do not work at all – in the distribution of
this increment? Their income will increase to the level of the least-paid full-time
worker, but workers on the whole will enjoy a higher proportion of the windfall,
even though it resulted not from their labour but from natural good fortune. Is
this not a bias towards those with a preference for paid work?

The point made here with respect to a natural windfall can be generalized
to all wealth and income that results not from labour but from external assets
such as land, and there is, van Parijs holds, 'a non-arbitrary and generally positive legitimate level of basic income that is determined by the per capita
value of society's external assets' (van Parijs, 1995, p. 99). This level

> must be entirely financed by those who appropriate these assets. If Lazy
> gives up the whole of his plot of land, he is entitled to an unconditional
> grant at a level that corresponds to the value of that plot. Crazy, on the
> other hand, can be viewed as receiving this same grant, but as owing
> twice its amount because of appropriating both Lazy's share of land and
> her own (van Parijs, 1995, p. 99).

There is a technical problem of how to assess the value of external assets,
which I set aside (van Parijs, 1995, p. 99). The key point is that, although some
wealth and income are due to labour, some result from the appropriation of
external assets which, from the standpoint of justice, are common to all, and
thus those who appropriate unearned wealth owe compensation to those who
do not, which compensation can take the form of unconditional basic income
(it could also be given to all in kind, as free education, free health care, and a
one-time lump sum grant, etc.). This income will typically fall between
Rawls's bias toward the Crazy and his earlier pro-Lazy bias.

Van Parijs's position has numerous precedents, notably Tom Paine's proposal
for a universal grant based on the rent of land, and Henry George's single tax,
again focused on land and rent. Van Parijs proposes to widen the basis of the
social dividend from land to include capital, and socially inherited technology.
But, he claims, once one adjusts for incentive effects (which for a Rawlsian
warrant inequalities when they are to the advantage of the least advantaged),
the amount of basic income per capita that would be generated would be
so small as not to be worth the trouble. (I think this conclusion may be too
pessimistic, but will not argue the point here.)

Van Parijs's principal innovation is to widen the basis for basic income
further to include jobs as assets.

> The crucial fact to notice is that, owing to the way in which our economies
> are organized, the most significant category of assets consists in jobs

people are endowed with. Jobs are packages of tasks and benefits. Of course, for jobs to count as assets, they must be in scarce supply. As long as jobs are scarce, those who hold them appropriate a rent which can be legitimately taxed away, so as substantially to boost the legitimate level of basic income (van Parijs, 1995, p. 90).

If jobs are treated as assets, the highest sustainable level of basic income could be very substantial in an affluent society.

But does justice require 'real freedom for all' – entailing the maximum feasible BI? Returning to Rawls, recall that he conceives of justice as a set of principles arrived at through agreement among members of a society who share in the benefits and burdens, who conceive of society as an ongoing cooperative arrangement. Does liberal neutrality really rule out as perfectionist the expectation that all able-bodied people be willing to work in exchange for their share of the benefits? Rather is it not central to the very idea of justice as a fair agreement that there be a bias toward the Crazies? And is it not to be expected that reciprocity be affirmed by moral traditions that form the overlapping consensus?

Interestingly, van Parijs is willing to concede this point, not by loosening his strict interpretation of neutrality, but by appeal to the conditions for social solidarity. With Rawls, he accepts as a requirement of a theory of justice that it possess 'stability' – that once justice is in place it should be reasonable to expect a just society to sustain and reproduce itself, with the necessary level of citizen allegiance and solidarity (Rawls, 1971, pp. 496–504). So he is willing to entertain the superiority of a 'participation income' – guaranteed basic income that is conditional on some form of public service – over an unconditional BI.

> But it must be clear that the argument is neither about economic viability (a compulsory public service of sizeable length would reduce the economic potential for financing a substantial basic income), nor about ethical justification but about the sociological conditions for widespread allegiance to solidaristic justice (van Parijs, 1995, p. 297, note 73).

In other words, the ethical justification still aims for neutrality between those who desire to contribute to society and those whose idea of the good life involves no such contribution, but in practice 'the sociological conditions for widespread allegiance' would dictate reciprocity. It then remains to be shown sociologically that social solidarity really depends upon a generalized work ethic.[9]

If one wants to argue more deeply that the core assumptions of the theory of justice should incorporate a bias toward the Crazies, one is in effect saying that Malibu surfers – the paradigmatic Lazies – lack moral standing in the community with respect to their conception of the good life, in the same way that murderers and rapists as such lack moral standing. The latter are beyond the pale in any moral tradition worthy of consideration. But is it so obvious that surfers are?[10]

Liberal neutrality does not – cannot – require neutrality towards any conception of the 'good' that includes violating the bodily integrity or liberty of others. The question is whether the Lazies – whom one might also be tempted to call parasites – are in some analogous way injuring, harming or stealing from others.[11]

The plausibility of this idea that non-contribution is harm may stem from the illusion that all of the wealth that results from labour is due only to that labour. (Even Marx, who holds that all exchange value is the result of labour, acknowledges that not all wealth is due to labour, since nature also contributes, sometimes lavishly and sometimes without any admixture of labour.) The illusion is compounded when labour is the principal source of wealth, but is combined with other assets that, in exchange, will yield to the worker (or whoever appropriates the product) more than the value of the labour expended (at equilibrium).

But once one grants that external assets also partially constitute and contribute to one's capacity for wealth creation, then the wealth that flows from labour employing these assets is only partly the fruits of labour and is also partly the consequence of others in society enabling the worker to produce.

Van Parijs effectively blocks the idea that the Lazies are merely parasites by arguing that their basic income is essentially not a handout but compensation for their letting-go of their *per capita* share of social wealth.

(This is not an argument for the capitalist's contribution. On the contrary, often the contribution of capital involves no contribution of the capitalist. From the standpoint of justice all such assets are collective property. Even when these assets are institutionalized in the form of private property, cooperative property, or State property, we must not lose sight of the requirement of justice to equalize the opportunities associated with control over such assets.)

> Crazy would be the 'invader' (in the broad sense of unfair taking from society) if she took the whole of (what looks like) her product instead of contributing to an endowment given to all in order to enable them as much as possible to pursue realization of their non-invasive (this time in the narrower sense of invasive) conception of good life.[12]

Eugene Torisky tries to make the case that the Lazies have an 'invasive' conception of the good life, not in the narrower sense but in the broader sense that everyone who receives support from society should give something in return. He thinks this idea of reciprocity is even-handed: 'What liberal justice denies the Crazies of society, the benefits of mutual cooperation without contributing to it, is precisely what it denies the Lazies' (Torisky, 1993, p. 296).

However, real libertarians might make an equally compelling claim to even-handedness: liberal justice denies equally to Lazies and Crazies any additional benefits (beyond BI) without some contribution. And the real libertarian will ask, what is the basis for denying the BI to everyone, if not a perfectionist work ethic?

Torisky tries to argue that the Lazies are injured alike with the Crazies without a reciprocity condition: An 'unconditional basic income ... goes too far, by exempting its recipients from the minimal cost of membership in society and thereby depriving them of the dignity and status of a member' (Torisky, 1993, p. 296).

But the recipients are free to participate – more free with a BI than without one. It is unclear how forced participation is more empowering and respectful than the mere freedom to participate. And, it might be said, BI, along with the affirmation of basic liberties and equality of opportunity, adequately affirms the dignity and status of each member.

As a final remark, anyone unpersuaded of the justness of BI with respect to liberal neutrality, either because of reasons favouring Rawls's position, or because of a rejection of liberal neutrality as a premise, may still be moved to support BI on pragmatic grounds.

Even if one were to favour a 'participation income' in principle, it raises questions of how to define participation, who will monitor it, what the cost of such monitoring will be, including the price paid in the dignity of the recipients.[13] Does raising children count? Political action? Writing poetry? Only good poetry? (Suppose James Joyce had written *Ulysses* while receiving a BI. Would he have been considered a free rider? Probably worse by those who initially judged his book obscene. On the other hand, it is seldom questioned whether a person making and selling landmines is contributing, because his product has a market.) Assuming that most people want to contribute to society, is it not better to endure a few real slackers in order to liberate the rest to contribute creatively and without surveillance, than to try to catch the slackers, burden bureaucrats with arbitrary judgments, and exclude many genuine and needy contributors? The current means-tested system errs in the opposite direction, failing to catch all the needy in the safety net. Should we not err on the side of generosity from the standpoint of a theory of justice that favours the least advantaged?

Notes

1 A significantly revised version of this chapter will appear in the *Review of Social Economy* under the title 'Basic Income, Liberal Neutrality, Socialism and Work', forthcoming.
2 University of Maine, USA.

3 Roemer estimates the annual dividend on non-financial, non-farm corporate and non-corporate wealth per adult in the 1980s to be about $1,200, if these assets were to be nationalized and distributed equally (pp. 133–43).
4 Marx makes this comment somewhere in *Capital*, but I do not have the precise reference.
5 A minor comment on Rawls: he does not favour a minimum, but the maximization of the minimum. The principle Schweickart attributes to Rawls is favoured by Galston (1991).
6 On the gendered welfare state, see Fraser (1989).
7 This book contains the articles in aforementioned *Boston Review* issue on basic income, with a foreword by Robert Solow and preface by *Boston Review* editors Joshua Cohen and Joel Rogers.
8 I myself once argued that such neutrality left the theory indeterminate with respect to some central questions of distributive justice (Howard, 1984).
9 Objections to a participation income, as attractive as it might seem in principle, are of a more pragmatic character (see below).
10 I am not sure which traditions they speak for, but there are many distinguished thinkers who have endorsed a right to unconditional income, including Bertrand Russell (*In Praise of Idleness*), Paul LaFargue (*The Right to be Lazy*), and Nobel economists James Tobin, Herbert Simon and James Meade. Thus it seems hazardous to maintain that anyone who thinks this way adheres to a conception of the good life that is beyond the pale of liberalism.
11 This objection is put forward by Torisky (1993).
12 Philippe Van Parijs, correspondence quoted in Torisky (1993), p. 296.
13 On these points see Barry (1996).

References

Atkinson, A. B. 1996. 'The case for a participation income', in *The Political Quarterly*, Vol. 67, No. 1 (Jan./March), pp. 67–70.

Barry, B. 1996. 'Survey article: Real freedom and basic income', in *Journal of Political Philosophy*, Vol. 4, No. 3, pp. 242–76.

Fraser, N. 1989. *Unruly practices: Power, discourse, and gender in contemporary social theory* (Minneapolis, University of Minnesota Press).

Galston, W. 1991. *Liberal purposes: Goods, virtues, and diversity in the Liberal state* (Cambridge, Cambridge University Press).

Gorz, A. 1992. 'On the difference between society and community and why basic income cannot by itself confer full membership', in P. van Parijs, *Arguing for basic income* (London, Verso).

Howard, M.W. 1984. 'A contradiction in the egalitarian theory of justice', in *Philosophy Research Archives*, Vol. X, pp. 35–55.

Larmore, C. 1987. *Patterns of moral complexity* (Cambridge, Cambridge University Press).

Marx, K. 1977a. 'Critique of the Gotha Programme', in D. McLellan. (ed.), *Karl Marx: Selected writings* (Oxford, Oxford University Press).

———— 1977b. *Capital, Vol. III*, excerpted in D. McLellan (ed.), *Karl Marx: Selected writings* (Oxford, Oxford University Press).

Musgrave, R. 1974. 'Maximin, uncertainty, and the leisure trade-off', in *Quarterly Journal of Economics*, Vol. 88, pp. 625–32.

Rawls, J. 1971. *A theory of justice* (Cambridge, Harvard University Press).

_____ 1988. The priority of right and ideas of the good', in *Philosophy and Public Affairs*, Vol. 17, pp: 251–76, also published as Ch. 5 of Rawls (1993).

_____ 1993. *Political liberalism* (New York, Columbia University Press).

Roemer, J. 1994. *A future for socialism* (Cambridge, Harvard University Press).

Solow, R. 1998. *Work and welfare* (Princeton, New Jersey, Princeton University Press).

Torisky, E. V. 1993. 'Van Parijs, Rawls, and unconditional basic income', in *Analysis*, Vol. 53, No. 4, October, pp. 289–97.

van der Veen, R. J. and van Parijs, P. 1986. 'A capitalist road to communism', in *Theory and Society*, Vol. 15, No. 5, pp. 635–55.

van Parijs, P. 1995. *Real freedom for all: What (if anything) can justify capitalism?* (Oxford, Clarendon Press).

_____ 2001. 'A basic income for all,' in P. van Parijs *et al.*, *What's wrong with a free lunch?* (Boston, Beacon Press).

Walzer, M. 1983. *Spheres of justice: A defense of pluralism and equality* (New York, Basic Books).

10

BASIC INCOME, COMMONS AND COMMODITIES: THE PUBLIC DOMAIN REVISITED

Michael Krätke[1]

1. Basic Income as a Right – To What and for Whom?

Basic income or the universal grant has been conceived as a citizens' right –
any citizen's right. In the European tradition, citizens' rights are non-alienable
and non-negotiable, even if we would no longer justify them in
Enlightenment terms as 'natural rights' or 'natural endowments'. Today, we
tend to share a belief in the creative powers of constitution-making instead.
The right to a basic income would be conceived of as a universal right belonging equally to everybody, without restrictions or subdivisions. It would also be
conceived of as a right belonging to individual citizens, not a collective right
referring to a community or body of citizens. The only restriction relates to
citizenship. To enjoy this right, you would have to become and stay a citizen
– a status that links individuals to the spiritual body of a nation State.

Even if this right were extended to 'legal residents' – already a well-
established practice in several European welfare states – we would draw a
dividing line between legal and illegal residents. Even if minimum qualifications for legal residence, such as a minimum length of stay, were easy to fulfil,
claimants would first have to cross the frontier and become part of the formal
economy and society of a country before they could enjoy any civil rights.

In the European State tradition (Dyson, 1980), citizens' rights used to be
linked to citizens' duties. The most important duties have been the duty to pay
taxes and the duty to serve the State in person, most frequently as a military
conscript. All sovereign States reserve the right to call their citizens to duty in
an emergency, and all legitimate Governments might expect the majority
of their citizens to report for duty when called upon (Krätke, 2000). A good

citizen was, and still is, not only law-abiding but doing his or her duty as a tax-payer, conscript soldier, jury member once in a while, even a polling officer if needed. Those duties have been codified in most countries and linked with citizens' rights in the process.

Although initially conceived of as natural rights, citizens' rights have at least implicitly been surrounded by various qualifications and reservations since the beginnings of modern constitutionalism. Citizenship, as it became a constitutional right, was categorized with the introduction of qualifications for the status of 'full' citizenship. A distinction between 'active' or full citizens and 'passive' citizens, between citizens who were part of the sovereign people and those who were not, although they were part of the nation, left its mark on our democratic constitutions as well as on the tradition of democratic thinking. Even now, the distinction is made, although the once established practice of excluding the poor from full citizenship is history. In this very history we find the link between the status of a full citizen, active citizenship and the right to public assistance in case of distress in the first republican constitutions of modern times (in several of the American republics and in the first French republic).

According to the European State tradition, civil rights used to be morally blind. Citizens' rights were not conceived as privileges for good citizens only, some revolutionary experiments to the contrary notwithstanding. Basic income schemes would fit well into this tradition, as grants would be distributed irrespective of desert or distinction. However, citizens' rights, with the exception of basic 'human rights', never fully acquired the status of unconditional and indisputable rights, although on the long road towards universal suffrage many qualifications – property, literacy, gender, and age – were either abolished or weakened.

In institutional terms, compared to the guaranteed minimum income arrangements that already exist in several welfare states (not only in Europe) (de Voogd *et al.*, 1995), basic income schemes would be free of means and morals tests of any kind and they would be open-ended. Unless someone left the country and the community of citizens, the guaranteed basic income would continue. Any such scheme looks rather generous today and runs counter to current trends to reintroduce and reinforce all types of means tests in social assistance to the poor and propertyless, to shorten the duration of benefits, to differentiate benefits between various categories of beneficiaries, and to strengthen conditionality by all means, more or less disguised and trumpeted as 'incentives'; in other words, to do everything to threaten and undermine the security and stability of social assistance. Basic income schemes are at odds with these prevailing trends in so-called 'modern' social politics.

What is more, a civil right to a basic income would constitute what is called a 'liberty' in the continental European tradition. Liberties are meant to engender freedom – a freedom to act, especially to participate in democratic decision-making and in the public life of a well-organized civil society. The founding fathers of democracies and republics in Europe and elsewhere were not naïve and certainly no textbook scholars; they knew perfectly well that the liberty of opinion or public speech would remain of little value if it was not supplemented by the liberty of the press and the liberty of association. One liberty depended upon another and *vice versa*. Hence the prevailing practice in democratic constitution-making not to mention single rights and liberties but to present whole lists, more or less exhaustive, of those rights. Although not explicitly linked to each other, civil rights used to come in pairs, even bundles, and for good reasons. Such practices mirror a simple process of learning-by-doing in the use one's civil rights or liberties, many of them being much older than modern constitutionalism: rights entail claims to more rights, liberties breed liberties. Liberties create real freedom only when they come in packages or bundles, as they do in all modern constitutions that try to define them. Basic civil rights, especially the liberties, entitling citizens to take action of their own, are complementary. This is true for all types of civil rights, be they 'human', 'political' or 'social' according to T.H. Marshall's terminology (Marshall, 1950). In the constitutional history of Europe and North America, the full scale of civil rights has only been attained by gradual extension – more often than not passing from one amendment to another or from one constitution to the next.

A similar case can be made regarding the right to a basic income. In isolation, it proclaims a liberty that could be fundamental for all other civil rights and liberties: a basic right to at least a minimal form of economic independence, not by granting everybody a piece of land but by granting everybody a basic income. As with its earlier and weaker, but not less contested brother, the 'right to work', which has been proclaimed only rarely, in short-lived exceptional cases, as every good citizen's right in a well-organized republic, it can be read as the late effect of a long-term learning process, responding to much of the criticism that haunted the idea of democratic self-government from its beginnings. If all people are to be regarded as equals in terms of humanity, they would still not be equal as citizens nor could they ever be, because some would be freer, more independent, more responsible, and more resourceful than others. That was simply a fact of life, especially of modern economic life in a rising capitalist market economy that had begun to spread around the world. All those people that were dependent upon others for their living, that were not their own masters but inevitably included in their masters, as James Mill put it, were not free to deliberate and judge even their own affairs and hence were unfit for participation in public deliberation and collective decision-making on the affairs of the State. A universal civil right to a basic income might thus be the solution, as it leaves nobody in a situation of dependency or bondage, even apparently voluntary contractual bondage or servitude.

At any rate, we can borrow quite a strong argument in favour of a basic income from the tradition of democratic political theory: if all human beings are members of society, if all are equally entitled to citizenship, except for the social state of dependency that will not only discourage but positively disable people as members of civil and political society, then we have for the sake of democracy to endow all potential citizens with the means to independence and self-determination in economic terms. As is well known from the history of universal suffrage, the traditional liberal concern about dependent people as full citizens was well founded, though not as a normative proposition. Poor people, such as farmhands, small retainers, tenants and shopkeepers, used to sell their votes to the local notables, establishing a practice of clientelism more or less profitable for all involved that still exists in many parts of Europe. So did the mass of domestic servants, and so did many home workers and even factory workers in the urban and industrialized areas. That is why the vote by secret ballot became such a big issue in the history of modern democracies, although it did not end the age-old practices of buying and selling votes by favours granted or denied by local 'masters' of all kinds. The justification was that we need special devices enabling people to make use of their constitutional rights. It is to the more or less silent intention of 'enabling' and 'empowerment' that we have to turn our attention if we want to understand what is necessary for the right to a basic income to develop into a full-scale liberty cherished by all good citizens.

2. Poverty Traps, Unemployment Traps – and Beyond

The right to be lazy used to be and still is a class privilege. You have to be a man or woman of means to enjoy it. When this very same right was proclaimed as a universal right – referring to a new regime of labour and leisure in the socialist world economy to come – it aroused outrage, not only among the well-to-do, but among workers as well. Nothing could be more provocative to the minds of socialist working men and women – even in France – than the idea that you could enjoy the right to be fed without more than a basic obligation to work. A claim to a right not to work, without suffering duress or poverty, must have appeared very strange indeed at a time when even the basic dividing line between labour and leisure time was heavily contested – as it was throughout the nineteenth century, and to a large extent still is today.

For most working people, in Europe and elsewhere, there is no 'free choice' of work and of hours worked. As a matter of fact, aside from a few specialists with very rare skills, workers are not in control even of their own individual 'labour supply'. Paul Lafargue's pamphlet, *Le droit à la paresse*, was first published in 1883 (Lafargue, 1989) at a time when the very concept of any 'paid absence from work' or holiday seemed a wild idea and not only to employers. Since then, it has been institutionalized and thoroughly entrenched in the welfare states of all advanced industrial countries. Even employers and managers, not to mention the tourism and leisure industry, would defend it as a fundamental economic freedom for everybody.

Basic income, on the contrary, has been propagated and justified in accordance with mainstream or orthodox thinking: it should, if well conceived and correctly implemented, avoid or abolish poverty traps and it should work according to the supposed logic of incentives and disincentives as depicted in the labour market analysis of conventional economics. The champions of basic income have done their best to demonstrate a fit with neoclassical labour market theory or at least that the possible impacts of a basic income can be analysed in such a framework. Of course, they can. But in the process, the original rich idea with all its vagueness and charming utopianism falls prey to the alleged 'rigour' of conventional economics. The goal, the overall conception of liberties and freedom, which form the very core of the original wild idea, is fundamentally compromised, even lost in the process.

In the view of conventional economics, ideologically flawed as it is, most welfare states have caught their good citizens in a series of 'traps' that they – unintentionally and unsuspectingly – have created for them. The 'poverty trap', the 'unemployment trap', the 'inactivity trap' and the like, all hold good citizens in a tight grip and deprive them of their freedom as labour market actors. Enlightened politics – that is, enlightened according to the prevailing dogma of neoclassical economics – should help people out this predicament and set them free. According to this new rhetoric of economic freedom, so dear to the worshippers of the 'activating' welfare state, the real freedom for all is nothing but 'employability' and labour market 'flexibility' fettered by the existing structure of welfare state arrangements. As the flexible labour market is where 'real freedom' prevails, the core idea behind a basic income is forgotten or swept aside in favour of the apparently and allegedly more 'pragmatic' concept of attenuating the built-in 'traps' of the unemployment benefit, social assistance and allied schemes. Basic income has thereby earned respectability and maybe even gained access to the political agenda of welfare state reform (van der Veen and Groot, 2000). I would rather say that many basic income supporters have adapted their concept to the prevailing logic of welfare state counter-reform as it exists in many European countries.

As a device of employment policy to make the unemployed more employable and reduce or avoid poverty and unemployment 'traps', a universal basic income that everybody would enjoy as an elementary civil right would not be very useful. A negative income tax would be much more suitable to serve these goals. In fact, only a negative income tax would generate labour market effects that could be measured and controlled, whereas the overall impact of a basic income would amount to a long-term cultural revolution with very few clear-cut labour market effects. A negative income tax fits perfectly well into the established logic of labour market policies – policymakers and recipients alike reacting directly to price (wage and income) signals and adapting their actions accordingly. The original basic income idea, however, is at odds with that logic, and is in fact an open affront to it, as basic income would engender unconditional and permanent independence from the labour market and its alleged 'logic'. If you switch to the negative income tax, you join the logic of labour market policy as it is, because you have to introduce various means tests and even morals tests in the process and give up the idea of a universal and unconditional grant. If you stick to the original idea, you are at odds with that logic as you proclaim that the labour market is not a market like any other and that human labour power is not a commodity like any other. Supporters of a basic income have increasingly come to make their peace with a much-reduced version of their original idea – the partial basic income. In this compromise, they can adapt to the logic of dominant employment policy discourse and still retain something of the original message referring to real freedom for all.

So, one of the crucial elements of the basic income idea has survived only in a rather rudimentary, crippled form in the course of many years of debate. Basic income has become a victim of its own success in winning respectability among policymakers, especially friends of 'activating' welfare state reforms. The idea of a permanent market was once regarded as a utopia, and a wild one. So was the idea of a guaranteed basic income for all. It was not conceived as a device to avoid or soften poverty and unemployment 'traps', to make people more employable and even more subject and submissive to the constraints of labour markets than they already are. It was meant to give as many people as possible a basic economic freedom, contrary to the conventional and dogmatic liberal creed; a freedom not merely framed in terms of the market but meaningful beyond the world of markets (van Parijs, 1995). That is why it was originally thought of as a universal civil right, an equal right for all citizens, and not just for the 'poor', 'unemployed' or 'jobless'. Hence, it carries a dangerous load for policymakers as it could be used as a right to 'voluntary unemployment' at the discretion of individual citizens, turning the real world of labour markets upside down.

3. The Concept of Poverty – An Exercise in Interdisciplinarity

Can the introduction of a basic income be a good, successful strategy enabling at least some people to avoid becoming trapped in poverty? The answer depends upon the concept of poverty we have in mind. If we have any concept of poverty apart from the common notion that lack of money or lack of income lies at the core of all the troubles affecting poor people, we have to look further than the world of markets. In a full-scale world of markets where – in the end and after a lengthy development – everything is for sale and everything must be bought, lack of money means temporary or lasting exclusion from the wealth of society presenting itself as 'an immense accumulation of commodities', as Marx put it (1990, p. 29). What started at the boundaries and affected only the very edges of communities has in the course of several centuries of 'capitalist development' pervaded the whole fabric of societies all over the world. Even if markets are still 'embedded', in a fully fledged market economy you will be poor as long as you do not have access to markets or are excluded from them for whatever reason. You may not belong there, as you have nothing to offer or do not command sufficient purchasing or bargain power to acquire a foothold in the market, you may never gain access, or you may lose the market position you had once you lose your marketable assets. For one reason or another, poor people are outside most markets, except some black and grey markets in the informal economy, the growing underworld of modern capitalism. Hence, a strategy of reform on behalf of the poor that would focus on access to official markets in the formal economy would make sense. But would it be sufficient to deal with poverty?

Poverty is a complex phenomenon, changing in historical time as 'social questions' do. What we have today in the social sciences is another example of abundance of measurements and data, and poverty of theory. Many efforts to chart and measure the phenomenon of lasting and reappearing poverty in the industrialized world have been undertaken in recent years – starting with the seminal work by Peter Townsend (1979) – and they have produced a now well-established practice of regular monitoring of poor people's condition in many countries. The official report on poverty, published by the German federal Government in 2001, could be regarded as a good, up-to-date example of the combined efforts of social researchers to document the known facts about poverty and poor people in their own country. The two reports on poverty in the member countries of the European Union in the 1970s and 1980s are others. Linking the many facts we know together and comparing them, we end up with a rather varied picture that does not easily fit together in one piece.

There are several kinds of poor people and gradations of poverty. Deprivations come in different guises at different times, some of which remain while others can be overcome in time. In order to understand this variety in the midst of rich societies with well-developed welfare states, social scientists have tried to identify various risks of poverty as well as strategies to cope with lasting and growing precariousness of subsistence. For a large group of people, increasing in numbers in recent years, poverty seems a temporary status from which they can escape. When they cannot, when poverty endures and even reproduces itself from one generation to another, more is at stake than just a lack of income. Somehow, the permanently poor are excluded from society or suffer from impediments in their relationships with a society that is officially quite 'open' and cherishes common values of liberty and equality. Today, poverty is regarded partly as the outcome, partly as the cause of a multi-faceted process of social exclusion – rendering 'the poor' a breed apart and even turning them into an 'underclass' insofar as it has a lasting impact. If the term 'underclass' has any analytical meaning, it can only refer to something that members of all 'classes' in modern bourgeois societies have in common – that is, their ability to engage in market exchanges of various sorts. Members of a true bourgeois society are typically engaged in an endless, repetitive series of market transactions with each other. Only those people who have no chance to do so, who have no stake in any market, who have nothing to sell and nothing to buy, who possess no marketable assets and are not regarded as creditworthy by anyone, whom nobody cares to hire, will fall out of the class system. Both the process and its effect can be deemed social exclusion, affecting employment, housing, education, basic living standards, mobility, health or the lack of it, just like the traditional picture of class inequalities in bourgeois societies. That is why the European Union, in pursuit of its official policy to combat poverty starting in 1990, publishes annual reports on social exclusion and has monitored the national policies of member countries which address it in regular annual reports since 1991 (Robbins *et al.*, 1994).

Would a basic income scheme be able to reduce various forms of social exclusion in favour of the excluded? It would certainly change the official status of welfare recipients thanks to the salient features of the grant – unconditional, that is, free of any kind of means and/or morals testing, and an undisputable and unalienable right of every citizen. It would reintegrate people into the formal economy of regular and legal exchanges. As buyers and customers, as creditors and debtors, as house-owners and tenants, they would retain a basic scope of action and a small level of discretion that recipients of social assistance benefits are normally deprived of. The enhanced status of a universal civil or citizen's right might, in the long run, even erode the moral stigma of poverty. But in a world of unfettered market competition and inequalities of income and wealth, living on a basic income only would still mean living in poverty, although no longer abject poverty.

So one might ask whether a basic income regime would not just introduce a 'respectable' form of poverty instead of a solution to the problem of poverty and underclass more generally. It would certainly not make any radical change regarding the lack of formal education, lack of skills, poor health, deplorable living standards, lack of mobility, inadequate housing, long-term unemployment and lasting alienation from regular, full-time well-paid jobs that the hard core of poor people are suffering from even in the most advanced welfare states. In order to change that, the introduction of a regular, stable, guaranteed and secure basic income for everyone would be just a first step, although an indispensable one. In order to remind ourselves of the hidden agenda of the 'enabling' strategy implicit in basic income schemes, we shall take a closer look at the implications of a viable basic income.

4. Welfare States and the Provision of Public Goods

Welfare states provide a large variety of public goods, although some welfare states are more service-orientated than others. First and foremost, however, they operate as money-transfer machines, shifting and redistributing large amounts of tax and insurance money. Health care is normally the most service intensive, including only a few monetary transactions between patients and medical personnel. Apart from sickness benefits, the bulk of the monetary transactions are not income transfers but payment for services already provided. Housing is another matter as most welfare states operate with a highly complicated mix of rents paid and subsidies transferred between various agencies. Public education and public transport could be added, although few countries provide the full range of services free of charge (including school textbooks, special transport and use of common sport and leisure facilities). Nonetheless, even in their present shape, battered and distorted by many waves of 'privatization', most welfare states continue to be important producers and providers of public goods and services.

It is useful to make a distinction between a broad concept of the welfare state as comprising all sorts of social welfare services, and a restricted concept of the welfare state as a social insurance or social security state, focusing on the monetary income transfers entailed by various public, social insurance and social assistance schemes. Some welfare states can be generous regarding their social insurance schemes while neglecting their equally important role as providers of public services, and *vice versa*. (A detailed comparison for instance of the British and Dutch welfare states would demonstrate the salience of this distinction.) The overall package has never been established according to a master plan and lacks coherence everywhere. But any larger reform, like the implementation of a basic income scheme, would affect the whole fabric of arrangements made in previous times.

Basic income schemes would turn policymakers' backs on the provision of public goods and services, making monetary income flows and the redistribution of purchasing power the key element for reform. The transfer machinery is where the action is and where the impact is expected to occur. On the other hand, basic income schemes do not fit well into the established fabric of social transfers. Until now, the debate on a feasible basic income scheme has focused on the impact it will probably have on social insurance and social assistance schemes. Who will benefit, who will lose and what? But this is only part of the story. In fact, the viability of a basic income superseding social insurance will depend upon what happens to the package of public goods and services provided by the welfare state.

Basic income schemes are completely tax financed, provided by some State authority and supply a basic public service – income security and stability of money income flows for everybody. The veil of insurance has been lifted, the cage of social assistance destroyed, the regulation of the poor has vanished. Fine. But who will bear the burden? As long as we do not take the logical step of regarding all citizens as collective owners òf a common wealth – say the totality of the productive resources of the country – and if we do not accordingly conceive of a basic income as a normal social dividend originating from this common wealth, we will run into trouble. The very notion of an unconditional basic income as a fundamental birthright of every citizen is at odds with the logic of exchange and, hence with the moral basis of modern capitalism. That has not changed, all the efforts to reconcile it with the dominant economic morals of bourgeois society notwithstanding. Basic income is just as provocative an idea as the notion of public goods and services, which is why they have been justified by accounts of market failures. Public finance has been built upon these accounts, most of which are myths according to the now prevailing wisdom in economics. Many of them are indeed myths, including the beloved stories on lighthouses that economists love to tell as evidence for the existence of public goods in a market economy (Coase, 1974). This does not mean that there is no case against privatization and in favour of public goods and services. It means simply that the case will be a political one as it always has been, and that the answers will be given by political economy, not by 'pure' economics.

5. The Importance of a Public Domain

Markets used to be great social events in earlier times – and they still are on the local level in many parts of Europe. As such, they are highly regulated and linked to specific times and specific spaces – the market place or market hall. They clearly belong to, and are in fact an integral part of, the public domain. Adam Smith used to invoke the supposedly firm business morals of good citizens who would not even think of abusing their market position to the detriment of their clients and competitors. Various pleas for *'laissez faire'* notwithstanding, most classical economists agreed that a market economy would not prosper if markets were left out of the public domain. In their enlightened view, the freedom of markets should be well ordered, controlled and regulated (Hirschman, 1992). This was a task for public authorities, a State in the modern sense that would replace the confused varieties of customs and rules by a unified, nationwide, comprehensive and clearly laid-out system of markets under the rule of law.

Some markets are more public than others. Many are surrounded by grey zones of informal and/or illegal economic activities, sometimes growing into full-fledged black markets. Even on the highest level, that of financial markets, the majority of transactions are OTC (over the counter) outside the highly organized and thoroughly regulated sphere of the official stock exchange. That does not make them illegal but keeps them effectively out of the control of market-regulating authorities. They still belong, however, to the public domain, as do all enterprises operating in an open market and dealing with the public. Basic income schemes presuppose a well-ordered world of markets where everybody's rights as a buyer and customer are equally respected – and where even the poor, the people living on their basic income alone, would be as fairly treated and get the same quality of goods and services at the same prices as the richest customers. This is a utopian idea, of course. But when debating a utopian idea like basic income, it is important to recognize that public authorities face a challenge here. A right to basic income would give everyone a common level of economic security only if all good citizens in fact enjoyed equal rights as customers, as buyers, debtors and consumers. The alleged market sovereign, his majesty the consumer, could use a little empowerment, in particular those consumers who can bring only modest purchasing power to bear.

Obviously, this is just the beginning. Although the two are not identical, the public domain is closely linked to what is conventionally called the 'public sector'. For the sake of the present argument, I refer to those goods and services that the welfare state provides and the resources it owns and uses. The standard theories about public goods and their counterpart, the standard theories about private goods, are both thoroughly flawed as they seek the reason for the public or private quality of a good in some 'nature of goods' referring to some 'natural', technical and/or economic properties of goods (Ostrom and Ostrom, 1977). Even if such qualities can be found, nothing can be inferred from this. Commodities, goods and services that are produced privately and for sale on a market, and that can be' privately appropriated and fully exchanged, are social constructions, not natural categories of 'things'. The process of their construction and 'commodification' can be analysed in terms of social conflicts, and so can the reverse processes of 'de-commodification' and 're-commodification'. In analytical terms, the concept of commodity has not one counterpart – the 'pure' public good – but several, four at least (Krätke, 2002). Any definition of the concept of commodity needs homemade or home-grown goods (including services) as a counterpart as well as the commons, non-commodities (prohibited goods and/or blocked exchanges), and public goods (most of them 'merit goods' in conventional public finance parlance). By means of these conceptual opposites, we are able to define 'contested terrains' where the battles about 'commodification' (and 'decommodification') are fought: battles about enclosing various sorts of commons, about privatization of public goods, about the marketization and commercialization of the gift and barter economy of the household and the neighbourhood. These contested terrains together with the provision of public goods, the governing of the commons and the marketing of commodities are all part of the public domain.

From the point of view of a basic income reform strategy, it matters little whether the goods and services provided by the public sector are truly public goods or not. What matters is whether those goods and services are accessible and useful. Even the most highly developed and service-intensive welfare states suffer from a built-in class bias, their structures and the nature of their services favouring middle-class clients and users. The well-known Matthews effect, that has frustrated efforts to redress inequalities of wealth and income through the operation of the welfare states, has to be blamed on the intrinsic patterns of unequal access to and use of public services such as health care and education. A basic income for all would not change this without some effort to reform provision of public goods and services.

Hence, a basic income scheme should be linked to a strategy of rebuilding and expanding the public domain. More and better public goods and services, less infected by class-bias or even freed of it, enhanced user participation – aspirations like these should reappear on the reform agenda, first and foremost with respect to public goods and services that are relevant for the majority of poor people. Fares, fees and charges are clearly a burden and a deterrent for those people, functioning as a rationing device and keeping them away from better-quality public goods and services. That is why in many welfare states, fees and charges are reduced or waived for categories of supposedly poor people (the retired, students, children, handicapped and so on). Public transport, public education, public health care and other services would all fare better, as would the majority of their clients, without the burdensome and wasteful contrivance of fees and charges. What is more, the real value of a basic income would rise immediately with each step towards complete tax finance in the public sector.

Even the friends of a partial basic income should agree: the larger the scope of public services provided free of charge for all, the lower the level of a basic income (partial or full) could be. A similar argument could be used regarding the stability and security of the universal grant: as a money income-flow its real purchasing power would depend upon variable prices in many markets. When supplemented by a wide array of public goods and services one could afford to worry less about the level of real income secured by the grant – on condition that the goods and services provided would be free of all charges or fees. Nothing else would be compatible with a truly universal grant to all citizens.

If we want to go a step further and reform the public provision of goods and services in order to redress the existing inequalities of life chances and enhance basic 'autonomy' for as many good citizens as possible, we will certainly look for more and new public goods and services. Free provision of access to information networks of all kinds (print, telephone, fax, computers and computer networks, internet) might be as important today as free access to schools, hospitals and urban transport. Regarding the overall concern with 'social exclusion' in contemporary 'wars on poverty', it might even be crucial. It would support the public domain in information exchange and communication and keep private market actors in check; in the longer run it might even be part of a long-term strategy aimed at enhanced economic self-government of citizens (Elson, 1988). But there is more. Apart from sustaining the provision of public goods and services, rediscovering and rebuilding the commons might be a supplementary strategy to follow.

6. Rediscovering the Commons – Rethinking Economic Governance

With the ascendance of private property the commons have disappeared all over Europe. Of course, the most popular story about this historical transformation, Hardin's 'tragedy of the commons' (Hardin, 1968), is thoroughly flawed. Set against the rich historical evidence on the process of 'enclosures' or the private appropriation of former commons in the countryside, Hardin's version is just a legend made up to support the ideological notion of the merits and superior quality of 'private property', the only means to prevent the destruction of all commons according to Hardin. In fact, there was no 'tragedy of the commons' as Hardin depicted it, at least as long as private property owners did not start to exploit the commons on their own behalf, expropriating the commoners and destroying the commons in the longer run (Cox, 1985).

Commons have to be used by many people. Obviously, this can hardly be done by conventional moral rules, by unwritten or 'common' laws; commons have to be governed. Even small-scale units, couples and families, need some established rules and some kind of governance to handle the use of their commons. Governing the commons means, if anything, self-government of the commoners regarding their common goods. Elinor Ostrom has demonstrated in a seminal study that associations, bodies of people cooperating to regulate and in govern the common use of the commons, preventing abuse and preserving the commons in most cases, do spring up at various places and times, local communities of fishermen being one of her most important examples (Ostrom, 1990).

Commons and public goods are not the same. To put it simply: commons cannot be left to the public; they are the common concern of a defined group of commoners sharing them and claiming a rightful share in using them for their own sake. User rights – e.g. the traditional mediaeval four: common of pasture, common of turbary (to cut turf or peat as fuel), common of estover (to take wood necessary for domestic furniture) and common of piscary (to take fish) – used to be even more restricted than the user rights we normally enjoy with regard to public goods and services. For both public goods and commons, the basic civil right is the right not to be excluded from access and/or usufruct. Regulations in both cases are meant to prevent misuse or abuse of all kinds, but in the case of commons the concept of misuse or abuse is more narrowly defined than for public goods. To use a commons and remain a good commoner you had to exercise a lot of restraint, following the common law rules, written or not. Those rules most certainly banned the good commoner from using the commons for his own private interest alone, especially from using the commons in order to make a private profit. Sharing and using a commons together was (and still would be) a basis for cooperation – for making a living, not for private entrepreneurship.

In terms of a basic income strategy, a link to a 'recovery of the commons', or some sorts of commons, has the great advantage of enhancing people's options. If given the chance of becoming commoners, people will acquire civil rights of considerable economic relevance – rights that are enabling and empowering by the same token, as a commoner does not only have more and better chances to earn a living but also a voice, a right to participate in the collective self-government of the commons he is sharing with others. Social insurance and allied services already enhance everyday autonomy, and basic income would increase that autonomy. A recovery of the commons, any commons fitting into the context of contemporary urbanized and industrialized societies, would add further autonomy gains (Krätke, 2002). As commoners and would-be commoners, people would need capacities and facilities enabling them to govern the commons recovered or reinvented, together with the civil rights empowering them to do so. Hence, for any enabling strategy based upon a basic income scheme, finding and establishing the right mix of public goods and common goods (and services) would be crucial. All would enhance the autonomy, the scope of choice and action, for good citizens. But some would be more important than others – free access for all to education, for instance, because you need educated, intelligent and resourceful people to govern the commons (Hardin and Baden, 1977), but also free access to a public information network, unfettered by the ever-growing variety of private toll or turnpike barriers now arising everywhere in the world of inter-networks.

Just follow the implicit logic of a reform strategy focused upon basic income and you get rather close to a highly sophisticated type of welfare state – one that not only provides stable income flows for all citizens but also a reliable and continuous supply of a variety of public goods and services, and a variety of common goods and services for various groups of commoners as well. Such a welfare state could easily do without most of the nuisances that make many a good citizen's life a misery in contemporary welfare states – the ever-growing number of fees, fines, fares, tolls and charges, the ever-growing bureaucracies, public and private, the ever-growing chaos of organized irresponsibilities shared by powerless public authorities and private providers that are accountable to nobody. But, of course, the advocates of the 'free market' as a universal device would not like that. They prefer and promote a strategy of ongoing privatization and marketization of the public domain, and they have inflicted a lot of damage in recent years. As a basic income would not be viable without a large public sector, requiring some rebuilding and even expansion of the public domain in several directions, the true supporters of a basic income should join the fray and give the public economy some serious thought again. The alternative is to give up and be content with some miserable form of poverty made 'respectable'.

Note

1   University of Amsterdam, Netherlands.

References

Coase, R. 1974. 'The lighthouse in economics', *Journal of Law and Economics*, Vol. 17, pp. 357–376.
Cox, S. 1985. 'No tragedy on the commons', *Environmental Ethics*, Spring, pp. 49–61.

de Voogd, J., de Koning, J. and others. 1995 *Guaranteed minimum income arrangements in the Netherlands, Belgium, Denmark, France, Germany and Great Britain* (The Hague, Dutch Ministry of Social Affairs and Employment).

Dyson, K. 1980. *The European state tradition* (Oxford, D.H. Robertson).

Elson, D. 1988. 'Market socialism or socialization of the market', *New Left Review*, No. 172, pp. 3–44.

Hardin, G. 1968. 'The tragedy of the commons', *Science*, No. 162, December 13, pp. 1243–1248.

_____ and Baden, R. 1977. *Managing the commons* (San Francisco, W.H. Freeman).

Hirschman, A. 1970. *Exit, voice, and loyalty* (Cambridge, Harvard University Press).

_____ 1992. *Rival views of market society* (Cambridge, Harvard University Press).

Krätke, M. R. 2000. *Taxation and civil rights*, Paper presented to the Eighth International Conference on Basic Income, Berlin, October 6–8, 2000.

_____ 2002. *The comedy of the commons*, unpublished manuscript, University of Amsterdam.

Lafargue, P. 1989. *The right to be lazy* (Chicago, Charles H. Kerr Publishers) (1883).

Marshall, T.H. 1950. *Citizenship and social class and other essays* (Cambridge, Cambridge University Press).

Marx, K. 1990. *Capital. A critical analysis of capitalist production* (London 1887, in Marx-Engels-Gesamtausgabe [MEGA] II / 9 (Berlin, Dietz Verlag).

Ostrom, E. 1990. *Governing the commons: The evolution of institutions for collective action* (Cambridge, Cambridge University Press).

_____ and Ostrom, E. 1977. 'Public goods and public choices' in E. S. Savas (ed.), *Alternatives for delivering public services. Toward improved performance* (Boulder, Westview Press).

Robbins, D. and others. 1994. *Observatory on national policies to combat social exclusion: Third annual report* (DG V, Lille, Commission of the European Communities).

Townsend, P. 1979. *Poverty in the United Kingdom* (Harmondsworth, Penguin Books).

van der Veen, R. and Groot, L. (eds.). 2000. *Basic income on the agenda* (Amsterdam, Amsterdam University Press).

van Parijs, P. 1995. *Real freedom for all* (Oxford, Clarendon Press).

11

'CALLING': A CHRISTIAN ARGUMENT FOR BASIC INCOME

Torsten Meireis[1]

1. Introduction

This paper outlines the preliminaries of a theological (Protestant Christian) argument for a basic income at the level of a decent minimum. It argues that the idea of 'vocation' or 'calling' (German: *Beruf*), developed by Luther and accepted by Calvin (Calvin, 1963, p. 467ff; see also Biéler, 1959, p. 397ff) and the Protestant tradition, can and should be reformulated under modern conditions to try to clarify what Christians understand as a good life.

To decide whether an activity is rightly understood as part of a vocation, Luther sketches two main criteria: the activity has to imply a service to one's neighbour and it has to be done in a spirit of love. A vocation in that sense and under modern conditions, however, cannot simply be identified with paid labour; it evidently transcends the range of gainful employment in a capitalist environment and thus can be understood to imply a basic income that makes it possible to follow that calling.

As Protestantism seems to be – at least according to Max Weber (1905) – partly responsible for the development that led to modern capitalism and the phenomenon of the 'labour-society', the dramatic changes which form one of the more important backdrops for the basic income debate, it might be of interest even to non-Christians to take a glimpse at the thinking and discussion in the Protestant community. As Martin Luther's ideas on work, expressed in the ideas of 'calling' and 'station', initiated that process, and have had a tremendous impact (not only in the Lutheran tradition) that is of systemic relevancy for Christianity still, they are worth a closer look.

To this end, four steps will be taken. First of all, Luther's ethical thought in its social and historical context is briefly sketched. Second, I reflect on the history of the reception of those ideas, which will show that Luther's concepts have been taken out of their social and historical context, resulting in serious misrepresentations. As a third step, a heuristic concept of 'work' is expounded: this is necessary to avoid such misrepresentation and to bridge the gap between theological insights won in a stratified, feudal society, largely based on agriculture and subsistence in a rural setting, and their application to a modern industrialized, urbanized labour-society in a process of change. Finally, I try to outline in which form the insights derived from Luther's doctrines may be of use in today's debates on the future of labour-society and welfare.

2. Calling, Office and Status – Luther's Ethical Thought in Context

Luther's basic theological insight is given in his doctrine of justification. In an interpretation of Paul's *Letter to the Romans* he argues that no man can justify himself successfully before God through words or deeds, but that God himself in Christ justifies all who believe him and in him. Faith, in the sense of trust in God's grace, is thus God's gift as well as the only proper attitude towards God.

Two ethical consequences from this doctrine can be stated: First of all, our good deeds and works cannot be seen as causes for God's attention, meriting God's love, but have to be understood, quite to the contrary, as results of God's love. The idea of doing good to bring oneself to the attention of God, and the pious pride behind it, is thus utterly rejected by Luther.

This theological demoting of good works before God leads – second – to a promotion of the work done in the course of daily life, because everything done in service of one's fellow man or neighbour motivated by love is seen by Luther as vocation or calling,[2] an activity sanctioned by God (see Luther, 1520, p. 206f but also 1531a, p. 377). The believer who wishes to be justified and reconciled with God freely and happily obeys Gods commandments, which are directed towards his neighbour's service, thus expressing his joy and disciplining himself.[3]

God's calling is understood to have two dimensions. As *vocatio spiritualis sive interna* it is directed at every man and woman through the Gospel. It leads to baptism and faith, through which Christians are incorporated into the body of Christ. This calling is directed to everybody and, equally, differences can only arise as the calling is accepted in varying intensity (Luther, 1531). As *vocatio externa*, bodily or worldly calling, it constitutes differences. It "*macht ein unterscheid, Est yrdisch, quanquam etiam divina. Ibi furst non rusticus, scholasticus non Magister, servus non dominus, pater non filius, vir non mulier*" (Luther, 1531, p. 307a), the German translates into English as "*makes a difference. It is earthly, even though it is divine at the same time. Here the duke is no peasant, the student no master, the servant no lord, the father no son, the man no woman*".

As the idea of calling is separated from certain works and their ecclesiastical sanction – e.g. becoming a priest, a monk or a nun, leading a life of contemplation, sponsoring mass, praying, going on pilgrimages – it becomes, in a way, more democratic. In its worldly dimension Luther binds it to the criteria of station (status, *Stand*)[4] and office (*officium, Amt*), which are in turn determined by love of and service toward one's neighbour given mutually. That, however, means that the idea of calling is not bound to some special experience, but to the everyday chores of Christians. In that respect, it is counter-intuitive. Luther thus tries to abolish the idea of a spiritual élite, which he thinks supercilious before God and thereby dangerous for the individual.

· Luther distinguishes three main stations: *politia, oeconomia, ecclesia*. He understands those as institutions of God's spiritual and worldly regime. Those stations do not constitute exclusive groups, they do not signify strata of society, but everybody is thought to belong to every station – although not in the same position (Elert, 1958, pp. 56ff). The positions – at least in *politia* and *oeconomia* – are understood to be hierarchically structured and stable, although a change of position is possible. As *ecclesia* is thought to belong to the spiritual regime operating solely through the Word, not by force, and implying equality of all, its offices do not constitute a special spiritual status, but are merely set up to guarantee a certain functional order, and are, in that respect, part of the worldly regime. Luther's concept of stations, however, which goes back to Aristotle's social philosophy, should not be understood as an empirical description of society's structure, but rather as a sketch of certain anthropological basics that allow for historical variability. For Luther and most of his contemporaries, a difference between theology, anthropology and theory of society implying human influence on the basic structures of society is simply unthinkable. Thus, Luther never states or insists normatively that noblemen should be at the top of society and peasants at the bottom. On the contrary, Luther understands and even advocates upward mobility (Luther, 1530, p. 578a ff), but this is not understood to change structures. This pre-modern attitude gives rise to a number of background presuppositions in Luther's thought. The first is a theological presupposition: Luther credits all earthly reality with a dignity stemming from the fact of God's providence. All misfortunes are understood to be a punishment for sin enacted by the Devil, whose workings are tolerated by God for a time. After all, to Luther the world is just a place of individual probation, and what really counts is God's kingdom to come, put individually: life after resurrection. For that reason, an improvement of the world is only possible in the sense of a more effective control of evil with the aim of conserving the world and humanity, so people can prepare for Judgment Day. In that vein, however, Luther was not simply what we would call conservative: thus, he strongly supported the aims of the peasants' movement before the beginning of violent turmoil (Luther, 1525, pp. 294b ff).[5] Second, Luther was, even for his times, a political pessimist.

Social and political change, implying militant action that does not proceed along the operating mode condoned by traditional order, to him is intolerable, since it can only be interpreted as anomie, violent anarchy and thus as disobedience against God's worldly regime. This does – third – extend to economic change and early capitalist developments: Luther criticizes the system of interest and the rising power of trading firms, in as much they transcend the comprehensible political order of feudal hierarchy.

The historical context of Luther's discovery is his struggle against monasticism and the Roman Church, which implies and enacts a spiritual hierarchy (Luther, 1521).[6] Since Luther argues against the idea that ordinary everyday activity is of less value than spiritual works that make extraordinary settings like monasteries and pilgrimages necessary, he stresses the duty to remain faithful to one's calling, which – to him – is bound to one's status (Luther, 1522a, p. 305ff). For that reason, the individual questioning of one's calling is always problematic – Luther sees this as resistance against God's providence. Thus, he reprimands all self-induced efforts to change one's social and political position in life as 'escape into alien works', works assigned to others, as motivated by a sinful spirit. This, of course, has to do with Luther's Augustine anthropology, to which 'autonomy' is an alien concept. Man is either, so to speak, 'theonomous' or 'satanonomous'; human reason that believes itself self-sufficient must necessarily fail and end in blindness and sin (Wingren, 1952, p. 61f). Thus, his promotion of everyday activity extending to and including even those activities and vocations which seem unimportant and bring little prestige (for instance, those of servant or maid), bears consequences that seem – in modern eyes – problematic. The implication of promoting the status of servant to an equal spiritual rank to that of lord consists in the obligation to accept this status as God's gift and assignment which is not to be shunned. Luther generally assumes that all, even the most different, vocations bring an equal amount of hardship and joy. Also he presumes that the mind-set accompanying work has noticeable effects, because every activity implies a certain freedom; this is of course based on the nature of activities and work at that time.

The individual's set of activities can be seen in two ways. To Christians, their station in life is an orientation provided by God to help them practise their happy and joyful obedience in service to their neighbour (Wingren, 1952, p. 43). Others[7] find their station in life obligatory, as it is ordained by some worldly authority.[8] The political and economical hierarchy of stations is – to Luther – a function of God's worldly regime extending to everybody and including the means of force, ultimately designed to preserve the world against the Devil's efforts. This helps to explain why in Luther's eyes the choice or change of trade can only be acceptable as ordered by the respective authorities. It also explains why Luther can exhort parents to follow the duty of their parental office and further the social promotion of their children by granting them the best education possible (Luther, 1530, p. 578a).[9]

Therefore, the Christian will not question but will obediently accept his station in life and the corresponding assignments as his calling, acting accordingly from a motivation of neighbourly love and in adherence to the Ten Commandments. Does that imply that any station will do? In Luther's view, the problem cannot – for reasons given above – be solved on an individual basis. Luther analyses the problem not in respect to 'calling' but concerning the concept of 'station', and subsequently develops criteria for godly and ungodly stations.[10] The main criterion for the discernment of godly and sinful stations is the accordance with or resistance to God's will as visible in the regimes of God. Sinful stations are those that either resist the spiritual regime by somehow obstructing the spreading of the Gospel or the worldly regime by resisting God's will to preserve the world. Any attempt to deduce from an isolated activity its relation to God's will meets with Luther's objection that only in the context of the function of a certain station does its significance show.[11]

3. Reception as Interpretation

It is a simple truth that Luther's categories of perception differ from those used today. For Luther, 'erbeit' (labour) means primarily strenuous physical labour. The issues we associate with the term 'work' or 'labour' are in his perspective expressed by the concepts of 'calling' (vocation) and 'station' (status). But that change of perspective goes farther and extends to core issues of theology as well. While in his time, Luther's theology was controversial because of his claim about the spiritual equality and religious maturity of all Christians, nowadays the presumption of Christianity's universality is no longer considered evident and is at least argued, even among theologians.[12] Luther distinguished between godly and sinful stations, but it was clear to him that even the unwilling and sinful are somehow instruments of God. Theology after the Enlightenment and after the Shoah finds the idea of God's toleration of evil hard to bear, which shows in theological attempts to do away with the idea of God's omnipotence (Groarke, 2001; Link-Wieczorek, 1999). While for Luther any autonomy is an illusion at best, modern theology and faith tend to accept the possibility of a harmony of theonomy, autonomy and self-realization.[13]

The idea of the imperfectability of society's structures, based on the idea of a hiatus between creation and redemption, has been replaced by the concept that a sensible political formation aware of its limits may find its criteria in God's will to redemption (Barth, 1946, p. 22ff). Whereas Luther counts on the immediate coming of Christ, making earthly life a mere time of probation, in modern times the significance of life before death has been far more highly valued. The background presuppositions of Luther's times, which are assumptions on which Luther's doctrine of stations and calling rests, have been widely replaced, and this is true for Lutheran Christians, too. Luther's pessimism concerning politics and the economy has lost plausibility; even contemporary critiques concerning the ideology of growth or naïve optimism concerning human progress usually do not aim to achieve a worldly condition short of European levels of moral autonomy, political democracy and economic wealth.

Transitions in theological thinking have to be understood in the context of social structure and structuration, as theology and Christian understanding are shaped by social structure and in turn affect that structure (Giddens, 1984).[14] Luther lives and argues in the context of a stratified, feudally organized and agrarian and rural society. There is a process of change going on, urbanization and the bourgeoisie are on the rise, but this process is still quite slow. The then predominant idea of social order – or better, order in the world – regards it as stable, linear, hierarchical and evident; it can be illustrated by 'status-trees' where the peasants populate the earth, while the upper branches are occupied by noblemen, dukes, kings, bishops, the Pope and so on.[15] Thus, Luther and his contemporaries do not expect rapid change by any earthly powers, but through the Second Coming of Christ. Phenomena of crisis or social transformation are thus usually attributed to God's or Satan's doing and understood as foreshadowing the Last Judgment (Wingren, 1952, p. 107f). As social structures in the artisan and agrarian society he lives in are embedded in relations largely based on face-to-face interactions and thus highly personalized, most activities and assignments usually imply some kind of freedom of judgment – if in no other sense than lack of controls. Unlike the last century's industrial worker, even most servants had some freedom of choice concerning the way they approached their chores, at least while the master was at some other task (Wingren, 1952, pp. 128f–138f).[16] This may well be one core explanation for the fact that Luther could declare the given situation individuals found themselves in as a signpost and guideline for a life led in the spirit of Christian freedom, like a *tertius usus legis* turned social structure.

However simple the truth may be that reception means interpretation, and even more so in a different historical context, it is often not observed. Prominently in the course of the nineteenth century, many representatives of the Lutheran tradition for various reasons[17] tried to meet the challenges presented by social and economic change through a historically uncritical, highly selective and methodologically problematic reception of Luther's insights. This led to arguments that were ideological in the worst sense of the word, leaving Lutheran social ethics as an instrument to preserve the power of the powerful.

- Thus Luther's doctrine of the two kingdoms and the two regimes of God were interpreted to signify a strict separation of 'church' and 'world'. Luther's distinction of two regimes is applied to a modern, functionally differentiated society in a way that transforms functional distinction into normative division.[18] While Luther holds it to be evident that God's will is predominant in both regimes and in the three stations of *ecclesia, politia* and *oeconomia*, and therefore could criticize those who to his mind opposed it, theologians now declare the realm of politics and the economy autonomous in a way that forbids any questioning from religious and theological motives, which are held to concern exclusively the psyche of the individual.

- The neo-Lutheran theology, which developed at the beginning of the twentieth century, interprets Luther's concept of stations as a doctrine of the orders of creation (Althaus, 1935; Althaus, 1953, p. 110f). Luther sees stations as spheres of life instituted by God and concerning every individual, and does so in the context of a world where social structures are usually comprehended as static. The idea of the orders of creation, on the other hand, operating in an era of obvious social change and growing insight into historical contingency, is designed to canonize certain social structures, like matrimony, people or State, by declaring them to be timeless – and therefore normative – institutions of God. This way, a certain type of social change was to be counteracted.

- Luther's warning against 'alien works', an individual choice of station or activity, has to be understood as part of his struggle against popular Catholic belief in the redeeming power of certain 'good works' on the one hand and against political spiritualism on the other. This thinking is situated in an agrarian society based on personal relationships, but many nineteenth-century theologians interpreted it out of that context. In a situation of economic dislocation and expropriation caused by developing industrial capitalism, they stressed Luther's warning against any self-induced pursuit of change and thus turned the idea into a weapon aimed at the victims of those processes. The industrial proletarians were then supposed to accept their miserable station in life as God's calling to them. Moreover, the idea of calling lost plausibility as the somewhat 'holistic' and often – at least to some extent – self-regulated jobs of artisans and farmers constituting Luther's world were increasingly replaced by tightly regulated industrial work, where personal judgment or freedom was neither necessary nor encouraged.[19]

Luther may – in a modern perspective – be described as ambivalent in terms of what we understand by autonomy and freedom of the individual. However, strong currents of the Lutheran tradition have given his ideas a blatantly ideological turn by taking them out of their social and historical context and thus effectively impeding a reception of those aspects in Luther's thinking that may be an inspiration even in our times. If that is to be achieved, a misrepresentation due to a lack of contextual understanding must be avoided. To that end, we need to look for the term that in modern times encapsulates those questions Luther treats under the labels of 'calling' and 'station'; evidently this is the concept of 'work' or 'labour'. Therefore, a closer look at the concept of 'work' should be helpful.

4. A Heuristic Concept of 'Work'

Rather than attempting a philosophical inquiry into the term 'work', I would – at this point – like to treat the concept heuristically, as a socio-cultural paradigm of interpretation,[20] rooted in everyday life and ordinary language, involving at least five areas of conflict in current north-eastern societies that are in one way or other associated when we use the concept.

A philosophically sound definition is problematic, precisely because the concept of 'work' is so tightly bound up with the development of modernity (Pankoke, 1990) – not only in social philosophy (Hegel, Marx, Weber, Marxism) but also in the emergence of modern industrialism, the design of welfare systems and, of course, the overall conception of the processes vital for the reproduction of any modern society.

- Existing definitions commonly used in theology are usually either too broad or too narrow; they are based on anthropology, signifying almost anything, or specify gainful employment only.[21]
- The concept of 'work' is deeply immersed in social contexts and thus in social change: there are ongoing debates in Germany as to what should be called 'work', the implication being that 'work' is the sort of activity that merits an income or at least some kind of social recognition or appreciation.[22]

In current social crises, and through the campaigning activity of social movements, the question of 'work' is involved in a number of debated issues:

- The unemployment crisis – or, in more liberal welfare states, the phenomenon of the working poor or rising imprisonment rates – has triggered debates on the character and the future of work,[23] sometimes extending to a debate on the aims of work in general in relation to the meaning of society and life (Gorz, 1994, p. 108ff).

- The feminist movement has drawn attention to the sexist (or gender) bias of the work place and, of family-based systems in general, and to the lack of recognition granted to activities of reproduction and human care (e.g. Hausen, 1993; Krebs, 1996).
- The ecological movement has criticized the idea of 'work' implying the processing, consumption and exploitation of natural resources thought of as plentiful and free of charge.[24]

Thus, 'work' may be seen as a key concept in at least five areas of conflict in (labour-) society:

1. Conflicts of **recognition:** The inflation of the use of the concept of 'work' — at least in German and Germany — may be seen as a strategy of acquiring recognition and implies that the only activities entitled to recognition are those that are regarded as legitimate 'work' in society. Recognition may take different forms, including prestigious 'social appreciation'[25] as an able citizen as well as recognition for entitlement to material resources.
2. Conflicts of **allocation** or **distribution:** Because the direct or indirect participation in some kind of 'work' — in the form of gainful employment — constitutes the main source of income and livelihood for the majority of citizens in capitalist societies, the idea of work is central to the distribution of wealth.[26]
3. Conflicts of **participation:** Political participation is — not de jure, but de facto — tightly knit into the fabric of social participation through educational and everyday involvement in the regular productive and distributive mechanisms of society, e.g. participation in gainful employment. Thus rising unemployment and/or increasing mobility implied in the change from Fordism to post-Fordism[27] links questions of the political organization of society to the organization of work.
4. Conflicts of **relations to the natural environment:** As economic growth, implying an idea and practice of work as processing and thereby consuming natural resources, is still seen as the route to universal well-being, sceptics are demanding new forms of management and work.
5. Conflicts in respect to the aims of work, culminating in conflicts concerning the **meaning of life:** In Fordism, many people were motivated by an ethos of hard work for the betterment of one's offspring. This, however, has changed.[28] People are not only interested in what they earn, but in what they do most of the day. Thus, the questions of what 'work' means in individual life, and what the aims of work are in general, are vibrant.

In our societies, the discussion, understanding and organization of what we usually call 'work' is central to these areas of conflict. This holds true, no matter how we otherwise analyse the structure of society. Thus, my thesis runs something like this: when looking for alternatives to the labour-society as we know it, or if we are interested in ideas on the subject generated in societies set up differently from ours, it makes sense to check those five areas, for the organization of which the concept of 'work' is central.

5. 'Calling' as Motivating a Christian Argument for a Basic Income

As it is my objective to study what, if anything, may be learned from Luther's ideas under the changed economic, social and cultural conditions of today, it is necessary to scrutinize them closely to avoid misrepresentations like those adduced above. Since Luther did not develop ethical criteria for the structure of society – which he thought remote from the influence of man – answers of that kind should not be expected from him. What Luther, in his time, thought about the problems of recognition, distribution, participation and the relationship to the natural environment may be sketched quite briefly.

- Social recognition, to Luther, has nothing to do with the person, but belongs to office and station. Christians have to refrain from any worldly recognition, since they live in Christ. What the modern age understands by 'personal identity'[29] is materially presumed by Luther. Modern insights on self-assurance, self-respect and a loving self-regard as necessary, if not sufficient conditions for the ability freely to act as a human person, are clearly beyond Luther's interests and, evidently, his cultural means.
- Questions of allocation are, similarly, of less importance. Participation in worldly goods is thought to be dependent on office and station. Up to certain limits it may be legitimately acquired through work, but this aim must remain secondary. The objective of worldly goods can only be seen in the context of the temporary preservation of earthly life to prepare for life eternal. In that vein, Luther can commend the institution of communal funds for the needy (Meireis, 2001).
- Concerning the question of political participation Luther follows Paul's ideas from *Romans* 13, categorizing political agents into rulers and subjects. He simply accepts the given order as prescription originating in divine providence. The idea of equality or democracy in the stations of *politia* or *oeconomia* is alien to him.
- The relationship towards the natural environment is seen in respect of *Genesis* 1.22, the so-called *dominium terrae*. Man is supposed to act as *cooperator dei* and in that function and dimension is seen to have a free will (Wingren, 1952, p. 23ff).

If Luther's ideas are interpreted in the context of individual and collective concepts on the meaning of life, reflecting the semantics of particular communities, the picture looks different. The insights connected to the concept of 'calling' can then be reframed for modern conditions. For if the Christian's activity is motivated by love and aimed at service for one's neighbour, then 'calling' can surely not be restricted to activities made possible by the current social order of labour-society, i.e. gainful employment. Since the questions of social structures and social order are in modern times understood to be questions of democratic choice, civic activity and, generally, human doing, ideas gained from Luther's thinking, while not granting us ready-to-use solutions, may help to open up the horizon of possibilities.

- In a Lutheran perspective, man's activity, his earthly calling, will not grant salvation, but is restricted to the achievement of his neighbour's well-being. The central idea of the doctrine of justification consists in the proposition that a person is not basically constituted or sufficiently described by what he or she does or by works (Giarini and Liedtke 1998, p. 233), but that there is always more than meets the eye. Luther's position has to be understood at a different level from the notion of the formation of identity and personality by socialization and routines described by the humanities. It may be rephrased, however, in terms of those transcendental conditions that make the idea of inalienable human dignity feasible.
- Luther's idea of 'calling', interpreting social conditions in a given society as guidelines for the Christian's life, helps to clarify that in a Christian perspective others are not only seen as limiting, but also as enabling individual and collective freedom (Huber, 1983; and also Marx, 1844, p. 365). Modern theological ethics are therefore challenged to integrate an adequate, theoretically consistent and empirically sound model of today's social formation into their reflections.
- The criteria developed by Luther in the context of his doctrine of stations and relevant for his understanding of 'calling' have to be reframed under modern conditions. A limitation of the criteria to the individual's intentions is bound to become ideological. Instead, they have to be applied to the activities in question. Thus, assignments, jobs, professions and all kinds of work should be designed so that they can be evidently done or fulfilled in a spirit of love and with the intention of serving one's neighbour.
- Luther's 'worldly' concept of vocation, aimed against the idea of an élite distinguished by a special experience of calling, may be interpreted as pertaining to a divine promise which implies that every Christian – and potentially, everybody – may trust that there is a place in active life where he or she may find (within the limits set by the human condition)

fulfilment through the service to his or her neighbour done in a spirit of love.

- The idea of 'calling' does not restrict the multitude of activities possible to individuals and determined only by individuality. Thus, a limitation to gainful employment is not plausible in this perspective. On the other hand, activities are not valued by efficiency or prestige, implying an anti-élitist stance.

Evidently, these ideas derived from Luther's concepts do not add up to a conclusive solution concerning the question of labour-society or basic income. Rather, they suggest a number of further questions.[30] Still, a provisional sketch of what those ideas might imply in a changing labour-society may be helpful.

- It seems not too far-fetched to suggest, that in western Europe's societies, distribution and political participation will increasingly result in some form of welfare pluralism (Evers and Olk, 1996), effecting income pluralism (Vobruba, 1999, p. 110, and 2000) and activity pluralism. The probability of holding a lifelong steady job will decrease, especially at the bottom of the income distribution range.
- As Christians live in those societies, they will partake in those pluralisms. The political question will be whether the emerging forms will allow for a certain freedom of the individual – presuming that freedom in that sense rests on income security, the possibility of earning a certain recognition, the ability to participate politically (implying an enabling education) and to lead one's life in accordance with values and goals pursued individually or by communities of choice. To Christians, this means, whether the social setting will allow pursuit of what they understand to be their calling, besides or instead of in gainful employment.
- As the division of labour is usually organized by the instrument of the market, this instrument appears to be necessary but not sufficient. For one thing, the market is blind to the moral demands of minorities without buying power; second, many activities necessary in society cannot sensibly be left to the organization of the marketplace.[31]
- Since Christian active life is to be characterized by serving one's neighbour in a spirit of love, a social order of distribution that condones only integration into gainful employment organized by the market (unless a person is independently wealthy or renounces all welfare) – denouncing other ways of life or stigmatizing those who are unable to fend for themselves – is not acceptable, not least because it effectively reduces the freedom to follow one's calling to a small élite.

• A basic income, covering the decent minimum (Sen, 1999, p. 92ff) in a given society, may well – in a Christian perspective – be a sensible instrument to grant that amount of freedom to develop one's abilities, necessary to follow one's calling individually, either in a job or out of a job. Of course, this cannot be the only instrument; others are necessary including a decent system of basic education and an improved system of political participation.

Notes

1 Theological Faculty, University of Münster, Germany.

2 This goes back to the Greek derived from 1 *Corinthians* 7,20. For a comprehensive analysis of Luther's thinking on those topics see Wingren (1952); Holl (1928); Elert (1958), Bayer (1995).

3 'Aber der glaub gleych wie er frum macht, ßo macht er auch [27] gutte werck. So dann die werck niemant frum machen, und der mensch zuvor [28] muß frum sein, ehe er wirckt, so ists offenbar, das allein der glaub auß [29] lauttern gnaden, durch Christum und seyn wort, die person gnugsam frum [30] und selig machet. Und das keyn werck, keyn gepott eynem Christen nott sey [31] zur seligkeit, sondern er frey ist von allen gepotten, und auß lauterer freyheit [32] umb sonst thut alls, was er thut, nichts damit gesucht seyneß nutzs oder [33] selickeyt, Denn er schon satt und selig ist durch seynenn glaubenn und gottis [34] gnaden, sondernn nur gott darynnen gefallen' (Luther, 1520a, p. 33). The necessity of discipline is rooted in Luther's anthropological dualism: The 'inner' man is justified by Christ and lives in Christ, but the 'outer' man – for whom the term 'flesh' is also used – is embedded not in divine but in worldly relations and has to be disciplined.

4 His use of the term 'station' is – as is often the case – not wholly consistent. He uses *Stand* for the three basic hierarchies in society, but also for certain jobs or offices (Luther, 1522a, pp. 305–323 and also Elert, 1958, p. 62ff).

5 For his turn against this revolt, Luther gives two arguments. First of all, he objects to war waged for religion's sake, because God's spiritual regiment must not use the sword. Second, he believes that a violent revolt against political order will necessarily end in anomie (Luther, 1522, p. 681 and 1528, p. 251b).

6 While he understands Roman Catholicism to be disobedient against God's spiritual regime, the representatives of the 'left wing' of reformation, the spiritualists, to him act against God's worldly regime.

7 The idea runs something like this: for true Christians, the worldly regime would not be necessary, but they gladly bear it for the sake of their brethren, so the world may be preserved and they have time to be reached by God's Word. However, as each Christian in Luther's view is always '*simul iustus et peccator*', justified by God but un-Christian sinner at the same time, both perspectives usually apply (Luther, 1520a, p. 20ff).

8 In that perspective Luther interprets his own biography, expressing relief that he was ordered to be a scholar and theological teacher – thus, he could be sure that his teaching was not his own or the Devil's doing (Luther, 1532, p. 522f).

9 Evidently, the parent's motive cannot include upward mobility as such – rather, parents should wish for their children to become useful instruments of God's love.

10 'Auch wenn [17] ich vom stand rede, der nit sundlich an yhm selb ist, meyne ich nit damit, [18] das yemand mug hie auff erden on sund leben, alle stende unnd weßen

[19] sundigen teglich, ßondern ich meyne die stend, die gott gesetzt hatt odder yhr [20] eynsatzung nit widder gott ist, als da sind: ehlich seyn, knecht, magd, herr, [21] fraw, ubirherrn, regirer, richter, ampleutt, bawr, burger &c.. Sundlichen stand [22] heyß ich reuberey, wucherhandell, offenttlicher frawen weßen unnd als itzt sind [23] Bapst, Cardinal, Bischoff, Priester, Munch, Nonnen stend, die nitt predigen [24] odder predigen horen. Denn diße stendt sind gewißlich wider gott, wo sie [25] nur mit messen und singen und mit gottis wort nit umbgehen, das eyn [1] gemeyn weyb viel ehr mag gen hymell kommen, denn dißer eynß' (Luther, 1522, p. 318f).

11 Thus, Luther sanctions the bloody trade of the soldier (fighting in a just war) by comparing it to the surgeon – the amputation of a limb, however cruel, is done to preserve the body: 'Obs nu wol nicht scheinet, das wuergen und rauben ein werck der liebe [27] ist, derhalben ein einfeltiger denckt, Es sey nicht ein Christlich werck, zyme [28] auch eym Christen nicht zu thun: So ists doch ynn der warheit auch ein werck [29] der liebe. Denn gleich wie ein guter artzt, wenn die seuche so boese und gros [30] ist, das er mus hand, fues, ohr odder augen lassen abhawen odder verderben, [31] auff das er den leib errette, so man an sihet das gelied, das er abhewet, [1] scheinet es, er sey ein grewlicher, unbarmhertziger mensch. So man aber den [2] leib ansiht, den er wil damit erretten, so findet sichs ynn der warheit, das [3] er ein trefflicher, trewer mensch ist und ein gut, Christlich (so viel es an yhm [4] selber ist) werck thut. Also auch wenn ich dem krige ampt zu sehe, wie es [5] die boesen strafft, die unrechten wuerget und solchen jamer anrichtet, scheinet es [6] gar ein unchristlich werck sein und aller dinge widder die Christliche liebe. [7] Sihe ich aber an, wie es die frumen schuetzt, weib und kind, haus und hoff, [8] gut und ehre und friede damit erhelt und bewaret, so find sichs, wie koestlich [9] und Goettlich das werck ist, und mercke, das es auch ein bein odder hand abhewet, [10] auff das der gantze leib nicht vergehe. Denn wo das schwerd nicht [11] werete und fride hielte, so mueste es alles durch unfride verderben, was ynn [12] der welt ist. Derhalben ist ein solcher krieg nicht anders denn ein kleiner, [13] kurtzer unfriede, der eym ewigen unmeslichem unfriede weret, Ein klein unglueck, [14] das eym grossen unglueck weret' (Luther, 1526, p. 626f).

12 In Protestant German theology, there is an ongoing debate on the extent to which theological motives should be introduced in public debates on justice. The influential statement of German churches on the questions of welfare and social issues in general, for instance, solved this problem by first summing up theological arguments and then trying to rephrase those ideas in a context of human rights, to argue their case for those who do not share a Christian background (*Rat der Evangelischen Kirche in Deutschland, Deutsche Bischofskonferenz*, 1997, pp. 39–67).

13 In the nineteenth century, liberal theological concepts – for instance, of A. Ritschl or W. Herrmann – went in that direction; in the twentieth century, liberation theology provides examples.

14 For an analysis from the perspective of sociology of religion, see Bourdieu (2000, p. 68f).

15 Linearity was thought to be universal, as documents by peasants in revolt at that time show. In these the peasants occupy the upper branches, while kings grovel in the dirt (Laube *et al.*, 1974, p. 219).

16 Otherwise social regulation was evidently much more rigid.

17 For an explanation of some of those reasons, see Tanner (1995).

18 For an example see Naumann (1911, pp. 71–534). For the problem in general, see Meireis (2001). Prien (1992, p. 232f) shows that Luther had different intentions.

19 Wingren acknowledges this contextual difference (1980, p. 657ff).

20 For this concept, see Meuser and Sackmann (1992), also Volz (1982).

21 Sometimes, both is the case. The term is introduced with anthropological breadth, but subsequently only used in the sense of gainful employment (paid labour). For an example, see Brakelmann (1980).

22 See Angelika Krebs' attempt (Krebs, 2002, p. 35ff.) to specify an 'institutional concept of work' aimed at an improved material and immaterial recognition of hitherto neglected forms of work that she – to my mind, adequately – argues are of significance for society as a whole. However, she has to go to great lengths to defend that concept whose range is supposed to be limited to existing labour societies.

23 As one of the more popular examples, see Rifkin (1995). For a discussion of the problems concerning the changing 'labour-society', see Offe (1984).

24 An attempt to model the consumption of resources in economic terms may be found in Immler (1989).

25 The term 'social appreciation' is supposed to be a translation of A. Honneth's term *soziale Wertschätzung* (Honneth, 1992, p. 148ff).

26 This thesis describes the everyday reality of the majority of citizens; it does not replace in-depth sociological, economic or political analysis or claim to be a normative proposition. It only contends that questions of distribution cannot be avoided whenever we talk about work.

27 For those terms, see Hirsch and Roth (1986).

28 As an example of this, see Sennett (1998) for a critical stance or, more as an appraisal, see Klages (2001).

29 For a brief summary, see Giddens (1991, pp. 35ff, 54f).

30 Those include – on the more theological side – the problem of human dignity in relation to the conflict areas of recognition, distribution, environmental relations and political participation, the problem of how Christian ethics are to consider sociological theory and empirical evidence, and in what way the concept of fulfilment has to be understood if it is to imply individual variety, human limitation and the relation to God. Closer to the problem of 'work', it has to be considered if and how the criterion of an activity evidently providing a service to one' neighbour motivated by love can be implemented in today's capitalist economies, since a certain efficiency is a prerequisite for that kind of freedom. Furthermore, the wide range of the idea of 'calling', which can be expressed by the use of the term 'activity' rather than 'work' has to be preserved to avoid losing touch with social reality or positively sanctioning any activity regardless. Last but not least, the question of 'unity' of action has to be considered. Is it possible to determine the unity of actions implied in the term 'calling' under the conditions of modern capitalist society? Those questions – among others – are the subject of an ongoing research project at Westfälische Wilhelms-Universität, University of Münster (see www.uni-muenster.de/ICGesWiss, also Meireis, 2001a).

31 For those reasons Krebs (2001, p. 80ff) pleads for a sufficient income distributed by the State to persons caring for children, the aged or the sick within the family.

32 Luther is quoted following the electronic full-text representation of the classical Weimar Edition, abbreviated WA and number of volume in question, easily accessible under http:\\luther.chadwyck.co.uk. The dates of original publication are given.

References

Althaus, P. 1935. *Theologie der Ordnungen* (Gütersloh, Bertelsmann).
_____ 1953. *Grundriß der Ethik*, (Gütersloh, Bertelsmann).
Barth, K. 1946. *Christengemeinde und Bürgergemeinde*, (Zurich, Theologishcer Verlag Zürich)

Bayer, O. 1995. 'Natur und Institution. Luthers Dreiständelehre', in O. Bayer, *Freiheit als Antwort. Zur theologischen Ethik* (Tübingen, Mohr).

Biéler, A. 1959. *La pensée économique et sociale de Calvin* (Geneva, Librairie de l'université).

Bourdieu, P. 2000. 'Genese und Struktur des religiösen Feldes', in P. Bourdieu, *Das religiöse Feld, Texte zur Ökonomie des Heilsgeschehens* (Konstanz, Universitätsverlag).

Brakelmann, G. 1980. 'Arbeit', in F. Böckle *et al.* (eds.), *Christlicher Glaube in moderner Gesellschaft* (Freiburg, Basel, Vienna, Herder).

Calvin, J. 1963. *Institutio christianae religionis*, Calvin, Institutio Deutsch, translated by O. Weber (Neukirchen, Neukirchener).

Elert, W. 1958. *Morphologie des Luthertums, Zweiter Band, Soziallehren und Sozialwirkungen des Luthertums* (Munich, Beck).

Evers, A. and Th. Olk. 1996. *Wohlfahrtspluralismus* (Opladen, Westdeutscher Verlag).

Giarini, O. and Liedtke, P. 1998. *Wie wir arbeiten werden* (Hamburg, Hoffmann und Campe) originally (1997), The Employment Dilemma and the Future of Work.

Giddens, A. 1984. *The constitution of society: outline of the theory of structuration* (Cambridge, Polity Press).

———— 1991. *Modernity and self identity: self and society in the late modern age* (Cambridge, Polity Press)

———— 1994. *Kritik der ökonomischen Vernunft, Sinnfragen am Ende der Arbeitsgesellschaft* (Hamburg, Rotbuch) originally (1989), Métamorphoses du travail. Quête du sens. Critique de la raison économique (Paris, Edition Galilée).

Groarke, L. 2001. 'Reconsidering absolute omnipotence', *The Heythrop Journal*, Vol. 42 (1).

Hausen K. (ed.) 1993. *Geschlechterhierarchie und Arbeitsteilung, Zur Geschichte ungleicher Erwerbschancen von Männern und Frauen* (Göttingen, Vandenhoeck und Ruprecht).

Hirsch, J. and Roth, R. 1986. *Das neue Gesicht des Kapitalismus. Vom Fordismus zum Post-Fordismus* (Hamburg, VSA).

Holl, K. 1928. 'Die Geschichte des Wortes Beruf', in K. Holl, *Gesammelte Aufsätze zur Kirchengeschichte Bd. III* (Tübingen, Mohr).

Honneth, A. 1992. *Kampf um Anerkennung, Zur moralischen Grammatik sozialer Konflikte* (Frankfurt am Main, Suhrkamp).

Huber, W. 1983. 'Freiheit und Institution, Sozialethik als Ethik kommunikativer Freiheit', in W. Huber, *Folgen christlicher Freiheit. Ethik und Theorie der Kirche im Horizont der Barmer Theologischen Erklärung* (Neukirchen-Vluyn, Neukirchener).

Immler, H. 1989. *Vom Wert der Natur, Zur ökologischen Reform von Wirtschaft und Gesellschaft* (Opladen, Westdeutscher Verlag).

Klages, H. 2001. 'Brauchen wir ein Rückkehr zu traditionellen Werten?', in *Aus Politik und Zeitgeschichte*, Vol. B29.

Krebs, A. 1996. 'Vom Aufmöbeln müder Männer und Kurieren kotzender Kinder. Eine begriffliche Analyse der ökonomischen Ausbeutung privater weiblicher Fürsorge', *Rechtsphilosophische Hefte*, Vol. 5.

———— 2002. *Arbeit und Liebe* (Frankfurt am Main, Suhrkamp).

Laube, A., Steinmetz, M., and Vogler, G. 1974. *Illustrierte Geschichte der deutschen frühbürgerlichen Revolution* (Berlin, Dietz).

Link-Wieczorek, U. 1999. 'Ist Gott wirklich allmächtig? Überlegungen im Rahmen einer neueren Theodizee-Diskussion', *Evangelische Aspekte*, Vol. 9 (2).

Luther, M.[32] 1520. *Von den guten werckenn D. M. L.* WA, Vol. 6.

———— 1520a. *Von der Freyheyt eynisz Christen menschen. Martinus Luther.* WA, Vol. 7.

———— 1521. *De votis monasticis Martini Lutheri iudicium.* WA, Vol. 8.

———— 1522. *Eyn trew vormanung Martini Luther tzu allen Christen, sich tzu vorhuten fur auffruhr unnd emporung*, WA, Vol. 8.

_____ 1522a. *Weihnachtspostille, Joh. 21, 19–24 Das Euangelium an S. Johannis tag Johan. vlt.* WA, Vol. 10,I,1.

_____ 1525. *Ermahnung zum Frieden auf die zwölf Artikel der Bauerschaft in Schwaben.* WA, Vol. 18.

_____ 1526. *Ob kriegsleutte auch ynn seligem stande seyn kuenden.* WA, Vol. 19.

_____ 1528. *Wochenpredigten über Joh. 16–20.*

_____ 1528–29. *Ex Euangelio Iohannis. Das XVIII. Capitel.* WA, Vol. 28.

_____ 1530. *Eine Predigt Mar Luther, das man kinder zur Schulen halten solle.* WA, Vol. 30,II.

_____ 1531. *90. Predigt am 17. Sonntag nach Trinitatis, nachmittags. A prandio.* WA, Vol. 34,II.

_____ 1531a. *97. Predigt am 21. Sonntag nach Trinitatis, nachmittags. Das Sechste Capitel der Epistel S. Pauli an die Epheser, Von der Christen harnisch und woffen, gepredigt durch D. Mart. Luther.* WA, Vol. 34,II.

_____ 1532. *Ein Brieff D. Mart. Luthers Von den Schleichern und Winckelpredigern. 1532. Dem gestrengen und vhesten Eberhard von der Cannen, Amptman zu Wartburg, meinem gonstigen herrn und freunde,* WA, Vol. 30,III.

Marx, K. 1844. 'Zur Judenfrage', in *Marx, Engels, Werke 1* (Berlin, Dietz 1958).

Meireis, T. 2001. 'Die Hungrigen füllt er mit Gütern und lässt die Reichen leer ausgehen. Reichtum als Thema evangelischer Theologie', in U. Huster and F.R. Volz, *Theorien des Reichtums* (Münster, Lit).

_____ 2001a. 'Money for nothing?! Oder: Arbeit ohne Ende?' in H.R. Reuter (ed.) *Übergang: 45 Jahre Institut für Christliche Gesellschaftswissenschaften* (Münster, Lit)

Meuser, M. and Sackmann, R. 1992. 'Zur Einführung: Deutungsmusteransatz und empirische Wissenssoziologie', in M. Meuser and R. Sackmann, *Analyse sozialer Deutungsmuster, Beiträge zur empirischen Wissenssoziologie, Bremer soziologische Texte Bd. 5* (Pfaffenweiler, Centaurus).

Naumann, F. 1964. 'Neudeutsche Wirtschaftspolitik', in F. Naumann *Werke, Bd. 3, Schriften zur Wirtschafts- und Gesellschaftspolitik* (Opladen, Westdeutscher Verlag).

Offe, C. 1984. *Arbeitsgesellschaft. Strukturprobleme und Zukunftsperspektiven* (Frankfurt am Main, New York, Campus).

Pankoke, E. 1990. *Die Arbeitsfrage. Arbeitsmoral, Beschäftigungskrisen und Wohlfahrtspolitik im Industriezeitalter* (Frankfurt am Main, Suhrkamp).

Prien, H.J. 1992. *Luthers Wirtschaftsethik* (Göttingen, Vandenhoeck).

Rat der Evangelischen Kirche in Deutschland, Deutsche Bischofskonferenz, 1997. *Für eine Zukunft in Solidarität und Gerechtigkeit. Wort des Rates der Evangelischen Kirche in Deutschland und der Deutschen Bischofskonferenz zur wirtschaftlichen und sozialen Lage in Deutschland* (Hannover, Bonn, Kirchenkanzlei).

Rifkin, J. 1995. *The end of work* (New York, Putnam).

Sen, A. 1999. *Ökonomie für den Menschen* (Frankfurt am Main, Vienna, Hanser) (originally 1999, *Development of Freedom*, New York, Knopf).

Sennett, R. 1998. *The corrosion of character* (New York, Norton).

Tanner, K. 1995. 'Der Staat des christlichen Gemeinwohls? Protestantische Staatsutopien und die Krise sozialstaatlicher Institutionen', in *Zeitschrift für Evangelische Ethik*, Vol. 39.

Vobruba, G. 1999. 'Income Mixes – die neue Normalität nach der Vollbeschäftigung', in *Jahrbuch Arbeit und Technik 199.9.*

_____ 2000. *Alternativen zur Vollbeschäftigung* (Frankfurt am Main, Suhrkamp).

Volz, F. R. 1989. 'Die « Arbeitsgesellschaft » – Bausteine zum Verständnis ihrer Elemente, ihrer Krise und ihrer Herausforderung für die theologische Ethik', in F.R. Volz and J. Harms, *Arbeit und Wirtschaft, Beiträge zu Ökonomie und Ethik* (Frankfurt am Main, Haag und Herrchen).

Weber, M. 1981. 'Die protestantische Ethik und der Geist des Kapitalismus', in J. Winckelmann (ed.), *M. Weber, Die protestantische Ethik I, Eine Aufsatzsammlung* (Gütersloh, Bertelsmann).

Wingren, G. 1952. *Luthers Lehre vom Beruf* (Munich, Kaiser).

———— 1980. 'Beruf II. Historische und Ethische Aspekte', in G. Krause *et al.* (eds.), *Theologische Realenzyklopädie Bd. V* (Berlin, New York, de Gruyter).

12

SOCIAL CREDIT AS ECONOMIC MODERNISM: SEVEN THESES

Alan Dyer[1]

1. Thesis One: Social Credit, Economic Democracy and the Self

The aim of this paper is to make a case for social credit on the grounds of economic democracy, using ideas from Thorstein Veblen, William James and William Carlos Williams. I use a very simple notion of social credit throughout the paper. Specifically, social credit derives from the belief that the provisioning capabilities of a country are a collective phenomenon based on the accumulation of generations of experience and accomplishment, and should be used in a democracy as a fund of credit from which each citizen is guaranteed an equal share in the form of a basic income.

While I begin with a consideration of the economic landscape of social credit, I end on psychological and aesthetic territory that may seem far removed from the political economy of the idea. But that is not the case. The conceivable effects of social credit can be used as a measure of the distance between corporate capitalism and economic democracy. However, it is not clear how this gap can be bridged using democratic means, since this would require many people valuing social credit while it is still an uncertain belief and an unrealized experience. What is clear to me, however, is that this uncertainty and unreality can be addressed by exploring psychological and aesthetic aspects of making the choice for social credit.

I do not consider questions of how such a system should be designed nor engage in technical arguments about the economic efficiencies of a social credit scheme. Instead, I show how Veblen, James and Williams have influenced my thinking in two ways. First, they have played a role in my understanding of social credit as a way to advance the goal of economic democracy at a time when even political forms of democracy in the United States are under pressure from powerful economic interests. Second, they have taught me the importance of defining a concept of the self that neither retreats into romantic nostalgia nor capitulates to the modern assault on the self. In other words, they have taught me the necessity of clarifying the boundaries of the self in a corporate-sponsored 'collectivist' world.

I show how social credit is relevant to what a number of recent authors describe as a loss of faith in the meaning of our economic efforts.[2] Economics contributes to this loss of meaning when it fails to engage seriously with issues like the loss of a clear distinction between luxury and necessity, the United States' disproportionate *per capita* consumption of the world's resources, and the near- impossibility of defining a life outside the precincts of the corporation. If economists do not help us understand better the dissonance between who we say we are and how we act, it contributes to the mystification of what our actions mean. In order to correct these shortcomings the focus of economics needs to be shifted away from the further elaboration of mathematical models of the economy and towards the institutional examination of the corporation. Modern economic relations, options and actions must now be understood in the language and rhythm of the corporation, not through those of the market. The way economists linger on the meaning of the market has only stretched the meaning of phenomena like market, choice and price until they blur into mathematics. To use Williams' language, modern economics fails to make contact with the flesh and bones of the corporation; it has lost touch with the modern economy.

The idea of social credit is relevant to developing what I call 'economic modernism', therefore, because it acknowledges several important facts of contemporary society. First, the modern economy is based on corporate and not market relations. Second, the corporation is essentially a financial organization that operates through an ingenious method of manipulating public credit for private gain. Third, society has lost its bearing, in part, due to the loss of meaning associated with the ways in which effort and reward are linked. Fourth, prolonged existence under these conditions produces a crisis of faith among people in their institutions and themselves.

2. Thesis Two: Economic Modernism

The single most influential person in my education as an economist has been Thorstein Veblen. The reasons for my attraction to him are: first, his critical stance towards the neoclassical dominance of economic thought; second, his belief that the corporation and not the market is the institution of primary economic importance in the modern era; and, third, his attempts to replace the hedonist and associationalist psychology introduced into economic analysis by the marginalists with a pragmatist social psychology. In turn, my own work explores the connections between Veblen's analytical style and assumptions with wider intellectual trends in the twentieth century.

To be honest, my work also shares Veblen's general reluctance to draw concrete policy conclusions from his analysis. If there is any policy implication in a Veblenian economics, it is a desire for democratic economic institutions. It is this desire, I believe, that motivates every explicit policy recommendation Veblen makes, whether sublime or ridiculous, ranging from his support of a General Strike in the United States to his controversial suggestion that the credit-based commercial control of industrial investment be replaced with a soviet of technicians.

In the interest of keeping this paper to a manageable size I am leaving out some of the thinkers who have influenced my attempts to revise the social psychology that grounds my Veblenian approach to economics. These thinkers include Norman O. Brown, Otto Rank, Ernest Becker, Harold Rosenberg, Philip Rieff and Christopher Lasch. I am drawn to each of them because of their interest in the question of whether or not there can be a meaningful concept of the self in modern social theory and, if there can, what exactly we mean by the self. From Rosenberg's un-Marxian proletariat to Rieff's therapeutic man and Lasch's élite in revolt, each of these thinkers has searched for a modern notion of the self as an integrated and self-determining phenomenon (Rosenberg, 1983; Rieff, 1987; Lasch, 1996). Their efforts have helped me to understand the difficulty of talking about a self-determining subject in a world of ever-present yet largely inaccessible technological know-how, large-scale corporate enterprise, and a culture in which the balance between Yes's and No's (control and remission mechanisms, as Philip Rieff calls them) no longer seems to provide sure answers to what we want as individuals and as a society.[3]

Veblen was one of the first economists to make a clear distinction between the industrial and financial aspects of the United States' economy (Veblen, 1942). He wanted to distinguish clearly those provisioning activities that contribute to the physical and conceptual manipulation of nature from the elaborate and, in his opinion, irrelevant pecuniary rituals we undertake in order to permit these provisioning activities to occur. In various writings he describes the psychological differences between people engaged primarily in industrial occupations and those engaged primarily in pecuniary ones.

The fundamental psychological difference is that industrial occupations instil an awareness of the impersonal and interdependent nature of productive activities. Pecuniary occupations, however, create specialists of the 'main chance' who seek better and subtler ways of manipulating property claims in order to enrich themselves (Veblen, 1964b, Ch. IV; 1975, p. 270). Clearly,

Veblen has simplified drastically the social psychology of a modern commercial industrial economy. But even if one thinks of these two personality types as the end points of a continuum, one can still find merit in the idea that there is a schizophrenic quality to the economy. The financial Jekyll is in control of the actions of the industrial Hyde. At times, their lives coexist in peace. At others, as we are learning once again in the United States, the response of the financial side to economic exigencies ends up sabotaging life on the industrial side. Veblen's point is that the economy has become too complicated and too much of a collective enterprise to allow this sort of commercial buccaneering to continue to disrupt the industrial provisioning processes of society.

Veblen saw clearly that the evolution of these games of pecuniary one-up-manship required a larger role in the economy for the credit system.[4] The increasingly sophisticated use of credit was instrumental, he argued, to the growing dominance of the corporate form of business enterprise and shifted control of the economy, in his words, from the Captains of Industry to the Captains of Finance (Veblen, 1964a, Ch. XII). He was under no illusion that new institutions, like the Federal Reserve in his day and later the Securities and Exchange Commission, could contain for long the financial psychoses that inevitably break out in a commercial economy (*Ibid.*, pp. 369–71; Veblen, 1975, pp. 164–74 and Ch. VII). It is not long, Veblen asserts, before novel and ingenious methods of 'getting something for nothing' are devised. Needless to say, he would have been quite sceptical that the recently legislated public regulation of the accounting industry in the United States will provide lasting pecuniary therapeutics.

Veblen's criticism of the pecuniary control of industry is clear and unwavering. His alternative to this way of organizing our provisioning activities, however, is vague and tentative (Veblen, 1964b, pp. 156–7 and 179–83). He sounds, at times, like a sixteenth century Anabaptist, calling for an end to pecuniary credit claims, or a twentieth century Sorelian, supporting the idea of a General Strike. And his one sustained argument for an alternative to finance capitalism – the creation of a soviet of technicians whose responsibility it would be to determine the most efficient way of producing the things society wants – today sounds more than a little naïve.

The one claim that safely can be made is that Veblen was not an advocate of social credit. Still, the spirit of his criticism is very much in the spirit of social credit. Behind the greed and masochism of pecuniary rituals, Veblen is bothered by the fact that modern credit institutions are designed to limit access to society's 'usufruct' of technical know-how to profit-making enterprises (Veblen, 1942a). By implication he favoured a new form of distributing the productive potential of this social inheritance (Veblen, 1964a. p. 413). Yet, at this point Veblen falls silent.

I have always wondered about Veblen's silence once he reaches the point in his analysis where the next logical question is, 'What is to be done?' After years of stewing over my frustration with him I quite independently learned about the social credit movement. My understanding of the history of this movement matured with the help of Walter van Trier's *Every One a King* (van Trier, 1995). When I came to wonder if social credit could serve as the logical policy conclusion that Veblen fails to draw, however, William James pulled me in a different direction. Namely, my goal cannot be to find the missing piece that 'completes' the logic of Veblen's analysis. Instead, James helped me to see that if I accept Veblen's diagnosis of the modern corporate economy and feel an attraction to the spirit behind social credit, I need to examine the question: what makes social credit a 'genuine option' for someone? How does a person whose life has been shaped by the experience of living in the schizophrenic economic world described by Veblen come to entertain social credit as a meaningful alternative?

3. Thesis Three: Pragmatism and the Problem of the Self

So far I imagine this paper sounds typically academic by raising an esoteric question like, 'How would a Pragmatist like William James make the case for social credit?' By the end of the paper I hope to have convinced you otherwise, showing that a Pragmatist case for social credit has very practical things to say about the psychological aspects of the political economy of social credit. As a start, let me discuss William James's place in my arguments.

Let me start with a riddle. What creature legally, politically, and economically constitutes an independent and self-acting bundle of rights and responsibilities yet, according to the best minds and research of its species, is largely defined by impersonal and largely uncontrollable forces of history, genetics, social class, and language? Answer: the human being.

The problem, as Harold Rosenberg argues in *The Act and the Actor*, is that 'the act' is the twentieth (now twenty-first?) century's 'outstanding riddle' (Rosenberg, 1983, p.6). He means that developments in philosophy, biology, psychology and political economy have undermined our sense of *action as the result of self-determining actors*. Applying Rosenberg's diagnosis to the problem of social credit means acknowledging that, while it promises a more democratic way of distributing access to the material grounds for self-exploration, the absence of a clear notion of a self-determining actor raises serious psychological questions about its contemporary relevance.

Another way of making this point is to say that the act has become problematic because modern culture no longer grounds the self in the actions of, take your choice, a Christian sinner, a capitalist climber, or a class hero. For a being with the singular distinction of being conscious of its own death, this is a serious psychological malady. It means that this culture no longer provides, in Rieff's words, those instruments that make us 'capable ... of controlling the infinite variety of panic and emptiness to which [we] are disposed. It is to control their disease as individuals that men have always acted culturally, in good faith' (Rieff, 1987, p. 3).

4. Thesis Four: James on Truth, Belief and Action

You may better understand now why I am more interested in the question of how someone would come to believe in the desirable effects of social credit rather than in refining the theoretical details of its form. Obviously, no one can know beforehand if these effects will come to pass. Therefore, though theory is important in imagining the effects of social credit, we must not confuse the certainty of theorizing with the uncertainty of acting on our beliefs in order to create a reality. Consequently, an important part in making the case for social credit is addressing why anyone should have faith in the idea of social credit.

I suspect that you are intrigued with my interest in the question of *faith*. Perhaps a quote from James will help to explain why I feel it is important to consider the role of faith. The quote is a concise summary of his view on the relation between faith, action and fact. Making the case that social theory must acknowledge that each member of society performs his or her duty in the faith that others will do the same, James concludes:

> There are, then, cases where a fact cannot come at all unless a preliminary faith exists in its coming. *And where faith in a fact can help create the fact*, that would be an insane logic which should say that faith running ahead of scientific evidence is the 'lowest kind of immorality' into which a thinking being can fall (James, 2000c, p. 214).

James has studied the relation between faith and religion in a variety of works. But he uses faith here to refer to a motivation that leads us to act when neither impulse, compulsion, nor reason will do the job. You may disagree with him that there are such instances. But James responds with the observation that each of us can recall examples from our own lives in which a 'fact' we desire comes about only if we first have faith in our desire and the actions necessary in order to realize it. 'Faith'means the capacity to 'stay the course' of action designed to realize an aim for which we have no prior assurances.

From a Pragmatic perspective it is impossible to compile enough arguments and evidence to prove *a priori* that the idea of social credit is true. As

James argued, this is because truth is neither an object nor a static quality of objects. It is, instead, a quality of a 'moment of experience through which we are led to other moments to which it is worthwhile to be led' (James, 2000b, p. 90). Thus, truth is a process that leads us to more and wider experiences that continue to respond to our cares and concerns. It is neither the universal and absolute quality of an object nor an agreement between an object and our thoughts about it. In this sense, the 'truth' of social credit can only mean a process through which it becomes clear over time that, by acting on the idea of social credit, its conceivable effects either do or do not ensue. Truth, for a Pragmatist, is always a work-in-progress. Thus, a pragmatic case for social credit will focus less on the 'truth' of it and more on the conditions necessary for people to take it seriously, which means much more than that they find it reasonable. It is only when enough people accept social credit as a serious option for organizing economic life that we begin to discover the truth of it.

In one of his more famous essays, 'The Will to Believe,' James wondered what makes a hypothesis a serious concern for someone. He calls this kind of hypothesis a 'genuine option' and says that for an option to be genuine it must have three characteristics: it must be live, forced and momentous (James, 2000c, p. 199). James means that only those hypotheses are genuine for which we cannot find an alternative to either accepting or rejecting the hypothesis; the results are unique, irreversible and hold a significant stake for us, and we are willing to act upon it.

We need to dip a little deeper, at this point, into James's notions of truth and belief. It is one of those quirks of intellectual history that William James's ideas about truth and belief should be so appropriate to a discussion of social credit. The quirkiness arises from what is called his credit theory of truth (Livingston, 1994, pp. 199–200). James explicitly says, in his essay 'Pragmatism's Conception of Truth',

> Truth lives, in fact, for the most part on a credit system. Our thoughts and beliefs 'pass,' so long as nothing challenges them, just as bank notes pass so long as nobody refuses them. But this all points to direct face-to-face verifications somewhere, without which the fabric of truth collapses like a financial system with no cash-basis whatever (James, 2000b, p. 91).

Closely related to truth are our beliefs, which,

> ... at any time are so much experience funded ... so far as reality means experiencable reality, both it and the truths men gain about it are everlastingly in process of mutation .... (*Ibid.*, p. 107)

James says that the beliefs we are willing to act upon are based upon unfinished truths that develop only as our action progresses. He was aware that this position would be criticized as implying, 'believe what you will; so long as nothing or no one forces you to change your mind you can make your own truth'. As he argued on many occasions, such a criticism misses the subtlety Pragmatists are trying to catch in the relation between belief, action and fact. He says:

> In the realm of truth-processes facts come independently and determine our beliefs provisionally. But these beliefs make us act, and as fast as they do so, they bring into sight or into existence new facts, which re-determine the beliefs accordingly. So the whole coil and ball of truth, as it rolls up, is the product of a double influence. Truths emerge from facts; but they dip forward into facts again and add to them; which facts again create or reveal new truth (the word is indifferent) and so on indefinitely. The 'facts' themselves meanwhile are not *true*. They simply *are* (James, 2000b, p. 99).

Let me bring the discussion back to social credit. Surely the 'fact' of credit may go through such a process of mutation. Why should our beliefs about credit be limited to those based on commercial 'truths'? What would happen if we were to broaden the range of possible 'facts' through which the truth of credit develops, for instance, that the ultimate 'cash-basis' of credit is society's collective technological know-how? Could not this fact move us further in the direction of the 'truth' that a democratic society should distribute this credit equally?

Despite the hope contained in questions like these, my earlier discussion of the self and the act should temper our enthusiasm. Namely, if people act on the basis of truths 'in progress', then part of what moves them must be faith in their beliefs, which are made up of these evolving truths.[5] Yet, if the modern self is ungrounded, as Rieff and others argue, is it not unrealistic to hope that people will treat the hypothesis of social credit as living, i.e., be willing to act on it?

These kinds of questions interested William Carlos Williams. I turn to him now in order to illustrate how one can make a Pragmatic case for social credit. Poetry is Williams's vehicle for making social credit a 'genuine option' for people living at the start of post-industrial America. In his effort to present an alternative form of credit that would release greater experimentation in economic lifestyles, Williams realized that one of the challenges he faced was whether or not the reader was willing to join him in his creative labour. He realized that he needed a form, as well as diction, that would make contact with his readers and encourage them to sort out the political, economic and social mess symbolized by Paterson, New Jersey.

5. Thesis Five: Williams and the Problem of 'Measure'

Before getting into the purely intellectual aspects of Williams's modernist case for social credit, it is useful to point out that he was an active supporter of the social credit movement in the United States. And though he and Ezra Pound exchanged ideas about social credit, Williams apparently first learned about the movement from Gorham Munson, editor of the social credit journal *New Democracy* (Mariani, 1990, Ch. 8; Weaver, 1971, Ch. 6). Williams was more than an 'armchair' supporter of social credit, joining the American Social Credit Movement and giving public lectures on the subject. According to Kenneth Burke, an influential literary critic and friend of Williams, 'each great poetic form ... [has] its own peculiar way of building the mental equipment (meanings, attitudes, character) by which one handles the significant factors of his time (Burke, 1984, p. 34)'. Alec Marsh's recent study of the connections between Williams's experiment with poetic form and his various political commitments details the 'significant factors' he felt the need to 'handle' by changing the 'measure' of his poetry (Marsh, 1998, Chs. 5 and 6). Specifically, Williams is suspicious of the effects that the increasing dominance of the corporation has in shaping people's imaginative possibilities. In turn, he is convinced that, through the commercial allocation of credit, corporations are able to widen their scale of operations and, therefore, their dominance of American life.

Williams, according to Marsh and others, sought a 'measure' for his poetry that was appropriate for people who live and work in a corporate society (*Ibid.*; Weaver, 1971, Chs. 5 and 7). His search for this form eventually paid off in *Paterson*, his epic poem about the local history of the post-industrial city of Paterson, New Jersey, and a fictitious citizen of that city, Dr Paterson (probably a symbol of his life as a physician in nearby Rutherford, New Jersey). In addition to its content, Williams believed that the form of *Paterson* must speak to his listeners.

Who were these listeners? Perhaps Williams's friend Kenneth Burke has captured best the character of this audience:

If food, comfort, and pleasant intercourse are desirable, and if money procures them, and if some dismal, unmuscular, unimaginative, and unbalanced kind of drudgery will procure money, one may actually see a person' eyes light up with hope when told that drudgery is to be permitted him. He 'got the job'. Eventually, he rounds out his values in keeping with such contingencies: He develops the emphases, standards, desires, and kinds of observation, expression, and repression that will equip him for his task. This is his occupation psychosis, a moral network, complex beyond all possibilities of charting (Burke, 1954, p. 238).

This 'drudgery' today consists of the filing and recording done in the cubicles of a typical corporation. The qualities of this 'work', to both Williams and Burke, do not demand adventure, risk or initiative. They represent instead a loss of contact with the work performed and the wider world in which the worker functions. Williams's similarly discouraging image of these citizens of the corporation sounds like this:

> At the
> sanitary lunch hour packed woman to
> woman (or man to woman what's the difference?)
> the flesh of their faces gone
> to fat or gristle, without recognizable
> outline, fixed in rigors, adipose or sclerosis
> expressionless, facing one another, a mould
> for all faces (canned fish) this.
>
> Move toward the back, please, and face the door!
> is how the money's made,
> money's made
> pressed together
> talking excitedly of the next sandwich.
> (Williams, 1995, p. 164)

Williams uses several devices, according to Marsh, in order to make *Paterson* appropriate to a corporate age. These include packaging his truths in discrete chunks of experience chipped from the local landscape, giving sound to the many strange and often conflicting voices he hears around him, and refusing to end up at any absolute and universal truths about society. He intersperses prose with poetry, newspaper facts with psychotic fictions, and makes line breaks that are exhausting to follow. Williams works out of the conviction that a good 'measure' creates sharp new boundaries that assist the self in differentiating its cares and concerns from foreign or imposed beliefs. In *Paterson* this meant serving up a wealth of local detail in a form that spoke to the citizens of a corporate society.

Generalizing, what does it mean to design a form that improves the comprehension of what we are trying to communicate? On one level, anyone who has tried to teach a group of moderately bright economics undergraduates the meaning of opportunity cost knows that giving them an abstract (i.e., inhuman) 'measure' of the concept often produces little meaning. Tell them, 'If you give up two widgets in order to get one more phalange, the opportunity cost of the phalange is the widgets you give up', and most of their eyes glaze over. However, change the 'proximity' of the 'units' in the example to something more local to the student's experiences, like turning widgets into 'ten exam points' and phalanges into 'all night beer parties', and the difference in comprehension is remarkable.

On another level, one may show the importance of 'measure' through historical example, as Williams does in his idiosyncratic American history book, *In the American Grain* (Williams, 1956). Many of the characters in this book illustrate the conflict between those who saw the new American landscape as grist for commerce on a massive scale and those who saw it as an opportunity to experiment with more democratic forms of contact with themselves, others and nature. The clearest example of this conflict between different 'measures' of economic life in America, according to Williams, is the contrast between Alexander Hamilton and Aaron Burr. The differences between them go beyond their conflicting views of the role of the central Government and the proper uses of raw natural forces. Williams shows how the personalities of these two men are metaphors for the impersonal and insatiable appetite of a mercantilist society (Hamilton), on the one hand, and the erotic, heroic and democratic preferences of an 'aesthetic' society (Burr), on the other hand.

Hamilton, a rather cold and socially inept person, embraced commerce as the surest means of guaranteeing the new country's growth and sovereignty and favoured a stronger central Government than many of the other revolutionaries wanted (*Ibid.*, pp. 195, 197). A stronger central Government was needed, according to Hamilton, in order to advance the country's commercial interests. Williams' conclusion is that the quantitative and calculating nature of commerce, as well as the bureaucratic routinization of local laws and customs to fit the central Government's broader interests, produced a more abstract and impersonal measure of the economic experiences of people in the new nation.

Burr, an outgoing and personable fellow, could not escape fast enough from the routinization of political and economic life he felt was spreading along the eastern coast of the country. These developments represented abandonment of the values of the revolution, according to him, limiting the range of local experiments in building democratic communities (*Ibid.*, pp. 196, 202–6). His attempts to start afresh somewhere west of the Mississippi River made him a pariah among the political establishment in the United States. Many consider Burr a throwback to the era of military aristocracy. Williams, however, emphasizes his interest in preserving the crude, unfinished nature of life in the new country so that people might experiment with a form of society nobler than one that simply copied Europe's mercantilist obsession with economic growth (Williams, 1969, pp.146–57).

6. Thesis Six: A Poetic 'Measure' of Social Credit

Williams' point in comparing Hamilton and Burr is to illustrate the importance of what I have called 'measure' in the assumptions of political economy. One 'measure', call it the Hamiltonian, passes over the unique and untested potential in an experience and forces it into an existing 'measure' for interpreting economic possibilities. The other 'measure', call it the democratic, pays careful attention to the qualities of the here-and-now, taps into local cares and concerns, and devises a new 'measure' that articulates all these aspects of the experience. Williams' explanation for the pollution and poverty he experienced in Paterson was that they are the long-term consequences of Hamilton's failed dream of creating an ideal mercantilist enterprise along the Passaic River. Interpreting the experience of the Passaic through the foreign 'measure' of government-supported commercial development, the virgin lands and waters around Paterson followed the typical commercial pattern of benefiting the few and leaving the many a sad and ugly place to call home.

Marsh shows how Williams shared the concern of other artists in the first half of the twentieth century with the effects of corporate society on the self.[5] However, unlike Ezra Pound and T. S. Eliot, Williams does not bemoan the loss of a romantic, historical ideal of self. Instead, he works to plumb the possibilities for the self in a corporate era and to identify sources of 'blockage' that keep this new self chained to outmoded nineteenth-century liberal beliefs about the economic foundations of the self (Heinzelman, 1980, pp. 267–75). These beliefs, which ground the self in the rights and responsibilities of private property, are dull 'measures' for marking the boundaries between the self and others, as well as between private and public spheres of care and concern in a corporate era. Williams' view of the effects of trying to live this spent vision of individuality is that it produces only ennui, resentment and perversion in the corporate self.

Paterson can be read as Williams' paean to the relativism, pluralism and, frankly, homelessness of the corporate self. He does not run from these 'local' conditions of modern life, but invites the individuals of a corporate society to learn all they can about their new station in society through contact with his poetry. It also serves as a reminder that we must perform for ourselves, as earlier generations have, the work of defining what it means to be virtuous, how we shall be 'married' to one another and the world, what we mean by 'labour' and, only then answering William James' question, 'Is life worth living?' *Paterson* is 'credit' issued by Williams on the basis of the truths of the poetical and historical experiences that 'fund' his composition. This credit is 'good' to the extent that it generates the 'interest' of his audience. That interest, in turn, is what sparks new beliefs and actions, new experiences.

Williams' interest in the effects of the corporation on the self is not to find reasons to resurrect an earlier version of the self. Rather, he engages this time of confusion about the self and looks for new 'measures' in order to define a modern self. And he insists that, in order to avoid the Hamiltonian error of importing a foreign 'measure' to help us find our way out of this confusion, we must first look at the contorted face, limbs and psyche of corporate man. It is only from the 'truth' of this reality that a meaningful alternative can be created.

If one problem for Williams was to invent a poetry that gave voice to the experience of everyday life in urban America, another problem was to invent an economics in which the accumulated wealth and know-how of society is expressed in a more democratic form. Just as he found classical 'measures' inadequate to the task of writing a modern poetry that was relevant to the everyday experiences of people, he found commercial 'measures' of credit inadequate to the task of democratizing society's collective economic inheritance. Just as a monopoly over the use of language can limit the amount and variety of poetry, it is obvious to Williams that monopoly control of credit limits access to society's fund of wealth and, consequently, limits the growth and variety of individual projects of self-expression. Finally, as Williams lent his voice to democratizing the number and types of voices in the commonwealth of poetry, he lent his voice as well to telling people that credit was a public possession, like their language, and not an object that belongs to private individuals for their private profit.

The evidence is that Williams did not put his labour as a poet in a different category of productive effort from his work as a physician (Heinzelman, 1980; Mariani, 1990). His attraction to social credit 'measures' his disappointment that so many local and idiosyncratic expressions of creative effort are denied a voice because the credit of society is channelled so completely into action that, literally, pays. His interest in social credit is ultimately an aesthetic one. It represents a chance to make up for the initial defeat of a vibrant local culture in the United States caused by the adoption of mercantilist beliefs about the proper form of a national economy. Social credit, he insists, could provide the economic independence that would encourage people to experiment with their lives, based on the local' truths they can discover from living in closer physical and psychic proximity to their cares and concerns. The kinds of experience social credit might encourage could provide a self-awareness and

self-confidence that make people unwilling to tolerate any longer economic
lives in which:

> ... in the tall
> buildings (sliding up and down) is where
> the money's made
> up and down
> directed missiles
> in the greased shafts of the tall buildings.
>
> They stand torpid in cages, in violent motion
> unmoved
> but alert!
> predatory minds, unaffected
> UNINCONVENIENCED
> unsexed, up
> and down (without wing motion) This is how
> the money's made using such plugs. (Williams, 1995, pp. 164–5)

7. Thesis Seven: Conclusion

If sixty years of history are any judge, Williams' attempt in *Paterson* to present
social credit as a genuine option must be called a failure. Yet it is difficult to
put an expiration date on the interest that may accrue to a poem. Certainly,
American capitalism and the global economy have both changed from the
time the poem was composed. Yet it is also true that Paterson was, in a negative sense, ahead of the curve in the United States, experiencing the loss of its
industrial base in the first half of the twentieth century, ahead of cities like
Flint, Michigan, and Youngstown, Ohio, in the second half.

Paterson, among other things, makes a Pragmatist case for social credit. It
does this by exploring truths 'in progress' about the effects of the corporate
organization of economic experiences on local natural, social and psychological environments. Written with a 'measure' that he believed would convey the
dissonance of modern life, Williams aimed to set people thinking about the
need to choose a new direction, their stake in economic change, and their
willingness to act on the uncertain promise of greater economic democracy
under social credit.

The fact that social credit and basic income have not been forgotten, but
resurfaced with new vigour in the past twenty years means that it still res-
onates in the imaginations of some. The next step for those of us in whom
these ideas resonate is to find the words and 'measures' that will make social
credit a 'genuine option' for a wider circle of people. The idea of this paper

is that the work of enlivening the hypothesis of social credit must include defining a concept of the self that emphasizes the importance of self-determination and experimentalism while acknowledging that the individualism of nineteenthth-century liberalism has died a corporate death.

Notes

1   Northeastern University, Boston, United States of America.
2   Christopher Lasch, in *The Revolt of the Elites*, and John Ralston Saul, in *Voltaire's Bastards*, analyse from different angles the breakdown of faith in the character building effects of economic behaviour as the corporate phase of capitalism developed in the United States. However, both emphasize how nineteenth-century beliefs about economic independence had turned into little more than cynical advertising copy, rhetoric used by chief executive officers at stockholder meetings, or political sound bites by the end of the twentieth century (Lasch, 1996; Saul, 1993).
3   Some claim that there is no need for a stable notion of the self in order to discuss or defend traditional western values like justice, rights, and freedom. Thinkers like Richard Rorty, for example, are suspicious of universal or absolute notions of the self because of the risk they pose for a return to political philosophies and movements that sacrifice the individual to social processes supposedly needed to 'safeguard' the self. As James Livingston argues, however, debates about democracy are empty (Bush's 'democratic' Palestine?) unless the question about where to draw the line between private and public cares and concerns is a central part of the debate. What sense does it make, he asks, to get worked up about rights and responsibilities unless one has a clear notion of a self in whom these rights and responsibilities supposedly reside? (Livingston, 1994, pp. 386–7, endnote 40).
4   See William Greider's *Secrets of the Temple* for an extensive and lively analysis of the evolution of the credit system in the United States from the 1890s to the 1930s, in particular. This evolution is closely tied to the rapid spread of the corporation as the dominant form of business enterprise during the same period. Greider also discusses the gradual eclipse of the idea of 'democratic money' during this period (Greider, 1989, Ch. 8).
5   This seems to me a serious issue for advocates of social credit. Given the generally deflated cultural grounds on which people make decisions of political economy today, we risk responding to this apathy (or worse, nihilism) by resorting to existing means of psychological and political persuasion – means that are of questionable democratic intent in my opinion.
6   Livingston calls this the problem of identifying a post-capitalist 'moral personality' (Livingston, 1994, Part 2).

References

Becker, E. 1973. *The denial of death* (New York, Free Press).
Brown, N. O. 1970. *Life against death: The psychoanalytical meaning of history* (Middletown, Wesleyan University Press).
Burke, K. 1954. *Permanence and change* (Los Altos, Hermes).
———— 1984. *Attitudes toward history*, 3rd edition, (Berkeley, University of California Press).

Greider, W. 1989. *Secrets of the temple: How the federal reserve runs the country* (New York, Touchstone).

Heinzelman, K. 1980. *The economics of the imagination* (Amherst, University of Massachusetts Press).

James, W. 1961. *The varieties of religious experience: A study in human nature* (New York, Collier).

———— 1968. 'The moral equivalent of war', in *Memories and studies* (New York, Greenwood Press).

———— 2000a. 'Is life worth living?', in G. Gunn (ed.), *Pragmatism and other writings* (New York, Penguin).

———— 2000b. 'Pragmatism's conception of truth' in G. Gunn (ed.), *Pragmatism and other writings* (New York, Penguin).

———— 2000c. 'The will to believe,' in G. Gunn (ed.), *Pragmatism and other writings* (New York, Penguin).

Lasch, C. 1991. *The true and only heaven: Progress and its critics* (New York, Norton).

———— 1996. *The revolt of the élites and the betrayal of democracy* (New York, Norton).

Livingston, J. 1994. *Pragmatism and the political economy of cultural revolution, 1850–1940* (Chapel Hill, University of North Carolina Press).

Mariani, P. 1990. *William Carlos Williams: A new world naked* (New York, Norton).

Marsh, A. 1998. *Money and modernity: Pound, Williams, and the spirit of Jefferson* (Tuscaloosam, University of Alabama Press).

Rank, O. 1958. *Beyond psychology* (New York, Dover).

Rieff, P. 1987. *The triumph of the therapeutic* (Chicago, University of Chicago Press).

Rosenberg, H. 1983. *Act and the actor* (Chicago, University of Chicago Press).

Saul, J. R. 1993. *Voltaire's bastards: The dictatorship of reason in the west* (New York, Vintage).

van Trier, W. 1995. *Every one a king*. Doctoral dissertation, Department of Sociology, Catholic University Leuven.

Veblen, T. 1942a. 'On the nature of capital: I. the productivity of capital goods', in *The place of science in modern civilization* (New York, Viking).

———— 1942b. 'Industrial and pecuniary employments,' in *The place of science in modern civilization* (New York, Viking).

———— 1964a. *Absentee ownership and business enterprise in recent times* (New York, Augustus M. Kelley).

———— 1964b. *The vested interests and the common man* (New York, Augustus M. Kelley).

———— 1975. *The theory of business enterprise* (New York, Augustus M. Kelley).

Weaver, M. 1971. *William Carlos Williams: The American background* (Cambridge, Cambridge University Press).

Williams, W. C. 1956. *In the American grain* (New York, New Directions).

———— 1969. *Selected essays* (New York, New Directions).

———— 1995. *Paterson* (New York, New Directions).

13

DELIBERATIVE DEMOCRACY AND THE LEGITIMACY OF BASIC INCOME

Jørn Loftager[1]

1. Introduction

The securing of democracy was an important general motive behind the development of the welfare state. Dearly bought experience from the preceding decades had revealed that neither the planned economy of State socialism nor free-market capitalism made up an adequate basis of democratic government. By means of the so-called 'demos strategy', including a politically regulated market economy and a basic measure of welfare for all (Korsgaard, 1999), the welfare state was supposed to lead society along a new and democratic *Third Way*. In a classic essay, T.H. Marshall outlined how an equal status of citizenship was progressing on the basis of universal civil, political and – especially – social rights in spite of the continuing prevalence of economic inequalities inherent in market capitalism (Marshall, 1950/1996; also see below).

After intensive discussions in the 1970s and 1980s dominated by Marxist and neo-liberal positions respectively, during the 1990s the problematic of democracy and capitalism disappeared to a large extent as a perspective and theme for discussions on the welfare state (Eriksen and Loftager, 1996). An immediate reason for that was no doubt the collapse of the former socialist regimes in the late 1980s and the ensuing almost complete consent to the institutions of liberal democracy. With one stroke, democracy became something trivial, something 'without enemies' (Beck, 1998), and correspondingly the question of the socio-economic conditions of democracy lost its relevance. From this 'taken-for-granted' premise, attention has concentrated instead on democratising the public sector on an institutional level by means of decentralization, user and customer influence on policy implementation and the managing of institutions (Eriksen, 1999).

However, such democratising remedies seem to concern effectiveness rather than democracy proper and, as far as I can see, there are still good reasons to maintain an interest in the relationships between the welfare state, capitalism and democracy. Generally, because the structural tensions between capitalism and democracy are still with us, and more specifically because of certain current trends concerning both 'what kind of democracy' and 'whose welfare we are talking about'. What I am thinking of is, on the one hand, a profound and growing interest in democracy as *deliberative* democracy, according to which the democratic role of the citizen is not merely that of expressing preferences, choosing and voting but also, and most importantly, that of taking part in public reasoning and deliberation; and the latter role is much more vulnerable to disturbances caused by socio-economic inequalities and asymmetric power relations than is the former. On the other hand, I am referring to the theory and practice of new welfare policies under headlines like 'from welfare to workfare' or 'from passive to active', which have been introduced as central parts of a (new) *Third Way* (Giddens, 1998; Rose, 1999). Although something like deliberative democracy seems to be endorsed by Third Way proponents, the delicate question is, I shall contend, whether this is a promising cocktail.

Against this background, the overall concern of the present paper is to discuss what kind of welfare system can nurture deliberative democracy. My basic contention is that the former Third Way does much better in that respect than to the present-day version of the Third Way.

In the first section of the paper I shall outline the idea of deliberative democracy by profiling it against the economic theory of democracy, with a special focus on the question of its socio-economic base. In the second section, Habermas' historical analysis of the decay of the public sphere is confronted with Marshall's theory of social class and citizenship. Referring to the Danish case it is argued that Marshall's vision of an equal status of citizenship to a large extent has been realized by the Nordic universal welfare state.

The third section briefly portrays the new Third Way, stressing how it introduces new ideas of community and of the proper relationship between the individual and the State. As an empirical case, I shall refer to the strategy of activation implemented under the Danish welfare reforms of the 1990s, and it will be shown how it embraces elements which challenge the ideals of equal citizenship.

The last section will briefly summarize some key results from analyses on the effects and basic assumptions of activation. I shall on this background speculate a little on possible alternative Third Way strategies.

2. Deliberative Democracy

The strong consensus after 1989 on the institutional content of democracy – the basic institutions and rights of liberal democracy – has not been followed by a similar agreement about the deeper meaning of democracy. On the contrary, the 'end of history' has given rise to widespread discussions on its 'regulative ideal' (Miller, 1993; Jakobsen and Kelstrup, 1999). One of the most significant theories is that of deliberative democracy. Even though this theory is represented by several different positions, they all focus on public reasoning and debate as the cornerstone of democracy. Likewise, although it has in no way won hegemonic status, the work of Jürgen Habermas serves as a common point of reference, and it is interesting to observe the expansion of the debate that followed the translation into English of Habermas' classic analysis on the public sphere published in 1962 (Habermas, 1989).

In this section I shall in a few words present some important features of deliberative democracy, stressing the way in which this theory differs from economic conceptions of democracy.

The phrase 'economic theory of democracy' was used by Anthony Downs as the title of his, also classic, book of 1957 (Downs, 1957). Its basic idea is that political man is identical to economic man. Voters are considered as consumers on the political market, choosing among commodities supplied by the political parties as producers. As a parallel to the capitalist company's motive of profit maximization, 'parties formulate politics in order to win elections rather than win elections in order to formulate politics' (*Ibid.*, p. 28). In his likewise classic account, Schumpeter similarly states: 'We must ... start from the competitive struggle for power and office and realize that the social function is fulfilled, as it were, incidentally – in the same sense as production is incidental to the making of profits' (Schumpeter, 1943/1976, p. 282).

Lacking a 'real' market mechanism in the political sphere, the basic problem of democracy on these premises is how to aggregate pre-given preferences in order to respect the principle of political equality – one man, one vote. And much of the debate within the tradition of *public choice* has been concerned with the question of constructing solutions to this problem of aggregation (Kurrild-Klitgaard, 1999).

However, the democratic ideal of what I prefer to call *mirroring* is not limited to positions that (explicitly) share the economic-man premises. It is a much more widespread ideal, also in the public at large, that democracy is fundamentally popular government, meaning that political decisions ought to be in accordance with the will or the preferences of the people or – in practice – its majority. For instance, the definitions of the grand old man of democratic theory, Robert A. Dahl points to 'the continuing responsiveness of the Government to the preferences of its citizens considered as political equals' (Dahl, 1971, p. 1).

In spite of its prevalence, the economic theory of democracy has several important limitations. On its own premises, the problem of aggregation is difficult and in principle impossible to solve, in the sense that there is no single voting procedure which can aggregate the preferences of the voters in an unambiguous and optimal way (Kurrild-Klitgaard, 1999). So there happens to be a necessary element of arbitrariness detrimental to the acknowledged values of democracy. Another limitation concerns the assumption of pre-given preferences. The problem is that the dynamics of preference shaping and opinion-formation, which seem to count a lot in real world democratic politics, are excluded by definition from the democratic process. The ideal of mirroring makes up a third problem, in the sense that this ideal is not only generally appreciated, but also highly contested. On the one hand, representatives should be responsive to the electorate and act according to its demands. On the other hand, populism, opportunism and 'Gallup politicians' are negative expressions, referring to quite another ideal of representation. A fourth challenge to the economic theory of democracy is that it makes no room for rational political reasoning and argumentation. Whereas the existence of ideals of dialogue and rational political debate cannot be denied, it can be maintained, of course, that such ideals are illusions and that, in the last instance, politics is essentially a game of power and interests and/or subjectively chosen preferences that will only allow for self-oriented strategic behaviour and pure instrumental rationality.

Precisely on this point the contrast *vis-à-vis* deliberative democracy is evident and pronounced. According to this theory, the regulative ideal and basic promise of democracy is *not* aggregation of preferences. Rather, the ideal is that political decisions should be based upon public reasoning, discussion and deliberation. Political man is not identical to the man in the economics textbooks; arguments rather than preferences make up the atoms of democracy. Of course, preferences, interests, attitudes etc. are there, but they are to be seen as results as well as starting points of political processes in which the force of the better argument ought to prevail.

Deliberative democracy is also different from the economic conception of democracy, in that it involves the presence of a political community or citizenship: reasoning – as opposed to mere choosing – presupposes someone to reason with. Furthermore, that kind of democratic interplay forms a positive-sum game somehow similar, for instance, to a scientific community of researchers. Problem-solving is the primary aspect of both types of conduct (Dewey, 1927).

Regarding the question of political participation, I myself find it important to stress that whereas economic theories of democracy to a large extent have focused on voting – in some cases just as an instrument of choosing among competing élites (Schumpeter) – the ideal of mirroring does not preclude extensive participation. 'Voice' is also a way of expressing preferences, for instance, by means of user boards in public institutions or grass-root actions, which seems to be fully in accordance with the premises of an economic conception of democracy. On the other hand, deliberative democracy is not participatory democracy in the sense that participation is considered as something good in itself. The crucial thing is that everyone should have the opportunity of taking part in the processes of political deliberation and reasoning.

Likewise, the notion of deliberative democracy that I am trying to expound does not consider political representation as a necessary second best compared to direct democracy. The public sphere is not a forum of governance, and it can fulfil its undertakings of deliberation, enlightenment and debate – and so function as a 'sounding-board' (Habermas, 1992) for social needs, problems and aspirations – only if there exists a distinct and separate formal governmental structure including elected representatives. Similarly, the kind of 'common good' that corresponds to the claim of political rationality must be understood as an *ironic*, 'for the time being' common good in the sense that the better argument will always and necessarily be the *provisional* better argument.

3. Socio-economic Conditions of Deliberative Democracy

Habermas' history of the structural transformation of the public sphere is a history of decay (Habermas, 1989). The public sphere in reality was never fully in accordance with its own ideal, but the analysis shows that in the late eighteenth century the British parliament had to give up its exclusivity and recognize the public as a partner of discussion. Moreover, although only a minority of the (male) population was included, at the time it was possible to believe in a future in which everyone would have the chance to fulfil the admission requirements in the form of property and general education or enlightenment (*Bildung*). However, in the course of the nineteenth century it became clear that the ideal of generalized possession of property would never be realized. Instead the political sphere was gradually opened to groups that did not meet conditions relating to economic independence and general education. As a consequence, politics proved *not* to be a matter of rational discussion and problem solving in order to realize a common good. Rather, it was essentially about conflicting groups fighting to promote their distinctive interests – in agreement with what would become the standard idea of politics in political science. History seemed to demonstrate the incompatibility between capitalism and (deliberative) democracy.

To make a long and complicated story very short, according to the early Habermas, the overall socio-political development during the twentieth century does not change this conclusion. In particular, he does not believe that the evolving social rights connected to the expanding post-war welfare state would be able to serve as a new basis for securing economic independence and autonomy for each citizen. Rather than neutralising class positions and securing an equal citizenship, the welfare state defines a new 'class' of dependent clients.

In that respect, the conclusion in Marshall's seminal essay on social class and citizenship is totally different. The basic message here is that the class inequalities of capitalism can be met by establishing an equal *status* of citizenship – 'the inequality of the class system may be acceptable provided the equality of citizenship is recognized' (Marshall, 1996, p. 6). According to Marshall, citizenship is constituted by three sets of universal rights: civil, political and social rights evolving in the eighteenth, nineteenth and twentieth centuries respectively. A crucial point is that the different rights make up a *system* of rights, so that the accomplishment of each of them presupposes the completion of the others. In particular, Marshall stresses how the equal fulfilment of civil and political rights is conditioned by the establishing of universal social rights. Whereas public support under the Poor Law resulted in *withdrawal* of civil and political rights the fundamental novelty of the twentieth century is that such support is given *as* rights:

> ... social rights imply an absolute right to a certain standard of civilization, which is conditional only on the discharge of the general duties of citizenship. Their content does not depend on the economic value of the individual claimant ... thus creating a universal right to an income, which is not proportionate to the market value of the claimant (*Ibid.*, pp. 26, 28).

The same universalism, which is constitutive for the State governed by law, should also characterize the welfare state. And it is precisely because social rights are given as universal rights of citizenship that the problems of stigmatization and clientelization are avoided.

> What matters is that there is a general enrichment of the concrete substance of civilized life ... Equalization is not so much between classes as between individuals within a population, which is now treated for this purpose as though it were one class. Equality of status is more important than equality of income (*Ibid.*, p. 33).

Now, comparing Marshall's hopes and visions to Habermas' pessimistic outlook, I would argue that the former are in much better accordance with the main trends during the last four decades than is the latter, especially if one thinks of the Nordic welfare state. As a matter of form, it should be added that in his later works Habermas changed his appraisals considerably

(Habermas, 1989; 199). However, with regard to the question of the basic conditions of a functioning political public sphere, I still find it more fruitful to refer to the original analysis.

In what follows I shall substantiate this assessment by referring briefly to the Danish experience, which seems to have accomplished Marshall's anticipations to a high degree. First, the Danish welfare state is an example of the universalistic model, where relatively generous social goods and services are tax-financed and given as rights of citizenship. Referring both to the political forces that brought about the Nordic welfare states historically and to their so-called de-commodifying qualities, it has been commonplace to label these states 'social democratic' (Esping-Andersen, 1990). However, at least regarding the Danish welfare state, I think that 'social-liberal' is a more appropriate designation. On the one hand, the liberal or bourgeois political parties have played a major role in important formative decisions (Nørgaard, 1999). On the other hand, and more importantly, the principle of universalism belongs basically to a *liberal* universe. And whereas it is important to stress the decommodifying aspects of social rights of citizenship, it is equally crucial to notice and recognize the market *conformity* characterising universalist rights and schemes.

Historically, the development of the Danish welfare state nicely illustrates Marshall's theory of a progressing citizenship (Bjørn, 1998; Loftager, forthcoming), but here we have to concentrate on the period since the early 1970s. In that period the Danish welfare system contributed to a practical 'universalization' in the specific sense that virtually all adult Danes have become individual income recipients, which amounts to no less than a basic historical novelty. The expansion of the public service sector played an important role by promoting a substantial increase in women's labour-market participation rate; so did the extension of the system of income transfers. The outcome was that almost all people without an earned income of their own were guaranteed an income from the State. In that respect, it is important to notice that various job-offer and educational schemes made it possible to regain entitlement to unemployment benefits without any time limit. A so-called principle of income replacement in the social security system was pointing in the same direction; so was an early-retirement scheme, which quickly became a universal right, financed by general taxes and covering most of the workforce. In addition, for some years a so-called transitional benefit allowed long-term unemployed people above 50 years of age to take (very) early retirement. At the other end of the age scale, the child allowance was universalized, in the sense that it was granted without an income test, and the same became true of the educational benefit system. Altogether, these developments indicated a scenario leading towards the ultimate universalistic welfare system, namely that of a basic or citizen's income given unconditionally as a right to every citizen (Goul Andersen, 1996; Loftager, 1996).

In a broad historical perspective, it seems both instructive and obvious to appraise the resulting securing of universal economic independence as a substitute for the general possession of property that was once a necessary – although not sufficient – requirement for a deliberative democracy based upon a status of equal citizenship. Certainly, Marshall did not imagine a Danish-type development, neither with respect to the size of the workforce, nor the large proportion – around 20 per cent – of the population on public transfer incomes. However, these conditions do not seem to be inconsistent with his ideal. This is self-evident with regard to the emergence of an independent basis of support for women, and it can be raised up as a rather serious problem in Marshall's analysis that he ignores the question of women's (previous) economic dependency. It might seem more difficult to bring a situation in which around 20 per cent of the population of working age live on transfer payments into accordance with a notion of equal citizenship. In principle, however, it is unproblematic. As mentioned above, the decisive thing is that a person's status is not determined by his or her market capacity but by universal rights of citizenship. It is quite another thing, of course, if receiving 'passive' support results in marginalization and exclusion. That has been a prominent perspective in the Danish political debate on welfare in general and a central argument behind the 'activation' reforms in particular but, as will be apparent below, it is an argument without firm empirical foundation.

4. The New Third Way of Activation

It is disputed how radical a change the activation strategy represents. Some argue that it accords well with traditional policies (Green-Pedersen *et al.*, 2001; Nørgaard; 1998); others find that it involves a significant tightening but not qualitative changes (Abrahamson and Oorschot 2002); and still others claim that the changes amount to a paradigm shift (Cox, 1998). My own conclusion is that it is in fact justified to talk about a radical change of paradigm. Although at present much looks the same as before, potentially far-reaching changes have been implemented, and a new discourse has clearly manifested itself (Jespersen and Rasmussen, 1998).

First and foremost and very simply: whereas so-called 'passive' support used to be an/the obvious general *solution* to the generic social-order problems of capitalist society, such public support is now conceived of as the basic *problem*. The inspiration behind this 'Copernican turn' clearly comes from the idea of workfare rather than welfare, which in turn forms a fundamental part of the politics of the current Third Way (Jordan, 1998; Rose, 1999). In that connection, it is important to stress that workfare is not concomitant with a neo-liberal minimal State strategy. Rather, it is coupled to communitarian concerns for community and inclusion accompanied by a strong conviction that it is both the right and the duty of the State to take responsibility for their protection (Mead, 1986, 1997; Etzioni, 1993). Second, however, the discourse of activation also includes economic-liberalistic notions of 'give and take' (Jespersen and Rasmussen, 1998; Nørskov Toke, 2002), and precisely the combination of neo-liberal supply-economic beliefs and a communitarian philosophy of community that appears to be characteristic of the present Third Way. For a more elaborate and general analysis, readers are referred to Nicolas Rose, who shows how notions of human and social capital make up mitigating elements in that they introduce 'etho-politics into economics through the capitalization of morality in the service of national economic advantage' (Rose, 1999, p. 282). Here I shall content myself with discussing the way in which this mixture appears in the Danish politics of activation.

It finds immediate expression in a typical duality of the concern for societal solidarity. That is to say, the concern does not only relate to the (asserted) negative consequences of welfare benefits for the recipients. It also concerns the legitimacy of the benefits in the eyes of taxpayers – how can one expect them to accept high tax levels in order to support people who do nothing in return?

The basic assumption of the activation strategy is that passive support is disqualifying as well as demotivating. It takes away the incentive to seek and accept jobs and so it produces marginalization from the labour market, which in turn results in further social marginalization and exclusion.

However, the answer should not be 'laissez faire, laissez passer'. Rather, the response should be what Giddens in his *The Third Way* labels 'generative policies' aiming at 'positive welfare' (Giddens, 1998). Whereas the old welfare state turned citizens into passive clients, the new Third Way welfare state will ensure that each individual becomes able to support himself and so contribute to the community. In that respect, the central instrument is the duty to do something immediately in return for any public support received.

But, one might object, is this something new? Has it not always been the case that the right to support is conditioned by an obligation to work? The answer, of course, is yes. The difference – and the difference that really makes a difference – is, that previously the duty of availability was a duty to accept an offer of a job on *ordinary conditions* on equal terms with everybody else. In other words, the difference is between duties and requirements that are universally in force and duties that are not known in advance and are not the result of a freely negotiated contract. General duties and obligations are totally in accordance with the liberal ideal of equal citizenship. Because of their universality, duties to pay taxes, go to school and perform military service etc. express *equality* of status. In contrast, the activation duties as they are defined – in the last instance – by the authorities signal and institutionalize differences and *inequality* of status.

Compared to other descriptions of activation policies, the above characterization may look rather biased. In his analysis, for instance, Torfing stresses how the Danish government has managed 'to detach workfare from its neo-liberal "origin" and to reformulate its content in accordance with the socio-political legacy in Denmark' (Torfing, 1999, p. 17). It is emphasized that the Danish success in fighting unemployment does not reflect an increasing number of 'working poor', and Torfing also gives a basically positive account of the activation measures and demands *vis-à-vis* each individual unemployed. In that respect, the so-called individual action plans are of crucial importance. They are plans that are prepared for each unemployed person in order to improve the effectiveness of their efforts. In accordance with the officially formulated intentions, Torfing stresses that the plans make it possible to target activities and demands in ways that are meaningful. He states that 'activation through participation in "futile work-for-the-sake-of-working projects" is limited, as the law does not aim at repressing and punishing the unemployed' (*Ibid.*, p. 18).

This is correct. At the same time, it must be added that no one has tried to disguise the fact that activation is not only about carrots; it is also about sticks. The authorities do not deny that the expected effect of activation, to a considerable degree, is due to the factor of motivation, which is connected both to the demand of activation and to the prospect of losing one's income for good (Arbejdsministeriet, 2000).

In some cases the element of targeting may result in greater effectiveness, and evaluation studies indicate that a majority of the involved persons express positive attitudes towards the activation projects (Hansen, 2001). Nevertheless, it appears to be more than doubtful to characterize the politics of activation in general, and the action plans in particular, as according well with the Danish socio-political legacy. The very idea that it is the responsibility and duty of the State to demand binding contracts with citizens on such far-reaching matters represents a paternalism that seems alien in a Danish context (Nørskov Toke, 2002). Certainly, in some cases paternalism might be in accordance with liberal premises, namely if the people in question have lost their autonomy, for instance, because of old age, illness or drug dependency. That is a very exceptional situation as far as unemployed people are concerned; so there has evolved an apparent discrepancy in Danish social policy between, say, compulsory treatment of drug addicts where the authorities have been very cautious not to encroach on the integrity and autonomy of the individual, and activation policies where this has hardly been an issue at all (*Ibid.*).

People in activation programmes are not only obliged to work in different and poorer conditions than people in ordinary jobs, in that they do not enjoy what Marshall termed 'collective civil rights' stemming from collective agreements. Another far-reaching change of the labour market reform of 1994 is that activation activities no longer mean renewed right to unemployment benefits. As a result, the previous guarantee upholding the status of the individual income receiver no longer exists. The period of support is limited to four years; after that unemployed people may qualify for social security payments, but these are tested against the family income so that even a rather modest income of the spouse eliminates the entitlement.

In this way (involuntary) private support has re-emerged as a socially recognized and legitimate form of support. In the light of communitarian ideals of strong family ties this may be judged a progressive step, but it seems difficult to reconcile with liberal ideas of equal citizenship.

In the Danish debate a prime argument against passive transfers is that they generate dependency on the State and undermine the ideal of taking care of oneself. However, apart from the fact that people on activation programmes still obtain their livelihoods from the State, what matters according a citizenship perspective is not dependency as such but different sorts of dependency. Again, from the perspective of the ideal of equal citizenship, the critical types of dependency are those that do not appear from general rules but stem from unpredictable bureaucratic discretion. In those cases there is a considerable risk of encroachment on the citizen's autonomy and integrity and so – ultimately – of weakened civil and political rights.

As mentioned above, according to the deliberative conception of democracy the opportunity of *public* participation in political reasoning and opinion-formation is of crucial importance, but such participation presupposes the presence of the kind of private autonomy that the course of activation potentially threatens. If your economic subsistence is dependent on the good will of the authorities, then this makes up a rather weak basis for (critical) political activity – parallel to the intimidation of electors by employers before the ballot was made secret (Elklit, 1989).

In addition to that kind of potential direct consequence, activation may also weaken the status of citizenship more indirectly by producing stigmatization; activated people are 'weak' people, who need special treatment and help in order to develop appropriate attitudes and personal qualities (Carstens, 1998). And activation as upbringing is, of course, a primary example of communitarian paternalism.

In general the difference between the previous and the new Third Way can be said to consist of two categorically different notions of community. Whereas Marshall's citizenship is to be understood as a liberal socio-political community of citizens with equal rights and duties, the community associated with the politics of activation is identical to the community of work. It appears – mechanically – as a reflex of everyone respecting the norm of doing paid work. So, activation is not merely a means to get more people into ordinary jobs, it is also an end in itself because it ensures 'that people are included in meaningful (work) communities. That is, participation in this connection is an aim in itself, because it considered to be good for the individual – even if it does not lead to self-support' (Socialministeriet, 2000, pp. 50–55 [my translation, JL]).

As shown in several analyses such communitarian arguments are widespread in the Danish discourse of activation (Jespersen and Rasmussen, 1998; Nørskov Toke, 2002). In relation to Durkheim's famous conception of solidarity, this indicates a mechanical understanding of solidarity, according to which inclusion is based on the sharing of common values and norms (Loftager, 2001). If one *defines* community as community of work, activation becomes a categorical imperative, i.e. a claim and a duty that does not need to be argued further by means of reference to specific consequences.

This interpretation accords well with the fact that belief in the principle of activation has not been disturbed by several studies which have questioned its results in terms of effects on employment and its basic assumptions in general. Serious doubt has been cast on the core supposition, that passive support produces marginalization and exclusion. Certainly, it has been well documented that there is co-variance between (long-term) unemployment and a lot of social problems and calamities such as problems of abuse, family dissolution, illness and early death (Nygaard Christoffersen, 1996). But what is the cause and what is the effect? Serious illness might equally well be the cause of long-term unemployment rather than the other way round. On the other hand, studies of people on public transfers indicate that passive support produces marginalization only to a very small degree. The striking and perhaps surprising observation is the extent to which the long-term unemployed and those on early retirement manage to continue their usual daily lives concerning habitation, contact with family and friends, and participation in various social activities (Goul Andersen, 1996, 2002; Lund Clement and Goul Andersen, 1999).

Likewise, the fear of shrinking solidarity among taxpayers towards the recipients of public transfer payments also seems to be unfounded (Goul Andersen, 1996).

It is commonplace to explain as an effect of activation policies the sharp reduction of the number of Danish unemployed persons during the 1990s. However, this does not tally with available facts and figures. A new overview of evaluation studies in the Netherlands and Denmark concludes that the employment effect of activation has been rather limited and in some cases even negative (Abrahamson and Oorschot, 2002). Furthermore, a panel study that followed a number of unemployed persons over four years casts strong doubt on the validity of the basic premise of unemployment as primarily *structural* unemployment. The study in question shows that to only a very small extent can renewed labour market integration be explained by the expected factors: the length of the period of unemployment, level of education and job motivation (Albrekt Larsen, 2002).

Finally, in addition to the much celebrated 57 per cent reduction of unemployment from 349,000 in 1993 to 150,000 in 2000 it is worth mentioning that the total number receiving public support in the same period was only reduced from 1,034,000 to 890,000, a drop of 14 per cent (Dansk Arbejdsgiverforening, 2001); and also that the employment rate for the age group 15 – 66 was the same in 1999 as it was in 1993, namely 73.5 per cent (Centre for Alternative Social Analysis, 2000).

5. Concluding Remarks: Beyond the (New) Third Way?

The realization of the ideal of deliberative democracy presupposes that everyone can take part in public reasoning and deliberation as autonomous and independent citizens. Originally, the fulfilment of this requirement was associated with the emergence of a market society, which in theory allowed every person to possess property. Thus the course of development marked by capitalist class divisions also moved in the direction of an equal citizenship, and the delicate relationship between capitalism and democracy became a recurrent preoccupation in political sociology. In the post-war period attention has, to a large extent, concentrated on the welfare state and its potential as a guarantor for democracy. The basic idea was that the establishment of social rights might constitute a basis for an equal citizenship. A key problem with this solution is, however, that the welfare state itself, depending on its structure and way of functioning, might create new dependencies detrimental to the preconditions of democracy and especially deliberative democracy.

Based upon general observations and theoretical arguments as well as Danish evidence, the main conclusion of this paper is that in this regard the former Marshall-like Third Way comes off better than the currently dominating Third Way. It should be stressed that the paper has not dealt with the actual deliberative working of democracy under the conditions of the new Third Way. Probably it would be very difficult to register any immediate effects of the shift of welfare paradigm. The focus has been on (one of) the pillars on which democracy rests, and it goes without saying that the consequences for democracy will appear only in the longer run.

It is not my ambition to forecast democracy's future development but this much seems certain: although democracy has become a democracy without enemies – if that holds true after September 11th 2001! – its prospects will still be dependent on socio-economic conditions.

To the extent that my conclusions are valid the interesting question is, of course, what kind of a future welfare system might nurture deliberative democracy. In line with the main argument of the paper, the general answer is that instead of following the current Third Way of selectivity it seems appropriate to suggest an expanded universalism as an obvious alternative. It is beyond the scope of this paper to assess the realism and practicality of a basic or citizen's income, but the generally positive Danish experience concerning 'passive' – but not passivity-inducing! – transfers could indicate that such an income is much more sensible and imaginative than the currently dominating discourse on welfare politics would lead us to believe. It might be an interesting new chapter in the history of expanding citizenship.

Note

1 Department of Political Science, University of Aarhus, Denmark.

References

Abrahamson, P. and Oorschot, W. v. 2002. *The Dutch and Danish miracles revisited: Comparing the role of activation policies within two different welfare regimes*, paper prepared for presentation at the 2nd European Cooperation in the field of Scientific and Technical Research (COST) Action 15 Conference, Oslo, April 2002.

Albrekt Larsen, C. 2000. *Det danske mirakel set fra jorden – en revurdering af grundlaget for aktiveringsstrategien*, Speciale, Administrationsuddannelsen, Aalborg Universitet.

_____ 2002. *Challenging the hegemonic discourse of structural unemployment*, Centre for Comparative Welfare Studies (CCWS) Working paper No. 2002–24, Aalborg University.

Arbejdsministeriet 2000. *Effekter af aktiveringsindsatsen* (Copenhagen, Arbejdsministeriet).

Beck, U. 1998. *Democracy without enemies* (Cambridge, Polity Press).

Bjørn, Ole. 1998. *Dengang Danmark blev moderne. Historien om den virkelige danske utopi* (Copenhagen, Gyldendal).

Carstens, A. 1998. *Aktivering – klientsamtaler og socialpolitik* (Copenhagen, Hans Reitzels Forlag).

Centre for Alternative Social Analysis (CASA). 2000. *Social Aarsrapport* (Copenhagen, Socialpolitisk Forlag).

Cox, R.H. 1998. 'From safety net to trampoline: Labour market activation in the Netherlands and Denmark', in *Governance*, Vol. 11, No. 4, pp. 397–414.

Dahl, R. 1971. *Polyarchy: Participation and opposition* (New Haven and London, Yale University Press).

Dansk Arbejdsgiverforening 2001. *Arbejdsmarkedsrapport 2001. Tal og diagrammer* (Copenhagen, Dansk Arbejdsgiverforening).

Dewey, J. 1927. *The public and its problems* (Chicago, Gateway Books).

Downs, A. 1957. *An economic theory of democracy* (New York, Harper and Row).

Durkheim, E. 1999. *Den sociale arbejdsdeling* (Copenhagen, Hans Reitzels Forlag).

Elklit, J. 1989. *Fra åben til hemmelig afstemning* (Århus, Politica).

Eriksen, E. O. 1999. *Is democracy possible today?* (Aarhus, Magtudredningen).

_____ and Loftager, J. (eds.). 1996. *The Rationality of the Welfare State* (Oslo, Scandinavian University Press).

Esping-Andersen, G. 1990. *The three worlds of welfare capitalism* (Oxford, Polity Press).

Etzioni, A. 1993. *The spirit of community* (London, Fontana Press).

Giddens, A. 1998 *The third way: The renewal of social democracy* (Cambridge, Polity Press).

Goul Andersen, J. 1996. 'Marginalization, citizenship and the economy: The capacities of the universalist welfare state in Denmark', in E.O. Eriksen and J. Loftager (eds.), *The rationality of the welfare state* (Oslo, Scandinavian University Press).

_____ 2002. *Coping with long-term unemployment: Economic security, labour market integration and well-being*, Centre for Comparative Welfare Studies Working paper No. 2002–23, Aalborg University.

Green-Pedersen, C., K.v. Kersbergen and A. Hemerijck. 2001. '"Neo-liberalism, the 'Third Way' or what?" Recent social democratic welfare policies in Denmark and the Netherlands', in *Journal of European Public Policy*, Vol. 8, No. 2, pp. 307–325.

Habermas, J. 1989. *The structural transformation of the public sphere* (Cambridge, MIT Press).

_____ 1996. *Between facts and norms* (Cambridge, MIT Press).

Hansen, H. 2001. *Arbejde, aktivering og arbejdsløshed* (Frederiksberg, Samfundslitteratur).

Holmes, S. 1995. *Passions and constraints* (Chicago, Chicago University Press).

Jespersen, S.P. and Rasmussen, S.L. 1998. *Fra velfærdsstat til velfærdssamfund – en analyse af 90'ernes velfærdsdebat*, specialeopgave, Institut for Statskundskab, Aarhus Universitet.

Jordan, B. 1998. *The new politics of welfare* (London, Sage).

Korsgaard. O. 1999. *Demosstrategien*, Arbejdspapir nr. 5, Forskningsprojektet Voksenuddannelse, folkeoplysning og demokrati (Copenhagen, Danmarks Lærerhøjskole).

Kurrild-Klitgaard, P. 1999. 'Demokrati, magt og kollektive valgs rationalitet', in U. Jakobsen and M. Kelstrup *Demokrati og demokratisering: Begreber og teorier* (Copenhagen, Forlaget Politiske Studier), pp. 238–282.

Loftager, J. 1996. 'Citizens income – A new welfare state strategy?', in E.O. Eriksen and J. Loftager (eds.) *The rationality of the welfare state* (Oslo, Scandinavian University Press), pp. 134–149.

_____ 2001. 'Émile Durkheim: Borgerrollen og det multikulturelle', in O. Korsgaard (ed.), *Poetisk demokrati* (Copenhagen, Gads Forlag), pp. 111–128.

_____ Forthcoming. 'Aktivering som (ny) velfærdspolitisk tredjevej', in *Politica*, årg. 2002, No. 3.

Lund Clement, S. and Goul Andersen, J. 1999. 'Ny marginaliseringsundersøgelse af før-tidspensionister mv.', in *NYT* (Institut for Økonomi, Politik og Forvaltning, Aalborg Universitet), No. 2, pp.1–2.

Madsen, P.K. 1999. *Denmark: Flexibility, security and labour market succes*, Employment and Training Papers 53 (Geneva, International Labour Organization).

Marshall, T.H. 1966. *Class, citizenship and the State* (New York, Doubleday), first published 1950.

Mead, L.M. 1986. *Beyond entitlement* (New York, The Free Press).

_____ 1997. Welfare employment in L.M. Mead (ed.) *The new paternalism* (New York, The Free Press).

Mik-Meyer, N. 1999. *Kærlighed og opdragelse i socialaktiveringen* (Copenhagen, Gyldendal).

Miller, D. 1993. Deliberative democracy and social choice, in D. Held, *Prospects for democracy* (Cambridge, Polity Press), pp. 74–92.

Nørgaard, A.S. 1999. 'Viden og videnskab om velfærdsstaten: er der én dansk velfærdsstat?', in *GRUS*, No. 56/57, 20 årg., pp. 6–39.

_____ 2000. 'Party politics and the organization of the Danish welfare state, 1890-1920: The bourgeois roots of the modern welfare state', in *Scandinavian Political Studies*, Vol. 23, No. 3, pp. 183–215.

Nørskov Toke, K. 2002. *Paternalisme i dansk socialpolitik – autonomi eller moralisme?*, specialeopgave, Institut for Statskundskab, Aarhus Universitet.

Nygaard Christoffersen, M. 1996. *Opvækst med arbejdsløshed* (Copenhagen, Socialforskningsinstituttet, 1996/14).

Rose, N. 1999. 'Inventiveness in politics', in *Economy and Society*, Vol. 28, No. 3, pp. 467–493.

Schumpeter, J.A. 1943/1976. *Capitalism, socialism and democracy* (London and New York, Routledge).

Socialministeriet 2000. *Socialpolitik som investering, Socialpolitisk Redegørelse 2000* (Copenhagen, Socialministeriet).

Torfing, J. 1999. 'Workfare with welfare: Recent reforms of the Danish welfare state', in *Journal of European Social Policy*, Vol. 9 (1), pp. 5–28.

14

MOBILIZING SUPPORT
FOR BASIC INCOME

Steven Shafarman[1]

1. Introduction

Here is a story told by political activists in the United States: during the Great Depression of the 1930s, when President Franklin Roosevelt was creating the many programmes and agencies of the New Deal, a delegation went to him with a proposal. He responded, 'Okay, you've convinced me. Now go on out and bring pressure on me!' (Alinsky, 1972, p. xxiii). Good ideas and arguments are not enough. Elected officials rarely act without strong, continuing pressure from their constituents.

In order to put pressure on elected officials, advocates for any reform have to organize effectively, in large numbers. Like the delegation to Roosevelt, advocates must be convincing, so they have to be educated. It is, however, impossible to educate people unless there are people who are interested in being educated. That means attracting people. A way to attract people is to present an idea, formulated clearly, that looks as if it will solve their problems. To summarize in order, here are the steps in a reform campaign: formulating, attracting, educating, organizing, and pressuring.

It is useful to see these steps as distinct and sequential. In practice, of course, every step provides insights that sometimes require campaigners to rethink their strategy, revise the formula, attract more or different people, and so forth. It helps if the people who initially formulate an idea do not retreat to an ivory tower but remain actively involved, so long as they are willing to revise.

A major challenge at every step, especially attracting potential supporters, is that people are quite busy. Providing for themselves and their families, trying to enjoy their lives, and other everyday matters usually, sensibly, come first. Relatively few people are really interested in political reform. Countless ideas, products, and services are constantly advertised through diverse media; all of these are competing for people's limited time and attention.

At the same time, reform proposals have to compete in the market place of ideas, have to compete not just with other reform proposals but also with the *status quo*. That playing field is far from level, especially when the proposed reform is something substantive, like a guaranteed basic income. The *status quo* is familiar, so it seems natural or even necessary. Substantive reform means changes that cannot be predicted, which makes it easy for opponents to attack reforms and scare people. Moreover, defenders of the *status quo* benefit from delays, such as studies and commissions, and often distract the public with reforms that are mostly cosmetic.

2. Formulating the Idea

Basic income has been defined as 'an income paid by government, at a uniform level and at regular intervals, to each adult member of society. The grant is paid, and its level is fixed, irrespective of whether the person is rich or poor, lives alone or with others, is willing to work or not' (van Parijs, 2001, p. 5).

Noteworthy in this definition is what it leaves out, starting with the actual amount of the basic income. It should be, most proponents say, adequate for subsistence in the state or country that implements it. Vagueness on this point is useful because it allows for beginning with a smaller amount, one that is more readily affordable. Also important and missing from this definition is any statement about varying the amount when economic conditions change.

Some proponents want to include all permanent residents; others would restrict it to citizens. And some proponents want to include children, although that raises many additional questions. Would the payment for children be the same amount, or less? Start at birth, or at some specific age like six months or seven years? Paid to the parents, or put into some sort of 'stakeholder' trust or 'baby bond' that can be cashed at age 18? What if parents are divorced and custody is disputed?

Discussions about the amount, who would be included, how to begin the programme, and other details are a way to engage and motivate potential supporters. Such discussions ought to be encouraged. However, it makes sense to defer specific answers until after the basic idea becomes popular.

3. Attracting People's Attention

In the United States, Republicans and most Democrats routinely oppose new grants, guarantees, entitlements and income supports, except those that are directly tied to work. Existing programmes – even for very poor mothers and their young children – are threatened or are being eliminated, as occurred with the 1996 law that ended welfare and replaced it with Temporary Aid to Needy Families. Despite that, at the Citizen Policies Institute, we have found two very effective ways to make basic income attractive. The first is to make the idea personal.

What could you do with the extra money? Would you change your job or other aspects of your everyday life? Your plans for education, vacations, retirement? Of course, your spouse and parents and adult children would also receive the basic income. What might it mean for each of them? For your family as a whole?

Advocates have to remember that they, too, will receive the money. And so will everyone they talk or write to, for, or about. Let us not be shy. Speaking personally may be unfamiliar, even uncomfortable, perhaps especially for academics who are more accustomed to lecturing and discussing ideas abstractly. Yet it can also be fun.

It is an axiom in marketing and public relations that people evaluate products, services or ideas according to perceived self-interest. Asking people what they might do with a basic income, what it might mean for them and their families, invites them to consider self-interest explicitly. Regardless of any more specific self-interest, almost everyone can use extra income.

Through personal questions and dialogue, advocates for basic income orient people toward the future and encourage a sense of hope. Hope is attractive. And it is missing from most conversations about politics and economics, which focus excessively on the present and often engender resentment, passivity, even despair. Too many would-be reformers ignore the advice of Brazilian educator Paulo Freire: 'We must never merely discourse on the present situation, must never provide the people with programmes which have little or nothing to do with their own preoccupations, doubts, hopes, and fears' (Freire, 1993, p. 77). Dialogue, he taught and showed, is an act of personal and social transformation. When it is authentic, participants are inspired and motivated.

Dialogue is also an effective way to respond to people's doubts and concerns, before they harden into objections. The most common of those is the assumption that some people will waste or misuse the money. Speaking personally transforms that conversation. Would you waste or misuse it? Would your friends or family members? Of course not, almost everyone asserts. Besides, what would be wrong with using the money for a vacation, or working fewer hours and spending more time with friends or family members?

Eliminating the fear of hunger and homelessness would leave intact all of the positive reasons to work, earn and save, to make a better life for oneself and one's family. Yes, some people will spend the money on drugs, alcohol and gambling. Yes, some will just sit in front of the television or play computer games. But some people do that today. With basic income, the lazy or irresponsible would be able to afford food and shelter, and therefore would not be impelled to beg or steal or depend on some charity or specific government programme. Dialogue and thoughtful questions can help people become aware of their own biases and prejudices; neither class, race, ethnicity nor national origin causes or explains laziness and irresponsibility.

There is another advantage to attracting potential supporters through dialogue: people can easily continue the conversations with their family members, friends, neighbours, and so on.

4. Educating Potential Supporters

The second thing we do to attract potential supporters also helps educate them. That is telling the story of previous proposals that are similar to basic income. It is a history that most Americans do not know. Briefly:

- In 1776, before writing the Declaration of Independence, Thomas Jefferson proposed to the Virginia legislature that it give land to any propertyless individual willing to farm it. Many states subsequently enacted homestead laws. In 1862, Abraham Lincoln called for, and the federal Government enacted, the National Homestead Act, which remained in effect until the early 1900s. In 1795, Tom Paine sought a cash payment to everyone at age 21 and yearly starting at age 50.
- During the Populist and Progressive movements of the 1890s, leading thinkers and authors included Henry George and Edward Bellamy. Each wrote a book that sold more than a million copies. Both wanted to guarantee everyone's economic security.
- The 1930s brought the passage of Social Security. It was, however, a weak response to two national movements, each of which had millions of supporters. The Townsend Plan called for monthly cash payments to the elderly. 'Share Our Wealth' demanded a more general and generous redistribution. Franklin Roosevelt subsequently proposed a 'Second Bill of Rights' that would guarantee everyone a decent home, medical care, education, and enough income for food and shelter.
- In the 1960s, Milton Friedman, James Tobin, Paul Samuelson, John Kenneth Galbraith, and other prominent economists endorsed 'guaranteed income' or a 'negative income tax'. Martin Luther King Jr. called for guaranteed income as an essential step toward ending racism. Richard Nixon presented a plan that passed in the House of Representatives with two-thirds of the vote, but was defeated in the Senate Finance Committee. In the 1972 presidential campaign, Senator George McGovern ran against Nixon and called for a 'Demogrant' that was very close to a basic income.

People like a good story, and the rhythm of this one gives it dramatic tension and suggests that resurgence is near. Most of the names are familiar, impressive, and therefore reassuring. We present this history in different ways, depending on the audience. For example, with people who are especially concerned about civil rights and social justice, it works well to start with Martin Luther King Jr. With conservatives, we quote Milton Friedman, plus F. A. Hayek and Peter Drucker, who are among the many significant individuals not mentioned here. In effect, we are inviting readers and listeners to join these figures in making history.

In Europe and elsewhere outside the United States, basic income advocates might use this history in another way. It seems that most people like Americans but resent or distrust the United States Government, particularly the Bush administration's unilateralism and militarism. Advocates might cite the 1960s' debates as evidence that the Government was, and perhaps still is, dysfunctional and out of touch with the people. A majority of Americans favoured Nixon's plan; public opinion polls showed that clearly, and the vote in the House confirmed it. Opponents in the Senate stalled until after the general election, and then defeated it in committee, avoiding the attention that comes with a full public debate.

This history also provides some important lessons. One is that advocates have to keep the pressure on. Another is that advocates have to be willing to compromise. In the Senate committee, moderate Democrats and Republicans voted for the plan. Voting against it were conservatives who opposed any aid to the poor and liberals who wanted something more generous. If the liberals and their supporters had been willing to compromise, it would have passed and they could have started working for an expansion. A third lesson, already learned, involves the specific formulation. Nixon's plan was to give cash payments only to very poor families. It was extremely complicated due to the means testing and the mechanics of reducing the payments to recipients who increased their earnings. In contrast, basic income is simple, universal and unconditional.

Soon after being introduced to the idea of basic income, many people ask if there is anything like it operating anywhere in the world. That question is an opportunity to talk about Alaska and the Permanent Fund Dividend. Residents receive close to $2,000 a year. That is news to almost everyone, and people sometimes joke about moving there. Also quite appealing is the logic of the plan: Alaska's oil belongs to the people, so royalties should be distributed directly, rather than used to fund Government.

5. Organizing Allies

Mobilizing support for basic income could take a long time if people are only attracted and educated at random. It makes sense to target our efforts. There are many individuals and organizations that can be valuable allies. Our task is to help them see how basic income can help them achieve their goals.

That is easy with organizations working to end hunger, homelessness and poverty. Conventional political approaches depend on creating jobs. There is, however, no evidence that there will ever be enough new jobs to make a significant difference. With basic income, everyone would have money for food and shelter. People can find or create jobs for themselves. The main obstacle to alliances with anti-poverty groups is that most focus on local, specific or short-term goals like funding shelters and soup kitchens or opposing cuts in particular government programmes; they may be reluctant to redirect their efforts. Even so, alliances are definitely worth pursuing. Many of those groups are large, well-organized, and skilful at lobbying, public relations and other ways to put pressure on politicians.

The issue of jobs suggests the possibility of alliances with labour unions. Employers have been reacting to globalization and new technologies by making greater demands on workers. It has become common for employers to keep people in part-time, contract or temporary jobs; such workers have few or no benefits, and are particularly hard to organize. Basic income would, in effect, provide every worker with a strike fund. Workers with basic economic security would be freer to join unions, organize, and demand better working conditions.

Civil rights organizations can emphasize the fact that the basic income would go to everyone without regard for race, gender, sexual orientation, ethnic background or national origin. The most basic civil right, after all, has to be the right to an income for food and shelter. When everyone has that, it will be much easier to focus on other aspects of social justice.

Other potential allies are environmentalists and their organizations. To reduce air pollution and slow global warming, the most effective thing we can do is cut fossil fuel consumption. But politicians balk because substantive cuts would bring widespread economic disruptions. However, the economic security of a basic income would make it easier for individuals to adapt as needed. Voters might even endorse higher gasoline taxes, particularly if the basic income also goes up. When consumers demand more efficient cars, homes, appliances, and so on, businesses will find it profitable to supply them. In that way, basic income will help individuals and businesses pursue our common interest in more sustainable lives and communities. Environmentalists will be better positioned to guide public policy.

Allies might come from many other organizations or populations. Senior citizens, for example, with their politically powerful associations, might see basic income as a way to supplement Social Security, and to make things better for their children and grandchildren. Education reformers could point out that parents with basic income would be able to spend more time meeting with teachers and helping their children with homework. Health care reform proponents might gather or produce research about the public health harms – and costs – associated with hunger and homelessness, which would be eliminated with basic income.

With this strategy of building alliances, basic income advocates can gain enormous leverage. There is no need for any major new organization.

Every reform organization engages in the tasks of formulating, attracting, educating, organizing and pressuring. Activists agree that the main struggle is to attract people, 'outreach'. Organizations that support basic income and integrate it into their formulations will be able to use it in their outreach efforts. After all, extra income is something we all want, especially if it comes without any work requirement or other conditions. By doing that, allied organizations can increase their membership and their effectiveness.

6. Pressuring Politicians

Conventional ways to put pressure on elected officials include petitions, pre-printed postcards, personal letters, phone calls, office visits, rallies, and demonstrations, and so on up to protests with civil disobedience. It is commonly suggested that activists begin courteously and escalate gradually.

Politicians routinely say they trust, respect and believe in voters, citizens, the people and us. On specific issues and generally, we hear such rhetoric from those on the political left and the right. We can use their statements: 'You say you believe in X, and want to do Y. Will you support basic income, which would help with X and Y?' With our allies, we can do that with poverty, workers' issues, civil rights, environmental problems, and other issues.

Typically, politicians initially refuse to commit themselves. Citing questions of cost and affordability, a common tactic is to suggest a panel or commission to study the idea. That is not good enough. Concerns about cost have to be challenged. When people say we cannot afford some reform, they are in fact fortifying the *status quo*. They are saying it is okay to leave people hungry and homeless, okay that workers lack economic security, okay that civil rights are violated and our environment is degraded. None of these is okay. It is the *status quo* that we cannot afford.

We can certainly afford basic income if we start with an amount that is less than needed for subsistence. After we win something, even if the amount is obviously too low, advocates can press for increases. We can pay for those increases by cutting government programmes that become superfluous. It may be necessary to increase taxes, yet it should also be easier to agree on tax policies because everyone will be more able to participate in the debates and everyone will have regular reminders that we are all stakeholders.

When elected officials hesitate – most will; they were elected, we have to remember, as representatives of the *status quo* – we have to be prepared to work for their opponents in the next election. Challengers are usually more willing to endorse new ideas. In most countries, two political parties dominate; our allies are likely to be Greens, Libertarians, members of other 'third' parties, and independent candidates. Basic income is a perfect issue for any third party in the United States. Candidates can talk about the 1960s and the popularity of Nixon's plan, while challenging Republicans and Democrats to explain why their parties abandoned the idea. Such a challenge might provoke an incumbent to endorse it. A goal is to get two or more candidates to debate the amount, mechanics and other details.

A crucial step in any campaign is to find even one elected official who agrees to sponsor legislation. Advocates can help write the bill, reformulating the idea as necessary. At the same time, advocates and allies have to renew their efforts to attract additional supporters, educate them and so forth, in preparation for public events when the bill is introduced. That is important because some political organizations only become involved when there is legislation.

In the United States, Germany, Canada, Brazil, and other countries with a federal structure, it may be possible for a state or province to implement a basic income; perhaps a city or county could do it. Candidates for governor or other offices might campaign for it, proposing that their state be the first to demonstrate what it could do and how it would work. For example, Alaskans could expand what they have into a 'Permanent Fund Dividend Plus'. Most new policies are enacted in cities or states before being implemented at the national level.

7. Citizen Policies

The Citizen Policies Institute plan contains several elements that are proving to be quite appealing to ordinary Americans. Each element could, of course, be modified as the plan moves forward. Each might also work in other countries and campaigns.

First, 'Citizen Policies' include only citizens. Basic income would be, many people fear, a magnet for immigrants. That concern is not simply a matter of discrimination or right-wing bias; we hear it from people around the country and across the political spectrum. Permanent residents would have an added incentive to become citizens.

Second, we include only adults. An additional amount for children makes sense, but would complicate things significantly and be much more expensive. Also, payments to parents would mean inequality with the childless. Having children is, after all, a choice. For single mothers, some or all of the father's basic income could be redirected to child support.

Third, perhaps because the United States is such a large country, many people ask about variations in the cost of living. There are places where a frugal adult can subsist on $400 a month; in some cities, however, it is hard to get by with twice that amount. We find it useful to say early on that a national programme would have to mean a national amount. And that cities or states could supplement it from local revenues and that the amount must be variable when economic conditions, such as fossil fuel prices, change.

Fourth, in return for the basic income, we propose that everyone contribute, say, eight hours a month to the community. Some form of reciprocity makes sense; many people are uncomfortable with the notion of 'getting something for nothing'. That phrase is common, and was also used by opponents of Nixon's plan. Universal community service seems to be especially important to young adults, a large percentage of whom already volunteer.

In our community service proposal, the only mechanism for regulation or enforcement is social pressure. Yes, some people will shirk. But would you? Would your friends and family members? When everyone is receiving the basic income, the social pressure to serve would be enormous. Besides, a regulatory bureaucracy would cost far more than any potential benefits.

Volunteerism has been widely promoted in the United States, by liberals and conservatives, particularly since the terrorist attacks on September 11, 2001. Many people, however, are so busy working to provide for themselves and their families that they cannot afford the time to serve. To them, even the call for volunteerism is an added burden and can induce stress, shame and guilt. Basic income would make universal service possible. The money would, in effect, pay for a portion of everyone's time. Universal community service would be a powerful way to unite and secure the nation.

In addition, community service activities could replace many tasks that are currently performed by local government agencies. The money saved can help pay for the basic income.

8. Transforming Politics

To be effective advocates for basic income, it is important for people to understand the idea and its power.

For most issues or problems – poverty, pollution, global warming, urban decay, racism, and so on – there are two conventional approaches, along with a middle position that often combines the worst features from both extremes. From the left, liberals think government programmes are necessary. From the right, conservatives want to cut government and rely on the market. Left versus right. Liberal versus conservative. Government versus markets.

As an example, to reduce poverty and associated problems, the left liberal approach is to have government build houses, provide food and create jobs. Right-wing conservatives want all of that to be done by the market; if we cut government and its regulations, they say, people will provide for themselves. (The 'moderate' alternative is to give government subsidies to private employers; that distorts markets and corrupts the political process.) Liberals and conservatives want to end extreme poverty, of course. Their disputes are about the means and priorities. Conservatives emphasize personal freedom, initiative, and responsibility, and say it is degrading for people to be dependent on government handouts, 'the dole'. To liberals, extreme poverty is far more degrading; their priority is to seek equality and social justice.

With basic income, everyone will have enough money for food and shelter, which can be purchased through the market. It will no longer be necessary for government to create jobs or provide food or housing; such programmes can be cut and the money used to pay for the basic income. Everyone will receive the same amount, so there would not be any loss of dignity in accepting it, in contrast with welfare payments that are need-based, means-tested, or conditional. And the distribution would be extremely efficient, with no welfare bureaucracy.

Markets and Government working together. Conservative means achieving liberal ends. Left and right forming a circle, no longer opposite poles on an ideological spectrum.

Some people, at least in the United States, think basic income sounds like socialism. On the contrary, it would preserve markets and private property. And everyone will still be free to earn as much money as one can. Other people do not worry about socialism, but struggle under capitalism. Socialist Governments, even with their inefficiencies and other problems, provide an absolute social safety net. So would basic income. The economic security of socialism combined with the individual freedom of capitalism: a synthesis.

'Democracies' will become more democratic. In many places, one political party dominates. Or there are two major parties that disagree only about certain issues or details, or that campaign mostly on the candidates' personalities. Basic income will give people something to vote for, rather than someone to vote against. Once enacted, it will ensure that everyone can afford the time to participate; for a healthy democracy, after all, voting is not enough. Everyone will have regular reminders that everyone is a stakeholder.

Many countries, of course, are not democracies or are only nominally democratic. And those are some of the poorest and most troubled by disease, pollution, exploitation, and military conflicts. The best that can be hoped for is peaceful revolution, such as occurred in the Philippines under Marcos, Romania under Ceausescu, Serbia under Milosević, and East Germany with the fall of the Berlin Wall. Even the most ruthless government cannot long endure when citizens refuse to cooperate. Perhaps the idea of a basic income will inspire people in undemocratic countries, and encourage them to make peaceful revolutions.

9. Moving Forward

Basic income, history suggests, is most likely to be enacted first in a poor country that has recently undergone some major political transition. A recent transition means people have experience with substantive reform, and those who profit excessively from the *status quo* are not so entrenched. Poverty means people with nothing to lose. There are many countries in Asia, Africa and Latin America that have recently undergone some economic collapse and political transition. In eastern Europe, it has been only a decade or so since the end of communism, and many countries are struggling with capitalism and democracy.

In the summer of 2002, the best prospect is South Africa, just eight years after the end of apartheid. A national commission has strongly recommended a Basic Income Grant of $10 a month to everyone starting at age seven. The report is awaiting action by President Thabo Mbeki. Advocates include labour unions, churches and diverse organizations working on issues affecting children, women, the elderly and AIDS. Other poor democracies where basic income is being considered, though not yet debated in their national legislatures, include Argentina, Colombia and Brazil. Several states in Brazil already provide a basic grant to parents to pay for their children's schooling.

Wealthier countries that have a functioning social safety net could introduce a basic income in stages. Existing grants and guarantees can be extended as conditions and restrictions are removed. Leading the way is Ireland, where a plan backed by the Green Party is being widely debated. Supporters held a mass march on parliament in the winter of 2002. The main anti-poverty programme in the United States is the Earned Income Tax Credit. It could be expanded into a negative income tax by removing the link to earnings, and could then be further expanded into a basic income.

Progress anywhere can help mobilize support everywhere. Implementation in any country can provide a model for other countries.

Here is another way advocates can attract potential allies: by encouraging conjecture about what basic income might mean for the Palestinians and the prospects for peace in the Middle East. Every year, a lot of international aid, mostly from Europe and Arab countries, goes to the Palestinian Authority. What if that money was distributed through a basic income?

For the 2.7 million Palestinians, *per capita* income has fallen in the past two years by at least 30 per cent. Almost half now live below the poverty line of $2 per person per day. A billion dollars a year distributed directly and equally would mean an extra dollar a day for everyone. That would not by itself bring peace, obviously. Grievances and problems go back years, decades, even centuries, so any resolution will require other reforms and time. But it would be a fundamental change.

Most Palestinians have never had economic security; with basic income, everyone would. People could use the money to rebuild their homes, businesses, schools and communities. The distribution would be a vehicle for establishing an effective and accountable government that can manage the distribution and related responsibilities. Such a government, built from the bottom up, would be much more capable of stopping terrorism, creating a viable State, and negotiating peace with Israel.

This is all conjecture, you say? Of course it is. But imagining and dreaming are a first step, the way we begin to formulate new ideas. And such conjecture can promote dialogue. Besides, when was the last time you heard anything hopeful about the Middle East?

The power of basic income is that it focuses on individuals and serves people directly. Every individual will have basic economic security guaranteed. As individuals, people will be encouraged to come together to decide what is best for their neighbourhoods and communities. As individuals and together, it will be easier for people to demand that government and markets serve their needs and interests. In contrast, conventional policies and political practices focus on government, the market, and other institutions or abstractions – while overlooking the fact that 'government' and 'the market' are aggregates of individuals.

Individuals are the key to progress regarding poverty, pollution, global warming, urban decay, racism, and other issues or problems, including war and terrorism. Our situation is clearly unsustainable. Our world is seriously troubled. The sooner we act, as individuals and together, the better it will be for everyone.

Basic income will make it easier for every one of us to participate and do what is necessary. Our children and grandchildren, and our world as a whole, are counting on us. What are we waiting for?

Note

1   Citizen Policies Institute, Washington D.C., USA.

References

Alinsky, S. 1972. *Rules for radicals* (New York, Vintage Books).
Freire, P. 1993. *Pedagogy of the oppressed* (New York, Continuum).
van Parijs, P. 2001. *What's wrong with a free lunch?* (Boston, Beacon Press).

Recommended

Moynihan, D. P. 1973. *The politics of a guaranteed income* (New York, Random House).
Spinosa, C., Flores, F. and Dreyfus, H. L. 1997. *Disclosing new worlds* (Cambridge, MIT Press).

15

A LEGITIMATE GUARANTEED MINIMUM INCOME?

Stefan Liebig and Steffen Mau[1]

1. Introduction

For a number of years academics and some political circles have been discussing the concept of the so-called guaranteed minimum income or basic income (e.g. Atkinson, 1996; Offe, 1995; Goodin, 1995; van Parijs, 1992, 1995). The basic ambition of this policy proposal is to depart from wage-centred, stigmatizing and selective forms of welfare provision and to arrive at an unconditional and universal mode of entitlement. Starting from the premise that the labour market and existing welfare systems cannot generate sufficient income security it has been suggested that a decoupling of basic income security and the beneficiaries' relation to the labour market is a promising alternative to the current arrangements (Standing, 1992; Vobruba, 1986). To those proposing the introduction of a basic minimum income it seems to be advantageous in many respects: it helps to tackle basic needs, assures the dignity of the poor, responds to the challenges of globalization and market liberalization, fills the welfare gaps left by insurance schemes and overcomes the flaws of the conventional organization of state welfare (Blasche, 1998, p. 152).

The animating and unifying idea of setting up a basic minimum income programme with strong elements of universalism and citizenship rights fleshes out some of the built-in principles of social assistance and cures some of its ills. It also gives priority to the prevention of poverty and the creation of a minimum income floor. However, it breaks with a particular notion of conditionality that demands that people reciprocate benefits by demonstrating their willingness to work. It is also to be distinguished from performance-based insurance entitlements since it is not tied to previous contributions and fosters a de-commodification of the status of individuals *vis-à-vis* the market at the minimum income level. Citizenship-based entitlements such as a basic income place emphasis on the coverage of 'basic needs' rather than on the protection of relative status (Offe, 1994). Ideally, such an arrangement should entitle people to an income as of right, independent of their household arrangements, their labour-force participation and any forms of bureaucratic monitoring and disciplinary controls.

There are numerous versions of the basic income proposal. The version most elaborated upon was put forward by Philippe van Parijs (1992), who suggested that a guaranteed minimum income should be paid unconditionally to all on an individual basis, without means-test or work requirements. Since it is paid to all citizens irrespective of their income resources, not only does it deal with socio-economic needs but also moreover it conveys an entitlement to a fair share in the national wealth. An affluent society owes its members a stake in the social surplus, which should be equally distributed amongst them. In van Parijs' vision, therefore, the basic income is not merely assigned to cover basic needs. The idea is that the basic income is granted as an unconditional entitlement to all, and that income from other resources will come on top of this. Other concepts rest on the notion of minimal conditionality, where a basic income is paid to all those with insufficient resources. Here, people would have to provide evidence that they lack resources, but household arrangements and work orientation would not be taken into account. Such a basic income would 'strive to secure people's autonomy by ensuring that people receive an income adequate to their needs, on terms which impinge minimally on their freedom of action' (Goodin, 2001, p. 17). This strategy has been coined as 'non-productivist' (Offe, 1994) or 'post-productivist' policy design (Goodin, 2001).

Four basic arguments in favour of a guaranteed social minimum can be identified. First, it is viewed as an efficient political device to eliminate income poverty and to give all citizens access to a decent standard of living (Blasche, 1998, p.144). According to its political protagonists, the level should be well above the level of social assistance and enable people to participate in the social and material welfare of society. A second argument in support of a guaranteed minimum income underlines its universalist aspect. From this perspective, the minimum income proposal fully develops the notion of social rights. Such provision comes close to the type of welfare arrangements envisaged by Titmuss:

> There should be no sense of inferiority, pauperism, shame or stigma in the use of publicly provided service: no attribution that one was being or becoming a 'public burden'. Hence the emphasis on social rights of all citizens to use or not to use as responsible people the services made available by the community (Titmuss, 1968, p. 129).

Third, the guaranteed minimum income can be regarded as a vehicle for the reduction of income inequality since it lifts up the income position of those on the bottom. The fourth argument suggests that the minimum income is a 'social dividend' or a collective surplus-sharing system that gives every citizen an individual stake in the national wealth. It is, in its deepest sense, a 'participation income' (Atkinson, 1996), providing everybody with a basic stake in the societal resources.

The more practical political concepts of the guaranteed minimum income do not fully match the philosophical accounts. Within the German context we find a variety of proposals ranging from a tax-financed basic pension (Meinhard Miegel and Kurt Biedenkopf), negative income tax (*Kronberger Kreis*), and a need-oriented minimum-security scheme (Social Democratic Party), to an unconditional basic income scheme (Green Party) and an existence income (*Bundesarbeitsgemeinschaft der Sozialhilfeinitiativen*). In some concepts the social minimum is assigned to supplement the contributory social insurance schemes and to replace only some tax-financed transfers (e.g. housing allowances, social assistance). More far-reaching, and for our paper more relevant, are the concepts that aim at replacing all social transfers, including insurance benefits, with a guaranteed minimum income. The basic aim is to provide a reliable, universal and non-stigmatizing safety net for those with insufficient resources. Such an equal income would represent a baseline sufficient to satisfy fundamental needs while facilitating some form of equal opportunity. There are hardly any political actors that would go as far as to call for a basic income that would be given to all irrespective of need, as proposed by van Parijs. Thus, the baseline condition the political actors stick to is that income from other resources should be taken into account. In some proposals, the basic income idea has been related to the idea of a negative income tax, where the State subsidizes incomes below a defined level and levies taxes on those above it (Scharpf, 1994). For those without an income the state grants a full basic income. With rising incomes the state subsidy diminishes and at a certain point the negative income tax becomes positive, that is, it becomes normal income tax. This system has the virtue of being in accord with labour market incentive structures.

The basic income concept is not uncontested. Some opponents doubt whether such a programme can be financed by the State budget,[2] while others question whether it is in accord with accepted justice principles. They cast doubt on whether the guarantistic and universalistic ethic of the guaranteed basic income can find social and political approval. It is seen as one of the fundamental requirements of implementation that the general public understands and approves the norms of justice incorporated in the guaranteed basic income scheme, without which it would risk lacking social and political legitimacy. Behind this consideration stands the fact that the guaranteed income proposal breaks with some of the fundamental principles of social security provision. This is especially salient in the German case, which is studied in this paper. The German Bismarckian system depends heavily on social insurance schemes with contributory financing and earnings-related benefits. Since welfare entitlements are closely tied to the contributory record and the employment position of claimants, the benefits are perceived as 'just' compensations for contributions made. Due to this institutional design most of the redistributions are horizontal redistributions that assist the individual to reallocate resources over his or her lifetime, to save when they are earning a market income and to claim social benefits when there is a loss of income, such as in periods of unemployment or when reaching retirement age. This system is morally undemanding since it gives participants the impression that interpersonal redistribution is prevented and that people get what they have paid for (Offe, 1990, p.4). The notion of 'deserved benefits' in such a system rests on norms of work and employment, where those who contribute accumulate entitlements while those less attached to the sphere of paid labour are less protected. That the norms of the 'work society' guide and govern the understanding of social entitlements was also vividly apparent during the 'shirker' debate in 2001 (Mau, 2001). However, as with most welfare states the German system can be characterized as a two-tier system with higher-level social security provided by social insurance existing alongside a lower-level social assistance scheme. Although this last-resort safety net provides benefits for those with insufficient income, it does not fully resemble the guaranteed minimum income proposal. The main difference is that it still requires people to make attempts to re-enter work, takes into account other income sources and savings within the household, and is paid to the family unit rather than to the individual. Hence, it is a conditional welfare provision in reserve rather than a universal grant.

2. The Guaranteed Minimum Income and Justice Attitudes

As the guaranteed minimum income proposal demands a departure from the well-entrenched principles of benefit entitlement, it makes sense to ask whether such a proposal can find social acceptance. Are the normative principles compelling enough to gain political support? Do the normative principles underlying the guaranteed minimum income correspond with people's sense of justice? On a theoretical level, some have argued that since everybody can appreciate the potential benefit of such a minimum income it would also be in accord with the rational interests of a large proportion of the electorate (Offe et al., 1996, p.214). The basic income is also supposed to respond to people's wish that the state guarantee a bottom line under which nobody should be allowed to fall (Pioch, 1996). Social justice research is highly supportive of the fact that arrangements that place priority on the basic security objective can find social recognition. It has been demonstrated that citizens exhibit a deep aversion to allowing people to fall below the poverty line (Alves and Rossi, 1978). Frohlich and Oppenheimer's experimental study (1992, p.59) confirms that a system with a guaranteed minimum income possesses a high moral attraction. They report:

> Groups generally choose a floor constraint. The groups wanted an income floor guaranteed to the worst-off individual. The floor was to act as a safety net for all individuals. But after this constraint was set, they wished to preserve incentives so as to maximize production and hence average income. Only occasionally was there a sustained interest in the imposition of a ceiling of incomes (a range constraint).

However, if one consults the empirical literature concerning the social acceptance of the welfare state the picture is less clear. Most of the research focuses on general support for the welfare state rather than on concrete principles and entitlement modes (e.g. Roller, 1992). It has been established that the German welfare state rests on a broad consensus that the State should be responsible for the policy areas of health, poverty, unemployment and pensions, and that nobody should suffer social hardship (see Andreß et al., 2000, p. 132; Mau, 1997). In addition, Lipsmeier (1999) has found that there is also a consensus with regard to a social minimum. People agree upon the question as to what should be supplied in order to enable people to live a decent life. However, these findings are somewhat inconsistent. While some studies report that in the mid-1990s over 80 per cent of the German population was in favour of low-income social support schemes such as housing allowance and social assistance (Lipsmeier, 1999), others report that a social minimum income was welcomed by only half of West Germans and 87 per cent of East Germans (Andreß et al., 2000, p. 118). At the same time, it can be shown that people support the idea that welfare benefits should be conditional upon an individual's readiness to move off benefits and gain market income (Lippl, 2001, p.11). This picture confirms the findings of social justice research, namely that people show a high commitment to the egalitarian notion of a minimum income while, at the same time, stick to the idea that goods should be allocated according to individual achievements and contributions (Wegener and Liebig, 2000).

However, this body of data and studies does not come to terms with the central question of this paper: how do people evaluate the guaranteed minimum income from a normative point of view? The problem with the existing studies is that they are too general and not complex enough to provide us with a full answer. Item-based research focuses on the social acceptance of single normative principles, while we get little information on how much income should be provided and under which conditions. Yet, this concrete information is necessary in order to grasp the chances for the minimum income proposal. People tend to combine and weigh up different principles when making justice judgements within specific situations (Leventhal, 1980). They are not prone to adhere to one single principle; rather, justice judgments blend different principles and concerns. Therefore, one needs to distinguish between order-related justice judgments and result-related judgments, with the former representing a type of evaluation that focuses on principles while the latter focuses on the actual outcome of an allocation rule (Wegener, 1999; Liebig, 1997; Liebig and Verwiebe, 2000). The plus side of asking people to evaluate the outcome of a distribution rule rather than the principle itself is that they can combine and mix different justice principles. Social justice research also stresses that people need sufficient information in order to make an unambiguous justice judgment (Boudon, 2001). Where this information is withheld, their judgments tend to be inconsistent and ramshackle. We can infer from this brief account that the question of how people evaluate the guaranteed minimum income from a normative point of view requires more sophisticated instruments. The simple question of whether people agree that the State should supply a basic income does not seem to be satisfactory, and research therefore runs the risk of dealing with rather dubious results. Hence, we are in need of an instrument that is able to record people's attitudes towards a social minimum in a more refined manner, and which gives respondents more specific information regarding the object of evaluation.

3. The Evaluation of the Guaranteed Minimum Income

The instrument we are using as an alternative approach to the research question is the factorial survey design.[3] It fulfils the requirement of enabling us to depart from item-based research and to reveal important qualifications and determinants of people's attitudes towards the minimum income. The factorial survey design asks the respondents to evaluate vignettes with descriptions of persons – age, employment status, sex etc. – with regard to a specific dimension. The vignette design has the major advantage that it does not ask for the degree of agreement or disagreement with an abstract principle, but translates issues of the allocation of goods into concrete situations. In many instances, people's attitudes are more informed and knowledgeable in a concrete situation where they have to judge how much injustice exists under the given circumstances. Vignettes make it possible to vary the attributes of persons and situations systematically so that one can specify how much weight a specific personal attribute holds in determining the justice evaluation. The procedure applied in our study permits us to establish the level of a just minimum income and the importance of different personal attributes in the determination of a just minimum income.

3.1 Data

The data basis of this study consists of a questionnaire that was posed to 121 employed persons in Germany. The sample universe consisted entirely of German-speaking employees eligible to vote in national elections living in private households. From this a stratified random sample was drawn up within the framework of the ADM (*Arbeitskreis Deutscher Marktforschungsinstitute*) master-sample.[4] Since the sample is rather small no conclusions can be made for the population. The computer-supported interviews were carried out between July 19 and August 2, 2000. Two instruments were used: a selection of 24 vignettes and a standardized questionnaire comprising a number of attitude questions and socio-demographic information. The average duration of the interview was 33 minutes of which the vignette question lasted 22 minutes. The description of the sample can be seen in Table 15.1.

Table 15.1 Description of the sample (N = 121)

	%
Age	
Mean	40.60
Standard deviation	9.97
Minimum	18.00
Maximum	65
Gender (%)	
Woman	37.27
Man	62.73
Education (%)	
School not completed	2.51
9 years	42.98
10 years	34.70
12 or 13 years	19.84
Occupational position (%)	
Self-employed	12.40
Civil servant	11.57
Clerk (non-manual occupations)	38.84
(Un-)skilled worker (manual occupations)	37.19

3.2 The Factorial Survey Design: Structure of the Vignettes

In the first part of the interview the respondents were asked to evaluate a given income transfer in terms of being just or unjust. Every vignette consisted of two parts: the description of the person receiving the minimum income and the amount of money transferred. For the description of the persons we used criteria that related to need and to achievement principles (Figure 15.1). For example, the number of children relates to the need criteria whereas the occupation can be interpreted as indicating a person's productive contribution. In order to capture people's attitudes towards the issues of work-orientation we distinguished between voluntary and involuntary unemployment. For income we have defined six classes from 0 up to 1,600 DEM. The second part of the vignette was the income subsidy, which ranged from 0 up to 3,000 DEM.

Figure 15.1 Vignettes

---

1. Introduction

In Germany we have a number of different types of social welfare payments which provide those who are needy with a decent standard of living e.g. unemployment payments, retirement pension, benefit payment, housing subsidies etc. Recently, politicians have been discussing different ways of simplifying the whole German system of social welfare transfers. One suggestion made within these debates was to replace the different types of payments with a general income subsidy. All citizens who are needy would get a fixed amount of money from the State and all other types of social welfare payments would be abolished. Those citizens who have a job but whose income is very low also get an income subsidy from the State. With this new regulation everybody in Germany would have a guaranteed minimum income.

The question now is, what should be the amount on income subsidy provided by the State and should these payments differ according to the individual situation of the person subsidized? In the following we are going to present you with a number of examples of fictitious persons who may get a State-financed income subsidy. We want to know if, in your opinion, the amount of income subsidy is just and fair or if you think the income subsidy is unjust. The only thing we are interested in is your personal opinion and your views on how just or unjust the particular income subsidies in the presented examples are.

---

2. Dimensions of vignettes
Dimensions
Values

Gender
Man, woman

Age
25, 40, 55

Marital status
single

Children
No children, 1 child, 4 children

Occupational position
Worker, self-employed

Employment status
Voluntarily unemployed, involuntarily unemployed, part-time job,
full-time job

Income before taxes
0 (for unemployed); 400; 700; 1,000; 1,300; 1,600

Income subsidy
0; 300; 800; 1,500; 3,000

3. Example of a vignette

A 25-year-old man,
With 4 children,
Was self-employed and had to close his business.
He has no income.

The vignette presented is a selection from the vignette universe, i.e. all possible combinations. At first, the universe of all eight dimensions was generated, the result being 4,320 different vignettes. From this sample 48 vignettes were drawn within which one part of the sample described an unemployed person and the other part an employed person. The selection was carried out in such a way as to vary all dimensions efficiently and to guarantee the orthogonality of the dimensions. Since 48 vignettes were regarded as too numerous we divided the vignette sample into two 24-vignette sub-samples by random distribution. The 121 respondents were also divided into two groups and confronted with either the first or the second vignette set. That meant that every respondent had to judge the income subsidy for 12 unemployed and 12 employed fictitious persons.[5]

3.3 Data Generation: Justice Evaluations

People were asked to evaluate the income supplement in terms of it being just or unjust. If the income supplement was perceived as unjust – either too high or too low – people were asked to express the extent of injustice using numbers chosen by them. The justice evaluations were not made on a classical scale – e.g. a Likert scale – but using a self-rated scale in which people could choose their own numbers in order to express the intensity of the feeling of injustice. This approach allows people to make a fine-tuned judgment rather than having to rely on a given scale. The central problem with using such an open measure is that people must learn how to use it and make adjustments to the scale (Wegener, 1980). Following the handling of the magnitude measure it became necessary to anchor the scale by fixing a reference point. This was carried out in three steps (Figure 15.2): at first respondents had to indicate the amount of money in DEM that would be necessary to afford the most basic things in life (clothing, housing, food). In a second step respondents had to practice the use of quantities. Therefore, they were asked to mark a starting number on a vertical line. Subsequently, the interviewer asked the

Figure 15.2 Evaluation task

1. Minimal income
'How much money does a single person need per month to afford reasonable accommodation, enough food and basic clothing? Please tell me the amount of DEM required.'

2. Building an individual scale for the vignette evaluation
A vertical arrow describes the degree of injustice a person feels. The interviewer points at one point on the arrow and asks what number the respondent would use to descibe this degree of injustice. The interviewer then asks for a number the respondent would choose to express a degree of injustice that is twice as high. Subsequently, the same procedure is repeated for half the initial degree of injustice.

Strong injustice

0 just

3. Building a reference point for evaluating the 24 vignettes

Evaluating the intensity of injustice for a reference case using the individual scale.

Reference:

A 40-year-old man, with no children, was employed as a worker and was laid off by his employer.
He has no monthly income.
He is paid a monthly income subsidy by the State of DEM (minimal income mentioned in step 1 minus 20%) and no other social welfare payments.

'Do you think the income subsidy which replaces all other kinds of social welfare payments is just, or do you think the income subsidy is unjustly too high or too low?'

{If unjust}:

'What is the extent of the injustice of this income subsidy? Please describe to me how great the degree of injustice is using those numbers, which best express your feeling of injustice. You can use and number. Some people take 10, others 50 or some people 100. The most important thing when using these numbers is that the particular number best expresses your feelings of injustice regarding the income subsidy for this 45-year-old man. What number would that be?'

4. Evaluating the 24 vignettes

{Description of a fictitious person (see Figure 1)}
'Do you think the income subsidy for the person described is just or unjust?'
{If unjust}: 'How would you express the intensity of injustice, using any number, if the injustice of the unemployed 45-year-old man in our example from the beginning was {XX}?'

respondents to indicate a number that expressed an injustice twice as great. In a third step, respondents were asked to evaluate a vignette, which was not part of the successive vignette module. In order for it to be recognized as 'weak injustice', the amount of State subsidy had to be 20 per cent lower than the value that people had given in the first step.[6]

The main part of the investigation comprised the 24 vignettes, which were presented to the respondents on a computer screen. In each case they were asked to indicate whether the given income supplement was just or unjust and, if the second case applied, whether it was too high or too low. Subsequently, they were asked to express the extent of the injustice with reference to the initial judgment (see Figure 15.2). The data were entered directly into the computer. If people stated that the State subsidy was just, it was coded as 0. Negative numbers reflect the feeling of injustice with regard to benefits being too small, whereas a positive number expresses the extent of injustice with regard to benefits being too high.

3.4 Data Processing: The Just Income Subsidy

Having acquired justice evaluations from our respondents we need to transform the data in order to obtain the amount of income subsidy regarded as just. This is possible by applying Guillermina Jasso's theory of justice (Jasso, 1978, 1990, 1998). According to this model empirical justice evaluations (J) can be reconstructed as the product of an individual expression coefficient (θ) and the logarithm of the ratio of the actual reward (A) and the just reward (C) a person should get. In our case the 'actual reward' (A) is the income subsidy presented in the vignettes and the 'just reward' (C) is the just income subsidy each respondent has in mind when judging the fictitious person presented in the vignettes (Equation 1).

$$\mathcal{J}_{ij} = \theta_i \ln\left(\frac{A_j}{C_{ij}}\right) \tag{1}$$

C = just income subsidy
A = presented income subsidy
$\mathcal{J}$ = justice evaluation
θ = individual expression coefficient
i = respondent
j = person described in a vignette

Two terms in equation 1 are known: the respondents' justice evaluation ($\mathcal{J}$) and the income subsidies presented in the 24 vignettes (A). The other two terms are unknown (θ and C). As we are interested in the amount of the just income subsidy we have to solve equation 1 for C (Equation 2):

$$C_{ij} = A_j \cdot \exp\left(\frac{J_{ij}}{\theta_i}\right)$$
(2)

C = just income subsidy
A = presented income subsidy
J = justice evaluation
θ = individual expression coefficient
i = respondent
j = person described in a vignette (recipient)

To obtain a measure for the second unknown term in this equation we have to estimate for each person his or her expressiveness coefficient. This can be done by running separate bivariate linear regressions for each respondent. The 24 justice evaluations (J) of each respondent are the dependent variables and the presented income subsidies (A) are the independent variables in the model. With a sample of 121 respondents we have to run 121 regression analyses. The estimated slope for each regression can be interpreted as the expressiveness of each respondent. In other words is the scaling coefficient, which reflects the use of the scale and the numbers when making the 24 justice judgments. Knowing for each respondent we have enough information to calculate the exact amount of the just income subsidy our respondents have in mind. We insert the presented income subsidy (A), the respondent's justice evaluation (J) and the estimated expressiveness coefficient (θ) into Equation 2 and calculate the just income subsidy (C) for each vignette.

Using descriptive statistics we may draw our first conclusions with regard to the variation of the just income subsidy. If our respondents favour a basic income paid equally to everyone we should not observe any variation over the presented vignettes. For each fictitious person described in the vignettes the same amount of income subsidy would be seen as just. In this case our respondents would not, for example, differentiate between the person who was made unemployed involuntarily and one who is unemployed by choice, or between those who are workers and those who are self-employed. Each person should then receive the same amount of income subsidy. To get an idea of whether or not our respondents prefer a basic income differentiated according to certain traits of the recipient, we can calculate the impact of the vignette dimensions on the just income subsidy. For this we ask, for example, how much the just basic income should be raised if the recipient has four children. To answer this type of question we estimate a regression model with the just income subsidies as the dependent variables and the dimensions of the vignettes as the independent variables. For each of the traits used in our vignettes we can then tell if it is relevant in defining a just income subsidy and how, if a person possesses this trait, the just income subsidy should be increased or decreased (Equation 3).

$$C_{ij} = a_j + \sum_{k=1}^{n} b_{k_i} X_{k_j} + \varepsilon_i \tag{3}$$

C = just income subsidy
i = respondent
j = recipient
b_{ki} = weighting by respondent
X_{kj} = recipient's traits: X_{1j} gender; X_{2j} age; X_{3j} number
of children; X_{4j} occupation; X_{5j} employment
status; X_{6j} income before taxes.

3.5 Results

Of the 121 respondents 102 made complete and meaningful statements for all 24 vignettes. We assumed that the evaluation of the single vignettes was dependent on the general attitudes towards welfare state activities. Therefore, we used a filter question where people could express their support for, or rejection of, a State-financed minimum income. In response to the question: 'Do you think that the State should grant every citizen a minimum standard of living?' 77 per cent answered 'agree' or 'agree fully' while 22.3 per cent were against or indifferent. Comparing the two groups shows that the justice judgments (J) of those against or indifferent are less determined by the traits of the single vignettes. By calculating a linear regression with the justice judgments (J) as dependent variables and the vignette traits as independent variables (Equation 3) the explained variance (R-square) is much lower than for the comparison group.

The more interesting results are reported in Table 15.2. The left side displays the results for those who are in favour of a State-financed social minimum. The right column reports the results for the remainder who did not supported State responsibility. The table shows the results of linear regression models. Departing from common procedures, the units of analysis are not the respondents but the 24 judgments of the vignettes. Accordingly, the sample of analysis consists of 24 judgments multiplied by 76 cases (those agreeing with the basic income scheme) or 24 cases (those who are indifferent or against). A dependent variable serves the just income subsidy, which was calculated for each judgment separately according to Equation (2). The independent variables are the traits of the vignette: sex, age, number of children, occupation and employment status and gross income. The reported coefficients for the independent variables can be interpreted as DEM sums.[7]

Table 15.2 Income subsidy and traits of the vignettes for respondents favouring or opposing a State-financed basic income (linear regression models)

	Just income subsidy			
	Only respondents favouring a State-financed basic income		Only respondents opposing a State-financed basic income	
	Amount of DEM (coefficients)	t-value	Amount of DEM (coefficients)	t-value
Gender (women)	n.s.	0.019	n.s.	1.134
Age (reference category: 25 years)				
40 years	201.24	2.361*	n.s.	1.752
55 years	468.56	4.302***	383.96	2.239*
Number of children (reference category: no children)				
1 child	1086.97	12.168***	968.15	5.559***
4 children	1892.15	16.946***	1633.95	10.147***
Self-employed (reference category: worker)	−219.97	−3.640***	n.s.	−1.022
Part-time (reference category: full-time)	−294.70	−2.080*	n.s.	0.547
Unemployed	731.96	2.540*	1208.49	3.175**
Voluntarily unemployed	−1034.28	−7.359***	−687.02	−2.887**
Income before taxes	−.732	−3.545**	n.s.	−0.599
Constant	1630.07	6.150***	n.s.	2.024
R^2	.263		.210	
Evaluations / Respondents	1824/76		624/26	

Note: Unstandardized regression coefficients; t-value based on robust standard errors to correct clustering for respondents (Huber regression). * pt < 0.05; ** pt < 0.01; *** pt < 0.001.

For those who are in favour of a State-guaranteed social minimum income all independent variables, apart from the gender variable, have a significant impact.[8] Higher 'just' income supplements are assigned to those who are older and have a greater number of children. A reduced level of transfers should be given to income earners, to people who have left paid work voluntarily and to those who are self-employed. In contrast to the very general statement that the State should supply a social minimum income, people tend to qualify their judgment on the basis of further information about 'who is the recipient', 'what are his or her circumstances' and 'is he or she responsible for his or her situation'. When looking at the level of provision one sees that, for most cases, it is significantly above the social assistance level.[9] This hints at the fact that people, when assigning a fair transfer income, expect the State to provide more than a residual benefit that protects from deep poverty, indeed, one on a level that enables people to live a decent life and to participate fully in the social and cultural life of society. For the subgroup, which did not agree with the State-provided minimum income, there are only a few significant independent variables. Not even the constant, which can be interpreted as the basic income, shows an effect. Only the dummy variables of number of children and unemployment (voluntary unemployment), as well as the second age variable (55 years old) are significant. Larger families, involuntary unemployment and higher age of the claimant lead people to believe that a higher level of benefits is just. All the other traits have no significant effect.

In Table 15.3 the judgments of those favouring a basic income have been divided into those vignettes where the justice judgments were made for people

Table 15.3 Regression results for employed and unemployed (only respondents favouring a State-financed basic income, linear regression model)

| | Just income subsidy | | | |
| | Unemployed | | Employed | |
	Amount of DEM (coefficients)	t-value	Amount of DEM (coefficients)	t-value
Gender (women)	n.s.	0.019	n.s.	0.019
Age (reference category: 25 years)				
40 years	201.24	2.361*	201.24	2.361*
55 years	468.56	4.302***	468.56	4.302***
Number of children (reference category: no children)				
1 child	1086.97	12.168***	1086.97	12.168***
4 children	1892.15	16.946***	1892.15	16.946***
Self-employed (reference category: worker)	−219.97	−3.640***	−219.97	−3.640***
Part-time (reference category: full-time)			−294.70	−2.080*
Unemployed	731.96	2.540*		
Voluntarily unemployed	−1034.28	−7.359***		
Income before taxes			−.732	−3.545**
Constant	1630.07	6.150***	1630.07	6.150***
R^2		.263		
Judgments / Respondents		1824/76		

Note: Unstandardized regression coefficients; t-value based on robust standard errors to correct clustering for respondents (Huber-regression). * $p_t < 0.05$; ** $p_t < 001$; *** $p_t < 0.001$.

currently employed (column 2) and those who are unemployed (column 1). The results show that a single unemployed person who is childless, 25 years old and who had previously been a worker should receive 2,362.03 DEM (constant plus coefficient). If a person has quit a job voluntarily, the State transfer should be reduced by 1,034.28 DEM. If the person was self-employed the constant was reduced by 219.97 DEM. Again higher age and children are reasons to raise the just State subsidy. For employees with low incomes the same type of calculation can be carried out focusing on the question of how the market income should determine the level of transfer a person is entitled to. What is decisive here is that the base benefit sum of 1,630 DEM decreases with a growth in income.

This result suggests that some of the features of the negative income tax (Scharpf, 1994, 1995) match the moral intuitions of our respondents. We can see that there is a lower threshold where the State should take action and that market income should be taken into account only proportionally. However, due to methodological limitations a degree of degression has not been estimated. We can calculate that a full-time employed worker, 25 years old and without children, should not receive state subsidies any more if his income is above the threshold of 2,226 DEM. Or *vice versa*: those who share these attributes and earn less should be entitled to state support. What is striking is that part-time workers and the self-employed should receive less.

4. Discussion of the Empirical Findings

The study aims to provide a more precise description of the attitudes towards a guaranteed social minimum and to reveal the determining principles of these attitudes by using the factorial survey design method. This has enabled us to move beyond the rather general statement that the State should provide a minimum income and investigate how people judge guaranteed income schemes in more detail. The vignette design allows us to construct examples that are closer to everyday experience than normal item-scales. For many people it is easier to make a justice judgment about the grant of resources than it is to evaluate abstract allocation rules (Liebig and Jäckle, 2001). The factorial survey design also provides a closer description of the allocative scenario and the relevant features. However, since it is not possible to confront the respondents with an unlimited number of vignettes, only a few dimensions could be covered. We believe that the 24 vignettes used in our study are within the limit of what is possible methodologically. Concerning the results, we could not only show the amount of minimum income regarded by a large majority as just, but we could also reconstruct the justice principles underlying people's reasoning.

Thus, our findings move beyond the rather general finding that the majority of people approve of State responsibility for a social minimum and asks what are the criteria and conditions that people use for determining a just level of income transfers. We have seen that only a minority of 22.3 per cent of the sample of German employees is indifferent or against a social minimum. For them, the criteria used to describe the vignettes (the welfare recipient) only have a significant impact on the just minimum income in a few cases. However, what is more telling are the results for the large majority that welcome the State taking action to guarantee a minimum standard of living. On the one hand, they argue for the right to a guaranteed minimum income; on the other hand, they regard different levels as just depending on social needs and the relation of the welfare beneficiary to the employment sphere. That the numbers of children as well as age are significant signals shows that people take seniority principles and arising needs into consideration.

We were able to establish that an unconditional granting of a uniform minimum income independent of people's productive contributions runs against the moral intuitions of our respondents. Moreover, voluntary unemployment and part-time work leads people to 'lower' the level of benefits regarded as just. The response patterns suggest that access to a guaranteed minimum income should not undermine the work incentive and that whether a beneficiary demonstrates his or her willingness to work is seen as a necessary precondition for a full social minimum income. Those who are suspected of drawing on social benefits without making efforts to be self-sustaining would face substantial deductions if our respondents were to determine the fair level of benefits. Obviously, those who are regarded as being responsible for their own fate, as in the case of the voluntary unemployed, are treated as less deserving. People seem to be suspicious of the idea of non-conditionality and it may be that the adjusted level of benefits serves as a precautionary measure intended to foster the work-orientation of the benefit recipients. We might conclude that they are not convinced that there is a 'relative preferability of employment' (Offe, 1994, p. 104) if everybody is able to call on the same level of support irrespective of willingness to work.

Our findings provide support for some of the arguments doubting the social acceptance of a substantial and unconditional basic income. Stuart White (1997), for example, has emphasized that a universal basic income paid irrespective of contributory activity undermines the reciprocity norm since it invites the exploitation of working and tax-paying citizens by those who choose to live on the dole. The claim to a share in societal wealth is perceived as unfair if citizens are not willing to cooperate socially and make some kind of effort. Conditionality, therefore, affirms the link between income entitlement and productive contributions and thereby safeguards the reciprocity requirements. From this perspective, 'doing one's bit' in return remains the crucial and decisive justification for granting welfare entitlements and the motivation of public support. The major outcome of our result is that the fundamental principle of equal resources is not fully compatible with the sense of justice of our respondents and that they make use of additional criteria in determining how much should be given. A uniform and fully unconditional welfare entitlement is not endorsed. Also, those who support the idea of a basic income make distinctions depending on which categories a person belongs to and whether he or she meets certain conditions. However, empirical research can neither verify nor falsify normative theories. The ambition of our study was rather to scrutinize people's 'sense of justice' when judging the minimum income scheme. The social acceptance of the justice norms incorporated into the guaranteed minimum income proposal can be seen as one important determinant that engenders its political legitimacy. The more profound the social consensus about such reform proposals, the more likely it is that political actors will put it on the political agenda. However, it must be conceded that most social policy innovations have been introduced as contested concepts. The existing justice attitudes are only one factor that could advance or impede new reforms.

Notes

1   Humboldt University of Berlin, Germany.
2   Countering the cost argument, protagonists of the basic income proposal highlight the cost-saving measures related to its introduction. Other welfare expenses in the areas of unemployment provision, housing allowance and social assistance would decrease significantly once the minimum income scheme was introduced (see Meinhard, 1996). A sceptical evaluation of the cost factor has been put forward by Hauser (1996) and Becker (1998), though their analyses assume that social insurance schemes are fully retained.
3   For a detailed description of this instrument see Alves (1982); Alves and Rossi (1978); Jasso (1978, 1990, 1998); Jasso and Wegener (1997, 2001); Rossi (1979); Rossi and Anderson (1982); Hox et al. (1991).
4   Three-level selection process with 40 sample points, random-route procedure and choice of the person with the next birthday. The 40 interviewers were given instructions via a written document. The fieldwork was carried out by a commercial institute.
5   In order to avoid a lack of clarity the family status was kept constant. Otherwise people would also have regarded the possible income of a partner.
6   If people regarded this reduced income as just, the interviewer continued lowering the income subsidy in 10% steps until people stated that it was unjust.
7   The 1,824 or 624 cases of these regression models are not completely independent because each person had to make 24 judgments. Therefore, the residuals are not statistically independent. Under these conditions, the estimated standard error of the coefficients can be distorted. Thus, we calculated a Huber regression that accounts for possible clusters of the judgments and estimates robust standard errors.

8   The units of analysis are the vignettes and not persons. Hence, significance on a 5 per cent level means that we would find the same effect if we carried out our analysis not only with the sample but also with the whole vignette universe.
9   However, a direct comparison is not possible since the vignettes vary other attributes than those relevant to the social assistance level (e.g. age of the children, housing and heating costs).

References

Alves, W.M. 1982. 'Modelling distributive justice judgments', in P.H. Rossi and S.L. Nock (eds.), *Measuring social judgments: The factorial survey approach* (Beverly Hills, Sage), pp. 205–234.

_____ and Rossi, P.H. 1978. 'Who should get what? Fairness judgments of the distribution of earnings', *American Journal of Sociology*, 81, pp. 324–342 .

Andreß, H.-J., Heien, T. and Hofäcker, D. 2000. *Einstellungen zum bundesdeutschen Wohlfahrtsstaat*. Bielefeld: Abschlußbericht des Projektes 'Wohlfahrtsstaatliche Maßnahmen und Einstellungen der Bürger', Universität Bielefeld.

Atkinson, A.B. 1996. 'The case for a participation income', *Political Quarterly*, 67, pp. 67–70.

Becker, I. 1998. 'Vergleich und Bewertung alternativer Grundsicherungskonzepte', in *Wirthschaft- und Sozialwissenschaftliches Institut (WSI) Mitteilungen*, 11, pp. 747–757.

Blasche, S. 1998. 'Gerechtigkeit, Mindestsicherung und Eigenverantwortung', in S. Blasche and D. Döring (eds.), *Sozialpolitik und Gerechtigkeit* (Frankfurt and New York, Campus), pp. 117–171.

Boudon, R. 2001. *The origin of values* (New Brunswick, New Jersey, Transaction Publishers).

Frohlich, N. and Oppenheimer, J. A. 1992. *Choosing justice* (Berkeley, University of California Press).

Goodin, R.E. 1995. *Utilitarianism as a public philosophy* (Cambridge, Cambridge University Press).

_____ 2001. 'Work and welfare: Towards a post-productivist welfare regime', *British Journal of Political Science*, 31, pp. 13–39.

Hauser, R. 1996. *Ziele und Möglichkeiten einer Sozialen Grundsicherung*, (Baden-Baden, Nomos Verlagsgesellschaft).

Hox, J.J., Kreft, I. and Hermkens, P. 1991. 'The analysis of factorial surveys', *Sociological Methods and Research*, 19, pp. 493–510.

Jasso, G. 1978. 'On the justice of earnings: A new specification of the justice evaluation function', *American Journal of Sociology*, 83, pp. 1398–1419.

_____ 1990. 'Methods for the theoretical and empirical analysis of comparison processes', in C.C. Clogg (ed.), *Sociological methodology 1990* (Washington, D.C., American Sociological Association), pp. 369–419.

_____ 1998. 'Exploring the justice of punishments: Framing, expressiveness, and the just prison sentence', *Social Justice Research*, 11, pp. 397–422.

Jasso, G. and Wegener, B. 1997. 'Methods for empirical justice analysis: Part I. Framework, models, and quantities', in *Social Justice Research*, 10, pp. 393–430.

_____ 2001. 'Methods for empirical justice analysis: Part 2. Basic research designs and analytic procedures', Unpublished Manuscript, (Berlin, Humboldt University).

_____ and Rossi, P.H. 1977. 'Distributive justice and earned income', *American Sociological Review*, 42, pp. 639–651.

Leventhal, G.S. 1980. 'What should be done with equity theory? New approaches to the study of fairness in social relationship', in K.J. Gergen, M.S. Greenberg and R.H.Willis (eds.), *Social exchange. Advances in theory and research* (New York, Plenum Press), pp. 27–55.

Liebig, S. 1997. *Soziale Gerechtigkeitsforschung und Gerechtigkeit in Unternehmen*, (Mering, Hampp)

_____ and Jäckle, N. 2001. 'Die Komplexität von Gerechtigkeitsurteilen und die Folgen für die Einstellungsmessung', Unpublished manuscript (Berlin Humboldt University).

_____ and Verwiebe, R. 2000. 'Ostdeutsche Einstellungen zur sozialen Ungleichheit: Plädoyer für eine doppelte Vergleichsperspektive', in *Zeitschrift für Soziologie*, 29, pp. 3–26.

Lippl, B. 2001. 'Soziale Sicherheit durch den Sozialstaat? Einschätzungen zu Rente, Arbeitslosigkeit und Krankheit in Ost- und Westdeutschland', in *Informationsdienst Soziale Indikatoren (ISI)*, 26, pp. 7 –11.

Lipsmeier, G. 1999. "Die Bestimmung des notwendigen Lebensstandards Einschätzung sunterschiede und Entscheidungsprobleme", *Zeitschrift für Soziologie*, 28, pp. 281–300.

Mau, S. 1997. *Ungleichheit- und Gerechtigkeitsorientierungen in modernen Wohlfahrtsstaaten. Ein Vergleich der Länder Schweden, Großbritannien und der Bundesrepublik Deutschland*, Working paper Forschungsschwerpunkt III 97/401(Berlin,Wissenschaftszentrum für Sozialforschung {WZB}).

_____ 2001. 'Die üblichen Verdächtigen. Mythen über die "Drückeberger" der Arbeitsgesellschaft', in *Frankfurter Rundschau* 2001/93, p. 7.

Meinhard, V. 1996. *Fiskalische Auswirkungen der Einführung eines Bürgergeldes. Gutachten im Auftrag des Bundesministeriums der Finanzen* (Berlin, Deutsches Institut für Wirtschaftsforschung).

Offe, C. 1990. *Akzeptanz und Legitimität strategischer Optionen in der Sozialpolitik*, Zentrum für Sozialpolitik Arbeitspapier Nr. 3, Universität Bremen.

_____ 1994. 'A non-productivist design for social policies', in J. Ferris and R. Page (eds.), *Social policy in transition. Anglo-German perspectives in the new European Community* (Aldershot, Avebury), pp. 87–105.

_____ 1995. 'Full employment: Asking the wrong question?', *Dissent*, 10, pp. 77–81.

Offe, C., Muckenberger, U. and Ostner, I. 1996. 'A basic income guaranteed by the State: A need of the moment on social policy', in C. Offe (ed.), *Modernity and the State. East, West* (Cambridge, Mass., MIT Press), pp. 201–221.

Pioch, R. 1996. 'Basic income: Social policy after full employment', in A. Erskine (ed.), *Changing Europe. Some aspects of identity, conflict and social justice* (Aldershot, Avebury), pp. 148–160 .

Roller, E. 1992. *Einstellungen der Bürger zum Wohlfahrtsstaat Bundesrepublik Deutschland*, (Opladen, Westdeutscher Verlag).

Rossi, P. 1979. 'Vignette analysis: Uncovering the normative structure of complex judgments', in R.K. Merton, J.S. Coleman and P.H. Rossi (eds.), *Qualitative and quantitative social research: Papers in honour of Paul F. Lazarsfeld* (New York, Free Press), pp. 176–186.

_____ and Anderson, A.B. 1982. 'The factorial survey approach: An introduction', in P.H. Rossi and S.L. Nock (eds.) *Measuring social judgments: The factorial survey approach* (Beverly Hills, Sage), pp. 15–67.

Scharpf, F. 1994. 'Negative Einkommenssteuer – ein Programm gegen Ausgrenzung', in *Die Mitbestimmung*, 3, pp. 27–32.

_____ 1995. 'Subventionierte Niedriglohnbeschäftigung statt bezahlter Arbeitslosigkeit', in *Zeitschrift für Sozialreform*, 41, pp. 66–82.

Standing, G. 1992. 'The need for a new social consensus', in van Parijs, P. (ed.), *Arguing for basic income. Ethical foundations for a radical reform*, (London and New York, Verso), pp. 47–60.

Titmuss, R. M. 1968. *Commitment to welfare* (London, Allen and Unwin).

van Parijs, P. (ed.) 1992. *Arguing for basic income* (London and New York, Verso).

_____ 1995. *Real freedom for all. What (if anything) can justify capitalism?* (Oxford, Oxford University Press).

Vobruba, G. 1986. Die Entflechtung von Arbeit und Essen. Lohnarbeitszentrierte Sozialpolitik und garantiertes Grundeinkommen', in M. Opielka and G. Vobruba (eds.), *Das garantierte Grundeinkommen. Entwicklung und Perspektiven einer Forderung* (Frankfurt am Main, Fischer), pp. 39–52.

Wegener, B. 1980. 'Magnitude-Messung in Umfragen: Kontexteffekte und Methode', in *Zentrum für Umfragen und Analysen (ZUMA)-Nachrichten*, 6, pp. 4–40.

_____ 1999. 'Belohnungs- und Prinzipiengerechtigkeit. Die zwei Welten der empirischen Gerechtigkeitsforschung', in U. Druwe and V. Kurz (eds.), *Politische Gerechtigkeit* (Opladen, Leske and Budrich), pp. 167–214.

_____ and Liebig, S. 2000. 'Is the "inner wall" here to stay? Justice ideologies in unified Germany', *Social Justice Research*, 13, pp. 177–197.

White, S. 1997. 'Liberal equality, exploitation, and the case for an unconditional basic income', in *Political Studies XLV*, pp. 312–326.

16

REPUBLICANISM AND BASIC INCOME: THE ARTICULATION OF THE PUBLIC SPHERE FROM THE REPOLITICIZATION OF THE PRIVATE SPHERE

Daniel Raventós and David Casassas[1]

1. Introduction

Republicanism is a longstanding tradition of political thought that first arose from the Socratic *ethos* and certain political aspects of the Athens of the fifth and fourth centuries B.C., after which it was to be the object of successive reformulations. First in Europe and subsequently in America, republicanism has always opposed obscurantism, tyranny, oppression and inequalities based on arbitrary interference. From the second half of the nineteenth century onwards, this tradition became increasingly invisible with the codification of liberal thought. Republican ideals were only present in some of the various manifestations of political socialism of the nineteenth and twentieth centuries, though the limits and vicissitudes involved ended up eclipsing them. Now, at the beginning of the twenty-first century, more attention is being paid to republicanism both in the academic milieu and in circles outside academia.

The core idea of the republican tradition is to approach the concept of freedom, 'republican freedom as non-domination', without overlooking the ideals of equality and fraternity; it is a programme of thought and action that opens up fruitful ways of analysing the economic, political and social challenges now facing mankind. Republicanism promotes the institutional mechanisms by means of which citizens may obtain the material and economic security that ensures that formal freedoms become a reality, so that individuals may be equipped to face different forms of domination. And this is of even greater importance in societies where the logic of the market and private accumulation impose a significant degree of inequality in terms of distribution of income and wealth. Basic Income (henceforth BI) is an extremely valuable instrument for achieving these goals because one condition of full citizenship is the universal and unconditional guarantee of the right to existence that it would establish.

It should be noted that any materialization of the republican ideal of freedom, understood as self-government, opposition to tyranny, and more recently conceptualized from the standpoint of the notion of freedom as non-domination, entails certain demands on social and political reality, among which the guarantee of security of income must be emphasized. A BI for everybody may be understood as the guarantee of material sufficiency and therefore of the socio-economic independence necessary to reduce the levels of domination that affect people belonging to the most significant groups of social vulnerability – wage-earning workers, women, etc. – and thereby to open up greater areas of freedom so that they may carry out their respective life-plans.[2]

The main aim of this paper is to highlight the importance given by the republican tradition to the role played by property – understood as socio-economic independence – as the basis of its attempt to construct a robust notion of civic virtue, which might then open up the doors to a social and political order that would make the republican ideal of freedom as non-domination a reality. Liberal thought, heir to the typically Roman distinction between the public and private spheres assumes that the latter consists exclusively of relations between individuals with equal rights before the law who establish strictly voluntary contracts. Power, from the liberal point of view, becomes apparent only within the sphere of public affairs. Republicanism, however, assumes that civil society – the private sphere – is profoundly asymmetrical in terms of distribution of resources and social privilege, which means that it is permeated by power relations. The republican public sphere must therefore be understood as an extension of the private sphere wherein the relations of dependence and domination that affect the participants in the processes of political decision-making have been abolished. Civic virtue is a mere chimera unless there is material independence.

First, we shall explore the link that the republican tradition has established, from Aristotle onwards, between the possibility of civic virtue and property – and here we will need to discuss what kind of 'property' we are talking about. This will be done by analysing the views of the political theorists of the time concerning the most significant phenomena that rocked Athenian political and social life during the fifth and fourth centuries B.C. We shall then go on to examine whether conclusions might be drawn from these views and applied to the circumstances that define present-day societies.

Second, we shall analyse the key points that shape republican ethical and political thought, with special attention to its 'proprietarian' nature. We shall particularly attempt to throw light on the link between its notions of freedom (the republican *libertas*), civic virtue, political participation and property, with a view to understanding what Philip Pettit, one of the leading current theorists of republicanism, means when he points out that 'if a republican State is committed to advancing the cause of freedom as non-domination among its citizens, then it must embrace a policy of promoting socio-economic independence' (Pettit, 1997, pp. 158–159). Next we shall analyse how far a BI might constitute the materialization of these postulates.

Third and finally, once we have looked into the question of why it might be affirmed that BI constitutes a highly valuable tool for fostering republican ideas, we shall go on to detail the essential features of the political institutions that republicans aspire to. We shall indicate the measure in which a BI might facilitate the basic elements necessary for the articulation and reproduction of these political institutions. In brief, in this final section we shall discuss to what extent the socialist assumption of the central role of property in articulating a non-vacuous notion of citizenship (and it is common knowledge that political socialism objects to the liberal dissociation between the public and private spheres) permits us to make a connection between this political tradition and the tradition of the democratic republicanism that once again erupted on to the political scene in 1789. It is well known that contemporary civil law universalizes the condition of citizenship, at least on paper. Given this fact, a consistent republican politico-institutional order would need to seek a mechanism for 'universalizing property' – material independence, 'self-ownership' – in order to ensure that this condition of citizenship goes rather deeper than mere legal stipulation with no real effects. Presenting BI as a suitable mechanism for achieving this goal of the necessary universalization of property means relating this measure to the core of the socialist tradition; this is the attempt to 'repoliticize' the private sphere, assuming that it is permeated by power relations. Facing this reality is an unavoidable condition for articulating an authentically democratic political sphere, which is understood, all things considered, as an expression of the most genuine democratic republicanism.

2. Civic Virtue and Property in Republicanism

2.1 The Sociology of Republican Politics and the Athenian Democratic Experience[3]

The Athenian plebeian revolution, led by the free poor men's party of Ephialtes and Pericles, and which triumphed in 461 B.C., gave rise, thanks to the 'Ephialtes' reforms', to a new political order that allowed significant reinforcement of the democratic mechanisms that Cleisthenes' Constitution of 508–507 B.C. had envisaged. Cleisthenes' Constitution had already provided the Athenians with the elements that ancient Greeks deemed necessary for full democracy and, though certain socio-economic privileges were still required for the holding of public office, all citizens had the right to vote in the sovereign assembly. Ephialtes' reforms went still further. In effect, the reforms of 461 B.C. implied certain modifications in the structure of political institutions so that they became decidedly more democratic. First, the political tasks carried out by members of juries and the council that prepared the order of the day of the assemblies were remunerated. Second, mere attendance at the assembly was also remunerated so that even the poorest citizens could play an effective, real part in the public life of the *polis*.

The plebeian revolt, then, is remarkable for the real inclusion – and not just on paper – of poor people (non-owners) in the deliberative processes that took place in the agora, as well as for the establishment and strengthening of typically Athenian democratic mechanisms: the rotation of public positions, decision-making by drawing lots, and other innovations. Herodotus himself praised this democratic system of the fifth century B.C., that opposed monarchy and oligarchy, stressing that in it '[leaders] must account for the power they exercise, and all deliberations are subject to public scrutiny.[4] Only 50 years later, however, the democratic regime was undermined as a result of both internal and external difficulties – the war against Sparta, for instance, was a heavy burden – and eventually collapsed with the oligarchic *coup d'état* of 411 B.C.

This does not mean that 'Athenian democracy' constitutes a historical period that is confined exclusively to these 50 years. In fact, the old democratic Constitution remained in force until 322–321 B.C., when Antipater, the regent of Macedonia, after stifling the Greek revolt against Macedonian domination that broke out with the news of Alexander's death (this revolt being proudly referred to by the Greeks as 'the Hellenic war'), compelled the Athenians to replace it with another Constitution of a markedly oligarchic nature. However, it was during the fifth century B.C. that the Athenian political institutions were at the height of their democratic vigour. Hence, the fifth century B.C. constituted a real testing ground for the next century's political theorists, whose thought is marked by these highly significant events. This is particularly the case with Aristotle, the real founder of the republican political tradition.

Aristotle's favourable opinion of the processes of public deliberation allows us to highlight the fact that the earliest republicanism approved of introducing mechanisms for promoting democratic participation, fostering what we would nowadays call 'participatory democracy'.[5] However, it should be said that Aristotle's dictum on deliberation refers to these mechanisms only as mechanisms *per se*, that is, regardless of the nature of their 'users'. Aristotle, then, understands the deliberative process as the transformation of a certain set of previously existing values and interests into a shared decision, which has been possible thanks to rational analysis of that set of prior values. In this sense, it might be said that individuals are virtuous insofar as they show their willingness, once persuaded, to relinquish their previous interests, always with a view to promoting the common good. Moreover, this exercise offers the possibility for individuals to mould their own characters, both individually and reciprocally.

The Aristotelian critique of the institutions of deliberative democracy appears with the possibility of opening them up to free people who lack their own resources, individuals who are non-proprietors and thus bound to others by ties of socio-economic dependence. Ownership thus appears as an essential requirement for enabling individuals to contribute towards ensuring that the processes of public deliberation achieve good results. First, property is understood as socio-economic independence and thus as self-ownership, endowing individuals – who are free from possible blackmail stemming from someone else's socio-economic privileges – with the necessary independence of judgment for promoting the best interests of both themselves and the community. Second, property, to the extent that it permits basic needs to be covered, enables individuals to leave strictly reproductive work – temporarily or permanently – and to cultivate virtues, creating for themselves excellent characters, both individually and mutually, through the practice of self-directed, non-instrumental activities. In short, material independence appears as a necessary condition for civic virtue.[6]

Aristotle, the true 'sociologist of Greek politics' (Ste. Croix, 1988), at once philosopher and social and natural scientist with a deep inclination for exhaustive and precise empirical investigations, did not overlook the fact that the socio-economic conditions affecting individuals profoundly determine their political behaviour. As Ste. Croix indicates:

> far from being an anachronistic aberration, the concept of economic class as a basic factor in the differentiation of Greek society and the definition of its political divisions fits surprisingly well with the approach of the Greeks themselves to this reality; and Aristotle, the great authority on the sociology and politics of the Greek *polis*, is always working with a class analysis as his starting point, which is to say, on the assumption that individuals will behave in the political sphere, as in any other field, according to their economic situation (Ste. Croix, 1988, p. 100).[7]

Technically speaking, oligarchy is the Government of very few people – the *oligoi* – while democracy is the Government of the majority or the *demos*.

However, in one of the outstanding passages of his *Politics* (1279b–1280a) Aristotle disregards the mere numerical difference between oligarchy and democracy, which he sees as incidental, to stress that the real determining factor of the difference between democracy and oligarchy stems from poverty and wealth respectively. He goes on to argue that he would still talk in terms of 'oligarchy' and 'democracy' even if there were many rich people and only a few poor. In short, the aristocrat Aristotle opts for oligarchy over democracy – an oligarchy made up by virtuous people – starting out from the assumption of the importance of material independence for the cultivation of public virtues. Nonetheless, Aristotle would not disapprove of a Government of the majority if, and only if, that majority could be constituted by owners – or, in other words, by self-owners.

So Aristotle, an aristocrat in the Athens of the fourth century B.C., does not go into normative considerations on the possibility of opening up the set of owners – the group of self-owners – to include the whole citizenry, regardless of sex, origin or social condition. Rather, Aristotle, the philosopher and social scientist, does not find ontological-existential reasons for denying individuals the possibility of using all the political rights that a Constitution might envisage, as long as they meet the necessary material conditions for being considered as full citizens. It is indisputable that the position of Aristotle the aristocrat is far from being that of nineteenth- and twentieth-century liberalism, which sees citizenship as being a reality once political rights have formally been guaranteed, independently of the living conditions of these so-called citizens. Aristotle, in undertaking his study of democracy as a form of government, points out that 'the true friend of the people should see that they are not too poor, for extreme poverty debases democracy; measures should therefore be taken so as to bring them lasting prosperity' (*Politics*, 1320a).

2.2 From Athens to Modern Times: The Question of Property Today

Republican emphasis on property has been a constant since Aristotle's times. The civil dependence of non-owners – of wage earners, for instance – on rich people or owners, which makes the former into mere instruments of the latter's thirst for wealth, has been viewed by all the different kinds of republicanism as the clearest sign of the impossibility of free civil society, and as the most unequivocal symptom of the decline of republican freedoms. Madison, to give one example, stressed, as did the majority of those present at the 1787 Philadelphia Convention, that complete political and civil equality is incompatible with free political life when a large part of the citizenry lacks property and must therefore engage in civil relations of dependence on others (Domènech, 2002).

A republican look at today's world makes us take this reality into account. It has been said that the first requirement for republican freedom is a certain level of material independence. The idea seems to be quite simple. In order to live reasonably well it is necessary to have access to a – finite and limited, in the words of republicanism (*Politics*, 1256b) – set of external resources or goods. If these resources are not fully guaranteed, individuals will be forced to do everything in their power in order to obtain them, accepting someone else's domination, selling their labour power – their freedom – and even suffering their own alienation.[8] Material independence, then, is a condition for political freedom. However, private property is distributed in a highly unequal and asymmetrical way. This is why certain forms of patrician republicanism were moved to exclude dependent individuals, or non-self-sufficient individuals – slaves, women, poor free people – from the political sphere and citizenry, and to propose a republic of owners, great and small, whose independence enabled them to exercise political freedom.

Democratic liberalism has also opted for a simplistic solution in accepting all adult individuals into full citizenship – men and women, rich and poor people – regardless of their property, wealth or sources of income. This was done at the price of eroding the idea of freedom, giving priority to its strictly formal nature and thereby 'depoliticizing' social life and removing the question of power and social domination – in the factory, at home, in the political party or in any other institution of civil society – from the political agenda (Francisco and Raventós, 2002). In fact, with nineteenth-century liberalism, economic science stopped being 'political economy' and economic relations were no longer seen as relations of power and domination but rather as aseptic and apolitical relations of voluntary exchange.

In contrast, democratic republicanism – both classical and modern – has opted for a more complex approach. Democratic republicanism is not satisfied merely with rights and formal inclusion since its main concern is freedom as non-domination, which will be explored in more detail below. This explains why democratic republicanism, from Jefferson to Marx, has consistently sought to 'repoliticize' social life. In other words, it has sought to include again on the political agenda the serious problems of domination – of lack of freedom – affecting the most disadvantaged social groups in contemporary societies, which are replete with all sorts of asymmetries of access to information, mechanisms for domination and power relations.[9]

Thus today, a democratic and inclusive republicanism that neither depoliticizes social life nor dilutes the idea of freedom into formal rights, and that does not exclude from full citizenship those without means, must promote alternative 'social-republican' forms of property and all the corresponding institutional measures that would provide all citizens of the political community with material and economic security. Such security would make formal freedom a reality and individuals would then be able effectively to confront the various forms of domination existing in both civil and political society.

Today then, the 'universalization of citizenship' demands the 'universalization of property'. Since we are dealing with an idea of political community which, far from being limited to a small group of owners, includes almost all the inhabitants of our countries (with the serious exception of immigrant residents without political rights), it is necessary to articulate new measures so as to universalize this 'condition of ownership' that republican theorists have correctly defined as the first step in allowing individuals to exercise political freedom. In short, without a well-founded idea of 'self-ownership', or the real possibility of articulating one's own life plans and putting them into practice, the notion of citizenship is impoverished to the point of becoming a mere mirage. Nothing less than new measures for 'universalizing self-ownership' are required (Casassas, 2002).

3. Republicanism, a Theory of Freedom and Government

3.1 'To be Ruled by None, if Possible, or, If this is Impossible, to Rule and be Ruled in Turns'

Freedom is the essence of republicanism. The republican approach to freedom has little to do with that of the 'modern' notion of freedom or 'liberal' freedom. The republican *libertas* is always defined by its opposition to tyranny and slavery. Slaves are submitted to the despotic authority of their masters, who can interfere at whim in their lives.[10] The master dominates the slave who is thus unfree. From the perspective of domination, it is all the same to the slave whether the master is benevolent and does not interfere *de facto* in his or her life or whether he does. The crux of the problem stems from the fact that the master has the power to interfere whenever he wants. Republicanism understands freedom as the absence of domination, meaning the absence of even the possibility of arbitrary interference.

More specifically, this absence of domination implies 'to be ruled by none, if possible, or, if this is impossible, to rule and be ruled in turns' (*Politics*, 1317b). To live under domination means being governed by someone else so that this someone else decides how an individual is to lead his or her life. On the other hand, those who are not dominated – those who are free – are able to govern themselves and decide for themselves how to act and, essentially, who to be. In accordance with these postulates, the republican ideal demands for government in the public sphere 'positive public freedom', or the participation of the people in collective self-government – individuals ruling and being ruled in turns, as Aristotle stressed. Otherwise, an individual or group could govern indefinitely, which would make power despotic and cause people to lose their freedom. The freedom of individuals, who are not asocial atoms but rather 'political animals', can only be achieved within the republic, the political community; in other words, they must become citizens who govern themselves, who promulgate their own laws, who jointly deliberate and make decisions on what they think fair and advisable.

But none of this is possible without an understanding of the role that a non-banal notion of civic virtue can play. In fact, freedom and virtue constitute two poles of mutual attraction (Francisco and Raventós, 2002). Even a first approach to Athenian republicanism immediately suggests a conception of the republic as a 'republic of reasons',[11] this being understood as a process in which people speak and make suggestions, where ideas are discussed and accepted or refused according to a principle of rationality. In this sense, civic virtue means nothing less than the disposition for detecting, or contributing towards detecting, with due deliberation, the general interests of the community, along with the will to promote them over time. But is republican civic virtue something that is within the reach only of the saintliest of beings? Is the notion of civic virtue compatible with the evidence of the motivational pluralism of human action or, in other words, the fact that the dispositions operating in human sociality are extremely diverse? At this point it is worth going somewhat deeper into the finer points of the republican conceptualization of civic virtue.

3.2 Civic Virtue and the Development of Personal Identity

Republicans stress that the virtuous citizen is one who, participating in collective self-government, is able to impose the best law in the interests of the republic on him- or herself. This law is the fullest expression of the common good, of general interest, of the 'universal', as Aristotle would say. On the other hand, citizens who, as victims of vice and ethical corruption, are governed by the tyranny of their own immediate passions, lose sight of their own overall private good. What is more, those who fall into the trap of particular interests or political factionalism, who systematically put their own interests before the public interest, are bad citizens. It is clear then, that, from the republican perspective, ethics and politics go hand in hand, that private good and public good are interdependent and that virtue acts as the bridge between the two spheres (Francisco and Raventós, 2002).

The heart of the matter lies in the fact that individuals find in political *praxis*, which implies the cultivation of civic virtues, the way to the unfolding of their own ethical identity, which is to say of their own personal identity. As Domènech (2000) has pointed out, there is good reason for thinking that the

notion of our earliest thinkers that individuals are driven by all sorts of inner
conflicts and disputes, that they constitute a set of 'multiple selves' dissemi-
nated in space and time, is essentially correct. Hence Aristotle considered that
separate and autonomous existence, the formation of the individual's character, is a fundamental ethical objective and that this depends, first, on individuals themselves, on their self-modelling, on their constructing themselves to
the extent that they are capable of selecting their wishes and resolving their
inner conflicts

> by the harmonious integration of their different selves and their becoming
> more *enkratic*. This is the only case in which it can be said that someone
> is a 'one and indivisible self', or an individual. On the other hand, an
> *akratic* individual, an intemperate and even wicked person, 'is not one
> self, but multiple selves, and he is so inconstant that he becomes another
> person in the same day'. All this leads the non-virtuous man to clash with
> himself, since the fact that his wishes and feelings are separate 'makes a
> man his own enemy' (Domènech, 2000, p. 31).[12]

The primary task, then, is individual; yet the separate and autonomous
existence of individuals also requires mutual modelling, reciprocal collaboration
in the identification and cultivation of individual excellence. The Aristotelian
link between virtue and friendship is as follows: friendship occurs among free
individuals who are seeking virtue or excellence and the formation of a good
character through mutual, and therefore, self-modelling. This is why Aristotle,
like most of the ancient philosophers, thought that there is symmetry in the way
in which individuals treat themselves and the way they treat others. Herein may
be found the deepest sense in Aristotle's celebrated words when he stresses that
man is a 'political animal'. All his relations, including those with himself, are
potentially political, which is to say that they are power relations, of authority
and of government, and the only way for man to become a separate and
autonomous individual is to cultivate his social relations.

So this is not a question of atomized individuals, like Leibniz's 'monads',
completely self-contained entities that are indifferent to all others, paradoxically devoting themselves to the cultivation of civic virtues which means regulating private good in favour of a priority common public good. Republican
anthropology moves in a different direction, assuming that articulation of the
self and the development of personal identity, although conditioned by certain prior ontogenetic factors, is essentially a social and collective task. It is
hardly surprising, therefore (but rather 'natural' that this should be the case),
that individuals in certain conditions opt to participate in the articulation and
reproduction of political institutions that may be seen as the expression of this

continuum between intra-psychic and interpersonal deliberation. Their own identity is clearly dependent on it.

3.3 Civic Virtue and the Guarantee of Libertas

A second factor that enables us to talk about civic virtue without appealing to outlandish anthropological suppositions is that individuals are conscious of the fact that the maintenance and vigour of republican political institutions constitutes the guarantee of their own *libertas*. Why can it be stated (Francisco, 1999) that, for republicanism, virtue is attainable only through the exercise of political freedom, conferred upon participating and co-deciding individuals? It is worth mentioning here the old republican idea that the active participation of citizens in decision-making processes is a necessary condition for freedom as non-domination or for ensuring that power does not become arbitrary. In other words, this *libertas* that is located at the heart of republican principles is not possible without opening out real channels for citizens' participation in the reproduction of republican political institutions. The participation of individuals in the *polis* must be understood from this perspective as a guarantee against those arbitrary interferences that might end up by eroding the individual's capacity for making a reality of his or her own freely-determined goals. First, the deliberative mechanisms themselves constitute an epistemic filter that selects those options that arise from correctly formulated beliefs, and this means rejecting both unfounded reasons and those which are simply imposed because of certain prerogatives and positions of power. Second, the smooth running of the political institutions that emanate from – and are responsible for the well-being of – these deliberative processes and institutions, whose stability depends on the constant presence of the individuals within them, makes it possible to avoid the grave danger of which Machiavelli warned:[13] without republican institutional devices, certain individuals may retain powerful positions from which they subjugate other citizens thanks to the coercive mechanisms made available by these positions and the forms of bribery permitted by their proximity to public funds.

It seems clear, then, that the republican tradition manages to articulate a robust and consultative notion of civic virtue without being based on impossible and naïvely optimistic anthropological notions. It is a fact that the

Republican tradition has never denied the importance, nor even the legitimacy, of self-interest in human action, from Aristotle's *sympheron*, Rousseau's *amour de soi* and Spinoza's *conservatio sui* through to Adam Smith's self-interest. What republicanism does object to – and very realistically – is the monopoly of this kind of motivation in explanations of human action (Domènech, 2000, p. 33).[14]

The republican tradition affirms, rather, that the design of political institutions can bring out civic virtue, to a greater or lesser extent and in different ways. In other words, the manner in which the design of political institutions is approached has a lot to do with the possibility of creating a 'climate of confidence' in these institutions and this has much bearing on their social and political success. Montagut (2001, p. 41) stresses that 'all participatory and respectful dynamics require a high level of confidence'. Again, she adds 'social confidence is based not only on interpersonal confidence, or that between individuals, but also on the confidence of individuals in government institutions'. The fact is that the existence of expectations of cooperation from others leads each individual to cooperate too, and this gives rise to a 'virtuous circle' (Putnam, 1993) that makes it possible to resolve the basic dilemmas of collective action. Montagut also points out that 'civic commitment constructs a communal political identity that provides citizens with experience of government and the ability to judge public affairs. Social capital thereby promotes good government and reinforces the articulation of demands to the benefit of all and in detriment of those that favour some members of society at the cost of others'. As we have already suggested, political participation is, at least to some extent, a very valuable mechanism for maintaining those institutions on which the possibility for individuals of carry out their autonomous life plans depends.

3.4 The Scope and the Meaning of Republican Freedom as Non-Domination: The Horizons of Basic Income

Nothing that resides within the basic republican claims is possible without the guarantee of material existence. When individuals lack their own means of support, or when they are obliged to sell their labour power – their freedom – in order to survive, republican virtues, and the concomitant happiness, the real objective of Aristotelian ethics and politics (Aristotle, *Nicomachean Ethics*, I), are no longer attainable. Hence the importance attached to the notion of freedom as non-domination in the republican scheme.

From the perspective of republican freedom as non-domination it is understood that X dominates Y if and only if X enjoys a certain power over Y and, in particular, the arbitrarily based power to interfere in Y's affairs. To be more precise, Pettit (1997) stresses that X dominates Y insofar as he or she (1) has the capacity to interfere; (2) arbitrarily; and (3) in certain choices made by Y. Not all interference is necessarily arbitrary. Interference is arbitrary inasmuch as it depends on the will of the one who is interfering, independently of the opinions, preferences and interests of those who are subjected to this interference. Even if X never interferes in actions chosen by Y – because of X's benevolence or because of Y's fawning, or whatever – we still need to talk about domination if X simply has the power to interfere at whim. A slave's master might refrain from 'interfering in his or her life out of kindness, for instance, but he still has the power to do so and hence there is domination. On the contrary, non-arbitrary interference is that which exists when there is basic equality between X and Y in terms of means and power and Y is aware of and shares X's reasons for intervening in his or her actions. Republicanism rejects arbitrary interference and is committed to defending freedom as non-domination, this being understood as the freedom enjoyed by those who live in the presence of others and, by virtue of certain social and institutional structures, none of these others has the slightest possibility of interfering arbitrarily in the decisions that they might make. Republican freedom as non-domination is therefore a highly demanding social concept since it requires that those people who could interfere arbitrarily in the lives of others are prevented from doing so.

At this point it is appropriate to consider again Pettit's assertion that 'if a republican state is committed to advancing the cause of freedom as non-domination among its citizens, then it must embrace a policy of promoting socio-economic independence' (Pettit, 1997, pp. 158–159). This implies a defence of the republican scheme in a world in which the condition of citizenship has now been extended to almost everybody – it has been 'universalized'. This in ·turn implies the definition of social and economic policies aimed at the 'universalization of this condition of (self-) ownership' which, as already noted, has been identified, from the true republican standpoint, as the main determining factor of the civic behaviour of citizens.

Could BI constitute the materialization of this republican aim of universalizing (self-) ownership? The main objective of this paper is to provide the basis for an affirmative response to this question.

4. Basic Income and Republican Freedom as Non-Domination

At this point we need to analyse to what extent the implementation of a BI could favour the normative requirements of republican theory. Since it is committed to the cause of freedom as non-domination, republicanism stands for the socio-economic independence of all citizens. Its main objective is to ensure that citizens are independent of charity – both public and private – and free from the possible arbitrariness of employers. Without socio-economic independence, the chances that individuals might enjoy freedom as non-domination are greatly reduced, both in terms of scope and intensity. It should be taken into account that the establishment of a BI would mean the achievement of a very significant socio-economic independence, much greater than that held by significant numbers of citizens in present-day societies, in particular the so-called 'groups of social vulnerability' – wage-earning workers, the unemployed, women and, in general terms, lower-income groups.[15] The implementation of a BI would expand the possibilities for republican freedom as non-domination, first in terms of scope, since citizens would be free in more spheres of their lives within which freedom is presently vetoed and, second, in terms of intensity because the currently consolidated spheres of freedom would be reinforced.[16]

What are these spheres of – republican – freedom that a BI might open up? It seems reasonable to think that only from a position of material independence might one choose freely. Thus, only material independence would permit a woman to choose not to be maltreated by her husband; a young person might choose to turn down a meagre salary or precarious job; an unemployed person might opt for non-remunerated work that could benefit society and thereby avoid the social stigma of being on the dole – where it existed; a poor person might aspire to a decent life; while a worker could choose from a range of gratifying occupations, even if it were for less pay (Raventós and Francisco, 2002; *Red Renta Básica*, 2002). Thus independence increases freedom, and a sufficiently generous BI would universalize a reasonable degree of independence.[17]

It should not be overlooked, however, that the proposal of a BI, taken from republican postulates, while it might play a crucial role in the spheres under discussion, does not stop there. A reduction of the asymmetries of power characteristic of labour markets, and the concomitant increase of freedom as non-domination of the workers, constitutes in itself a highly valuable goal. At the same time, it should be seen as an underpinning for further social and political ends: the construction of a republican social domain. The effects of BI on the labour market should therefore be analysed, as noted above, with reference to the significance that ownership – of oneself – has in the articulation of republican political institutions. This would constitute an analysis of the reinforcement of freedom as non-domination, as the fruit of introducing BI, and it should be carried out in the awareness that this 'repoliticization of the private sphere', that goes into effect from the moment that there is an attempt to reconsider the basic socio-economic conditions that affect the participants in the exchanges of civil society, is oriented towards the 'articulation of a public sphere' that is full and vigorous.

4.1 The Articulation of the Public Sphere from a Repoliticization of the Private Sphere

It has been stated from very beginning: the Aristotelian critique of democratic institutions appeared when the possibility was raised that these institutions might be occupied by any individuals who were free but lacked their own resources, by individuals who were not proprietors and thus were restricted by bonds of socio-economic dependence on other people. Ever since the times of Aristotle, republicanism has denied that there is any sense in conceiving of a citizenry that lacks material independence. This is the essential condition for being able to develop the civic disposition stored in individuals. Without material independence citizens (if they might be called such in this case), as prey to the factional interests that are fed by the forms of servitude to which they are submitted, would not be capable of giving priority to the common good over private gain or of understanding that they are required to engage in a task that is constitutively human, consisting in fostering the interests of the republic with the prior understanding that one's own freedom is positively and reciprocally related to that of the citizenry as a whole.

It is in this sense that BI has been presented as a privileged instrument for promoting republican freedom as non-domination or, in other words, for correcting, at least partially, the asymmetries of power characteristic of civil society and thereby to confront the task of constructing the public sphere on solid foundations. Far from conceiving the republican tradition as a political theory with which certain economic principles might be related, it should be presented as true political economy, which is to say as a body of doctrine that, starting out from an investigation into the impact of socio-economic conditions on human motivations, reflects upon the best way of articulating political institutions that would be capable of guaranteeing the freedom of citizens as a whole. Ste. Croix stated it very clearly (1988, p. 95): 'Aristotle's analysis of political activity in the Greek city started out from an empirically demonstrable premise that he shared, not only with other Greek thinkers, but also with [the republican] Marx, this being that the main factor that determines the political behaviour of the majority of individuals is economic class, as this is still the case today'.[18] The aim, therefore, is that which has already been stated: to 'repoliticize the private sphere' – in the sense of accepting and confronting the levels of power that operate therein – 'in order to articulate the public sphere'.

Why do we need to speak of 'repoliticization'? As noted above, the discontinuity between the private and public spheres, between individual and social ethics that is at work within liberalism is, in good part, heir to the line of demarcation drawn between public and private spheres in Roman civil law. At this point, we should point out the significance of the process of progressive neglect by economic science, after David Ricardo, of the question of power, of the bonds of economic dependence between individuals, which had previously been of central concern in classical political economy. This set out from an analysis of the relations of production and was also concerned with theorizing on good government. At the same time, it still shared republican concerns about the *continuum* between the public and the private spheres and also used a notion of freedom that was frequently close to the republican idea, so that this freedom was one that embraced more aspects that its mere formal guarantee.

One should analyse, then, to what point a republican approximation to the proposal of a BI permits a recovery of the political, 'proprietaria' spirit of economic science prior to the nineteenth century. It is highly probable that this would be one of the main contributions that a republican perspective could make to the normative social science of our times, which is more concerned with questions pertaining to the subjective evaluations that individuals might make of society's goods – their own or those of others – than with the influence exerted by the socio-economic base and power relations on the relations between individuals.

4.2 From Basic Income to Republican Political Institutions

Though they take ethical and philosophical postulates as their starting point, republican ideas are ultimately directed towards the political process. The republic's imperative of self-government and its rejection of despotic or tyrannical principles require that decision-making must necessarily respond to a process that is deliberative by nature. Where there is tyranny or a despotic Government, decisions are taken from a position of absolute power, immediately and incontestably. In contrast, the political decisions taken by a collective of citizens in a free republic are 'mediated' and 'contestable' decisions (Pettit, 1997)[19], which is to say they are – and here it is worth returning to the formula employed earlier – the result of a process of deliberation in which proposals are made and discussed and ideas are talked about, accepted or rejected according to a principle of rationality. It follows that the domain of oratory has been central for the republican tradition. 'In a republican nation', writes Jefferson, 'whose citizens are to be led by reason and persuasion and not by force, the art of reasoning becomes of first importance'.[20]

Again, this deliberative political rationality is geared to the good, not of any particular individual or faction of the *demos*, but of the republic as such. This is also the logical result of the process of deliberation itself, for deliberation is not the negotiation of pre-established interests but rather it is to participate in a process in which reasons are given with respect to matters of general – and not particular – concern. Through reasoning it is hoped to convince others of the soundness of one's own position. Anything else would be to force or impose – in short to dominate. Deliberation, which is a requirement of republican freedom, imposes two conditions on the political process.

- The preferences of individuals should not be exogenous to the political process (Sunstein, 1988), and they should not be fixed by a supposedly selfish or sinful human nature that is given priority over an immutable social life and is therefore unfit to be the basis of interaction between individuals. On the contrary, the political process is understood as a 'constitutive' element of the preferences themselves, as a setting where it is possible to modify them on the basis of the best reasoning that is proffered in the process of deliberation.

- The regulative ideal of the political process should be the 'consensus' that results from deliberation, and not the balance of interests that might be derived from a process of negotiation. To deliberate intrinsically means to aspire to convince.

Furthermore, for deliberation and consensus to be possible, an additional condition that affects the political process also seems necessary: the condition that Francisco and Raventós call the 'dispersion' or 'non-accumulability' of political power. It is here that two of the main lines of classical republican thinking converge: the doctrine of 'separation of powers' and that of 'checks and balances'. First, as is known, the doctrine of division of powers states that a concentration of the three great powers of State – legislative, executive and judicial – in the same hands inevitably leads to tyranny. Second, the doctrine of checks and balances is inspired, in the heart of the republican tradition, by the same anti-tyrannical principle. As the Founding Fathers of the 1787 United States Constitution saw it, power without checks and balances tends to become all embracing. Thus, democratic republicanism that is free of the elitist and anti-majority biases of the republicanism of certain historical periods must strive for the institutional materialization of the principle of the dispersion of political power, to be designed in such a way that the interests of the better organized groups of social and economic power cannot undermine it. In particular, in the present-day process of globalization, it is extremely difficult to prevent these economic interests from colonizing the political process, even in political frameworks where, to some extent, systems of checks and balances and separation of powers have been included. There are always fissures that are unforeseen in institutional engineering through which the buying and selling of favours and traffic of influences might slip. So the only reliable formula for avoiding or minimizing this colonization is democratic reinforcement: to ensure that democracy is effectively participatory, to see that a robust and well organized citizenry exercises self-government, controlling the political class by means of effective mechanisms of accountability and obliging the political process to respond to its needs. This means opening up spaces for deliberation, generating a mesh of associations, and so on (Francisco and Raventós, 2002).

Once again, it should be made clear that citizens without guarantees of a certain level of material sufficiency, of economic security, which BI guarantees by definition, are ill-furnished to engage in political action and democratic participation. Without the right to material existence, there can be no full citizenship. This is to say that a guaranteed basic material level constitutes the condition – which, while it may not be sufficient, is at least necessary – for the possibility of full citizenship. The great appeals for a strengthening of democracy and citizens' participation may frequently be brilliant intellectual and political exercises, and they are almost always well-intentioned but, in the absence of a guarantee of material existence, there is not the slightest possibility of access, at least by a good part of the citizens, to the improvements that are called for.

The basis for such an assertion has been outlined above in our discussion of republican ideas. In a few succinct words and going straight to the point, Gargarella states,

> it seems reasonable to think that those people who lack the material resources for ensuring their daily subsistence must have greater problems when it comes to participating in politics. To put it crudely, it does not seem inappropriate to conjecture that the poorest people must have less time, less power of negotiation, less intellectual capacity than rich and better-educated people (1995a, pp. 146–47).

If citizens can enjoy the security of a stable and constant income it should be possible to foster their disposition to participate in deliberative processes. In short, a BI confers on the members of political community levels of economic independence that are not in the least discreditable with respect to those of other individuals. This would make it possible to increase autonomy of judgment (individuals could contribute their best reasoning towards the processes of deliberation, and govern themselves effectively according to criteria of rationality in making decisions, so that it would be possible then to discard questions of opportunity raised by economic dependence on other participants in the political process). BI would also increase the responsibility of citizens (the choice of personal projects would be more autonomous so that individuals would be in a position to justify their preferences and their proposals, always with the promotion of the common good as their end). This is simply to suggest that a BI would make the cultivation of civic virtue, and the disposition for the development and reproduction of republican institutions that must guarantee freedom as non-domination for the citizens as a whole, a much less fanciful proposition. Of what kind of citizenship can we speak when, of all the citizens of the United States, the richest 1 per cent controls 70 per cent of all the wealth generated since the mid-1970s (Frank, 1999)?

4.3 The Universalization of Citizenry and 'Universalization of Property'

As noted above, republicanism's 'proprietarian' concerns have been a constant since the times of Aristotle. The great republican tradition, that of freedom, which, since Aristotle's times, has rejected all political forms of tyranny, without overlooking the tyranny that settles into the very interstices of social relations, has clearly called for material independence as a criterion of full citizenship, this giving it its highly 'proprietarian' nature. To go no further, a democracy of small – and large – producers was Jefferson's dream, a dream that the modern industrial world swept away in creating a huge army of individuals excluded from the property of capital – and of the earth. This is at the root of the great transformation so formidably described by Karl Polanyi (1944) as the creation of an army of wage earners, of 'free' workers. As Raventós and Francisco (2002) say, it is no accident that nineteenth- century liberalism should have ended up separating the ideal of citizenship from the condition of independence. Modern liberalism universalized civil and political rights without taking the property and wealth of individuals into account. With this operation it created not only a vulnerable and dependent citizenry – that is also dependent on State protection – but it also gave juridical and constitutional legitimacy to social inequality between citizens who were formally free. In contrast, the proposal of a BI, in recovering the ideal of independence for everyone, links up with the republican tradition of freedom. From this standpoint, BI must be understood as the right to social existence, as a universal assignment that enables citizens, especially the most vulnerable and disadvantaged, to be effectively free citizens (Raventós and Francisco, 2002).

Republicanism, whether it be democratic or aristocratic, has therefore understood that in the *polis*, or in the heart of a social system regulated by republican political institutions such as those described above, man is capable of self-realization – of making his own nature a reality, to put it in Aristotelian terms – because only in the *polis* does the division of labour allow the needs of individuals to be covered. It is on this basis that the precise, rational, intersubjective encounter takes place whereby individuals may discern what they are and what they want to be. Here we are concerned with establishing the limits of such a *polis*. This issue, pertaining to the limits of the *polis* – and, it follows, of citizenship – is what makes it possible to establish that, historically, there have been radically democratic and profoundly aristocratic republicanisms. It also makes it possible to see how one should approach an application of republican ideas in a world, today's world, whose principles supposedly bestow the condition of citizenship on almost the totality of individuals.

Today, it is only by resorting to weird, unsustainable and even aberrant psychological-social, anthropological or historical-political considerations that it is possible to argue for the deprivation of citizens' rights for any segment of the members of a society. In fact, hardly anyone would contemplate depriving part of the population of the rights and guarantees enshrined in the law. Citizenship is seen as universal. If the aim is to provide this notion of 'citizenship' with all the vigour which an exploration of the postulates of the republican tradition reveals it might have, a coherent consideration of republican normative ideas requires that formulas should be articulated with a view to 'universalizing the condition of ownership' for these supposed citizens.

This is also the basic intuition of the nascent socialism that appeared in the nineteenth century as an extension of the radical democratic ideas, which, at least for a while, inspired the French Revolution of 1789. If nineteenth-century legal systems were progressively bestowing on all individuals, without consideration of social extraction, the same civil, and subsequently political, rights, why could not these same individuals also enjoy full freedom in the civil sphere? Why did they have to continue to be dependent on others in order to live? Why did they have to live only with the 'permission' of the owners of the means of production?[21] Why, to use Marxist terminology, did they have to be 'alienated' in civil terms if, at least on paper, they enjoyed the same rights that the well-to-do classes enjoyed? The 'proprietarian republican' nature of political socialism was, at least during its genesis, clear enough. The immense mass of the dispossessed generated by capitalism as a result of the 'great transformation' – especially the demographic transformation – consisted of men who had been freed from the feudal yoke but not from proprietors and who, as good republicans, called for full civil freedom because they were well aware that, without it, the much-vaunted civil and political freedom and equality offered to them *de jure* by liberalism were meaningless. They understood the importance of property when it came to talking about true political freedom. In essence, this was the central intuition that fuelled democratic socialist – and one might add 'republican' – political thought. It this was a hard blow for the general line of the normative discourse of liberalism, and also for the more intransigent forms of political elitism, a blow that was frequently met with the harshest of responses.

The Kantian idea that everyone should be fully responsible for his or her own destiny is frustrated when circumstances beyond the control of individuals determine the kind of life they must lead (Gargarella, 1995b). It is highly probable that one of the main tensions in modern moral philosophy arises from the instability of some ideals of autonomy and responsibility that have been expounded at the limits of a negative and strictly formal conception of freedom; this has eroded the real space for the realization of these ideals.[22] If it is true that, after Kant, moral philosophy once again began seriously to consider the possibility, contemplated in ancient philosophy and neglected after its decline, that the individual creates him- or herself (Domènech, 1989), it is no less exact to say that this possibility vanishes in the absence of certain social and economic guarantees. These are now being strangled by the modern-liberal conception of liberty, anchored as it is in a strictly formalist concern with eliminating interferences which may act as obstacles to voluntary contracts. In this sense, an institutional system that assumes as its own a non-trivialized notion of this – very modern – autonomy would need to attend to the socio-economic circumstances of individuals in such a way that the life of each one of them would be the product of their own choices alone. In other words, it would mean careful treatment of the notion of 'freedom as non-domination'. Proposing a BI at this point would have a great deal to contribute.

'To articulate the public sphere from the repoliticization of the private sphere' is then the true task and measure of a BI. This means assuming the existence of power relations that traverse civil society and then providing the weakest parties in these relations with the necessary resources so as to cope with the processes of decision-making in an equality of conditions. On this goal depends the successful functioning of a number of political institutions oriented towards attaining the common good – the promotion of freedom as non-domination for the citizens as a whole – on the basis of the disposition of the members of the political community to come together in these institutions, to foster them and reproduce them from a position of rationality and good judgment that is made possible by the absence of domination. In short, the doses of civic virtue that are necessary for the proper functioning of republican political institutions depend on it.

Notes

1 University of Barcelona, Spain.
2 The notion of 'group of social vulnerability' is precisely defined in footnote 14.
3 The classicist Ste. Croix (1988) has provided us with a detailed historical analysis of this period.
4 Quoted by Domènech (1998).
5 The epistemic virtues of deliberative processes are clearly emphasized in his *Politics* (III, 11).
6 A detailed account of the Aristotelian analysis of the link between virtue and property can be found in Domènech (2002).
7 Translated from the Spanish edition.
8 It is worth mentioning that the Marxist theory of alienation – and self-realization – has a clear basis in the republican tradition.
9 Francisco and Raventós (2002) have contrasted the patrician nature of certain forms of historical republicanism with the main features of democratic republicanism – both classical and modern.
10 For an analysis of the philosophical significance of this reality, see Domènech (1999).
11 This concept, which was coined by Sunstein (1993), has also been defined more precisely by Domènech (2000).
12 The Greek *enkrateia* could be translated as 'willpower' or 'strength of will'. This then indicates the chance of bringing to bear a whole second-order rationality that regulates

the primary wishes that appear in individuals. On the other hand, *akrasia* could be translated as 'weakness of will'. The quotations in Domènech's text have been taken from Aristotle's *Nicomachean Ethics*.

13 Machiavelli's well-known *Discorsi sopra la Prima Deca di Tito Livio* constitutes not only one of the founding texts of modern political theory, but also one of the high points of the republican tradition.

14 For a republican reading of Adam Smith's thought, see Aguiar (2002) and Rae (1965).

15 A 'group of social vulnerability' is a set of people sharing the possibility of being submitted to arbitrary interference by the same mechanisms, or as a result of the same causes or reasons. There are many groups of social vulnerability, for instance, those consisting of poor people, women, homosexuals, certain immigrants or wage-earning workers. t is worth quoting here a passage from one of Marx's last writings, *riti e o the otha Pro ramme* (19 1) ' if the only thing that a man has at his disposal is his labour power, he will inevitably become, in any social context and stage of civili ation, the slave of those men owning the material conditions of work. And he will be unable to work and, therefore, to live without their permission to do so' (translated from the Spanish edition). The republican echoes of this statement are, again, very clear the assumption of the need for ownership so as to construct a solid and non-banal notion of freedom is evident. t is well known that the salaried worker's essential 'vulnerability' did not go unremarked in Marx's analysis.

16 et we must go beyond that. The republican aim is to ensure that specific policies that provide citi ens with specific needs do so in terms of basic rights and not at the discretion of a overnment or group of government employees (Francisco and Ravent s, 2002 Ravent s, 2000). The aim, then, is to avoid the establishment of other forms of domination whereby government institutions respond to citi ens' needs. n other words, it is necessary to establish the highest possible guarantee of the provision of these socio-economic resources. t has even been indicated that constitutional guarantees of would add scope and intensity to freedom as non-domination (Ravent s, 2000).

1 A detailed analysis of the mechanisms whereby the aforementioned social groups would have expanded republican freedom as non-domination is beyond the scope of this paper which aims to focus on matters that are strictly confined to normative philosophy.

1 Translated from the Spanish edition.

19 t is the principle of 'contestability' that, according to ettit, must guide a political system that aims to minimise domination. owever, it should be pointed out that this assertion is not incompatible with consensus continuing to be the basic regulative ideal in a republican deliberative process. ' onsent' and 'contestability', then, are not necessarily opposing principles (Francisco and Ravent s, 2002).

20 ited by Richard (1995).

21 See footnote 14.

22 The analysis of hilippe van ari s (1995) is in keeping with these considerations.

Aguiar, F. 2002. ' n Adam Smith republicano ', in A. Domènech and A. de Francisco (eds.), *ep licanismo* (in press).

Aristotle 1995. *Nicomachean ethics*, the revised Oxford translation, edited by onathan arnes (rinceton, rinceton niversity ress).

_____ 1995. *Politics*, revised Oxford translation, edited by Jonathan Barnes (Princeton, Princeton University Press).

Casassas, D. 2002. 'Nuevos instrumentos para una nueva ciudadanía. Balance del Primer Simposio de la Renta Básica', in *El Vuelo de Ícaro. Revista de Derechos Humanos, Crítica Política y Análisis de la Economía* 2–3 (Madrid, Liga Española Pro-Derechos Humanos).

Domènech, A. 1989. *De la ética a la política. De la razón erótica a la razón inerte* (Barcelona, Crítica).

_____ 1998. 'Ocho desiderata metodológicos de las teorías sociales normativas', in *Isegoría. Revista de Filosofía Moral y Política* 18 (Madrid, Consejo Superior ' de Investigaciones Científicas).

_____ 1999. 'Cristianismo y libertad republicana', in *La Balsa de la Medusa* 51–52 (Madrid, Ediciones Antonio Machado).

_____ 2000. 'Individuo, comunidad, ciudadanía' *Contrastes. Revista interdisciplinar de filosofía*, Supl. 5 (Málaga, Universidad de Málaga).

_____ 2002. *Democracia, virtud y propiedad*, in press.

Francisco, A. de 1999. 'Republicanismo y modernidad', in *Claves de Razón Práctica* 95 (Madrid, Progresa).

_____ and Raventós, D. 2002: 'Republicanismo y renta básica', in A. Domènech and A. de Francisco (eds.), *Republicanismo* (in press).

Frank, R. 1999. *Luxury fever* (New York, Simon and Schuster).

Gargarella, R. 1995a. *Nos los representantes. Crítica a los fundamentos del sistema representativo* (Buenos Aires, Ciepp/Miño y Dávila Editores).

_____ 1995b. 'El ingreso ciudadano como política igualitaria', in R. Lo Vuolo (ed.), *Contra la exclusión. La propuesta del ingreso ciudadano* (Buenos Aires, Ciepp/Miño y Dávila Editores).

Machiavelli, N. 2001. *Discorsi sopra la Prima Deca di Tito Livio* (Roma, Salerno Editrice).

Marx, K. 1981. 'Crítica del programa de Gotha', in K. Marx and F. Engels, *Obras escogidas* (Moscú, Progreso).

Montagut, T. 2001. 'Republicanismo y Estados de Bienestar', in *Claves de Razón Práctica* 112 (Madrid, Progresa).

Pettit, P. 1997. *Republicanism. A theory of freedom and Government* (Oxford, Oxford University Press).

Polanyi, K. 1944. *The great transformation* (Boston, Beacon Hill).

Putnam, R. D. 1993. *Making democracy work: Civic traditions in modern Italy* (Princeton, Princeton University Press).

Rae, J. 1965. *Life of Adam Smith* (New York, Augustus M. Kelley).

Raventós, D. 2000. 'El salario de toda la ciudadanía', in *Claves de Razón Práctica* 106 (Madrid, Progresa).

_____ and Franciso, A. de. 2002: 'Republicanismo y Renta Básica', in *Veualternativa* 192 (Barcelona, Esquerra Unida i Alternativa).

Red Renta Básica 2002. *La renta básica* (Barcelona, Red Renta Básica).

Richard, C. 1995. *The founders and the classics* (Cambridge, Mass., Harvard University Press).

Ste. Croix, G.E.M. de. 1988. *La lucha de clases en el mundo antiguo* (Barcelona, Crítica).

Sunstein, C. 1988. 'Beyond the Republican revival', *Yale Law Journal* 97.

_____ 1993. *The partial constitution* (Cambridge, Mass., Harvard University Press).

van Parijs, P. 1995. *Real freedom for all: What (if anything) can justify capitalism?* (Oxford, Oxford University Press).

17

WORKING POOR IN EUROPE: A PARTIAL BASIC INCOME FOR WORKERS?

Wolfgang Strengmann-Kuhn[1]

1. Introduction

While the problem of the working poor is widely discussed in the United States, there are very few empirical investigations of the working poor in Europe; and this group barely features in the public and political debate about poverty. In Europe it is typical to think of 'the poor' as non-workers such as the unemployed, pensioners and children, or as people whose ability to work is restricted, such as single parents. However, this paper will show that a substantial share of the poor work, and that the majority of the poor in Europe live in households with at least one household member working.

The question thus arises of what mechanism can prevent workers from falling into poverty. Since the working poor have an income, albeit insufficient, a partial basic income (PBI) could be a means of fighting poverty for this group. I will propose a model for a partial basic income for workers and discuss its consequences, advantages and disadvantages.

2. The Working Poor in Europe

For the discussion it makes sense to have some basic empirical background information about the working poor in Europe. For several years a comparable data set has been available for all countries in the European Union except Sweden. Using this data set I will answer some simple questions, such as: how many working poor are there in the EU and its member states, and what are the causes of poverty among the working poor?

2.1 Definition and Measurement of Poverty

The first question, however, is: what is poverty and how is it measured? There are a variety of poverty definitions and measures (see Atkinson, 1998, pp.10ff.; Hagenaars, 1986; Strengmann-Kuhn, 2000; Van den Bosch, 1999). Though the alternatives cannot be discussed here in detail, the following outlines the approach used for the investigations presented in this paper.

One basic distinction is the difference between direct and indirect measures of poverty (see Ringen, 1988; Sen, 1981). Indirect measures are based on what is known as the resource definition of poverty; that is, people are poor if they lack resources, and are not poor if they have sufficient resources, independent of their use. Direct measures of poverty are based on the observation of an individual's current living standard and supply of goods. Most international comparative investigations, including those for this paper, use indirect measures based on income.

When an income definition of poverty is used a number of questions have to be answered regarding measurement. The first is what income should be used: the income period (monthly, yearly or weekly income), the kinds of income sources (especially if non-monetary income can be included), gross or net income, and so on. Another question is the income unit. Typically, household income is used. Thus it is presumed that income is equally distributed within the household or – more precisely – that income is distributed in such a way that the welfare of each household member is the same. This assumption can be criticized (see Jenkins, 1991; Ruspini, 1998; Burri, 1998), because intra-household transfers may not actually take place or ensure that everyone in the household has the same welfare. Nevertheless, it cannot be observed how income is distributed within a household, and the assumption that income is not distributed within the household is even less plausible than the equal distribution assumption.

Besides the problem of unequal distribution within the household, household income itself is not a good measure for welfare. A more obvious measure would be *per capita* income. But this neglects economies of scale: a two-person household does not need twice the income of a single-person household, and children do not need as much as adults. The solution to this problem is to calculate an equivalent income using a weighted equivalence scale. One customary scale, used in this paper, is the (original) OECD scale, where the weight of one adult is one, the weight of other persons in the household aged 15 years or older is 0.7, and each child under 15 years has a weight of 0.5. The equivalence scale is then calculated by dividing the household income by the sum of weights of the household.

Finally, there is the question of the poverty threshold. Usually the poverty line is defined as a percentage of average income. Here, too, several points must be clarified. The first is whether national averages or a Europe-wide standard are used (see Atkinson, 1998, pp. 27ff.; Vos and Zaidi, 1998). Typically, poverty is defined by a national standard, which corresponds to the poverty definition used by the Council of the European Union. The second is the percentage of the average to be used: typical choices are 40 per cent, 50 per cent or 60 per cent. The third is how to calculate the average. There are several possibilities, each of which has advantages and disadvantages (see Hagenaars et al., 1994). Usually the median or the (arithmetic) mean is used. The median is the point at which exactly 50 per cent have a higher income and 50 per cent a lower one. The mean, which is higher than the median, is the income if there were to be equal distribution. In this paper I use 50 per cent of the mean as a poverty threshold, a threshold also used by Eurostat (Eurostat, 1997). In more recent publications, Eurostat changed this to 60 per cent of the median (Marlier and Ponthieux, 2000; Mejer, 2000; see also Atkinson et al., 2002). However, both thresholds are roughly the same for all member states of the EU (see Hauser et al., 1999).

In summary, in this paper I will use the following poverty measure: a person is poor if she or he lives in a household with a monthly net equivalent income below 50 per cent of the mean equivalent income (MEI), with the original OECD scale used as the equivalence scale. However, the European Community Household Panel provides the possibility of using several other poverty measures (Strengmann-Kuhn, 2000). Results for the working poor using alternative measures of poverty can be found in Strengmann-Kuhn (2002). These alternatives are

- yearly instead of monthly income;
- the subjective poverty line, where both the poverty line and the equivalence scale are estimated empirically; and
- a poverty line based on a welfare function that is dependent on both income and direct measures of welfare.

2.2 Definition of the 'Working Poor'

The next step is to clarify what is meant by 'working poor', a term which remains rather ambiguous both in political discussions and in the academic literature. One possibility is to define as working poor persons whose individual wage lies below a certain threshold (Schäfer, 1997); this threshold may be a poverty line, a percentage of the average wage or determined in some other way. In this case, however, the term 'poor' is misleading: workers with a low wage are not necessarily poor, because they may receive income other than wages, or other household members may have an income high enough to keep the household out of poverty.

Another possibility is to define the working poor as all workers who are poor – that is, according to the definition of poverty used in this paper, all workers who are living in a poor household. Following the ILO (International Labour Organization), the term 'worker' designates all who worked at least one hour in the week before the interview. In the literature on the working poor this definition is sometimes restricted further to certain types of workers. But in some studies the definition of the working poor is extended to all household members who live in a poor household with at least one worker (Knöpfel, 1999; Caritas Schweiz, 1998). In this paper four different definitions are used:

- all workers living in a poor household;
- all full-time workers living in a poor household;
- all people living in a poor household with at least one working household member (working poor household);
- all people living in a poor household with at least one full-time working household member (full-time working poor household).

2.3 Database: The European Community Household Panel (ECHP)

The database for the following empirical results is the European Community Household Panel (ECHP). The ECHP is a data set provided by Eurostat, collected in the countries of the European Union since 1994. The ECHP is a panel study, i.e. the same households are interviewed each year. In 1994 it covered 12 countries that were then EU members; Austria was added in 1995 and Finland in 1996. Sweden does not take part in the ECHP. The aim of the ECHP is to acquire comparable data for all countries using a similar questionnaire. The advantage of this data set for poverty research is that it includes detailed data on income and a number of additional indicators, which can be used for poverty measurement. This paper analyses the data from 1996, the third wave.

2.4 Empirical Results

In the following only some basic findings about working poor in Europe are presented (for further results see Strengmann-Kuhn, 2001 and 2002). The first question is: what are the poverty rates of workers? The results are shown in Figure 17.1. In all countries the poverty rates of workers are below the

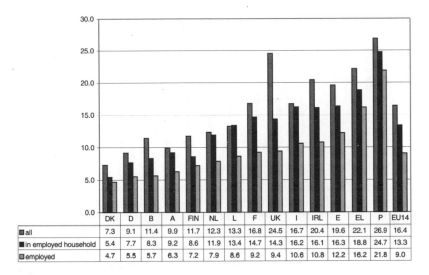

	DK	D	B	A	FIN	NL	L	F	UK	I	IRL	E	EL	P	EU14
all	7.3	9.1	11.4	9.9	11.7	12.3	13.3	16.8	24.5	16.7	20.4	19.6	22.1	26.9	16.4
in employed household	5.4	7.7	8.3	9.2	8.6	11.9	13.4	14.7	14.3	16.2	16.1	16.3	18.8	24.7	13.3
employed	4.7	5.5	5.7	6.3	7.2	7.9	8.6	9.2	9.4	10.6	10.8	12.2	16.2	21.8	9.0

Source: European Community Household Panel (ECHP) (1996), author's calculations
Note: DK = Denmark; D = Germany; B = Belgium; A = Austria; FIN = Finland; NL = Netherlands; L = Luxembourg; F = France; UK = United Kingdom; I = Italy; IRL = Ireland; E = Spain; EL = Greece; P = Portugal.

Figure 17.1 Poverty rates in the member states of the European Union (%)

average poverty rates. Across the EU (except Sweden) the poverty rate is 16.4 per cent in the whole population, but 'only' 9 per cent of all workers are poor. The poverty rate in employed households, that is, households with at least one employed household member, is higher than for the worker alone in all countries. For the EU this poverty rate is 13.3 per cent, which is still lower than the general poverty rate. This is typical for all member states; only in Luxembourg is the poverty rate in employed households slightly higher than for the whole population.

Workers have the highest poverty rates in Portugal (24.7 per cent) and Greece (18.8 per cent), followed by Spain, Ireland and Italy with poverty rates between 10.6 per cent and 12.2 per cent of all workers and about 16 per cent in employed households. This means that the poverty rates connected with employment are particularly high in southern Europe and in Ireland. These are also the regions with the highest general poverty rates. At the bottom of the ranking are the countries in which poverty rates are also low for the whole population, namely Denmark, Germany, Belgium, Austria and Finland. In general there is a correlation between the poverty rate for the whole population and the rate for the employed. The most striking exception is the United Kingdom, which has the second highest poverty rate for the whole population but poverty rates for employed located in the middle of the ranking.

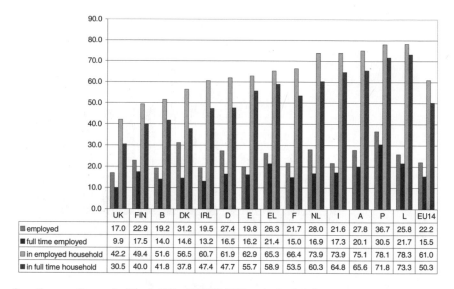

	UK	FIN	B	DK	IRL	D	E	EL	F	NL	I	A	P	L	EU14
▨ employed	17.0	22.9	19.2	31.2	19.5	27.4	19.8	26.3	21.7	28.0	21.6	27.8	36.7	25.8	22.2
▪ full time employed	9.9	17.5	14.0	14.6	13.2	16.5	16.2	21.4	15.0	16.9	17.3	20.1	30.5	21.7	15.5
▨ in employed household	42.2	49.4	51.6	56.5	60.7	61.9	62.9	65.3	66.4	73.9	73.9	75.1	78.1	78.3	61.0
▪ in full time household	30.5	40.0	41.8	37.8	47.4	47.7	55.7	58.9	53.5	60.3	64.8	65.6	71.8	73.3	50.3

Source: European Community Household Panel (ECHP) (1996), author's calculations.
Note: UK = United Kingdom; FIN = Finland; B = Belgium; DK = Denmark; IRL = Ireland; D = Germany;
E = Spain; EL = Greece; F = France; NL = Netherlands; I = Italy; A = Austria; P = Portugal; L = Luxembourg.

Figure 17.2 Shares of the working poor among all poor in the member states of the European Union (%)

As a consequence, the share of the working poor among the poor is lowest in the UK. Only 17 per cent of the poor in the UK are employed and only 10 per cent of them are working full-time (see Figure 17.2). Nevertheless, even in the UK, 30.5 per cent of the poor live in a full-time working poor household and 42.5 per cent in a working poor household. In all other countries the majority of the poor live in a working poor household: in Portugal and Luxembourg this proportion is over 80 per cent; in the Netherlands, Italy and Austria it is over 70 per cent and in Germany, Spain and France it is between 60 per cent and two thirds. In the EU as a whole, 50.3 per cent of the poor live in households in which at least one member works full-time. If all kinds of employment are included, this percentage increases to about 61 per cent. The shares of employed persons themselves among the poor are somewhat lower, between 17 per cent (UK) and 36.7 per cent (Portugal). Between 9.9 per cent (UK) and 30.5 per cent (Portugal) of the poor are full-time workers.

These percentages refer to all poor including children and the elderly. Focusing on people in the primary working-age group (25 to 55 years), more than a third of the poor in the EU work full-time; an additional 10 per cent work less than full-time (see Figure 17.3). Compared to the 43.3 per cent who

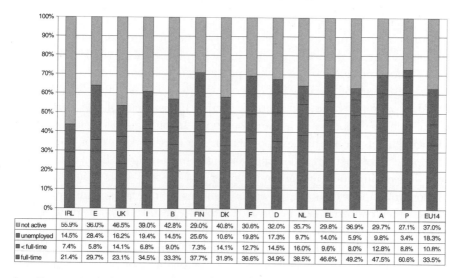

	IRL	E	UK	I	B	FIN	DK	F	D	NL	EL	L	A	P	EU14
not active	55.9%	36.0%	46.5%	39.0%	42.8%	29.0%	40.8%	30.6%	32.0%	35.7%	29.8%	36.9%	29.7%	27.1%	37.0%
unemployed	14.5%	28.4%	16.2%	19.4%	14.5%	25.6%	10.6%	19.8%	17.3%	9.7%	14.0%	5.9%	9.8%	3.4%	18.3%
< full-time	7.4%	5.8%	14.1%	6.8%	9.0%	7.3%	14.1%	12.7%	14.5%	16.0%	9.6%	8.0%	12.8%	8.8%	10.8%
full-time	21.4%	29.7%	23.1%	34.5%	33.3%	37.7%	31.9%	36.6%	34.9%	38.5%	46.6%	49.2%	47.5%	60.6%	33.5%

Source: European Community Household Panel (ECHP) (1996), author's calculations.
Note: IRL = Ireland; E = Spain; UK = United Kingdom; I = Italy, B = Belgium; FIN = Finland; DK = Denmark;
F = France; D = Germany; NL = Netherlands; EL = Greece; L = Luxembourg; A = Austria; P = Portugal

Figure 17.3 Employment status of the working-age poor in the member states of the European Union (%)

are employed, the 18.3 per cent share of the 25- to 55-year-olds who are unemployed is relatively low. Portugal has the highest employment ratio of the poor. More than 70 per cent of the working-age poor are employed and more than 60 per cent of them work full-time. In all of the other countries, less than half are full-time workers. However, nearly half the poor in Austria, Luxembourg and Spain work full-time; when workers who are employed less than full-time in these countries are included, the majority of the poor between 25 and 55 years are working. In the Netherlands, Germany, France and Denmark about half are employed, but with a relatively high share of part-time workers, such that about 40 per cent of all working-age poor are employed full-time. This is nearly the same percentage as in Italy, Belgium and Finland, but in these three countries there is a lower additional share of poor part-time workers. The lowest employment ratios of working-aged poor are found in Ireland, Spain and the UK. The percentages are below 40 per cent (in Ireland below 30 per cent). The lowest percentage of full-time workers among the working-age poor is found in the UK and Ireland, with a higher additional share of part-time employment in the UK. It must be emphasized that in all countries more working-age poor are employed full-time than are unemployed.

To gain a final impression of the extent of the working poor in the countries of the European Union, working poor rates are calculated – that is, the percentage of the working poor in the population as a whole (see Figure 17.4). Since Portugal has the highest poverty rate with employment, as well as the highest share of working poor among the poor, it is not surprising that the working poor rates are also highest. Nearly 10 per cent of the Portuguese population work but live in a poor household. Including household members, 20 per cent of the Portuguese population live in a working poor household, 19.3 per cent of them in a full-time working poor household. In all other countries the working poor rates are much lower. In Greece, 5.8 per cent of the population work and are poor; in all other countries the rate is less than 5 per cent. These other countries can be divided into two groups. Ireland, Italy, Spain, France, Luxembourg, the UK, and the Netherlands have relatively high working poor rates. Between 3.4 per cent (Luxembourg) and 4.2 per cent (UK) are employed and are poor, and about 10 per cent of the population lives in working poor households. But it must be noted that there are different reasons for these relatively high working poor rates. While in the UK and Ireland the working poor share among the poor is relatively low, but poverty rates relatively high, the reverse applies in Italy, Luxembourg and the Netherlands.

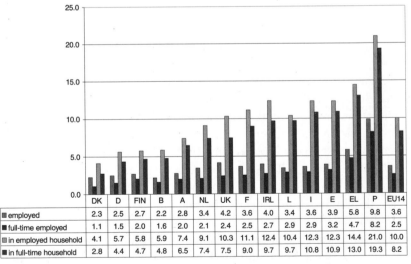

	DK	D	FIN	B	A	NL	UK	F	IRL	L	I	E	EL	P	EU14
employed	2.3	2.5	2.7	2.2	2.8	3.4	4.2	3.6	4.0	3.4	3.6	3.9	5.8	9.8	3.6
full-time employed	1.1	1.5	2.0	1.6	2.0	2.1	2.4	2.5	2.7	2.9	2.9	3.2	4.7	8.2	2.5
in employed household	4.1	5.7	5.8	5.9	7.4	9.1	10.3	11.1	12.4	10.4	12.3	12.3	14.4	21.0	10.0
in full-time household	2.8	4.4	4.7	4.8	6.5	7.4	7.5	9.0	9.7	9.7	10.8	10.9	13.0	19.3	8.2

Source: European Community Household Panel (ECHP) (1996), author's calculations.
Note: DK = Denmark; D = Germany; FIN = Finland; B = Belgium; A = Austria; NL = Netherlands; UK = United Kingdom; F = France; IRL = Ireland; L = Luxembourg; I = Italy; E = Spain; EL = Greece; P = Portugal

Figure 17.4 Working poor rates in the member states of the European Union (% of the population)

In the remaining countries – Austria, Belgium, Finland, Germany and Denmark – the working poor rates are comparatively low. Less than 3 per cent of the population work and are poor, and less than 7.5 per cent live in a working poor household. Nevertheless, even in these countries the problem of the working poor is not to be overlooked. For example, in Germany, a rate of 2.5 per cent of the whole population means that two million workers are poor. In total, 10 per cent of the EU population live in a working poor household; 2.5 per cent are employed full-time and poor.

In the final part of this section, we will look at the causes of poverty. For this it makes sense to analyse the income distribution process by looking at each stage at which income falls below the poverty line, that is, 50 per cent of MEI. The first stage is individual earnings, and the question is whether the wage would be high enough to avoid poverty if the worker were living alone. If that is not the case, I call it a poverty wage. The second stage is household earnings. Then the question analysed is whether the household earns enough to avoid poverty if there was no other income e.g. from capital or State transfers. Some workers rise from or fall into poverty between the first and second stages. Workers with a poverty wage may rise out of poverty because household earnings are above the poverty threshold; workers with a better than poverty wage may fall below the poverty line because other household members have no or insufficient earnings. The final stage is net household incomes, taking into account other income. If these fall below the poverty line then the household is poor.

Figure 17.5 illustrates this process. One can see that there are two ways for workers to become poor. The first is that the worker has a poverty wage and poverty cannot be avoided by earnings of other household members or other income like State transfers. Then the reason for poverty is low pay. The second way to become poor is that the worker has a sufficient income, but falls below the poverty line because of the household context.

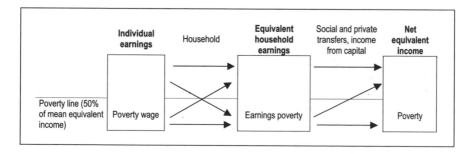

Figure 17.5 The income distribution process and poverty

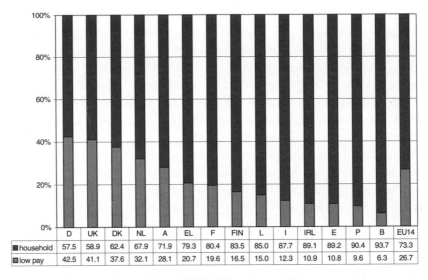

	D	UK	DK	NL	A	EL	F	FIN	L	I	IRL	E	P	B	EU14
■ household	57.5	58.9	62.4	67.9	71.9	79.3	80.4	83.5	85.0	87.7	89.1	89.2	90.4	93.7	73.3
▨ low pay	42.5	41.1	37.6	32.1	28.1	20.7	19.6	16.5	15.0	12.3	10.9	10.8	9.6	6.3	26.7

Source: European Community Household Panel (ECHP) (1996), author's calculations.
Note: D = Germany; UK = United Kingdom; DK = Denmark; NL = Netherlands; A = Austria; EL = Greece;
F = France; FIN = Finland; L = Luxembourg; I = Italy; IRL = Ireland; E = Spain; P = Portugal; B = Belgium

Figure 17.6 Causes of poverty of workers in the member states of the European Union (% of working poor)

Now we analyse which of these two causes (household context and low pay) can be found more often in each country. The working poor are distinguished between those who have a poverty wage and those who do not, revealing that the majority of the working poor falls below the poverty line due to the household context (Figure 17.6).

The highest percentages of low pay as a cause of poverty can be found in Germany and the UK (a little over 40 per cent), Denmark (37.6 per cent), the Netherlands (32.1 per cent) and Austria (28.6 per cent). In all other countries at least four-fifths of the working poor become poor due to the household context.

3. A Partial Basic Income for Workers?

3.1 Goals of Anti-poverty Policy

Before presenting and discussing a partial basic income as a means to prevent poverty among the employed, the goals of anti-poverty policy need clarification. Obviously the reduction of poverty is one goal. For this it would be sufficient to increase *a posteriori* the income of a person or household with an income below the poverty line, for example, by State transfers. The target is thus the last stage of the income distribution process described above. However, it is also an aim of social policy that people can receive an income of their own that is sufficient, independent of social or private support. Here, earlier stages of the income distribution process become targets for measures to fight poverty.

A point of discussion is whether the worker's own wage should be sufficient to avoid poverty. In former times when the male breadwinner model was typical, the answer to this question would be a clear 'yes'. Since this model belongs to the past – at least as the only model – the answer is not so obvious. The changing employment behaviour of women has several consequences. On the one hand, a man does not need to earn an income that is also sufficient for his wife, on the assumption that she does not have her own income. On the other hand, women's earnings in many cases still provide only additional income, often from part-time employment.

Therefore there are two points to discuss. The first is the extent to which the household context should be taken into account in fixing a target for a poverty-avoiding wage. The second is whether a poverty-avoiding wage should apply to all kinds of employment. It could be argued that in cases where the partner has a sufficient income, the wage need not necessarily be above the poverty line, because poverty could be avoided by intra-household transfers. However, it is not certain that these transfers actually occur. Furthermore, it was argued above that an aim of social policy is to make it possible for every individual to receive a sufficient income independent of private or social transfers, and there is no reason why this should not be the case with regard to private intra-household transfers as well. So, if a wage above the poverty level could be guaranteed, dependency (especially of women) on a partner could be decreased. Therefore a goal could be that the individual wage should be above the individual poverty line, that is, the poverty line of a single-person household.

The second question is whether this should be a goal for all kinds of employment. Should people who work only one hour per week receive a wage that is above the poverty line? I expect most people would answer this question with 'no'. One argument would be that the resulting hourly wage rate would be too high. So, what could be an employment threshold above which an individual income over the individual poverty line should be received? Surely there is a consensus that a full-time worker should receive a wage that is sufficient to avoid poverty. If part-time workers should also receive an individual income above the individual poverty line, then the following could be a sensible threshold. Germany has instituted what is known as *Geringfügige Beschäftigung* (minor employment), which is employment for fewer than 15 hours per week with a monthly wage less than €325. Such employment is usually seen as additional employment and not intended to secure a subsistence wage. Therefore it would make sense to say that a wage for employment that is more than a *Geringfügige Beschäftigung* should be higher than the individual poverty line. Incidentally, the €325 threshold is about half the German poverty line, measured as half of mean equivalent income. Thus this goal can be generalized for other countries: workers who have a wage of more than half the poverty line should receive an additional income taking them above the individual poverty line.

3.2 A Partial Basic Income for Workers

Means to reach this goal could be wage subsidies or a partial basic income (PBI) that looks like the following (see Figure 17.7). Each worker who earns more than a quarter of the mean equivalent income, or half the poverty line, would have the right to receive a PBI at the level of half of the poverty line. That would guarantee that all of these workers have an income of their own above the individual poverty line.

To limit the costs for this PBI it should be constructed in such a way that the net payment will decrease with increasing earnings. Figure 17.7 shows an example with a marginal tax rate of 50 per cent. Here only workers with earnings between 25 per cent and 75 per cent of average income, or 50 and 150 per cent of the poverty line respectively, would take advantage of the PBI.

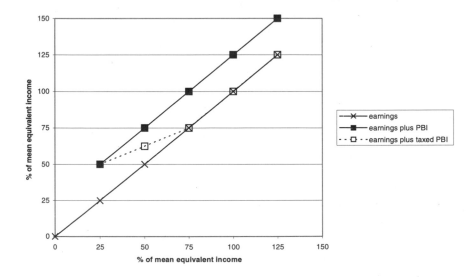

Figure 17.7 A model for a partial basic income for workers

Naturally, this tax rate could be higher (or lower). Then fewer (more) people would have a benefit from the PBI and the costs would be lower (higher).

As generally for basic income, this PBI could be constructed in two ways. One is to pay the PBI like a social dividend; everyone who has the right to receive it would get the PBI only by proving that her or his earnings were high enough. At the end of the year, the PBI would be taxed along with other income. People who earned more than 75 per cent of mean income would pay 100 per cent of the PBI as a tax, and below this income the tax would be 50 per cent of the difference between gross earnings and the PBI, as shown in Figure 17.7.

The advantage of this type of social dividend is that everyone who is eligible receives the PBI; there is no problem of non-take-up. The disadvantages are that the gross costs are relatively high and a large amount must be redistributed by the tax authorities. The second alternative is that the PBI be paid like a negative income tax or like a transfer. In this case, only workers with an income between 25 per cent and 75 per cent of the mean income would be eligible and they would only receive the difference between the PBI and the 'PBI tax'. Then the gross costs would be much lower, but the earnings would have to be checked, which might lead to non-take-up of the PBI. Beyond transaction costs, the costs are equal for both of these alternatives.

3.3 Discussion

A principal argument against a full basic income – a basic income at least as high as the poverty line – is that it is too expensive. A partial basic income obviously has much lower costs. This is not only because the payment for each person is lower, but also because the number of persons who are eligible for a net payment is reduced substantially. A full basic income at the level of 50 per cent of mean income and a marginal tax rate of 50 per cent would make a net payment to everyone with an income below the mean. The majority of people would receive a net payment, which is the main reason for the high costs of a full basic income. With a PBI as described above, only people with earnings between 25 per cent and 75 per cent of the mean income would receive a net payment, which limits costs.

What would be the effect on labour supply of the above model? There are three kinds of incentive. First, it is worthwhile for non-active persons of working age to become employed, particularly women. This is obviously positive. Second, there would be a benefit for workers who have only a *Geringfügige Beschäftigung* if they increase their employment above the 25 per cent threshold. This can also be judged as positive. Third, there is an incentive for workers above the 75 per cent line to decrease employment. This is positive in the sense that it would serve as an incentive for part-time work, which has positive effects on the reduction of unemployment. It might be argued from a feminist point of view that this reduces the link to the labour market for part-time workers, presumably more women than men. However, the other labour-supply effects are positive even from a feminist point of view and may compensate for this.

The third point of discussion is the effect on poverty reduction. The proposed PBI guarantees that the individual income of workers who earn at least half of the poverty line is above the individual poverty line. This reduces dependence on other household members, the State or other organizations, and thus the poverty risk. But it does not guarantee that the household income is above the household poverty line; the subsistence level of the other household members must also be satisfied. As shown in the empirical part of this paper, only a minority of the working poor, albeit in some countries a large minority, have earnings below the individual poverty line. The majority becomes poor because other household members have either not enough income or no income at all. However, for households in which one worker earns above the poverty line and another earns below the poverty line, a PBI for workers would help reduce the poverty risk. Furthermore, one frequent reason why workers become poor due to the household context is that their partners, in most cases women, are not working. Since the described PBI has a positive effect on labour-market participation, there would be another, indirect effect operating to reduce the poverty risk of workers. Nevertheless, to avoid the possibility of workers falling below the poverty line due to the household context, non-working household members must also be able to cover their individual subsistence needs, particularly children and the unemployed.

4. Conclusion: A Partial Basic Income – Not Only for Workers?

Not only in the USA, but also in the member states of the European Union, there is a high number of working poor. Among the poor more people are employed than unemployed, and a majority of the poor live in working poor households. It is not necessary for the working poor to receive a full basic income, because they have some income of their own. For workers whose earnings are at least half of the poverty line, a partial basic income as proposed above would be sufficient for them to reach their individual subsistence level. Compared to a full basic income it has much lower costs. Furthermore, there are mainly positive labour supply effects and the poverty risks of workers would decrease.

To guarantee that workers will not be poor, not only they but also other household members of a working poor household must have an income above their individual subsistence level. Children usually do not receive any State allowance reflecting their subsistence level, which is about the half the poverty line. One financially viable and effective model to guarantee that every child receive this subsistence level was proposed by Hauser and Becker (2001) and adopted by the German Green party (see Otto, 2002, Otto *et al.*, 2001), which calls it *Kindergrundsicherung* (basic income for children). Poverty then can arise only if the adults in the household do not have sufficient income. This prompts the thought of applying the idea of a partial basic income for workers to other groups as well. Like workers, non-working adults usually have an individual income such as unemployment benefits or retirement pension. Thus, an individual partial basic income at the level of half the poverty line for all children, and for all adults who have an individual income of more than half the poverty line, would greatly reduce poverty. For example, it would guarantee that single parents who have their own income – including individual social transfers – at half the poverty line would no longer be poor.

Finally, the question arises of why adults with an individual income below half the poverty line should not be eligible for the PBI. Two reasons for this are that the costs would be much higher and that the labour-supply incentives would not be as strong as those described above. More important, however, is that many of them do not need aid. Many of them are voluntarily unemployed or are voluntarily earning only a small amount, for example because they have a partner with a high income. It is not reasonable for the State to subsidize these individuals. Finally, resistance against a basic income would be lower if it were paid only to those who make a contribution to society, and if the recipients' own income were higher than the basic income. Of course, in the case of a partial basic income rather than a full basic income it would be necessary to have something like means-tested social assistance for those who are not making ends meet even though they receive a partial basic income. But these would be only exceptional cases.

Note

1   University of Frankfurt, Germany.

References

Atkinson, A. B. 1998. *Poverty in Europe* (Oxford, Blackwell).
_____, Cantillon, B., Marlier, E. and Nolan, B. 2002. *Social indicators: the EU and social inclusion* (Oxford, Oxford University Press).
Burri, S. 1998. *Methodische Aspekte der Armutsforschung* (Bern, Stuttgart, Vienna, Haupt).

Caritas Schweiz. 1998. *Trotz einkommen kein Auskommen: Working poor in der Schweiz* (Luzern, Caritas-Verlag).

Eurostat. 1997. *Income distribution and poverty in Europe – 1993*, Statistics in Focus: Population and Social Conditions (Luxembourg, Eurostat), 6/1997.

Hagenaars, A. J.M. 1986. *The perception of poverty* (Amsterdam, Elsevier).

————, de Vos, K. and Zaidi, M.A. 1994. *Poverty statistics in the late 1980s: Research in microdata* (Luxembourg, Eurostat).

Hauser, R. and Becker, I. 2001. 'Lohnsubventionen und verbesserter Familienlastenausgleich als Instrumente zur Verringerung von Sozialhilfeabhängigkeit', in H-C. Mager, H. Schäfer and K. Schrüfer (eds.) *Private Versicherung und Soziale Sicherung. Festschrift zum 60. Geburtstag von Roland Eisen* (Marburg, Metropolis Verlag).

————, and Nolan, B. with Hock, B., Mörsdorf, K. and Strengmann-Kuhn, W. 1999. *Changes in income poverty and deprivation over time. A comparison of eight European countries from the mid-eighties to the mid-nineties with special attention to the situation of the unemployed*, Working paper No. 21, Personelle Einkommens- und Vermögensverteilung in der Bundesrepublik Deutschland (EVS-Projekt- http//www.wiwi.uni-frankfurt.de/professoren/hauser/AP21.zip) (Goethe University Frankfurt/Main).

Jenkins, S. 1991. 'Poverty measurement and the within-household distribution: Agenda for action', in *Journal of Social Policy*, Vol. 20(4), pp. 457–483.

Knöpfel, C. 1999. 'Working poor: Stand des Wissens in der Schweiz', in R. Fluder *et al.* (eds.), *Berichterstattung zur Armut. Aktueller Stand und Perspektiven aus der Sicht der Statistik* (Neuchâtel, Bundesamt für Statistik).

Marlier, E., Ponthieux, S. 2000. 'Low-wage employees in EU countries', in *Statistics in Focus: Population and Social Conditions*, Theme 3–11 (Luxembourg, Eurostat).

Mejer, L. 2000. 'Social exclusion in the EU member States', in *Statistics in Focus: Population and Social Conditions*, Theme 3–1 (Luxembourg, Eurostat),.

Otto, B. 2002. *Die sozioökonomischen Folgen eines einkommensabhängigen Kindergeldzuschlags. Eine Mikrosimulation der Grünen Kindergrundsicherung*, DIW discussion paper No. 273 (Berlin, Deutsches Institut für Wirtschaftsforschung).

————, Spiess, K. and Teichmann, D. 2001. *Berechnung des Grünen Kindergrunsicherungsmodells und einer Gegenfinanzierung durch ein Ehegattenrealsplitting. Kuzgutachten des DIW Berlin für die Bundestagsfraktion von Bündnis '90/ Die Grünen* (Berlin, Deutsches Institut für Wirtschaftsforschung).

Ringen, S. 1988. 'Direct and indirect measures of poverty', *Journal of Social Policy*, Vol. 17(3), pp. 351–365.

Ruspini, I. 1998. 'Women and poverty dynamics: The case of Germany and Britain', *Journal of European Social Policy* Vol. 8(4), pp. 291–316.

Schäfer, C. 1997. 'Working poor: "Inequitable" wages in Germany and Europe – (higher) minimum wages as an instrument of justice?', in N. Ott and G. Wagner (eds.), *Income inequality poverty in Eastern and Western Europe* (Heidelberg, Physica).

Sen, A. K. 1981. *Poverty and famines. An essay on entitlement and deprivation* (Oxford, Clarendon Press).

Strengmann-Kuhn, W. 2000. *Theoretical definition and empirical measurement of welfare and poverty: A microeconomic approach*, Paper presented at the 26th General Conference of the International Association for Research on Income and Wealth (IARIW), August 27 to September 2, Cracow, Poland.

———— 2001. 'Erwerbstätige Arme in den Ländern der Europäischen Union', in I. Becker, N. Ott and G. Rolf (eds.) *Soziale Sicherung in einer dynamischen Gesellschaft. Festschrift für Richard Hauser zum 65. Geburtstag* (Frankfurt am Main, Campus).

_____ 2002. *Armut trotz Erwerbstätigkeit. Analysen und sozialpolitische Konsequenzen* (Frankfurt am Main, Campus).

Van den Bosch, K. 1999. *Identifying the poor, using subjective and consensual measures* , Proefschrift voorgelegt tot het behalen van de graad van Doctor in de Politieke en Sociale Wetenschappen aan de Universiteit Antwerpen.

Vos, K. de and Zaidi, M. A. 1998. 'Poverty measurement in the European Union: Country-specific or union-wide poverty lines?', in *Journal of Income Distribution*, Vol. 8(1), pp. 77–92.

18

BASIC INCOME, SOCIAL POLARIZATION AND THE RIGHT TO WORK

José Noguera[1] and Daniel Raventós[2]

1. Introduction: Two Classic Objections to Basic Income and Two Kinds of Conditional Benefit

Ever since basic income (BI) first emerged on the academic and political agenda, two objections of principle have been levelled by critics across the political spectrum. These objections, which have often led to the defence of a conditional income guarantee (CIG), may be posed as follows:

- why should we pay a BI to those who have enough income of their own, including the rich?
- why should we pay a BI to those who do not want to work, even if we understand 'work' in a broad sense?

The questions raise two central issues – the distribution of income and the distribution of work, paid or not. Critics of BI argue that any income guarantee should be based upon some entitlement condition beyond pure citizenship:

- an income, and perhaps a wealth, condition for entitlement to a public income guarantee;
- a work condition based on past, present or future participation in paid work: claimants must have worked a certain number of years – as in contributory schemes, or are expected to work if they are offered the opportunity, and/or to seek that opportunity, and/or to participate in activities to enlarge their employability – as is the case in social assistance and unemployment benefits. The work requirement may also consist of being currently in paid work as a condition for tax credits, for instance.

Some critics of BI may support both conditions and, in fact, in most advanced countries they apply together in many of the existing benefit schemes. However, they are in principle independent from one another:

- the existence of a means test does not necessarily imply a work requirement: some means-tested benefits do not require any work condition, for instance disability benefits, non-contributory pensions, child benefits or, in some countries, social assistance for poor or unemployed people;[3]
- conversely, the existence of a work requirement does not necessarily imply the existence of a means test, as with contributory benefits.[4]

This independence can be seen in Table 18.1, which classifies social and tax benefits according to their entitlement conditions.[5] The table includes traditional social benefits such as those mentioned above, but also tax benefits and allowances and other income-support measures:

- workfare – in the form of a 'right to work', or 'guaranteed work' – would require a work contribution as well as a means test;[6]

Table 18.1 Social and tax benefits according to entitlement conditions

| | | Work requirement | |
		Yes	No
Means-test or income condition	Yes	Non-contributory unemployment benefits Social assistance Tax credits and other in-work benefits Workfare or 'right to work'	Non-contributory pensions Child benefits Negative income tax (NIT) Income-conditioned CIG (social assistance without work requirement) Some income tax allowances (including 'life-minimum')
	No	Contributory pensions Contributory unemployment benefits Universal tax credit or tax allowance for employed people 'Chosen-time' subsidies (parental or sabbatical leave, early retirement, reduced working time) Participation income (PI)	Universal pensions Universal child benefits Basic income (BI)

- a negative income tax entails a means test but no work requirement;
- a CIG might require a means test but no work contribution. This is conceptually the same as a negative income tax, the only difference being that the benefit is claimed and paid not through the tax system but through the social services administration (that is, we would not have a tax-benefit integration). In fact, some European countries are very close to this 'extended social assistance' model; the Basque Country in Spain is the closest example;
- a participation income as proposed by Atkinson (1996) implies a work requirement – though in a broader sense than any workfare scheme – but no means test;
- finally, BI does not require any work or income condition.

The two objections mentioned at the beginning of this paper have been challenged in various ways by advocates of BI. However, these debates have centred on normative notions of equity, equality or reciprocity, as well as efficiency considerations. Here we want to examine such objections from a different point of view, that of social polarization. In Section 2, we will define this concept and outline how it may be related to those objections. Section 3 will deal with the claim that social polarization in the distribution of income would be better tackled by an income-conditioned CIG than by a BI. In the same way, Section 4 will consider whether social polarization in the distribution of work may be better reduced by a work-conditioned CIG than by a BI; in addition, the specific CIG analysed here is a 'guaranteed job' or 'right to work' approach. Finally, Section 5 will raise the normative question of why social polarization should be combated at all.

2. The Concept of Social Polarization

The concept of social polarization as distinct from social inequality has been refined by Esteban and Ray (1994). Although their attention has focused on applying the concept to the analysis of income distribution, it may also be applied to the distribution of work, rights or any other 'primary good'.[3] Esteban and Ray proceed as follows: inequality can be measured with the help of tools like the Gini coefficient (or many others – see Sen, 1997), or by comparing percentiles or income groups. However, a society S may be very unequal but not very polarized; conversely, a society S may be very polarized but not very unequal. This is because polarization relates to how the population forms broad clusters. The relevant attributes or characteristics such as income, wealth, jobs or rights of the members of each cluster are very similar, but different clusters comprise members with very different attributes. In other words, we can speak of social polarization when we face large groups or social classes that are internally very homogeneous but very heterogeneous in relation to the others. As Esteban and Ray point out, polarization appears when 'each cluster is very "similar" in terms of the attributes of its members, but different clusters have members with very "dissimilar" attributes' (Esteban and Ray, 1994, p. 819). Polarization entails a high degree of homogeneity within groups, and a high degree of hetero geneity across groups.

Esteban and Ray add a third condition: that the number of significantly sized groups must be small. Then, when in a society S the population forms two groups – rich and poor, for instance – which are very different from each other, but inequalities within these groups are low, we can speak of polarization without high inequality. By contrast, when in a society S the income of the better-off is much higher than the income of the worse-off – so that the value of the Gini coefficient is high – and the population does not form distinct groups but income varies along a continuum, then we can speak of relatively high inequality without polarization – taking income as the relevant attribute. So inequality does not require polarization, but polarization requires some degree of inequality even if low.

It follows from this definition that the difference between polarization and inequality may also be understood in dynamic terms: a given decline in inequality is fully compatible with an increase in polarization, and vice versa. As far as BI is concerned, even if it is shown that it would produce a decline in social inequality, it does not follow that it will reduce social polarization; in fact, it could increase it. Quite often the two mentioned objections against BI have to do with the concept of social polarization:

- the income condition is necessary, according to some critics, in order to stop the rich from taking more; in that case, even if a BI would reduce income inequality, a CIG would better reduce income polarization (Aguiar, 2001).
- the work condition is necessary, say some critics, because otherwise society would be polarized between two groups, those in and out of work; this would encourage parasitism, create social conflicts, and weaken incentives to social participation for those out of paid work (Krebs, 2000; White, 1997; Riechmann, 1996; Gorz, 1992; Elster, 1986).

In discussing these two statements, we should keep in mind that to say that BI can combat social polarization better than a CIG of any sort is not to answer the question of why we should combat social polarization as such. This question will be addressed in section 5; for the moment, we will simply assume that social polarization, either of income or of work, is unjust and should be reduced.

3. Basic Income and Social Polarization in the Distribution of Income

The first criticism of BI relates to its income-unconditional nature: why pay an equal amount to everyone including the rich, and not just those in need? This objection raises one of the traditional controversies of modern social policy, already considered by Beveridge and Titmuss: should we focus our resources on the needy or universalize social services and transfers? The debate has not ended and it is not our aim to study it here. But it is this same debate that underpins the opposition between CIG and BI: CIG relies on a philosophy of targeting, of focusing help only on those who need it.

In Spain, Fernando Aguiar (2001) has supported the idea that BI is not 'well-armed' to fight social polarization, because it is also paid to the well-off; a CIG paid only to those under a specified income level or out of employment would perform better.[4] Aguiar does not deny that, so far as income inequality is concerned, BI can be at least as effective as any form of CIG. It is well known (van Parijs, 2000b) that a CIG in the form of a negative income tax may produce exactly the same income distribution as a BI plus a sufficient tax rate, flat or progressive. But by the same token, it follows that social polarization is also unaffected by the conditional or unconditional nature of BI: it rather depends on the amount of BI and on the sort of tax system and rates that go with it.

Aguiar also did not bear in mind that one of the keys to understanding BI proposals is tax-benefit integration; virtually all costed BI proposals assume such integration, so that the well-off pay more in taxes than they receive by virtue of BI, and the less-well-off get better off – because their BI is higher than the taxes they pay. This is – or should be – obvious for BI proponents, or at least for egalitarian ones. We have shown that exactly the same income distribution may result from either CIG or BI: it is just a matter of properly adjusting parameters such as the amount of benefit, tax rates and the income threshold for tax exemption (Noguera and Raventós, 2002).

We can give an example and some implications in a more formal way. Our claim is that, given an income distribution (D), if we want to achieve a less polarized distribution (D'), we can do it in three equivalent ways:

(a) introducing a CIG of amount A paid only to the less well-off, plus a system of tax rates T paid by the well-off – Aguiar's proposal;
(b) introducing a BI of the same amount plus tax rates T' for the well-off, such that for them the difference between paying T and T' is equal to A; with a BI, there are always some tax rates T' whose effect on polarization is equivalent to that of the first option;

(c) introducing a BI of amount A', higher than A, plus some tax rates T for the well-off; that is, there is always a BI of amount A' whose effect on polarization is equivalent to that of option (a).

The distributive equivalence of these three options in terms of polarization may be clearly seen in the hypothetical example we present in Table 18.2. We suppose a polarized society S where the population is broadly divided into four income groups, two of them poor and the other two rich. The two poor groups comprise 50 per cent of the population, while the rich groups make the other 50 per cent. The table shows the average income of each group (in 'imaginary' income units) under the three reform alternatives. The column on the right displays a 'polarization index', which expresses the quotient between the income of the two poor groups and that of the two rich ones: as the index approaches 1, polarization declines. We can easily see that polarization does not depend on the conditional or universal nature of BI: choosing (a), (b) or (c) makes no difference to polarization; choosing (a) or (b) also makes no difference to inequality, for the simple reason that, in distributive terms, raising benefits is exactly the same as cutting tax rates, and vice versa.

Table 18.2 Equivalence between three different ways of reducing income polarization

	(A) Very poor	(B) Poor	(C) Rich	(D) Very rich	Polarization index
	Average income (units)				(A+B) ÷ (C+D)
Initial income distribution	10	20	150	300	0.066
Option (a) CIG, paid only to A and B Amount =15 Tax rates: 25% for C and 35% for D	25	35	112.5	210	0.172
Option (b) BI Amount = 15 Tax rate: 35%, with total exemption for A and B	25	35	112.5	210	0.172
Option (c) BI Amount = 16.5 Tax rates: same as in (a)	26.5	36.5	129	236.5	0.172

Therefore, if we have to choose between CIG and BI, polarization in the distribution of income is not a relevant criterion. Our conviction is that BI is preferable because CIG would require complex bureaucratic controls, additional to those implied by the tax system alone; besides, these controls would bear on the poor and not on the rich, and would hence promote well-known effects of stigmatization, non-take-up and poverty traps; furthermore, as van Parijs has convincingly argued (van Parijs, 2000b), CIG would have to be paid *ex post*, so it would leave many claimants unprotected during the often lengthy periods during which applications are handled and controls carried out. It is much more transparent and equitable to give the benefit to all, and afterwards withdraw it through the tax system from those above a defined income level.

4. Basic Income and the 'Right to Work'

4.1 Social Polarization in the Distribution of Work

The second objection we address relates to the polarization of work that BI would allegedly produce. This is more difficult to answer than the question of distribution of income, because it was easy to show that income distribution does not depend on the conditional nature of benefits. The distribution of work, however, is not a matter of adjusting tax and benefit parameters, but of people's expected behaviour. So we can say that the relationship between BI and social polarization is not so much about income, as about work.

Are the critics' fears justified? To start with, they overlook the fact that BI is precisely intended to fight the effects of social polarization in the present distribution of jobs – that is, the polarization between people in and out of the labour market, and also between 'good' jobs (well-paid, stable, with social rights, and with opportunities to develop a professional career and search for personal fulfilment) and 'bad' jobs (temporary, low-paid, without social protection rights, and without any opportunity of fulfilment or career development) (see Offe, 1992; De Wispelaere, 2000; van Parijs, 1995 and Groot and van der Veen, 2000). BI is designed to tackle the unequal and polarized distribution of 'employment rents' in a non-Walrasian labour market (van Parijs, 1995) and the benefits linked to employment. If we take 'work' as meaning something more than 'employment', BI seems to be better than the present situation: with a BI people would be likely to work in a more heterogeneous way, in and out of the labour market; the diversity of work life and styles would be much higher, and this would reduce and prevent polarization. As a result of economic security combined with labour market flexibility, BI would probably lead us to a less polarized society than the present one, as far as the distribution of work is concerned.

An extended income-conditioned CIG, because of its stigmatization and unemployment-trap effects, would perform worse than BI with regard to social polarization; in fact, it may reinforce the polarization between people in and out of paid work.[3] But this is not the case for other conditional proposals (such as a participation Income), which could have similar positive effects as those expected from BI. Other schemes, such as a legally guaranteed right to work, may even claim to correct directly the distribution of jobs while BI tries simply to 'compensate' for it in a monetary way. It is thus with these two forms of work-conditioned income guarantee that BI has to be compared in terms of social polarization.

Consider first a participation income (PI): would it prevent (or reduce) social polarization more than BI? If it was introduced, the most likely effects would be: (a) some people with 'bad' jobs would move to non-market activities; (b) that a number of employed people (whether in 'bad' or 'good' jobs) would probably reduce their market work-time to make it compatible with other activities or with more free time; (c) as a result of (a) and (b), some unemployed people would fill in the gaps, partially compensating for the movement from employment to non-market activities. The barriers between being in and out of work, and between paid and non-market activities would then partially blur. What difference could BI make in this scenario? Very little, it could be argued. It might well increase slightly the tendency to move from market to non-market work, but that could be all. In that case, polarization would increase slightly compared to the PI scenario. The difference would be small, we think, because with a PI the work-condition would be extremely difficult to enforce and control, and fraud could be as easy as 'pretending' to be a student, a caregiver or a volunteer. The cost of administrative checks would make the work condition extremely weak in practice. So we can consider that PI and BI would have almost equivalent effects on social polarization.

Consider now the 'right to work' or 'guaranteed work' approach (henceforth RW), as another possible form of CIG. It seems likely that RW would produce a more polarized situation than PI and BI, because it would tend to concentrate the working population in two – and only two – groups: those with market jobs and those with state-guaranteed jobs. Non-market activities would tend to be commodified or statised – unless a substantial reduction in working time went together with the RW, something that does not seem very probable. Thus, the polarization a RW would produce would be even higher than in the present situation, or a situation with an extended income-conditioned CIG.

We have so far considered the distribution of work only in a 'quantitative' way; but if we include in our analysis the quality of work, that is, the satisfactions and pains of different kinds of work, then the comparison is again quite favourable for BI. A guaranteed RW would have to reduce in some degree the free choice of work by individuals, and most state-guaranteed jobs could not be expected to offer a very promising field for personal fulfilment. In contrast, BI would enhance individuals' choices of any combination of any kind of work, and would make it possible for them to reject arduous and unpleasant jobs, which do not offer adequate compensation. So from the standpoint of work quality, BI (or PI) would also perform better than RW in avoiding a high degree of social polarization.

In short, the most plausible hypothesis seems to be that social polarization in the distribution of work (whether in quantitative or qualitative terms) would be increased by RW proposals, and reduced in a similar way by BI or PI proposals. So the work-condition objection to BI on grounds of social polarization appears as untenable. Note that, even if this were not the case, it would not necessarily constitute a reason to reject BI in favour of RW, because BI could still be better on other grounds or in relation to other valued ends. As Fitzpatrick (1999) or Groot and van der Veen (2000) have made clear, a comprehensive comparison between BI and other policy options has to reflect a complex set of policy aims. Even if BI performs worse than other measures on each of these aims, its overall performance may make it better than any other option. In the next sub-section we will leave for a while the polarization issue, in order to compare BI and RW on other grounds.[4]

4.2 Basic Income or Guaranteed Work?

As we have said, BI may have to be compared with a guaranteed right to work (RW) on grounds other than social polarization. One of us has tried to make this comparison (Noguera, 2002). Here we will offer a brief summary of arguments against RW and in favour of BI from a pragmatic viewpoint, without entering into the philosophical foundations of the debate on parasitism and reciprocity.

The advocates of the RW approach rely on two main arguments to prefer it to BI: first, a RW would avoid parasitism and, second, it would grant the right to social participation, as a necessary foundation of personal self-esteem. BI would allegedly not satisfy these two conditions: it would reproduce barriers to social participation and encourage parasitism. But what would a 'right to work' mean? What would it consist of exactly if it were to be institutionalized? We think that proponents of this measure have not yet answered these questions with enough precision. Let us mention, to start with, three conditions that any RW approach has to meet if it aims to be a real alternative to BI.

First, as Elster (1988) has convincingly argued, if the RW is to be a coherent proposal, it should be presented as the right to something more than an income, be it recognition, reciprocity, self-esteem, or something similar. This is implied by the adduced rationale for the RW: to grant social participation and/or to avoid parasitism. Otherwise, if the only objective were to secure an income for every citizen, there would be no reason to reject BI.

Second, we are speaking here of a 'right to work' in the sense of State-guaranteed employment of last resort for those who cannot find it by themselves in the labour market. This is so even if some activities which today are not paid – such as most care-giving and some kinds of community work – are included as guaranteed jobs in the programme. When we talk about a right to work, we are talking about paid work, otherwise the idea would not make any sense: we would be defending the right to work for free, which is absurd and, in practice, does not seem necessary to defend at all.

Third, recall that we are speaking of working as a condition to receive an income; so it is the 'duty' – and not only the right – to work that is advocated (provided you are able to work and want to receive some income from society). This is required if RW is to be consistent with the parasitism objection to BI. Of course, here 'duty' may be understood in two different ways: as a coercive legal duty – which we would like to think that nobody is proposing – or as a condition of obtaining something valuable, for example rights or income. Otherwise, the RW would not be an alternative to BI, but fully compatible with it, because there is conceptually no problem in having a BI and, at the same time, a right to a state-guaranteed job for those who freely claim it. This 'duty' component of RW proposals is somewhat surprising, because many left-wing advocates of this approach are at the same time fierce opponents of workfare and active welfare measures: the contradiction seems obvious.[5]

Providing the right to an employment of last resort, as a condition of receiving an income, would at first sight satisfy the two conditions avoiding parasitism (every citizen able to work would be given employment) and granting the right to social participation through employment provided by the State. But let us think how the State could implement such a right. In the first place, if an RW has to stand as an alternative to BI from a left wing and egalitarian point of view, then it has to satisfy certain conditions. A RW cannot be the right to any kind of work; for the proposal to be defensible from the Left, (a) it should guarantee decent jobs (with sufficient wages, proper labour conditions and social rights); (b) these jobs would have to satisfy some ethical conditions (it would not be acceptable to achieve full employment by producing weapons or polluting the country); and (c) they would have to make some sense for the worker (the question of whether the right to put stamps on envelopes for seven or eight hours a day is a right to work worth having).

We can now evaluate this RW approach in relation to BI. Proponents should show that RW is at least as feasible or desirable, or both, as BI.

However, this has never been demonstrated in detail due, in our view, to the difficulty of designing a feasible institutional structure for the RW that does not have inefficient or ethically undesirable effects. Indeed, the problems an RW would have to face are considerable:

- to start with, the net economic and organizational costs of implementing an RW – for example, in Spain – would be much higher than those of BI. It makes one dizzy to think of the number of decent and socially useful jobs that would have to be created, even if many of them were part-time. For example, today in Spain there are about 12 million people able to work who are not in paid employment. If we add those who have temporary or bad-quality jobs, that number could easily rise to 15 or 16 million. To provide all these jobs – with their entire wage, training, infrastructure and supervision costs – would be unthinkable without a social revolution or the imposition of an authoritarian regime (or both).
- What would be the entitlement conditions for having a State-guaranteed job? Should those jobs be 'appropriate' for claimants' qualifications, interests or careers? Could the State ask claimants to change residence or to travel? What degree of competence or productivity would it be fair to demand in 'guaranteed jobs'? How would the State monitor and supervise the whole project?
- It would be necessary to establish some normative criterion to decide which activities are to be considered 'socially useful'. However, this would lead to contradictions: for instance, why demand 'social utility' for the 'guaranteed jobs' and not for paid work in the market? This may be caprice, but why should weapons producers or property speculators has more rights and fewer controls than community workers and caregivers?
- There is another serious problem with the RW approach: the different quality of the jobs the state would be able to offer, that is, the equitable distribution of arduous or unpleasant jobs. A lot has been said in recent years about 'job sharing', but very little on the equitable sharing of the satisfactions and pains produced by different types of work. Solving this problem in a non-authoritarian way should be one of the main aims of any egalitarian defence of the RW; but we still have no clarification of this aspect from its proponents.
- How should the State deal with those who refuse to accept 'guaranteed jobs'? To force them to work would lead us back to the Poor Laws or the work camps, while to give them an income would be very close to BI. So the only coherent policy for those who defend the RW would be to do nothing, that is, to leave these people to fend for themselves. However, such a policy is problematic: first, it would discriminate by comparison with rentiers or speculators, who can live without working, so that the rationale for RW

proposals crumbles; second, and more importantly, the RW would not have ended poverty in our society. A consistent and sensitive egalitarian government would have to implement some form of income transfer for those individuals, so how far – or how close – would it be from BI?*

- Finally, it has been repeatedly argued and demonstrated that any guaranteed-work policy, which aims to offer 'social recognition' and 'self-esteem', has self-defeating results, and tends to frustration, disappointment and lack of motivation for many workers. Additionally, it tends to create a second tier of 'artificial' and 'charity' jobs that are often socially stigmatized. As Elster (1988) or van Parijs (2000a) have made clear, social recognition, like love, cannot be granted as a right.[6]

To sum up, the RW cannot be supported as an alternative to BI whether in terms of economic feasibility or on normative or ethical grounds. Maybe we should agree with Elster when he says that any RW we may reasonably create would not be a RW worth having. By contrast, proponents of BI have shown that it could be much more efficient and feasible way of raising the number of people in employment, and at the same time fostering a more equitable distribution of work – paid or not – and a higher degree of social reciprocity, without administrative control and without linking survival to paid work. In a complex post-industrial society, the RW remedy could be worse than the disease it aims to heal.

5. Conclusion: Should we Fight Social Polarization?

We have argued that BI proposals are at least as good as an income-conditioned CIG in fighting income polarization, and much better than a work-conditioned CIG or RW in fighting work polarization. But to finish this paper we could ask the following question: what is wrong with social polarization? Should we fight it *per se*? Nothing has been said about this question so far. Even when we speak of social inequalities, it is not clear that all of them are unjust. Usually, only those inequalities that come from circumstances not chosen by individuals are considered unjust, not those that come from circumstances which individuals are responsible for (Rawls, 1971; van Parijs, 1995; Domènech, 1996). It might seem that the same would be true for social polarization, which is only another sort of inequality.

Esteban and Ray (1996) have suggested a reason to fight social polarization *per se*, as distinct from social inequality: polarization is often at the origin of serious social conflict. Their contention is that 'polarization is closely linked to the generation of tensions, to the possibilities of articulated rebellion and revolt, and to the existence of social unrest in general' (Esteban and Ray, 1994, p. 820). But this is just a stability claim: it says nothing about why polarization is unjust. Some social conflicts or tensions may be unjustified as such in moral-distributive terms – think, for instance, of envy and anger against the Jews in Europe through the centuries – and, conversely, it is not totally clear why 'social unrest' or 'social conflicts' – and even 'revolutions' – should always be avoided, prevented or combated – think of a revolt against dictatorship, or how some groups of the radical Left have for many years regarded social conflict as a political aim in itself.

The reason suggested by Domènech (1996) seems more tenable: polarization is unjust because it has a harmful effect on social participation, civic virtue and active citizenship. As far as we assume some degree of republicanism, or some concern for 'public good' and 'civic virtue', then we must fight social polarization. To non-republican egalitarian liberals, this may sound like begging the question: the neutrality of liberal-egalitarian theories of justice may be seen as a problem for these theories or, a reason to be indifferent towards social polarization (as different from unjust inequality).

Furthermore, the two arguments might be somewhat conflicting: if Esteban and Ray are right and polarization leads to social unrest, then we could expect from a polarized situation a high degree of social mobilization and participation in public life – even if not institutional or 'deliberative'. Of course this kind of 'participation' and 'active citizenship' may not be of the same sort as Domènech was thinking of. The decrease in social conflict produced by lower polarization may well be the foundation on which republicans want to build a strong participatory public life, and an active conception of citizenship and civic virtue. There is no doubt that, if one subscribes to the republican ideal, then combating polarization, as distinct from unjust inequality, is desirable.

But this republican justification of the fight against polarization raises another problem, this time related to BI. If we really value social participation and active citizenship as ends in their themselves, then why should we not prefer a RW or, better a participation income (PI), more than an unconditional BI, which seems to be more sympathetic to liberal neutrality (see White, 2000). We could reply that, as BI reduces polarization better than RW (see Section 4.1.), and to fight polarization is a genuine republican aim, and then BI is not at odds with republicanism. However, this argument would not stand up against PI for, as we saw, a PI could be expected to fight polarization slightly better than BI. So it may appear that PI is a more 'republican' approach, while BI is a more 'liberal' one. Of course, for republicans this is not necessarily a reason to support PI rather than BI, because, as we already said, it is the overall performance of these measures against a complex set of different goals that should be considered.[7]

Let us go back to our first question: should we make the fight against polarization a specific aim of social policy, distinct and independent from the fight against unjust social inequalities? Or does this latter aim alone exhaust and include the former? Let us think again in a pragmatic way, and imagine some possible or real polarization situations, for example, the disappearing middle classes, the 'feminization of poverty', or ethnic segmentation of the labour market. These situations would certainly not pass the test of a Rawlsian liberal-egalitarian idea of distributive justice – not to mention van Parijs, Sen or Dworkin. So, if it is empirically the case that most social polarization situations are already targets of the fight against social inequality, why should we bother to categorize them separately? Think about the 'feminization of poverty': poverty, feminine or not, is something to be tackled *per se* from any liberal-egalitarian point of view – and even from some non-egalitarian ones, like Hayek's. Another, different issue is what kind of policy instruments are more appropriate to fight each kind of poverty, but on normative grounds, it is not the 'feminization' that provides the reason for fighting poverty as such.

Are we then concluding that BI proponents should not be too worried about social polarization, but just about compensating unjust inequality and securing real freedom, as van Parijs argued in *Real Freedom for All* (1995)? From a pragmatic point of view, it is not evident we should give more attention to fighting polarization than to fighting unjust social inequality. But, if we have to fight the first as well, we are convinced that BI can do this as well as any other form of income guarantee, and probably better than some of them.

Notes

1　Autonomous University of Barcelona.
2　University of Barcelona, Spain.
3　Or between people entitled to contributory social protection and those who are only entitled to an income-conditioned assistance (see Noguera, 2001).
4　This comparison is significant for us because the main opposition to BI from a left-wing point of view often comes from the idea that it would be better to grant paid work to all.
5　In Spain, for example, left-wingers who reject BI because of its work-unconditional nature have gone on strike against government measures, to tighten the work-requirement for unemployment benefits. However, it should be said that critics of BI from the Left have often supported something like 'basic work', that is, the just distribution of socially necessary work, paid or not, among all citizens able to work (Krebs, 2000; Riechmann, 1996). The feasibility of this idea seems near to zero in a complex modern society, and it would require an unthinkable degree of authoritarism and State control over the economy and the life choices of citizens (see Noguera, 2002).
6　In Spain we have recently witnessed the failure of 'charity jobs' in the form of a work-farist 'active income' policy for long-term unemployed with dependent children. During the two years this programme has been running, very few people have applied.

The reasons can easily be imagined; the wages are so low, the jobs so unpleasant, and the means test so tight, that it is better for unemployed workers to seek income in Spain's extended shadow economy.

7   On the relationship between BI and republicanism, see Raventós (1999).

References

Aguiar, F. 2001. 'Renta básica universal y polarización', in D. Raventós (ed.), *La renta básica* (Barcelona, Ariel).

Atkinson, A. 1996. 'The case for a participation income', *The Political Quarterly*, Vol. 67, No. 1, January-March.

De Wispelaere, J. 2000. *Universal basic income: Reciprocity and the right to non-exclusion*, Citizens Income Study Centre Occasional Paper (London, CISC).

Domènech, A. 1996. 'Desigualdad, responsabilidad, ciudadanía y polarización', in *Perspectivas teóricas y comparadas de la desigualdad* (Madrid, Fundación Argentaria).

Elster, J. 1986. 'Comment on van der Veen and van Parijs', *Theory and Society*, Vol. 15, pp. 709–22.

———— 1988. 'Is there (or should there be) a right to work?' in A. Guttman (ed.), *Democracy and the welfare state* (Princeton, Princeton University Press).

Esteban, J. and Ray, D. 1994. 'On the measurement of polarization', *Econométrica*, Vol. 62, No. 4, July.

Fitzpatrick, T. 1999. *Freedom and security. An introduction to the basic income debate* (London, Macmillan).

———— 1996. 'Polarización y conflicto', in *Perspectivas teóricas y comparadas de la desigualdad* (Madrid, Fundación Argentaria).

Gorz, A. 1992. 'On the difference between society and community, and why basic income cannot by itself confer full membership of either' in P. van Parijs (ed.), *Arguing for basic income* (London, Verso).

Groot, L. and van der Veen, R. 2000. 'How attractive is a basic income for European welfare states?', in L. Groot and R. van der Veen (eds.), *Basic income on the agenda. Policy objectives and political chances* (Amsterdam, Amsterdam University Press).

Krebs, A. 2000. 'The humanitarian justification of basic income', paper presented at the 8th Basic Income European Network (BIEN) Congress (Berlin, October).

Noguera, J. A. 2001. 'La Renta Básica y el principio contributivo', in D. Raventós (ed.), *La renta básica* (Barcelona, Ariel).

———— 2002. 'Renta básica o 'trabajo básico'? Algunos argumentos desde la teoría social, *Sistema* (Madrid, Fundación Sistema), No. 166, January.

———— and Raventós, D. 2002. 'La renta básica de ciudadanía: acerca de su justicia, el derecho al trabajo y la polarización social', *Claves de razón práctica* (Madrid, Progresa), No. 120, March.

Offe, C. 1992. 'A non-productivist design for social policy', in P. van Parijs (ed.), *Arguing for basic income* (London, Verso).

Raventós, D. 1999. *El derecho a la existencia* (Barcelona, Ariel).

Rawls, J. 1971. *A theory of justice* (Oxford, Oxford University Press).

Riechmann, J. 1996. "Sobre trabajar, comer, holgar y liberarse: el debate acerca del subsidio universal incondicional', *Mientras tanto* (Barcelona, Icaria), nº 64.

Sen, A. K. 1997. *On economic inequality*, Second edition (Oxford, Oxford University Press).

van Parijs, P. 1995. *Real freedom for all* (Oxford, Clarendon Press).

_____ 1996. '¿Cuándo son justas las desigualdades?', in *Perspectivas teóricas y comparadas de la desigualdad* (Madrid, Fundación Argentaria).

_____ 2000a. 'Real freedom, the market and the family. A reply', in *Analyse und Kritik*, Vol. 22, No. 2.

_____ 2000b. 'Basic income: Guaranteed minimum income for the 21st century', in *Papers de la Fundació Rafael Campalans* (Barcelona, Fundació Rafael Campalans), No. 121.

_____ Jacquet, L. and Salinas, C. C. 2000. 'Basic income and its cognates', in L. Groot, and R. van der Veen (eds.) *Basic income on the agenda. Policy objectives and political chances* (Amsterdam, Amsterdam University Press).

White, S. 1997. 'Liberal equality, exploitation, and the case for an unconditional basic income', *Political Studies*, Vol. 45.

_____ 2000. 'Rediscovering republican political economy', *Imprints*, Vol. 4, No. 3, Spring.

19

POPULAR SUPPORT FOR BASIC INCOME IN SWEDEN AND FINLAND

Jan Otto Andersson[1] and Olli Kangas[2]

1. Introduction

The Scandinavian countries are widely respected for their universal social policy. 'Universalism' in this context means that the right to social security is guaranteed on the basis of citizenship or residence. Social security in central Europe – Germany, for example – is more closely tied to an individual's position in the labour market, whereas in Anglo-Saxon countries – in Australia and New Zealand in particular – benefits are primarily distributed on the basis of need.

Because of the large rural population and the strong political representation of agrarian interests, social insurance schemes in Scandinavia were extended far beyond the traditional working class. Elements of universalism were already implanted in the agrarian structure of Nordic societies. The initial social security programmes in central Europe were worker insurance schemes, whereas 'national insurance' or 'people's insurance' was the underpinning idea in Scandinavia.

A basic income (BI), which would be automatically distributed to each individual, is the clearest example of a universal benefit. It could be seen as an extension of the unconditional child benefits and people's pensions that have been central components of Scandinavian welfare regimes. However, only in two of the Scandinavian countries – Denmark and Finland – has the idea of a basic income received serious attention. The discussions in Sweden and Norway have been relatively sporadic and utopian (Andersson, 2000).

In this study we are not focusing on the intensity and character of the discussion, but on the views of ordinary citizens. Are there also large differences in popular opinion in Sweden and Finland? How do people in general react to ideas related to a BI? Which forms, if any, are the most popular? Who supports and who dislikes different BI schemes? Do the old political lines of demarcation play any role? Is it possible to explain attitudes towards basic income by looking at different background variables and at people's views on the causes of unemployment and poverty?

The study is based on nationwide and representative opinion surveys conducted in Finland and Sweden. Gallup in Finland collected the data in May 2002 through telephone interviews of 800 respondents representing the Finnish population aged 15–80. TEMO[3] collected the data for Sweden in June 2002, also through telephone interviews of 1,000 Swedes aged 16 years and above.

2. The Questionnaire

In our surveys, we tried to formulate the questions so that they would pertain to the two main models of basic income:

- the negative income tax model; and
- the unconditional basic or citizen's income model.

In addition to these basic income questions, we asked four questions by which we tried to discover the way people would like to encourage employment. In one of these questions, we wanted to know how the respondents reacted to the idea of giving the unemployed a basic income, which they could keep even if they earned additional income. A positive answer to this question can be interpreted as support for a 'participation income' of the type suggested by Atkinson (1998). We also asked respondents to indicate a monthly level of BI that they thought appropriate.

The three other ways of encouraging employment we asked about were:

- public subsidy for low-paid jobs;
- stricter conditions for unemployment benefits; and
- creating jobs – including outside the ordinary labour market – tailored to the qualifications of the unemployed.

The first of these has been used in the United States in the form of an Earned Income Tax Credit (EITC). The EITC was introduced after the Negative Income Tax (NIT) experiments in the 1970s. The second and third questions reveal the position of the respondent towards workfare. BI has been supported as an alternative to workfare, but some BI proposals have been linked to job creation in the informal or 'third' sector, outside the ordinary labour market.

One question that lurks behind all debates on the proper degree of public involvement in the distribution of resources through various welfare-state measures is how rightful the individual's need is perceived to be, or how inescapable the social risks from which the need emerged are. If we see the need as unavoidable, such that the sufferer cannot remove it through his or her own actions, we generally support the giving of help. If we perceive the difficulties to be caused by people themselves we become more stringent. They have brought their misfortunes on themselves – why should others have to help them? (see e.g. Kangas, 2002) Instead, they should be whipped to work. In his studies of opinions on selectivity and universality in the Netherlands, van Oorschot (1997 and 1997) concluded that the first question the Dutch public is likely to ask before giving benefits is: 'Why are you needy?' Two main answers were offered. The first described the source of need as beyond the control of the individual, holding that society should be blamed. The second emphasized individual choices, meaning that the individual should be blamed. On the basis of previous studies it seems reasonable to suppose that these two aspects, 'social blame' and 'individual blame', play a crucial role in people's attitudes towards welfare measures. Therefore, we also included these dimensions in our surveys in order to see if they significantly affected opinions on basic security.

We were also interested in how different background variables affected support for basic income. These included gender, age, education, income, residence, socio-economic and labour market status, and in the Swedish case unionization and family size. We were especially interested in how political party affiliation affected attitudes towards BI.

Our questions on people's opinions on basic income and negative tax models were as follows:

1. NIT: 'What do you think about a system in which taxes and benefits are integrated so that those with very low incomes would automatically receive an income transfer (a so-called negative income tax) and those with high income would pay taxes as normal on their income over a certain limit?'
2. BI: 'What do you think about a system that would automatically guarantee a certain basic income to all permanent residents?'
3. 'How much should such a basic income be?' (in *kronor* or *markka* per month).

The respondents could choose between five options: very good idea; good idea, bad idea, very bad idea, no opinion/do not know. The amount of unconditional basic income was asked in former Finnish *markka*, since it is still easier for people to reason and calculate in *markka* than in euros.

Another set of questions was formulated in argument form. In the case of questions 4 to 10 the answering options were: totally agree, agree, disagree, totally disagree, no opinion/do not know.

4. PI: 'The unemployed should be encouraged to get jobs by paying them a basic income that they could retain even if they obtained additional income.'
5. 'The unemployed should be encouraged to get jobs by subsidising low-paid jobs.'
6. 'The unemployed should be encouraged to get jobs by tightening the qualifying conditions for unemployment benefits if they refuse offered jobs.'
7. 'The unemployed should be encouraged to get jobs by creating jobs tailored for them, even outside normal labour markets.'

The individual blame (8 and 10) and social blame (9) questions were constructed as follows:

8. 'Unemployment is the fault of the unemployed person him/herself.'
9. 'Unemployment is caused by social deficiencies.'
10. 'Poverty is caused by the fact that poor people are not enterprising enough.'

Previous studies (e.g. Rasinski, 1989; Kangas, 1998) on the impacts of wording indicate that results from opinion polls are sensitive to the way the question is posed. In order to evaluate to what extent, if any, some of our questions are word-sensitive, Finnish data also included an additional sample of 500 respondents where two of the ten questions were presented slightly differently. In terms of background variables (age, gender, etc.), the two samples were identical. In this smaller 'framed' sample the basic income question was presented as follows: 'What do you think about a system that would automatically guarantee a certain basic income (*citizenship wage*) to all permanent residents?' The other framed question dealt with attitudes to higher qualifying conditions: 'The unemployed should be encouraged to get jobs by tightening the qualifying conditions for unemployment benefits if they refuse offered jobs *even if those jobs did not correspond to their skills.*'

3. A Survey of the Results

In this section we shall present the results in simple tables comparing Sweden and Finland. In the next section we will analyse the relationships in order to find some causal explanations.

3.1 Negative Income Tax (NIT)

'What do you think about a system in which taxes and benefits are integrated so that those with very low incomes would automatically receive an income transfer instead of paying a tax (a so-called 'negative income tax') and those with high incomes would pay taxes as normal on their income over a certain limit?'

3.2 Basic Income (BI)

'What do you think about a system that would automatically guarantee a certain basic income to all permanent residents?'

3.3 Participation Income (PI)

'The unemployed should be encouraged to get jobs by paying them a basic income that they could retain even if they obtained additional income.'

Independently of how the question is framed, a majority of Swedes are critical of a basic income. In Finland a clear majority favours all three forms of basic income. Finns are especially attached to a 'participation income',

Table 19.1 Negative income tax

	Sweden (%)	Finland (%)
Good idea	13	76
Bad idea	47	14
Do not know	10	9

Table 19.2 Basic income

	Sweden (%)	Finland (%)
Good idea	46	63
Bad idea	48	32
Do not know	10	5

Table 19.3 Participation income

	Sweden (%)	Finland (%)
Agree	44	79
Disagree	50	17
Do not know	7	4

where a link is kept between the basic income and willingness to work. When we reframed the question on BI in the second smaller Finnish sample, using the term citizen's wage (CW), a clear majority (59 per cent) still supported the idea.

In both countries the differences between the sexes are insignificant. Young people are more enthusiastic than old. In Sweden 59 per cent of those aged 16–29 supported a BI. In Finland 78 per cent of the age bracket 15–24 years support both a BI and a CW. In both countries support tends to diminish somewhat with education and more clearly with income. In Finland, students (80 per cent, 78 per cent) and unemployed (93 per cent, 91 per cent) are strong supporters of both an NIT and a BI. We do not have figures for these categories in Sweden, but both are included in the group 'others', which significantly supports both an NIT (52 per cent) and a BI (54 per cent). In both countries those living in low-income households are most in favour, and those in the highest income bracket most against a BI.

In both countries people living in the countryside tend to favour a BI. The difference between cities and sparsely populated areas is somewhat stronger in Sweden (44 per cent and 57 per cent) than in Finland (61 per cent and 68 per cent). In Sweden lone parents were significantly in favour of both a NIT (58 per cent) and especially a BI (69 per cent). We do not have the corresponding figures for Finland.

When we look at political party affiliation we find some interesting results.

Proportion Responding Positively According to Political Affiliation

In both countries conservatives tend to be more critical than the others. In Finland, the supporters of the Left and the Greens are the most pronounced adherents, which is understandable since both parties have supported the idea in their party programmes. In Sweden the relatively high support from the Social Democrats and the Left (as well as from the Danish Confederation of Trade Unions – LO membership) is surprising, since both parties have turned down BI-initiatives, whereas the Greens, who have promoted the idea, do not seem to have such strong support among their voters.

That the Finns are more thrilled by the idea than the Swedes becomes evident by comparing the lowest support in Finland with the highest support in Sweden. Some 63 per cent of Finnish conservatives like the NIT model, whereas only 52 per cent of the Swedish Greens do so. 73 per cent of the Finnish conservatives support a PI, in contrast to 50 per cent of Swedish Liberals. Regarding a BI, however, the 65 per cent support from the Swedish Left beats all Finnish parties except the Left and the Greens.

Table 19.4 Sweden

Party	% positive response to:		
	NIT	BI	PI
Conservatives (M)	29	30	40
Liberals (Fp)	43	51	50
Centre (C)	42	32	47
Christian (Kd)	45	42	38
Social Democrats (S)	47	52	43
Left (V)	42	65	47
Greens (Mp)	52	37	38

Table 19.5 Finland

Party	% positive response to:		
	NIT	BI	PI
Conservatives (kok)	63	48	73
Centre (kesk)	79	61	80
Others (kd, sfp, etc)	83	59	89
Social Democrats (sd)	82	60	74
Left (vas)	86	85	88
Greens (vihr)	82	70	92

Table 19.6 Earned income tax credit

	Sweden (%)	Finland (%)
Agree	49	66
Disagree	50	28
Do not know	7	6

3.4 Earned Income Tax Credit (EITC)

'The unemployed should be encouraged to get jobs by subsidising low-paid jobs.'

The difference between Swedes and Finns is repeated when they are asked about a subsidy to low-paid work. EITC is a workfare-type measure, but it could be constructed in a way that resembles a PI. In both countries an EITC gets more support from women than from men, and from young than from old.

3.5 More Stringent Conditions

'The unemployed should be encouraged to get jobs by tightening the qualifying conditions for unemployment benefits if they refuse offered jobs.'

Both Swedes and Finns favour more stringent measures towards the unemployed if they turn down a job offer. We reframed the question in the second Finnish sample asking how the respondent would react if the work offered did not correspond to the qualifications of the unemployed. The acceptance of more stringency in such a situation diminishes, but it is still surprisingly high (61 per cent)

The difference between those employed and those unemployed is large: 75 per cent and 39 per cent respectively in Finland. For Sweden this difference seems to be smaller since the group 'others', which includes the unemployed, differs only marginally from the average.

3.6 Third-sector Employment

'The unemployed should be encouraged to get jobs by creating jobs tailored for them, even outside normal labour markets.'

Swedes are somewhat more sceptical of the possibility of deviating from the normal labour market.

3.7 Individual Responsible for Unemployment

'Unemployment is the fault of the unemployed person him/herself.'

3.8 Society Responsible for Unemployment

'Unemployment is caused by social deficiencies.'

Table 19.7 More stringent conditions

	Sweden (%)	Finland (%)
Agree	77	74
Disagree	22	24
Do not know	2	2

Table 19.8 Third sector employment

	Sweden (%)	Finland (%)
Agree	49	55
Disagree	43	36
Do not know	8	9

Table 19.9 Individual responsible for unemployment

	Sweden (%)	Finland (%)
Agree	16	14
Disagree	82	85
Do not know	2	1

Table 19.10 Society responsible for unemployment

	Sweden (%)	Finland (%)
Agree	64	70
Disagree	32	27
Do not know	4	3

Table 19.11 Individual responsible for poverty

	Sweden (%)	Finland (%)
Agree	22	26
Disagree	75	71
Do not know	3	3

3.9 Individual Responsible for Poverty

'Poverty is caused by the fact that poor people are not enterprising enough.'

The differences between the two countries are negligible in these three questions. A large majority among both Swedes and Finns tends to blame society rather than the individual.

Women are less likely than men to blame the individual and more likely to blame society. In Sweden young people, people with only basic education and people not belonging to a trade union are prone to blame *both* the individual and society. In Finland the youngest and the oldest, farmers and entrepreneurs tend to blame the individual. Those with a low education blame both the individual and society.

3.10 Level of Basic Income

'How much should such a basic income be?' (SEK or FIM converted to euros)

The table shows the percentage of all respondents, including those who did not respond because they did not think any BI would be a good idea. Those proposing a zero BI have been left out. The Swedes are clearly more generous than the Finns, but the average in both countries is high compared to the

Table 19.12 Level of basic income

Euros per month	Sweden (%)	Finland (%)
Less than 500 (F) or 550 (S)	16	33
500 (550) to 670 (F), 770 (S)	6	13
More than 670(F) or 770 (S)	46	25
Mean €/month	€970	€620
(No suggestion or zero)	32	39

existing lowest benefits and to the amounts (€250 – €500) that have been proposed in the political debates.

In general, men and older people propose a higher BI than women and youngsters. In Finland the proposed amounts rise with urbanization, but this does not seem to be the case in Sweden. In both countries those affiliated to the Left propose the highest amounts, and those with the Greens the lowest.

4. Explaining Attitudes Towards Basic Income

The tables presented above gave a rough overview of attitudes towards basic income. We can refine the analysis by looking at more complex relationships between different variables. Can we explain the attitudes towards basic income using the background variables and the variables expressing how the respondents tend to blame individuals or society? How are the proposed BI levels related to the attitudes towards BI and to the background variables?

Using the answers to the NIT, BI and PI questions, we constructed a composite measure for the attitude towards basic income: ATTIBAS. The answers to these three questions have high factor loadings in both countries and we calculated ATTIBAS as a sum of the attitudes towards NIT, BI and PI. The range of ATTIBAS goes from 1 (the most negative attitude) to 7 (the most positive attitude).

We also constructed another composite measure, INDIBLAM, using the two questions related to individual blame. The range of this measure goes from 1 (blames the individual least) to 3 (blames the individual most). We did not include the question on social blame in this composite measure, since in both countries its factor loadings were surprisingly low.

After these transformations we analysed the data using methods of path analysis. On each 'path' we looked for explanatory models which on the one hand gave the highest degree of explanation, and on the other only contained variables that were statistically significant. After much experimenting we could not find a structure that was adequate for both countries (one reason being that we did not have the same labour status data for the two countries). We started by looking for variables to 'explain' ATTIBAS, although it is questionable if this is a continuous variable. One variable that has some significance in both countries was INDIBLAM, and we also tried out explanations for this variable (which only takes on three values). In the Finnish case both party affiliation and socio-economic status seem to explain some of the variance in INDIBLAM. We then used ATTIBAS and other variables to explain the suggested amounts of BI. This type of analysis has its drawbacks, and the degrees of explanation tend to be low. However, we find the results to be worth reporting. The relationships are not counter-intuitive, and they point to some interesting differences between Finland and Sweden.

The explanatory models we ended up choosing were the two outlined in Figure 19.1. The thickness of the arrows expresses the statistical significance of each explanatory relationship.

The degree of explanation is somewhat higher in the Finnish case. One reason may be that we did not get the responses of the unemployed in Sweden separately. In Finland the labour market status and the individual-blame variables are good predictors of the attitudes towards BI. In Sweden income and age are the best predictors (low income or young age increases ATTIBAS). It is possible that income and age in Sweden act as proxies for the labour-market status variable in Finland. Either individual blame or residence adds to the explanation in Sweden. Blaming the individual or living in cities decreases ATTIBAS. In Finland the socio-economic status affects ATTIBAS only indirectly through INDIBLAM.

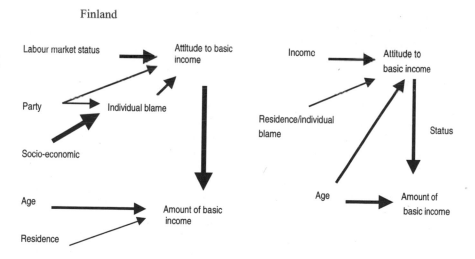

Figure 19.1 Explanatory models for basic income in Finland and Sweden

In Finland party affiliation affects ATTIBAS both directly and indirectly through INDIBLAM. In Sweden we could not find a similar relationship. This may be because the debate in Finland has differed from that in Sweden. The political parties have either endorsed or rejected the idea. We also found in the Finnish case that those who were sure of voting for a certain party also tended to agree more strongly with the party line on basic income (compared to more lukewarm supporters of the same party).

Age affects the proposed amount of BI in both countries. Young people are satisfied with a lower level and so are those living in the countryside in Finland.

The Finns are much more thrilled by a basic income than are the Swedes. The reasons may be sought on the individual level, but clearly there are some important differences in the economic, social and political situation, which are more interesting explanations. Factors we believe to be important are:

- the relatively low levels of unemployment in Sweden;
- the stronger adherence to the insurance principle (*inkomstbortfallsprincipen, standardtrygghet*) in Sweden;
- the stronger influence of the Centre, Left and Green parties in Finland, all of which have been relatively eager supporters of universal benefits that are not dependent on labour-market status;
- the lower level of basic security in Finland;
- Finns are less afraid of toying with new, even 'crazy', ideas.

Notes

1   Åbo Akademi University, Finland.
2   University of Turku, Finland.
3   A leading Swedish opinion poll firm.

References

Andersson, J. O. 1998. 'Inkomst utan arbete? Debatten om medborgarlön i Finland och Sverige', in *Historisk Tidskrift för Finland*, No. 2, pp. 356–377.

_____ 2000. 'The history of an idea: Why did basic income thrill the Finns but not the Swedes?', in R. van der Veen and L. Groot (eds.), *Basic income on the agenda* (Amsterdam, Amsterdam University Press), pp. 224–237.

Atkinson, A. B. 1998. *Poverty in Europe* (Oxford, Basil Blackwell).

Forma, P. 1999. *Interests, insititutions and the welfare State. Studies on public opinion towards the welfare state* (Helsinki, Stakes).

_____ and Kangas, O. 1999. 'Need, citizenship or merit: Public opinion on pension policy in Australia, Finland and Poland', in S. Stefan and P. Taylor-Gooby (eds.), *The end of the welfare state: Responses to State retrenchment* (London and New York, Routledge), pp. 161–189.

Kangas, O. 1997. 'Self-interest and the common good: The impact of norms, selfishness and context in social policy opinion', in *Journal of Socio-Economics*, Vol. 26, No. 5, pp. 475–494.

_____ 2000. 'Muurahaiset ja heinäsirkka: australialaisten ja suomalaisten mielipiteet oikeudenmukaisista sosiaalieduista', in *Yhteiskuntapolitiikka*, Vol. 65, No. 5, pp. 406–421.

Rasinski, K. 1989. 'The effect of question wording on public support for government spending', *Public Opinion Quarterly*, Vol. 53, pp. 388–390.

van Oorschot, W. 1997. *Who should get what, and why? On deservingness criteria and the conditionality of solidarity among the Dutch public*, Working papers 04/ Onderzoekschool Arbeid, Welzijn, Tilburg, Sociaal Economisch Bestuur.

20

THE PRINCIPLE OF UNIVERSALISM: TRACING A KEY IDEA IN THE SCANDINAVIAN WELFARE MODEL

Nanna Kildal[1] and Stein Kuhnle[2]

1. Introductory Questions

When the Holy Roman Empire of the German Nation was headed for dissolution it was neither particularly holy, specifically Roman, or much of an empire. How well does the concept of the Scandinavian welfare model describe the reality of the Nordic countries? Scandinavian? Welfare? Model? What makes whatever it is Scandinavian? And is 'whatever it is' headed for dissolution?

Basically we subscribe to the view that there is such a thing as a Scandinavian welfare model or type (or welfare regime), characterized among other things by the general adoption of the principle of universalism. The questions we shall discuss are: What is meant by universalism? When did the (defined) principle of universalism become embedded in the Scandinavian welfare states? Why did it become so important in Scandinavia? Who promoted the principle, with what arguments? Is universalism still intact following recent social and welfare policy reforms in Scandinavia?

Scandinavian welfare policies have undergone both minor and major changes during the 1990s, some of which imply stricter, others more generous, welfare policies. Interpretations of the reforms, which consist mainly of incremental changes, are varied and even conflicting. In 1990, Kuhnle' raised the question: 'Is the welfare state in the process of creating new divisions and conflicts? Could it be that we are moving towards what I shall call the segmented welfare society?' (Kuhnle, 1990, p. 17). The question was asked on the basis of the apparently or allegedly growing relative importance of fiscal welfare arrangements and employment- and work-related welfare schemes and benefits.[3] Today, in the field of social welfare policies proper, referring to Titmuss'

(1958) conceptual map, the move towards a possible dualism or segmentation has gained more attention in socio-political debates. In Norway the issue of targeting has come to the fore as poverty is on the agenda of the centre-right 'cooperation government' formed in October 2001 (Hatland, 2001). Thus, some argue that a process of convergence is pushing diverse European welfare states towards 'a corporate welfare model' and a dualization of welfare protection (Abrahamson, 1999, p.55). 'The flight from universalism' and 'a shift of paradigm' are characteristics that sum up the latter position (Sunesson *et al.*, 1998; Cox, 1998; Kildal, 2001). On the other hand, it has been claimed that in spite of changes and reforms during the last decade the institutional characteristics of the Scandinavian universal type of welfare state are likely to remain basically intact for the foreseeable future (e.g. Kuhnle, 2000).

An important question is, however, whether seemingly insignificant piecemeal changes may be understood as merely pragmatic adjustments or rather as indications of fundamental normative trends in the development of social policies. In fact, these piecemeal changes can be seen as evidence of a lack of reflection on the welfare state's normative basis. Especially in times of reform, it is essential to clarify changes in policies and principles of distribution, entitlements and eligibility in order to evaluate possible normative changes with long-term social, political and institutional consequences. With the aim of exploring this issue our paper focuses on the normative principle of universalism as a guiding principle in Scandinavian welfare policies, in contrast to the distributional principles of residualism and reciprocity.

2. The Conception of a Scandinavian (Welfare) Model

The concept of the Scandinavian model has gained wide acceptance in the social science literature as well as in journalistic essays. It can probably be traced to observations outlined in the book *Sweden: The Middle Way* which Marquis Childs, an American reporter, published in 1936. He argued that Sweden had found an admirable middle way between bolshevism and unregulated *laissez-faire* capitalism. Although the Swedish case was then, and during most of the period since the Second World War has been identified as the empirical embodiment of the Scandinavian model, in fact all five Nordic countries took off in the same developmental direction during the 1930s. All the Nordic countries won their crisis compromises in that decade, leading to new tension-reducing institutional solutions for mediation between agricultural and industrial interests as well as between the interests of organized labour and employers. This is the Nordic *Sonderweg*: crucial steps, unique in Europe, towards building a broad political consensus on a platform of a State-regulated socially-modified capitalism were taken before the Second World War.[4]

According to Erikson *et al.* (1987), the core of the Scandinavian model 'lies in broad public participation in various areas of economic and social life, the purpose of which is to promote economic efficiency, to improve the ability of society to master its problems, and to enrich and equalize the living conditions of individuals and families. In social policy, the cornerstone of the model is universalism.' By this is meant that the Scandinavian countries – 'at least on paper' – have set out to develop a welfare state that includes the entire population. In summary:

> global programmes are preferred to selective ones: free or cheap educa-tion for all in publicly owned educational institutions with a standard suf-ficiently high to discourage the demand for private schooling; free or cheap health care on the same basis; child allowances for all families with children rather than income-tested aid for poor mothers; universal old-age pensions, including pension rights for housewives and others who have not been in gainful employment; general housing policies rather than 'public housing' (Erikson *et al.*, 1987, pp. vii-viii).

Kuhnle (1990) lists 11 components of welfare systems which, taken together but with partial exceptions, set Scandinavian/Nordic countries apart from other welfare states. Among these are the relative size of government welfare provision; size of welfare employment (broadly speaking); public employment as proportion of total employment; redistribution; high legitimacy for State/public welfare provision; and universal citizenship-based social rights. 'Their universal embrace has anchored the Scandinavian welfare states' claim to a special status' (Baldwin, 1990, pp. 51–52). However, the principle of uni-versalism is also part of the Beveridge post-war development in the United Kingdom and, indeed, Scandinavian post-war developments were partly inspired or spurred by Beveridge (1942) and the introduction of the National Health Service in the UK in 1948.

Esping-Andersen and Korpi (1987) label the Scandinavian welfare states institutional welfare states in contrast to 'marginal' or 'residual' welfare states and the 'corporatist' or so-called 'reciprocal' ones, based on earlier attempts at classification of welfare state models (see e.g. Wilensky and Lebeaux, 1958; Titmuss, 1974). A few years later Esping-Andersen (1990) renamed the vari-ous categories of welfare state models, and replaced the title 'institutional' with that of 'social democratic'. The underlying view is that the institutional alias social democratic model prescribes the welfare of the individual as the responsibility of the social collective: all citizens should be equally entitled to a decent standard of living; and full social citizenship rights and status should be guaranteed unconditionally (Esping-Andersen and Korpi, 1987, p. 40).

The hallmark of the contemporary Scandinavian institutional welfare state is expressed in terms of three essential features: social policy is comprehensive; the social entitlement principle has been institutionalized (social rights); and social legislation has a solidaristic and universalist nature.

3. What is Universalism?

The concept of universalism is central in different European traditions of thought. In theology it connotes a religious view that asserts the ultimate salvation of all souls (*inter alia* in opposition to Calvinist predestination). In moral philosophy the concept denotes different moral theories arguing for principles of universal validity, independent of particular traditions, cultures or relations. In sociology, universalism is primarily attached to Talcott Parsons and the universalising of citizens' relationships during the nineteenth century, replacing particular groups of membership. In the area of politics, the principle of universalism was initially expressed in the eighteenth-century idea of human rights. In welfare policy, universalism as a distributive principle has been discussed since the nineteenth century. It is associated with some kind of equity and redistribution; yet the content of universal ideas in welfare policies remains somewhat unclear. Universal welfare policies are often contrasted with selective policies of a residual, means-testing kind, targeted at the poor. However, it is important to bear in mind that selective policies include insurance-based, reciprocal programmes targeted at individuals who cannot provide for themselves, as well as programmes restricted to the working population. While in general there are striking conceptual confusions in welfare policy and theory, the conceptual polysemy regarding universalism may be due partly to its different dimensions. Two of these are of special importance – membership and principles of allocation.

3.1 Membership

Democratic governance has, so far at least, been closely interconnected with the nation state; just as the democratic constitutional State guarantees equality before the law and equal political status for all citizens, the main characteristic of a universal welfare state is the high degree of population coverage; people are attributed rights by virtue of membership in a particular community. The whole population, or to be more precise, all members of a population category (e.g. people beyond a certain age, sick people, families with children, etc.) are, as a matter of right, beneficiaries of schemes that cover certain politically-defined need situations. A problem of definition remains, however: What is 'the whole population'? According to Kuhnle (1990, p. 15) and Hatland (1992, p. 23; 2001, p. 35), citizenship appears to be the basis for membership in universal social security systems. Others define membership according to residence: 'The Nordic countries have established a universal model of social protection, where benefits and services based on residence are combined with earnings-related social insurance programmes' (Palme, 1999, p. 9). Residence is obviously the most comprehensive principle and the most generous to immigrants, guest-workers etc.[5] In addition to the confusion produced by mixed definitions of membership within a universal welfare state, between welfare states this mix may produce serious gaps in social protection systems.[6] In a world of increasing migration, these gaps represent a challenge to principles of justice for all democratic governments – especially for welfare states that claim to be universal.

3.2 Allocation of Benefits

How welfare benefits and services are allocated is another dimension of universal welfare policies. This issue is even more intricate than the membership one.

Universal Versus Discretionary Benefits?

A distinction is frequently made between universal and discretionary allocation of benefits. Universal policies are contrasted with selective ones in which gatekeepers, often based on integrity-violating investigations and discretionary evaluations, determine the eligibility of applicants (see Rothstein, 1998, p. 21). However, no comprehensive universal welfare state manages without discretionary allocations. Certainly, the ideal-typical universal allocation is the distribution of an unconditional 'basic income' to all residents in a defined area. Yet, this universality is restricted in all known welfare policies; the benefits are generally allocated by category, related to politically defined needs arising at different stages of life. More importantly a just universal welfare state that is not only aiming at achieving a basic security for all, but also at compensating for social and natural inequalities, is compelled to include discretionary evaluations. As Titmuss noticed some 30 years ago:

> Universalism is not, by itself alone, enough: in medical care, in wage-related social security and in education. This much we have learnt in the past two decades from the facts about inequalities in the distribution of incomes and wealth... (Titmuss, 1968, pp. 134–35).

He therefore advocated a particular infrastructure of universal policies that incorporated 'positive selective discrimination' in income maintenance, housing, health care, and education – that is, complex professional discretionary assessments of needs. Individual discretionary assessments may thus be a precondition for fair treatment within universal welfare systems.[7]

Differentiation of Needs

Hence, the distinction between objective and discretionary assessments of needs is not essential to identify universal welfare policies. A distinction between types of need is, however, important for the demarcation between universal and selective policies. A primary function of the welfare state is to protect its members against social risks. It is characteristic of the development of the Scandinavian welfare states that an increasing number of risks, such as unemployment, illness and the like, have been recognized as matters of public responsibility. Thus, the categories of citizens with legitimate needs for protection have gradually expanded. Risks that have not been granted this recognition are subsumed under residual social support mechanisms like the Social Assistance Acts. As a consequence, a demarcation line is drawn between the testing of legitimate needs based on professional norms, without concern for the person's economic circumstances, and the testing of economic needs ('means'), i.e. of the ability to pay. Only the latter should be classified as selective 'since they select in relation to individuals' economic standing' (Rothstein, 1998, p. 20). Thus, professions and local administrators, i.e. the welfare state's gatekeepers, are granted a considerable discretionary power to decide who should be supported by the universal welfare state; the criterion for receiving support within selective welfare policies is lack of means. In this case, selective policies are targeted at the economically weakest part of the population. Insurance-based policies for the economically active population are also selective, targeted at those with the ability to pay. However, we should search for another (sub-)concept to distinguish between these two qualitatively different forms of selectivity.

Another necessary distinction is that between different kinds of assessments of economic needs. Means testing may be carried out according to quite precise rights-based rules or with a high degree of professional or bureaucratic discretion. Most benefits fall somewhere in between, but the distinction is important.

Graduated Universalism

As a preliminary last point in this conceptual discussion, universality and selectivity are clearly graduated along different dimensions: the concepts of universalism and selectivity are often used as entries to different ideological perspectives on welfare policy rather than as useful analytical tools (Hatland, 1992, p. 22). For instance, schemes that are universal in terms of population coverage normally have certain filters such as eligibility (age, years of employment, income earned, etc.) and benefit formulas (e.g. equal benefits or benefit amount based on certain criteria). Some of these filters may have become more important over time. For example, during the period 1959–1967 the Norwegian old age pension system was at its most universal, taking various dimensions of the concept of universalism into account. All those beyond a certain age received a pension, irrespective of work history, and, significantly, the size of the pension was equal for all beneficiaries. After 1967, pension benefits became unequal as the filter of work history was introduced – though from the early 1990s documented unpaid care work was added as an additional criterion for earning a supplementary pension beyond the minimum pension. Thus Scandinavian welfare states are not necessarily universal if by universal is meant equal benefits. Flat rate or uniform benefits were in one period considered especially egalitarian because they were regarded as an indication of the State's refusal to perpetuate market inequalities (Baldwin, 1990, p. 52).

4. Universal Welfare – When?

If we consider education as part of the welfare state, the Nordic countries stand out as relatively early proponents of universal education. An early step towards democratization and universalization of education was the demand for general literacy for all, women as well as men. This 'need' or 'demand' was in principle created in the sixteenth century when with the coming of the Reformation, the two Nordic kingdoms of Denmark-Norway-Iceland and Sweden-Finland became Evangelical Lutheran. The Church took responsibility for making the population literate.[8] Introduction of a general and compulsory system of elementary education came in the nineteenth century: provision of elementary schools was a duty of local authorities, and every citizen had the right to an elementary education of a certain length and of a broader secular content than the former church schools had offered (Sysiharju, 1981, pp. 420–21). Denmark was first, with a Public Education Act of 1814 which introduced seven years of compulsory education and obliged all municipalities to set up primary schools (Flora, 1983, p. 567); compulsory elementary education (length not specified) was introduced by law in Sweden in 1842 (ibid, p. 613); compulsory education for all children from the age of seven to confirmation (about age 14) was legislated in 1848 in Norway (ibid, p. 608); and a system of general elementary schools was by legislation established in principle in 1866 in Finland (Sysiharju, 1981, p. 421). Elementary education for all citizens was introduced partly under the influence of ideas behind the American and French revolutions.

Before the idea and institution of social insurance came firmly onto the agenda in European countries after the introduction of relatively comprehensive social insurance legislation in Germany in the 1880s, the welfare responsibility and role of States and governments was since the sixteenth century, to develop and maintain State-supported welfare or poor relief programmes. By the seventeenth century, virtually every European state had some sort of centrally established public welfare programme (Leichter, 1979, p. 22), among which the Elizabethan Poor Law of 1601 is probably the best-known case. The motivation was not always simply paternalistic or moral/religious, but also to maintain law and order. Early welfare measures, particularly health, were also related to the doctrine of mercantilism; thus the 'national interest' required State intervention in the area of public health (*Ibid.*). A healthy population was considered good for the creation of national wealth and strength.

Public health was one of the first areas in which the State began playing an active role, motivated not least by the empirical fact that epidemic diseases such as cholera, typhus and smallpox tended to be socially indiscriminate, affecting rich and poor alike. Some of the first positive exertions of State authority came in the area of public health; the first public health laws were introduced in 1832 in France and 1848 in England (Leichter, 1979, p. 31). The provision of free, State-supported and State-administered medical assistance to the needy was introduced as a reaction to industrialization and urban-related health problems in the nineteenth century. In England, such assistance was supplied under the Poor Laws, but at a social and political price: until 1885, to request free medical assistance resulted in pauperization (i.e. losing one's political rights and being subject to placement in a work-house). France was one of the first nations to provide free medical treatment and hospitalization for the needy, with the 1893 National Law for Free Medical Assistance (Leichter, 1979, p. 32). Sweden and Norway were among the countries which by the latter part of the nineteenth century employed doctors to provide free or inexpensive medical services to the needy, i.e. those without means, and to supervise public health programmes (Leichter, 1979, p. 32). This early selective legislation for the needy can – at least *post factum* – be looked upon as a step towards universalizing public health care.[9] The Nordic countries have a long tradition of health and medical services. Denmark passed a health law in 1858, followed by Norway in 1860, Sweden in 1874, and Finland in 1879 – all laws introducing control over and regulation of health and hygiene by local authorities (Kuhnle, 1981b).

After 1850, *die Arbeiterfrage* or the 'social question' frequently appeared in parliamentary discussions and deliberations in Denmark, Norway and Sweden. Though modest attempts at worker insurance following the emergence and growth of industrialization had been attempted in several countries, it was Germany under Bismarck which introduced a new concept of state-legislated social insurance in 1883, with all industrial workers being insured against sickness in a compulsory programmes.[10] This law was only one in a series of social insurance schemes to be implemented in Germany in the 1880s. The shift from the concept of Poor Law relief to the idea of social insurance was a dramatic and significant change in attitudes to public responsibility for certain types of risks or individual misfortunes. Scandinavian debates, and to some extent social policy developments, were influenced by the German legislation (Kuhnle, 1981a, 1996), but decisions varied as to priority of insurance needs, forms of organization, extent of population or worker coverage and whether insurance should be voluntary or compulsory.

Of particular interest here is coverage or membership of schemes. All the early laws were limited in terms of coverage, except the Swedish old-age and disability pension law of 1913 which, with minor exceptions, was universal in scope, although with varying rules of eligibility for different benefits (e.g. means testing). All early pension laws in the Nordic countries prescribed income-tested pensions. Not until after the Second World War was the right to receive a national pension independent of a means test instituted, thus making the schemes truly universal (1946 in Sweden, 1957 in Norway and Finland, 1964 in Denmark and 1965 in Iceland) (Kuhnle, 1981b). The Danish pension scheme of 1891 has been described as universal (Knudsen, 2000, pp. 9, 21), but that stretches the concept of universality too far: only deserving poor people aged 60 or more – who had not received poor relief during the previous 10 years – were entitled to a pension (Kuhnle, 1981a).[11]

Industrial accident insurance, first introduced in one form or another between 1894 and 1903, covered only industrial workers (in Iceland it included fishermen), but was gradually extended to cover all employees (Denmark 1916, Sweden 1927, Finland 1948, Norway 1958, Iceland 1965) (Kuhnle, 1981b). Sickness insurance was made voluntary in the first legislation in Denmark and Sweden in 1892 and 1891, respectively. Norway started out with a compulsory insurance scheme which in principle covered all wage earners below a fixed, relatively high income limit, thus proving much more supportive of the principle of universality than legislation in the other Nordic countries. The principle of universality was even more emphatic: Norway was the first country in the world to introduce, in 1909, the family-friendly principle in sickness insurance that the spouse (in practice, the wife) and children of the employee/worker were automatically insured without having to pay an extra premium (Kuhnle, 1983). Thus, a much larger part of the population was covered than statistics on the insured would indicate. Other European countries introduced corresponding family-friendly schemes from the 1930s onwards. Only after the Second World War, however, were all Nordic schemes were made truly universal, encompassing all citizens (Sweden 1955, Norway 1956, Iceland 1956, Denmark 1960, Finland 1963). With the exception of Norway, unemployment insurance has been voluntary in the Nordic countries and so less universal than other schemes. Unemployment insurance in Norway has been compulsory since 1938, adopted for nearly all wage earners, and organized by the State. However, any unemployed person in the other Nordic countries can claim economic assistance based on some kind of means test.

It was during the post-war period that the cornerstones of the modern welfare state were laid. Where previously Scandinavia had hardly differed from international trends, the new period gave rise to a uniquely Scandinavian model. This model is characterized by 'considerable inter-Nordic convergence' (Esping-Andersen and Korpi, 1987, p. 47).

The post-war construction of the welfare state went through two phases: the first was characterized by the general acceptance and establishment of universal population (or relevant category of population) coverage with a flat-rate benefit system; the second phase from the 1960s is marked by the introduction of earnings-related benefits, and thus also maintenance of status (and income) achieved in gainful employment.

5. Why Universal Welfare?

Originating in Europe at the end of the nineteenth century, the development of public health and social security has spread worldwide. The evolution of welfare states, in one form or other, is a universal phenomenon. But universal social programmes are less common, and were for a long time the hallmark of the Nordic and British welfare states. However, universal social security programmes from the early post-1945 period in Britain offered very low benefit levels, in practice, as intended by their 'architect' Beveridge, giving the market relatively more space than in Scandinavia. Though we have stressed that by universalism we refer to population coverage of programmes, and that the Nordic countries and Britain show similarities in this respect, a careful comparison would remind us that other aspects of social security and welfare programmes can be conducive to the development of institutionally very different types of welfare states, with Britain often placed in the category of 'residual', 'marginal' or 'liberal' welfare states. The Scandinavian–British contrast is not a topic to be pursued here. Rather, we shall focus on: Why was it that the idea of universal welfare and social security programmes, relatively generous although not always 'adequate' (variously defined) in terms of benefit levels, developed earlier and more strongly in the Nordic countries than elsewhere? Why did citizenship (or resident) status become as important as employment status in northern Europe, but not elsewhere? What possible structural factors were conducive to the emphasis on one or the other principle of membership of State welfare programmes?

5.1 Arguments Supporting Wniversalism

Goul Andersen (1999) has listed arguments that have been used in debates on universal (general, adequate) welfare schemes. Arguments against are that universal schemes are too expensive; require high taxes which have negative effects on the market; achieve less social equality; lead to inefficient priorities; create dependency cultures; increase transaction costs; and create excessive expectations among citizens. Arguments in favour of universal programmes have been (or are) that such programmes are market-consistent (create fewer negative incentives for saving, employment, etc); administratively simpler; remove incentives for abuse; create greater social equality; are non-stigmatizing; create and support community feeling and social cohesion; and support and increase citizens' resources and thus their autonomy.

Many of these arguments can be found in political debates and government documents at various times in the Nordic countries. At this stage we shall try to order them in distinct, broader categories and only briefly discuss some arguments that have been used in favour of universal programmes. Then we list some possible structural and contextual factors that may have been conducive to universalism.

The basis for universalistic Nordic welfare states, empirically a post-Second World War phenomenon, can be traced to idealistic and pragmatic ideas promoted and partly implemented in many early examples of social insurance legislation immediately before and after the turn of the twentieth century. Arguments in favour may tentatively be grouped in four main categories.

Community-building

Early social security programmes were initiated concomitant with political and economic 'modernization', in an era where State- and nation-building topped the agenda of European political leaders, and national identity- and community-building were important. New social groups pressed for political inclusion and, whether this fight was successful or not, social inclusion was considered important both by authoritarian State leaders (e.g. Germany, Austria) and more democratically oriented leaders (e.g. Scandinavian countries). Early programmes did not include all groups (although the Swedish pension law of 1913 came close), groups were excluded on different grounds (non-employed; economically well-off; morally 'unworthy' people), but an idea of universalism can perhaps be said to have been at least a latent element of the 'nation-building' project. In Norway, the concept of a 'people's insurance' appeared around 1900, and although 'people' and 'all citizens' (or 'all residents') were not synonyms at the time, an (intended or unintended) seed was sown. The first parliamentary workers' commission formulated among its proposals in 1894 that 'because of the greatness of the cause and the interest it has aroused, the pension scheme should cover the entire population' (Hatland, 1992, p. 55, our translation). In the far-off days before the First World War, important voices considered welfare and national efficiency complementary; welfare was supposed to prevent waste of human resources in a highly differentiated, unequal and 'class-saturated' society.[12]

Risk Exposure

The protection against social risks caused by a century of turmoil, war and change, and the novel idea of prevention, contributed to the recognition of the ideas of social rights and universalism (Titmuss, 1968). 'We are all in the same boat' is a normatively impregnated description of this risk-situation: every citizen is potentially exposed to certain risks and all capable citizens should share responsibility for meeting welfare needs arising from such risks. For instance, in 1918, the non-socialist Norwegian government's proposal for an old-age and disability pension covering all workers, rich and poor, was justified by the society's risk pattern; very few citizens could afford a lengthy loss of income, and thus nearly the whole population had an interest in the equalizing of risks. In this respect, the Norwegian non-socialist parties went against the international trend – the implementation of 'class insurance' for the less well off (except for Sweden) (Hatland, 1992, p. 56). Moreover, the high degree of universalism in population coverage was not supported by the Norwegian social democratic party, which, as late as 1946, proposed an old-age pension restricted to workers below a certain income limit. Soon afterwards, however, in the same year, the social democratic idea of a 'people's insurance' was transformed into a universal idea and implemented as a universal child allowance (*Ibid.*, p. 70).

It can be claimed that socialist or social democratic parties in the 1880s had a solidaristic vision of universal social programmes. For instance, in 1885 it was claimed 'the State should guarantee a general old-age pension with State subsidy for all classes of society' (*Det Norske Arbeiderparti*, 1918, p. 11, authors' translation). However, at that time it implied improving (selectively) the life chances of workers and the poor; it was not based on an idea of all classes and citizens being part of public programmes offering benefits to everybody, which has become part of post-Second World War social democratic programmes.

The famous Beveridge report, *Social Insurance and Allied Services* (1942), sought to establish a universal set of principles for social security – not merely against physical wants, but against all five giant evils of peace: poverty, disease, ignorance, squalor and idleness (1942, para. 456). The universalistic ambition of the report – the aim to expand the risk-pool from particular classes to all citizens – made it an immediate success. It inspired, for instance, the design of the Norwegian White Paper on a National Insurance Scheme that was presented in 1948 (Seip, 1994, pp. 152–53).[13]

Human Dignity

Early social programmes tended – without much controversy at the time – to exclude 'unworthy' people from coverage (beggars, drunkards, 'lazy good-for-nothing people'). Only after the Second World War did the concept of 'unworthy' people lose ground concomitant to the rise of the concept of human rights (civil, political, social rights) with the United Nations Universal Declaration of 1948: all citizens are 'equal' or of equal worth. According to Titmuss, an essential historical reason for adopting the twin concepts of social rights and universalism in welfare politics was to remove the humiliating loss of status, dignity and self-respect that goes with exclusion from programmes and entitlements. 'There should be no sense of inferiority, pauperism, in dignity or stigma in the use of a publicly provided service; no attribution that one was being or becoming a "public burden"' (Titmuss, 1968, p. 129).

According to Jose Harris (1994), Beveridge's biographer, the Beveridge proposals largely resulted from his long-term aversion to the Poor Law, selectivity and all forms of means-tested benefits. He fought the ethic of 'clientage, concealment, and calculated improvidence' that he assumed would ultimately corrupt the whole society (Harris, 1994, p. 26).

In the Norwegian socio-political debates too, the dignity argument was salient, expressing first and foremost a deep dissatisfaction with the existing poor relief system that offered little help to a heterogeneous group with quite different problems in a highly paternalising and stigmatising way. On several occasions in the 1950s, the Norwegian social democratic Prime Minister Einar Gerhardsen justified his proposal for moving from a means-tested to a universal old-age pension with dignity arguments; old people's self-respect and social standing were more important than economic equalization (Hatland, 1992, p. 74). This argument was also prominent in the justification of a universal child allowance in 1946, which noted the positive effects of not distinguishing between children of poor and rich families.

The other main argument was more pragmatic – the administrative costs of keeping the wealthy outside the system would eat up the resources saved by income limits – an argument that belongs to our forth and last group.

Economic and Bureaucratic Inefficiency

The principle of universal social programmes, i.e. no selectivity on moral or economic grounds, has also been promoted on a pragmatic basis. In Norway in the 1950s the Conservatives and other non-socialist parties pressed for reform of the means-tested old-age pension in favour of a universal (flat-rate) pension because as many as 75–80 per cent of all old people received means-tested pensions. To make pensions universal – a matter of citizen's rights – it was argued, would save huge amounts in administrative costs. The Conservative Party (*Høire*) in Norway was the first party to include in its pro-gramme, in 1949, the aim of a universal pension scheme (Sejersted, 1984, p. 528). Other arguments (often heard in these debates) were the claim that means-testing penalizes the will to work and save, and the problem linked to the demarcation line; different municipal practices undermined the legitimacy of the means-testing arrangements.

5.2 A Social Democratic Myth

Political actors are seldom consistent over time, and parties of similar ideo-logical predisposition have not always advocated the same arguments across countries. Several authors (e.g. Seip, 1981; Bull, 1982; Esping-Andersen, 1985; Bergh, 1987; Marklund, 1988) have claimed that universalism is a par-ticularly strong idea within the social democratic movement. This was not always so (Hatland, 1992). Social democratic parties were long in favour of means-testing of the wealthy both before and after reaching government, partly for class solidaristic reasons, partly for economic reasons (too expensive) and partly as a matter of principle (affluent people do not need public bene-fits) (ibid, p. 62). According to Hatland, their main contribution to universal social security in Norway was their struggle for means-tested insurance schemes, which seem to have a stronger inherent potential to develop into sys-tems of universal social insurance schemes than insurance originally estab-lished for certain occupational groups (see footnote 7). However, since the 1960s, social democratic parties, now with substantial experience as govern-ment parties, have tended to make the universal welfare state part of their image and trademark. They have become the great defenders of the univer-sal, solidaristic welfare state in which the rich and middle classes are con-sciously included as members and beneficiaries of uniform public programmes to promote egalitarianism and fight social differentiation, and as a means to underpin broad social and political support for the welfare state. The argument has been that universal programmes make for a 'better', more generous welfare state than selective, means-tested, stigmatizing programmes which the middle classes and well-off are assumed to take little or no interest in paying taxes to maintain (see e.g. Rothstein, 1998). 'Forced solidarity', it is argued, produces a better welfare state for economically, socially and politically weak groups than 'selective solidarity', even though in principle this latter should result in more economic resources being available for weak groups.

5.3 Universalism: A Vision, a Compromise or an Overlapping Consensus?

As we have shown in this preliminary analysis, different kinds of argument have been used in favour of universalism. Even though this analysis is tentative and must be substantiated through a closer analysis of historical documents, we have not found a clear social democratic vision behind the political initiatives towards universalism. At the same time, universalism can hardly be conceived of as a pure interest-based compromise, a result of a bargaining process. The interpretation that we will suggest, and which will be further explored, is that universalism was a result of a long, dynamic argumentative process developing towards an 'overlapping consensus' (cf. Rawls, 1993, lecture IV). Political actors were critical of different parts of the traditional social security system, and universalism was the alternative they gradually came to agree on. The driving force seems, in other words, to have been the same as that which inspired Beveridge's proposals for universalism – a deep discontent with the existing selective system.

5.4 Structural and Contextual Factors Conducive to Nordic Universalism

Can it be that certain social-structural conditions have been conducive to arguments in favour of universalism? Let us indicate four possible 'causal' factors, which, independently or in combinations, may have favoured a social and political climate for universalism in the Nordic countries, or have more easily put the Nordic countries on the track of universalism:

- *Historical institutional prerequisites*: The early fusion of the church and State bureaucracies since the Reformation in the 1500s made for a more unified and stronger public interest in and responsibility for welfare matters in general; citizens would direct their welfare demands towards government (central and/or local). Local communities had a long, pre-Reformation history of responsibility for poor relief or support. There was no 'competition' between State and church for provision of education and health services in the modern State- and nation-building period, as was the case in many other countries of Catholic Europe. And there was limited space for market and other non-governmental solutions. Development of universal programmes later on can also be interpreted as a result of piecemeal, pragmatic learning from experience of policies and their shortcomings. But, and this may be important, some early institutional solutions for social security programmes may have been more conducive to being transformed into universal programmes than other early solutions. For example, early means-tested pension schemes were easier to transform into universal citizenship based programmes than pension schemes based on employment record (Palme, 1999; Hatland, 1992; see footnote 7). Thus, early institutional solutions and structures made some later reforms, adjustments and extensions easier than other kind of reforms, and help explain strains of 'Nordic exceptionalism'.

- *Egalitarian pre-industrial society*: Nordic pre-industrial society was characterized by relatively egalitarian pre-industrial social structures; early predominance of independent or relatively independent peasants; historically early enfranchisement of peasants; the formation of separate agrarian political parties creating party systems distinct from those of other European countries and giving such parties a key role in formulating public policies in general, including welfare/social policies. Peasant farmers gained a relatively strong political role, and a more important role as taxpayers and potential beneficiaries of public policies. They were critical of public outlays in general, and particularly on outlays or programmes from which they would be excluded, so it was more difficult to draft social security policies covering only industrial workers. The socialist or social democratic forces were weak at the time of the industrial take-off and the political setting was more conducive to searching for and defining universal solidaristic welfare solutions rather than class-solidaristic solutions (e.g. first old-age relief/pension laws in Iceland (1890), Denmark (1891), Sweden (1913), Finland (1936), Norway (1937); first sickness insurance law in Norway (1909) – although elements of selectivity and means-testing were present, and 'unworthy citizens' were excluded).
- *Cultural homogeneity*: The combination of relatively egalitarian social structures, small and relatively homogenous populations in terms of ethnicity, religion and language, and a long historical tradition of public/communal responsibility for welfare issues, made universal social programmes more likely than in inegalitarian, culturally heterogeneous and fragmented societies. But over time, the idea of universalism gained strength beyond the Nordic countries, circumstances changed and lessons from historical and foreign examples could be learnt. Changing social structures, changing patterns of public-private interplays over time, may also weaken univeralist ideas and institutions in societies in which the majority of the population can be defined as well-off.
- Extraordinary crises: Although the idea of universal social security programmes was vented to some extent in the late 1800s, and was promoted in International Labour Organization (ILO) documents and in parliamentary committee reform proposals in Norway in the 1930s, it was only after the Second World War that universal programmes were actively and

comprehensively introduced in Scandinavia (and also in Britain, see above). The war experience itself has been mentioned by many (e.g. Titmuss, 1968; Seip, 1986; Goodin and Dryzek, 1987) as an important driving force for solidáristic, universal social policy solutions; the devastating war brought leading political opponents closer together in their fight against Nazism and occupation and was conducive to forming a broader platform of common values for the prospective peace era.

6. Welfare Reforms of the 1990s: *quo vadis* Universalism?

In 1945, no Norwegian social benefits had universal coverage (Hatland, 1992, p. 78). As of the early 1970s, all Nordic countries had established universal coverage of old-age pension systems, sickness insurance, occupational injury insurance, child allowance and parental leave schemes. Unemployment insurance was in principle universal and compulsory in Norway only, while only union members were selectively covered in the other countries (Kuhnle, 2000, p. 388). The same overall institutional pattern was in place at the time of the international recession around 1990, and at the end of the 1990s, although with some modifications. The introduction of a partial income-test of the 'pension-supplement' part of the basic old-age pension in Denmark in 1994 can be seen as a potentially significant change towards means-testing, but in this case, it was means-testing at the top of the income scale, not the bottom. Similar means-testing of the top income earners was introduced as part of the 1998 pension reform in Sweden, and in the Finnish reform of 1996–97: the hitherto universal minimum national pension is offered only to pensioners with employment-derived (earnings-dependent) pensions below a certain income limit (which is set high) or to people beyond pensionable age who have not been employed (Kuhnle, 2000, p. 388).

These are interesting novel examples of tendencies towards introducing selectivity in the allocation of benefits in universal membership schemes in Nordic welfare states – interesting precisely because the very few at the top of the income pyramid are excluded from some benefits. Simultaneously, the insurance or reciprocity principle has been strengthened in the Swedish and Finnish pension reforms by establishing a closer link between what is paid into the system and what can be taken out. In the Norwegian case, this link was weakened during the 1990s in the national pension scheme, but incentives for taking out private pension insurance have been maintained. Thus the overall effect of policy changes has been to strengthen the insurance principle in Norwegian pension policy. Proposals to retract from the principle of universalism in the allocation of benefits have been discussed, but not implemented, in the field of child allowances, using a similar method of means-testing to that for pensions.

An important arena for changes in thinking and reform of the western and Nordic welfare states has been employment policies. Unemployment and worklessness are firmly on the agenda, and even in Norway, with little experience of high unemployment rates, the issue of non-work has been given much political attention during the last decade. A general feature of European welfare policy reforms in this area is the trend towards active measures rather than passive, negative sanctions rather than incentives, duties rather than rights. Other trends include a public-contract approach rather than a rights-based approach and an emphasis on selectivity rather than universality (Ferrera and Rhodes, 2000, p. 4–5). In this area, at least, a kind of convergence seems to be evolving, both in terms of the interpretation of political challenges and in terms of the political answers, irrespective of national institutional preconditions and political colour of the government.

The primacy of work has always been central to Scandinavian welfare legislation. Characteristic for these welfare states is the close relation between the institutions of welfare and work; the Scandinavian countries stand out as both 'strong work societies' and 'strong welfare states'. Thus, an 'active labour market policy' and the 'work approach' have been cornerstones of welfare policy since the Second World War, especially in Norway and Sweden. Yet, during the 1990s, new 'work' and 'activity approaches' emerged that tightened eligibility criteria and reduced periods and levels of support (Kildal, 2001). For instance, all four countries have introduced stricter qualifying conditions for unemployment insurance. In Norway, stricter medical criteria for disability pension were introduced in 1993. Qualifying conditions for sickness insurance benefits were tightened in Finland and Sweden (Kuhnle, 2000, p. 389).

The duration of social security support for single parents in Norway has also been reduced dramatically, from ten to three years, to encourage – or compel – single mothers to seek (re)employment. However, the most distinctive difference between the 'new' and 'old' work approaches is the introduction of a quite new kind of requirement: an immediate 'duty to work' in return for benefits in the lowest tier of the income maintenance system (Kildal, 1998).[14] It is this workfare element of welfare policies in Scandinavia which may be regarded as a new trajectory, different from the rights-based income security policy which can be said to come close to a 'citizen's wage trajectory' (Goul Andersen, 2000, p. 80). In Norway, the workfare element of the new 'work approach' is limited to the social assistance programme.[15] Still, as the qualifying criteria for receiving unemployment benefits have become stricter, unemployed newcomers to the labour market increasingly have to apply for the less favourable social assistance benefits. In 1997 the minimum income requirement for receiving unemployment benefit was nearly doubled, and in 1998 eligibility criteria were further tightened; from that year the obligation to accept any work that the employment office might find 'suitable' anywhere in the country was reinforced.

In assessments of the last decade's welfare policy developments, it is sometimes stressed that neither Norway nor other Nordic countries have moved towards convergence with a 'neo-liberal' model of social protection (e.g. Swank, 2002, p. 152). By the mid-1990s at least, Norway had enjoyed more continuity of welfare state programmes than other Nordic countries. Some non-market-related benefits have also been introduced during the 1990s, such as cash support measures for parents with small children (since 1998).

Yet several trends in Norwegian welfare policy suggest at least some modifications of its basic principles, not least the new 'work approach', which consists of various initiatives to increase labour market participation by strengthening the link between contributions and benefits; this strengthens the norm of reciprocity at the cost of the principle of universalism. The consequence is that more people are directed into the means-tested social assistance system, which is another move towards selectivism.[16] That the issue of targeting in welfare reforms has become a key concept both in Norwegian and international debates confirms this interpretation, together with trends towards greater use of user charges in the public system as well as towards more private providers of social and health services.

7. Concluding Remarks

In this paper we have primarily been concerned with the normative basis of Scandinavian welfare policy, mostly with Norwegian references. More precisely, we have been concerned with the definition and justifications of one of its characterizing traits, the principle of universalism: what is the meaning of this principle? What is the origin of it? Why did it gain a foothold in our welfare states? Which values and ideas are expressed though universal arrangements? What significance do reasons for universalism have in current Scandinavian welfare policies? Relating to the current convergence debates, the question in focus is whether the inherent norms of recent western welfare reforms, for one reason or another, are becoming more alike, and if so, what consequences these shared norms may have for future development of national welfare reforms. However, for us the basic issue has been to reconstruct the varieties of argument that prepared the ground for universal welfare policies and to re-assess the status of these arguments in current welfare debates.

In our far from finished, conceptual and historical analysis, the preliminary conclusion is, first, that the arguments that supported the introduction of the principle of universalism were more indirect and pragmatic than current conventional political and academic wisdom tells us. It was rather a question of moving away from a social policy that had become normatively unjustifiable and economically inefficient than a vision and aim of expanding the risk-pool from particular classes to all citizens, although such visions were present. Thus, the principle of universalism seems to have been a result of a kind of 'overlapping consensus'. Second, the frequently heard claim that the social democratic movement was the driving force for the adoption of a principle of universalism has not been corroborated. Many social policies developed before social democratic parties reached power, and other parties often, for various reasons, advanced the idea and practice of universalism of one kind or another. Finally, a peculiar observation seems to be that the arguments that are used to support more targeting and means-tested policies today are similar to arguments once used – 50 to 70 years ago – to support the introduction or adoption of universal policies (human dignity, efficiency, incentives etc).

Notes

1 The Stein Rokkan Centre, University of Bergen.
2 University of Bergen.
3 For a recent comparative study of the changing importance of fiscal welfare, see Ervik (2000).
4 In the context of analyses of welfare state development it makes sense to stretch the concept of 'Scandinavian' to 'Nordic', although intra-Scandinavian as well as intra-Nordic differences in social policy development can be identified. 'Scandinavia' and 'the Nordic countries' are used interchangeably in this paper, referring to all five Nordic countries.
5 Strange as it may seem, most political rights are attributed by virtue of citizenship while social rights, which sometimes incur substantial public expenditures, are more often attached to residence.
6 The main principle in the Norwegian National Insurance Scheme – *Folketrygden* – is residence. A resident is a person who has resided 12 months or more in Norway; citizenship, work participation or ability to pay has no significance in the attribution of rights and duties (§ 1-3). Yet, according to the European Economic Area (EEA) agreement that came into force in 1994, only employed citizens may bring with them pension rights when moving to another EEA country. This excludes citizens from a third country (a non-EEA country) as well as non-working citizens of EEA countries. Another group denied membership in the Norwegian pension system is asylum-seekers, as the grant of political asylum or residence permission is required for pension rights.
7 Obviously, from a normative perspective, there is a significant difference between the allocation of benefits based on objective standard criteria and welfare allocations based on discretionary assessment of individual needs. While a just allocation of benefits requires impartial treatment of everyone, elements of arbitrariness, unpredictability and uncertainty are brought into the process of allocation wherever the professions act as the welfare state's gatekeepers. Hence, justly designed welfare institutions that aim at compensating people for individual bad luck may very well conflict with fair implementation of welfare policies.

8 Tim Knudsen (2000) has searched for the genesis of the Scandinavian universalistic welfare state. He repudiates the common social democratic explanation, or explanation by other political groups for that matter, and concentrates on the role of the State. A main focus is the State's capacity to conduct a welfare policy. This was built up by the Protestant Church, which became the kingdom's instrument in its new caring duties for the poor and sick after the Reformation.

9 Based on work by Palme (1990) and Goodin and Le Grand (1987), Hatland discusses the development of the pension system according to the allocation principles of 'need', 'work history' or 'citizenship', and reports that no European States provided universal benefits in their first social security legislation (Hatland, 1992, pp. 104–8). Moreover, he states that universalism was first developed in countries that initially legislated means-tested benefits and services – seldom in countries with initial legislation based on work history.

10 Bismarck very much favoured compulsory social insurance for workers, with provision financed by the State and not by worker contributions. This came to be an element of the legislation passed in the *Reichstag* in 1883. He argued, based on practical Christianity and conservative paternalism, for a social reform that assigned a greater responsibility to the State for the protection of the working class. He favoured compulsory insurance because he considered it unrealistic and out of touch with real life to require that workers should insure themselves against needs caused by illness, invalidity and failing capacity for work in old age (Svenstrup, 2000, p. 115).

11 Iceland was first among the Nordic countries to introduce an old-age (and disability) relief or pension law: in 1890 the parliament enacted a means-tested scheme for old and weak persons outside the poor relief system. This law has also been seen as a model for the Danish law of 1891 (Berner, 1894).

12 The nation-building argument has in recent years been extended to reach beyond the borders of national communities, especially in Western Europe where a 'European identity' is consciously being nurtured in the headquarters of the European Union. Already in the mid-1950s a Nordic social union was established, among other things to promote a Nordic identity, but also for the pragmatic purpose of promoting a common Nordic labour market.

13 Lowe (1994) claims that, contrary to conventional historical accounts, the report's success was only short-lived, both in Europe and in Britain; a remarkable disparity exists between the report's ideal of a welfare system where ordinary people could experience freedom of poverty guaranteed as a right to adequate resources without means-testing, and its practical implementation. The new social security system's six main pillars (Beveridge, 1942, para. 17) were never implemented (the 'adequacy of benefit' and 'the unification of administrative responsibility'), were soon abandoned (flat-rate contributions and benefits) or were heavily qualified (comprehensiveness and classification) (Lowe, 1994, pp. 120–23). Although the rejection or failure of implementation of many of the report's recommendations may be sought in the inconsistencies of the report itself, a not unimportant reason may also be of a structural kind relating to the normative basis of British society – the lack of a cultural sounding board, which may have existed in Scandinavia where Beveridge's ideas, more or less openly referred to, gained stronger support in practice.

14 'Workfare workers' are priced lower than other workers; they have no bargaining power, nor rights to sickness or unemployment benefits, vacation etc.

15 About 25–50 per cent of municipalities have put the scheme into practice in ways that, not surprisingly, vary in the use of sanctions (positive or negative), working hours, age

PROMOTING INCOME SECURITY

groups etc. (The percentage of the municipalities varies according to the definition of workfare). The content of the work activity may vary too, from activities aimed at 'lifestyle changes' to work in the ordinary labour market. Thus, the duty to 'work in exchange for benefits' is not a standard condition, but is adjusted individually and regionally to local labour market schemes (Lødemel and Trickey, 2000).

16 This development is in concordance with Lawrence Mead's description of current western welfare policies as a change from a notion of 'rights' to ideas of 'social contract' and reciprocity: 'the needy should receive aid, but only in return for some contribution to the society' (Mead, 1997, p. 221).

References

Abrahamson, P. 1999. 'Activation and social policies: Comparing France and Scandinavia. Introduction', in The Research Mission (MiRe) *Comparing Social Welfare Systems in Nordic Europe and France* (Paris, Drees).

Baldwin, P. 1990. *The politics of social solidarity; Class bases of the European welfare states 1875–1975* (Cambridge, Cambridge University Press).

Bergh, T. 1987. *Storhetstid. 1945–65. Arbeiderbevegelsens historie i Norge, Vol. 5* (Oslo, Tiden).

Berner, H. E. 1894. 'Arbeiderforsørgelsen i de nordiske lande', in *Statsøkonomisk tidsskrift*, pp. 115–139.

Beveridge, Sir W. H. 1942. *Social insurance and allied services* (London, Cmd. 6404, His Majesty's Stationery Office).

Bull, E. 1982. 'Velferdsstaten i historisk perspektiv', in Stjernö, S. (ed.) *Velferd eller nöd?* (Oslo, Pax).

Childs, M. 1936. *Sweden: The middle way* (New Haven, Yale University Press).

Cox, R. H. 1998. 'The consequences of welfare reform: How conceptions of social rights are changing', *Journal of Social Policy*, Vol. 27, No. 1, pp. 1–16 .

Det Norske Arbeiderparti 1918. *Folkeforsikring eller Folkepension* (Kristiania, Det Norske Arbeiderpartis Forlag).

Eriksson, R., Hansen, E.J., Ringen, S. and Uusitalo, H. (eds.), 1987. *The Scandinavian model: Welfare states and welfare research* (New York, M. E. Sharpe).

Ervik, R. 2000. *The hidden welfare state in comparative perspective: Tax expenditures and social policy in eight countries*, doctoral dissertation, (Department of Comparative Politics, University of Bergen).

Esping-Andersen, G. 1985. *Politics against markets: The Social Democratic road to power* (Princeton, New Jersey, Princeton University Press).

——— 1990. *The three worlds of welfare capitalism* (Cambridge, Polity Press).

——— and Korpi, W. 1987. 'From poor relief to institutional welfare states: The development of Scandinavian social policy', in R. Eriksson *et al.* (eds.), *The Scandinavian model: Welfare states and welfare research* (New York, M. E. Sharpe).

Ferrera, M. and Rhodes, M. 2000. 'Recasting European welfare states: An introduction', in M. Ferrera and M. Rhodes (eds.) *Recasting European welfare states* (London, Frank Cass).

Flora, P. *et al.* 1983. *State, economy, and society in western Europe 1815–1975. A data handbook. Volume I: The growth of mass democracies and welfare states* (Frankfurt, Campus Verlag).

Goodin, R. E. and Dryzek, J. 1987. 'Risk-sharing and social justice: the motivational foundations of the post-war welfare state', in R.E Goodin and J. Le Grand (eds.), *Not only the poor* (London, Allen and Unwin).

_____ and Le Grand, J. (eds.), 1987. *Not only the poor: The middle classes and the welfare state* (London, Allen and Unwin).

Goul Andersen, J. 1999. 'Den universelle velferdsstat', *Grus*, No. 56/57, pp. 40–62 .

_____ 2000. 'Welfare crisis and beyond: Danish welfare policies in the 1980s and 1990s', in S. Kuhnle (ed.), *Survival of the European welfare state* (London/New York, Routledge).

Harris, J. 1994. 'Beveridge's social and political thought', in J. Hills *et al.* (eds.), *Beveridge and social security* (Oxford, Clarendon Press).

Hatland, A. 1992. *Til dem som trenger det mest? Økonomisk behovsprøving I norsk sosialpolitikk* (Oslo, Universitetsforlaget).

_____ 2001. 'Mer målrettet velferdspolitikk?', in *Confederation of Norwegian Businesses and Industries (NHO) Horisont*, No. 4

Kildal, N. 1998. 'Justification of workfare: The Norwegian case', *Critical Social Policy*, Vol. 19, No. 3.

_____ 2001. *Workfare tendencies in Scandinavian welfare policies*, SES paper series No. 5 (Geneva, International Labour Office InFocus Programme on Socio-Economic Security).

Knudsen, T. (ed.), 2000. *Den nordiske protestantisme og velfærdsstaten* (Århus, Aarhus Universitetsforlag).

Kuhnle, S. 1981a. 'The growth of social insurance programmes in Scandinavia: Outside influences and internal forces', in P. Flora and A. J. Heidenheimer (eds.), *The development of welfare states in Europe and America* (New Brunswick and London, Transaction Books).

_____ 1981b. 'Welfare and the quality of life', in E.Allardt *et al.* (eds.), *Nordic democracy* (Copenhagen, Det Danske Selskab).

_____ 1983. *The development of the welfare state: Norway in a comparative perspective* (Bergen, Olso, Universitetsforlaget).

_____ 1990. 'Den skandinaviske velferdsmodellen – skandinavisk? velferd? modell?', in A.R.Hovdum, S. Kuhnle and L. Stokke (eds.), *Visjoner om velferdssamfunnet* (Bergen, Alma Mater).

_____ 1996. 'International modeling, States and statistics: Scandinavian social security solutions in the 1890s', in D. Rueschemeyer and T. Skocpol (eds.), *States, social knowledge, and the origins of modern social policies* (Princeton, Princeton University Press).

_____ 2000. 'The Nordic welfare state in a European context: Dealing with new economic and ideological challenges in the 1990s', *European Review*, Vol. 8, No. 3, July, pp. 379–398.

Leichter, H. M. 1979. *A comparative approach to policy analysis. Health care policy in four nations* (Cambridge, Cambridge University Press).

Lowe, R. 1994. 'A prophet dishonoured in his own country? The rejection of Beveridge in Britain (1945–1970)', in J. Hills *et al.* (eds.), *Beveridge and social security* (Oxford, Clarendon Press).

Lødemel, I. and Trickey, H. 2000. *An offer you can't refuse. Workfare in international perspective* (Cambridge, The Policy Press).

Marklund, S. 1988. *Paradise lost? The Nordic welfares States and the recession 1975–85* (Lund, Arkiv).

Mead, L. 1997. 'Citizenship and social policy: T.H. Marshall and poverty', *Social Philosophy and Policy*, Vol. 14, No. 2, pp. 197–230.

Palme, J. 1990. *Pension rights in welfare capitalism. The development of old-age pensions in 18 OECD countries 1930 to 1985*, Dissertation series 14 (Stockholm, Swedish Institute for Social Research).

_____ 1999. *The Nordic model and the modernization of social protection in Europe* (Copenhagen, Nordic Council of Ministers).

Rawls, J. 1993. *Political liberalism* (New York, Columbia University Press).

Rothstein, B. 1998. *Just institutions matter. The moral and political logic of the universal welfare state* (Cambridge, Cambridge University Press).

Sejersted, F. 1984. *Høyres historie 3: Opposisjon og posisjon 1940–1984* (Oslo, Cappelen).

Seip, A-L. 1981. *Om velferdsstatens fremvekst* (Oslo, Universitetsforlaget).

_____ 1986. 'Velferdsstaten Norge', in L.Alldén, N. Ramsöy and M. Vaa (eds.), *Det norske samfunn* (Oslo, Gyldendal).

_____ 1994. *Veiene til velferdsstaten* (Oslo, Gyldendal).

Sunesson, S., Blomberg, S., Edebalk, P.G., Harrysson, L., Magnusson, J., Meeuwisse, A., Petersson, J. and Salonen, T. 1998. 'The flight from universalism', *European Journal of Social Work*, Vol. 1, No 1, pp. 19–29 .

Svenstrup, T. 2000. 'Den etiske socialisme. Biskop Martensens samfundssyn i 1870'erne', in T. Knudsen (ed.), *Den nordiske protestantisme og velfærdsstaten* (Århus, Aarhus Universitetsforlag).

Swank, D. 2002. *Global capital, political institutions, and policy change in developed welfare states* (Cambridge, Cambridge University Press).

Sysiharju, A-L. 1981. 'Primary education and secondary schools', in E. Allardt *et al.* (eds.), *Nordic democracy* (Copenhagen, Det Danske Selskab).

Titmuss, R. M. 1958. 'The social division of welfare' in *Essays on the Welfare State* (London, Allen and Unwin).

_____ 1968. *Commitment to welfare* (London, Allen and Unwin).

_____ 1974. *Social policy*, (London, Allen and Unwin).

Wilensky, H. and Lebeaux, C. N. 1958. *Industrial society and social welfare* (New York, Russel Sage Foundation).

21

WOMEN'S POLITICS AND SOCIAL POLICY IN AUSTRIA

Sabine Stadler[1]

1. Introduction

The conservative populist government in Austria, which has established a successful austerity programme on budgetary and social policy, can refer to a number of European Union directives, especially relating to women's work and the payment for childcare. Of the social policy innovations introduced by the Freedom Party, most controversial has been its take-over of the formerly socialist ministry for social security and generation, which has given the Freedom Party direct influence over policies for the elderly, disabled, women and children as well as over all kinds of labour regulations. Moreover, for the first time in Austrian history, a man has been appointed as a minister for women, a post that was criticized from the first.

EC guidelines and directives on social policy and the fight against poverty were welcomed by the Austrian Government because they focused on the extent of poverty in member States and their attempts to follow austerity programmes. The EU's comparative approach aimed to achieve a common goal for social policy within the Union based on the experience of existing programmes of member States (European Union, 2001).

The EU's unifying idea is social cohesion, which 'relates to the degree to which individuals and groups within a particular society are bound by common feelings of consensus, share common values and goals and relate to one another on a co-operative basis' (*Ibid.*, p. 13). The criteria are the extent of inequalities in income, health and other living conditions, the effective reduction of these inequalities and trends in social participation, as well as the impact of existing patterns of inequality on macro-developments and trends towards greater individualism.

Uncertainty, family benefits, individualism and immigrants are the key words for the EU's social situation. The data relate to work and employment, social dialogue, participation of civil society and volunteering, and the increasing share of the social economy. If trust in political institutions and social organizations is a sign of a good political system, Austria scores highly on percentage of voters in organized membership of political parties.

With regard to gender, the EU notes, 'equal opportunity between men and women is still an important issue. The number of women in education has improved and their participation in the labour market has risen in the last decade. Nevertheless they still tend to have lower pay and to be underemployed compared to men' (*Ibid.*, p. 17).

An analysis of low-income households provides the basis for a commitment to poor women and children: 'On average, 40 per cent of unemployed persons have a low income. The proportion is just over 50 per cent in the United Kingdom. In Ireland and the United Kingdom, the unemployed are around eight times more likely than those people with a job to have a low income. For the Union as a whole, 9 per cent of those at work fall into the poor category' (*Ibid.*, p. 96).

Italy has the lowest risk of poverty, while Ireland has the largest number of poor people. 'Looking at income below the poverty line identifies those persons in income poverty, but does not show how severe this poverty is. Measuring the gap between the level of income of "the poor" and the poverty line (poverty gap) provides an insight into the severity of income poverty' (*Ibid.*, p. 96). The poverty rate of employees in the EU is 8 per cent, and the existence of working poor is attributed to wage polices. Further, gender-related poverty is connected to education level, working hours and higher female unemployment. The EU suggests that inequality is worse at high rather than low income levels: 'Pay differences between men and women appear to increase with the level of education although the picture is far from homogenous between member States. In Belgium, Denmark, Spain, France, Italy and the Netherlands, the highest qualified women are the most unequally paid compared to their male colleagues' (*Ibid.*, p. 102). And as the report does not compare member States, it implies that the unequal treatment of men and women can be solved with political means.

Employment and social policies in the EU were modernized from 1999 to 2001 under the key words social cohesion and training. 'The dynamic development of economy, employment and social affairs' is the nucleus of the social agenda adopted at the Nice summit in December 2000, nine months after heads of government met in Lisbon, to create a 'dynamic and competitive' European Union for the twenty-first century (European Commission, 2001b, p. 13). The European Commission decided that modernization would take place no matter what the political conditions along three main axes:

- maximization of employment potential;
- modernization of social protection; and
- encouragement of social dialogue.

For the EU, the fight against discrimination and inequality comprises integration into the labour market, measures against racism, enterprise formation, the social economy, life-long learning, adaptation to change, work-life balance, reduction of gender-related discrimination, and the social and labour-market integration of asylum seekers.

The conclusions of the Stockholm summit highlight the importance of old people and the need for pensions including pensions mobility to facilitate the movement of workers. Protection of the rights of old people is combined with the aim of increasing the numbers in paid work; the creation of new jobs is a priority to achieve full employment.

To monitor the creation of jobs in a knowledge society, the EU set up an observatory, which studies trends in this area. Meanwhile, the European

Table 21.1 Women's average earnings as a percentage of men's, 1998

	Industry and services	Services only
EU-15	77	72
Belgium	84	80
Denmark	82	95
Germany	77	76
Greece	73	79
Spain	76	76
France	80	81
Ireland	70	73
Italy	77	81
Luxembourg	84	74
Netherlands	72	78
Austria	69	65
Portugal	73	72
Finland	79	81
Sweden	82	92
United Kingdom	72	70

Note: 1995 is date for Belgium, Greece, Ireland and Luxembourg (Industry and services) and Italy (all data).
Source: Eurostat.

Commission has focused on regulating tele-work in order to achieve rights such as labour-status guarantees, equal treatment, rights to information, labour protection and working hours, protection of privacy, and rights of payment and access.

The publication series of the European Foundation for the Improvement of Living and Working Conditions shows a widespread interest in gender discrimination. 'Gender segregation at the workplace remains prevalent. This is

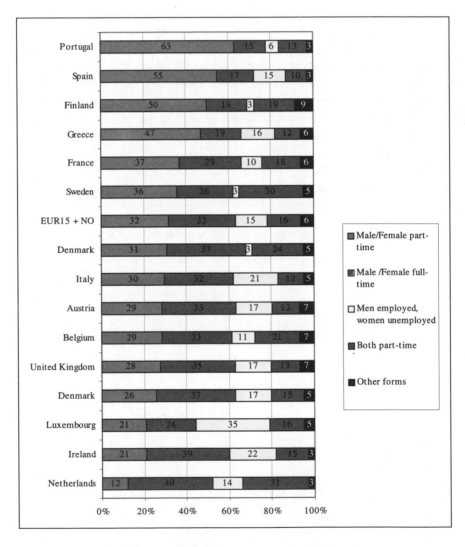

Figure 21.1 Preferred modes of distribution of paid work between partners in two-adult households (couples with at least one of the partners in paid employment), %

evident not only in the occupational structure, where men and women do not occupy the same jobs, but also within the jobs, where men generally occupy more senior positions' (European Foundation, 2000a, p. 6). Noting that 'the average working time of dependent employees varies between 33.7 hours in the Netherlands and 41.4 hours in Austria', the Foundation says: 'The average figures conceal the differences between men's and women's working times, since women in each country continue to shoulder the main burden of unpaid domestic and family work and for this reason tend to devote less time to paid work than men' (*Ibid.*, p. 2). The results show the wish to equalize the working time for men and women; when both work the combination of two full-time jobs is preferred, but a general reduction of working time is desired. (Figure 21.1 shows the preferred modes of distribution and paid work between partners in two-adult households.) Otherwise, the preference is for a part-time and full-time combination, countering the breadwinner model.

2. Austrian Social Policy Under the Conservative Populist Government

Austrian social policy has been extensively analysed by many scholars. Gächter (1996) shows development of social policy since 1971 as a function of economic changes, based on different uses of company profits:

* used by the enterprise;
* extra profit for the enterprise;
* higher pay for employees;
* shorter working time;
* taxed by the state;
* put into a social fund of the enterprise; or
* used to lower prices to the consume (Gächter, 1996, p. 85).

The poverty and the debts of the country were also compared for the years 1995–2000. Private debt was estimated at 733 billion Austrian Schillings, one-third of all Austrian households were creditors and high-income households had higher transfer payments. Meanwhile, 420,000 Austrians were living in poverty – defined as living in poor conditions, on low incomes, lacking means to buy basic goods.

Of these households, 60 per cent did not own a car and nearly half had an income of no more than 6,000 Austrian Schillings. Trade unions compared these figures with the balance sheets of leading Austrian enterprises, which show a total absence of any contribution towards the fight against poverty. Thus, the State together with non-governmental organizations has the responsibility to tackle poverty. And the means adopted demonstrate clear discrimination against women compared to men, as well as the dependency of women on transfer payments.

Already, under the previous Klima Government, a hostile social policy marginalized women. The abolition of the birth grant was followed by discussion of the supply of kindergarten places and by abolition of payment for maternity leave. The maternity leave payment was replaced by the childcare allowance, which was promoted by the Freedom Party but contested by the opposition because it was not an insurance benefit but applied also to women in agriculture and to students.

Emmerich Talos (2001) describes the situation after the Social Democrats fell out of government. At great speed the conservative policy was published, including exclusion measures in case of abuse (*Treffsicherheit*), and financial measures such as:

- abolishing spouse's insurance;
- taxing injury pensions;
- allowing seasonal employment in tourism;
- reducing family assistance payments; and
- demanding more efficiency in the unemployment benefit system.

All these measures were taken without consulting the trade unions. Another highly controversial debate took place on the reforms of the Austrian pension-system, which rests on the three pillars of private, company and State pension. The three together make up the pension payments at the age of 60 for women and 65 for men.

In his analysis of Austrian social policy, Talos (2001) summarizes 'the new social policy' as:

- a remarkable redirection of social policy measures;
- an application of authoritarian tradition;
- adoption of an austerity policy; and
- showing disregard for many socially necessary systems.

Hammer and Österle (2001) categorized social policy in Austria as neoliberal, an expression of Foucault's, in which freedom of market participation is guaranteed by a system of high individual payments for the individual instead of supply by the State. A lack of jobs and care-homes for the disabled is answered by a disablement benefit to buy the goods and services. The same principle was adopted for the childcare benefit: when kindergarten places are lacking the answer is to make payments for childcare.

The neo-liberal government is a reproduction and confirmation of existing class and gender relations, as the institution of the family is confirmed and the housewife role of the woman is maintained and paid. The dream of a service society is combined with a family and household society, where income and roles can change – e.g. who goes to work and who stays at home to care for the disabled. The debate on the respective roles of the private and public sectors has also been noteworthy, as the Government has sought to introduce public-private partnerships and convert large state-owned enterprises into private monopolies.

Böheim, Hofer and Zulehner (2002) analysed the incomes of men and women between 1983 and 1997 due to different qualifications and education, and working hours. Only 24 per cent of women say they have made a career, compared with half of men. Men's income was 23 per cent higher than that of women, adjusted for working hours. In general, the situation of women did not change from 1983 until 1997, but differences were narrowed or eliminated in the public sector where the trade unions fought against gender discrimination. The authors found that education level, shorter working hours and so on could not explain all of the divergence in incomes, pointing clearly to gender discrimination.

Austria's national action plan against poverty and social exclusion is in fact the reverse of what it claims to be. It envisages a reduction of the highest tax rates, payment for ambulances and universities and the reduction of many social policy obligations. The integration package for immigrants envisages labour market participation only after completion of a German language and integration course, a similar attitude to that of the Swiss 20 years ago – the film *Der Schweizermacher* and the book *Das Boot ist voll* both illustrate the same restrictive thinking.

> The approximately 740,000 foreigners living in Austria (9 per cent of the population) contribute a great deal to the welfare of the country. At the same time unemployment has increased and social exclusion has deepened. Whereas the unemployment rate of citizens is about 5.7 per cent in 2000, foreigners have an unemployment rate of 7.5 per cent. A higher risk applies to certain groups of foreigners. The government accordingly foresees as a principal aim the integration of foreigners living in Austria, and then the integration of newcomers (*European Public Social Platform*, 2001, p. 16).

The anti-poverty policy extends to the long-running debate on equalizing levels of social assistance payments in the nine federal states of Austria and the strengthening of health care and care at home. *Pflegevorsorge* involves giving the cared-for person his own income in order to buy care instead of being hospitalized; about 320,000 people are Pflegegeldbezieher, receiving a payment after medical checks and classification. Measures to fight violence against women are also prolonged though the austerity policy has sharply reduced funding for voluntary women's centres.

3. *Das Kinderbetreuungsgeld*: Childcare Benefit in Austria

The childcare benefit is a family assistance payment of €435 per month. No proof of employment is needed and the money can be obtained on production of a birth certificate. Only one payment is made in the case of twins or a second birth within three years. Childcare benefit is paid only for one parent, not for both, until the child is 30 months old. The parents receiving the benefit are allowed to earn up to €14,600 a year, or €1,133 a month.

Mothers under 18 years who are apprentices have the right to receive part-time payment, alongside the childcare benefit. Parents can also receive help with medical insurance costs. In case of high unemployment benefits, no childcare benefit or other social assistance benefit is paid. For the first 18 months, the childcare benefit counts towards the pension system.

The right to return to the previous job is maintained only for two years. However, prolongation of job protection is possible when the father takes over the care after 18 months for six months, after which the mother can stay at home for a further year.

One of the main reasons for introducing the childcare benefit was to increase Austria's birthrate, which has been shrinking steadily year by year. In June 2001, the Austrian statistical office announced that births had risen for the first time in three years.

The results of the populist measures have not yet been evaluated, but they are not the objects of public protest or court challenges. Since the beginning

Table 21.2 The impact of the introduction of childcare benefit as family income (Austrian Schillings per month)

	2000	2001	2002
Childcare payment	5565	5643	6000
Family assistance for 2nd child	663	400	0
Assistance payment for 3rd child	663	400	0
Payment for further child	400	400	500
Total	7291	6843	6500

Shortfall: 791 Austrian Schillings a month.
Source: Austrian trade unions/Chamber of Labour (2002a).

of 2002, other payments have been stopped, whch has undermined people's welfare.

4. The Abolition of the Prohibition on Night-Work by Women

Austria's Night-Work Act was introduced as a direct social policy intervention to protect women's health, family life and childcare. Its abolition had been contemplated since Austria joined the EU in 1994. The European Court decided on July 25, 1991, 'the principle of prohibiting night-work for women is not in accordance with the demand for equal treatment of men and women concerning working conditions' (Moser, 1999, p. 12).

This decision became a guideline for equal treatment cases in the European Union and for the abolition of the prohibition of night-work for women. The case for prohibition was mostly argued from the perspective of the threat to women's health and safety. But the European Commission argued that there was no real risk provided appropriate precautions were taken. Austria asked for a delay until 2001, though in 1997 a compromise was reached allowing the work of women at night on condition that they received preferable treatment for day work and the recognition of the obligation of childcare up to the age of 12 years.

After the introduction of night-work for women at the beginning of 2001 the trade unions started a campaign for more health and safety precautions at the workplace and asked for more control by the elected representatives of night-work conditions. These include:

- gender-neutral and non-discriminating regulations for night-work;
- no obligations to do night-work against the wishes of the worker;
- medical examinations, and regular checks during night-work;
- to return to a day job;
- provision of food or transport;
- use of a positive time-account system for the worker;
- participation rights for representatives (ÖGB/AK, 2002b, p. 9).

Neither numbers nor any qualitative studies are available to indicate how many women already do night-work, how many night-work jobs for women have been created, and the repercussions on health and family life. The fact is too new and up to now an object of political debate. The law is strongly criticized by the Social Democratic Party in Austria, which argues that social standards are far too low.

Note

1   Vienna, Austria.

336   PROMOTING INCOME SECURITY

References

Böheim, R., Hofer, H. and Zulehner, C. 2002. 'Lohnunterschiede zwischen Frauen und Männer in Österreich. Ein Vergleich zwischen 1983 und 1997', in *Kurswechsel*, Vol. 1, pp. 50–57.

Bundesministerium für soziale Sicherheit und Generationen (BMSSG). 2001. *Nationaler Aktionsplan für die Bekämpfung von Armut* (Wien, Nationaler Aktionsplan für die Bekämpfung von Armut).

European Commission 2001a. *The social situation of the European Union* (Brussels, Office for Official Publications of the European Communities).

_____ 2001b. *Die Beschäftigungs-und Sozialpolitik der EU 1999–2001* (Luxembourg, Office for Official Publications of the European Communities).

_____ 2001c. *Europäische Rahmenbedingungen für die soziale Verantwortung der Unternehmen* (Green Book, Brussels, Office for Official Publications of the European Communities).

European Foundation for the Improvement of Living and Working Conditions. 2000a. *Ten years of working conditions in the EU* (Dublin, European Foundation for the Improvement of Living and Working Conditions).

_____ 2000b. *Employment and working time in Europe* (Dublin, European Foundation for the Improvement of Living and Working Conditions).

_____ 2000c. *Gender, employment and working time preferences in Europe* (Dublin, European Foundation for the Improvement of Living and Working Conditions).

European Public Social Platform. 2001. Republic of Austria – National Action Plan for Social Inclusion (Brussels, Office for Official Publications of the European Communities).

European Union. 2000. *Charta der Grundrechte der Europäischen Union* (Brussels, Office for Official Publications of the European Communities).

Gächter, A. 1996. 'Sozialpolitik im normalen Kapitalismus', *Kurswechsel*, Vol. 3, pp. 75–87.

Hammer, E. and Österle, A. 2001. 'Neuliberale Governmentalität im österreichischen Wohlfahrtsstaat. Von der Reform der Pflegevorsorge 1993 bis zum Kinderbetreuungsgeld 2002', *Kurswechsel*, Vol. 4, pp. 60–70.

Moser, S. 1999. *Nachtarbeitsverbot für Frauen und Gleichheitssatz sowie seiner Konformität zum EU- Recht* (Salzburg, Salzburg University).

Österreichischer Gewerkschaftsbund/Bundesarbeiterkammer (ÖGB/AK). 2002a. Gestern Karenzgeld – heute Kinderbetreuungsgeld (ÖGB Frauen, Wien, ÖGB/AK).

_____ 2002b. *Schutz und Sicherheit bei schwierigen Arbeitsbedingungen*, No. 9 (Vienna, ÖGB/AK).

Schlager, C. 1999. 'Verteilung in Österreich – some basic facts', *Kurswechsel*, Vol. 4, pp. 52–65.

Talos, E. 2001. 'Sozialpolitik zwischen konservativen Traditionalismus und neoliberaler Orientierung. Eine Ein-Jahresbilanz der ÖVP/FPÖ-Regierung', *Kurswechsel*, Vol. 1, pp. 17–31.

22

BIO-ECONOMICS, LABOUR FLEXIBILITY AND COGNITIVE WORK: WHY NOT BASIC INCOME?

Andrea Fumagalli[1]

1. Introduction

Labour flexibility relates to the functioning of labour markets. The majority of the economic literature, according to the general equilibrium paradigm,[2] maintains that exchange in the labour market is free and *solvable*.[3] In a theoretical context in which there is individual private property and economic activity is directed towards maximizing agents' welfare, only solvable exchanges are analysed.

> Definition 1: *An exchange is as defined solvable when it implies the passage of property rights of the commodity against its value (price): the seller gives up the property rights and the buyer purchases the property rights.*

It follows that the private exchange is an exchange of competing goods; otherwise there is no property rights exchange. In fact, the value of a good and its *solvability* derives from its exclusivity in use (public goods are not here considered).

> Definition 2: *A private solvable exchange is defined as free when the following two conditions hold:*

- *The two parties are autonomous agents with equal potential and effective decision-making power. Behavioural differences are due to different subjective preferences and to a different degree of uncertainty.*[4]
- *There is total price flexibility, that is, neither party is able to impose a price on the other.*

2. The Solvability of the Labour Market Exchange

Not all private markets deal with solvable exchanges. The most relevant exception is the credit market. The existence of *seignorage rights* implies that money exchange has nothing to do with property rights. Money is the property of a supra-individual board (the State and the central bank) and money is actually 'sign money' – that is, social convention. In the macroeconomic textbooks credit markets are usually not considered (only financial markets, where transfer of property rights occurs – see, for instance, Blanchard, 2000).

The question of exchange solvability is relevant even in the labour market, where the issue of whether work availability is separate from the human being is a matter of some controversy.

> Definition 3: *Work availability is defined as the working time supplied by agents in order to gain a monetary income.*

Work availability is something different from labour activity.

> Definition 4: *Labour activity is defined as the different ways with which work availability is used or exploited according to the degree of alienation.*

> Definition 5: *Alienation is defined as the degree of separation between the worker and the content (object, result) of his work.*

When the separation reaches the highest level, that is, when the work object or result is completely expropriated from the worker, then we talk of *total alienation.*

> Proposition 1: Labour exchange can be defined as solvable if and only if work availability and not labour activity is exchanged.

> Corollary: labour exchange is solvable if and only if there is alienation.

In neoclassical theory, the law of demand and supply holds in all markets, the labour market included. Hence, the monetary wage is determined on the basis of the theory of scarcity. Neoclassical theory states that labour supply in terms of working hours (that is, work availability) is the result of the agent's choice in resolving the trade-off between the need for income and the loss of 'leisure time' (defined as not working time → labour disutility). The characteristics and content of labour activity do not play any role in solving this allocation problem. They are incorporated in the preference structure of the agents. This implies that in neo-classical economic thinking the concept of alienation does not exist.

Nevertheless, labour is different from other goods because 'work availability' is not physically separable from the agent who owns it (as it is for vehicles or potatoes). In the labour exchange, what happens is not an effective transfer of property rights (power) but rather of availabilities (potentialities). If we consider the labour exchange as a whole, it is not possible to separate work availability and labour activity. Thus, the solvability of labour exchange is questionable. Consequently, the law of demand and supply in determining the value of labour cannot be completely applicable to the labour market.

Proposition 2: The value of work availability (that is, the price → the monetary wage) is not only dependent on its scarcity, but should take into account labour activity (in other words, the degree of alienation), on the basis that there is no physical separation between the object of work and the agent who offers it.

That means that the degree of alienation should enter into the determination of wage level.

Proposition 3: The law of demand and supply is inapplicable to the labour exchange as a whole.

Proposition 4: The labour market cannot be analysed as just another market.

Hence, most of the dominant labour economics theories can be thrown away.

3. Is the Labour Market a Free Market?

The existence in the labour market of the two conditions for free market equality between the parties and price flexibility, according to the law of demand and supply, has been discussed above. We will now attempt to further substantiate the argument.

Definition 6: *Labour supply is defined as work availability. It depends on the trade-off between the marginal disutility of labour (loss of leisure time) and the monetary income that the agent is able to gain from labour activity (monetary wage).*

It follows that labour supply is subject to a budget constraint.

Definition 7: *Labour is required by entrepreneurs, and labour demand consists of both work availability and labour activity.*

In the manufacturing sector, labour and machinery (physical capital) are separate – the first is the property of workers, the second of entrepreneurs) – and they need to be joined to start production. This decision is taken by entrepreneurs, not by workers. Labour demand depends on two principal factors:

- investment decisions, on the basis of expected demand and profit;
- labour productivity, according to the existing technology.

Thus, labour demand is subject to a technological constraint and to an expectation constraint, not a budget constraint.

The difference between these constraints gives rise to *ex ante* discrimination between the two parties in the labour market. The labour exchange does not involve equal opportunities for the parties. Budget constraints, in fact, are more relevant than the technological ones. In a monetary economy, it is possible to live without technical change, but not without money. The discrimination between workers and entrepreneurs depends on the fact that entrepreneurs have the property (or the control) of the means of production whilst workers do not.

> Proposition 5: In the labour market, by definition, there is no free, solvable exchange. The labour market is a particular market, which is structurally subject to constraints. It cannot be 'flexible'.

4. Rivalry in the Labour Market Exchange

The separation between the worker and his work availability implies that labour, as a product separated from the producer, is a rival good. If work availability is offered to one entrepreneur, it cannot be simultaneously offered to another. Thus, rivalry in the labour market exchange implies total alienation. The level of alienation varies according to two main parameters:

- the extent of control over duties, which depends on the type of labour activity;
- the degree of routinized behaviour in the labour activity.

> Definition 8: *Manual work is defined through the prevalence of body-energy intensive activity over brain activity, due to the separation between labour activity and labour contents. Manual work is different from artisan work.*

Manual work is characterized by a *formal subsumption*[5] of labour under capital, based on the separation between labour activity and work availability. It represents a high level of alienation.

Definition 9: *Cognitive work is based on the constant use of all the brain faculties such as relationship, mnemonic, cognitive, learning activities and so on.*

Cognitive work is characterized by a *real subsumption*[6] of labour under capital both in work availability and labour activity (what is called today *adaptability*)[7], tending to eliminate the separation between them and reduce to the minimum the degree of alienation. In a hypothetical ranking from manual to cognitive work, it is reasonable to assume a reduction in the degree of control and routinized work. Consequently, the level of alienation also decreases. Given these definitions and coming back to the question of rivalry in the labour exchange, the following point can be made:

Proposition 6: In manual work, labour exchange implies rivalry. In the case of cognitive work, rivalry tends to diminish to nothing.

To discuss more fully the qualitative changes introduced by the spread of cognitive work, it is necessary to highlight the deep structural transformations of the labour market in the last 20 years. We start from the decline of the so-called Fordist-Taylorist-Keynesian paradigm. According to several analyses on the transition to post-Fordism (or, better, 'flexible accumulation paradigm'), some broad facts have become evident as far as rich western countries are concerned:

- Added value in production is no longer based only on materials and energy-intensive inputs but increasingly on immaterial inputs — intangible factors that are not easily measured and whose production depends on brain intensive labour (see Marazzi, 1997).
- Added value is no longer based on a homogenous and standardized form of production and labour organization, independent of the type of output. Production activity can use different forms of organization, characterized by a network structure, thanks to information and communication technologies (ICT) and changes in transport technologies. The unique production unit (large enterprise) has given way to the spread of different intra-firm chains based both on subcontractor and cooperative networks.
- Labour activity has changed in structure from both a qualitative and a quantitative point of view. As far as material conditions and work are concerned, there has been an increase in working time and, often, an accumulation of more duties, a reduction in the separation between working and leisure time, and a prevalence of individual bargaining over collective bargaining. Furthermore, labour activity is increasingly characterized by immaterial factors such as relationships and interpersonal activities that

need education, competences, knowledge and attention. The separation between brawn and brain, typical of the traditional Taylorist organization, has become a divide between highly routinized work on one side and deep involvement in and adaptability of work on the other. To the traditional labour division based on different duties has been added the new labour division based on know-how and knowledge, with the effect of increasing the degree of labour subordination. This subordination is no longer imposed by command in a disciplinary way, as in the Fordist era, but is injected by social and generally accepted customs, thanks to the spread of conformist behaviours resulting from a sort of *social self-control*.[8] Individual bargaining becomes the natural institutional picture, inside which competition and emulation represent the guidelines for work behaviour.

When we discuss *cognitive capitalism* or the *knowledge society*, we mean the production of money not only through commodities, but by means of knowledge and through the exploitation of those faculties which relate to brain and attention activities (cognitive labour).

Since the brain (considered as the faculty of accumulating knowledge) is by definition individual and the principal element of identity definition thanks to memory and language,[9] cognitive work cannot be considered homogenous. It is bio-economic, that is, it depends on individual biology. In order to make it productive, cognitive labour needs a strong relational activity as a tool for transmission and decoding of the accumulated knowledge. It follows that cognitive labour needs 'space' to develop a network; otherwise, if it remains incorporated in a single person, it cannot be valorized. In other words, it does not become *exchange value* but only *use value* for the single agent. *Cognitive capitalism*[10] is by definition 'network capitalism', and the hierarchies are within different nodes constituting the same network: these new hierarchies are complex and linked to different factors and subcontractor relationships, depending on the technological and financial power structure (see Castells, 2000).

5. Manual and Intellectual Labour (*excursus*)

The traditional and Fordist division between manual and intellectual labour needs to be revised. The spread of flexible technologies linked to ICT structurally changed the way of working.

Manual labour now needs more attention and individual involvement in the work activity to check, modify and programme the flexible manufacturing systems with different degrees of automation. The possibility of communication between machines thanks to informatics implies an increase of skilled education and professional training. The level of routinized work tends to decrease, even if the degree of exploitation does not. In fact, if the work becomes less Taylorized, the speed of many technical operations increases together with the number of tasks the worker must perform (lean production). We define this as *corporeal work*.

From the other side, 'intellectual labour' has been modified in a deeper way. If once it was remunerated according to the type of activity and the degree of education, now the standardization of cognitive procedures and language codification have highlighted an increase of routinized behaviour and a Taylorist organization of 'creative' working time. In many cases, intellectual labour deals with salaried brain intensive activity, which is subject to different constraints and timetables like a new type of cerebral assembly line. That is why we prefer to call it *cognitive work* instead of intellectual work. Of course, this argument cannot be enlarged to include every type of cognitive work. Since cognitive work, as already discussed, is individual work, it is possible to have a wide range of different activities, which cannot be analysed in a homogenous way. By definition, cognitive work has to do with knowledge and learning processes (by doing or by using). Nevertheless, we can distinguish two categories of knowledge which play an important role in classifying cognitive work: codified and tacit knowledge.

Codified knowledge is defined as all those competences and know-how that are transmittable and can be easily spread with no prohibitive transaction costs thanks to informatics and communication technologies (ICT). They constitute the most important tool for the spread of new technologies and they represent the 'core' of professional training. The more this knowledge is spread, the more the people who have it can be substituted without loss of know-how for the firms. Thus, in the presence of individual bargaining on the labour market, this type of knowledge represents a disadvantage for workers, diminishing their individual bargaining power. Codified knowledge is spread more widely in technology-receiving industries, which adopt technology from outside and are not on the technological frontier.

Tacit knowledge is defined, conversely, by the competences and know-how that are incorporated in the experience of the worker for a more or less limited time and cannot be spread outside since individual experience cannot be transmitted at all. In this case, the labour experience and incorporated knowledge represent the 'elite' of the labour market. It is this knowledge that is protected by patents and is not exchangeable on the information market. The worker, if he is conscious of it, has strong individual bargaining power; moreover, tacit knowledge lies at the core of technological competitiveness of the firm and only constant investment activity is able to generate and maintain it. It represents the 'essence' of technological control and concentration characteristic of industries on the technological frontier. Further, it needs to be reproduced every time and whoever owns it must constantly regenerate it if he wants to keep his bargaining power intact.

6. Production of Money by Means of Knowledge

The capitalist system is able to reduce to *exchange value* (in order to get surplus-value) as much as is technologically possible. The first industrial revolution of the late eighteenth century made labour free and thus productive. Thanks to the French revolution, labour activity became free but, paradoxically, it needed to be remunerated and so the labour market was born. Since labour is the only input able to induce accumulation, labour activity itself, according to the technology used, is the core of economic growth.

Is this a case of the production of money by means of commodities (M-C-M) where what is exchanged in the labour market is only work availability and not the agent? (When labour was not free in the pre-capitalist system, there was the production of commodities by means of commodities, C-M-C.) There is in some ways a separation between the 'object' of labour (the final commodity) and the 'subject' of labour (worker). That is the situation described by Marx with the word 'alienation'.

We have already discussed the problem of rivalry in the labour market. Generally speaking, according to the economic theory, tangible goods are rival, while intangible goods are not. A theoretical model, for instance, is not a rival intangible good; it is an 'idea'. If a good is rival, its production cost and, consequently, its price is positive and constant for every user. For a non-rival intangible good, the production cost is the same, independent of the number of customers – that is, it is zero for the second user and beyond. It is important to notice that non-rival goods are normally incorporated in a material support, which is a rival good. The point is that the cost of material support is not related to the cost of the intangible good incorporated in it. The Paretian efficiency principle would say that the right price for non-rival intangible goods should be zero, but at zero price there is no incentive to produce.

It is clear, now, why protection of intellectual property is fundamental to capitalism whose main output is more and more 'knowledge'. Thanks to copyright and patents, a copy of an intangible good has a positive price, even if its production cost is zero, since only the work that went into the original good (and not into the copy) is paid. Of course, the author's right – the remuneration of his cerebral activity – is something different from the copyright or patent – the exclusivity of the exploitation of the cerebral activity – which has nothing to do with the author.[11] The labour commitment in writing a book or in the creation of new software does not vary according to the number of sold copies.

Proposition 7: In a context of corporeal labour, labour exchange implies a 'particular' exchange of property rights and rivalry.

The worker, during his working time, cedes his time availability in order to earn a monetary wage (hence, there is an exchange of property rights as far as the worker's lifetime is concerned) and, at the same time, if this time availability is at the disposal of one entrepreneur, it cannot be made available to another entrepreneur. That is, there is rivalry in its use and economic results.

With the spread of production of money by means of knowledge, the nature of labour activity changes structurally in the market for cognitive labour, and the exchange assumes a different meaning: if, from one side, it is still possible generally to assume that cognitive work availability still implies an exchange of the respective property rights, nevertheless, this change occurs neither in a linear nor in a forced way. Cognitive activity is not separable from the body, and the content of labour activity, the 'idea' (a logistic solution and/or intangible services), cannot be alienated from the owner. Moreover, it generates cumulative learning processes thanks to circulation and general exchanges of knowledge and know-how. It is at this point that it becomes necessary to cede the rights to knowledge (as copyrights or patents), that is, the property rights on the result of the cognitive activity. But, in contrast to material production and corporeal labour, the supply of 'knowledge' implies a process of accumulation of knowledge, which cannot be alienated from the cognitive workers as the object of labour was alienated previously from manual workers. The result is that 'knowledge' is not a rival good. The traditional ways of monitoring labour activity through disciplinary actions no longer play a role. Thus, it is necessary to highlight new more sophisticated mechanisms to monitor cognitive capacity. Some trends in this direction seem to be evident:

- juridical trend: individual bargaining has become increasingly prevalent, and not only in Anglo-Saxon countries. This trend has been facilitated by the process of *individualization* of labour activity, due to the linguistic characteristics of cognitive labour, which, by definition, are individual;
- socio-cultural trend: stronger control of information and a concentration of mass media both at national and international level, together with the building of positive and individualistic imagery, lead to a self-discipline and self-repression of unorthodox behaviour with negative effects on a critical and autonomous cultural capacity (*society of control*). This situation is worsened in some segments of the labour market and in an organizational context in which the practices of bullying and individual competitiveness are increasing;
- inside the production process (material and immaterial), the communication of knowledge tends to be increasingly subject to routinized procedures, which are codified and exchangeable independently of the type of input. Only tacit knowledge is able to preserve its autonomy and bargaining power.

Proposition 8: Labour flexibility,

- when it has to do with corporeal labour, implies wage reduction or an increase in labour productivity (that is, in both cases, increased labour exploitation);
- when it has to do with cognitive but routinized labour, implies new forms of control and, finally, the indirect expropriation of the (intangible) output of labour activity, mainly through practices of self-control;
- when it has to do with cognitive but tacit labour, increases the bargaining power of the worker.

7. First Conclusion

We have argued the following:

- Labour exchange is a particular exchange, which cannot be likened to a solvable exchange of any other commodities.
- In particular, the two necessary and sufficient conditions for a solvable exchange – exchange of property rights and rivalry in the use of labour – are not always present. The exchange of property rights holds only if the commodity 'labour' is considered as pure work availability, by assuming complete separation between the same work availability and the labour supplier – in other words, if there is labour alienation. But this separation should also affect the price of labour, whose level hence, cannot be determined only according to the laws of demand and supply.
- In the case of total alienation, there is rivalry in the use of labour. Even if a solvable exchange is possible under certain circumstances, the labour exchange is not a free exchange, since the different constraints affecting the two parties imply *ex ante* differences in their behaviour.
- If we consider an economy in which the production is mainly obtained through cognitive work and immaterial input, the labour exchange no longer involves rival goods.
- The relevance of relationship, learning, experience, language, individual character and personal expectations within labour activity makes it impossible to separate this activity from the quality of labour. What in the Taylorist paradigm was called 'intellectual work' – professional work, highly skilled work, remunerated not in terms of salary but in terms of results and performance and whose productivity was difficult to quantify – is today, in the flexible accumulation paradigm, called 'cognitive work'; in most cases (with the exception of tacit knowledge) it is characterized by routines, is quantified and salaried.

The production of money by means of knowledge and the centrality of cognitive work are realities in modern western economies. What in the Taylorist era was the *oeconomicus* today tends increasingly to appear as *bio-oeconomicus*, where all activities are useful for and employed in production, able to produce added value. The classic distinctions between production and reproduction, leisure time and working time, consumption and output tend to lose their original meaning.

> Definition 10: *Bio-economy is that economic process which involves a real subsumption (not only formal) of the whole human being, with the aim of achieving monetary accumulation.*

In this context, labour exchange moves outside the realm of traditional economic analysis and cannot be any longer likened to the exchange of tangible goods or explained by market theory. In a bio-economic process, labour exchange tends to be individually defined, without mediation groups such as trade unions. However, unless the worker is in a monopsonist situation due to the possession of tacit knowledge, labour exchange is totally subsumed in the productive process and in the hierarchies established by the bio-power structure[12]. It follows that labour exchange is no longer solvable and does not involve a rival good. Thus it cannot be treated as a free market exchange.

> Proposition 9: The first paradox of labour exchange in bio-economics is that just when labour exchange becomes individual, and could be analysed according to the premises of methodological individualism, it no longer makes sense to speak of a solvable exchange in a free market.

> Proposition 10: In bio-economics, labour exchange becomes unmeasurable and cannot be reduced to private exchange. Labour becomes a *common good*.

8. Second Conclusion: Why not Basic Income?

The labour market is a different and special market, since labour is not a private good. We have defined it as a *common good*. A common good is different from a public good. A public good is owned by the State, that is, a supra-individual entity. Labour is by definition individual, since it cannot be separated from the individual human being.

Since men and women are social animals, they are used to sharing their lives in communities, whether in families or in other structures. Human experience, relational activities, and the learning process depend on the social connections that characterize the community. In other words, labour activity and practices are social entities. Hence:

> Definition 11: *A common good is the result of social procedures in production, or, in other words, is the result of a cooperative process at social level.*

In modern post-Fordist economies, the new realities of bio-political production (bio-economy) cannot be understood within the traditional frameworks for analysing time. In the Taylorist context, time was programmed and divided in order to increase and measure labour productivity through the allocation of processes and jobs. Working time and the job performed were strictly defined and separated from leisure time and activities. Thus, it was possible to measure the labour supply and the intensity of labour. The determination of labour value (wage) was the result of the two components of working time and labour intensity (productivity) determined by collective bargaining between employers' associations and trade unions. Wages were determined in a collective way but privately distributed, since each worker's commitment (in terms of effort and time) was measurable. On the distribution side, labour was considered as a private good.

In a bio-economic context, however, the production of added-value (wealth) comes ever closer to the production and reproduction of social life itself: it thus becomes ever more difficult to distinguish productive, reproductive and unproductive labour. Labour – material, immaterial, cognitive or corporeal – produces and reproduces social life. The progressive blurring of the line between production and reproduction highlights the incommensurability of time and value. The clearest example is provided by cognitive work, in which the power of science, knowledge and their communication is fundamental for productivity, but whose source is social rather than individual. It is the result of what Marx names the 'general intellect' (see Marx, 1973, part 32). According to Marx, at a certain point in capitalist development (which Marx glimpsed as the future), the powers of labour are infused by the powers of science, communications and language. *General intellect* is a collective, social intelligence created by accumulated knowledge, techniques and know-how. General intellect is a common good, whose value becomes unmeasurable.

> Proposition 11: As labour moves outside factories, and life is incorporated into production (bio-economy), it becomes increasingly difficult to maintain the fiction of any measure of the working day and thus to separate production time from reproduction time, or work from leisure time.

There are no time clocks to punch in the realm of bio-political production.

Proposition 12: In this context, since the most important input for production becomes life itself, the right remuneration for bio-political inputs is remuneration for existence: in other words, a *basic income* and a *guaranteed income for all*.[13]

Basic income stands opposed to the family wage. Basic income extends well beyond the family to the entire population, even those who are unemployed, because everyone produces. In post-Fordist society, labour power has become increasingly collective and social. The old Fordist slogan 'equal pay for equal work' can no longer be supported when labour cannot be individualized and measured.

Proposition 13: The second paradox of labour exchange in bio-economy is that labour exchange is subject to a process of individualization (outside the free market), but that its remuneration should be determined socially.

Notes

1 University of Pavia, Italy.
2 Most economics textbooks treat the labour market as a normal free market, which can be analysed with the traditional tools of supply and demand analysis (see, for instance, Varian, 1992). Even those in the neo-Keynesian tradition do so, though Keynes does not treat labour analysis in this way, since he neglects labour supply (see Keynes, 1936). For a heteredox interpretation of labour flexibility and its effects and social costs, see Standing (1999).
3 The type of economy considered here is a production economy with private property.
4 General equilibrium theory, the mother of modern neo-liberalist theory, is based on methodological individualism. Only individual agents are considered and only micro-economic analysis is relevant. But, in order to model individual behaviour, very strict assumptions are made: the maximizing hypothesis of behaviour states that each agent has different preferences but is equal in terms of opportunities for acting. It follows that agents will act in the same way, since they are potentially equal and no discrimination *ex ante* is possible. Only conformist behaviour is rational, which is a paradoxical result for a theory that aims to highlight diversity among human beings.
5 Marx uses the term 'formal subsumption' to name processes whereby capital incorporates under its own relations of production labouring practices that originated outside its domain. The processes of formal subsumption are thus intrinsically related to the extension of the domain of capitalist production and capitalist markets. On the formal (and real, see note 5) subsumption concept in Marx, see primarily Marx (1976, Vol. 1, pp. 1019–1038).
6 The concept of 'real subsumption' is the result, in Marxian thought, of the growth of the capitalist economy. As capitalist expansion reaches its limit, the processes of formal subsumption can no longer play the central role.

7 One of the four pillars of the European Employment Strategy resulting from the Luxembourg Summit of 1997 has been designated as adaptability, which applies to both workers and to firms. As far as workers are concerned, it means that the workers must consider the requirements of firms better to obtain a job to match labour supply and demand.

8 The concept of social self-control recalls the societal concept of control and bio-power. On these topics, see note 10.

9 On human identity defined as memory and language, modern thought is still inspired by Locke (see Locke, 1690).

10 See Moulier-Boutang (2002).

11 On this topic, see the wide debate on free software and the question of 'copy-left' (see, among others, Scelsi (ed.), 1994.

12 The concept of bio-power is Foucault's. 'Biopower is a form of power that regulates social life from the interior, following it, interpreting it, absorbing it and rearticulating it. Power can achieve an effective command over the entire life of the population only when it becomes an integral vital function that every individual embraces and reactivates of his or her own accord' (Hardt and Negri, 2000, pp. 23–24). As Foucault says: 'Life has now become … an object of power' (Foucault, 1994, p. 1979). Therefore, the concept of bio-power is closely linked to that of the *society of control*: they are the two faces of the same coin. For a deeper analysis of these concepts, see Dreyfus and Rabinow (eds.) (1992, pp. 133–172).

13 For a deeper discussion of the definition of basic income in an post-Fordist economy, see Fumagalli (2000).

References

Blanchard, O. 2000. *Macroeconomics* (Upper Saddle River, Prentice Hall).

Castells, M. 2000. *The rise of the network society* (Oxford, Blackwell).

Dreyfus, H. and Rabinow, P. (eds.), 1992. *Michel Foucault: Beyond structuralism and hermeneutics* (Chicago, University of Chicago Press).

Foucault, M. 1994. 'Les mailles de pouvoir', in *Dits et Ecrits* (Paris, Gallimard), Vol. 4, pp. 182–201.

Fumagalli, A. 2000. 'Ten propositions on basic income: Basic income in a flexible accumulation system', in A. Fumagalli and M. Lazzarato (eds.), *Tute bianche. Reddito di cittadinanza e disoccupazione di massa* (Roma, Derive Approdi).

Hardt, M. and Negri, T. 2000. *Empire* (Cambridge, Mass., Harvard University Press).

Locke, J. 1690. *An essay concerning human understanding* (Italian translation, *Saggio sull'intelligenza umana*, Bari, Laterza, 1994).

Keynes, J. M. 1936. *The general theory of employment, interest and money* (London, Macmillan).

Marazzi, C. 1997. *Il posto dei calzini* (Casagrande, Bellinzona).

Marx, K. 1973. *Grundrisse* (New York,Vintage).

———— 1976. *Capital* (New York,Vintage).

Moulier Boutang, Y. (ed.), 2002. *L'età del capitalismo cognitivo* (Verona, Ombre Corte).

Scelsi, R. (ed.) 1994. *No copyright: nuovi diritti nel 2000* (Milan, Shake Edizioni Underground).

Standing, G. 1999. *Global labour flexibility* (London, Macmillan).

Varian, H. 1992. *Microeconomics analysis* (New York, Norton).

23

EXPLORING WAYS TO RECONCILE FLEXIBLE EMPLOYMENT WITH SOCIAL PROTECTION[1]

Pascale Vielle and Pierre Walthery[2]

1. Introduction

In a context marked by growing international competition, the disappearance of exchange rates as an economic policy tool for counterbalancing variations in productivity (at least within the European Union (EU)), the gathering strength of shareholder capitalism (Aglietta, 1998) and moderate productivity improvements in economies now centred on services, we are witnessing some distortion of the main post-war macroeconomic equilibria, generally known as 'the Fordist compromises' (Boyer, 1986; Boyer and Durand, 1993) or 'welfare capitalism'. These changes are evident in both the welfare state's traditional prime areas: social protection and its various sectors, and employment policies in labour markets characterized by stable forms of contract that Castel used to term the 'wage society'.

For a long time, European welfare states used a variety of strategies to achieve or maintain the 'full employment' that was essential to their financing and an instrument for securing a satisfactory level of well-being among citizens/workers. In many EU countries, the above-mentioned changes have given rise to calls for a lowering of costs from employers, who are contending with sharper international competition than in the past, and a need to match production rhythms to fluctuations in demand. This has gradually led to the development of atypical or flexible forms of labour and employment.

Flexible work (also known as internal flexibility) refers to changes in the organization of production tasks within a firm. Flexible employment (or external flexibility) concerns the status of workers, their contract and the constraints/advantages associated with it (de Nanteuil, 2000; Goudswaard and de Nanteuil, 2000). These atypical forms display extremely heterogeneous characteristics, so much so that it is impossible to identify clearly one single model. Their sole common feature is probably that they call into question the traditional benchmark of 'typical' employment (i.e. a full-time employment contract without a time limit), its legal elements (subordination, one single employer) and even the notion of the workplace (in the case of telework). We are therefore faced with a situation of 'employers without employment', in the sense of typical employment, or of 'jobs without an employer' where the very notion of subordination becomes increasingly elusive (Kravaritou-Manitakis, 1987).

The most frequently encountered forms of flexible employment discussed in this paper are part-time work (about 17 per cent of the European working population), fixed-term contracts (10 per cent), temporary work (between 0.2 per cent and 2 per cent)[3] and self-employment (15 per cent) (European Commission, 2001a and 2001c). Although of marginal significance, new forms of employment like on-call work or telework are increasing. In all, about a third of the European working population is involved in one or more of these forms (Eurostat, 2001).

Although atypical employment affects the labour force as a whole, it is most prevalent among women, young workers, low-skilled workers and/or immigrants. While flexible employment is chiefly found in the most vulnerable categories of workers whose jobs often display several characteristics of flexibility simultaneously (Fagan, Rubery and Smith, 1994), it also exists, albeit to a much lesser extent, among certain categories of the most competitive workers on the labour market (Marsden, 2000 and 2001). Hence flexibility is not necessarily synonymous with economic and social insecurity. Similarly, not all firms are framing flexibility strategies, or identical strategies when they do so (Boyer, 1986). Although flexible employment is spreading in response to employers' needs to sustain productivity, trim wage costs as best they can and cope with fluctuating demand, that is not the only cause. Some employment policies (especially in the public sector) and, even if this has been less clearly proved, workers' demands themselves can also encourage flexible employment.

As far as 'social protection' is concerned, these mutations are resulting in budgetary difficulties due to a deterioration in the ratio of workers to non-workers, falling revenue (above all in systems financed by employment-based contributions, rising expenditure for reasons inherent in welfare states (e.g. the cost of technical advances in health care), cultural changes making for greater individualization of benefits and, lastly, a greater demand for services and care to compensate for the responsibilities traditionally shouldered by women who did not go out to work. In many EU countries, the constraints imposed by the economic convergence criteria have led to a linear reduction in public funds for social protection. One of the clear objectives of the European employment strategy is the reduction of social security expenditure by the 'activation' of certain categories of the jobless.

A distinction must, however, be drawn between these pressures, depending on the welfare-state regimes or 'worlds' identified in previous research (Esping-Andersen, 1990; Ferrera, 1996): the social democrat regimes of the Scandinavian and Anglo-Saxon countries that were heavily influenced by Beveridge's thinking, and the corporatist regimes on the continent which were mainly inspired by Bismarck's ideas. The analysis should also take in the Mediterranean regimes, which are a mixture of both. The same pressures are expressed in different terms in the various types of welfare state and give rise to different problems and political responses. While the Scandinavian universalist schemes, which are financed by taxation, seem to be less pressurized by current changes, the continental welfare states' margin of manoeuvre is restricted by their employment-based funding which, in turn, directly affects wage costs.

2. Security and Insecurity

In order to deal with the issue of security in a pertinent manner, we must investigate the forms of security generally provided by welfare states. According to Esping-Andersen (1990), this security was historically anchored in the decommodification of social protection, in other words by 'the degree to which individuals or families can maintain a socially acceptable standard of living without participating in the labour market'. In welfare states, decommodification can result from individual providence (private insurance), employment-related social insurance with a fairly high redistributive effect, or universal social rights based on citizenship and with fixed benefits more or less linked to wages. While these various forms offer a picture of how the whole system initially hung together, they are a less satisfactory explanation of subsequent developments, especially the growth of benefits subject to needs, which took place in many welfare states, or the spread of employment-related insurance in the social democrat welfare states. These modes of decommodification offered security essentially based on maintaining income, or a significant proportion of it, for a specified period and/or the provision of more or less universal care or services (usually health care, personal assistance or family care).

From the point of view of employment policies, this temporary, relative income security was accompanied by government guarantees to preserve the economic and legal conditions promoting full employment, if not for life then for a relatively long period, or at least conditions that would make it easy to find employment again, when it was not protected. Employment policies therefore added a dimension of temporal stability to the notion of income security. The respective roles played by the market and redistribution could vary enormously from one welfare-state regime to another.

The alterations to which we have referred undermined this compromise and the attendant notion of security. New ideas about security are being entertained. Since neither policies nor the macroeconomic environment (especially against a background of the constraints stemming from European Monetary Union) are able any longer to guarantee full employment or income security for an ever larger category of workers, new notions of security, coinciding with the emergence of a new social ill, social exclusion (Castel, 1995; Lødemel and Trickey, 2000; Paugam, 2000), are coming into existence. They include career security, according to which the role of the welfare state is to help each worker to find a job through social integration measured by participation in the labour market, generally by means of active labour market policies, throughout a person's life cycle. The fashioning and implementation of this compromise is a, if not the, big challenge facing social policy in the next few years. We will come back to this point later. At present, the only conclusion to be drawn is that the relationship between social protection and flexibility is ambiguous.

- The first reason is that in many cases social protection regimes do not, or do no longer, guarantee flexiworkers a level of security (of income, employment or career) comparable to that of other workers. The standards for calculating benefits, access rules and eligibility are implicitly predicated on an employment model (white male breadwinner) which corresponds less and less to the experience of most workers and certainly not to that of flexiworkers (Scharpf and Schmidt, 2000; Esping-Andersen *et al.*, 2001). Furthermore, there is a risk that the labour market will split into two and that the gulf will widen between the shrinking circle of protected workers and the circle of insecure workers whose jobs display one or more forms of flexibility and whose rights to social protection will therefore become more fragile.
- The second, correlated reason is that social protection regimes probably tend to permit less flexibility than in the past. As active labour market policies subject workers to heavier economic pressures and growing insecurity, they deprive them of the requisite basis for acquiring independence and autonomy and make them less well placed fully to develop their productivity. Conversely, one may ask whether the encouragement of forms of flexibility such as temping do not foster emotional disengagement and opportunistic behaviour (Marsden, 2001), 'employment zapping' and, ultimately, lower output.
- The third reason is linked to the fact that social protection systems can themselves fuel individual insecurity because of the nature of some of the activation measures they use. These include creating or encouraging jobs for pay lower than guaranteed minimum wages and creating hybrid statuses

somewhere between unemployment and employment, which do not give rise to contributions, do not necessarily provide entitlement to certain social benefits and offer none, or only some, of the protection traditionally associated with the right to work (for example, ALE[4] contracts in Belgium) (Vielle and Bonvin, 2002).

These three observations indicate several unsatisfactory features that exist to varying degrees in the various types of welfare state.

3. Prospects for Security and Capability

The ambiguous relationship between social protection and flexibility, and the growing dissatisfaction it occasions among beneficiaries, employers and trade unions, may be pushing some welfare states towards major changes that could call into question their underlying policy paradigms (Hall, 1993).

At the political level, several international actors, after recommending full-blown flexibility, have recently tried to mark out new standards in an attempt to combine individual flexibility with career security for workers. Unlike the notion of decommodification, the idea behind career security implies that, in some circumstances, it is legitimate to breach income security (for example, by not maintaining the amount of unemployment benefit), so long as a worker's long-term security of existence is preserved (for example, that person's ability to find a job). One example of this is the promotion of 'decent work' by the International Labour Office, or the European Union's incorporation of the idea of 'quality employment' in the Luxembourg process and the guidelines for employment.

In the scientific field, several avenues have been suggested, including the idea of a *contrat d'activité*, put forward by Jean Boissonnat (Boissonnat, 1995), the 'occupational status' advocated in the Supiot report (Supiot, 1999) and the transitional labour markets proposed by Günther Schmid, Bernard Gazier and the research network of the *Wissenschaftszentrum Berlin für Sozialforschung* (Schmid, 1998; Schmid and Gazier, 2002). Boissonnat and Supiot try to imagine a continuous working status partly dissociated from the notion of continuous employment. This post-Fordist employment status would be accompanied by social drawing rights, which could be used at any point in a wage earner's career. This proposal probably fits in better with the reality of welfare states where employment is regulated by central governments. The other notion, which is similar in principle, focuses on the right to both mobility (moving from one form of employment to another and entering and leaving the labour market on occasions) and career security (understood to mean the maximization of possibilities for joining the labour market during one's life cycle), while at the same time concentrating the public authorities' attention on transitions between different situations on the labour market. This would make it possible to ensure a kind of full employment calculated on the basis of an average working week of 30 hours spread over the whole occupational life cycle (Schmid, 1998).

All these proposals tend to be subsumed under the heading of 'flexicurity' because they try to establish a 'good' compromise between flexibility and security (Wilthagen, 1998). However, some of them raise issues with regard to their practical application, since the rules are, by definition, set in a decentralized fashion in at least two respects (Supiot, 1999; Coutrot, 1999): first with regard to the definition of the common characteristics making up worker security (the body of minimum individual social rights) and second, with regard to negotiating procedures and the guarantees of access to negotiations that are offered to the most vulnerable workers or groups of workers, for example, workers not represented by a trade union. In the same spirit, the notions of decent work (ILO) or quality employment (EU) should be clarified, especially with a view to securing social security rights for flexible forms of employment. Hence, as the Supiot report suggests, it might be quite possible to envisage a progressive interlocking of rules, the most general of which would be formulated at the European level, with the final detailed terms and conditions being established at the level of firms.

The purpose of a study we are conducting for the European Foundation for the Improvement of Living and Working Conditions is an overall critical appraisal of these new theoretical approaches. But, since any reform is by nature normative, we consider it important to make a prior detailed examination of the criteria of distributive justice that might guide political responses to a number of basic questions. What must a welfare state accomplish? What type of justice and equality must it try to achieve? This debate is all too often stifled, or at least the normative groundwork of the propositions is rarely explained or discussed objectively. The notion of 'decommodification' put forward by Esping-Andersen (1990) cannot alone supply (or has perhaps never supplied) a normative criterion for evaluating welfare states, *a fortiori* in the context of the above mentioned mutations. It is therefore necessary to construct another principle or basis on which changes to the political balance between social protection and the security derived from participation on the labour market could rest (Vielle and Bonvin, 2002).

At this stage of our work, we suggest the use of the notion of *capability* developed by Amartya Sen, winner of the Nobel Prize for Economics (Sen, 1990, 1992 and 1995), where justice and equality are defined in terms of *effective freedoms* (capabilities) to accomplish 'functionings'. A functioning is described as one means among others for attaining a good life (good health, enough income to lead a full life in society). Some basic functionings are essential (for example, food or access to health care or education). In addition to these, the author deems it advisable to consider the different functionings available to an individual as 'baskets of goods', between which he or she must be able to choose. Individual well-being and security are therefore measured by the extent of a person's freedom to choose between various opportunitities. The quantities and qualities of the latter are related to the characteristics of individuals themselves and of their surrounding environment.

This approach differs from other, more widespread notions because it is underpinned by the *informational basis of ethical choice*, in other words by the scope of the substantial freedoms offered to individuals, which must be maximized. In this, it diverges from utilitarian conceptions, which, in practice, usually consider only individuals' aggregate incomes and equate them with the satisfaction that they derive from them. It also departs from Rawlsian concepts of justice based on primary goods (the seed capital), which disregard unequal capabilities to turn these goods into effective functionings (Vielle and Bonvin, 2002).

This approach opens up new prospects and can pose some problems with regard to the relationship between flexibility and security.

- For our argument, its main interest is that it offers a dynamic view of individual accomplishment. As far as capabilities are concerned, the aim of a welfare state is not necessarily to guarantee the same income (or even a job at any price) to individuals throughout their career but, on the contrary, it is at all times to maximize their freedom of choice between several possible accomplishments, i.e. various opportunities. In return, this wider horizon of possibilities for personal development must be seen as potential, or a factor adding to flexibility (Supiot, 1999; Castel and Haroche, 2001). Similarly, the 'old' ideas of security, resting solely on the provision of a 'decommodifying' allowance, fail to take account of unequal personal ability to turn these allowances into functionings. Since some aspects of the new active labour market policies afford workers more numerous training possibilities, they may be deemed to develop their capabilities (Lødemel and Trickey, 2000; Vielle and Bonvin, 2002).
- Consequently, this approach maintains freedom of choice, especially in activation policies. Once constraint is introduced, individuals' capabilities and therefore their security of existence are reduced by it. For this reason, some avenues for reforming social assistance through versions of 'workfare' or 'learnfare', which necessarily imply constraint, are harder to justify in a capability-based approach.
- The focus of attention of public policies must therefore shift from a purely quantitative vision of the labour market (measured, for example, in terms of employment rates), or from the notion of human capital, to a more

quality-centred view of the individual worker. The very notion of capability presupposes that there is no *per se* contradiction between flexibility and greater individual freedom.

- It goes without saying that the emphasis on capabilities is not a legitimate ground for abandoning income security in favour of a policy of developing one aspect of these capabilities (vocational training, for example). On the contrary, income security is justified, as it makes it possible to accomplish the basic functionings required for a fulfilled individual life.

- Since capabilities are related not only to individual preferences but also to characteristics, which have to do with individuals' membership of communities, categories or groups, the 'decentralized' nature of this notion of equality may be regarded as a boost to flexibility (because logically it stems from the decentralization of the choice between various sets of capabilities). In some cases, it may also be viewed as an obstacle to security, if decentralized negotiation does not encompass corrective procedures to offset unequal power in, or access to, decision-making. This is particularly true in countries, sectors or regions where trade unions are under-represented. In other words, the fact of considering the dialectic of flexibility and security from the angle of capabilities does not dispose of the issue of establishing (by whom and how?) substantive and procedural collective rights for all workers. This comes back to the complex issue of definite guarantees mentioned in the Supiot report.

As this preliminary examination shows, the idea of capability is quite useful for evaluating proposed reforms and the missions that welfare states accomplish or could accomplish. This theory must, however, be further operationalized. It was originally expounded in relation to concerns for development and, in the context of analysing social protection in the countries of the North, it can sometimes give rise to some ambivalence owing to its very general nature (Standing, 2002). This line of enquiry is being currently pursued by several research teams who are trying to employ capability as a more objective instrument for assessing public policies. Further work on this subject is expected in the near future (Salais, 2002; Standing, 2002; Lewis, 2002; Kazepov, 2002; etc).

We intend to continue the debate by linking it more systematically with the other above-mentioned approaches, such as transitional markets or the ideas of 'occupational status'.

Notes

1   For the final report of this research, please see 'Flexibility and social protection' by the European Foundation for the Improvement of Living and Working Condiitons, Dublin (2003).

2   University of Louvain, Belgium.
3   With a rapid growth rate over the last 10 years.
4   *Agences locales pour l'emploi* (local employment agencies), set up as part of policies to provide entitlement to unemployment benefit.

References

Aglietta, M. 1998. *Le capitalisme de demain*, Note de la fondation Saint-Simon, No. 106 (Paris, Fondation Saint-Simon).

Barbier, J.-C. 2001. *Welfare-to-work policies in Europe. The current challenges of activation policies* (Noisy-le-Grand, Centre d'étude de l'emploi).

Beattie, R. 2000. 'Une protection sociale pour tous, oui, mais comment l'assurer?', in *Revue Internationale du Travail*, Vol. 139, No. 2, pp. 141–161.

Beffa, J.-L. *et al.* 1999. *Les relations salariales en France* (Paris, Fondation Saint-Simon.

Bellofiore, R. 2000. 'Le sens des mots dans le débat sur l'après-fordisme ou le capitalisme fin-de-siècle au-delà des mythes', *Economies et société*, Vol. 11, No. 1, pp. 5–31.

Boissonnat, J. (Rapporteur). 1995. *Le travail dans vingt ans* (Paris, Odile Jacob).

Bourdieu, P. (ed.) 1993. *La misère du monde* (Paris, Seuil).

Boyer, R. (ed.) 1986 *La flexibilité du travail. Une étude comparative des transformations du rapport salarial dans sept pays de 1973 à 1985* (Paris, La Découverte).

_____ 2000. *The French welfare: An institutional and historical analysis in European perspective*, paper prepared for the conference on 'The role of private and public sector in the social security system', Kyoto University, Japan, Aug 28–29.

_____ and Durand J.-P. 1993. *L'après-fordisme* (Paris, Syros).

Cadiou, L. *et al.* 2000. 'Disparités institutionnelles et flexibilité des marchés du travail dans l'UE', in *Economie et statistique*, Vol. 2/3, Nos. 332–333, pp. 49–63.

Castel, R. 1995. *Les métamorphoses de la question sociale. Une chronique du salariat* (Paris, Gallimard).

_____ 1999. 'Droit du travail: Redéploiement ou refondation?', in *Droit social* (5 May 1999), pp. 438–442.

_____ and Haroche, C. 2001. *Propriété privée, propriété sociale, propriété de soi. Entretiens sur la construction de l'individu moderne* (Paris, Fayard).

Coutrot, T. 1999. '35 heures, marchés transitionnels, droits de tirage sociaux. Du mauvais usage des bonnes idées', in *Droit social* (7/8 July 1999), pp. 659–668.

de Nanteuil, M. 2000. 'Flexibilité et travail: Esquisse d'une théorie des pratiques', *Cahiers du Laboratoire de Sociologie du Changement des Institutions*, June, p. 34.

Dupeyroux, J.-J. and Ruellan, R. 1998. *Droit de la sécurité sociale* (Paris, Dalloz).

Esping-Andersen, G. 1990. *Les trois mondes de l'Etat-providence* (Paris, PUF) (1999).

_____, Gallie, D., Hemerijck, A. and Myles, J. 2001. *A new welfare architecture for Europe?*, Report submitted to the Belgian Presidency of the European Union (Brussels).

European Central Bank. 2002. *Labour market mismatches in euro area countries* (Frankfurt am Main, European Central Bank).

European Commission. 1999. *Women and work – Report on existing research in the European Union* (Luxembourg, Office for Official Publications of the European Communities).

_____ 2000. *Proposal for a Council decison on guidelines for Member States' employment policies for the year 2001* (Luxembourg, Office for Official Publications of the European Communities.

_____ 2000a. *Towards a community framework strategy for gender equality (2001–2005)* (Luxembourg, Office for Official Publications of the European Communities).

_____ 2000b. *Gender use of time* (Luxembourg, Office for Official Publications of the European Communities).

_____ 2000c. *Reconciliation of work and family life for men and women and the quality of care services – Report on existing research in the European Union* (Luxembourg, Office for Official Publications of the European Communities).

European Commission 2001. *Report by the Employment Committee. Indicators of quality in work* (Brussels).

_____ 2001a. *Employment in Europe 2001. Recent trends and prospects* (Luxembourg, Office for Official Publications of the European Communities.

_____ 2001b. *MISSOC 2001 – Evolution of social protection in the European Member States and the European Economic Area* (Luxembourg, Office for Official Publications of the European Communities.

_____ 2001c. *European Employment Observatory Review – Spring 2001* (Luxembourg, Office for Official Publications of the European Communities.

European Foundation for the Improvement of Living and Working Conditions. 1997. *New directions in social welfare. Report of a Conference of the Irish Presidency of the European Union* (Luxembourg, Office for Official Publications of the European Communities).

_____ 1999. *Linking welfare and work* (Luxembourg, Office for Official Publications of the European Communities).

_____ 2001. *For a better quality of work. Report of a Conference of the Presidency of the European Union* (Luxembourg, Office for Official Publications of the European Communities).

Eurostat 2001. *European social statistics – labour force survey 2000* (Luxembourg, Office for Official Publications of the European Communities).

Fagan, C. and McAllister, T. 2001. *Gender, employment and working time preferences in Europe* (Dublin, European Foundation for the Improvement of Living and Working Conditions).

_____, Rubery, J. and Smith, M. 1994. *L'évolution des modalités d'emploi et de la durée du travail et l'impact sur la force de travail des deux sexes* (Brussels, European Commission {DG V/A/3 - Equal Opportunities Unit}).

Ferrera, M. 1996. 'Modèles de solidarité, divergences, convergences: Perspectives pour l'Europe', in *Revue suisse de science politique*, Vol. 2, No. 1, pp. 55–72.

Friot, B. 1996. Le régime de la contrepartie dans la logique salariale', in *Revue Française des Affaires Sociales* (3, July–September), pp. 65–87.

Goudswaard, A. and De Nanteuil, M. 2000. *Flexibility and working conditions. A qualitative and comparative study in seven EU Member States* (Dublin, European Foundation for the Improvement of Living and Working Conditions).

Hall, P. A. 1993. 'Policy paradigms, social learning, and the State', in *Comparative Politics*, Vol. 25, No. 3, pp. 275–297.

Hetru, E. *et al.* 1998. *Les conséquences sociales de l'externalization et de la sous-traitance* (Brussels, Office de recherches sociales européennes).

Kazepov, Y. 2002. *Social assistance and activation measures in Europe*, European Cooperation in the field of Scientific and Technical Research (Cost A15) Second Conference: Welfare Reforms for the 21st Century (Oslo).

Klammer, U. 2000. *On the path towards a concept of 'flexicurity' in Europe* (Dusseldorf, Wirtschafts und Sozialwissenschaftliche Institut (WSI) in der Hans-Böckler-Stiftung).

Kravaritou-Manitakis, Y. 1987. *Nouvelles formes de travail: Aspects de droit du travail et de sécurité sociale dans la communauté européenne* (Dublin, European Foundation for the Improvement of Living and Working Conditions).

Legoff, J.-M., Malpas, N. and Vielle, P. 2000. *Intégration de l'égalité des chances pour les femmes et les hommes dans les politiques de l'emploi et du marché du travail. Un inventaire critique des indicateurs statistiques en vue d'une évaluation des politiques de l'emploi et du marché du travail en terme de genre* (Brussels, Office for Official Publications of the European Communities).

Lewis, J. 2002. *Gender and welfare state change*, European Cooperation in the field of Scientific and Technical Research (Cost A15) Second Conference: Welfare reforms for the 21st Century (Oslo).

Lilja, R. and Hämäläinen, U. 2001. *Working time preferences at different phases of life* (Dublin, European Foundation for the Improvement of Living and Working Conditions).

Lødemel, I. and Trickey, H. 2000. *An offer you can't refuse. Workfare in international perspective* (Bristol, Policy Press).

Marsden, D. 2000. *Can the right kinds of labour institutions create jobs? Europeanization of industrial relations* (Brussels, Université Libre de Bruxelles).

⸻ 2001. 'L'adaptation des institutions du marché du travail à celle de la nouvelle donne économique', in J.-P. Touffut (ed.) *Institutions et croissance. Les chances d'un modèle économique européen* (Paris, Albin Michel), Vol. 1, pp. 61–92.

Merllié, D. and Paoli, P. 2000. *Dix ans de conditions de travail dans l'Union européenne* (Dublin, European Foundation for the Improvement of Living and Working Conditions).

Michon, F. 1999. *Temporary agency work in Europe* (Dublin, European Foundation for the Improvement of Working and Living Conditions).

Moene, K. O. and Wallerstein, M. 1995. 'How social democracy worked: Labour market institutions', in *Politics and Society*, Vol. 23, No. 2, pp. 185–211.

Organization for Economic Cooperation and Development (OECD). 1995. *La flexibilité du temps de travail: Négociations collectives et intervention de l'état* (Paris, OECD).

Palier, B. 2002. *How can we analyse the process of welfare state reforms in Continental Europe?*, European Cooperation in the field of Scientific and Technical Research (Cost A15) Second Conference: Welfare reforms for the 21st Century (Oslo).

Paoli, P. 1992. *First European survey on the work environment 1991–1992* (Dublin, European Foundation for the Improvement of Living and Working Conditions).

⸻ and Merllié, D. 2000. *Third European survey on working conditions 2000* (Dublin, European Foundation for the Improvement of Living and Working Conditions).

Paugam, S. 2000. *Le salarié de la précarité. Les nouvelles formes de l'intégration professionnelle* (Paris, Presses Universitaires de France).

Peña-Casas, R. 2002. *Indicators of quality of employment in the EU* (Brussels, European Social Observatory).

Pochet, P. 2000. *Union monétaire et négociations collectives en Europe* (Brussels, Presses Interuniversitaires Européennes-Peter Lang).

Room, G. 2000. 'Commodification and decommodification: A developmental critique', in *Policy and Politics*, Vol. 28, No. 3, pp. 331–351.

Salais R. 2002. 'Work and welfare. Towards a capability-based approach', in J. Zeitlin and D. Trubek (eds.) *Governing work and welfare in a new economy. European and American experiments* (Oxford, Oxford University Press).

Sarfati, H. and Bonoli, G. 2001. *Marchés du travail et protection sociale dans une perspective internationale: Parallélisme ou convergence?* (Geneva, International Social Security Association).

Scharpf, F. W. and Schmidt, V.A. (eds.), 2000. *Welfare and work in the open economy* (Oxford, Oxford University Press).

Schmid, G. 1998. *Transitional labour markets: A new European employment strategy* (Berlin, Wissenschaftszentrum Berlin für Sozialforschung).

_____ 2001. L'activation des politiques d'emploi: combiner la flexibilité et la sécurité dans les marchés du travail transitionnels, in J.-P. Touffut, *Institutions et croissance. Les chances d'un modèle économique européen* (Paris Albin Michel), Vol. 1, pp. 61–92.

_____ and Gazier, B. 2002. *The dynamics of full employment. Social integration through transitional labour market* (Cheltenham, Edward Elgar).

Schömann, K., Flechtner, S., Mytzek, R. and Schömann, I. 2000. *Moving towards employment insurance – Unemployment insurance and employment protection in the OECD* (Berlin, Wissenschaftszentrum Berlin für Sozialforschung).

Seifert, H. 1999. *Job security: A new topic of collective bargaining* (Dusseldorf, Hans-Böckler-Stiftung).

Sen, A. 1990. 'Welfare, freedom and social choice: A reply', in *Recherches Economiques de Louvain*, Vol. 56, Nos. 3–4, pp. 429–450.

_____ 1992. *Inequality reexamined* (New York, Oxford University Press).

_____ 1995. 'Rationality and social choice', in *American Economic Review*, Vol. 85, No. 1, pp. 1–23.

_____ 2000. 'Travail et droits', in *Revue Internationale du Travail*, Vol. 139, No. 2, pp. 129–139.

Standing, G. 1997. 'Globalization, labour flexibility and insecurity: The era of market regulation', in *European Journal of Industrial Relations*, Vol. 3, No. 1, pp. 7 –37.

_____ 2002. *CIG, COAG and COG: A comment on a debate*, Paper presented at the Real Utopias Fifth Conference: Rethinking redistribution: Designs for a more egalitarian capitalism, Madison, Wisconsin, May 3–5.

Storrie, D. 2002. *Temporary agency work in the European Union* (Dublin, European Foundation for the Improvement of Working and Living Conditions).

Supiot, A. 1994. *Critique du droit du travail* (Paris, Presses Universitaires de France).

_____ (ed). 1999. *Au-delà de l'emploi. Transformations du travail et devenir du droit du travail en Europe* (Paris, Flammarion).

Sykes, R., Palier, B. and Prior, P.M. 2001. *Globalization and European welfare states. Challenges and change* (Basingstoke, Palgrave).

Taylor-Gooby, P. (ed.). 2001. *Welfare states under pressure* (London, Sage).

Traxler, F. and Woitech, B. 2000. 'Transnational investment and national labour market regimes: A case of "regime shopping"?', in *European Journal of Industrial Relations*, Vol. 6, No. 2, pp. 141–159.

Verly, J. 2000. *Les rouages de l'emploi: Relations collectives du travail et protection sociale* (Louvain-la-Neuve, Academia-Bruylant).

Vielle, P. 1997. *Le coût indirect des responsabilités familiales. Sa reconnaissance en droit comparé, européen et international de la sécurité sociale dans la perspective de l'égalité des chances entre femmes et hommes* (Florence, Institut Universitaire Européen).

_____ and. Bonvin, J.-M. 2002. *Activation policies: A capabilities perspective*, Paper presented at the Real Utopias Fifth Conference: Rethinking redistribution: Designs for a more egalitarian capitalism, Madison, Wisconsin, May 3–5.

Visser, J. 2002. *Is employment the answer to social policy?*, Paper prepared for the European Cooperation in the field of Scientific and Technical Research (Cost A15) Second Conference: Welfare reforms for the 21st Century (Oslo).

Webster, D. 2002. *Unemployment: How official statistics distort analysis and policy, and why*, Paper presented at the Radical Statistics Annual Conference, Newcastle, University of Northumbria.

Wilthagen, T. 1998. *Flexicurity: A new paradigm for labour market policy reform?* (Berlin, Wissenschaftszentrum Berlin für Sozialforschung).

Yeates, N. 2001. *Globalization and social policy* (London, Sage).

24

ON A PATH TO JUST DISTRIBUTION: THE CAREGIVER CREDIT CAMPAIGN

Theresa Funiciello[1]

1. Caregiver Credit Campaign Briefing

Billions of people worldwide – mostly women – do the work of caring for children, ensuring the very survival of the species, without pay. Women also comprise the vast bulk of those who give care to adults in need. The seeming invisibility of this 'gender apartheid' not only fails hands-on care-givers, but also negatively affects their wages in the market. After all, if you are worth zero when not in the market place, how much is your paid labour worth?

The Caregiver Credit Campaign speaks to families who confront the tension between caregiving and earning a living. It also speaks to all those who want to achieve a more human-centred society in the twenty-first century. Social Agenda is the catalyst. The campaign works in part because it is a practical way to engage people in sweeping but winnable issues: redefining work and value, counting traditional 'women's work' in gross domestic product, and obtaining social and economic benefits for care-giving performed or purchased by families.

The Caregiver Credit Campaign is a populist model of national, state and local networks. It educates participants, is educated by them, and provides a forum for ideas and emerging leadership. It is multi-partisan and constitutes a majority bloc of caregivers, people who need care and supporters. The campaign unites the need for social, political and economic support for low-income single mothers, middle-income married homemakers, grandparents raising their children's children, those caring for spouses and partners dying of cancer or living with AIDS or disabilities, professionals juggling two careers and the needs of aging parents, and even affluent caregivers whose work is often essential but undervalued in the home and community.

2. Fundamentals

Caregiving is as essential to human life as land, water or air. It is as important as paying jobs at McDonalds, Ebay or Boeing. Without caregivers, no one would be alive today.

Caring work within families is an essential component of economic, social and political well-being. It is largely unacknowledged, usually unpaid. Yet, from the moment caregivers 'leave home' for the marketplace, the former nurturing work is extracted from the nation's economic resources by way of day-care centres, fast food outlets, nursing homes, etc. This exchange may be in the best interests of many families and society, but certainly is not always.

In the United States and worldwide, well over 90 per cent of all caregivers are women. Traditional 'women's work' is represented as altruistic and falling outside the marketplace, as if rendered valueless. Every nation is tethered to this 'free' or unpaid labour. The market is believed to operate apart from it but actually competes for human resources formerly devoted to it. Despite the fact that caregiving is key to every nation's economy, political and corporate leaders have been reluctant to acknowledge the true economic value of caregivers or to recognize the role of interdependence in a just society.

Interdependence is a central and informing value as well as a key structural element of society. It virtually defines families and is what transforms groups of families from isolated units into communities. Interdependence underlies the will to subsidize the smooth functioning of the economy by funding social and physical infrastructure, e.g. public schools, sewerage systems, or social security payments to limit poverty among the elderly. At present, neither the burdens nor benefits of interdependence are broadly or equitably distributed.

Families of blood or choice are the building blocks of community. Optimal nurturing tends to occur within families and ideally produces happy, healthy, active, engaged children (society's 'replacement parts') and preserves the dignity of adults in need of continuing care. People, who choose to work at caregiving, full- or part-time, still need the means to survive. Those who give care need productive choices to decide rationally when or whether to enter or leave market (paying) jobs, and whether to give care directly or purchase care services outside the home. The ability to make sane caregiving decisions in the best interests of the family applies to rich and poor people alike.

Most caregivers agree. A recent survey by Social Agenda shows that 95 per cent of respondents across race, gender and class 'agree' or 'agree strongly' that caregivers of children and adults ought to receive income support. In addition, eighty per cent of responding parents between the ages of 20 and 39 chose family time as their top priority in a Radcliff Public Policy Centre poll. Furthermore, a Democratic Leadership Council poll of likely voters showed that 85 per cent of all parents would prefer it if one parent did not have to work outside the home full-time. As far back as the mid-1980s, a *New York Times* poll showed that the majority of lower- to middle-income mothers would prefer to raise their children full-time, if money were not an issue. In 2000, 72 per cent of respondents in a *Parent* magazine poll said they would rather raise their children than 'work' [outside the home].

The time/poverty gap of single-parent families is most stark. Single fathers are time-stretched to the limit, though few will be income-poor. Equally time-deprived, single mothers lack income equity when in the market-place. Most often their wages alone are insufficient to meet any semblance of a decent living standard. As often as not, single-mother families are income- and time-poor with or without paying jobs.

Families with children and/or disabled, ailing or aged adults who need the regular attention of a (preferably loving) human being have two options. One is a paid alternative to a 'mother'; the other is mother (or father, sister, partner, etc.). Quality alternatives are expensive and often unavailable even to those who can afford the cost. The home caregiver option means diminished or no paid work and an effective income opportunity cost of 100 per cent, hour-for-hour, of that person's time. Either way families pay. Society can ill afford to ignore their need for recompense.

Estimates of US savings resulting from home caregiving to frail elderly parents or disabled or dying family members were pegged at $200 billion in 1999. Similarly, replacing a good 'mother' with all the 'intangibles' is all but impossible and very expensive. Current annual estimates range from $100,000 to over $500,000 to substitute enough quality paid help for one mother. If caregiving were not done within families of blood or choice, the cost to society of substitute care would be huge. A fully refundable Caregiver Credit would set us on a political trajectory toward 'just distribution,' beyond a corporatist/unionist version of work and life.

3. Three Practical Goals

3.1 Our First Win: Making the Child Tax Credit Refundable

The child tax credit minimally supports caring for most children directly in the home or through purchased alternative care. Until 1992 it was not refundable so low-income families were unable to take advantage of it in part because they did not make enough money to owe taxes. In the very first year of the Caregiver Credit Campaign the many thousands who participated in the effort with us succeeded in making it refundable. For those in the refundable category, checks are mailed from the Inland Revenue Service (IRS). Universal refundability is not yet in place to cover all children (including the very poorest) but we are getting there. It was increased 20 per cent from $500 to $600 in 2002, and will rise to $1,000 over the next few years. As a result of our campaign, millions of low-income families are now eligible for a substantial share of an estimated $9.2 billion in new money, including an overall increase in the per child value of the credit to all qualifying families ($10,000 to $150,000 annual income for two parents). The credits are low and still cover only children, but they are clearly susceptible to popular pressure.

3.2 Convert the Child Tax Credit to a Caregiver Credit

Phase Two of the campaign in which we are now engaged is to seek conversion of the credit to cover care of adults in need as well as children, and to shift the focus of the credit to the giver of care, not the qualifying individuals. The psychological and sociological effects of rewarding the caregiver cannot be underestimated.

3.3 Increase the Value of the Credit

The value of the credit should be increased more reasonably to represent the actual cost of giving care. Caregiving is not free to the giver. Those who sacrifice part or all of their market income to do caring work that individuals and society need ought not to suffer severe economic deprivation.

4. Advantages of the Caregiver Credit

- It is 'mommy neutral', applying equally to at-home and employed mothers.
- Caregivers tending to the needs of other adults are a large and growing part of the population that will increase as baby boomers' aging parents become needy, followed in mere decades by their own aging concerns. This group has and will continue to have substantial political clout.
- If the benefit were offered at a reasonable level, the potential for community-based reforms to the service delivery system for families with children and adults in need would expand exponentially.
- Its range of appeal is intergenerational, gender and sexual-preference neutral, class-, ethnicity-, ability-, and race-balanced, and multi-partisan.
- Caregiver credits can be implemented at federal, state and/or local levels, commensurate with varying fiscal needs and levels of consensus.

5. Next Steps

- Increase the critical mass of people for change.
- Promote individual and family activism. In 2002 we expect to launch a two-year pilot project to maximize application for, and receipt of, the child tax credit.

- Capture the vast bulk of the mainstream women's movement from all political parties to engage in a dialogue on the political benefits of inclusiveness of mothers and other caregivers, and on the social and economic benefits of counting unpaid care-giving labour in the gross domestic product.
- Generate state-by-state press coverage to influence opinion-leaders and decision-makers, and provide a feedback loop for polishing our tactics to build on initial public policy achievements.
- Continue recruiting intellectuals, celebrities and other prominent individuals to form host committees and participate in ways they best can. For instance, in 2002 a 1960s teen rock star, Lesley Gore, performed at the first of several fund-raising events.
- Influence political polls. Already, the issue scores high – above even crime and education.
- Promote the economic development basis of the campaign. A universal caregiver credit benefits local economies. Money is spent in communities, circulates fast and creates paying jobs along the way.
- Put people in place to assist and encourage formation of state groups.
- Hold regional meetings, leading to a national convention.

The New Economy has profound implications for Americans – less job security, more time between paying jobs, more hours of formal education, more involvement in politics, more financial investment skills, more expertise in health insurance coverage and administration. Some argue, implausibly, that there should also be more time for child rearing. Even functioning at superhuman capacity, people have no more than 24 hours in a day. Where can the time come from? 'Faster-smarter-better' works to produce things, but it still takes 18 or so years to raise children successfully. Robots may soon be able to sweep our floors, but when will they be able to teach our children ethics or comfort the dying?

6. Observations

Access to the means (currently money income) through which necessities are normally acquired is indispensable to the proper functioning of a democracy. The relative monetary muscle of the elderly (whose poverty rates have dropped precipitously since the 1930s, due to Social Security), their extraordinary stake in public policy, and the availability of leisure time help explain why such a high proportion vote and are active in political associations.

The universality of Social Security confers the often asserted but rarely achieved 'inalienable' right of equality on recipients, homogenizing not so much income as regard. By public policy, beneficiaries are equal simply because they are human. One need only look at the price of cinema tickets to see how this goodwill towards perfect strangers has extended to private behaviour. We know nothing of their integrity, motivations, sex lives or work habits. We do not know whether they were good younger people by any definition, but we deliver them collectively from the bell-jar of public scrutiny.

Having conferred and sustained a measure of social and economic justice by law, policy and culture upon them the nation has been justly rewarded. Liberated from having to appraise the relative merit of each supplicant, we leave reckoning to a higher power.

Can the nation support caregivers and those they care for fairly, too? Is there another way to build a secure and civil society based on common human decency? If you think the nation can, and do not have a better idea for how to get on an appropriate political trajectory, join the Caregiver Credit Campaign. If not, ask some questions. Let us see if we can convince you. If you have a better idea, try and convince us. We are all ears.

Note

1   Social Agenda, Inc., New York, USA.

25

A CARE-WORKER ALLOWANCE FOR GERMANY

Michael Opielka[1]

1. Introduction

That in modern welfare states financial transfers for the work of childcare and child-raising in the private family sphere could be paid in the form of a parental wage – or more generally, a 'carework salary' – would have seemed unthinkable just a few decades ago.[2] Of course, in the feminist discussion of the 1970s, the introduction of 'wages for housework' was proposed, but this never reached the general social policy debate, and was very controversial in feminist circles, too (for an overview see Leipert and Opielka, 1998). However, in recent decades the options in the social-policy arena have changed considerably. The superficial reasons for this are above all the demographic upheavals in almost all western European OECD States which, on the one hand, increasingly cannot guarantee care for older persons in the 'natural' way within the family, and on the other hand, have increasingly allowed children to become a scarce resource. This presents problems above all for financing old-age security and medical insurance programmes.

The decline in the 'natural' reproduction process in families has other, socio-cultural causes, above all in connection with changes in gender self-image. While women still do feel primarily responsible for family tasks, their educational and occupational background is increasingly comparable with that of men. In a subsequent and successful integration into the world of work, this clearly creates a situation of multiple obligations. Women's response has been to withdraw from family carework to a societally significant extent, by avoiding living with (and taking care of) parents (and/or in-laws), and by practising contraception. From the point of view of payment for in-family carework, however, the two problems mentioned here should be kept separate. The care of the elderly is dependent on different social policy preconditions and consequences than the home care of children.[3]

This paper focuses on the discussion surrounding the introduction of payment for childcare within the family, and references in the following to family carework mean childcare. It also concentrates on Germany and the discussion-taking place there. This discussion would nevertheless seem to have more general – and perhaps because of the historical specificity – even paradigmatical relevance: as through a magnifying-glass, the changes in work within the family and the attendant socio-political issues come to a focus in the German debate as recent comparative studies of European family policy show (Pfau-Effinger, 1999; Carling *et al.*, 2002).

The question of the value-relation between work in the family and work in market-based employment is being currently raised anew.[4] The old dichotomy is in a practical and theoretical crisis. That dichotomy viewed work in the family not as economically productive but as reproductive activity, one of the many non-monetary requirements of the money economy – like peace, natural resources or economically friendly ethics. The practical crisis is apparent above all in falling birth rates and their dramatic demographic consequences. The theoretical crisis is revealed by the fact that the feminist criticism of traditional disregard for important carework performed mainly by women has now reached the core of contemporary democratic and economic theory; the old market-capitalistic dichotomy is being challenged by newer theories stressing the role of social capital created in and by the family.

To get a better overview, we shall proceed in two steps. The first step looks back to the three historical way-stations of German social policy, which were unique in the world in their cumulative effect: that particular family-policy pathway leading from the motherhood cult of National Socialism, to the duality of the idyllic conservative family ideal of post-war West Germany on the one hand, and the socialistic work-religion of East German society on the other, to the remedial modernization of united Germany. In the second step, the German family policy situation one decade after reunification is examined in the context of a new orientation for the welfare state.

This leads finally to a position that requires a new historical compromise for social policy progress, where work in the employment sphere and work in the family sphere are treated as qualitative equals. Three transaction streams are redirected out of the familial and into the State and/or societal sphere: 1) the care of children and other care-dependent people (through professionalization); 2) assuring adequate coverage of living costs (by financial transfers for children and carers); 3) regulation of the time available for family and jobs (through appropriate labour policies). The reshuffle changes the welfare state itself: it adds the universalistic principle of 'guarantor' to the existing three system principles (social insurance, social assistance and social care).[5]

2. Germany – A Family Laboratory

Reconciling family and employment is problematical in countries other than in Germany, but there it is especially so, not least for historical reasons. As mentioned earlier, German social and family policy followed a particular path, beginning with the Nazi regime and its image of the woman, leading to the two separate systems of the German Democratic Republic and Adenauer's West Germany, and finally to Germany as a united country since 1989 seeking its place in the international community.

2.1 The Nazi Mutterpflicht

One often reads that the housewife marriage model in Germany first became dominant with the policies of the Nazi regime. 'Of course the objection to this is that the housewife marriage model (...) already appeared significantly earlier at the centre of the gender arrangement', writes Birgit Pfau-Effinger in her lucid study of the cultural bases of women's employment in Europe (Pfau-Effinger, 2000, p. 114).[6] In fact, since the second half of the nineteenth century, all societal groups in Germany favoured the family model of the male breadwinner marriage. This model, initially a development of the urban bourgeoisie, was successively adopted by the workers' movement and the Social Democrats – at first in contradiction to fact, because among the working class the gainful employment of women was still necessary and usual in the twentieth century up until the 1950s (Hausen, 1993).

'The first, best and proper place for the woman is in the family', exclaimed Joseph Goebbels in his opening speech on the occasion of the exhibition 'The Woman' in March 1933 (Mühlfeld and Schönweiss, 1989, p. 61). Nevertheless, the family policies of the Nazis did not lead to the exclusion of women from paid work, although many of their policy measures sought to promote the idea of the full-time housewife. More typical was this paradox: women were to be reinforced in their identity as housewife and mother, but were also available for work outside the home, while at the same time their traditional legal position in marriage and family was destabilized. The regime's racist objectives subjected women to marriage adeptness tests and forced sterilizations, but above all reduced men to their reproductive function and promoted social and sexual irresponsibility on the part of fathers (Czarnowski, 1991). Marriage was made a State function; the private bourgeois model was rejected. Motherhood became a national and racist-ideological duty.

Nazi family policies there have left a particular legacy: the housewife model of marriage and, more generally, the recognition of mothers' (work) contribution was seen in post-war Germany – and above all for many intellectuals after 1968 – as a product of fascist motherhood ideology. This was historically false, and theoretically serious: motherhood began to be politically suspect.

2.2 German Democratic Republic: The Right to and Duty of Employment

In the Soviet occupation zone, women's policies, under the influence of the Soviet military administration, were consciously and radically dissociated from those of the Nazi regime. Drawing on the Marxist traditions of the German workers' movement, a new image of the woman was propagated which, with repeated modifications, was to remain valid until the end of the German Democratic Republic (Bast and Ostner, 1992). The 'Women's Question' as a social problem was held to be resolvable only with the abolition of private property. Gender equality would be reached only when the woman could be freed from enslavement in the family and her economic dependence on the man, and integrated as an independent economic agent into societal production.

The overriding objective of GDR social policy was securing full-time female employment in order to respond, given the chronic shortage of labour, to the threat of increasing female part-time work. From 1976 a 'baby-care year' was introduced for those with a second child, and other benefits were improved, to bring about an increase in birth rates. Fathers at first could take neither the baby-care year (this right was granted only from 1986) nor the housekeeping day: 'The special privileges of employed women (shorter work periods, longer employment interruptions) meant a new reassignment of women's duties to mothers' (Schäfgen, 2000, p. 109). Employing women came to be a risk for management, and consequently women faced discrimination in their careers. This contradiction between postulated gender equality and actual discrimination was answered by women in the GDR with reduced reproduction. From the beginning of the 1980s the model of the three-child family was propagated with new intensity: from 1986 the baby-care year could be taken for the first child, and after the birth of the third child this was extended to 18 months.

Despite these measures the GDR birth rate fell in the 1980s from 1.94 in 1980 to 1.57 in 1989 (Wendt, 1997, p. 119), approaching the even lower rates of West Germany. Remarkably however, the number of childless women in the GDR also fell continuously, so that more women were giving birth to fewer children. Children and marriage in the GDR were part of normal existence; the family played a central role. Wendt speaks of the 'standardized family' and 'standardized motherhood' in so far as other family models, besides the double-earner marriage, were discriminated against socially and legally. Family forms besides the nuclear one, such as cohabitation or single parenting, nevertheless also increased in the GDR, at least in the 1980s (Wendt, 1997, pp. 148f.).

In sum, the GDR policy of combining family and occupation has been aptly described by Hildegard Nickel as a 'combination arrangement'. Double employment of the marriage partners was combined with State childcare; but the concept of full labour-market integration of women was tied to the woman's primary responsibility for the household and childcare. In the new (i.e. eastern) *Länder* of the Federal Republic of Germany, women are today still trying to live up to this model (Pfau-Effinger, 2000, p. 128).

2.3 The Adenauer Era: From Complementarity to Partnership

The policies of the Federal Republic of Germany (FRG), in contrast to East Germany, openly supported the bourgeois family model of the housewife marriage, which since the beginning of the twentieth century had been culturally at the core of the gender arrangement.

In the 1950s it was actually practised on a wide scale in West Germany as in the US. Not being employed was seen generally as an indicator of a house-wife's position of prosperity and privilege (Kolinsky, 1989, p. 24). In spite of the plausible feminist criticism of FRG policies on the relationship between family and occupation, which were relatively conservative in European terms, those policies do not seem to have been so far detached from people's needs, at least in the longer term. Then and now, it was characteristic for West German women to have a dual-career arrangement based on reduced working-hours. In an opinion poll by Allensbach in 1996, 46 per cent of women preferred being mothers and part-time employed, and 33 per cent wanted to be exclusively a housewife and mother; the latter were older women, so that a decline in preference for that model is probable in the future. Only 8 per cent of West German women wanted to be full-time employed mothers, and only 9 per cent stated that they would like to become or continue to be childless career women (Pfau-Effinger, 2000, p. 126).

These attitudes are in no way unrealistic. West German men – like their East German counterparts – have only to a very limited extent increased their attention to children and especially childcare. In the public debate in Germany, especially among the male leaders of all parties, the problem of compatibility of family and occupation is above all seen as a problem for women, not for men.

2.4 From 1989: Joining the Modern Europe

German reunification saw a collision of gender-political differences between East and West. Even now the attitudes of women in the 'old' and 'new'

German *Länder* differ with regard to full-time employment, although they do show a certain convergence in the direction of Western models, according to the principle of 'equality within the difference'. One could describe the situation, simplified, as follows: in the main, women want children, and so do men. Since children cause work, the question arises, who is going to do it. In the western *Länder* the majority of women do not see the solution as lying in the professionalization and institutionalization of childcare for the first three years of life; in the East this proportion is markedly lower. But even with a high level of childcare professionalization, a lot of work, and the necessity of being present and available, remains, especially with small children. Who is to make this investment of time, and when? Men do not want to change their employment behaviour significantly, and women also support this. Thus, work in the family is left for the women to do. Certainly, this is a simplified description, but it is supported by the data: 'In the vast majority of families the responsibility for housework, by common consent, seems to lie with the women, while the participation of men in housework is interpreted as a helping role' (Kaufmann, 1995, p. 127).

This is not just the case in reunified Germany, but also in other countries, and even in 'more modern' Scandinavia. Men there consider their participation in housework as 'voluntary help', their 'demonstration of love', which is 'highly dependent on the emotional stability of the partnership relation' (*Ibid.*). Furthermore, men show more verbal commitment to housework and child raising than in their behaviour. This indicates a certain inconsistency between consciousness and deed, but also surely some important objective obstacles. The longer the female partner has held the main paid position in the family – though the partners may be similarly qualified – the more the husband is likely to be motivated to do housework.

The initial family policy situation in the 'new' Germany was particularly interesting. After the Nazis' racist motherhood ideology, the post-war split into an 'equality ideology' in the East, and a 'difference ideology' in the West, the united Germany now – in the twenty-first century – joins modern 'average' Europe (Table 25.1).

3. The Political Parties: Women's Employment and Childcare Allowances

Family policy, after a lengthy marginal existence, seems to have been revitalized. Not only in Germany but in other (western) countries too, the family has become a political problem (Gauthier, 1996; Ringen, 1997). In the US, for example, it has been recognized that the situation of American children, and with them the future of the whole society, is endangered by the newer phases

Table 25.1 Typology of family models and policies in Germany [7]

Model	Wife	Husband	Family policy	Gender arrangement	Historical dominance in Germany
Natalism (L1)	Mother ('racially pure')	Patriarchy	Demographic orientation, selectivity	Difference	Nazi period (1933–1945)
Double breadwinner marriage (L2)	Full time employed + mother	Full-time employed + father in free time	Public childcare promotion of women	Equality	GDR (E. Germany)
Male breadwinner (L3)	Housewife + mother + low-level employment	Family provider, moderately patriarchal	Marriage- and provider-centred	Moderate difference	FRG (W. Germany) (until 1990s)
Partnership-based family (L4)	Compatibility of family and occupation		Public Childcare 'childcare salary'	Sharing, participation	2002..?

of the globalization process (Kamerman, 1998), and that the US in the past has spent too little on childcare.

The compatibility of family and employment has remained a 'woman's dilemma'. 'Since the 1980s this dilemma ascribed to women has appeared in newer packaging: in the face of the increasing employment orientation of women, programmes supporting the family were not imposed as family or men's – but rather women's – promotion programmes' (Hausen, 2000, p. 350; see also Ostner and Lewis, 1998)

This appears to be changing. In wide-ranging programme papers the two large German parties, the Social Democrats (SPD) and the Christian Democrats (CDU), have made an effort to address the issue of the family. It is worth examining their positions more closely, because they define the dilemmas and in part come up with fundamentally differing answers.

3.1 Social Democratic Party: Compatibility Through Employment Integration

SPD alternative Chairperson Renate Schmidt initiated a party commission which, immediately after the party came to power in 1998, and under the general watchwords 'Future of the Family and Social Cohesion' and 'Forum on the Family', formulated basic questions on a re-evaluation of the family and obtained the opinions of SPD-linked academic specialists and organizations (*SPD-Projektgruppe*, 2000). A document presented at the SPD party congress in Nuremberg in November 2001 proposed a new orientation for family policy. The departure from all feminist anti-family overtones was remarkable: instead, there is the realistic formulation: 'Family, in the classical form the nuclear family, i.e. an adult couple with biological children, has revealed itself (...) more stable than suspected (...) divorce and separation occur largely in childless couples (..)' etc. (SPD-Parteivorstand, 2001, p. 4). The authors have recognized the importance of the family in the 'middle' of society, which the SPD is trying to win over. At the same time, they complain of an 'increasing division of society (...) into family and non-family sectors'. The reasons why the desire for children and its realization often do not coincide are seen as the unsolved incompatibility of family and employment.

How should this problem be tackled? Two packages of measures are suggested: an 'all-day supervision infrastructure for children of all ages' (*Ibid.*, p. 13), and the further development of a compensation scheme for family work, in the direction of a change in the child-raising allowance, such that 'for one year it can function as salary replacement' (*Ibid.*, p. 15). The hope is that fathers will become engaged more intensively in the care of small children, since fathers 'today, because they earn more than mothers, and want to provide for their families' economic security, largely forgo this opportunity' (*Ibid.*, p. 16). That is a somewhat exaggerated interpretation of scientific findings on the reluctance of fathers to claim childcare leave (or the newer term: 'parenting time'). Even with equal incomes, men and women tend to stick with the traditional gender arrangement, which suggests deeply anchored cultural norms (Vaskovics and Rost, 1999).

How is the proposed SPD package to be assessed in the light of German family policy generally? First, it is noticeable that both instruments – all-day child supervision and parenting allowance as salary replacement – have been taken from the Scandinavian as well as the GDR family policy schemes. Their main idea is gender 'equality'. But because men are not taking on female roles, the solution to the problem lies in the socialization of family tasks, while assuring continued occupational progress of women (based on the male model). In contrast to the GDR, the SPD has approved part-time work solutions and flexible work hours, thus emulating Scandinavian countries, which have had such family policies in place since the 1990s. Their experience shows that male behaviour patterns hardly change, or at best extremely slowly. Thus the 'compatibility of family and employment' in the SPD party programme will also remain, for the moment anyway, a project for mothers, who nevertheless should expect significantly more societal support.

This rather critical assessment of the employment-oriented family concept of the SPD may be relativized by taking a wide European perspective. Birgit Pfau-Effinger has observed, in the welfare states whose policies were based on the housewife model of the male breadwinner marriage – among which she includes post-war Germany – a transformation of the 'gender arrangement' (Pfau-Effinger, 2001). During the Christian/Liberal coalition in the 1990s, as a reaction to cultural change, decisive steps were taken to individualize claims to family benefits, allowing a greater independence of mothers from male providers (child-raising leave included in public pension insurance, etc.). The 'Red/Green' coalition has, since 1998, in particular with the Parental Leave Law in force from the beginning of 2001, undertaken further steps towards a 'cultural modernization of the male breadwinner model': parenting leave and child-raising allowance claims can be combined with part-time work of up to 30 hours; one year of the parenting leave can be delayed until the end of the child's eighth year; fathers and mothers can take parenting leave simultaneously; but, above all, a parent is given the legal right to switch to part-time work, at least in firms with more than 15 employees. Parenthood is thus taken a step further out of the exclusively private sphere and into the realm of societal responsibility.

The SPD programme just mentioned aims beyond the long-overdue modernization measures towards an extension of women's freedom of choice – but this means above all the choice of employment and children. Taking up the terminology of Pfau-Effinger, the programme can be defined as the 'double breadwinner model with State childcare' (Pfau-Effinger, 2001), for decades the dominant family- and gender-policy model in Scandinavia and France. The SPD demand for the abolition of the German tax-splitting model for spouses, and an extension of all-day supervision facilities for children fits in along this path of development. The increase of the child allowance to a level covering minimum needs has, by contrast, its political source in the wish to redistribute wealth in order to bring about social justice. The SPD is attempting with this to achieve a kind of guaranteed basic income for children, which does not conflict with the party's central emphasis on employment, as would a guaranteed income for persons of working age. The SPD remains thus true to its historical roots: a citizen becomes a citizen by gainful employment, and that applies also to women. As for the obvious dilemma for women that employment and family tasks become a double burden, making the expectation of a full career realistic only by renouncing reproduction, the SPD tries to resolve this by broadening public child supervision and fatherhood campaigns, in which fathers are encouraged voluntarily to do more work within the family.

3.2 Christian Democratic Union: Compatibility Through Family Allowances

With the loss of its long-held governing position in 1998, the CDU also gained a breathing space in which it could examine its ideological assumptions anew for their basis in reality. In family policy this means above all recognizing the plurality of forms of family life and accepting this as a practically unalterable political fact. While the SPD programme begins with the presumption of the 'normality' of the nuclear family, the point of systemic revision for the CDU lies in the broad recognition of 'non-normality': 'Therefore we recognize the family anywhere where parents have responsibility for children, and children for parents' (CDU Federal Board, 2001, p. 39) The CDU also sees the compatibility of family and employment as a 'key question' in assessing the child-friendliness of a society. Their strategy for solving this question differs significantly from that of the SPD.

In order to understand the difference, it is worth looking at the diagnosis: 'The desired family-life model today is, for the majority, the simultaneous occupational activity of both partners. There are, however, still many women who wish to devote themselves exclusively to the family and child raising. This must also remain possible in the future; the CDU stands for the principle of freedom of choice' (*Ibid.*, p. 39). The SPD would not use this formulation, at least not if it is a matter of benefit claims which result from said the freedom of choice.

While the SPD demands an 'all-day infrastructure' for the supervision of children, the analogous CDU proposal of 'need-based construction of all-day schools' (CDU Bundestag parliamentary group, 2001, p. 7) sounds more restrained, though in essence similar. The difference is to be found in the monetary transfer systems for families (*Familienlastenausgleich*). While the SPD – arguing for women's integration into employment and less paid work by fathers – is betting on a combination of employment and transfer systems, the CDU wants to replace the existing child allowance and child-raising allowance with a 'family allowance' which would be tax- and social contribution-free[1] and – remarkably – unaffected by employment and/or income level. The amount quoted for this allowance is about €613 per month for each child under three years, about €307 for each child between three and 17, and about €154 for older children while still attending school (*Ibid.*, pp. 10ff.; CDU Federal Board, 2001, pp. 41–43). At the same time, as a broadening of the existing system, a 'time account' for 'family time' of three years within the first eight years of a child's life has been suggested, which could be extended to 3½ years as an incentive for fathers, if both partners share the family time.

The costs of such a measure are naturally considerable: the CDU parliamentary group has calculated that €25 billion extra would have to be spent annually. Armed with an expert opinion from IIFO (assuming a lower family allowance level; Werding, 2001), the group nevertheless expects only limited refinancing to be necessary due to employment and growth effects. This measure thus represents a far-reaching reorganization project, and an investment in families.

How is the proposal of a 'family allowance' (*Familiengeld*) to be assessed, above all in its effect on reconciling family and employment? A look back at the controversy surrounding the proposal of a 'Child-raising salary' in 2000 (*Erziehungsgehalt*, 2000; Leipert and Opielka, 1998) might help (Tünnemann, 2000). That proposal differed in some aspects from the CDU model (the amount suggested for the child-raising salary was 2000 DM, i.e. about €1,000 per month; only modest supplements would be paid for each additional child; the salary would be social contribution-free but not tax-free, i.e. taxed like any other income). But both proposals have in common the absence of any relation to employment or income of the claimant; the family allowance is meant to honour the work accomplished in family and child-raising. It is not clear that the existing tax-free, minimum living-cost income allowed by law would continue in addition to the family allowance (Werding, 2001, p. 5).

In theoretical terms, the social-policy innovations are contained in the side-remarks, for example, in an accompanying strategy paper of the CDU parliamentary group. Its discussion of the family allowance, in the context of an employment-promoting policy implies that the allowance is seen as something other than a simple 'financial transfer'. 'The difference between the minimum income guaranteed by social assistance and minimum wages (*Lohnabstand*) must be increased. Those who work must on principle earn more after taxes than those who do not, but receive transfer benefits. By means of the family allowance too, this difference will be upheld' (CDU Parliamentary Group, 2001, p. 16) Perhaps the authors did not realize how far-reaching their discussion would be, but they seem to have conceived of the family allowance as a source of primary income just like wages and salaries. If we suspend the convention of looking at the total national economic balance-sheet, we can see here a new concept of the politically directed revaluation of societal work: the family allowance (like the 'child-raising salary') is seen neither as compensation for lost wages, like contribution-equivalent social insurance, nor as a welfare benefit linked to need, like social assistance. In so far as the CDU proposal envisages integrating into the family allowance the present child allowance, the latter's social-policy logic – i.e. the principle of care (*Versorgung*) on the basis of special status (familiar from the special legal status of civil servants or war victims) – would extend to it. One can thus see, in the idea of the family allowance, the nucleus of a 'guaranteed basic income' for child-raising persons and, later, for children and youth (Opielka, 2000a).

Whether the family allowance would help or hinder the reconciliation of family and employment is not easy to judge. At first glance, it would seem to help, as the family allowance would be received as a supplement to earnings. Advocates and measures to promote full-time careers by both partners will nevertheless criticize the fact that the family allowance would encourage part-time or irregular work; in the first three years of a child's life, and in two-parent families, some low-level employment may suffice when material needs are relatively modest. In contrast to the SPD proposal – i.e. a child-raising allowance as a wage replacement – the family allowance (on a child-raising salary) would favour the mixing of various income sources. There is evidence of an existing trend in this direction; Georg Vobruba has recently argued convincingly that any future labour policy that does not accommodate the mixing of income sources will be a failure, since permanent full-time employment for all is neither probable nor desirable (Vobruba, 2000).

4. Carework Salary as Guaranteed Minimum Income?

In the preceding discussion of child-raising salary (or family allowance) there is almost no mention of proposals for a guaranteed minimum income (Opielka, 2000a). This has to do with the different contexts within which the discussion takes place. The family-policy debate has been – at least until now – carried on among experts; it has only recently been widened as a result of concerns over the results of the OECD comparative educational study 'PISA 2000', as well as the demographic developments mentioned earlier, which for the first time are being publicly associated with deficiencies in family policy.

By contrast, the discussion over a guaranteed minimum income in Germany has been stimulated above all by labour market and tax policy considerations, and is still highly controversial. Clearly a child-raising salary – depending on its actual form – has the same effect as a selective basic guaranteed income, limited to those raising children. The German welfare state is particularly oriented towards wages. The introduction of carework salaries, in the form of a child-raising salary or family salary, would establish a new way of 'earning a living' for persons raising children. One can see in this a step in the direction of a universal citizen-based family policy, the legitimacy of which will be a precondition for a general, freely available basic guaranteed income (Opielka, 2000a, 2002b). To that extent, the prospective family-policy reorientation in Germany, together with similar developments in other EU states such as France or Norway (Leipert, 1999), direct attention to the possible introduction of guaranteed basic income models.

Notes

1   University of Jena, Germany.
2   Abbreviated versions of this paper have been published under the title 'Familie, Beruf und Familienpolitik', in Forum Familie der SPD (ed.), (2002) *Mit Kindern leben*. Berlin, Schriftenreihe Zukunft Familie, Heft 2, SPD Bundesvorstand, pp. 104–120, as well as under the title 'Familie und Beruf. Eine deutsche Geschichte' in *Aus Politik und Zeitgeschichte*, B 22–23 , 2002, pp. 20–30.
3   The need for care for older family members is unpredictable, depending on their self-sufficiency skills and the existence of appropriate family relationships.
4   For an overview of specific family-policies, see Leipert (1999), as well as relevant passages in studies on family policy in a European context with reference to: the welfare state (Fahey, 2002); on change in socio-cultural patterns, above all in the 'male bread-winner' model (Lewis, 2001, 2002; Ostner and Lewis, 1995, 1998; Pfau-Effinger, 1999; Gottfried and O'Reilly, 2002, who observe a similar discussion in Japan); the political value of public childcare (Waldvogel, 2001); the general perspective of State family-policy formation (Gauthier, 1996); and the socio-philosophical context (Krebs, 2002).
5   In German social policy, State-run transfer systems which are based neither on contributions (social insurance), nor on need (social assistance), are categorized as a third system type called *Versorgung* (social care).
6   All translations from the German are by the author (M.O.).
7   The abbreviations after the models (L1 to L4) indicate a socio-theoretical advance in logical complexity comparable to the increase of complexity in Talcott Parsons' Adaptation, Goal Attainment, Integration, Literacy (AGIL)-scheme (for a more detailed discussion of the sociological theory behind this, see Opielka, 1996, 2002a).
8   So there may be an element of taxability.

References

Bast, K. and Ostner, L. 1992. 'Ehe und Familie in der Sozialpolitik der DDR und BRD – ein Vergleich', in W. Schmähl (ed.), *Sozialpolitik im Prozeß der deutschen Vereinigung* (Frankfurt and New York, Campus), pp. 228–270.

Carling, A., Duncan, S. and Edwards, R. 2002. *Analysing families. Morality and rationality in policy and practice* (London and New York, Routledge).

CDU-Bundesvorstand (Federal Board). 2001. *Freie Menschen. Starkes Land. Antrag des Bundesvorstands an den Dresdner Parteitag im Dezember 2001* (Berlin).

CDU/CSU-Bundestagsfraktion (Parliamentary Group). 2001. *Faire Politik für Familien. Eckpunkte einer neuen Politik für Familien, Eltern und Kinder* (Berlin).

Czarnowski, G. 1991. *Das kontrollierte Paar. Ehe und sexualpolitik im nationalsozialismus* (Weinheim and Basel, Beltz).

Fahey, T. 2002. 'The family economy in the development of welfare regimes: A case study', *European Sociological Review*, Vol. 18, pp. 51–64.

Gauthier, A. H. 1996. *The State and the family. A comparative analysis of family policies in industrialized countries* (Oxford, Clarendon Press).

Gottfried, H. and O'Reilly, J. 2002. 'Reregulating breadwinner models in socially conservative welfare systems: Comparing Germany and Japan', *Social Politics* , Vol. 9, No. 1, pp. 29–59.

Hausen, K. (ed.). 1993. *Geschlechterhierarchie und Arbeitsteilung. Zur Geschichte ungleicher Erwerbschancen von Männern und Frauen* (Göttingen, Vandenhoeck).

_____ 2000. 'Arbeit und Geschlecht', in J. Kocka and Offe, C. (eds.), *Geschichte und Zukunft der Arbeit* (Frankfurt and New York, Campus), pp. 343–361.

Kamerman, S. B. 1998. *Does global retrenchment and restructuring doom the children's cause?*, University lecture, Columbia University.

Kaufmann, F-X. 1995. *Zukunft der familie im vereinten Deutschland* (Munich, Beckders).

Kolinsky, E. 1989. *Women in West Germany. Life, work and politics* (Oxford, New York and Munich, Berg Publishers).

Krebs, A. 2002. *Arbeit und Liebe. Die philosophischen Grundlagen sozialer Gerechtigkeit* (Frankfurt, Suhrkamp).

Liepert, C. (ed.) 1999. *Aufwertung der Erziehungsland. Europäische perspektiven einer strukturreform der familien- und gesellschaftspolitik* (Opladen, Leske and Budrich).

_____ and Opielka, M. 1998. *Erziehungsgehalt 2000. Ein Weg zur Aufwertung der Erziehungsarbeit* (Bonn, Institut für Sozialökologie).

Lewis, J. 2001. 'The decline of the male breadwinner model. Implications for work and care', *Social Politics* , Vol. 8, No. 2, pp. 152–169.

_____ 2002. 'Individualization, assumptions about the existence of an adult worker model and the shift towards contractualism', in A. Carling *et al. Analysing families. Morality and rationality in policy and practice* (London and New York, Routledge).

Mühlfeld, C. and Schönweiss, F. 1989. *Nationalsozialistische familienpolitik* (Stuggart, Enke).

Opielka, M. 2000a. 'Grundeinkommenspolitik. Pragmatische Schritte einer evolutionären Reform', in *Zeitschrift für Gemeinwirtschaft* , Vol. 38, Nos. 3–4, pp. 45–59.

_____ 2002b. 'Zur sozialpolitischen Theorie der Bürgergesellschaft', in *Zeitschrift für Sozialreform* , 4.

Ostner, L. and Lewis, J. 1995. 'Gender and the evolution of European social policies', in S. Liebfried and P. Pierson (eds.), *European social policy. Between fragmentation and integration* (Washington D.C., Brookings Institution), pp. 159–193.

———— 1998. 'Geschlechterpolitik zwischen europäischer und nationalstaatlicher Regelung', in S. Leibfried and P. Pierson (eds.), *Standort Europa. Europäische Sozialpolitik* (Frankfurt, Suhrkamp), pp. 196–239.

Pfau-Effinger, B. 1999. 'Change of family policies in the socio-cultural context of European communities', in *Comparative Social Research* , Vol. 18, pp. 135–159.

———— 2000. *Kultur und frauenerwerbstätigkeit in Europa. Theorie und Empirie des internationalen Vergleichs* (Opladen, Leske and Budrich).

———— 2001. 'Sozialkulturelle Bedingungen staatlicher Geschlechterbedingungen', in B. Heinze (ed.), *Geschlechtersoziologie. Sonderband der KZfSS* (Opladen, Westdeutcher Verlag), pp. 487–511.

Ringen, S. 1997. *Citizens, families and reform* (Oxford, Clarendon Press).

Schäfgen, K. 2000. *Die Verdopplung der Ungleichheit. Sozialstruktur und Geschlechterverhältnisse in der Bundesrepublik und in der DDR* (Opladen, Leske and Budrich).

SPD-Parteivorstand 2001. *Kinder-Familie-Zukunft. Antrag F1, SPD-Bundesparteitag Nürnberg*, November (Berlin).

SPD-Projektgrupe. 2000. 'Zukunft der Familie und sozialer Zusammenhalt', in P. Mackroth (ed.), *Zukunft Familie* (Berlin).

Tünnemann, M. 2002. *Der verfassungsrechtliche Schutz der Familie und die Förderung der Kindererziehung im Rahmen des staatlichen Kinderleistungsausgleichs* (Berlin, Duncker and Humboldt).

Vaskovics, L. A. and Rost, H. 1999. *Väter und Erziehungsurlaub* (Stuttgart, Kohlhammer).

Vobruba, G. 2000. *Alternativen zur Vollbeschäftigung* (Frankfurt, Suhrkamp).

Waldfogel, J. 2001. 'International policies toward parental leave and child care', in *The Future of Children* , Vol. 11, No. 1, pp. 9–111.

Wendt, H. 1997. 'The former German Democratic Republic: The standardized family', in F-X. Kaufmann (ed.), *Family Life and Family Policies in Europe* , Vol. 1 (Oxford, Clarendon Press), pp. 114–154.

Werding, M. 2001. *Das 'Familiengeld'-konzept der CDU/CSU-Bundestagsfraktion. Ergebnisse einer ifo Studie zu Wirkungen der reformpläne der Opposition* (Berlin, CDU-Bundestagsfraktion).

26

FEMINIST ARGUMENTS IN FAVOUR OF WELFARE AND BASIC INCOME IN DENMARK

Erik Christensen[1]

1. Introduction

The extensive social science research on women and welfare rarely offers feminist political arguments in favour of guaranteed basic income or citizens' wage. This is surprising in view of the convincing arguments that many women would benefit from a basic income scheme. It would: (1) lead to equal treatment of men and women on the labour market and in the social sphere; (2) express recognition of unpaid work; (3) guarantee income outside the labour market and thus strengthen family life; (4) give many people more incentive to work; (5) ensure economic independence within the family; and (6) perhaps encourage a more equal division of labour in families (McKay and Vanevery, 2000; McKay, 2001).

Women's research generally agrees that the Scandinavian welfare states are among the most 'women-friendly' societies, but that gender-related injustice still exists. 'There are still fundamental contrasts between work life and family life, and women earn less than men at the same level. In addition, women rank lower than men in the job hierarchy, and they have less power and influence in society than men' (Borchorst, 1998, p. 127). It therefore seems odd that basic income has not attracted more attention.

Considering that some feminists (Siim, 2001) are calling for new equality and solidarity visions for women in relation to other marginalized social groups, it seems obvious to ask why many feminists find it hard to see and accept basic income as an ideal long-term solution to gender inequality and injustice.

With reference to the debate in Denmark, I will argue that:

- One reason for the modest feminist interest in basic income is that women's research and the women's movement have been locked into Wollstonecraft's dilemma, named after Mary Wollstonecraft (1759–1797), the pioneer of the British women's movement (Pateman, 1989, pp. 195–204; Christensen and Siim, 2001, pp. 19–20). The women's movement has worked, on the one hand, for equality and a gender-neutral society, and, on the other hand, for recognition of women's differences from men, their special abilities and needs. There seem to be two different and contradictory paths to gender equity; hence the dilemma. In modern society, the dilemma is often formulated as follows. Following the path of equality, women will tend to join the dominant, male wage-work norm. Following the path of difference by prioritizing women's carework over wage-work, women will continue to be marginalized in relation to men on the labour market.

- Wollstonecraft's equality/difference dilemma is not a real conceptual dilemma, but rather a 'double bind' defined by the dominant, patriarchal power structure. Like other gender-political dilemmas –commodification/decommodification, dependence/independence and wage-work/care – it can be broken down by a critical, deconstructive analysis.

- It can also be solved or softened theoretically by adding conceptual nuance to the equality and difference concepts, as American philosopher Nancy Fraser has done. She suggests that a universal basic income or citizens' wage would fulfil the desire for both equality and difference, combine decommodification and commodification, and create a new type of economic independence that could be a basis for new dependence relations.

- The modest interest in basic income in Danish and international women's research is a result of a greater focus on increasing women's participation in the labour market (commodification) than on securing economic independence in relation to the labour market (decommodification). In addition, attempts to accommodate care needs have been met with scepticism because they might keep women in the traditional gendered division of labour. Unconditional basic income has been seen as utopian or dangerous in the short term because it might keep some women from entering the labour market.

- Danish feminists have nevertheless developed theoretical understandings of the relation between wage-work and care that open the way for new arguments in favour of basic income.

2. Towards a New Breadwinner Model – But Which One?

The last 30 years have brought about a revolution in society's gendered division of labour. All welfare states have abandoned the old 'male breadwinner model' with its clear distinction between the male wage-worker and the female care-worker in the family. Many women have entered the labour market, and the family's role in relation to children and the elderly has changed as new public and private care systems have expanded.

However, although the breadwinner model has been abandoned, we can still use it as a benchmark, which is what Ilona Ostner and Jane Lewis have done (Ostner, 1996; Lewis and Ostner, 1994). They created the concept of 'male breadwinner model' as a reaction to Gösta Esping-Andersen's (1990) typology of liberal, corporatist and social democratic welfare states, which has decommodification as the key concept.

They argue that women, and thus the gendered division of labour, disappear in Esping-Andersen's analysis because he focuses on State and market and ignores unpaid work. As a reaction, they construct what they call a 'strong male breadwinner model'. This aims to define some qualitative and quantitative measures for the degree to which welfare states liberate women from family obligations, i.e. in what sense the welfare state individualizes women. They give individualization two dimensions:

- economic independence – women's opportunities to earn their own money;
- independence from family obligations – society as caregiver and real choice for women in terms of care-work in the family.

This concept is the basis for Ostner and Lewis' classification of European welfare states, which distinguishes between strong male breadwinner states (England and Germany), moderate male breadwinner states (France), and weak male breadwinner states (the Scandinavian countries).

The 'ideal typical' male breadwinner model has a clear gender-dualistic division of labour. The husband has full-time wage-work; the wife is full-time homemaker and caregiver for children and the elderly. In the weak male breadwinner model, both husband and wife have wage-work, which is possible because the State has assumed a significant share of the childcare and care for the elderly that was previously done by women.

Danish researchers use different concepts to describe the Danish welfare state from a gender perspective. The Ostner and Lewis model describes it as a 'weak male breadwinner model' because women, according to their indicators, still lag behind men in terms of economic independence measured by participation rates. Likewise, there is a weak dependency in the legislation. The individual principle has been implemented in Danish social legislation to a large extent, but not completely.

Birte Siim (2000) describes the Danish welfare model as a 'dual breadwinner model' or an 'adult worker model' according to which all adults, regardless of gender, are expected to have wage-work and be self-supporting.

388 PROMOTING INCOME SECURITY

In that sense, the modern Danish welfare state is widely regarded as gender neutral.

Two factors explain the progress in the Danish and the other Nordic welfare states: the rise in the female participation rate and the expansion of public child-care and eldercare facilities. These are preconditions for women's liberation from the homemaker role and private care-work and their entry into wage-work.

Despite the increased equality, Danish society is still far from giving completely equal status and justice in the gendered division of labour. Unpaid house- and care-work is not equally divided, and inequality in the labour market is significant both in terms of wages and jobs. The result is a high level of gender segregation, with a majority of women among the low-paid and publicly employed. Moreover, more women than men are unemployed or receiving income transfers.

3. The Danish Debate on Leave Schemes and Equality Between Work and Care

In 1994, Denmark introduced a new labour market policy with three leave schemes: childcare leave, educational leave and sabbatical leave. At the time, unemployment was very high in Denmark (12 per cent), and the main objective of the schemes was to reduce unemployment through job rotation and job sharing. Another objective was to enhance the qualifications of the work-force and improve the balance between family and work through better possibilities for paid care-work (Jensen, 2000).

In the Danish gender-political debate on the leave schemes, the arguments concerning the relationship between wage-work and care-work stayed within the boundaries of an equality/difference dilemma similar to Wollstonecraft's classic formulation of women's choices. The women's movement and the Equal Status Council (*Ligestillingsrådet*) supported the new leave schemes, although they did express criticism and concern about equality in the labour market. It was also noteworthy that the leading women politicians on this occasion rejected pay for informal care-work.

Two high-ranking women from the Socialist People's Party, Christine Antorini and Margit Kjeldgaard, expressed scepticism about the new parental leave in a newspaper article before the new labour market reform was implemented (*Informatio*, December 21, 1993). They were particularly worried that granting a right to parental leave would weaken women's position in the labour market. In their view, the prime target should be labour market inequality, followed by the division of labour in families.

In that same period, Britta Foged, chairwoman of the Danish Women's Society, rejected pay for work and childcare performed in the home, saying: 'I am fundamentally opposed to paying people for staying at home' (*Informatio*, October 7, 1993). She was supported by Anne Grete Holmsgård, chairwoman of the Equal Status Council, who said, on the same occasion: 'I don't see the logic in receiving money for staying at home and taking care of one's children.'

These unambiguous statements were made in connection with the rejection of a proposal from the Christian People's Party for a general subsidy to parents who take care of their own children. Interestingly, Foged called the proposal 'statification of an area the State should not interfere in'. Anne Grethe Holmsgård 'felt bad about turning family work into productive work.' She would like housework to be 'appreciated', which required a 'change in attitude', but 'I don't see why we have to put money on the table for that reason'.

In 1994, the Equal Status Council published *The Equality Dilemma*, a discussion anthology (Carlsen and Larsen, 1994). The main theme was dual-income families with children in day care institutions: the norm in the labour market tends to prioritize work life over family life, which goes against the priorities of most women who are thus disadvantaged in the labour market. The objective was to 'introduce new ideas and launch new discussions'.

The anthology's title and preface suggested a dual equality objective:

- creating balance (equality) between work and family life;
- creating balance (equality) between men and women in the labour market.

The Equal Status Council's activities mainly focus on this latter form of equality. It remained unclear whether the call for innovative thinking and reassessment of old strategies was aimed at labour market equality or equality between family and work life. However, there was a clear sense that gender equality in the labour market was the primary goal.

A specific topic of discussion was whether the old strategies of helping parents in full-time work – part-time, flexible hours, extended maternity leave – were adequate. While they may have improved the balance between work and family life in the individual family, they also seemed to have led to new labour market inequalities. The old methods could, as the editor of the anthology said, 'threaten the form of equality that preconditions women's self-support through paid work outside the family' (*Ibid.*, pp. 10–11). This statement contained a latent criticism of the parental leave scheme that had just been introduced.

4. Deconstructing Some Gender-political Dilemmas

The theoretical debate on the nature of the Danish welfare model, and the political debate over the prioritization of wage-work and care-work, demonstrates the need for a theoretical deconstruction and reflection on various conceptual pairs that are used in both discussions.

4.1 Equality / Difference

Carole Pateman has reformulated Wollstonecraft's dilemma as follows:

> On the one hand, they [women] have demanded that the ideal of citizenship be extended to them, and the liberal-feminist agenda for a 'gender-neutral' social world is the logical conclusion of one form of this demand. On the other hand, women have also insisted, often simultaneously, as did Mary Wollstonecraft, that as women they have specific capacities, talents, needs and concerns, so that the expression of their citizenship will be differentiated from that of men. Their unpaid work providing welfare could be seen, as Wollstonecraft saw women's tasks as mothers, as women's work as citizens, just as their husbands' paid work is central to men's citizenship (Pateman, 1989, p. 197).

According to Pateman, the patriarchal understanding of citizenship, which links citizenship to the public sphere (State and market) in contrast to the private sphere (family), makes the two demands incompatible. Either women become like men in order to become full citizens, or they continue their informal care-work, which has no value for their citizenship. Escaping this dilemma requires a paradigm shift, because the concepts of citizenship, work and welfare must all be redefined.

Ruth Lister (1995) shares this view, but she is more explicit than Pateman in stating that the equality/difference dilemma must be seen as a logical, a conceptual and political one. She leans on Joan W. Scott (1988), who performed a model deconstruction of this conceptual pair. The problem is that the two elements are often perceived as binary opposites, and there is often a latent ranking in the concepts.

When the relationship between wage-work and care-work is discussed within an equality/difference perspective, the equality concept is tied to wage-work, and the difference concept to care-work, which by itself implies a ranking. The fact that wage-work is male-dominated, and women dominate care, gives the concepts a specific, gendered connotation.

In addition, difference is assumed to be an antithesis to equality, and equality is presented as an antithesis to care. However, these are false opposites: the antithesis to equality is inequality and not difference, and the antithesis to difference is uniformity or identity and not equality. Equality does not entail an elimination of difference, the creation of uniformity, and difference does not necessarily threaten equality. So it is possible to join equality and difference, or we can say that equality and difference feed on each other. The demand for equality is often based on a desire to protect difference.

Presenting equality/difference as dichotomous choices makes it impossible for feminists to choose. If they accept equality, it looks as if they accept that difference is its antithesis. Conversely, if they choose difference, they admit that equality is unattainable. Either way, they are punished.

Feminists cannot give up on "difference", which is a creative analytical tool. Nor can they give up on equality, because it represents fundamental principles and values in the political system.

Kathleen Hall Jamieson (1995) has shown that 'double-bind' rhetoric remains prevalent in the ideological suppression of women. She defines it as follows: 'A double bind is a rhetorical construct that posits two and only two alternatives, one or both penalizing the person being offered them. ... The strategy defines something "fundamental" to women as incompatible with something the woman seeks – be it education, the ballot, or access to the workplace' (*Ibid.*, pp. 13–14). Jamieson lists the typical ideological double-bind arguments, one of which is the equality/difference dilemma (No. 3):

1. Women can exercise their wombs or their brains, but not both.
2. Women who speak out are immodest and will be shamed, while women who are silent will be ignored or dismissed.
3. Women are subordinate whether they claim to be different from men or the same.
4. Women who are considered feminine will be judged incompetent and women who are competent, unfeminine.
5. As men age, they gain wisdom and power; as women age, they wrinkle and become superfluous (*Ibid.*, p. 16).

A double bind disempowers those who are forced to choose. They are faced with a quandary, and the only way out is to reject the dominant ideological (discursive) definition of options and identity. The situation in the modern labour market can, to a large extent, be seen in this light. If women cannot support themselves on the labour market, the only options are 'family support' or 'State support.' However, 'State support' is negatively charged and perceived as a burden, while 'family support' is old-fashioned and also negatively charged.

How to resolve the double bind? Jamieson has different suggestions, all with one thing in common: they reject the dualistic dilemma, and demand a new definition of the choices (in her words, 'reframing, recovering, recasting and reclaiming'). In this connection, we could also talk of a paradigm shift, which is characterized by a new perspective.

4.2 Commodification / Decommodification

Another conceptual pair that has given rise to different interpretations and misunderstandings is commodification/decommodification. Claus Offe (1996) explains that decommodification, the antithesis of commodification, is a neologism that was created in 1974 in a discussion with Gösta Esping-Andersen. Both have used it since, and it is especially known from Esping-Andersen's welfare regime typology.

As mentioned earlier, Ostner and Lewis reacted to Esping-Andersen's conception of decommodification. Esping-Andersen saw it as defining liberation from the market, and the labour movement's goal in contrast to that of employers. It was therefore also seen as an objective for the welfare state and as a special trait of the social democratic welfare state.

He defines it as follows: 'Decommodification occurs when a service is rendered as a matter of right, and when a person can maintain a livelihood without reliance on the market' (Esping-Andersen, 1990, pp. 21–22). He later emphasizes that the concept implies a choice and consequently that: 'Decommodifying welfare states are, in practice, of very recent date. A minimal definition must entail that citizens can freely, and without potential loss of job, income, or general welfare, opt out of work, when they themselves consider it necessary' (*Ibid.*, p. 23).

In this definition decommodification is synonymous with what we understand by basic income or citizens' wage, and he does, in fact, mention a guaranteed citizens' wage as an example of ideal decommodification (*Ibid.*, p. 47).

Opposite decommodification, which is positive, Esping-Andersen places commodification as a negative. Referring to Marx, he says it leads to alienation (*Ibid.*, p. 35), and weakens the individual worker (*Ibid.*, p. 36). Decommodification is therefore indispensable in collective labour actions (*Ibid.*, p. 37).

Ostner and Lewis point out that decommodification and independence from the market are gendered concepts. Due to the gendered inequality in the division of paid/unpaid work, decommodification and independence from the market are not necessarily positive for women, among other things because decommodification will increase the burden of unpaid work. Ostner says, 'feminist scholarship insists that commodification is prior to decommodification. In order to be granted exit options from the labour market and respective wage replacement or subsidies, one has first to be fully commodified' (Ostner, 1996, p. 3).

This shows that decommodification can be perceived in different ways. In 1990, Esping-Andersen saw it as an objective of liberation, while Ostner and Lewis saw it as an expression of dependence. Ostner and Lewis talk about 'individualization' (in terms of economic and social norms), understood as freedom from family obligations, as a goal for woman-friendliness. Consequently, commodification is seen as liberation.

Whereas Esping-Andersen and Ostner and Lewis are one-sided in their use of the concepts, Claus Offe highlights their dialectic character. He sees decommodification as a fundamental trend in welfare state capitalism that works simultaneously with a contrary commodification process. Capitalism and the welfare state seem to contradict each other, but at the same time one cannot exist without the other (Offe, 1984, p. 153). In Offe's interpretation, the State form implies a structural tendency to create commodification, and at the same time the commodification process also requires non-commodified forms. The labour movement has also been marked by this duality; the movement has strengthened the labour force by working for economic growth and full employment, while through its demands for reduced working hours, it has supported decommodification. The labour movement has, in other words, attempted to create dual freedom: both freedom *to* wage-work and freedom *from* wage-work.

This is in contrast to Esping-Andersen, who only focuses on the labour movement's decommodification goals, freedom from the market, and Ostner and Lewis, who are especially keen to highlight freedom from wage-work.

4.3 Dependence / Independence

The debate about commodification/decommodification as 'freedom to/ freedom from' also reflects divergent views on dependence/independence. Just as Offe uncovers the dialectic and contextual character of the decommodification concept, so Nancy Fraser and Linda Gordon have shown, through a linguistic analysis of the concept of dependence, how the words dependence/independence historically have undergone a radical change, and that they have a gender dimension (Fraser and Gordon, 1994).

In pre-industrial society, dependence was perceived as the norm, and independence as deviant. In industrial society, wage-work and democracy became the norm. Wage-work became increasingly associated with independence, and those who were excluded from wage-work were regarded as dependent.

The conceptual pair dependence/independence has been associated with numerous hierarchical dichotomies: 'The opposition between the independent and dependent personalities maps into a whole series of hierarchical oppositions and dichotomies that are central in modern culture: masculine/feminine, public/private, work/care-giving, success/love, individual/community, economy/family, and competitive/self-sacrificing' (*Ibid.*, p. 22).

In Esping-Andersen's definition, decommodification creates choice and independence in relation to wage-work whereas Ostner and Lewis see commodification as creating independence. According to Fraser, it is important, in the emerging post-industrial society, to reshape dependence and create a balance between dependence and independence.

5. Nancy Fraser's Redefinition of and Solution to the Gender-Political Dilemmas in the Welfare State

In addition to her deconstructive analysis, Nancy Fraser has also examined the concepts in the context of other conceptual pairs, and applied her critical deconstructive analysis as a tool in a normative reconstructive project.

Fraser wants to be more than just analytical and deconstructive in relation to the welfare state. While most feminist researchers refuse to be normative or political, and prefer to give their research a purely scientific look, her goal is to outline an emancipatory vision for a new social and gender order.

> We should ask: What new, post-industrial order should replace the family wage? And what sort of welfare state can best support a new gender order? What account of gender equity best captures our highest aspiration? And what vision of social welfare comes closest to embodying it? (Fraser, 1994, p. 593).

To answer these questions, she constructs a normative ideal type for gender equity and attempts to measure two political feminist visions in relation to this ideal.

5.1 Two Ideal Types: 'The Universal Breadwinner Model' and 'The Care-giver Parity Model'

One model is based on the preference of many European and American feminists, namely the universal breadwinner model, which implies a universalization of wage-work. The goal is to increase women's participation in wage work along with a marketization and statification of childcare and care for the elderly.

The other model, the caregiver parity model, is mainly based on the implicit praxis and vision of some European feminists. The dual breadwinner model is more common in Europe than in the US, and it is therefore a priority to ensure that care-giving has the same status as wage-work. The caregiver parity model thus attempts to equalize care-giving with wage-work through publicly supported care-giving in the form of maternity, parental and other forms of leave, and through more flexible wage-work conditions for women.

Fraser's definition of gender equity is interesting because it shows how she perceives the dualisms of the industrial society (e.g. commodification/decommodification and dependence/independence) and approaches the two general norms of equality and difference.

She breaks down the dualism and double binds in the gender-political dilemmas through a redefinition process that can be seen as a form of dialectic synthesis or paradigm shift. In practical terms, her method is to dissolve the two mega-norms of equality/difference and replace them with a more complex concept with five value dimensions that contain different forms of equality as well as economic, political and social/cultural dimensions:

- *Anti-poverty principle*: fulfilment of basic needs.
- *Anti-exploitation principle*: prevent exploiting dependence on family, market and state.
- *Equality principle*: obtain a certain equality in terms of
  - income;
  - leisure time;
  - respect.
- *Anti-marginalization principle*: equal participation in different social spheres.
- *Anti-androcentrism principle*: change traditional gender norms.

Fraser points out that the five principles may contradict each other, and reminds us that there are other important goals in society, for instance 'efficiency, community and individual liberty'. However, she does grade the two political strategic models based on their fulfilment of the principles (the equality dimension being further measured on its three separate dimensions). She concludes that both models are inadequate, with both scoring highly on two dimensions, fair on three dimensions, and poorly on two dimensions.

The breadwinner model is considered good in terms of preventing poverty and exploitation, fair when it comes to income equality, equality of respect and equal participation, but poor in terms of leisure-time equality and changing traditional gender norms. In comparison, the caregiver model is also considered good in terms of preventing poverty and exploitation, fair in terms of

Table 26.1 Fraser's two ideal types for a post-industrial welfare state

	Universal breadwinner	Care-giver parity
Anti-poverty	Good	Good
Anti-exploitation	Good	Good
Income equality	Fair	Poor
Leisure-time equality	Poor	Fair
Equality of respect	Fair	Fair
Anti-marginalization	Fair	Poor
Anti-androcentrism	Poor	Fair

Source: Fraser (1994, p. 612).

leisure-time equality, equality of respect and changing traditional gender norms, but poor in terms of ensuring income equality and equal participation.

The breadwinner model primarily aims to stimulate women to adapt to male norms and specifically emphasizes market equality. The caregiver model prioritizes care in the family, but has no real aim to change gender roles.

5.2 A Utopian Idea: 'The Universal Caregiver Model' with 'A Universal Basic Income Scheme'

Fraser suggests that to overcome the contradictions between these two models we combine the best from the two models and discard the rest. This model is based on extended social citizenship and contains 'a universal basic income scheme' (Fraser, 1994, p. 615). It represents a deconstruction of the opposed gender roles in both the universal breadwinner model and the caregiver parity model, and thus also deconstructs the opposition between a bureaucratic, public institutional model and a private family model.

In a later version of the 1994 article (Fraser, 1997), she names this model the 'universal caregiver model'. The purpose is not only to balance wage-work and care-work, but also to dissolve the opposition between what she calls the 'workerism' of the universal breadwinner model and the 'domestic privatism' of the caregiver parity model. The universal caregiver model puts much more emphasis on civil society and stimulates men to emulate women.

The key is that you cannot change a dualism without changing both elements. Fraser calls her third strategy a deconstructive strategy for many of the dualisms in industrial society, which would include gender.

Fraser does not say much the specific design of a basic income. She admits that it will probably be expensive, 'and hence hard to sustain at a high level of quality and generosity'. Some social scientists worry about free-riding, which Fraser rejects as a typically male concern: 'The free-rider worry, incidentally, is typically defined androcentrically as a worry about shirking paid employment. Little attention is paid, in contrast, to a far more widespread problem, namely, men's free riding on women's unpaid domestic labour' (Fraser, 1994, p. 615). Basic income would be a good way to stop this widespread free-rider problem. It is noteworthy that her reference to basic income in the 1994 article has 'disappeared' in the 1997 version.

Elsewhere, Fraser talks about basic income as 'a fully social wage' (Fraser, 1993), and about developing Marshall's idea of social citizenship based on genuine rights so that 'benefits must be granted in forms that maintain people's status as full members of society entitled to "equal respect"' (Ibid., p. 21). On the other side, we find the neo-conservatives with an 'anti-social wage', and the neoliberals with a 'quasi-social wage'. Both are based on a heightened obligation to work in return for social benefits ('workfare').

The vision of a universal caregiver model with a basic income is 'highly utopian', as Fraser says. But when she calls it as 'a thought experiment', she does so because the universal breadwinner and caregiver parity models are not utopian enough. With reference to André Gorz, Fraser sees the basic income model as implying radical social change.

6. Overtures to a Feminist Basic Income Discussion in Denmark

From 1992 to 1995, as the basic income debate raged in Denmark, the idea received support neither from prominent women politicians as a political discourse, nor from gender researchers as a scientific paradigm (Christensen, 1999 and 2000). This was despite the fact that an opinion poll from that period showed that the idea was widely supported by women, the middle-aged and unskilled workers (Andersen, 1995).

In general, it appears that a large part of the women's movement is locked into a rigid wage-work and equality paradigm. On the one hand, the idea that women should be paid for taking care of their own children was clearly rejected, which conforms to the dominant tradition in Danish social law. On the other hand, there was no rejection of the new parental leave scheme that was introduced on January 1, 1994. There was a clear understanding among feminist scholars that the equality principle on the labour market functioned on men's terms and did not lead to equality between work and care. At the same time, there was growing concern that the new leave schemes could hurt equality on the labour market.

Many in the women's movement were caught in the classic double bind. As described by Nancy Fraser, they faced a dilemma of a breadwinner model versus a care model, and were unable to find a new understanding that transcended both models. As a consequence, many gave priority to the breadwinner model.

However, some feminist scholars rebelled against the breadwinner paradigm in the Equal Status Council's anthology (Carlsen and Larsen, 1994). For example, the basic imbalance between work and family life was discussed in two theoretical articles by cultural sociologist Lis Højgaard and legal expert Hanne Petersen.

6.1 Prioritizing and Recognizing Reproductive Work: A Cultural Revolution?

Højgaard describes how recent theories of patriarchy explain the unequal gender division of work; they emphasize the correlation between labour market, family and State and call it a 'patriarchal capitalism', in which the men mainly work in production (the economy), while women still mainly work in reproduction (outside the economy). Capitalism is the basic structure and dynamic of society, it is exercized in patriarchal forms, and production is superior to reproduction (Højgaard, 1994, p. 21).

Her perspective is a prioritization and recognition of reproductive work in the family. Højgaard concludes that, until reproductive work is ascribed the same social value as productive work, and power and remuneration reflect this, both class inequality and gender inequality will persist.

However, the gendered productive/reproductive division of labour has undergone some changes in modern society, and there is no longer the same unequivocal correlation between women's oppression in the family, on the labour market and in the State. Inequality in housework and care work still exists but, according to Højgaard, that alone does not explain inequality in the labour market and inequality in politics. Other women theorists find an explanation of the unequal gendered division of labour in the modern welfare state's mode of functioning, which secures patriarchal relations through its family, labour market and welfare policies. Højgaard is here close to Carole Pateman's idea that citizenship must be based on wage-work as well as the unpaid care work performed by women.

According to this perspective, women can only achieve 'full citizenship' if the separation of care-work and wage-work is abolished, and new definitions of independence, work and welfare are constructed. A democratic citizenship must encompass both the content and the value of women's contributions, and it must be defined so that citizens are both autonomous and mutually dependent (Højgaard, 1994, p. 25). The exact meaning of this statement is not explained.

Højgaard hopes for a 'cultural revolution' to resolve the conflict between work and family life, i.e., that men participate equally in housework and child-care and fight for this right on the labour market. This could be the kick-off for a change in the prioritization of productive and reproductive work. She describes a 'push' process: the leave schemes give women a position in the family from which they 'can push the men to make a change on the labour market, from where the men – freed from the heavy breadwinner burden – can win rights for the family' (*Ibid.*, p. 28).

6.2 Beyond Status-work and Wage-work?

Hanne Petersen uses different concepts to describe the conflict between work and family. She applies a historical perspective to the relationship between the status-conditioned obligation that regulates care work in the family, and the contract law that regulates wage-work. 'Status-determined life' (family life) is characterized by inequality and difference and is based on values like care and mutual dependency. This goes against the 'contract-determined' life's (the labour market's) demand for equality, uniformity and standardization, which is based on values like freedom, independence and growth (Petersen, 1994, p. 45). Historically, wage-work has always had women's care work (status-work in the family) as a precondition and companion. Wage-work and care work have never been equal or balanced.

Hanne Petersen is more direct and provocative in her analysis of how to promote equality. She thinks that, due to the labour market fixation, modern equality policy privileges a few women without benefiting the many. She therefore asks whether we have not reached the point where we need – particularly from women's point of view – to re-assess the necessity and importance of the work that is being performed in society, regardless of who does it, or its legal form. In other words, how much care-work do we need in a society (and for whom and what), and how much production and other material and immaterial goods do we need (*Ibid.*, p. 51)?

Such a perspective requires combating the idea that wage-work is a means of liberation for women (and perhaps fighting against the liberation and equality ideal itself) and combating the idea that care-work is a private matter, which families – i.e. women – have to perform in cooperation with a low-paid and poorly esteemed public sector.

She then poses a couple of new questions: 1) Whether the contract as a form of regulation, including labour market regulation through bargaining, should be subjected to a rational of care, balance or sustainability? 2) How can the courts reduce the polarization between family life and wage-work? She does not offer an answer to these questions, and not one word about basic income!

6.3 Towards a New Understanding of Basic Income?

Once you have a good and concise problem formulation, you are halfway to solving your problem; you know part of the answer. This is true for Lis Højgaard and Hanne Petersen. They both formulate the problem in such a way that basic income emerges as the natural, logical answer.

In Højgaard's case, a new universal right to a basic income will create 'full citizenship'. Reproductive work will become visible and receive the same social value as productive work. Citizenship will have two legs to stand on, and the 'new definitions of independence, work and welfare' which she calls for will emerge.

Basic income is also the obvious answer to Hanne Petersen's proposal for a fundamental re-assessment of wage-work as the (only) means to liberation.

It will create the institutional balance between work and family life by redefining the work and breadwinner concept.

6.4 Money and Care Support – Work Duty and Care Duty

Danish feminist scholars have also developed a broader theoretical apparatus, in which basic income appears as a logical solution, if the goal is equality and justice in the gendered division of labour. Kirsten Ketscher, a Danish legal expert, describes how rules in the labour market and social system systematically focus on wage-work and discriminate against care- work (Ketscher, 1990, 2001). She distinguishes between money support and care support, and links it to a distinction between the different social spheres (State, market, family). Support is defined as procuring the means necessary for the individual's survival, and each person needs both care support and money support (Ketscher, 1990, p. 33).

Care support is the work involved in cooking, cleaning, washing, shopping, etc. – in other words, everything we normally think of as housewifely duties (*Ibid.*, p. 40). Money support is the activity that aims to procure the necessary funds. Money support has three major sources: wages (from the market), support through marriage (from the family), and social benefits (from the State). Likewise, care support comes from family support, public support and market support. In money support the labour market is the central source, and in care support the family is the major source, but public support is gaining ground in both. However, it is important to keep in mind that men and women combine these support systems in different ways.

Earlier, men were in charge of money support via the labour market, while the women handled care support in the home. In the modern welfare state, money support has become significant for both genders, although many men support women financially for a while. Conversely, many men receive a lot of care support from women.

Money support is linked with a legal availability and work duty in relation to both market and State, whereas care support is linked to a legal care duty in relation to children, and for married couples in relation to each other. But whereas money support requires a personal presence, care support can be handled by a substitute (e.g. public childcare institutions).

Self-support is the leading principle in §75 of the Danish constitution and § 6 of the Social Assistance Act; when it is not possible, a right to State support applies. For married couples this self-support duty is supplemented by the mutual obligation to support each other (§6 of the Social Assistance Act), and for parents the obligation to provide for children under 18 (§13 of the Child Act and §6 of the Social Assistance Act).

However, with women's increasing participation in wage-work, the problem of double work has arisen: women still have the main responsibility for care support *and* contribute to money support. According to Ketscher, this means that they have been forced to choose between two legal obligations: the obligation in the work contract (work duty) and the obligation to care for their children. The difference between the two obligations is that the work duty, in contrast to the care duty, requires personal presence. And the obligation to fulfil the wage contract and the obligation to provide for the family are not equal. Current rules put 'the work duty' before 'the support duty.'

6.5 Justice in the Support Triangle: Basic Income as an Option

So how can the modern welfare state resolve the conflict between the work and the care duty and, based on the support triangle, distribute time, money and care fairly between the genders?

Ketscher does not bring basic income into her analytical model (the support triangle), but Norwegian feminist legal expert Tove Stang Dahl does. She is the founder of the support triangle paradigm (Dahl, 1985, Vol. I, pp. 85–93; Dahl, 1987). Dahl distinguishes between reciprocal justice and distributive justice. Reciprocal justice has to do with reciprocity and balance between parties, with a reciprocal right and duty as the central element. Distributive justice concerns distribution of values based on an entity, a distributor (e.g. the State), where the recipients are made as equal as possible.

Dahl does not think that reciprocal justice is enough to strengthen women's position in the market, arguing that we also have to establish distributive justice in terms of money above the State. She suggests dissolving the relationship between social assistance and wage-work to ensure women direct access to money, and discusses three paths:

- a care wage;
- abolishing qualification requirements for access to unemployment benefits and social assistance;
- a guaranteed minimum income for all adult citizens.

She does not see any of these proposals as utopian, but rather as central to the women's movement's active participation in a discussion. Perhaps basic income will turn out to be the uniting idea (Dahl, 1985, Vol. II, p. 246).

The basic income perspective thus emerges as a logical possibility of the support triangle paradigm. A basic income would make money support and care support equal and partially remove the opposition between the two. By partly decoupling (as far as basic income is concerned) the work duty in relation to the labour market, the new element in money support (basic income) would be available for all types of care. Basic income would therefore constitute recognition of care work, which Ketscher is asking for, and ascribe to it a value in itself.

Although there are signs that the women's movement and feminist scholars are changing their view on the normative function of wage-work, the idea of a basic income has always seemed remote and provocative to many feminists. They prefer to think within a division of labour strategy rather than an alternative basic income strategy.

7. Conclusion

My initial claim was that gender research has almost ignored the basic income concept. This is only partially true. Some Danish feminists seem to be breaking with the wage-work and labour market fixation in the gender political debate and seem to acknowledge the systematic discrimination against care-work in favour of wage-work in the current social and labour market system.

The support triangle paradigm developed by Dahl and Ketscher is fruitful in a basic income perspective, because it demonstrates that the only way to justice is to secure women economic independence by giving them a right to money.

Dahl and Ketscher are in line with Ostner and Lewis in their description of how women's work/support has changed from being mainly determined by the marriage contract (the family) to being determined by the work contract (the market). The result is liberation from one type of dependence, but the creation of a new type of dependence, namely dependence on wage-work and the State (transfer income and the resulting clientification), a situation they share with men. The right to independence from family, State and market is not for women only, but for all citizens, and it can be secured through basic income.

The international feminist debate is showing some interest in this perspective. Carole Pateman (1989, pp. 202–203), who has described the modern welfare situation of women as a version of Wollstonecraft's dilemma, is also one of the few to point out that the way out of this double bind is to redefine terms and, make a paradigm shift with a basic income as a possible element. Recently, Alisa McKay (with Jo Vanevery, 2000; McKay, 2001) has argued that basic income might be an important tool in furthering a gender-neutral social citizenship in what is called a 'post-familial' society.

Other prominent feminist scholars are more sceptical. Ruth Lister (1995) briefly mentions basic income as a possible solution to the gender-political dilemmas, but expresses concern that it could also strengthen or maintain the traditional gendered division of labour, unless it is combined with other reforms. Jane Lewis (2001) expresses sympathy for the idea. However, she finds that a 'participation income' is more realistic than a pure basic income scheme.

Nancy Fraser's analysis of different welfare strategies opens up the possibility that the basic income concept could climb up the gender-political agenda in the future. She demonstrates how to perform a deconstructive ideology analysis, i.e. to historicize and contextualize various concepts (dependence, exploitation, marginalization, equality and citizenship) by recognizing the gendered aspects. Generally, she examines how to cancel and/or unite/balance oppositions and dualisms through a more positive assessment of female roles and concepts and a re-assessment of male roles and concepts. She is also interested in finding concepts and strategies for joining the oppositions between the old class interest in a redistribution of resources (creating equality) and the new social movements' demand for recognition of their identities (recognition of difference).

In terms of values, Fraser is contributing to the development of a justice concept that includes the social gendered division of labour. To Fraser, justice is not only determined by market conditions; though it is about creating a certain equality in income and jobs on the labour market, it is also about creating autonomy in relation to State, family and civil society. Therefore, her justice concept includes dimensions like recognition of female identity, equal status and equal resources to participate in politics and civil society.

Fraser's analysis is helpful in developing the political strategic aspects of the basic income concept. She sees that changes in social institutions take place through a political battle between different political discourses, created in the public sphere through debates among social movements, experts and State institutions. She therefore finds it important to influence the women's movement's political discourse on the future of the welfare state.

When Nancy Fraser succeeds in theoretically escaping Wollstonecraft's dilemma it is because she, unlike many other feminists, is explicitly normative in her theory formation. Whereas Ostner and Lewis' typology of welfare state regimes mainly has a descriptive-analytical objective, but is normatively based on an historic rejection of the male breadwinner model, Fraser looks ahead with a positive normative goal. She is one of the few to offer a new vision for creating equality and solidarity, which Danish feminists are also calling for (Siim, 2001).

Note

1 Aalborg University, Denmark.

404   PROMOTING INCOME SECURITY

References

Borchorst, A. 1998. 'Køn, velfærdsstatsmodeller og familiepolitik', in J. E. Larsen and I. H. Møller (eds.) *Socialpolitik* (Viborg, Munksgaard).

Carlsen, S. and Larsen, J.E. (eds.), 1994 *The equality dilemma. Reconciling working life and family life, viewed from an equality perspective – the Danish example* (Copenhagen, Munksgaard).

Christensen, E. 1999. 'Citizen's income as a heretical political discourse: The Danish debate about citizen's income', in J. Lind and I. H. Møller (eds.), *Inclusion and exclusion: Unemployment and non-standard employment in Europe* (Aldershot, Ashgate), pp. 13–33.

———— 2000. *Borgerløn. Fortællinger om en politisk ide* (Århus, Hovedland).

Christensen, A-D. and Siim, B. 2001. *Køn, Demokrati og Modernitet. Mod nye politiske identiteter* (Gylling, Hans Reitzels Forlag).

Dahl, T. S. (ed.), 1985. *Kvinnerett I og II* (Oslo, Universitetsforlaget AS).

———— 1987. *Women's law. An introduction to feminist jurisprudence* (Oslo, Norwegian University Press).

Esping-Andersen, G. 1990. *The three worlds of welfare capitalism* (Oxford, Polity Press).

Fraser, N. 1993. 'Clintonism, welfare, and antisocial wage: The emergence of a neoliberal political imaginary', *Rethinking Marxism*, Vol. 6. No. 1, pp. 10–23.

———— 1994. 'After the family wage. Gender equity and the welfare state', *Political Theory*, Vol. 22. No. 4, pp. 591–618.

———— 1997. *Justice interruptus. Critical reflections on the 'postsocialist' condition* (New York and London, Routledge).

Fraser, N. and Gordon, L. 1994. '"Dependency" demystified: Inscriptions of power in a keyword of the welfare state', *Social Policy*, Spring, pp. 4–30.

Goul Andersen, J. 1995. 'Arbejdsløshed, polarisering og solidaritet', *Social Politik*, No. 4, pp. 5–15.

Højgaard, L. 1994. 'Work and family – Life's inseparable pair', in S.Carlsen and J.E. Larsen (eds.), *The equality dilemma. Reconciling working life and family life, viewed from an equality perspective – the Danish example* (Copenhagen, Munksgaard), pp. 15–28.

Jamieson, K. H. 1995. *Beyond the double bind. Women and leadership* (Oxford, Oxford University Press).

Jensen, Per H. 2000. *The Danish leave-of-absence schemes. Origins, functioning and effects from a gender perspective*, CCWS Working paper No. 2000–19, Center for Comparative Welfare State Studies, Department of Economics, Politics and Public Administration, Aalborg, University of Aalborg.

Ketscher, K. 1990. *Offentlig børnepasning i retlig belysning* (Gylling, Jurist og Økonomforbundets Forlag).

———— 1995. 'Offentlig og privat i socialretten', in L. Adrian *et al.* (eds.), *Ret og Privatisering* (Copenhagen, GadJura), pp. 137–158.

———— 2001. 'From marriage contract to labour contract: Effects on care duties and care rights', in K. Nousiainen (ed.), *Responsible selves. Women in the Nordic legal culture* (Dartmouth, Asgate).

Lewis, J. 2001. 'The decline of the male breadwinner model: Implications for work and care', *Social Politics*, Vol. 8 (1), pp. 152–181.

———— and Ostner, I. 1994. *Gender and the evolution of European social policies*, Zentrum für Sozialpolitik (ZeS)-Working Paper No. 4/94, Centre for Social policy Reseach (Bremen, University of Bremen).

Lister, R. 1995. 'Dilemmas in engendering citizenship', in *Economy and Society*, Vol. 24 (1), pp. 1–40.

McKay, A. 2001. 'Rethinking work and income maintenance policy: Promoting gender equality through a citizens' basic income', in *Feminist Economics*, Vol. 7, No. 1, pp. 97–118.

———— and Vanevery, J. 2000. 'Gender, family, and income maintenance: A feminist case for citizens basic income', *Social Politics*, Summer.

Offe, C. 1984. *Contradictions of the welfare state* (Cambridge, Massachusetts, MIT Press).

———— 1996. *Modernity and the State East West* (Cambridge, Polity Press).

Ostner, I. 1996. *Individualization, breadwinner norms, and family obligations. Gender sensitive concepts in comparative welfare*, (Aalborg, Feminist Reseach Centre).

Pateman, C. 1989. *The disorder of women. Democracy, feminism and political theory* (Cambridge, Polity Press).

Petersen, H. 1994. 'Law and order in family life and working life', in S. Carlsen and J.E. Larsen (eds.), *The equality dilemma. Reconciling working life and family life, viewed from an equality perspective – the Danish example* (Copenhagen, Munksgaard), pp. 41–52.

Scott, J. W. 1988. 'Deconstructing equality versus difference: Or the uses of poststructuralist theory for feminism', in *Feminist Studies*, Vol. 14 (1), pp. 33–50.

Siim, B. 2000. *Gender and citizenship. Politics and agency in France, Britain and Denmark* (Cambridge, Cambridge University Press).

———— 2001. *How to achieve gender equality?* Keynote speech, Cost A13 Conference, Social Policy, Marginalization and Citizenship, Aalborg University, Denmark, November 2–4.

Wollstonecraft, M. 1997 (1792). *The vindications: The rights of man; The rights of woman*, D.L. Macdonald and K. Scherf (eds.), (Peterborough, Broadview Press).

27

PUBLIC SUPPORT FOR BASIC INCOME SCHEMES AND A UNIVERSAL RIGHT TO HEALTH CARE: WHAT THE FRENCH PEOPLE THINK

Christine le Clainche[1]

1. Introduction

The issue of public acceptance of basic income has only just begun to be raised. From a theoretical point of view – particularly in the political philosophy literature – it is argued that the acceptability of social organization principles established by political theory can be found through investigating people's opinions about what a good society is (van Parijs, 1991; Miller, 1992, 1999; Swift, 1999; Demuijnck, 2002). Thus, it is important to study the nature of preferences that might legitimate redistributive schemes such as basic income. A crucial aspect affecting the efficiency of public action, lies in the identification those factors that lead people to oppose or favour a particular method of redistribution.

If we subscribe to the assumption of self-interest, as in optimal taxation models, for example, we believe that people who draw or expect to draw net benefits from a redistribution scheme will favour it; in contrast, people who think they will lose in the 'game of redistribution' will oppose it. However, some studies are at variance with the self-interest hypothesis, demonstrating other motivations such as altruism, reciprocity and social rivalry. Indeed, it appears that attitudes towards redistribution depend on the public values people support (Kluegel and Smith, 1986; Piketty, 1995; Fong, 2001; Cornéo and Grüner, 2002; Boarini and Le Clainche, 2002). Cornéo and Grüner (2002), like Piketty (1995), found that social mobility experienced by individuals could explain support or opposition to redistribution. The former use another argument, the so-called 'social rivalry' effect: an individual's preferences for redistribution depend upon her relative social position in the distribution of incomes. When groups of individuals, because of taxes and contributions, have incomes close to those of lower social strata who benefit from public assistance, they will tend to oppose redistribution because their position in the income distribution is lower than their perceived social status. It is thus interesting to know more about the motivation of people who favour basic income schemes.

Support for basic income and the universal right to health care can be linked to the 'undominated diversity' principle proposed by van Parijs (1995):[2] a universal right to health care is a transfer that everyone thinks should be granted to people who are considered by everyone to be the worst-off. That means that unanimity is obtained concerning both the transfer and the recipients. A way to observe whether unanimity might be possible is through a specific survey questionnaire.

This paper aims to provide evidence on French support for basic income schemes and the universal right to health care. I use data from the French survey 'Opinions on Social Welfare' conducted by *Direction de la recherche, des Études, de l'Évaluation et des Statistiques* (DREES) on a sample of 4,000 individuals in 2001. In the first part of the paper, I introduce the data set, the questions selected and method used. The second part of the paper is devoted to presentation of the results, while the third part provides a discussion of the main findings and conclusions.

2. Data Set and Methodology

The data from the survey 'opinions on social welfare' include responses to questions about social protection and possible reforms of the social protection system, as well as data relating to the socio-demographic characteristics of respondents (see Appendix). I focus on opinions relevant to basic income and a universal right to health care (*Couverture Maladie Universelle – CMU*).

2.1 Main Questions Used

The question relating to basic income is formulated as follows:[3]

> Basic income is a principle of income redistribution within society. It aims at replacing a certain number of social minima in order to encourage the resumption of employment. It would consist in giving to each person, via the State, a basic income of about 2,000 francs per month, whatever the other sources of income. What would you say about this?

Basic income is:
a. morally acceptable and economically viable;
b. morally acceptable but economically non-viable;
c. morally unacceptable but economically viable;
d. morally unacceptable and economically non-viable.

I also processed the answers to another question, relating to support for the principle of a universal right to health care, which could be combined with basic income in the perspective of van Parijs' 'undominated diversity' principle.

This question is framed as follows:[4]

The authorities have established a universal right to health care, ensuring full payment of health costs for people with a low income (for example, less than 3,500 francs per month for a single person). This measure is financed by income taxation and by a tax on mutual insurance and insurance companies. Are you personally:

a. favourable to;
b. fairly favourable to;
c. fairly unfavourable to;
d. unfavourable to this measure?

Lastly, I have used a reference question, which makes it possible to evaluate the position of individuals in society and, therefore, their inclination to accept possible reforms of the welfare system. This question relates to the 'justice of French society' and it is formulated as follows:

Does French society today appear to you:

a. just,
b. fairly just,
c. fairly unjust,
d. unjust?

The answers to these questions constitute the basis for constructing the latent variables to construct regression models of the logit type. In the following sub-section, I describe the methodology, including the various explanatory variables reflecting either self-interest or social preferences following, for example, Fong (2001), or related to collective values as in the research of Cornéo and Grüner (2002).

2.2 Models to Estimate: Self-interest and Social Values

The answers to the question relating to support for basic income are synthesized in a dichotomic variable 'Y' separating the first answer (a: morally acceptable and economically viable) from the others. A regression of the logit type is then performed. In addition, two 'sub-variables' distinguish answers endorsing the moral character of basic income (variable 'Y$_1$') and answers endorsing the economic character or effectiveness of basic income (variable 'Y$_2$'). The very few 'don't know' observations are dropped. Each of these variables is dichotomic, and two specifications of the logit-type model are estimated.

The answers to the question relating to support for the principle of a universal right to health care (CMU) are synthesized so that the variable 'Y$_{3a}$' is dichotomic; the 'don't know' observations are also dropped. A regression model of the logit type is thus implemented whose latent variable is Y*$_{3a}$. I also proceed to a regression on the whole sample according to an ordered probit model. Insofar as the relevant values are framed in a natural order, the latent variable is then 'Y*$_{3b}$'.

The answers to the question about 'the justice of society' are used as a reference point indicating a general inclination towards social protection reforms and are synthesized in a dichotomic variable 'Y$_4$', where 'don't know' observations are dropped.

I thus estimate a model with different specifications:

$$Y^*_i = \alpha_i X_i + \mu_i$$

In the logit model, 'Y*$_i$' is thus the latent variable, 'Y$_i$' is the observed variable (response to one of the various questions), equal to 1 for the individual 'i' if Y*$_i$ > 0 and if the individual agrees with the fact that the basic income is moral and effective (the first specification of the model) or agrees with the principle of the CMU, and 0 if not; 'X$_i$' is the vector of the variables which approach the effects mentioned above and m$_I$ are the residuals.

In each of these models, following Cornéo and Grüner (2002) or Boarini and Clainche (2002), 'X$_1$', indicates socio-demographic characteristics (gender, age and educational level); 'X$_2$' is then a proxy of self-interest, and I use household income and a variable in the database which reflects proximity to precariousness (see Appendix) as objective attributes of the individual.

Finally, as an indicator reflecting the 'collective values' of the individual, 'X$_3$' includes opinions relating to the French guaranteed minimum income scheme (*Revenu Minimum d'Insertion – RMI*), the causes of poverty, as well as the particularly unacceptable nature of certain inequalities compared to others (see Appendix). I thus test various specifications of the model (see above) to evaluate the explanatory capacity of determinants other than those positing self-interest with regard to support for redistribution.

3. Results and Comments

Before commenting on the results of each regression, I present some tables of descriptive statistics in order to take a measure of the percentage of the answers realized by each variable.

3.1 Response Distributions

The view of basic income as ethical but nonviable attracts the most support.

Table 27.2 shows the percentage of respondents affirming the ethical character of a basic income scheme while Table 27.3 gives the percentage of respondents endorsing its economic viability.

Table 27.1 Support for the basic income proposal (response %)

Variable "Y"	%	Cumulative %
Moral and economically viable	18.3	18.3
Moral and non-viable	30.9	49.2
Morally non-acceptable but viable	11.6	60.8
Morally non-acceptable and non viable	26.1	86.9
Don't know	13.1	100.0

Source. DREES (2001), 'Opinions on social welfare.'

Table 27.2 Is basic income morally acceptable (response %)?

Variable "Y_1"	%
Morally acceptable	49.2
Morally unacceptable	37.7
Don't know	13.1

Source: DREES (2001), 'Opinions on social welfare.'

Table 27.3 Is basic income viable (response %)?

Variable Y_2	%
Economically viable	29.8
Not viable	57.1
Don't know	13.1

Source: DREES (2001), 'Opinions on social welfare.'

Table 27.4 Support for a universal right to health care (CMU)
(response %)

Variable "Y_3"	%	Cumulative %
Very favourable	40.8	40.8
Fairly favourable	41.7	82.6
Fairly unfavourable	9.0	91.6
Very unfavourable	3.9	95.5
Don't know	4.5	100.0

Source: DREES (2001), 'Opinions on social welfare.'

Table 27.5 Is society just or not (responses %)?

Variable "Y_4"	%
Just	26.9
Unjust	68.3
Don't know	4.8

Source: DREES (2001), 'Opinions on social welfare.'

A large majority believes that the basic income proposal is not economically
viable. Perhaps the lack of indication of how it would be financed explains the
distribution of responses. Table 27.4 presents the percentage of respondents
favourable or unfavourable to the CMU, which has been implemented and is
explained more precisely in the survey questionnaire.

More than 80 per cent of the respondents are thus favourable to the CMU. In
a first approximation, one can say that the 'undominated diversity' principle could
be valid because there is almost unanimity about CMU transfers. But this is only
an indirect way to reveal support for the 'undominated diversity' principle. A
direct way would require (a) asking people to rank the situation of potential
CMU recipients with respect to others in society (i.e. ranking people by income
access); (b) letting them propose who could receive CMU and how much money
each recipient should receive, given the wealth of society and the amount of
basic income granted; (c) comparing the amount of money granted to each
recipient to what, theoretically, the 'undominated diversity' principle requires.

Finally, Table 27.5 summarizes opinions on the justice of the society in
which they live:

A great majority regards French society as unjust. Obviously, these descriptive statistics are not enough to characterize precisely the opinion of individuals. The regression analyses carried out here, enable me to refine the opinion
profiles and more particularly, to check the importance of the 'social values'
effect to explain support for public intervention.

3.2 Regression Results for Model Various Specifications

In what follows, I present the regressions modelling individual attitudes towards redistribution, represented by the basic income proposal and by CMU. The same socio-demographic control variables are introduced into each regression, and the reference is the same each time;[5] the constants are not presented in the tables and the 'don't know' observations are also dropped so that the final sample before weighting comprises approximately 2,900 individuals.

Regressions Relating to the Principle of Basic Income

The latent variable is Y_i^*; the observed variable Y_i (responses on the morality and viability of basic income) is equal to 1 for the individual 'i' if $Y_i^* > 0$ and if the respondents agree with the proposition that basic income is moral and economically viable.

Table 27.6 shows the results for various specifications of the model. Let us start by studying the traditional determinant of support for redistribution – self-interest. In logit (1) the effect of self-interest is initially captured by income. A negative sign means that individual 'i' in a specific income category is more likely than the reference individual to think that basic income is moral and economically viable. One observes a negative and strongly significant coefficient for the very low-income group only; the coefficients for the other income groups are positive but not significant. This result is partly confirmed for the other regressions (logits {3} and {4}), where the coefficient for very low incomes is also strongly significant.

A 'transfers-and-taxation' assessment for the various income classes indicates that those on very low incomes would benefit from redistribution. One cannot thus reject the assumption of self-interest. However, in logits (3) and (4), the coefficients for very high-income groups are also negative, which suggests that self-interest is not the only determinant of support for redistribution.

Another way of testing the effect of self-interest is to use the variable measuring proximity to precariousness (see Appendix): the closer the individual is to precariousness the more she is likely to benefit from transfers and be favourable to them. The signs of the coefficients are those expected but they are significant only for the individuals furthest away from precariousness, who are less favourable than the reference individual to the basic income proposal.

Let us come now to the 'social values' effect. It is captured by the variables relating to the RMI, the causes of poverty and the particularly unacceptable character of income inequalities compared to other types of inequality. In certain specifications of the model, responses were added relating to the CMU and opinions about the fairness of society. With regard to the control

Table 27.6 Basic income regression (variable 'Y')[6]

Explanatory variables: Preferences for redistribution and socio-demographic variables	Logit (1): With income	Logit (2): With precariousness	Logit (3): With income and precariousness	Logit (4): With income, precariousness and CMU
Incomes (*ref. medium income*)				
Very low income	-0.4658** (0.1838)		-0.3792** (0.1931)	-0.3847** (0.1922)
Low incomes	0.00320 (0.1580)		-0.0166 (0.589)	0.000267 (0.1599)
High income	0.1103 (0.1460)		0.1114 (0.1478)	0.1182 (0.1478)
Very high income	0.0609 (0.2939)		-0.0401 (0.2959)	-0.0622 (0.2979)
Don't know	0.1950 (0.1348)		0.1487(0.1365)	0.1202(0.1373)
Awareness of precariousness – knows a person in a precarious situation (*ref. precariousness in the family*)				
*Him/herself in such a situation		-0.0920 (0.1900)	-0.0497 (0.2021)	-0.0411 (0.1975)
*Somebody far from the family		0.2828** (0.1144)	0.2522** (0.1162)	0.2491** (0.1164)
*Nobody		0.3975** (0.1430)	0.4039**(0.1458)	0.3602**(0.1465)
*RMI should not exist (*ref. RMI should exist*)	0.5067** (0.1695)	0.4808** (0.1695)	0.4575** (0.1703)	0.3410** (0.1725)
Obligations for RMI (*ref. yes*)				
*No	-0.2410** (0.1190)	-0.2410**(0.1189)	-02204* (0.1207)	-0.2005* (0.1213)
Causes of poverty				
*Do not want to work (*ref. no*)	0.0604 (0.0976)	0.0645 (0.0974)	0.0474 (0.0985)	0.0123 (0.0992)
*No, missing family help is not a cause (*ref. yes, this is a cause*)	-0.1043 (0.1021)	-0.1018 (0.1021)	-0.0873 (0.1034)	-0.1202 (0.1043)

	(1)	(2)	(3)	(4)
Opinion about the CMU (ref. favourable)				
*Not favourable	1.0897**(0.1790)			
Least acceptable inequalities				
*Income compared to others (ref. no)	−0.2429**(0.1059)	−0.2227*(0.1051)	−0.2419**(0.1036)	−0.2287**(0.1036)
Education level (ref. 2 years university diploma)				
*Low	−0.3543**(0.1414)	−0.2882**(0.1407)	−0.3734 (0.1350)	−0.3094**(0.1389)
*Professional qualification	−0.2337*(0.1407)	−0.2343*(0.1401)	−0.2399 (0.1375)	−0.2187**(0.1385)
*Postgraduate	−0.3595*(0.1857)	−0.3864**(0.1849)	−0.3815 (0.1823)	−0.3502*(0.1840)
*Don't know	0.3774 (0.6258)	0.4115 (0.6238)	0.5020 (0.6220)	0.5206 (0.6197)
Female (ref. male)	0.0302 (0.1015)	0.0272 (0.1021)	0.00212 (0.0992)	0.0230 (0.2081)
Age (ref. 35–49)				
*18–24	−0.4219**(0.0270)	−0.3982**(0.1894)	−0.4589**(0.1884)	−0.4256**(0.1885)
*25–34	−0.1303 (0.3665)	−0.1472 (0.1465)	−0.1483 (0.1424)	−0.1537 (0.1427)
* 50–64	0.00399 (0.9795)	0.00345 (0.1391)	−0.0152 (0.1518)	−0.0168 (0.1523)
*Over 65	0.0216 (0.1944)	0.0134 (0.1376)	−0.0227 (0.1897)	0.0215 (0.1899)
Marital status (ref. married)				
*Single	0.1107 (0.1633)	0.0988 (0.1625)	0.0901 (0.1606)	0.1256 (0.1617)
*Widowed	0.2136 (0.2461)	0.2527 (0.2374)	0.2375 (0.2405)	0.2868 (0.2423)
*Divorced	−0.2372 (0.1810)	−0.2849 (0.1790)	−0.3262*(0.1751)	−0.2850 (0.1771)
Size of family (ref. Couple)				
*One	−0.1414 (0.1689)	−0.1352 (0.1702)	−0.2130 (0.1659)	−0.1427 (0.1663)
*Three or four persons	0.00666 (0.1350)	0.00567 (0.1291)	−0.0115 (0.1324)	−0.0309 (0.8166)
*Five or more	0.1658 (0.1753)	0.1567 (0.1593)	0.1443 (0.1720)	0.0997 (0.1732)

** Coefficient significant at the 5% level; *Coefficient significant at the 10% level. The same convention is adopted for the other regressions.
(.) Standard error.
Source: DREES (2001), 'Opinions on social welfare.'

variables, one notes that for all the selected variables, there is a strong effect of education level and age: more highly educated and younger people are likely to favour basic income.

Here, the characteristics of the coefficients are those expected for the validation of a 'social values' effect. This appears particularly in responses on the RMI and, to a lesser extent, on the need or otherwise for the recipient to undertake contractual obligations. When the opinions on the CMU are introduced, one notes that those who are less favourable to it are also those who are less favourable to basic income. In Table 27.7, I give the results of the regressions when the variable to be explained is endorsement of the moral character of basic income, whatever the opinion on its economic viability.

Roughly speaking, the same effects as before are found. However, the coefficients relative to very low incomes and low education level lose their significance. In addition, for logits (3) and (4), individuals with high incomes are more convinced than the reference individual of the moral character of basic income, while individuals far from a situation of precariousness are less likely to endorse its moral character.

The effect of 'social or public values' appears here through responses to the question on the contractual obligations of RMI recipients: those who think that the receipt of RMI should not come with obligations are also those more likely than the reference individual to think that the basic income proposal is moral. The CMU effect is negative: those who are not favourable to the CMU are also more likely to think that the basic income proposal is not moral.

Table 27.8 shows the results of the regressions when the variable to be explained is endorsement of the economic viability of basic income. In contrast to the results of the preceding regressions, the effect of 'obligations of the RMI' disappears and, between income groups, only those on very low incomes endorse the viable character of the basic income proposal. However, if control variables are used, in particular educational level, whatever the level of education, viability is endorsed. Divorced persons also take this view.

Regressions Relative to CMU

Table 27.9 presents the results relating to support for the French universal right to health care (CMU). Similar to the basic income analysis, the observed variable is Y_{i3a}, equal to 1 for the individual 'i' if $Y^*_{i3a} > 0$ and if the individual is favourable to the CMU.

The effect of self-interest appears less strongly here and in a negative way: those who refuse to mention their level of income, like those who are not aware of precariousness, are more unfavourable to the CMU. The effect of social values runs through almost all the explanatory variables used as proxies.

Table 27.7 Basic income: Moral (Y_1)

Explanatory variables: Preference for redistribution and socio-demographic variables	Logit (1): With income	Logit (2): With precariousness	Logit (3): With income and precariousness	Logit (4): With income, precariousness and CMU
Incomes (*ref. medium income*)				
Very low income	-0.0760 (0.1612)		-0.0560(0.1649)	-0.0765 (0.1675)
Low income	0.0611 (0.1268)		0.0640 (0.1276)	0.0714 (0.1293)
High income	-0.1271 (0.1123)		-0.1440 (0.1129)	-0.1354 (0.1142)
Very high income	-0.4104 *(0.2286)		-0.5284**(0.2356)	-0.5680**(0.2384)
Don't know	-0.1821*(0.1030)		0.1828*(0.1042)	0.1524(0.1055)
Awareness of precariousness – knows a person in a precarious situation (*ref. precariousness in the family*)				
*Him/herself in such a situation		0.1473 (0.1616)	-0.1313 (0.1657)	-0.1589 (0.1678)
*Somebody far from the family		0.2379**(0.0886)	0.2321** (0.0898)	0.2347**(0.0908)
*Nobody		-0.0273 (0.1058)	-0.0184 (0.1069)	-0.0716 (0.1087)
*RMI should not exist (*ref. RMI should exist*)	-0.0650 (0.1157)	-0.0625 (0.1158)	-0.0894 (0.1167)	-0.2230 * (0.1205)
Obligations for RMI (*ref. yes*)				
*No	-0.5103**(0.0988)	-0.5084* (0.0985)	-0.5093**(0.0996)	-0.4979**(0.1008)
Causes of poverty (*ref. no*)				
*Do not want to work	-0.1123 (0.0765)	-0.0816 (0.0763)	-0.0870 (0.0770)	-0.1385* (0.0782)
*No, missing family help is not a cause (*ref. yes, this is a cause*)	0.0225 (0.0808)	0.0213(0.0807)	0.0334 (0.0816)	0.00397 (0.0826)
Opinion about the CMU (*ref. favourable*)				
*Not favourable				0.8226**(0.0837)

Table 27.7 (Continued)

Explanatory variables: Preference for redistribution and socio-demographic variables	Logit (1): With income	Logit (2): With precariousness	Logit (3): With income and precariousness	Logit (4): With income, precariousness and CMU
Least acceptable inequalities				
*Income compared to others (ref. no)	-0.1115 (0.0831)	-0.1042 (0.0830)	-0.1172 (0.1618)	-0.1368 (0.1073)
*Society is just (ref. just; society is unjust)			0.0125 (0.1322)	
Education level (ref. 2 years university diploma)				
*Low	-0.0746 (0.1070)	-0.0416 (0.1039)	-0.00639 (0.1062)	-0.0950 (0.1092)
*Professional qualification	-0.0257 (0.1058)	0.00304 (0.1049)	-0.0365 (0.1067)	-0.0305 (0.1079)
*Postgraduate	0.1200 (0.1447)	0.0639 (0.1432)	0.1145 (0.1459)	0.1392 (0.1470)
*Don't know	-0.2659 (0.3763)	-0.1355 (0.3760)	-0.2795 (0.3850)	-0.3207(0.3856)
Female (ref. male)	-0.0466 (0.0779)	-0.0418 (0.0776)	-0.0756 (0.0781)	-0.0453 (0.0795)
Age (ref. 35–49)				
*18–24	-0.5002**(0.1525)	-0.4818**(0.1522)	-0.5291**(0.1514)	-0.4731**(0.1551)
*25–34	-0.2169*(0.1108)	-0.1987* (0.1105)	-0.2811**(0.1112)	-0.1958* (0.1127)
*50–64	0.00159 (0.1175)	0.0136 (0.1173)	-0.0105 (0.1185)	-0.00862 (0.1200)
*Over 65	0.4078**(0.1480)	0.4456**(0.1481)	0.3089* (0.1505)	0.4265**(0.1520)
Marital status (ref. married)				
*Single	0.0473 (0.1269)	0.0612 (0.1260)	-0.0168 (0.1270)	0.0318 (0.1294)
*Widowed	-0.3223*(0.1845)	-0.3111* (0.1838)	-0.1729 (0.1786)	-0.3216* (0.1900)
*Divorced	-0.2255 (0.1472)	-0.2135 (0.1458)	-0.2840* (0.1473)	-0.2055 (0.1503)
Family size (ref. Couple)				
*One	-0.0116 (0.1336)	-0.0228 (0.1331)	-0.0550 (0.1352)	-0.0341 (0.1370)
*Three or four persons	-0.0652 (0.1043)	-0.0666 (0.1037)	-0.0664* (0.0989)	-0.0656 (0.1063)
*Five or more	0.1574 (0.1332)	0.1477 (0.1324)	0.0630 (0.1277)	0.1894 (0.1356)

Source: DREES (2001), 'Opinions on social welfare.'

Table 27.8 Basic income: Economically viable (Y_2)

Explanatory variables: Preferences for redistribution and socio-demographic variables	Logit (1): With income	Logit (2): With precariousness	Logit (3): With income and precariousness	Logit (4): With income, precariousness and CMU
Incomes (ref. medium income)				
Very low income	-0.4540**(0.1650)		-0.4044**(0.1702)	-0.4121**(0.1690)
Low income	0.0450 (0.1369)		0.0356 (0.1387)	0.0409 (0.1401)
High income	0.0151 (0.1225)		0.0251 (0.1245)	0.0288 (0.1267)
Very high income	-0.0448 (0.2447)		-0.0597 (0.2456)	-0.0716 (0.2464)
Don't know	-0.00011 (0.1117)		-0.0254 (0.1134)	-0.0464 (0.1152)
Awareness of precariousness – knows a person in a precarious situation (ref. precariousness in the family)				
*Him/herself in such a situation		-0.0725 (0.1691)	-0.0288 (0.1701)	-0.0273 (0.1711)
*Somebody far from the family		0.0323 (0.0949)	0.0172 (0.0965)	0.0132 (0.0976)
*Nobody		0.2716** (0.1178)	0.2869**(0.1182)	0.2597**(0.1187)
*RMI should not exist (ref. RMI should exist)	0.1605 (0.1284)	0.1450 (0.1285)	0.1323 (0.1289)	0.1167 (0.1293)
Obligations for RMI (ref. yes)				
*No	-0.0497 (0.1044)	-0.0422 (0.1042)	-0.0304 (0.1050)	-0.0169 (0.1053)
Causes of poverty				
*Don't want to work (ref. no)	0.0918 (0.0825)	0.0880 (0.0823)	0.0817 (0.0831)	0.0552 (0.0836)
*No, missing family help is not a cause (ref.: yes, this is a cause)	-0.0796 (0.0867)	-0.0798 (0.0867)	-0.0700 (0.0875)	-0.0922 (0.0881)
Opinion about the CMU (ref. favourable)				
*Not favourable				0.6268**(0.1237)

Table 27.8 (Continued)

Explanatory variables: Preferences for redistribution and socio-demographic variables	Logit (1): With income	Logit (2): With precariousness	Logit (3): With income and precariousness	Logit (4): With income, precariousness and CMU
Least acceptable inequalities				
Income compared to others (ref. no)	−0.0966 (0.0890)	−0.1057 (0.0890)	−0.1021 (0.0895)	−0.1038(0.0904)
Educational level (ref.: 2 years university diploma)				
*Low	−.3552**(0.1167)	−0.3876**(0.1135)	−0.3580**(0.1165)	−0.3971**(0.1178)
*Professional qualification	−0.2220*(0.1164)	−0.2342**(0.1154)	−0.2358**(0.1167)	−0.2371**(0.1189)
*Postgraduate	−0.3487**(0.1555)	−0.3723**(0.1540)	−0.3652**(0.1554)	−0.3489**(0.1567)
*Don't know	0.1369 (0.4403)	0.0860 (0.4415)	0.0278 (0.4423)	0.00582 (0.4434)
Female (ref. male)	0.0300 (0.0842)	0.0117 (0.0838)	0.0262 (0.7557)	0.0369 (0.6651)
Age (ref. 35–49)				
*18–24	−0.2130 (0.1615)	−0.2419 (0.1611)	−0.2132 (0.1621)	−0.2033 (0.1630)
*25–34	0.0211 (0.1200)	0.0272 (0.1197)	0.0236 (0.1205)	0.0400 (0.1210)
*50–64	0.2371* (0.1288)	0.2289*(0.1285)	0.2035* (0.1289)	0.2668**(0.1293)
*Over 65	0.0719 (0.1578)	0.0249 (0.1578)	0.0242 (0.1579)	0.0772 (0.1580)
Marital status (ref. married)				
*Single	0.0767 (0.1372)	0.0475 (0.1361)	0.0612 (0.1376)	0.0717 (0.1379)
*Widowed	0.2725 (0.2030)	0.2308 (0.2012)	0.2297 (0.2032)	0.2141(0.2037)
*Divorced	−0.3253**(0.1534)	−0.3580**(0.1517)	−0.3242**(0.1539)	−0.2965* (0.1542)
Family size (ref. couple)				
*One	−0.0361(0.1428)	−0.0543 (0.1420)	−0.0368 (0.1430)	−0.0320(0.1434)
*Three or four persons	0.0642 (0.1128)	0.0628 (0.1121)	0.0625 (0.1128)	0.0850 (0.1132)
*Five or more	0.0832 (0.1436)	0.0980 (0.1427)	0.0929 (0.1437)	0.1212 (0.1441)

Source: DREES (2001), 'Opinions on social welfare.'

Table 27.9 Adhesion to CMU (Y_{3a})

Explanatory variables: Preference for redistribution and socio-demographic variables	Logit (1): With income	Logit (2): With awareness of precariousness	Logit (3): With income and precariousness
Incomes: (*ref. medium income*)			
Very low income	0.0263 (0.2202)		−0.00507(0.2285)
Low income	0.0311 (0.1731)		−0.0869 (0.1772)
High income	−0.0001(0.1559)		0.0124 (0.1568)
Very high income	0.2971 (0.3041)		0.2018 (0.3203)
Don't know	0.2632*(0.1352)		0.2299*(0.1374)
Awareness of precariousness – knows a person in a precarious situation (*ref. precariousness in the family*)			
*Him/herself in such a situation		0.1330 (0.2207)	0.1484(0.2328)
*Somebody far from the family		0.0777(0.1214)	0.0664 (0.1237)
*Nobody		0.3297**(0.1341)	0.3034**(0.1362)
*RMI should not exist (*ref. RMI should exist*)	0.9459**(0.1296)	0.9233**(0.1297)	0.9079**(0.1315)
Obligations for RMI (*ref. yes*)			
*No	−0.2611*(0.1319)	−0.2591*(0.1377)	−0.2000 (0.1387)
Causes of poverty			
*Don't want to work (*ref. no*)	0.3437**(0.1043)	0.3470**(0.1042)	0.3237**(0.1060)
*No, the missing family help is not a cause (*ref. yes, this is a cause*)	0.2768**(0.1058)	0.2613**(0.1058)	0.2714**(0.1073)
Least acceptable inequalities			
*Income compared to others (*ref. no*)	0.2336**(0.1084)	0.2280**(0.1084)	0.1860*(0.1089)
*Society is just (*ref. society is unjust*)			−0.2104*(0.1210)

Table 27.9 (Continued)

Explanatory variables: Preference for redistribution and socio-demographic variables	Logit (1): With income	Logit (2): With awareness of precariousness	Logit (3): With income and precariousness
Education level (*ref. 2 years university diploma*)			
*Low	0.3260**(0.1433)	0.2892**(0.1393)	0.2981**(0.1458)
*Professional qualification	0.0193 (0.1466)	−0.00852 (0.1457)	−0.00539 (0.1497)
*Postgraduate	−0.2900 (0.2203)	−0.2730 (0.2183)	−0.2882 (0.2297)
*Don't know	0.2439 (0.4765)	0.2142 (0.4762)	0.2299*(0.0942)
Female (*ref. male*)	−0.1009 (0.1045)	−0.1022 (0.1041)	−0.0877 (0.4812)
Age (*ref. 35–49*)			
*18–24	−0.00516 (0.2100)	−0.00366 (0.2092)	−0.0116 (0.2129)
*25–34	−0.0974 (0.1539)	−0.1059 (0.1536)	−0.0388 (0.1553)
*50–64	0.0473 (0.1568)	0.0534 (0.1570)	0.0769 (0.1594)
*Over 65	−0.0364 (0.1921)	−0.0392 (0.1924)	−0.00647 (0.1960)
Marital status (*ref. married*)			
*Single	−0.0562 (0.1761)	−0.0613 (0.1748)	−0.0516 (0.1780)
*Widowed	−0.0938 (0.2456)	−0.0963 (0.2441)	−0.1175 (0.2525)
*Divorced	−0.2513 (0.2075)	−0.2643 (0.2064)	−0.2350 (0.2119)
Size of the family (*ref. couple*)			
*One	0.0591 (0.1851)	0.0437 (0.1840)	0.0196 (0.1896)
*Three or four persons	−0.0272 (0.1415)	0.000519(0.1411)	−0.0219 (0.1429)
*Five or more	−0.0716 (0.1804)	−0.0278 (0.1798)	−0.0602 (0.1823)

Source: DREES (2001), 'Opinions on social welfare.'

Moreover, the signs of the coefficients are those expected, except for the coefficient relating to 'incomes inequalities are among the least acceptable'. With regard to educational level, the least educated appear less favourable than others to the CMU, which seems difficult to explain.

The number of 'don't know' observations on the survey is highest in relation to income (undoubtedly, individuals among the highest income classes) and for educational level. In the regressions, the 'don't know' observations have been retained only for the objective variables (not for the subjective variables) in order to limit the loss of sample numbers. To try to evaluate the impact, I ran a regression dropping 'don't know' responses on incomes and educational level. This regression was carried out within the framework of an ordered probit model and the results appear in Table 27.10 (by contrast with the preceding regressions, coefficients with a negative sign here mean less support for the scheme):

The results here generally corroborate the results obtained with the logit model, but the coefficient relating to 'low educational level' is no longer significant. Other variables also have coefficients which are no longer significant, such as 'lack of family assistance is not a cause of poverty' or even 'the particularly unacceptable character of income inequality compared to other types of inequality'. On the other hand, the fact of being divorced appears strongly significant for a favourable judgment on the CMU. The exclusion of 'don't know' responses thus modifies the results but without upsetting the broad trends. Perhaps one explanation is that these individuals have more interest in cash services than services in kind.

To finish presentation of the study, I turn now to the judgment of individuals on the 'degree' of justice in society. Social values and self-interest can be mixed here, according to whether respondents make an impartial judgment or voice their own satisfaction or dissatisfaction with their personal situation in society.

Regressions Relative to the Justice of Society

Table 27.11 shows the results of two regressions. In the second, logit (2), opinions on the CMU and the basic income proposal are introduced.

The descriptive statistics revealed that a large majority of respondents considered the society in which they lived as rather unjust. The results of the regressions tend to show that individuals answer according to their relative position in society (a negative sign for the coefficient means greater support for the idea that society is just). Thus, whereas those on low incomes regard society as rather unjust, those with high incomes regard society as quite just. In the same way, people who are distant from experience of precariousness

Table 27.10 Support for CMU (Y_{3b}) ('don't know' responses on income and education level dropped)

Explanatory variables: Preference for redistribution and socio-demographic variables	Probit
Incomes (*ref. medium income*)	
Very low income	0.13774 (0.09700)
Low income	0.03999 (0.07366)
High income	0.02651 (0.06516)
Very high income	−0.06609 (0.13123)
Awareness of precariousness – knows a person in a precarious situation (*ref. precariousness in the family*)	
*Him/herself in such a situation	−0.04663 (0.07277)
*Somebody far from the family	−0.08413 (0.07147)
*Nobody	−0.29947** (0.07320)
* RMI should not exist (*ref. RMI should exist*)	−0.57626** (0.07511)
Obligations for RMI (*ref. yes*)	
*No	0.14166** (0.06469)
Causes of poverty	
*Don't want to work (*ref. no*)	−0.17924**(0.05109)
* No, the missing family help is not a cause (*ref. yes, this is a cause*)	0.06602 (0.05354)
Least acceptable inequalities	
*Income compared to others (*ref. no*)	−0.01985 (0.05831)
Educational level (*ref. 2 years university diploma*)	
*Low	−0.11812 (0.07277)
*Professional qualification	0.00896 (0.07147)
*Postgraduate	0.10239 (0.09655)
Female (*ref. male*)	0.02550 (0.05244)
Age (*ref. 35–49*)	
*18–24	0.01316 (0.10106)
*25–34	0.00786 (0.07361)
*50–64	0.01098 (0.07922)
*Over 65	0.05085 (0.09882)
*Single person (*ref: married*)	−0.08932 (0.08429)
*Widowed	−0.05396 (0.12444)
*Divorced	0.24437**(0.10304)
Family size (*ref. coulple*)	
One	−0.18838**(0.09048)
*Three or four persons	0.01471 (0.07009)
*Five or more	0.11024 (0.08332)

Source: DREES (2001), 'Opinions on social welfare.'

Table 27.11 Society – just or injust? (Y$_4$)

Explanatory variables: Preference for redistribution and socio-demographic variables	Logit (1)	Logit (2): With CMU and basic income
Incomes (*ref. medium income*)		
Very low income	0.4277**(0 .1925)	0.4252**(0.1928)
Low income	0.2236(0.1442)	0.2255 (0.1443)
High income	–0.0264 (0.1231)	–0.0266 (0.1231)
Very high income	–0.5975** (0.2323)	–0.6047 (0.2326)
Don't know	0.3408**(0.1178)	0.3353** (0.1179)
Awareness of precariousness – knows a person in a precarious situation (*ref. precariousness in the family*)		
*Him/herself in such a situation	– 0.1316 (0.1913)	–0.1353 (0.1915)
*Somebody far from the family	–0.2594**(0.0988)	–0.2596**(0.0989)
*Nobody	–0.2556**(0.1195)	–0.2623**(0.1197)
*RMI should not exist (*ref. RMI should exist*)	0.3887**(0.1388)	0.3596**(0.1400)
Obligations for RMI (*ref. yes*)		
*No	0.0813 (0.1100)	0.0857 (0.1102)
Causes of poverty		
*Don't want to work (*ref. no*)	0.00177 (0.0859)	–0.00717 (0.0861)
*No, the missing family help is not a cause (*ref. yes, this is a cause*)	0.0584 (0.0910)	0.0499 (0.0912)
Opinions about basic income (*ref. moral and viable*)		
* Rest together		–0.0348 (0.1107)
Opinion about CMU (*ref. favourable to*)		
*Not favourable to		0.2063*(0.1199)
Least acceptable inequalities		
*Income compared to others (*ref. no*)	0.3822**(0.0970)	0.3745**(0.0972)
Education level (*ref. 2 years university diploma*)		
*Low	0.5581**(0.1171)	0.5481**(0.1174)
*Professional qualification	0.8275**(0.1205)	0.8272 (0.1207)
*Postgraduate	–0.0518 (0.1484)	–0.0471 (0.1486)
*Don't know	0.1656 (0.3988)	0.1626 (0.3993)
Female (*ref. man*)	0.2995**(0.0874)	0.3030**(0.0875)
Age (*ref. 35–49*)		
*18–24	–0.0386 (0.1691)	–0.0396 (0.1693)
*25–34	–0.0848 (0.1255)	–0.0824 (0.1256)
* 50–64	0.00525 (0.1341)	0.00369 (0.1342)
*Over 65	–0.2061 (0.1655)	–0.2047 (0.1657)

Table 27.11 (Continued)

Explanatory variables: Preference for redistribution and socio-demographic variables	Logit (1)	Logit (2): With CMU and basic income
Marital status (*ref. married*)		
*Single	−0.1128 (0.1419)	−0.1108 (0.1419)
*Widowed	−0.2346 (0.2054)	−0.2303 (0.2056)
*Divorced	−0.2414 (0.1661)	−0.2371 (0.1663)
Family size (*ref. couple*)		
*One	0.0201 (0.1491)	0.0164 (0.1492)
*Three or four persons	−0.0193 (0.1175)	−0.0210 (0.1175)
*Five or more	−0.0715 (0.1510)	−0.0701 (0.1511)

Source: DREES (2001), 'Opinions on social welfare.'

are more likely to regard society as just. With regard to the control variables, those with low education level regard society as more unjust, and so do women relative to men. In addition, the people who think that income inequalities are among the least acceptable are significantly more likely to say that society is unjust. This opinion is shared by those who are rather unfavourable to the CMU and who think the RMI should not exist, though the interpretation of this result could be ambiguous. Is the explanation the following: 'if the RMI or CMU did not exist because of eradication of poverty and precariousness, society would be less unjust', or is it rather: 'the distribution represented by the RMI or CMU is unjust'?

If a regression is performed dropping 'don't know' responses for income and educational level, the results change somewhat. The coefficient relating to the CMU loses significance while that relating to whether the RMI should exist strongly decreases and, although significant, is lower than before. The two interpretations sketched above can perhaps exist together. However, the respondents who refuse to indicate their income level are also, undoubtedly, those who are less favourable to redistribution.*

4. Conclusion

This study shows that self-interest and the social values supported by individuals can explain their attitudes towards redistribution. The basic income proposal, however, deserves a better presentation to respondents than it was given in the survey supplying the data. By comparison, the 'social value' effect appears more important to explain support for a universal right to health care than the self-interest effect. However, to determine the real nature of social judgments, survey questionnaires could usefully be supplemented by experimental questionnaires for example, to check acceptance of the 'undominated diversity' principle, which is here revealed only in an indirect way. In such an experiment, questions would be formulated in order to minimize the ambiguities which sometimes lie in larger scale survey questionnaires. The information related to the proposed redistribution to be evaluated is clearly specified so that individuals can make precise moral judgments.

Appendix. Description of the Data Set

The principal socio-demographic variables retained in the study are gender, age, educational level, marital status, and family size.

Age

* 18–24 years old
* 25–34
* 35–49 (reference)
* 50–64
* more than 65

Education Level

Five levels of educational attainment used:

* Persons with no qualifications or with only a junior high school diploma;
* Persons with a professional diploma or high school certificate;
* Persons with two years university diploma (reference);
* Persons with postgraduate degree;
* Don't know.

Marital Status

* Single
* Married (reference)
* Divorced
* Widowed

Family Size

* One adult
* Two adults (reference)
* Household with three or four persons
* Household with five or more persons

Variables that are Proxies for Self-interest

The variables used as proxies for self-interest are household income and awareness of precariousness.

Income

Six monthly income levels were used (in French francs)

- Less than 5,000
- From 5,000–7,500
- From 7,500–12,500 (reference)
- From 12,500–25,000
- More than 25,000
- Don't know

Proximity to Precariousness

This is constructed from responses to the following question: 'Do you know anyone in your family or in your entourage other than family who is in a precarious situation or, conversely, can you say that you know anybody in this situation?'

- In your family (reference)
- Somebody not in the family
- Nobody
- Yourself (not suggested)
- a jobless person with assistance
  - a jobless person without any assistance
  - a person without fixed residence
  - a single-parent with an income lower than the French guaranteed minimum wage (*salaire minimum interprofessionnel de croissance* – SMIC)
  - a disabled person
  - a recipient of guaranteed minimum income (*revenu minimum d'insertion* – RMI)

Variables Reflecting Social Values of Individuals

The variables reflecting the social values of individuals are derived from questions on the causes of poverty (responsibility of individuals or of society – see Kluegel and Smith, 1986; from questions on 'the particularly unacceptable character of certain forms of inequalities compared to others'; and finally from questions about the need for the French mean-tested minimum income (RMI), about the need for obligations on the part of the recipients, about its level and so on.

The Least Acceptable Inequalities

The question is framed as follows:
'There are several types of inequality. Among the following, which seem to you the least acceptable today in French society?' (Only one possible answer)

- Income inequalities
- Housing inequalities
- Inequalities relating to family inheritance
- Inequalities relating to type of employment
- Inequalities relating to school studies
- Inequalities relating to access to health care
- Inequalities relating to having or not having a job
- Inequalities relating to ethnic origin
- Don't know

In the regressions, I initially use a synthetic variable targeting income inequalities compared to the others, because the former is most frequently cited. Later, I constructed a variable where 'inequality relating to access to health care' was opposed to the others in order to introduce it into the regressions relating to the CMU. This variable was, however, never significant: that is why the regressions presented here only include the income inequalities compared to other types of inequalities.

Poverty

The question is framed as follows:
'Here are a number of reasons which can explain why people are in a situation of exclusion or poverty. For each one of them, tell me if you agree, quite agree or if you don't agree' (one answer).

- They are deep in debt
- They do not want to work (reference)
- They are victims of redundancy
- They lack qualifications to find a job
- They did not have opportunities
- There is not enough work for everyone
- They could not benefit from family assistance

Because the variable relating to the proposition 'they do not want to work' is not correlated with the others, I use it as the reference in the regressions. It particularly represents the 'responsibility' of the individual for his situation of poverty.

RMI: Existence, Evolution and Counterparts

The three following questions are used:

A) 'The RMI is paid to people in difficulty. In your opinion, does it have to be....?' (Yes or No)

- Permanent until the person has a sufficient income again;
- Subject to obligations on the part of the recipient.

B) 'But finally, does the RMI have to exist?' (Yes or No)
C) 'Today the RMI is approximately 2500 F per month for a single person. Do you think ...

- it is necessary to increase the RMI?
- it is necessary to decrease the RMI?
- the RMI is at the right level?' (not a suggested answer)

As this variable is correlated with the others, I introduce it as an alternative way into the regressions; the results presented here do not include it.

Notes

1 Ecole Normale Supérieure de Cachan, Labores, Catholic University of Lille, France.
2 Dominance corresponds to the following idea: if the situation of individual 'i' is judged by all as worse than that of 'j' then the situation of 'i' is dominated. The absence of domination can constitute a realizable ethical design. The application of this principle is relevant for the case of a person – or group of persons – who cannot meet their health needs because of lack of income. This is precisely the role of the French universal right to health care.
3 This is a curtailed presentation: the amount of basic income received would depend on the tax rate and which social minimum it replaced. Moreover, incentives are also difficult to assess (see Atkinson and Sutherland, 1989; Atkinson, 1995; van Parijs and Gilain, 1995).
4 The formulation of this question is better because the measure is in place and known. Moreover, the financial implications are better known than for the preceding question on basic income, which makes it easier to interpret the responses.
5 The choice of reference is, for subjective variables, guided by the highest frequencies collected while, for objective variables (income, education level), the choice depends upon average values to make the comparison with other categories easier.
6 Here, the variable Y is modelled so that $\Pr(Y=1)$ is the probability that the individual regards basic income as morally acceptable and economically viable; conversely $\Pr(Y=0)$ means that the individual does not support this proposal. We thus interpret a coefficient with a negative sign as meaning support for the proposal provided the coefficient is significant. In addition, for all the regressions, reliability is validated by the

usual statistics (Score, Wald, rate of agreement etc.; this last exceeds 60 per cent for all the regressions).

References

Atkinson, A. B. 1995. *Public economics in action, The basic income/flat tax proposal* , The Lindhal Lectures (Oxford, Clarendon Press).
_____ and Sutherland, H. 1989. 'Analysis of a partial basic income scheme', in A.B. Atkinson *Poverty and social security* (Hemel Hempstead, Harvester Wheatsheaf).
Boarini, R. and Le Clainche, C. 2002. *Social preferences and public intervention: An empirical Investigation*, Mimeo, Communication to Sesame, Aix en Provence, September.
Bresson, Y. 1994. *Le partage du temps et des revenus* (Paris, Economica).
Cornéo, G. and Grüner, H.P. 2002. 'Individual preferences for political redistribution', in *Journal of Public Economics* , Vol. 83, pp. 83–107.
Demuijnck, G. 2002. *A positive approach to norms to distributive justice*, Mimeo, Laboratoire de Recherches Économiques et Sociales/Economic (LABORES), Fédération Universitaire et Polytechnique de Lille (Fupl).
DREES (Direction de la Recherche, des Études, de l'Évaluation et des Statistiques). 2001. Opinion on Social Welfare (Paris, Research Department, Ministry of Social Welfare).
Fong, C. 2001. 'Social preferences, self-interest, and the demand for redistribution', in *Journal of Public Economics* , Vol. 82, pp. 225–246.
Kluegel, R. and Smith, E. 1986. *Beliefs about inequality: an American's views of what is and what ought to be* (New York, Aldyne de Gruyter).
Lehmann, E. 2001. *Evaluation de la mise en place d'un système d'allocation universelle en présence de qualifications hétérogènes. Le rôle institutionnel de l'indemnization du chômage et du salaire minimum* (Cahiers de la Maison des Sciences Economiques, Eurequa, Université de Paris I).
Miller, D. 1992. 'Distributive justice: What the people think', *Ethics*, April, pp. 555–593.
_____ 1999. *Principles of social justice* (Cambridge, Mass., Harvard University Press)
Piketty, T. 1995. 'Social mobility and redistributive politics', in *Quarterly Journal of Economics*, Vol. 110, pp. 551–584.
Swift, A. 1999. 'Popular opinion and political philisophy: The relation between social-scientific and philosophical analyses of distributive justice', in *Ethical Theory and Moral Practice* , Vol. 2, pp. 337–363.
Van der Linden, B. 2002. 'Is basic income a cure for unemployment in unionized economies? A general equilibrium analysis' , in *Annales d'Economie et Statistique*, No. 66, April – June.
van Parijs, P. 1991. *Qu'est-ce qu'une société juste?* (Paris, Le Seuil).
_____ 1995. *Real freedom for all. What (if anything) can justify capitalism?* (Oxford, Clarendon Press).
_____ and Gilain, B. 1995. *L'allocation universelle: un scénario de court terme et son impact redistributif*, document de travail de la Claire Hoover d'éthique économique et sociale (DOCH) No. 19, Université Catholique de Louvain, Belgium.

28

ACTIVATION OF MINIMUM INCOME AND BASIC INCOME: HISTORY OF A COMPARISON OF TWO IDEAS[1]

Gianluca Busilacchi[2]

1. Basic Income and Selective Measures: Contrast or Co-existence?

Among the Nobel prize winners for economics most often quoted in recent years are James Tobin, Amartya Sen and Herbert Simon. All three have dedicated a large part of their research the fight against poverty, focusing in particular on measures to guarantee for every individual a minimum of resources necessary for survival.

While Sen's work in this field is well known, less is known about the work of the other two. Tobin's name is mainly connected with a financing system (the Tobin tax) – but one of his essays was a pioneer study on basic income in contemporary economic science (Tobin, 1966). Even less was known about Simon's views on this issue until, shortly before he died, the father of limited rationality theory wrote an article on basic income for the *Boston Review* (Simon, 2000).[3]

Since then, the debate on poverty and minimum income policies has intensified for a number of reasons, two of which are of a political and institutional nature internal to the transformations of the welfare system.

On the one hand, many European welfare systems clearly require reforms that will deliver a better distributive and financial balance, especially in the field of social protection; on the other hand, a new form of governance in European Union social policies will permit comparison of the various minimum income systems now instituted in almost all the EU member States (Heikkilä and Keskitalo, 2001; Saraceno, 2002).

Other reasons can be found in the socio-economic transformations of the last decades. The crisis of the traditional model of work and the family has aroused a new interest in basic income and working time. This interest has been fuelled by the appearance of new forms of poverty and marginalization in the world's richest countries. Finally, the dynamics and dilemmas of globalization underline the contradictions of a world where one third of the population lives in a situation of extreme poverty and a child under five dies of starvation every two seconds, while 20 per cent of the world uses more than 80 per cent of available resources. This simplified picture allows us to understand why politicians, intellectuals and supporters of international cooperation are trying to find more effective measures to fight against poverty.

In Europe, there has been renewed interest in conditional minimum income policies targeted on the poor, selected on the basis of means testing, and usually implying the individual's inclusion in the world of work. The empirical support for these policies is the strong correlation in Europe between unemployment and poverty. Therefore the combination of money transfers and job opportunities seems to be the best way to limit social exclusion.

In the dominant political culture, these measures have become increasingly popular. The failure of Margaret Thatcher's economic liberalism on one hand and communist egalitarianism on the other has narrowed the range of ideologies legitimized by broad consent.

In comparison with a few decades ago, the differences between European social policies seem to lie more in their implementation than in their theoretical underpinnings. The inexorable advance of 'one current of thought' of liberal inspiration, although differently interpreted by Right and Left, is orientating these policies in the direction of a form of meritocratic egalitarianism, combining equality of opportunity and economic efficiency by promoting individual employment.[4]

Another debate in Europe has centred on the idea of basic income, unconditionally granted to all individuals to guarantee their material subsistence. This proposal was long regarded as anachronistic but later became a utopia 'abreast of the times' (van Parijs, 1996) and is now politically feasible. A basic income scheme has existed for about 20 years in Alaska, where all citizens are granted about $2,000 a year by the public administration, independent of their age, work status, income, gender etc. Many authors have decided to propose a similar scheme for Europe.[5]

At first sight the idea of a basic income appears to be antithetical to means-tested measures targeted on the poor and characterized by a work inclusion programme. The schemes differ both in their underlying ideologies and in their political and macro-social frameworks incorporating a different conception of the relationship between capital and labour, and between work, poverty, exclusion and citizenship.

This dichotomy does not necessarily mean there is no complementarity between the two. It is possible to think of coexistence between them,[6] or to see one as the natural evolution of the other. However, our purpose is to underline their differences rather than the similarities.

In recent years confused terminology has meant that the same name has been given to different measures, and the same concept has been called different names. If it is true that social dividend, basic or citizenship income (or wage), and universal subsidy are the same thing or at least have much in common, they have nothing to do with the 'basic income' introduced by the Basque Country (Raventós, 2001) nor with the concept of the minimum wage.

Our main purpose is therefore to sort out the muddle in order to compare the two kinds of measure and their relative advantages both in terms of economic efficiency and their effectiveness in hitting targets. In the next section we will review the history of basic income, trying to understand where and how the different definitions originated and on what ideologies they were founded. This will allow us to understand their normative justifications.[7]

In the third section we will analyse the 'state of the art' existing measures – the minimum income policies adopted in Europe – underlining both the good and the bad points of these policies. This will allow us to compare the two varieties of policy in economic and social terms and to conclude with a feasible though utopian proposal.

2. Which Minimum? History of Ideas on the Need for an Unconditional Basic Income

Even with respect to the elementary definition of basic income there are varying positions concerning the basic amount, its coverage and the form of provision.[8] The fundamental concept underlying basic income is that of a guaranteed income unconditionally granted to any member of a community, so as to allow him/her to live with dignity and achieve Sen's defined *functionings.*[9]

A first set of differentiations concerns the term *base*. According to some authors it is to be meant as a guarantee of the resources for subsistence. In this sense basic income would mean a survival income covering food, shelter, medicines, and so on. In truth, all social protection systems in Western countries already guarantee this kind of support, through social services, the third sector, traditional and local schemes, and health services. This provision, however, does not represent a right.

In this paper the term *base* will be used to mean a foundation upon which the individual can build his/her own life. This implies a base for the accumulation of other sources of income. The problem is that in almost all languages the term means both foundation and essentiality. Nor is the expression 'conditions for a dignified life' of help. Does this refer to physiological needs only or to the social dignity belonging to the community? Obviously the $2,000 granted to each citizen in Alaska will only cover the need for food, not the complex 'functionings' of an American citizen.

A second problem concerns *coverage*. A first sight it would seem obvious that a basic income would be granted to all individuals. More ambiguous is the French or Italian expression *citizenship income*, which includes income among the fundamental rights of a citizen but does not say whether the provision should be granted to resident non-citizens. This aspect is often neglected, although it is not a minor issue in a period characterized by an increase in mobility and population flows. To avoid *assistance shopping*[10] a minimum period of time should be considered, for example a year. Obviously supranational income schemes are not subject to this limitation (Genet and van Parijs, 1992; Bauer and Schmitter, 2001).

Besides the term base, the word *income* also deserves clarification. An income is an amount of money granted in time at a regular interval. Is this characteristic essential to define basic income? For example, money could be granted in a lump sum. These measures share some of the characteristics of basic income but they are not basic income.

Some confusion is also often due to the context: for example, expressions like *social dividend* are now in fashion, are connected to a particular historical period or a country's tradition – hence the popularity of the term *citizenship income* in the Italian and French debates of the 1980s. Before focusing on variations it is useful to present an historical overview in order to eliminate the characteristics connected with a specific historical context and its cultural and expressive trends.

Although in his *Utopia* of 1516 Thomas More referred to the State's involvement in the fight against poverty,[11] the first mention of basic income goes back to his friend Jean Luis Vives who, in a letter to the mayor of Bruges,[12] speaks about the need to guarantee a minimum income to all citizens, not only to the deserving poor. However, we are far from a basic income as the provision was to be granted to the poor (like a guaranteed minimum income) together with a job so that 'being busy and engrossed in their work they will abstain from those wicked thoughts in which they would engage if they were idle'.

Three centuries were to pass before Thomas Paine relaunched the idea in *Agrarian Justice* (1796): he was the first to envisage an unconditional income, which combined a definite proposal with an ideological justification. Paine speaks of the need for 'an equal share of the value of nature's gifts'. As the land-owning system does not guarantee the natural heredity of each person, he suggests that this injustice should be compensated for with a national fund, out of which a small sum of 15 pounds would be paid to each 20-year old person and an annual income of 10 pounds would go to each person over 50. While the second benefit is very similar to a universalistic form of pension, the first can help to offset the unfair distribution of advantages at birth in such a way as to guarantee the presuppositions of a regular market where all individuals, once they become of age, start from the same line (Magri, 1978). A sort of liberal justification laid the foundations of basic income (although it was an estate rather than an income).

Some decades later the mathematician Cournot proposed a negative income tax (NIT), in his *Recherches sur les principes mathématiques de la richesse* (1838).

The idea of a basic income began to take form in the works of some French social utopians; among them was Charles Fourier, under whose inspiration Joseph Charlier wrote *Solution du problème social* (1848), in which he defended the idea of ['a territorial dividend for each citizen based on the co-ownership of the national territory' (quoted by van Parijs, 2000b). Fourier's influence also spread across the Channel. In a critical review of his ideas, John Stuart Mill (1849) suggested a two-stage distribution of the national product: first by assigning a minimum amount of resources to all citizens in order to grant them subsistence, while at a second stage the distribution would depend on the person's contributions in terms of work, capital and talent.

In the twentieth century proposals for a minimum income passed from the academic debate to the political one. The reason was a change in public policies in the welfare field, from the charitable residualism of the previous centuries (when there was no intervention other than the Poor Laws and the workhouse) to the programmes of Bismarck's welfare state in Germany.

The rhythm of the debate was later set by Lord Beveridge and John Maynard Keynes. In *Social Insurance and Allied Services* (1942), which could be regarded as the basis of the modern welfare state, Beveridge wanted to create a system which would guarantee all individuals a minimum subsistence level by uniting the liberal tradition to a sort of State collectivism.[13] This was to be implemented by a system of public intervention in which the separation between social insurance and residual assistance was the foundation of a cooperation pact between State and people; intervention was balanced so as to preserve work incentives. Influenced by Keynes (Cutter, 1986), Beveridge attributed an economic stabilization function to the system of income without specifically proposing unconditional minimum income. The idea was advanced in those years by other Keynesians of the Cambridge group, among them James Mead, Jean Robinson and Abba Lerner.[14] Interpreting some passages of Keynes' *General Theory* (1963) as a signal that the introduction of basic income would allow reconciliation of social and macro-economic policies, Robinson proposed a social dividend,[15] later taken up by Mead (1936).

On the other side of the Atlantic, Lady Rhys-Williams published in 1942 the first American study on basic income. Her proposal for a negative income tax aimed to guarantee basic resources to all individuals, thus replacing all other instruments of assistance and tax exemption. With significant exceptions[16] the *laissez-faire* approach of American economists was opposed to the English welfare tradition of those years, and the guarantee of a minimum income would in the US have reduced welfare-state intervention to the negative income tax. This idea enjoyed great popularity in the US in the 1960s when changed macro-economic conditions increased inflation and poverty, and drove both President John Kennedy and President Lyndon Johnson to launch campaigns against poverty.[17] The policies adopted were strongly influenced by the opposition to government intervention typified by the Chicago School (Friedman, 1962). The negative income tax, although never applied, became the ideal flag under which to reconcile the fight against extreme poverty and the fight against the growth of bureaucracy, while keeping work incentives.

Some authors, however, began to focus on the relationship between minimum income and poverty traps (Tobin, 1965, 1967) rather than on welfare residualism, and supported a minority trend favourable to the expansion of the welfare system in the fight against poverty (Lampman, 1969).

A few years later the effects of negative income tax on poverty rates began to be studied in the United Kingdom (Barr, 1975; Kakwani, 1977). In the 1980s the crisis of the assumptions on which Keynesian proposals were founded, and in particular the government fiscal crisis, opened the way to the dismantling of welfare policies. However, minimum income programmes became increasingly popular in countries where such policies already existed; they represented an outlet for a difficult situation to which the contributory model could offer no solution simply because it had not been devised for that purpose (Room, 1991). The evidence of this is the increasing number of people who have been granted non-contributory income support in recent years (Clasen, 1997; Gough, 2000) and the introduction, in many countries, of new measures to combat poverty (Aguilar, Gaviria and Laparra, 1995) – second-generation minimum income based on a closer link between availability of resources and the world of work.

So far we have been talking about selective, means-tested policies. Since the 1980s, however, awareness of the failure of the Keynesian model, and of the contributory welfare system based on Fordism and the nuclear family, has stimulated fresh debates on minimum income. Many proposals for an unconditional basic income has been made that could, on one hand, help fight against poverty and, on the other hand, effectively redistribute job opportunities and freedom of life.

3. Unconditional Incomes

3.1 Basic Income

'A basic income is an income paid by a political community to all its members on an individual basis, without means test or work requirement' (van Parijs, 2000a).

This definition has the advantage of immediately presenting the concept although, in its simplicity, a variety of meanings are included. In this approach basic income and citizenship income are synonyms. However, such a general expression may cause problems. Being centred on the principle of a right rather than on the nature of the payment, it could cause misunderstanding as to its variations (NIT and social dividend), which might be considered basic incomes in a broad sense as they also guarantee a minimum income to all.

Our analysis by contrast aims to classify those measures that guarantee this right but which differ from each another in their technical-procedural characteristics. From this perspective, basic income is defined as a universal payment made at a regular intervals, unconditionally, to all individuals in a community.

Something needs to be said at this point about *participation income*. Some authors use this expression and basic income interchangeably, as in their opinion participation, like citizenship, means belonging to a community with the right to unconditional money transfers.[18] For other authors, participation has a narrower meaning implying a commitment to a work activity in return for an income from the State (Atkinson, 1993). In this case, we would be in the presence of an anomaly because an instrument with all the characteristics of a basic income in terms of provision and financing, and with a possible advantage in terms of 'defamilization' and equality of training opportunities lacks its main prerequisite – unconditionality. However, none of these differentiations can be found in practice, so that clarifying the taxonomy depends on subtle interpretative acrobatics.

If the analytical variables are the form of financing and the form of provision the distinction between pure basic income and its variations is easier. The first guarantees some cash at regular intervals and is paid on an individual basis, thus solving the problem of the *isolation trap* (van Parijs, 2000a), which characterizes measures aimed at families.[19]

The forms of *financing* employed to provide a basic income vary considerably depending on whether the amount is the threshold of poverty or higher. In the first case the objective would be the fight against poverty and would require fewer resources.[20] In some countries, the rationalization of public spending combined with other policies could be sufficient.

To guarantee more generous provisions allowing greater freedom in allocating time between work, care and leisure, higher income taxes or the introduction of new taxes (for instance, on property) would be necessary. Proposals include new non-fiscal taxes such as a tax on energy consumption (Genet and van Parijs, 1992) or on financial transactions (Tobin tax). On this we will present a modest proposal at the end of this paper.

The problems of financial sustainability, like the objectives to be reached with basic income, depend on its amount. As van Parijs says (1995), many justifications may be at the origin of a basic income, founded on 'the principles of equality and freedom, efficiency and community, the common ownership of the land and an equal participation in the benefits of technical progress, the flexibility of the labour market and the dignity of the poor, the fight against unemployment and inhuman work conditions, interregional differences and ... the promotion of adult education or workers' autonomy'.

The ethical spheres commonly involved are those of freedom and equality. Access to a secure income frees individuals from several conditioned choices. They are free to decide how much time to dedicate to work and what job to do. In this way the link between the need to earn a living and unskilled work would be broken for the working poor. Therefore a policy of this kind contains a high level of *decommodification* (Esping-Andersen, 1990) but also other benefits. Women would most enjoy the benefits of this policy. For example single mothers, a group that more than others risks social exclusion, could more easily reconcile care work with a part-time job, without being penalized by loss of benefits.[21] Inside the nuclear family, women would be less dependent on the husband's income (*defamilization*).

Compared with other minimum income measures that depend on workfare, basic income would provide emancipation from an ethical State, which compels beneficiaries to participate if they do not want to lose benefits (*depaternalization*). A second form of liberation would apply by comparison with minimum income schemes subject to 'multidimensional' selectivity – when access to a benefit, besides being means-tested, depends on many other conditions, and officials may enjoy some discretion in interpreting the rules. With the elimination of these conditions people would be free from the control of requisites (*debureaucratization*), which can be a source of social stigma.

In political philosophies the question of a just sharing of common resources is confronted in two ways: one has Marx's imprint, according to which a part of the social product must be divided among individuals, independently of their merits, as the legacy of common work (Van der Veen and Van Parijs, 1986). The other is rooted in maximalist liberalism. One of the basic principles of this doctrine is the inviolability of property. Nothing must modify the original appropriation of resources (Nozick, 1974). Then how can the fruit of the common property of natural resources be divided?

Steiner (1992) maintains that the best possible way to distribute this common property is through a universalistic income, and the same idea is shared by those who find in social capital the justification of a basic income: all individuals participate in intellectual growth and economic progress, therefore all of them have a right to participate in the results. However, initial endowments of social capital, as well as its transmission, are distributed at random and are therefore unfair, requiring a new balance through a universal basic income (Simon, 2000).

Another normative justification is the *republican* one (Raventós, 2001; De Francisco and Raventós, 2002). According to this doctrine, freedom is to be seen as the absence of any form of domination and interference of an individual in the life of another: the socio-economic independence that the basic income provides prevents these forms of domination in general, as regards the exploitation of the working poor and, in particular, due to reduced dependence of an individual on his/her boss, husband, a bureaucrat or the State, depending on the situation.

The main criticism of basic income is two-fold. First, in order to achieve results, basic income must be high and thus costs will be high.[22] The second and main attack, however, is against the ethics of basic income, which is accused of breaking the principle of reciprocity according to which payments financed with public money should correspond to duties by the beneficiaries.

In reality, as Widerquist (1999) emphasizes, basic income 'not only respects reciprocity but it is necessary for reciprocity to be achieved', for two reasons:

- The principle 'no work, no food' is not valid in a society without basic income where people born of a rich family can choose not to work while the others do not enjoy such freedom. Basic income would eliminate this violation of reciprocity by extending the possibility of a choice to all.
- With a basic income everybody has the same chance to work. Those who decide not to will enjoy benefits that are at the disposal of the others as well, both in terms of money and personal satisfaction (it is difficult for a lazy person to have a high rate of utility although he/she is maintained by the community).

3.2 Negative Income Tax (NIT)

Negative income tax (NIT) might produce results very similar to those obtained with basic income. The main difference is that NIT uses the fiscal system to redistribute income. An equilibrium income is fixed, to be defined as the threshold at which the individual is indifferent to the presence or absence of a transfer scheme (Granaglia, 2001). The people enjoying this income are neither net beneficiaries nor net contributors (R_1). The people below this threshold receive a subsidy equal to: $NIT = t\ (R_1 - R_0)$, where R_0 is the original income of the individual and t is the tax rate applied. Higher incomes are taxed at a rate equal to $t\ (R_0 - R_1)$.

In 2001 Visco proposed a flat tax, of t = 33 per cent, a rate which remained the same irrespective of income, with the exception of a higher tax on very high incomes.[23] Flat-rate taxes are often associated with the NIT proposal, both out of a desire for fiscal simplicity and because a first redistribution would have already occurred by financing subsidies to the poor with taxes on incomes of the rich. Also the latter would be guaranteed a 'basic income' in the form of a fiscal credit. In conclusion, all taxpayers would be able to enjoy an income of at least of R_1 every year as money payment or as fiscal exemption.

From the redistribution point of view, however, the type of taxation to be applied to NIT can make all the difference. If 't' is the same for every income bracket, the normative justification of a basic income founded on greater social justice would become groundless. An ordinary system of progressive tax rates would guarantee a better redistribution of resources.

Moreover, according to van Parijs (2000b), there are two other disadvantages in comparison with the basic income proposal:

- NIT being an *ex post* payment, it is necessary to complement it with another programme of minimum support for the poor in order to allow them to live with dignity until the time of the fiscal tax return, when fiscal debits and credits are calculated. No such a problem occurs when a basic income is granted *ex ante*;
- In contrast to basic income, which is directed addressed to the individual, NIT addresses the fiscal subject and therefore the family. Thus the level of defamilization is lower; however, NIT's effects on intra-family income equity are unknown.

Another problem can be due to ineffective fiscal control. This may cause two further negative effects – public money given to tax evaders and an incentive for people just above the threshold to continue to do 'black' work (*trap of black work*). For these people the marginal tax rate is unfair, passing from 0 per cent to 33 per cent for each extra unit of income $(R_0 - R_1) R_1$.

Therefore we cannot agree with those who consider NIT as the best policy short of basic income. The presence of characteristics like unconditional universality, simple operation and lack of stigma are not enough to overcome the difference of principle. It is not by chance that this model has found favour with thinkers who value the economic efficiency of basic income more than its solidarity towards the weakest members of a society. The normative justifications advanced by NIT supporters mainly focus on technical rather than ethical aspects, like, for example, the absence of disincentives to work.

3.3 Social Dividend [24]

The term social dividend has been used to indicate a variety of concepts including, recently, NIT. What we mean by it here (following both Paine and Mead) is a basic amount of resources to be guaranteed to the individual as the natural heritage of the community's social production, shared by all its members. The boundaries between social dividend and basic income vary according to the variable used, but it is important to remember that the two measures are very similar both in purpose and in their technical aspects.

According to some authors, what differentiates social dividend from other basic income programmes is above all the form of provision. In this case a small amount of capital, a lump sum, is paid once, for example at the time of birth (Meade, 1989) or when the individual comes of age. This sum can be invested to obtain an income, or spent on education or even wasted in Las Vegas. Other authors have focused on the form of financing of the measure (Morley-Fletcher, 1989), while a few identify the uniqueness of the social dividend in its normative justification. According to them people would receive something in exchange for the co-sharing of the natural and social wealth of a community (Ackerman and Alstott, 1999).

The expression 'social dividend' thereby takes on a more precise meaning, that is to say, that of a natural income coming from production which belongs to everybody and nobody. It is not by chance that some authors speak of 'social heredity' (Morley-Fletcher, 1989).

As Ackerman and Alstott (1999) underline in their review of Paine's original proposal,[25] a social dividend would guarantee the establishment of a 'participants' society' and would represent the sense of belonging to and participation in a community, where the connotation given to the term participation is very different from its equation with work activity discussed earlier (Section 3.1).

In Ackerman and Alstott's proposal the dividend would be financed through an annual tax on health (2 per cent) or through the reimbursement of the sum on the death of the individual, as if each single share of the social heritage should return to the community once its function is over.

The American culture of the grant seems to underlie this proposal. The authors argue that this considerable sum of money would offer 20 year-olds 'unprecedented opportunities: he/she could go to college, choose where to live, whether to get married or how to pick up economic opportunities. Someone might fail... but less than now' (Ackerman and Alstott 1999, p. 5).

What differs is the *ideological root*. In this sense the social dividend finds its origin in a sort of liberalism that we could define 'right wing', not to place it in a precise political context but to differentiate it from the sort of liberalism that van Parijs derives from Rawls.[26]

The philosophical liberal tradition in the USA has become a fertile ground for the support of basic income, in the literature on social capital: the sharing not only of natural resources but also of the culture of a community allows productive, economic and social development for which each individuals should be rewarded.

In conclusion, the two elements that allow us to distinguish social dividend from basic income seem to be its property basis and its different normative justification. Theoretical problems arise when the two aspects combine, as in the only basic income scheme now existing in the world. How should we classify it in our taxonomy?

Since 1982 all citizens in Alaska have been granted an unconditional payment ($1,680 per year in 1999), which has all the characteristics of a pure basic income. The theoretical problem arises because these payments are financed by 22 per cent of the sale proceeds from oil extracted in Prudhoe Bay, which the authorities have decided to subdivide proportionally among the people who have been living in Alaska for at least one year. It is a real dividend, which, besides varying according to the level of oil production and prices, implies the idea of natural heredity already underlined. Although this payment is considered a form of basic income, the definition of social dividend seems to be more correct.

The main advantages of a social dividend are two-fold. From an ethical point of view, each individual feels he/she is participating in the social growth of a community and is being compensated for this participation. Moreover, this aspect might create an incentive to increase collective production. From a technical point of view, the property basis of the measure means that the availability of a large sum of money would allow investments, which would not be possible if the money was granted periodically (purchase of a house, access to Harvard University etc.).

On the other hand, a young person given a large lump sum may not use it rationally for the needs of his life cycle. This could be particularly true of those who are most at risk of poverty. The particular attention recently paid to the dynamic longitudinal aspects of poverty (seen as a condition that one can escape and fall into periodically) seems to show that the guarantee of a basic income, paid at regular intervals, is more effective in decreasing this risk.

In conclusion, we have seen that there are different forms of basic income, which cannot be precisely classified in a taxonomy (NIT excluded) because of overlapping technical (financing, form of provision, etc.) and ideological variables. The same proposal may have the support of heterogeneous alignments of political philosophers with different ethical justifications. Obviously it is necessary to analyse better the relationships between the philosophical roots and the political culture of the various groups.

4. Activation Policies and Guaranteed Minimum Income (GMI): Implementation

Over the last century, while the debate on basic income was going on, most European countries were developing social welfare programmes, which included systems to guarantee minimum income. However, none of these systems is characterized by the universality and unconditionality of Alaska's basic income. We cannot explain the reasons for the choice of selectivity in all European countries, including 'universal' welfare states. Besides the difficulties that social welfare programmes encounter in terms of consent and social legitimation,[27] financial constraints and the attempt to fight poverty and unemployment simultaneously through targeted instruments also play a role. This last aspect has favoured policies specifically targeted on socially excluded citizens, based on a combination of payments and work projects.

The history of minimum income policies can be divided into three phases (Ayala, 2000). The first corresponds to the expansion of welfare systems with the introduction of income protection policies of the Bismarck or Beveridge type, that is, policies integrated into an insurance system of social protection.[28] Minimum incomes do not have a life of their own and even in the most generous countries they function as a last resort.[29]

It was in this phase that Family Income Support was introduced in England for the families of poor workers together with Supplementary Benefit for unemployed people. Although in Denmark the law recognized the right to economic security in 1891, the modern version of the *Social Bijstande* only dates back to 1974.

During the 'Golden Age' of the welfare state in the post-war period, minimum income policies were introduced in Germany (1961), but these decentralized schemes were still influenced by the contributory social insurance policies to which they were linked. Similarly in Austria, the minimum income measure is so residual and secondary in welfare programmes as to represent a stigma for the small number of beneficiaries.

In northern Europe welfare policies are totally different and minimum income schemes more generous, as in Sweden and Finland. In 1963, Holland introduced its two-tier system of *Social Bijstande* (for laid-off workers and others), which grants beneficiaries an income very close to the minimum wage.

The second wave of minimum income policies arrived in the 1970s, in a situation of economic crisis and increases in poverty and unemployment. In many countries there was a sharp rise in the number of needy people passing from contributory to social assistance schemes, which had previously been considered emergency measures. When the emergency became constant some countries decided to introduce minimum income measures independently located in the social welfare system. In 1977, Ireland adapted a model similar to the English one and in 1973 Belgium introduced *Minimex*, though this was not very successful due to its residual character and the high level of decentralization.

The crisis in public finances and the growing problem of unemployment demonstrated the ineffectiveness of all these programmes and paved the way for new policies to fight both poverty and social exclusion. This third wave of minimum incomes schemes included the *Revenu minimum garanti* in Luxembourg in 1986, but especially the French *Revenu minimum d'insertion of* 1988, which were the pioneers of a series of guaranteed minimum income schemes in which payment was accompanied by a programme of social and work inclusion for the weakest citizens.[30]

In the 1990s the French example was followed by some countries in southern Europe which until then had been characterized by the weakness of their welfare system, both 'plethoric and fragmented' according to Italy's Onofri Commission for the Analysis of Macro-economic Compatibility of Social Expenditure (*Commissione per L'analisi delle compatibilità macroeconomiche della spesa sociale*, 1997).[31]

To date only Portugal has completed the transition to a full system of minimum income policies (Guibentif and Bouget, 1996). In Spain no national programme exists and the management of the *renta minima* is entrusted to the *autonomas communes*. Italy is even further behind: the experiment of *reddito minimo di inserimento (RMI)* began in 1998, but its prospects remain uncertain. Meanwhile, Greece continues to be the only EU member country where no income support programme exists.

From an analytical point of view we will continue with the same classification as for the unconditional basic incomes, introducing two subdivisions of the 'pure' GMI: the 'minimum insertion income' and the scheme ensuring protection for the families of the working poor through the fiscal system with a mechanism similar to that of NIT.

5. Conditional incomes

5.1 Guaranteed Minimum Income (GMI)

Unlike basic income GMI is granted to needy people and is means-tested. In this case it is also necessary to distinguish between a broader meaning, that is, the right to have some resources at one's disposal,[32] and the instrument implied in it, consisting of a payment whose amount differs according to the resources of the beneficiary, so that what is guaranteed is the final amount, the target being a certain threshold income. This value is usually determined by the official poverty threshold of each country or, more often, a percentage of it. Thus the guarantee relates to the final economic condition of the individual and not the provision of the benefit. This is the main difference between GMI and basic income, besides the selectivity of the measure, which is aimed only at people with an income below the given threshold.

The income test concerns the household and not the individual. The payment is usually monthly, its amount is proportional to the size of the household calculated using equivalence scales, and it is financed through taxation.

In the classification of minimum income measures according to the different systems of welfare (see Table 28.1), GMI has been associated with the Scandinavian social democratic model because, although it is means-tested, it has a universal character as it is targeted at all the poor without their being asked for anything in return. This measure does not have any link with the labour market nor is it connected to any particular group. Moreover, the countries in which GMI has been introduced are all in northern Europe.

The efficiency of targeting is certainly one of the factors in favour of GMI together with its economic sustainability. The most serious disadvantage seems to be the social stigma connected with the selectivity of the measure. Moreover, means-testing implies high transaction costs for two reasons: first, it is more difficult to publicize this instrument than one addressed to the whole population, and some of the potential beneficiaries may never receive the information or act upon it (low take-up); second, verifying eligibility entails administrative costs.

Another possible consequence of targeting is the well-known poverty trap. People close to the threshold would have no incentive to work because the income gain due to work would make them ineligible for GMI, and their economic situation might not improve or could worsen. In addition, they would incur the opportunity cost of lost free time.

Less can be said about disincentives to honesty. Black work and tax evasion are devices often used to gain inclusion in the group of beneficiaries by those whose incomes would otherwise exceed the threshold. In a time of flexible jobs and families, other traps are likely to appear, like the 'isolation' trap (see footnote 17) or the 'dequalification' trap. The latter indicates dependence on the measure, similar to the poverty trap, which gives no incentives to the beneficiary to move out of a low-income situation.

5.2 Minimum Insertion Income (MII)

The minimum insertion income has characteristics very similar to those of GMI, of which it is a subdivision. The only difference lies in workfare programmes for beneficiaries. This greater distance from the unconditionality of basic income can be read in two ways: as a request for something in exchange, that is, a further condition for access to benefits, or as another opportunity for weaker members of society to achieve social inclusion. In the second case, it would be an attempt to promote social participation more efficiently than with a GMI.

In order to receive the payment, the beneficiary is required to attend training courses or enter social inclusion programmes of a workfare type.

Table 28.1 Taxonomy of minimum income schemes

NAME	Condition	Financing	Provision: from beneficiary	Reference model,[a] countries of implementation	Ideological root	Normative justification	Advantages	Disadvantages
Basic income (or citizenship)	No	Redistribution of social expenditure; property or fiscal	Income provided at regular intervals (monthly); individual	Universalism - Social democratic Not applied	Liberalism according to Rawls (Sen, van Parijs); Marxism	Left wing liberalism -ensures complete freedom in life choices; Republican - prevents domination	Protection against poverty in all cases; in case of high income, effects on work redistribution, more free time, flexibility and job creation; elimination of traps and stigma; administrative simplification	Relative inefficiency in provision to rich people; high cost for provision with full effects; cultural resistance (society of work and meritocracy)
Participation income	Work	Property or fiscal	Individual, monthly income	Universalism Corporative; non applied	(Atkinson)	Liberal, with a tendency towards meritocracy	like the previous one, with less emphasis on the effects of the liberation from work	Exclusion of people who can't and do not want to work: no great freedom of choice
NIT	No	Fiscal	Tax credit; family	Universalism liberal-residual; unapplied	Liberalism of the Nozick type (Friedman)	Liberal efficiency Residualism, against the State	Automaticity of the system, simplicity, protection from poverty, no stigma	Unfair for people just above the threshold; unemployment trap; black work
Social dividend	No	Property; dividend of common resources	Lump sum (e.g. on coming of age)	Universalism liberal; Alaska	(Paine, Meade, Simon)	Right-wing liberal, as a right to the sharing of common resources	Income types -: the same as BI; property - more possibility of choice in spending a big sum	In the property forms, it creates uncertainty for future incomes

Guaranteed minimum income	Means-testing	Fiscal	Family, monthly income	Social democratic selectivity: UK, Sweden, Finland, Denmark, Austria, Ireland, Germany, Netherlands, Belgium[b]	Efficiency in the fight against poverty	Stigma and poverty trap; sometimes both coverage and performance are low
Minimum insertion income	Means-testing, work inclusion	Fiscal	Family, monthly income	Corporative selectivity France, Portugal, Luxemburg, Spain, Italy	Efficient provision of resources, activation of beneficiaries, more possibility of inclusion	Low coverage and performance, high administrative costs; problem of controls
Tax credit for workers	Means-testing	Fiscal	Tax credit Workers' families	Liberal selectivity; UK, USA, France	Administrative simplification, no particular bureaucratic costs	Only for the working poor, it does not cover the very poor, nor women's emancipation

[a] This classification is obviously theoretical for universalistic models which cannot be found in Europe. It is based on normative justifications, which seem to reflect a fully inclusive philosophy only in the case of basic income. The welfare model most similar to this is the social democratic one (in this case we use typologies where the political element is too strongly marked). The 'labour' spirit which characterizes the participation income leads us to see it as very close to corporative models. In the same way the residualistic principle present in many justifications of NIT suggests a similarity with those welfare models. The division is, however, only theoretical and it has neither historical foundations nor generalizing intentions.

[b] This is a spurious case as people under 25 must sign an inclusion contract as happens with MII.

The advantages are the active participation of the beneficiary, and the opportunity for him/her to fight against social exclusion. But these advantages are counterbalanced by the risk of his/her eligibility being subject to means-testing and job involvement. It has been seen that this combination may increase the number of low-skilled low-paid jobs, which allow the beneficiary to do his/her duty without any corresponding increase in income (dequalification trap). Very often access is hindered by too many conditions and this is the reason for a low take-up, that is, a low proportion of potential beneficiaries receiving a minimum income under these schemes (see Table 28.2).

It is also true that the conditions discourage opportunistic behaviour and encourage people to do their best to achieve social inclusion; workfare, a term which often carries negative connotations, can also have a positive impact, provided its application is not too strict. In reality, as recent studies on these programmes have shown (Saraceno, 2002), it is the beneficiaries themselves who see the measure as an opportunity rather than as a duty. This attitude, which makes measures more effective, obviously depends on the initial situation of the beneficiary and his/her determination to fight social exclusion.

5.3 Tax Credit

More oriented towards the world of work are the measures which go under the name of 'tax credits for workers'.[33] This is the case of the English *Working families' tax credit* (WFTC), introduced by the Blair Government based on US President Bill Clinton's pro-labour programmes. It is not by chance that such measures are adopted in those countries in which the ratio of unemployment to poverty is low.

The instrument consists of a tax credit for the families of the working poor. Workers whose wages are below a certain threshold will receive incremental fiscal bonuses according to household size and economic circumstances. The income of these families thereby exceeds both the poverty threshold, and unemployment benefits and social assistance subsidies, creating a strong incentive to work. However, Samuel Brittan has pointed out that, what in the intentions of its promoters should be the first step towards a basic income seems to be a 'labour market participation income' (*Financial Times*, August 17, 2000), that is, a measure which only protects workers' families. It is a sort of guaranteed minimum wage, which offsets tax debits and credits like the negative income tax, but has not much connection with basic income seen as a right of citizenship.

In theory this kind of intervention should reconcile minimum income protection with a strong incentive to work; in practice it has been demonstrated that it creates a disincentive to work over a certain number of hours

Table 28.2 Minimum income schemes in Europe

Country	Name and year of introduction[a]	Kind of policy	Context	Duration	Beneficiaries	Numbers and take-up (%)[b]	Obligations
UK	(Family Income Support 1948) Family Credit 1987	Tax credit for workers	National	Unlimited	National, EU citizens bilateral agreements; Over 18 years; Family	5,600,000 (74.1%)	No
	(Supplementary Benefit 1948), Income Support 1987	Guaranteed minimum income					
Denmark	Social bistand 1974	Guaranteed minimum income	National	Unlimited	Resident applicants, and husband or wife	95,743 (100%)	Supporting wife and children
Sweden	Social bidrag 1982	Guaranteed minimum income	Local and national	Unlimited	Residents; husbands (wives) and partners; single people	753,100 (100%)	Supporting husband (wife) and children
Finland	Toimeentulotuki 1982	Guaranteed minimum income	Two levels according to the municipality of residence	Unlimited	Residents Family	609,700 (100%)	No
Netherlands	Sociale bijstand 1963	Guaranteed minimum income	National	Unlimited	National, EU citizens and refugees; residents; 18 years (with exceptions); applicant and partner	489,200 (100%)	No
Germany	Sozialhilfe 1961	Guaranteed minimum income	Länder	Unlimited	National, EU citizens and refugees; residents; applicant and partner	3,484,818 (92.1%)	No

Table 28.2 (Continued)

Country	Name and year of introduction[a]	Kind of policy	Context	Duration	Beneficiaries	Numbers and take-up (%)[b]	Obligations
Austria	Sozialhilfe; different dates according to Länder	Guaranteed minimum income	Länder	Unlimited	Residents (in some Länder and also nationals); Applicants dependents	120,000 (28%)	No
Belgium	Minimex 1973	Guaranteed minimum income	National	Unlimited	National, EU citizens and refugees; residents; 18 years old (with exceptions); husbands and wives or cohabitants, single people	80,119 (20.7%)	Inclusion measures/ quarterly for people under 25
Ireland	Supplementary Welfare Allowance 1977	Guaranteed minimum income	National	Unlimited	National, EU citizens and refugees; residents; 18 years old; applicant and people living with him/her	143,784 (28.5%)	No full time job
Luxembourg	Revenu minimum guaranti 1986	Minimum insertion income	National	Unlimited	10 years of residence; 30 years old (with exceptions) cohabitants	10,098 (100%)	Inclusion measures
France	Revenu minimum d'insertion 1988	Minimum insertion income	National	3 months with renewal, max. 1 year	Residents; 25 years (with exceptions); applicant and people living with him/her	1,835,275 (60.8%)	Inclusion measures

Portugal	Rendimento minimo garantido 1996	Minimum insertion income	National	12 months, automatic renewal	Residents; 18 years old (with exceptions); Family	55,897 (39.7%)	Inclusion measures
Spain	Rentas minimas (de inserción) 1989–1993 according to commune	Minimum insertion income	Autonomous communes	12 months with renewal	Residence in the commune up to five years; 25–65 years old (with exceptions for people under 25); family	63,000 (6.3%)	Inclusion measures
Italy	Reddito minimo di inserimento 1998	Minimum insertion income	National (experiment)	Limited but renewable	Residence; Family		Inclusion measures

[a]. The date of introduction refers to the last important legislative modification; in the case of the UK we underlined its pioneering nature as the first in Europe.
[b]. Latest year.
[c]. Values in PPP (purchasing power parity) and in per cent in relation to that country's poverty threshold. Data partially processed by Ayala (2001) and European Commission (1999), *Report on Minimum Income Schemes*, Brussels.
[d]. Although in Italy RMI is only an experiment, its characteristics have been analysed; as for data those in square brackets refer to the averages of the *minimo vitale* implemented in some regions.

(Jordan *et al.*, 2000) and to look for good jobs (Brittan, quoted above). In 2003 WFTC is due to be split into two programmes: *Employment Tax Credit* and *Integrated Child Credit*. But, however implemented, this kind of scheme is constrained by the decision to bind work income to the negative income tax model. Such scheme can work universalistically only if it is accompanied by other measures of social protection, which extend the intervention to unemployed and other disadvantaged people.

The names of these schemes show their 'labour-based' orientation. In the USA, where Clinton extended nationally a measure introduced in Louisiana 25 years ago, it is called the *Earned Income Tax Credit*. In France the *Prime pour l'emploie* (PPE) has recently been introduced, whose reference model is that of the tax credit. Paradoxically, in France different and sometimes opposite policies coexist; a measure like PPE operates alongside the *Revenu minimum d'insertion* and other policies for the elderly (like *Minimum vieillesse*), or single-parent families.

Apart from the legislative confusion created by the different forms of intervention in the same sector (in the identification, informing, and control of the beneficiaries of each measure), the confused and confusing political choice of mixing two different models, of showing both sides of the same coin, reveals some ambiguity: either it is a strange coin or someone is cheating.

6. A Comparison of the Efficiency of Basic Income and Guaranteed Minimum Income

Comparing poverty to a disease is sad but appropriate. One can be born poor or become poor more or less accidentally, and one can also die of poverty. Like diseases, poverty also has its own medicines – such as redistribution by the government or community or third-sector solidarity.

Here we are dealing with a specific remedy, that of minimum income policies. Having analysed the various forms of basic income and guaranteed minimum income from an historical and analytical point of view, we will assess their effectiveness by comparing basic income with minimum insertion income (MII). MII has been chosen because of its ability to combat social and work exclusion and because it has recently been implemented in a large number of European countries.

First, however, it is necessary to decide whether the results of the two measures can be compared – whether, apart from cost, their success in terms of effectiveness concerns the same dependent variable. In short, do these two medicines aim to cure the same disease?

As we know, poverty may mean different things. We cannot here enter into the debate, which would imply categorizing the concept of poverty and differentiating it from the concept of exclusion (Gordon and Townsend, 2000;

Silver, 1994). Here we simply want to distinguish between absolute poverty, meant as lack of the income necessary for subsistence, and multidimensional poverty, a more complex concept, less clear than that of social exclusion, which involves deprivation of both economic and non-economic goods (social, cultural and relational goods such as level of education, position on the labour market, access to particular technologies, and so on).

The minimum insertion income is a measure aimed at fighting against the second kind of poverty, although it does not have all the necessary instruments. However, the emphasis on work inclusion targets lack of income through access to the labour market. It is more difficult to identify the social risk basic income is designed to combat, especially since this depends on the model and its nature, scope and objective. This is why we wonder whether it is correct to use the same term 'liberal' for normative justifications which are very different from one another, such as those of van Parijs and Steiner, which, although belonging to liberalism, express the opposing philosophies of Rawls and Nozick.

We need to start from the realization that for some liberals the desired target is meritocratic egalitarianism while others are against this principle. The differences lies in a different vision of poverty and of the aims of public intervention, ranging from the anti-welfare idea of 'no work, no food' to the charitable residualism of support for those left behind, to an attempt to guarantee real freedom in life-choices. Only in the last case is the idea of freedom connected with that of social justice.

If the justification of basic income was simply the elimination of extreme poverty, its amount might be limited. The objective would be worth reaching but this would imply the acceptance of inequality and the distribution of resources by the market. Those who think that what should be granted is equal access to Sen's 'functionings' want to uproot poverty in a more complex sense. They question the present relationship between capital and labour, and see the idea of freedom as connected with redistribution both of resources and work.

It is the different interpretation of the role of work, together with the different ideas of poverty, that constitute an interesting variable for evaluating the impact of basic income and MII. Like the forms of basic income that implicitly consider the individual's participation in work as a social 'duty' (and as necessary to guarantee the efficiency of economic production), the minimum insertion income is based on a meritocratic labour-oriented vision in which the solution of the problem of poverty and that of unemployment go together.

Most supporters of basic income, instead, want to redefine the idea of labour and see a link between the fight against poverty and freedom not to work. Apart from the reasons used to justify the two measures, a comparison between basic income and MII cannot overlook their differing impacts in terms of economic efficiency. This impact can only be studied through simulation models, as basic income schemes have not been implemented in reality.

According to Pinilla (2001), the efficiency of a minimum income policy can be analysed using three parameters: the overall impact on the economy, the push to economic growth and therefore the possibility for the measure to sustain itself, and its efficiency compared with that of similar social assistance policies.

With regard to the first parameter, a basic income would make labour more flexible and human, with an indirect benefit for the economy as a whole and a direct benefit for the poor (Pinilla, 2001, p. 162). A possible decrease in minimum wages as a consequence of the introduction of basic income would increase the elasticity of the labour market. Mobility would also increase and there would be greater redistribution of jobs. The certainty of an income not coming from work would allow greater freedom of choice, oriented not towards wages but other factors (like hours, job satisfaction, etc.)

In this way the wages of less-good jobs would increase while the wages of the better ones would decrease. A microeconomic evaluation would recognize the increase in systemic efficiency triggered by this process, in terms of congruence between individual likes and behaviours. Apart from its effect on efficiency, this last aspect would decrease income inequality and the correlation between the minimum wage and survival needs would no longer be a central issue.[34]

As for economic growth and financial sustainability in the long term, the decreased perception of future risks due to a guaranteed income and lower costs for firms (wages and human capital) would certainly increase consumption and development. It should be added, however, that this would not guarantee the financial sustainability of any level of basic income. A high basic income would not guarantee a flow of marginal benefits from the economy equal to its costs.

Finally, in comparison with other public programs like MII, a basic income eliminates the traps of poverty, unemployment and isolation that accompany the minimum insertion income.

In the debate on basic income there is a tendency to justify it by virtue of the low efficiency of selective measures in terms of take-up by beneficiaries (Granaglia, 2001).[35] This kind of technical justification is not enough and basic income deserves to be supported from another perspective. As basic income is a measure against absolute poverty, rather than income inequality, there would not be strong disincentives to work in the sense that an individual may be driven to look for high earnings by the perception of other people's wealth.

The avoidance of all the traps of the GMI and the defeat of extreme poverty would be a technical justification to better evaluate basic income from the point of view of efficiency compared to selective measures.

Basic income would also reduce administrative costs,[36] especially control and transaction costs, both evident (more difficulty in the information take-up process, more bureaucracy) and non-evident. Among the latter is the misuse of a conditional measure like MII due to favouritism or familism involving a disincentive to work for the wife of a man subjected to means-testing.

In general, we have already seen that a basic income would guarantee more defamilization than a MII, resulting from the greater economic independence of women and children, and the higher overall income of big families where each member enjoys a basic income.[37]

Moreover, the universality of the instrument could generate a feeling of 'social responsibility' towards public money and fraud would be more easily punished.

We conclude with the results of two simulations comparing the efficiency of minimum insertion income and basic income for the Italian case. The Centre for European Reform (CER) recently effected a simulation in order to compare the efficiency of a conditional measure of the GMI family (like the Italian RMI) with a basic income of the NIT type (De Vincenti and Pollastri, 2001).

Assuming that other benefits were eliminated, the authors found a saving of about €28.5 billion which, together with an *imposta sul reddito delle persone fisiche* (IRPEF – tax on personal income) reform, would finance €3,100 worth of basic income or alternatively a GMI with a threshold value of €8,264.[38] In both cases the economic situation for all Italian families would improve,[39] especially for the families of the poor, and inequality would be reduced.

The GMI would favour very poor families (with annual incomes below €7,748) and middle-high incomes. Basic income being less selective, would favour poor families (between €7,748 and €15,496) and middle incomes; both policies would benefit families without elderly people, especially NIT, but while GMI would favour mono-nuclear families in redistribution, the basic income would be higher for big families.

The second study uses an econometric model, which considers work participation as an endogenous variable and evaluates the effects that the intro-duction of the basic income could have on it and on employment displacement (Serati, 1999).

The author assumes that basic income can have three effects: elimination of unemployment benefits, higher taxation and an increase in money transfers of the population.

If the effects of these aspects on work participation are assessed, the conclusion is that a basic income does not create disincentives to work either in absolute terms or in comparison with GMI. As a matter of fact, if the aggregate result of the three components is analysed, the values of the impact coefficients on work participation are positive. The only problem would be a temporary displacement of work for women in the south of the country due to increased mobility, but these effects would disappear in the long term, in particular due to the high significance of the positive values of the coefficients connected with the decrease of unemployment benefits (up to + 0.793) for a male worker in the south. This provides empirical confirmation of the avoidance of the various 'traps'.

7. Basic Income: A Utopia Which can Come True

While the second generation of GMIs began to appear on the European scene, strengthening the social protection system in the European Union and laying the foundations for greater stability and homogeneity on which the new forms of governance of social policies (like the Open Method Coordination) could be based, another debate on minimum income policies – that on basic income – continued to spread underground.

This time, however, perhaps spurred by the introduction of GMI systems in the member countries, the debate on basic income did not remain confined to the philosophical sphere. The proposal of Schmitter and Bauer (2001) for a European dividend, for example, contains features that appear to be financially feasible. The debate that followed in the *Journal of European Social Policy* showed that the basic income discussion was maturing and the ideas were beginning to be culturally acceptable. Both public opinion and institutions began to consider income as a possible right of citizenship.

In this paper we have used two focal variables for a comparative study of minimum income policies – poverty and work. At the dawn of a new millennium poverty is still far from being defeated, not only in the Third World but also in more developed countries.[40] The concept of poverty varies from poor societies to rich ones and its causes are different too. In the former, deprivation concerns the basic means of subsistence. In Sen's words the level and number of functionings are elementary, while in the rich world there is an increase in the causes of social exclusion and the risk of poverty appears to be longitudinal (one can enter this condition and leave it many times)

The old distributive welfare system founded on Keynes' ideas, whose function was to protect people from social risks when no labour-market protection was possible, is anachronistic at a time when living beyond 70 is common (Ferrera, 1998). Considering the money now spent on social security, especially in southern Europe, we could say that old age is a social risk overprotected by European welfare systems, especially in comparison with poverty.

If we consider that on average the rich live longer than the poor, the issue is not only one of intergenerational equity but of equality and social justice.

In this case a basic income could solve both the problem of extreme poverty and that of inequality, especially if the provision took the form of an income (not property) so as to reduce the risk of poverty in the long term. Basic income could be justified on the grounds that in an ever richer world, extreme poverty is no longer acceptable, nor can social exclusion be tolerated in rich societies where this is caused by illness, old age or precarious working conditions, in short, by situations of risk.

How can a society which produces more, redistribute its new added value in the best way? If inequality increases it is because redistribution mechanisms are less and less transparent. A basic income would partly modify this situation. In particular, the all-inclusive universalism of basic income seems to be a better solution than guaranteed minimum income, especially considering the limited success that GMIs have had in Europe so far, which concern only a limited number of potential beneficiaries, with peaks of exclusion in southern Europe. We know that, unlike in the USA, in Europe poverty is closely related to an individual's position on the labour market. This explains the usefulness of minimum income instruments like MII, which make it easier for a person to enter the job market.

We have also pointed out that the basic income solution joins the fight against poverty and liberation *from* work. Basic income, unlike MII, questions the 'work society' and does not try to find solutions inside it. It aims at achieving targets not only from the point of view of social justice and individual freedom but also from a general economic perspective.

In order for basic income to be successful, however, its amount should reach a certain level. The conclusions of this paper on the sustainability of basic income are that, while a high level of basic income does not seem to be feasible, its partial and gradual introduction would be possible. This would not mean giving up either a full extension of its use in the future or the possibility of obtaining immediate effects. Even a less generous measure would help to defeat poverty and offer individuals more choice.

However, a quasi-basic income should be accompanied by conditional measures for those who are more at risk (elderly, women, unemployed, big families, working poor). We have seen that the impact of the basic income is more homogeneous for type of income and family than the GMI. Therefore complementarity exists between a universalistic measure and selective instruments for very low incomes (under €7,748) as well as for particular socially disadvantaged groups. In the latter case, some social inclusion projects could be useful.

This two-level solution would be more pragmatic and easier to introduce than a radical introduction of basic income, which would be difficult to legitimize in a work-oriented society. The main difference between the two options is that a partial basic income takes for granted the present labour market situation and prepares the ground for change. Introducing a basic income from the very start would mean refusing today's concept of work and proposing an alternative model. To date there are no political groups capable of proposing this social and cultural revolution to their electors. It would be wise, however, to start presenting the elements that justify its introduction both from the point of view of economy and effectiveness.

Basic income creates more occupation and frees part of a person's time, creating flexibility in the labour market. 'Flexicurity', by which is meant the combination of flexibility and social security, can thus derive from basic income policies and not only from policies that annul workers' rights. There is no evidence that jobs can be increased by increasing job precariousness. Weakening the position of insiders (apart from the special privileges of a few) does not seem to be the way to a more just society.

For these reasons, basic income remains a feasible proposal and one to be hoped for. Several ethical reasons would justify its introduction, related to the right to freedom of life choices for all and more job opportunities with a consequent improvement of women's condition. It is feasible because it is effective from the point of view of the economic situation in general and economic and labour growth (it would prevent disincentives to work).

We conclude with a proposal deriving from what has been said so far. We have seen the partial failure of European experience with guaranteed minimum income policies due to the low level of the subsidies and the small number of beneficiaries able and willing to meet the many conditions. However, a basic income proposal would meet great opposition at a national level, and is difficult to defend in a still meritocratic society, which considers work as the only mechanism of income distribution. This society is also founded on the *do ut des* principle (the principle of reciprocity), particularly dangerous if it is the only value on which social policies are based. It is dangerous because it does not take into account differences in the starting positions of individuals and protects the more corporative and lobbyistic aspects of the welfare state.

A plan of action at a supranational level would be more likely to succeed. Several authors have proposed basic income for all European citizens. Considering the growing capacity of intervention of EU institutions and its resources, this proposal would be easier to realize although less useful than one involving the poorer parts of the world.

Among the problems commonly debated at international political meetings, the poverty of underdeveloped countries is one of the most alarming together with the demography problem, the environmental situation and fatal contagious diseases like AIDS. A global basic income could help solve at least two of these problems, if it was financed through the taxation of waste. The richer countries would contribute more to this global redistribution.

If there were international political institutions with a sufficient capacity of governance they would have two reasons to propose this solution: the fight against poverty and the prevention of a world ecological catastrophe. Countries would have to pay according to their level of pollution; they could recoup this by charging the industries responsible for pollution and favour non-polluting behaviours with tax exemptions. It would not be difficult to find a technical and at the same time an economic justification.

The problem is the capacity of intervention of supranational institutions; this problem does not concern basic income only. Which international institution would be strong enough to propose or to impose a solution of this kind? Theoretical arguments and studies of empirical simulations on basic income can help promote its cultural and ethical acceptance, not support it politically. It seems we are in front of Zenone's famous paradox: although scientific debate has wings to soar, the impression is that it will never affect political and institutional power.

Notes

1 A similar version of this chapter was published in 'Redditi di base e misure selettive di attivazione: antitesi o convivenza?', in *L'Assistenza sociale*, No. 3–4, July-December 2002.

2 University of Ancona, Italy.

3 Simon's interest in basic income was known in 1998, from a letter he sent to the organizers of the 7th Congress of the Basic Income European Network (see *Basic Income*, No. 28, February 1998). In the following number of this BIEN newsletter there is a conversation with Tobin ('James Tobin, the demogrant and the future of US policy'). This newsletter is available on the BIEN internet site, http://www.bien.be

4 Obviously, there are enormous differences in the ways in which policies are understood and put into practice. What we want to underline here is the hegemony of liberal thinking, as Michele Salvati said ('Reformers at the window, waiting for Godot" *Repubblica*, June 17, 2002). The problem is the labelling as 'liberal' those authors who are antithetical to each other, such as the liberal-conservative Robert Nozick and John Rawls, the supporter of democratic egalitarianism.

5 See the debate in the *Journal of European Social Policy*, started by Bauer and Schmitter (2001) and by the reactions of van Parijs and Vanderborght (2001) and Matsaganis (2001).

6 For instance, it is possible to combine a quasi-basic income providing a minimal floor and a second level of income protection for the working poor or similar groups.

7 In the third section we will limit ourselves to the ethical arguments underlying basic income. Its technical justifications will be dealt with in the fourth section better to compare existing basic income schemes from the point of view of efficiency and feasibility.

8 By 'elementary' definitions are meant the broad definitions usually adopted by the international associations of basic income supporters. For BIEN (Basic Income European Network), founded in 1986, basic income is 'an income unconditionally

granted to all on an individual basis, without means test or work requirement'. Equally general is the definition of the UK's Citizen Income Research Group (founded 1984), which underlines the 'inalienable right of all citizens independent of age, sex, faith, relationship with the labour market to a completely unconditional income'. These very general explanations leave space for different interpretations as to the amount, form of provision and ethical justification.

9 This term coined by Sen seems to be the only one capable of indicating the satisfaction of a person's needs making it possible for him/her to live with dignity in the community he/she belongs to. This concept has to do with individual perception of the results achieved in space and time and not with the opportunities at the individual's disposal (which Sen calls *capabilities*, often translated into Italian as *capacità* or *capabilità*). We will deal later on with the relationship between this important distinction and the right to basic resources.

10 This phenomenon occurs when the generosity of benefits attracts potential beneficiaries who do not live in the area.

11 More or less the same view was shared by T. Campanella in his *City of the Sun*. In the philosophical debate, Hobbes' vision – according to which the State should provide for poor citizens – is still present in later years in many authors, from Montesquieu to the social utopians (Morley-Fletcher, 1981).

12 See *De Subventione Pauperum, Sive de humanis necessitatibus* dated 1526, collected in the French edition of *De l'Assistance aux pauvres*, Bruxelles, Valero et Fils, 1943.

13 In the definition of subsistence Beveridge included, besides food, basic expenses for rent, fuel etc.

14 For a vision of Keynes' ideas on basic income, see Mead (1938).

15 These proposals were later collected in Robinson (1937).

16 For instance, the work of Tobin (1967) who, rather than dismantling the welfare state, is interested in combining the guarantee of a basic income with labour incentives.

17 For an interesting review, see Ayala (2000).

18 van Parijs (2000b), for example, considers it as a basic income with an ideologically liberal matrix, here called 'social dividend' with reference to the 'participants'society' on which Ackermann and Alstott's proposal is based (1999).

19 This happens when a household breaks up in order to be granted benefits. For an analysis of one such case in the Italian experience of Guaranteed Minimum Income, see Busilacchi (2000).

20 We do not think that amounts lower than the poverty threshold can be taken into consideration, at least from a theoretical point of view, although a *quasi basic income* may be useful from a political viewpoint to win over ideological resistance.

21 For an interesting analysis of the relationship between demand and supply for care-work connected with women's greater or smaller participation in the labour market, see Gorz (1994).

22 Groot's impossibility theorem (1999) states that basic income is too expensive to produce results and a basic income which is low enough to be financed would not be enough to create freedom in a person's life choices.

23 For a survey of the debate, see Busilacchi (2001).

24 We use this popular term in spite of doubts expressed elsewhere on its appropriateness (Busilacchi, 2001). The concept of dividend combines the co-ownership of a good offering a varying flow of resources with the sharing of those same resources. The basic income granted in Alaska is a perfect example of social dividend.

25 Like Paine these two authors present a proposal for a basic pension for the elderly (8,000 dollars a year to people over 67) and an amount of 80,000 dollars to each citizen over 21.

26 It may be confusing to put together under the label of liberal people like Rawls, Sen or van Parijs (who defines himself a left-wing liberal) on one hand and Ackermann, Nozick or Milton Friedman on the other. See note 3.

27 A culture of work seems to prevail not only in electoral majority groups but in Western society in general. This culture decidedly refuses to guarantee an income as a right.

28 In spite of the huge differences between the two approaches, neither system gives an autonomous role to minimum income policies but tends to guarantee income protection with other policies. Unlike Bismarck, Beveridge envisages a combination of insurance schemes and social assistance programmes, giving the latter a marginal role.

29 Beveridge himself saw minimum income as a target to be hit through social policies rather than through a particular scheme. Social democratic welfare programmes, which today follow the universalistic model, also see minimum income schemes as a marginal supplement to the labour market and a system of social services that already guarantee income, redistribution and social justice.

30 In Aguilar *et al.* (1995), the first two waves are merged into one. The minimum insertion incomes are classified as the 'second generation' of guaranteed minimum income schemes.

31 This characteristic is so egregious that it has been considered enough to identify the new southern European welfare system (see Leibfried, 1992). On the particular weakness of the welfare state of these countries, see also the classification of Gough (1996).

32 If we refer to the right to a 'minimum income', the term GMI paradoxically becomes synonymous with basic income.

33 We include this instrument in our taxonomy with some theoretical straining. It is actually a measure closer to the measures on minimum wages and social security cushions than to basic income. However, its technical similarity to NIT makes it possible to include it among the other minimum income models.

34 The consequence would be the end of the relationship between humble jobs and low wages together with the elimination of poverty. Nobody would be looking for a job simply to earn a living.

35 'Using Akerlof's terminology according to which there are no labels to indicate abilities', Granaglia analyses the possibility of the *target efficiency* degeneration of GMI policies, in which it is impossible to avoid a certain number of 'false positives, that is people who have access to payments without being eligible for them and of false negatives, that is people who have a right to benefits but no access to them' (Granaglia, 2001, p. 202).

36 It would be interesting to know how efficient GMI is from this point of view. How much of the money allocated fills the pockets of the poor and how much goes on administration? I am grateful to Daniel Raventós for making me think about it.

37 This phenomenon can be easily demonstrated empirically: all the equivalence scales adopted in the implementation of GMIs employ multiplication coefficients which assume economies of scale in family consumption. Therefore the total subsidy for a family, say, of four people will never be four times the subsidy for a single person.

38 In the case of the GMI all fiscal brackets would be reduced by about three percentage points, while the NIT would be accompanied by a two-rate system : 33 per cent for incomes up to €15,496 and 40 per cent for higher incomes.

39 Except for those with annual incomes between €60,950 and €71,797 in the case of the basic income.
40 The methodological instruments used focus on the relative dimension of poverty (and so they concern inequality more than deprivation) and do not isolate the time variable. In the presence of a generalized increase of *per capita* income, income inequalities can also increase, even if there is an absolute decrease in poverty.

References

Ackerman, B. and Alstott, A. 1999. *The stakeholder society* (Yale, Yale University Press).
Aguilar, M., Gaviria, M. and Laparra, M. 1995. *La caña y el pez. Estudio sobre los Salarios Sociales en las Communidades Autónomas* (Madrid, Fundación Foessa).
Ayala, L. 2000. *Las rentas mínimas en la reestructuracion de los estados de bienestar* (Madrid, Consejo Económico y Social de España – CES).
Atkinson, A. B. 1993. 'Participation income', in *Citizen's Income Bulletin*, No. 16, pp. 7–11.
_____ 1995. *Public economics in action. The basic income/flat tax proposal* (Oxford, Oxford University Press, Italian translation {1998} *Per un nuovo Welfare State* {Bari, Laterza}).
Barr, N. 1975. 'NIT and the redistribution of income', *Oxford Bulletin of Economics and Statistics*, Vol. 37, No. 1, pp. 29–48.
Bauer, M. W. and Schmitter, P. C. 2001. 'A (modest) proposal for expanding social citizenship in the European Union', *Journal of European Social Policy*, Vol. 11, No. 1, pp. 55–65.
Brittan, S. 1995. *Capitalism with a human face* (Aldershot, Edward Elgar).
_____ and Webb, S. 1991. *Beyond the welfare state. An examination of basic incomes in a market economy* (Aberdeen, Aberdeen University Press).
Busilacchi, G. 2000. 'RMI e means testing: il caso di Massa', *L'Assistenza sociale*, 3–4, pp. 139–167.
_____ 2001. 'Dividendo sociale e reddito di cittadinanza: una rilettura critica', in *Prisma*, 19/20, pp. 85–108.
Clasen, J. 1997. *Social insurance in Europe* (Bristol, Policy Press).
Commissione per l'analisi delle compatibilità macroeconomiche della spesa sociale. 1997. *L'istituto del minimo vitale: esperienze e proposte d riforma*, (Allegato al documenti di base n.3, a cura di Bosi, P., Ferrera, M. and Saraceno, C. Roma, Presidenza del Consiglio dei Ministri.
Cutler, T., Williams, K. and Williams, J. 1986. *Keynes, Beveridge and beyond* (London, Routledge and Kegan Paul).
De Francisco, A. and Raventós, D. 2002. 'Republicanismo y Renta Básica', in G. Pisarello (ed.), *Razones para una Renta Basica* (Madrid, Ed.Trotta).
De Vincenti, C. and Pollastri, C. 2001. 'Per un nuovo welfare: due 'universalismi' a confronto', in C. De Vincenti (ed.), *Famiglia, assistenza, fisco. Materiali per un welfare universalistico, 11th Report, CER-SPI* (Roma, Ediesse).
Esping-Andersen, G. 1990. *The three worlds of welfare capitalism* (Cambridge, Polity Press).
_____ 1999. *Social foundations of post-industrial economies* (Oxford, Oxford University Press; Italian translation {2000} *I fondamenti sociali delle economie post-industrial* (Bologna, Il Mulino).
Ferrera, M. 1998. *Le trappole del welfare* (Bologna, Il Mulino).
Friedman, M. 1962. *Capitalism and freedom* (Chicago, University of Chicago Press).
Genet, M. and van Parijs, P. 1992. 'Eurogrant', in *Basic Income Research Group Bulletin*, No. 15, pp. 4–7.

Gordon, D. and Townsend, P. (eds.) 2000. *Breadline Europe: The measurement of poverty* (Bristol, Policy Press).

Gorz, A. 1994. *Il lavoro debole* (Roma, Edizioni lavono).

Gough, I. 1996 'Social assistance in southern Europe', in *South European Society and Politics*, Vol. 1, No. 1, pp. 1–23.

_____ 2000. *Human capital, global needs and social policies* (Houndmills, Palgrave).

Granaglia, E. 2001. *Modelli di politica sociale* (Bologna, Il Mulino).

Groot, L. F. 1999. *Basic income and unemployment* (Amsterdam, Netherlands School for Social and Economic Policy Research).

Guibentif, P. and Bouget, D. 1997. *Minimum income policies in the European Union* (Lisbona, Uniao das Mutualidades Portuguesas).

Heikkilä, M. and Keskitalo, E. (eds.) 2001. *A comparative study of minimum income in seven European countries*, Synthesis Report (Brussels, European Commission).

Jordan, B., Agulnik, P., Burbidge, D. and Duffin, S. 2000. *Stumbling towards basic income* (London, Citizen's Income Study Centre, London School of Economics).

Kakwani, N.C. 1977. 'Redistributive effects of alternative negative income tax plans', in *Public Finance*, Vol. 32, No. 1, pp. 77–91.

Lampman, R.J. 1969. 'Expanding the American system of transfers to do more for the poor', in *Wisconsin Law Review*, 2.

Leibfried, S. 1992. 'Towards a European welfare state', in S. Ferge and J. Kolberg (eds.) *Social policy in a changing Europe* (Boulder, Westview Press), pp. 279–345.

Magri, T. 1978. 'Thomas Paine e il pensiero politico della rivoluzione borghese', in T. Magri (ed.), *I diritti dell'uomo* (Roma, Editori Riuniti).

Matsaganis, M. 2001. 'The trouble with the Euro-stipendium', *Journal of European Social Policy*, Vol.11, No.4, pp.346–348.

Mead, J. E. 1936. *Economics analysis and policy* (Oxford, Oxford University Press).

_____ 1938. 'Consumers' credits and unemployment', *Economic Journal*, March.

_____ 1989. *Agathotopia: The economics of partnership* (Milano, Feltrinelli).

Mill, J.S. 1987{1849}. *Principles of political economy*, 2nd edition (New York, Augustus Kelly).

Ministero del Tesoro, Ufficio per l'informazione e i Rapporti con la Stampa 2000. *Il dividendo sociale*, dattiloscritto 15 dicembre.

Mirabile, M.L. (ed.) 1991. *Il reddito minimo garantito. Il Welfare tra nuovi e vecchi diritti* (Roma, Ediesse).

Morley-Fletcher, E. 1981. 'Per una storia dell'idea di "minimo sociale garantito"', in *Quaderni della Rivista Trimestrale*, ottobre 1980 – marzo 1981, pp.279–321.

_____ 1989. 'Un'ipotesi di eredità sociale', *Politica ed Economia*, 6.

Nozick, R. 1974. *Anarchy, State and utopia* (Oxford, Blackwell; Italian translation {1981} *Stato e utopia* {Monnier, Firenze}).

Pinilla, R. 2001. 'Es posible una Renta Básica eficiente? Evaluación económica de la Renta Básica', in D. Raventós (ed.) *La Renta básica* (Barcelona, Ariel).

Raventós, D. (ed.) 2001. *La renta bàsica* (Barcelona, Ariel).

Rawls, J. 1971. *A theory of justice* (Harvard, Harvard University Press; Italian translation {1991} *Una teoria della giustizia*, quarta edizione, {Milano, Feltrinelli}).

Robinson, J. 1937. *Essay in the theory of employment* (Oxford, Basil Blackwell).

Room, G. (ed.) 1991. *National policies to combat social exclusion. 1991 Report* (Bath, Centre for Research in European Social and Employment Policy –CRESEP).

Saraceno, C. (ed.) 2002. *Social assistance dynamics in Europe. National and local poverty regimes* (Bristol, Policy Press).

Scharpf, F. W. 2000. 'Basic income and social Europe', in L. Groot and L. J. van der Veen (eds.), *Basic income on the agenda. Policies and politics* (Amsterdam, Amsterdam University Press).

Sen, A. K. 1992. *Inequality reexamined* (Oxford, Oxford University Press; Italian translation {1994} *La diseguaglianza. Un riesame critico* {Bologna, Il Mulino}).

———— 1999. *Development as freedom* (New York, Alfred A. Knopf).

Serati, M. 1999. 'Reddito di cittadinanza: un'opportunità o una trappola insidiosa per l'occupazione? Una verifica empirica per il caso italiano', in *Liuc Papers*, No. 60, Serie Economia e Impresa, 17, gennaio.

Silver, H. 1994. 'Social exclusion and social soldarity: Three paradigms', in *International Labour Review*, Vol. 133 (5–6), pp. 531–578.

Simon, H. 2000. 'UBI and the Flat Tax', *Boston Review*, October-November.

Steiner, H. 1992. 'Three just taxes', in P. van Parijs *Arguing for basic income: Ethical foundations for a radical reform* (London, Verso).

Tobin, J. 1966. 'The case for an income guarantee', *The Public Interest*, Vol. 4, pp. 31–41.

————, Pechman, J. and Mieszkowski, P. 1967. 'Is a negative income tax practical?', *Yale Law Journal*, 77, pp. 1–27.

van der Veen, R. and van Parijs, P. 1986. 'Una via capitalista al comunismo', in *Zona Abierta*, No. 46–47.

van Parijs, P. 1992. *Arguing for basic income: Ethical foundations for a radical reform* (London, Verso).

———— 1995. *Real freedom for all. What (if anything) can justify capitalism?* (Oxford, Oxford University Press).

———— 1996. 'Il sussidio universale contro la disoccupazione', in *L'Assistenza sociale*, 2, April–June, pp. 23–36.

———— 2000. *Basic income: A simple and powerful idea for the 21st Century*, paper presented to the 8th Congress of BIEN (Basic Income European network), Berlin, 6–7 October.

———— 2000b. 'A basic income for all', *Boston Review*, Oct–Nov.

———— and Vanderborght, Y. 2001. 'From Euro-stipendium to Euro-dividend', *Journal of European Social Policy*, Vol. 11, No. 4, pp. 342–346.

Widerquist, K. 1999. 'Reciprocity and the guaranteed income', *Politics and Society*, Vol. 33, No. 3, Sept.

29

THE UNIVERSAL GRANT
AND INCOME SUPPORT IN SPAIN
AND THE BASQUE COUNTRY

Luis Sanzo-González[1]

1. Introduction

Throughout the 1980s and 1990s southern European countries gradually introduced universal income support systems, generally along the lines of the French jobseeker's minimum income allowance (*revenu minimum d'insertion*). In Spain, the Autonomous Communities were the driving force behind this process, which was initiated in the Basque Country (*Comunidad Autónoma de Euskadi*). However, in view of problems entailed by the RMI-type of income protection, it is worth studying the possibility of moving from a traditional income support model to a system centred on a universal grant. This paper analyses the implications of introducing a universal grant in Spain (or in the Basque Country, which can set its own fiscal and social policies).

2. Traditional Income Support Systems

2.1 The Introduction of Income Support Systems in Southern Europe

France was the first Southern European country to introduce a universal income support system with the adoption in December 1988 of the Law on the Jobseeker's Minimum Income Allowance (RMI). This scheme was to have a decisive influence on the subsequent course of social policy in France.

The French RMI was the first example of a new type of income support that evolved in western countries during the 1980s. In contrast to the systems established in central and northern Europe and in North America, the RMI not only had the traditional aim of guaranteeing a minimum income for people without adequate resources, but also a social objective, that of securing the social integration of beneficiaries.

This new principle of social integration linked to the provision of income support, reinforced after the introduction of the French RMI, had a decisive influence on the ideas formulated by European institutions. For example, in 1992, Recommendation 92/441 of the EEC Council of Ministers invited member States to recognize a person's basic right to sufficient, stable and reliable resources and social assistance as part of a consistent overall policy for combating social exclusion. The right to adequate resources and social assistance was therefore to be backed by measures promoting economic and social integration, especially in the fields of health, housing, training and access to employment.

Subsequent initiatives in other southern European countries were also modelled on the French RMI, such as the *Rendimento Minimo Garantido* approved in Portugal in 1997 or the *Reddito Minimo d'Inserimento* introduced as an experiment in 39 local authorities in Italy in 1999.[2]

In Spain this process began much earlier, in 1989, at the initiative of the Autonomous Communities following the Basque Country's experiment, which also drew some of its inspiration from the French RMI.[3] It is noteworthy that, unlike all the other southern European countries, Spain has opted for a strictly regional income support system. The central Government's marginal role in this area of social policy is limited to possibly coordinating regional action.

2.2 The Disadvantages of Traditional Systems: The Universal Grant as an Alternative

The Spanish example shows that, when regional income support systems have a substantial economic and demographic impact, as in the Basque Country and the Madrid region, they become entrenched. This is then used to justify the income support policy, providing evidence that it is both needed and viable.

The RMI-type of protective system nevertheless raises awkward issues. One is the vast amount of red tape needed to check on beneficiaries in order to ascertain their income and assets, to decide not only whether to grant social assistance, but also to their continued eligibility for it. These measures are designed to prevent fraud, which tends to spread as income support systems are strengthened and, in the long term, leads to beneficiaries becoming heavily dependent on allowances.[4] This explains the political authorities' obsession with social integration and preventing idleness, which is reflected in the creation and spread of programmes to check on availability for work.

These management methods, essentially defined by the idea of supervision, often cause potential beneficiaries to drop out of social assistance networks so as to assert a modicum of independence and personal dignity *vis-à-vis* institutional services.[5]

The substantial economic and social costs resulting from this cumbersome and often repressive method of managing income support policies cannot be justified economically or socially. Studies conducted in the Basque Country show that fraud occurs on a fairly small scale – between 5 per cent and 16 per cent of the total cost of an income support system with only a very limited impact on GDP (generally around 0.25 per cent, with a maximum of 1 per cent in some Nordic countries). At the same time, the effort to curb fraud and dependency contrasts with the financial restrictions placed on the social services' positive steps to promote social integration.

Another problem, especially in countries with high unemployment and casualization of labour, is the difficulty of guaranteeing the whole population, particularly young people, sufficient financial stability through traditional income support systems. In the countries of southern Europe, these programmes are designed to meet the financial needs of families, not individuals. They therefore fail to deal with one of the thorniest social issues – support for access to an independent life for younger generations hit by unemployment, job insecurity and/or low wages. Studies on poverty in the Basque Country have revealed the magnitude of hidden poverty among the young and the relationship between this social ill and the structural demographic crisis that has taken hold since the 1980s.[6]

The predominant reaction to the limitations of traditional programmes has been, at least in the Basque Country, a growing demand for universal protection and social assistance for individuals rather than households. One of the principal features of the recent trend in income support in the Basque Country, which has the most highly developed model in Spain, has indeed been an approach gradually tending towards universal, individual allowances.

In this context, characterized both by pressure to individualize benefits and by a bureaucratization of public services scarcely justifiable in social terms, it makes sense to study the possibility of moving from a traditional income support model to a system centred on the universal grant. We can consider several arguments.

First, in relation to eligibility for income support, a universal grant system obviously has the advantage of sparing potential beneficiaries the control procedures that typify traditional schemes. Unlike these schemes, which demand continual proof of inadequate resources, the universal grant implies the *ex ante* unconditional provision of the means necessary to realize the universal right to existence. This approach has the merit of not creating any inducement to fraud and preventing the stigmatization of beneficiaries, thus avoiding feelings of humiliation and being different from the rest of society.[7]

From an administrative viewpoint, the decision to forgo any attempt to evaluate beneficiaries' assets and income, or to check on their willingness to work, also helps to simplify and rationalize the management of social policy. In countries like Spain, where management of the income support system is the responsibility of the social services, they could then turn their attention to more general measures to meet social integration needs.

Lastly, given the particular demographic situation in southern European countries, the introduction of a universal grant might help young people to become independent. As the universal grant would establish a universal system of economic support for individuals, and would guarantee a regular adequate source of income, it might encourage the setting-up of many new young households and thereby remove current obstacles to social and demographic regeneration. The introduction of a universal grant could therefore play a vital role in a strategy to stimulate population growth in some regions of southern Europe.

The absence of central government intervention in this area of social policy, to which we referred earlier, might paradoxically favour introduction of a guaranteed income for the whole population. This is because no set relationship has been defined between economic, fiscal and social policies, which, on account of inbuilt inertias, could cause difficulties and delay the emergence of new patterns of social assistance. Hence the Spanish situation makes it possible not only to theorize about an alternative to RMI-type income support, but also to think of completely new approaches to social policy such as the introduction of a universal grant.

3. The Characteristics of an Alternative to Income Support that would be Based on the Model of a Universal Grant

The central thesis of this paper is that it is now possible in Spain (or in the Basque Country, since the Autonomous Community has the power to devise fiscal and social policies), to establish a universal grant that would replace regional income support programmes. It is, however, necessary to examine the implications of instituting a universal grant so as to ensure that it would be consistent with the main objectives of current social policy and poverty alleviation measures, and with fiscal policy that is either already in place or under discussion in Spain or the Basque Country. I will therefore try to identify the main elements which should be investigated when formulating a precise proposal to bring in a universal grant.

3.1 An Initial Goal – Poverty Alleviation (Subsistence Guarantee)

In the long term, efforts to introduce a universal grant must certainly be directed towards establishing adequate levels of well-being and possibly even towards freeing people from the need to engage in a productive activity on the market in order to achieve these levels of well-being. The final objective of the universal grant is, after all, to ensure real individual freedom by permanently supplying the financial resources people require to attain economic independence and develop their own personal design for life.

In the short and medium term, however, it seems more prudent to direct efforts at the less ambitious, albeit especially important, goal of combating poverty. Caution is recommended not only because the measure must be financed, or because of the necessarily experimental nature of the introduction of a universal grant, but also because social policy should be targeted on the most destitute.

The proposed approach has two main consequences. First, when defining the model, account must be taken of the need to focus social expenditure on the most disadvantaged sections of the population so as to ensure that public resources are allocated with maximum efficiency. Second, the universal grant should initially be quite small and its aim should be no more than to provide the whole population with a sufficient income to cover subsistence and essential requirements.

Before specifying the possible amount of the grant required to meet subsistence needs in Spain (or the Basque Country), we must first consider what the universal grant would have to cover.

3.2 At the Outset a Mixture of a Household and an Individual Grant

In its classic form, the universal grant is envisaged as a standard amount paid to every individual. This approach is an extension of the principle of citizenship and of common and equal participation in the capital stock produced by society, which in turn ushers in the prospect of a universal right to a living and real economic freedom. The principle of an individual right is essential and implicit in any approach involving the universal grant.

Nonetheless, the principle of individual freedom should be inseparable from the equality of rights in both the theory and the practice of the universal grant. It is therefore necessary to take account of the economies of scale associated with the cohabitation typical of most households in any country. As living together under one roof can take various forms, the initial uniformity of the universal grant would in fact result in inequalities in real economic capacity. This *de facto* inequality affects freedom in that the personal freedom associated with access to the universal grant, i.e. the actual value of this freedom measured as capacity to meet vital needs, differs greatly according to cohabitation mode.

The solution to this problem cannot lie in formulae which necessarily entail a preference for one form of cohabitation over another, at least not if the principle of personal freedom of decision is to be respected. Ways must therefore be found of making it easier for individuals to take genuinely independent decisions, irrespective of whether they choose to remain single, marry or live with someone.

Consequently, if the aim is to launch a measure that can coherently combine personal freedom and equality, a universal grant that is truly uniform and equal for the whole population (in the sense of ensuring that the freedom it guarantees is really equal in value) can be devised only by neutralizing the differential effect introduced by the mode of cohabitation. It is vital to find an answer to this conundrum when introducing a necessarily small universal grant.

The solution we propose is the introduction of a household grant, in addition to the individual grant, which would cover the average level of expenditure common to all cohabiting units irrespective of their size.[8] The central element of this proposal is therefore the introduction of a mixed, two-part universal grant consisting of an individual and a household component.[9]

Studies of poverty in the Basque Country suggest that, at the outset, a universal grant covering essential subsistence requirements in Spain (or the Basque Country) could be based on the following:

- an annual household grant of €3,120 (€260 per month) applicable to all households, including people living alone;
- an individual grant of €2,160 (€180 per month).

The aforementioned individual level would be adjusted for dependants under 25 (for example, €1,020 annually for youngsters aged between 14 and 24 and €780 annually for children under 14). In a lone-parent family, the first dependant, irrespective of age, would be treated like an adult and would therefore receive an annual grant of €2,160.

We provide some examples of the way in which the guaranteed level of the universal grant in various cohabitation situations would compare with the income support currently provided by the Basque Country, which is the most generous in Spain.

Available statistics indicate that this system would make it possible to ensure that the whole population had an income sufficient to cover basic needs[10] and

Table 29.1 Level of the universal grant for various cohabitation situations[11] (euros per month)

Universal grant	Household unit	Individuals (aggregate amount)	Total universal grant	Present situation Basque Country[a]
Cohabitation situations				
Single person	260	180	440	408
Couple	260	360	620	537
Couple + child < 14	260	425	685	588
Couple + child < 14 + child > 14	260	510	770	640
Single parent + child < 14	260	360	620	537
Single parent + 2 children < 14	260	425	685	588
Three adults	260	540	800	588

(a) Means-tested income support under the present system.

would, at the same time, facilitate access to income equivalent to the minimum wage, even for single persons (€440 per month as against €442.20, the present minimum wage in Spain).

Given that Spain is one of the countries with the lowest per capita GDP in Europe, the proposed levels of the universal grant might serve as a reference for a European minimum guaranteed income, an aspect to which we will return later.

3.3 A Policy to Promote Access to Employment

One fundamental aspect of the universal grant is its unconditional nature. No *quid pro quo* is required for the grant and no specific action has to be taken to instil certain personal behavioural patterns. Nor does it depend on specific conditions regarding economic activity. It is not necessary to be available for employment, or to seek paid work, in order to receive the grant.

Most proponents of the unconditional nature of the universal grant nevertheless believe that prevailing social attitudes would normally lead to greater participation in socially beneficial activities in the commercial or non-commercial sector. These attitudes would be encouraged by the possibility of obtaining income additional to that earned from an economic activity.

Nevertheless, as the universal grant would constitute a guaranteed basic income, it is possible to imagine a hypothetical scenario in which no one would see any reason to participate in the requisite productive activities. That would happen if the level of the universal grant was so high that it would cover not only personal subsistence, but also a satisfactory level of well-being. In that case, the possible lack of enough human resources to sustain the productive system and the attendant loss of economic wealth should be borne in mind.

The problem is not so much one of parasitism versus participation as that of the disparity between participation in desired activities and participation in the activities needed for social and economic regeneration. Clearly many of these activities are not very stimulating and do not therefore give rise to any sense of commitment unless an added attraction exists.

Although this problem should not arise if the initial universal grant is fairly low, it should be considered from the beginning. It is a problem also found in traditional income support systems, which are often discredited because they are unable to reintegrate recipients into economic activity and employment.

One option might be to espouse Gorz's call (1985) to make active collaboration in the creation of wealth a condition for a citizen's entitlement to the universal grant. In view of the fact that this proposal would entail some restriction of personal freedom, it would, however, seem wiser to think of indirect mechanisms ensuring, for example, that those responsible for safeguarding economic regeneration and the functioning of the economic system have appropriate financial incentives.

Several measures could be contemplated to that end. The first line of action might consist in introducing a supplement to the universal grant for persons who, through their productive activity, help to regenerate and improve knowledge and social capital. This supplement would not, strictly speaking, form part of the universal grant itself, but in practice it would probably be combined with it. In this context, a formula for encouraging people to take a job (reminiscent of the incentive built into Basque income support) might be as follows:

Incentive or employment bonus = (25% earned income + [10% earned income − (2* individual universal grant)])

Nevertheless, two limits would have to be set – an upper limit for the deduction and a minimum for the bonus. The purpose of the first limit, which in Spain might amount to €3,000 a year, would be to avoid an excessively large sum being deducted from high incomes. The aim of the second limit would be to boost the smallest incomes by guaranteeing a minimum bonus of about €1,000 a year.

One of the advantages of the proposed formula is that final disposable income will generally tend to go up in proportion to earned income, thereby avoiding too much distortion of the general mechanism for determining the price of labour on the market.

The second kind of measure to encourage people to find a job and shun the black economy is linked to the retention of contributory pensions based on individual contributions during working life, which could be drawn in addition to the universal grant (in the same way as earned income).[12]

A third type of measure might go more in the direction of some degree of capitalization of available time devoted to work, which would vary according to the period of labour that had been built up. Any time worked by a citizen over and above a certain stint fixed by the public institutions would give rise to specific economic compensation in the form of an increase in the guaranteed individual universal grant.

The underlying purpose of the three proposed incentives to work would be to compensate persons who, through their labour, not only help to finance part of their own grant, but also that received now or in the future by the rest of the population. These employment incentives are therefore predicated more on the principle of recognizing personal contributions to society than on the idea of a *quid pro quo* or even of civic duty.

If the proposed measures are insufficient to secure the correct functioning of the economy and society, we should consider the possibility of introducing an obligation to participate in social regeneration, defined as a minimum period of time contributed to work or to other socially productive activities, as suggested by Atkinson (1996) or, before him, Gorz (1985). Once the original form of the universal grant became established, above all as a full guarantee of individual freedom, it might actually become an indispensable means of maintaining economic production.

The various proposals discussed are not inconsistent with the principle of egalitarian access to the universal grant in terms of participation in the capital and knowledge accumulated by society throughout its history. This justification remains valid only if the recipient of the grant contributes in turn to the regeneration and/or amplification of this capital and knowledge. We should not therefore reject an approach which would take account of a differential contribution to this process of regeneration and accumulation.

3.4 The Complementarity of the Universal Grant and Social Policy

Although in some radical proposals the introduction of the universal grant would be accompanied by the complete elimination of all other welfare benefits, most advocates of this measure propose merely a simplification or scaling down of the present system of benefits. Indeed, it would seem prudent at first to retain as much as possible of the general system of protection existing when the universal grant is brought in, so as to ensure that its introduction constitutes a real and effective step forward in the redistribution of the social product.

This implies the retention not only of the system of contributory pensions as we have suggested, but also of various non-contributory benefits of a structural nature (especially those awarded to the disabled or elderly), which are a way of introducing the principles of the universal grant in some sections of the population. The spread of the universal grant should thus complement existing non-contributory protective mechanisms without replacing them. The aim would be rather to adjust existing allowances so that they square better with the principles of universality and unconditionality of access that characterize the universal grant.

The introduction of the universal grant must in all events be compatible with the maintenance and expansion of general public services, especially the health, education and social services. When introducing the universal grant, it would therefore be essential to preserve the general and specific foundations of the welfare state.

3.5 Fiscal Management of the Universal Grant

It is normally assumed that the universal grant will be distributed by the competent political institution through a monthly cheque to each member of the population. In a country like Spain it would, however, be simpler to handle basic income by means of negative income tax.

An approach based on negative tax has two main advantages. The first is that it forges a direct link between social revenue and social expenditure within a policy on income security. The devising and management of fiscal policy and social policies including the universal grant will inevitably have to be coordinated in order to avoid social revenue and social expenditure getting out of step.

The second advantage relates to an argument advocated by proponents of the universal grant, at least in Spain: tax should absorb the additional income derived from the universal grant by the most favoured social classes, so that its introduction does not undermine the national redistribution of income. In the present situation, characterized by widespread poverty and the absence of well-being, the aim is to improve the circumstances of the most disadvantaged groups rather than those of the whole population, or even of the majority. The universal grant must reduce rather than accentuate the Mathieu effect of social policy under which the more affluent derive greater benefit from social policies than the poor (Deleeck, 1979).

If the principle of the fiscal neutralization of most universal grants is accepted when they are first introduced, there is little sense in distributing a monthly cheque since, in most cases, the State would claw back the sum through taxation. Annual tax settlement, accompanied by a policy of periodically withholding some income, seems much more realistic.

Of course, it is possible to object that, in these circumstances, the social vision behind the entitlement to a universal grant disappears, but two factors militate against this. First, the share corresponding to the universal grant is deducted in all cases from the basic amount of tax payable. Second, anyone can decide at any time to live temporarily or permanently solely on the income obtained from the universal grant and to organize their life around that possibility. It is precisely that possibility which makes the universal grant an element that genuinely widens people's range of options.

The suggestion that the universal basic income should be received through an annual tax payment does, however, raise other issues for consideration. The first difficulty lies in the organization of the two types of grants proposed (individual and household, i.e. covering several persons). A simple solution would consist in accompanying individual tax returns, which might attract negative tax and therefore income transfer, by an additional collective declaration relating to all the independent adults in the household.

The second much larger difficulty occurs when considering the situation of people who urgently require their universal basic income for subsistence. In such cases, an annual tax assessment would not seem appropriate.

This problem can, however, be easily resolved by combining the principle of an annual tax return with the possibility of regularly collecting the universal grant unconditionally at any time. Persons in need should therefore be allowed to apply for an advance on their universal grant and their share of the household grant. These advances would be provided by the relevant tax authorities on an automatic, unconditional basis and recipients should be permitted to choose between monthly or quarterly payments which could be kept up regularly, should the people concerned so request.

Where people have no access to other forms of income (wages or contributory pensions) the universal grant could be distributed through the payment of a monthly cheque, as for the non-contributory pensions or allowances that now exist in most European countries. This system would also apply to the payment of the grant for dependent minors. If advance payments are made (through non-contributory pensions or applications for advances on the universal grant proper), an annual tax settlement would ultimately sort out each individual situation by taking account of all income obtained, including advances. The model outlined thus combines the application of the principles of negative tax with the possibility of regular, unconditional access to the grant as foreseen in the classic approach.

In Spain, the current personal income tax system already makes allowance for individual and family subsistence levels, which would facilitate the approach put forward in this paper. However, it does not apply the principles of negative tax by compensating persons with inadequate income. Since the subsistence-level system in fact applies only to persons filing tax returns, whose income is above that level, it introduces the typical Mathieu discrimination effect mentioned by Deleeck (1979).

3.6 The Role of a Complementary but Residual Income Support System

Those who champion the idea of a universal grant argue that it would be a more effective means of combating poverty than traditional protective measures. This assertion indulges in too much wishful thinking. We must not reject the hypothesis that a general system of protection, even if based on the introduction of a universal grant, might still be insufficient. The often restrictive manner in which the central government adjusts benefits to inflation is apparent in the fact that some contributory or non-contributory allowances or pensions tend to lose value and end up below the poverty line.

If only for that reason, it would probably be necessary to maintain a complementary system of traditional, means-tested, family-based income support. This system should make it possible to check, as a fundamental duty, that essential needs were really covered and that certain groups who might initially be excluded from the universal grant (some categories of immigrants, for example) were protected.

Above all, this control function should serve to detect any malfunctioning of the general social welfare model and, more particularly, of the universal grant and, if any faults were found, to refashion the grant. The universal grant should therefore be constantly adjusted so as to equal the maximum quantitative and qualitative impact of traditional programmes of income security. All the aspects that might influence the effective coverage of basic needs (size and composition of households, special personal needs due to disability, for example, local or regional differences in price levels, additional transport costs, etc.) should be borne in mind when defining the general model of the universal grant.

In this context, the main problem is certainly the treatment of housing costs. One alternative might consist in retaining the present means-tested housing allowances. This option would, however, force the most disadvantaged sections of the population to remain economically dependent on the social services. A more attractive option might be to provide a tax credit on top of the universal grant in order to meet additional housing costs within predetermined, standardized limits.

Over and above the various aspects we have considered, the traditional income support system must continue to fulfil some socially important functions, irrespective of whether the universal grant is introduced. In particular, it must endeavour to meet the exceptional needs of the population (emergency support) and to ensure a minimum standard of living and well-being, by facilitating access to the goods, equipment and facilities required in order to maintain an appropriate environment, especially with regard to housing conditions.

Action to promote social integration, which today centres on guaranteeing income, must also be pursued in view of the success observed in this field after the introduction of RMI-type income support systems. The need to concentrate social work on integration is precisely one of the reasons for arguing that, essentially, income should be guaranteed by general protective mechanisms (universal grant) and not through traditional income support schemes.

At the same time, given that income support has allowed some people to realize certain social rights and to participate in individual integration strategies, efficient mechanisms should be provided so that access to the social services can still be facilitated once income security is chiefly managed through the universal grant. In this connection, it must be remembered that exclusion processes are not solely economic in origin.

One practical solution consists in making it possible for applications for an advance on the universal grant, to which we referred earlier, to be submitted not only to the tax authorities, but also to the social services as recognized intermediaries. This would be a means of preserving the most disadvantaged groups' access to all their social rights.

3.7 A European Framework for the Universal Grant

One of the fundamental aspects of the universal grant is that it should be automatically available to all members of a given society, including non-citizens who are entitled to permanent residence. In view of the implications for immigration or economic competitiveness (impact on wage costs), it would certainly be necessary to think of a universal grant system resting on common bases throughout the European Union (EU).

We can give two further reasons in favour of a European approach. First, it would turn the principle of social intervention by the EU into a reality by means of a specific measure that would offset the devil-take-the-hindmost rationale underpinning the total liberalization of markets. Second, European-wide introduction of a universal grant would provide a basic mechanism for redistributing resources to the poorest countries in the EU.

As the universal grant would be a mechanism for fostering European social integration, it would be desirable for some of the cost of establishing it to be financed by the EU, for example, 50 per cent of a European guaranteed basic income. The member States should then finance the remaining 50 per cent as well as any supplements to the European minimum level. Regional authorities could also adapt the level of the universal grant in their area, while at the same time extending the residual traditional income support system. In this way, the principle of compatibility between the various levels of solidarity (European, national and regional) would become a reality in decentralized States.

4. Conclusion

The model we have just described in detail is generally consonant with classic proposals for a universal grant. Nevertheless, it displays some particularities.

The household grant might give rise to some doubts in view of the principle that the universal grant should be individual and standard in nature but, as we have emphasized, this measure is necessary in order to safeguard an egalitarian approach to social policy. Once the universal grant is established, there would be nothing to prevent a strengthening of the individualist principle, if that was what most of society wanted, for example, by increasing the individual share of the universal grant while keeping the level of the household grant more or less stable.

The proposal to use taxation to manage basic income also entails checking on the composition of households, which would not arise if a strictly individual approach were adopted. It is a moot point, however, whether in an inclusive social and economic system, manifestations of a lack of solidarity, such as fraudulent declarations regarding cohabitation, would be on a sufficiently large scale to create insurmountable dysfunctions requiring cumbersome tax inspection. Social attitudes stigmatizing fraud would be a vital means of prevention.

Another problem linked to the use of taxation to manage basic income would mean that, in its initial phases, the grant would in reality be accessible to only part of the population (chiefly households with inadequate incomes, but also adults without individual incomes in economically well-situated households). The essential purpose of the model of the universal grant we advocate is not so much to guarantee every person a net sum to be added to existing income, but rather an unconditional, individual, universal right to a guaranteed income, the full amount of which would be available to anyone without resources. The vital feature of this right is that it would enable all citizens to plan how they wanted to live in the knowledge that they could at any time obtain an increase that would obviate the risk of poverty no matter what lifestyle had been chosen.

The inherent advantage of the proposed model is its economic and financial viability. Compared with more ambitious versions of the universal grant, it would entail an admittedly high, yet reasonable economic cost, which could therefore be borne in the medium term by the relevant public institutions.

The cost would amount to approximately 2.7 per cent of GDP in the Basque Country, which is well below the cost of traditional models of the universal grant.[13]

Unlike restrained versions of the universal grant (for example a standard, individual grant of €200 or €300), the proposed model provides a general solution to the problem of poverty and avoids the need for additional recourse to a traditional income support system.[14] It therefore constitutes an alternative to the dilemma that advocates of the universal grant have faced from the very beginning: to propose a grant at a level which would be financially insufficient to avert the risk of poverty, or to introduce an adequate grant which would be difficult to finance.

Notes

1 Department of Justice, Employment and Social Security, Spain.

2 For the moment, Greece seems to have decided against the establishment of a universal income support system.

3 The first income support scheme, the *Ingreso Mínimo Familiar*, introduced in the Basque Country in 1989 was replaced a year later by the *Ingreso Mínimo de Inserción*. Although the Basque Country's approach was prompted by the RMI, it is not an automatic application of the French scheme.

4 Dependency is, however, a complex issue. In Spain, we note that the proportion of recipients who are dependent on the benefit in the long term (for more than one year, for example) rise with the strengthening of new support programmes. At the same time, most of the people who have received these benefits at some time in the past are no longer dependent on them (between 70 per cent and 80 per cent in Madrid and the Basque Country). This finding calls for some qualification of conclusions as to the 'dependency' effect of income support benefits, although it must be accepted that some recipients do in fact become dependent on them for long periods.

5 This can be less of a problem when the management of income support systems is relatively open. In the Basque Country, for example, the take-up rate among potential beneficiaries is fairly high (92 per cent in 2000).

6 Research in the Basque Country since the mid-1980s has demonstrated the existence of a link between the demographic crisis, the risk of poverty and/or the absence of well-being among young adults. This situation worsened during the 1990s, partly owing to soaring unemployment and partly owing to increasingly insecure working conditions and the sharp rise in the cost of housing. The process of becoming independent has thus been delayed and consequently there has been an unprecedented structural drop in marriage and birth rates. With regard to this phenomenon in the Basque Country see *Encuesta de Pobreza y desigualdades sociales 1996 y 2000*, Vitoria-Gasteiz, Departamento de Justicia, Trabajo y Seguridad Social.

7 This is a formidable problem. In the Basque Country, for example, about 30 per cent of beneficiaries of income support programmes say that they feel humiliated or different from the rest of the population.

8 An approach with some points in common with the argument put forward in this paper has been proposed by Sally Lerner in Canada (Lerner, 1999).

9   The introduction of a mixed-model universal grant does not change the essentially individual nature of eligibility for the grant. In the case of independent adults the universal grant would always be paid to them individually. The level of the grant available to each person would differ depending on the mode of cohabitation and would thus comprise the individual grant plus a proportion of the household grant (calculated by dividing the value of the household grant by the number of independent adults making up that unit).

10 See in this connection Sanzo (2001) which confirms the model's ability to secure a large enough income to eliminate the risk of poverty.

11 The levels proposed can be compared with purchasing power in other countries. In order to achieve parity in European Union countries, the following weightings should be applied: Austria 1.27, Belgium 1.18, Denmark 1.46, Finland 1.31, France 1.30, Germany 1.31, Greece 0.92, Ireland 1.17, Italy 1.06, Luxembourg 1.31, Netherlands 1.16, Portugal 0.82, Sweden 1.41 and the United Kingdom 1.23. (These coefficients were calculated from PPS indicators defined by Eurostat for 1998.)

12 The proposal to retain contributory pensions should, however, apply exclusively to the real economic value of funded contributions (and would not therefore take into consideration non-contributory supplements).

13 If a more traditional approach, based on a standard, individual, universal grant, were chosen and if, at the same time, the principle of covering the poverty risk in all types of household were accepted, it would be necessary to establish the level of the grant at about €420 in Spain, according to recent trade union recommendations in Catalonia. If we accept the basic hypothesis that, after taxation, the universal grant would result in real compensation equivalent to the net difference between personal income and the level of the grant, the annual cost would work out at 10.2 per cent of GDP, or 52.4 per cent of all social expenditure excluding education. If the grant were distributed gross and not offset by tax the cost would be three times higher, with an impact of 30.2 per cent on GDP. These estimates do not take account of the additional expenditure occasioned by the introduction of an extra housing allowance.

14 Obviously a grant of €200 or €300 would have only a limited impact on poverty alleviation in the case of persons living alone, who are one of the main groups at risk in Europe. Traditional protective arrangements would inevitably have to be kept in normal operation.

References

Atkinson, A.B. 1996. 'The case for a participation income', *Political Quarterly*, Vol. 67, pp. 67–70.

Deleeck, H. 1979 'L'effect Mathieu', *Droit Social*, November.

Gorz, A. 1985. *Paths to paradise: On the liberation from work* (London, Pluto Press).

Lerner, S., Clark, C.M.A. and Needham, R. (eds.) 1999. *Basic income: Economic security for all Canadians* (Toronto, Between the Lines).

Sanzo, L. 2001. *Líneas de actuación para el impulso de una Política de Garantía de Ingresos*, first Conference of the *Red Renta Básica*, Barcelona.

30

THE IMPACT OF BASIC INCOME ON THE PROPENSITY TO WORK: THEORETICAL GAMBLES AND MICROECONOMETRIC FINDINGS

Claude Gamel[1], Didier Balsan[2] and Josiane Vero[3]

1. Introduction

1.1 Comprehensive View

A mere list of the multiple disadvantages stemming from the present arrangement of minimum welfare benefits is enough to suggest an equally long list of arguments in favour of harmonizing these various benefits, or even combining them into a single basic income paid to everyone with no conditions attached.

Although such a proposition is firmly anchored in the philosophy of 'real libertarianism' (van Parijs, 1995), it is commonly regarded as too daring because of two major objections, one relating to the way it would be financed and the other to its possible incentive to idleness. This paper focuses on the second objection and employs the economist's and econometrician's toolbox in an attempt to predict how individuals might use their newfound freedom.

First we analyse the theoretical uncertainties surrounding the changes that the unconditional nature of the grant might induce in the behaviour of workers on low wages. Although the universal grant eliminates any distortion due to the substitution effect, not only the level but also the direction in which the income effect works is indeterminate, since everything depends on whether the individuals in question consider free time to be a normal good.

An econometric analysis of replies to an *ad hoc* questionnaire, used by the French Centre for Research on Education, Training and Employment

(CEREQ) in interviews with the 'youth measures' panel study sample group in 2000, makes it possible to reduce these margins of uncertainty. The drawing of a monthly grant of FF2,000 (approximately €300) would not trigger a huge reduction in labour market participation rates. Social integration through work means more than simply earning an income, and severing the connection between work and income would rarely prompt the young people in the sample group to 'experiment' with other modes of integration.

1.2 Relevant Facts

Since the 1997–98 winter of discontent among the unemployed, and the Join-Lambert report (1998) which tried to provide a stop-gap analysis, the question of reforming minimum welfare benefits[4] has been on the agenda in France, as is shown by the growing number of studies on the subject (Bourguignon and Bureau, 1999; Belorgey, 2000). Attempts to eliminate the 'unemployment trap', the pernicious effect of existing arrangements, led in 2001 to the introduction of the *prime pour l'emploi* or 'employment premium' reserved for the 'working poor'.

The idea of establishing a basic income has been discussed in Europe since the mid-1980s and has been warmly championed in intellectual and university circles by Atkinson and Meade, for example. But the winter of discontent and its aftermath prompted a wider debate by the general public and in governmental decision-taking circles.[5] The purpose of the basic income is to guarantee everyone a lifelong minimum income irrespective of occupational situation, civil status or income from other sources. It would therefore replace not only all the existing minimum welfare benefits designed to offset sundry vicissitudes of existence (unemployment, scant resources, single parenting, disability, old age), but also family allowances.

In order to gain a more accurate picture of the role played by such a proposal in the current debate, we should remember that the present minimum welfare benefits are the by-product of successive layers of French social welfare, built up over more than 50 years. As time has gone by, the goal of providing social security coverage for all, which goes back to 1945, has proved to be less and less compatible with the even older 'Bismarckian' tradition inherent in the French system that rests chiefly on the principle of solidarity among workers and families (the worker and the persons who are eligible for benefits through him):[6]

- A great effort was made by means of the initial minimum welfare benefits, which were introduced over a period beginning before the 30-year post-war boom (1945–1975) and ending just after it, to fill each of the unavoidable gaps in the system (old age, widowhood, disability, etc.);

- During the 'crisis' years of the last quarter of the twentieth century, it then became necessary to cope with the rising number of cases of 'new poverty', as access to employment became difficult or even impossible (the RMI was created in 1988). Nevertheless, the implicit point of reference of the system has always remained permanent, full-time employment, a situation reflected in the differential nature[7] of the RMI;
- Yet this point of reference ignores the fact that a part-time minimum wage earner receives little more than the maximum amount of the RMI (406 Euros per month for a single person without means) and might therefore be tempted to remain idle. In other words, the spread of part-time work, encouraged by the difficulty of finding a job and changing habits, was not taken into account until the recent establishment of the employment premium (*prime pour l'emploi*);
- This plugging of gaps, which has gone on ever since minimum welfare benefits first saw the light of day, has also encountered a fourth, more recent obstacle linked to the crisis in family life and couples' relationships. The granting and/or the amount of certain minimum welfare benefits (old-age pension, RMI and disabled adult's allowance) are still calculated on a family basis, whereas the instability of the family unit, and the rising number of lone-parent families and step-families, calls for social welfare to become increasingly or even entirely individualized. The continuity of entitlement for adults and children alike would be more securely guaranteed if the amount of minimum welfare benefits was not affected by changes in personal circumstances.

The above comments show that the present arrangement of minimum welfare benefits combines three sets of disadvantages: it is ill-suited to the instability of employment and to the diversification of access to it; rights can be lost because some allowances are family-based; and the tangle of conditions for granting the various benefits is much too complicated and unintelligible for the target sections of the population.

These disadvantages are alone enough to prompt arguments in favour of harmonizing these various minimum welfare benefits, or amalgamating them in a single basic income. Such a move would result in streamlining and lower administrative costs. Most importantly, the fact that this grant would be given unconditionally[8] as a fixed sum to each individual would mean that it would be unaffected by the ups and downs of working life (thus doing away with any unemployment trap)[9] or by a change in personal circumstances (it would be neutral as far as remaining single or the number of offspring was concerned).[10] Basic income is, however, obviously regarded as much too daring a proposition to form the real backbone of any reform of minimum social benefits.

Two main criticisms are generally levelled against it, both of which are related to its unconditional nature:

- first, handing out the same sum to everyone, including those at the top end of the income distribution scale who do not need it, would make financing the grant extremely difficult and would lead to a waste of public money, some thing that does not occur with existing, targeted minimum social benefits;
- second, handing out the same sum to everyone, whether or not they work, might cause some people to work less or not at all; such a severing of the link between work and income is at odds with the present-day mindset, which sees work as the principal route to social integration.

The philosophical foundations of basic income, especially the most sophisticated thesis of 'real libertarianism' of van Parijs (1995), are not lacking in arguments to counter these criticisms: basic income is not an attempt to meet certain needs, nor is it a passive response to any hypothetical 'end to work', far from it. The aim of such a grant is to give the idea of freedom real substance, over and above its formal aspects, by offering to all the means of running their lives as they think fit (marketable, non-marketable or even domestic activities) within the limits of the society's resources. That would legitimize the universal and unconditional nature of basic income.

This article is an extension of the philosophical line of argument of van Parijs, although both its scope and analytical method are restricted. As regards the scope of the paper, we have left aside the first of the two main criticisms[11] and concentrated on the second, relating to the alleged incentive to idleness that an unconditional grant might provide. What follows is also an attempt to answer this question using economic and econometric tools with the greatest of care, since we must not underestimate the methodological obstacles to be overcome. Our paper endeavours first to assess the magnitude of theoretical uncertainties surrounding possible changes in the poorest people's behaviour. If the arrangement contains no deliberate incentive will they, for example, give up work completely, or only work part-time? Once these changes had been identified, we tried to remove the margins of uncertainty through an econometric analysis of the replies to CEREQ's questionnaire. The sample group comprised young adults likely to face marginalization or exclusion and who would therefore be affected by the plan to bring in a universal basic income.

2. Theoretical Uncertainties Surrounding Changes in Behaviour

At first sight, a reform of minimum welfare benefits in which basic income would replace the RMI and thereby remove any unemployment trap should facilitate a person's return to the labour market by making it easier for them to accept part-time jobs. Conversely, workers might be tempted by the 'godsend' of the grant to reduce their working hours. That view does, however, overlook the lessons of microeconomic theory on labour supply. Since the price of 'leisure' time (the wage rate) would remain unchanged by basic income, the effect of the resultant rise in income ultimately depends on whether leisure time is perceived as a 'normal good' or not. It is only if it is not perceived as a normal good that the non-working individual will feel the incentive to work. But this second eventuality cannot be taken for granted: leisure time must be an 'inferior good' in order for its consumption to fall as income increases. Conversely, for workers to scale back their working hours presupposes that they regard leisure time as a normal good, whose amount they seek to increase.

The essential question for our thesis is therefore whether the poorest people consider leisure time to be a normal or an inferior good. In this connection, the introduction of basic income is an interesting textbook case; of all the methods for effecting social transfers, it alone simplifies analysis by eliminating the distortion due to the simultaneous existence of the substitution effect (section 2.1). Individual behaviour then alters solely according to the income effect, the positive or negative influence of which has still to be determined (section 2.2).

2.1 The Particularity of Basic Income – The Absence of a Substitution Effect

We will focus our analysis on the case of a generic individual initially working part-time, whose attitude to work might be affected by the introduction of a redistributive transfer guaranteeing a minimum income (G) more or less equivalent to the income they earn from their part-time job. We will study in turn a differential allowance (like the RMI), a degressive allowance (negative income tax) and uniform basic income. We will then compare these three arrangements with the American Earned Income Tax Credit (EITC) which, although it does not guarantee a minimum income, targets all assistance at a return to work by the poorest people (the same principle is behind the French employment premium). Here in section 2.1, we will limit our study to the substitution effect generated by the transfer. The income effect – common to all the systems under review – will be discussed later in section 2.2 to determine whether it has a positive or negative influence.

Figures 30.1 and 30.2 illustrate our analysis: those social transfers that generate a negative substitution effect in terms of incentive to work are shown first.

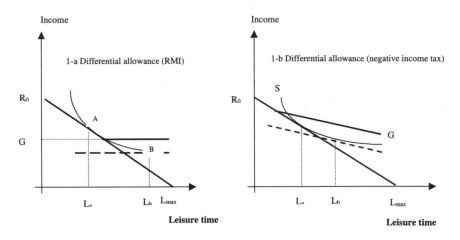

Figure 30.1 Negative substitution effects (on incentive to work) of differential and degressive allowances

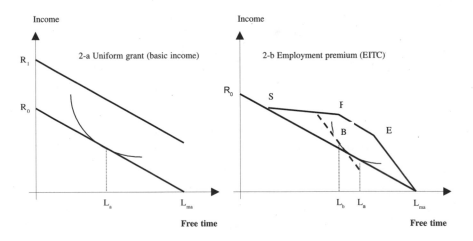

Figure 30.2 The zero substitution effects of the universal grant and positive substitution effects of the EITC

Differential and degressive allowances both trigger negative effects that are reflected in the graph by more leisure time (L_aL_b). Nevertheless we note that, quite logically, the intensity of the effect is not identical:

• The differential allowance (RMI) makes the opportunity cost of leisure time zero, owing to the confiscatory marginal tax rate (100 per cent) for individuals at or below the guaranteed minimum (G). As the straight line of income becomes horizontal in Figure 30.1-a, the individual can retain the same level of satisfaction while working much less (point B on the indifference curve); the disincentive to work (L_aL_b) is very strong and encourages the individual virtually to withdraw from the labour market.[12]

- The degressive allowance (negative income tax) is purposely designed to make this unemployment trap smaller by establishing a negative marginal tax rate of less than 100 per cent. In Figure 30.1-b, between the points G (maximum level of unemployment benefit) and S (threshold for entitlement to the benefit), the slope of the straight line of income and therefore the opportunity cost of leisure time, is no longer zero. Nevertheless, they are still lower than the price of leisure time which would have been recorded in the absence of negative income tax (slope of the initial straight line of income R_oL_{max}). Hence, the substitution effect (L_aL_b), while still negative, is considerably smaller. The disincentive to work is much weaker than in the case of a purely differential allowance.

Basic income and EITC will differ substantially from the above two cases because they virtually eliminate any disincentive to work, as is shown by Figure 30.2.

As far as basic income is concerned, the analysis could not be simpler: as Figure 30.2-a demonstrates, the introduction of such a transfer where the marginal tax rate is zero simply entails an upward shift of the income constraint. Since its slope and therefore the opportunity cost of leisure time remain unchanged, we see that there is no substitution effect. This characteristic, which has been underscored by microeconomic analysis, confirms the basic neutrality of basic income, which, in keeping with its 'libertarian' roots, brings with it neither an incentive nor a disincentive to work. The only purpose of the lump-sum transfer is to offer each individual the means to run their life as they see fit.

Among redistributive transfers, the EITC is the absolute opposite to differential or degressive transfers. The EITC establishes an employment or activity premium reserved for persons who start work again. This premium, which is added to the wage of the person concerned, is initially proportional to earned income and grows with it up to a specified ceiling, where it turns into a fixed sum (like basic income) before decreasing (like negative income tax) once a given level of income has been exceeded. Hence the straight line broken into three segments which, in Figure 30.2-b, illustrates the successive phases experienced by a person who has started work again and whose income grows.

All in all, three lessons can be drawn from a comparison of the substitution effects generated by these four types of redistributive transfer:

- All things being equal, because of its neutrality, basic income in fact gives rise to a stronger incentive to work than the other transfers, except during the initial phase ($L_{max}E$) of the EITC (see Figure 30.2-b), where the incentive to work is positive. Both the intermediate phase $E - F$ of this arrangement and basic income do away with any substitution effect;

- The previous remark also gives the lie to a received idea that is often put forward, namely that basic income would encourage idleness. In its own way, the Belorgey report (2000, p. 295) helped to fuel this doubt since, after an excessively imprecise microeconomic comparison of the four types of transfer, it concluded with reference to basic income that 'the incentive to work would go in the same direction as negative income tax or differential allowance, yet theory predicts that it must be less'.

- If the income effect is reintroduced into the analysis, there is certainly nothing to guarantee that the establishment of basic income will, all things considered, encourage individuals to go back to work. The opposite behaviour might even be observed if most people regard leisure time as a normal good that one seeks to enlarge. Nevertheless, should that happen, the intensity of the reaction would be lower with basic income than with degressive or purely differential allowances because, in the case of these allowances, the negative income effect on incentive to work will reinforce a substitution effect that is already negative.

The question of the neutrality of basic income with regard to work therefore boils down to the income effect that the introduction of such a transfer might produce. Even if this simplifies the analysis of neutrality, it is still very difficult to dispel fundamental theoretical uncertainty about the direction in which this income effect works.

2.2 The Direction in Which the Income Effect Works: The Uncertainty that must be Dispelled

The uncertainty that will be discussed here goes deeper than that normally mentioned in connection with the labour supply. In this case, if leisure time is regarded as a normal good, income and substitution effects have opposite influences in the case of a change in wage rate, and the only uncertain factor is the relative intensity of the income effect. The fairly general consensus is that 'a plausible graph for depicting labour supply' (Cahuc and Zylberberg, 1996, p.27) involves the idea of a turning point:

- In the case of the lowest wage rates, the negative substitution effect on leisure time is deemed to be greater than the positive but small income effect: a person with plenty of leisure time gives priority to increasing purchasing power and the labour supply curve tends upwards when the wage rate increases;

- Above a certain threshold of remuneration peculiar to each individual, the opposite occurs: the person in question prefers to have more leisure time than a higher income. Labour supply begins to decrease when the wage rate increases beyond this threshold.

If transposed as it stands to our investigation of the impact of basic income on behavioural patterns, analysis of the relative strength of the income effect would not give rise to any uncertainty, since the absence of any substitution effect makes it possible to conclude immediately that, as basic income raises income by a fixed amount, the persons concerned reduce their labour supply, since they regard leisure time as a normal good.

We feel, however, that it is indeed the validity of the latter hypothesis which needs to be re-examined. Is any improvement in income always reflected in a fairly strong preference for leisure time? In a society where work is still highly valued, is it not necessary to tone down the prevailing microeconomic hypothesis that work is tiresome and a source of disutility? These general questions are acutely relevant for the poorest social classes, where the receipt of basic income would signify a larger relative increase in purchasing power than for any other category. In that case, if standard microeconomic theory holds that the income effect is only slightly positive for the lowest wage rates, it makes sense that this income effect should become negative and leisure time should be regarded as an inferior good, when these population groups are on the margins of society, or on the verge of exclusion. In other words, it is the positive or negative direction, and not the strength, of the income effect that is rather uncertain here.

To be more precise, consideration of whether leisure time is regarded as a normal or an inferior good can be taken further by examining at least four different characteristics affecting the social bases of self-respect, without which 'nothing may seem worth doing' (Rawls, 1971, p. 440). In this case, it all depends whether an individual values participation in the labour market:

- Leisure time will be perceived as a normal good if the work available to the individual is tiresome and tedious (monotonous task, oppressive hierarchy, etc.), but it will be seen as an inferior good if, on the contrary, the job itself is satisfying (independence and creativity of a self-employed craftsman, for example);
- Leisure time will be a normal good if other people's attitudes give individuals such a poor opinion of their own work that they feel that it is of little value or below them. On the other hand, this 'stigmatization' effect will be reversed, and leisure time will be an inferior good, if the person feels ashamed of not working;

- If a person's social integration primarily rests on non-market networks (family, associations, etc.), leisure time will obviously be a normal good. But if working relations are more important, having a job will take priority and leisure time will be an inferior good;
- Lastly, from a more economic angle, leisure time will be a normal good when a full-time investment in seeking employment incompatible with any wage-earning activity is contemplated (setting up one's own firm, for example). But it will be perceived as an inferior good if discovering the best opportunities initially requires joining an occupational network and therefore taking a first job. More generally, an investment in training might give rise to the same dichotomy, depending on whether it necessitates full-time studies (leisure time is a normal good) or on-the-job training (leisure time is an inferior good).

The depth of the problem mentioned here, in connection with the impact on behaviour of a basic income, which is still purely hypothetical, seems to be confirmed *a priori* by sociological findings from a different, albeit closely related field. For example, the survey conducted by Bernarrosh (2000) among persons in receipt of the RMI and long-term jobless who had fallen into the unemployment trap, emphasizes the wide variety of relationships with work apparently displayed by the people she encountered. Only one person in 40 exactly matched the expected profile of being affected by the financial aspects of the unemployment trap and accordingly refusing work. The reasons given by the others for turning down job offers, or not seeking work, were many and various.[13]

Arguably, as the establishment of an unconditional basic income would eliminate the unemployment trap, it would be bound to add to the diversity of attitudes to work. Moreover, only individual attitudes to the supply of labour are touched on here, but it is important to look at them in the context of a household where the arbitration relations between men and women make any predictions even more hypothetical.

The challenge is therefore one of using microeconometric approaches and studying the responses of 'sensitive' population groups who would be directly concerned, in an attempt to foresee how they might react to the introduction of basic income.

3. Young Adults' Responses Regarding Basic Income

How can we measure and predict young people's reactions to a reform of minimum welfare benefit that would be based on basic income? In order to disperse uncertainties on that count, the ideal solution would probably be to conduct an experimental project in real conditions for long enough and on a sufficiently large scale, as was done for the first time between 1969 and 1972, for negative income tax in the US state of New Jersey. A comparison of the behaviour observed among beneficiaries and the reference population revealed the impact of negative income tax on the propensity to work. Persons other than the head of a family (spouses and young people on the labour market) had a much lower propensity in the beneficiary group than in the reference group.[14] Quite apart from the inherent limitations of the process (observation undoubtedly alters the phenomenon being observed), the cost of such an experiment is clearly prohibitive. For that reason, it might be possible to think about testing reactions to the plan for basic income by means of a less expensive method using the standard tools of experimental economics. But the complexity of the latter and the goal of gaining a better understanding of the laws governing individual behaviour seem *a priori* make the gathering of information from an 'uninitiated' public an unsuitable course of action.

That is why we felt that for the time being a much more modest microeconometric analysis of an *ad hoc* questionnaire added to the fifth wave of questions (February–May 2000) put to CEREQ's third 'youth measures' panel might supply a substantial amount of information (see Appendices). The specific traits of the group questioned (young people aged under 25 who had left school in 1994 with qualifications equal to or lower than the baccalaureate) make the survey all the more pertinent, bearing in mind the difficulties these individuals have encountered in the school to work transition. Originally, we sought to compare the behaviour of two sub-groups: the unemployed and the employed. The difficulties encountered in handing out the questionnaires meant that only 455 responses from persons in employment in February 2000 could be used for econometric analysis, since the 94 utilizable responses from the unemployed were insufficient in number.

The whole questionnaire from the 'youth measures' panel survey was used to construct explanatory variables. Generally speaking, gender, family situation (living as a couple, children), present job (wage, part-time, present employment status), transfer income, spouse's income, subjective perception of one's financial situation, occupational pathways (length of time spent in the different stages of the labour market), level of education and the highest diploma obtained were the explanatory variables whose influence on reactions to basic income was tested. An attempt has been made throughout to link these sets of variables to the replies to the supplementary survey on basic income. Only the variables which are of minimum statistical significance, are, however, shown for each model.[15]

One main question connected with the above-mentioned theoretical issues runs through the whole survey: how would these employed persons react to the payment of a monthly basic income of FF2,000 (default value assumed throughout the questionnaire)? If the payment of the basic income results in a drop in the labour supply, it may be considered that leisure time is a normal good. Conversely, when behaviour towards employment remains unchanged, leisure time can no longer be regarded as a normal good, since its consumption is not rising. In this connection, it is perhaps regrettable that the answer 'work more' was not included among the possible responses to question BI1 (see below), since this would have made it possible to discern the strength of the perception that leisure time is a strictly inferior good. In order to simplify the 5th wave questionnaire, it was however assumed that an insignificant number of persons already in employment would display such behaviour and that anyone tempted to choose that option would plump for the nearest option 'You would not change anything with basic income'.

3.1 Leisure Time is not Strictly Speaking a Normal Good for Two Thirds of the Sample

On perusal of the distribution of replies, we find that the majority response is 'no change' (55 per cent for option 8 of question BI1). This is in itself a major finding of this research, giving the lie to frequently expressed fears that an unconditional basic income would naturally encourage beneficiaries to work less.

Question BI1. Today you have a job, if you were automatically paid this universal grant, would you be prepared first to[a] ...

Option	Number	%
1. Work less	77	16.9
2. Stop work	2	0.4
3. No longer do undeclared work	8	1.8
4. Change jobs	8	1.8
5. Obtain training through a system such as a skilling contract (contrat de qualification)	33	7.2
6. Resume your studies	18	4.0
7. Engage in an interesting activity (sport, rock group, etc)	57	12.5
8. You would not change anything with basic income	252	55.4
9. Don't know	0	0.0
Total	455	100.0

[a] Only the first choices are analysed here, since very few respondents expressed their second choice (only those individuals who did not select item 8 as their choice were asked for their second choice.)

This initial finding is further confirmed when we take account of the gradation in the responses opting for change. Overall, 136 persons (30 per cent) selected the options of 'work less', 'stop work' or 'engage in an interesting activity'. In their case, it is quite legitimate to consider that the additional leisure time caused by the payment of basic income is immediately 'consumed'. For these people, leisure time is unambiguously a normal good.

Responses 4, 5 and 6 (13 per cent) seem to express a point of view midway between neutrality and immediate consumption. The leisure time that BI provides is invested in improving human capital ('obtain training through a system such as a skilling contract' or 'resume studies') or in looking for another job ('change jobs'). In both cases, labour supply is deferred. It dwindles in the short term but should increase in quality in the long term. Without adopting a strictly normative position, it already appears possible to describe this effect as 'positive', since it increases the stock of human capital and thereby contributes to economic growth (endogenous growth). Be that as it may, the margin of 'real freedom' offered to an individual by basic income might thus also be of benefit to the community as a whole. All in all, for two-thirds of the sample (68.4 per cent for options 4, 5, 6 and 8) leisure time is not, strictly speaking, a normal good to be consumed immediately.

Having come to this overall conclusion, we must investigate the characteristics of the persons within this general profile. To do so, a two-stage procedure is used:

- First, we estimate a model which compares the 'no change' option to all the other options;
- Then, among the people who indicated they would be in favour of a change, we distinguish between two categories according to whether this change results in an immediate reduction in labour supply (consumption behaviour) or a postponement thereof (investment behaviour).

3.2 The 'No Change' Probability is Stronger When the Employment Situation is Stable

The level of education does seem to have a significant impact on the probability of responding 'no change' if basic income were paid (see Table 30.1).[16] Persons at level IV[17] would be less inclined to change their behaviour towards the labour market if a basic income of FF2,000 were paid to them.

It is possible to arrive at an interpretation which is confirmed by the effects of the other variables and by other models. Persons with level IV education (deliberately chosen as the highest level of initial education in the sample) are more often on the primary labour market, outside a zone that may be termed 'hybrid' or 'secondary'.

Table 30.1 The model comparing 'no change' with the other options (question BI1)

Variable	Coefficient	T value
Constant	−0.01	−0.05
Level IV education	0.59*	2.48
Level V education (diploma)	Ref.	
Level V education (no diploma)	Ref.	
Level Vb and VI education	Ref.	
Full-time employment at present	0.39**	1.67
In receipt of transfer income	−0.52*	−2.41
Fixed-term contract at present	−0.27	−1.03
A different employment situation at present	−0.45	−1.44
Number of months unemployed	0.01	1.29
Number of months of inactivity	−0.04	−1.18
Log-likelihood	−293.2	
Proportion of matching pairs	60.6 %	

* Significant at 5% level.
**Significant at 10% level.

In this secondary zone, we tend to find people in a precarious situation, in jobs that are not very secure, often part-time and poorly paid. In this type of situation, the persons concerned might well react to the payment of a basic income amounting to FF2,000, for this sum would represent a substantial share of their total income. This seems to be all the more true when we consider not the income of the person, but that of the household. Another marker of belonging to this 'hybrid' zone is receiving transfer income (housing allowance, minimum income guarantee RMI, family allowances, etc.). The fact of receiving such transfers is associated with a higher probability of plumping for a change if basic income were to be paid.

Conversely, people in full-time jobs are also more likely 'not to change anything with basic income', which corroborates this same interpretation. In other words, if basic income introduces an incentive to withdraw from the labour market, this tendency is less marked among persons in full-time employment than among persons in part-time employment: the situation of the latter is more likely to be 'endured' than 'chosen' if they are in this secondary zone on the fringes of the labour market.

It therefore appears that persons in employment for whom leisure time is not a normal good are more often found among persons with level IV education, working full-time and not receiving any transfer income. Lastly, we should note that the variables describing the family situation and gender of the person, and information about their career path, do not seem to bear any correlation to the fact that they say that they 'would not change anything' in the event of basic income payments of FF2,000.

At this stage, it is interesting to supplement the analysis by drawing a distinction among those who would be in favour of a change between those for whom labour supply is deferred (investment behaviour) and those for whom leisure time is a normal good (consumption behaviour).

3.3 Investment Behaviour is More Often Displayed by Persons in a More Precarious Situation

A logit model was estimated for the sub-set of individuals who indicated they would make a change in question BI1. This was done by modelling the probability of reducing labour supply. The results set out in Table 30.2 show that persons in the hybrid zone of the labour market have a greater tendency to select options corresponding to an investment, whereas those in a more settled situation, when they choose to react, tend more towards the adoption of a consumerist mode of behaviour.

In fact, variables indicative of more settled situations (living as a couple, with children, full-time job) are associated with a greater probability of reducing labour supply in order to have more leisure time. On the other hand, a low level of education (VI and Vb) and/or a fixed-term contract more usually go hand in hand with the selection of an option oriented towards investment (human capital or a new job).

All in all, when reactions to the establishment of basic income take the form of a change in behaviour, they would result in more rational economic behaviour: consumption of leisure time for people who are apparently employed in a satisfying job, and reinvestment for those who consider their job to be insecure.

Table 30.2 Model comparing consumption and investment behaviour (question BI1)

Variable	Coefficient	T value
Constant	0.37	1.01
Living as a couple	0.94*	2.45
One or more children	0.92**	1.66
Level IV education	Ref.	
Level V education (diploma)	Ref.	
Level V education (no diploma)	Ref.	
Level Vb and VI education	−0.94*	−2.18
Full-time job at present	0.77*	2.06
Fixed-term contract at present	−0.91*	−2.15
In a youth employment scheme at present	−0.63	−1.26
Log-likelihood	−99.9	
Proportion of matching pairs	70.2 %	

* Significant at 5% level.
**Significant at 10% level.

4. Conclusion

The most important finding to emerge from our research is that, contrary to the frequently asserted objection, the receipt of basic income would not trigger a massive reduction in labour market participation rates. Most the people questioned would not alter their behaviour with regard to employment. Such an attitude was more the prerogative of the people who were best integrated in society and on the primary labour market. Persons who, on the contrary, would take advantage of the 'real freedom' that would be offered by basic income to alter their behaviour would do so in very different ways depending on whether or not they were well integrated into working life.

This relatively stable behaviour among the best-integrated individuals is also confirmed by further results of our survey, which cannot be described in detail here. For example (see question BI3 below), persons who opted not to change their occupational situation, even if they were paid a monthly grant of FF2,000, are deeply attached to their job for non-pecuniary reasons (more than 60 per cent of responses to options 1 and 2). For young people who have not been employed for very long, social integration through work plainly means more than just earning an income and the severance of the link between work and income that the introduction of basic income would bring would rarely tempt them to 'experiment' with other modes of social integration (scarcely 30 per cent of respondents selected the 'consumerist' options of question BI1). Basic income even arouses some suspicion among more than one-fifth of the sample (see option 6 of question BI3), especially among youngsters in job-creation schemes,[18] who do not grasp why they do not have to do something in exchange.

Question BI3. (*If BI1 = 8*). Why would you not change anything in your professional situation if you were paid the sum of FF2, 000? Because in your present situation (*only one reply possible*)

Option	Number	%
1. Your job is interesting	143	56.8
2. Your job allows you to avoid feeling isolated	13	5.1
3. You want to go on doing undeclared work	0	0.0
4. You have no other choice apart from your present job	29	11.6
5. FF 2,000 is not enough	13	5.2
6. You think that it is suspicious or abnormal to be paid FF 2,000 without having to do anything in return	53	21.0
7. Don't know	1	0.4
Total	252	100.0

The behaviour that some people would contemplate if they were paid the basic income also depends on its amount. If it were under FF1,500, the unconditional nature of basic income is seemingly not sufficient to offset the smallness of the sum and to trigger significant changes in behaviour, either consumption or investment of leisure time. It should be noted, however, that the people who decided that they would reduce their labour supply even with an allowance of scarcely FF500 tend to be on the secondary labour market rather than in presumably better situations (full-time, stable job, etc.).

More research in a number of directions could be done on these initial findings. In particular, two paths, which we had to ignore for various reasons, still have to be explored:

- In the event of BI being introduced, would the stronger tendency for part-time employees to withdraw from activity be compensated by a greater propensity for inactive individuals or active jobseekers to accept part time work?
- If there is a 'minimum' amount below which the effect of basic income becomes significantly more neutral, is it also true that there is a 'ceiling' somewhere above 2000 Francs, above which the majority of recipients would change their general behaviour or even adopt an exclusively consumerist attitude to leisure time?

For this reason, the results of this research and the various ways in which it could be continued can only reinforce the fundamental aim pursued here: to take plans for basic income seriously, as they are in most European countries, and to back them with more credible arguments in the French debate about minimum welfare benefits, where up until now they have been mainly treated as utopian, or a baleful ugly vision.

Appendix 1. CEREQ's 'Youth Measures' Panel Survey (1994–2000)

In 1996, the French Centre for Research on Education, Training and Employment (CEREQ), in collaboration with the Department of research and statistical surveys (Dares) of the Ministry of Employment and Solidarity, carried out a third panel study of 'youth measures' among a sample group of 3,500 young people who had left school in 1994 with initial education lower than or equivalent to the baccalaureate. The main purpose of this survey was to provide data on the use of youth programs to ease the school to work transition.

The sampling frame was based on lists of former pupils gathered from secondary schools (*lycées* and *collèges*) and on apprenticeship contracts supplied by the Ministry of Employment and Solidarity. The panel survey comprised five annual waves of interviews between 1996 and 2000. Each wave of interviews was performed using the Computer Assisted Interview Procedure (CATI).

The themes broached during the interviews concerned initial education, occupational pathways (month-by-month progress report after leaving the educational system in order to avoid memory bias), family background, and income and living conditions.

Some figures regarding the survey:

	No. of respondents	Attrition rate (%)
Wave 1 (1996)	3 469	
Wave 2 (1997)	2 957	15
Wave 3 (1998)	2 627	11
Wave 4 (1999)	2 297	13
Wave 5 (2000)	1 928	16

Appendix 2. The Supplementary Survey on Basic Income (2000)

In 2000, CEREQ and the *Groupement de recherche en économie quantitative d'Aix-Marseilles* (Greqam), a research team specializing in quantitative economics research, carried out a supplementary survey in addition to the panel survey on 'youth measures'. This supplementary survey was designed to meet the specific needs of a research project financed by the *Commissariat général du plan*. Its chief purpose was to study a radical reform of the present system of minimum welfare benefits through the introduction of a basic income. The comparison of such a scheme with the possible extension of the RMI to the under-25s was initially envisaged, but usable data on this second aspect were insufficient for an econometric analysis.

The initial sample used contained all the respondents to wave 5 of the 'youth measures' panel survey. The scope of the study was, however, restricted to young people who where either employed or unemployed in February 2000 and whose wages or unemployment benefit amounted to less than FF7,000 per month.

The method employed for collecting responses was similar to that of the 'youth measures' panel survey, namely Computer Assisted Interview Procedure (CATI). The telephone interview took place one week after the principal survey. In the meantime a written version of the questionnaire on basic income had been sent by post to volunteers.

The main subject broached in the survey by means of three sets of questions concerned envisaged changes in behaviour prompted by the hypothetical introduction of a universal grant.

A few figures regarding the supplementary survey:

	Employed	Unemployed
No. of individuals in the initial sample	960	232
No. of respondents	455	94
Response rate	47%	41%

Notes

1 University of Aix-Marseille, France.
2 Former Minister of Employment and Solidarity, France.
3 French Centre for Research on Education, Training and Employment (CEREQ).
4 This term refers to a set of eight means-tested allowances: minimum old-age pension; minimum disability pension, disabled adult's allowance; specific solidarity allowance *(allocation de solidarité spécifique)*, aimed at long-term unemployed people no longer eligible for unemployment benefits; integration benefit *(allocation d'insertion)*, aimed at categories of unemployed people ineligible for unemployment benefits (released prisoners, asylum-seekers,..); RMI or 'minimum income guarantee' *(revenu minimum d'insertion)*; lone parent's allowance; and widower's or widow's pension. All of these are paid to persons who are unable to obtain sufficient resources from past or present work.
5 For example, at the *Commissariat Général du Plan*, the theme of one of the three workshops of the Belorgey (2000) think tank was precisely 'Basic income and reforms of minimum welfare benefits'.
6 This 'Bismarckian' idea of social insurance for workers contrasts sharply with Beveridge's notion of universal welfare for any citizen in need. In the French system, which is to a great extent a hybrid, the minimum income guarantee (RMI), for example, falls under the latter notion.
7 An allowance is 'differential' when each Euro of income earned by an individual reduces the allowance they receive by the same amount. The 'marginal tax rate' (through lowering benefits) is 100 per cent, a confiscatory level which is at the root of the 'unemployment trap'. The RMI is the prime example of this (if we disregard transitional profit-sharing mechanisms that just postpone taxation). The marginal rate of taxation is even higher than 100 per cent when a person stops collecting the RMI, given the loss of associated rights (full housing allowance, suspension of residence tax, etc.).
8 The only remaining criterion restricting its award would be a minimum requirement of residence or nationality.
9 Unlike the 'differential' RMI, where the marginal tax rate (in principle, 100 per cent) is confiscatory, the 'lump sum' basic income attracts a zero marginal tax rate for the beneficiary. 'Negative income tax' offers a wide range of fairly 'degressive' compromises according to the marginal tax rate chosen (between 0 and 100 per cent).
10 The economies of scale permitted by married or family life (all the personal allowances of each spouse or child can be drawn simultaneously without any reductions) would, however, supply a financial argument in favour of safeguarding these lifestyles.
11 Replies obviously exist to this first objection if the same analysis includes social transfers and income tax, according to the method recommended in the Bourguignon and Bureau report (1999, pp. 30–41). For a fuller discussion see Gamel (2001, pp. 99–112).
12 The reasoning we illustrate with the graph is obviously in the nature of an approximation and tends to underestimate the strength of the disincentive to work. As it is

drawn, the indifference curve has, as an asymptote, a horizontal straight line which, strictly speaking, it could meet only at infinity. In practice, however, leisure time L_b is very close to its maximum L_{max}.

13 These reasons can, however, be grouped under four headings: 'demanding relationship with work' where occupational ambitions are incompatible with the acceptance of a more lowly job; 'rejection of exploitation prompted by a revulsion against injustice' ensuing from the experience that promises of turning a fixed-term contract into a with-out-limit-of-time contract were not kept; refusal to accept any work, but not motivated by any occupational ambitions (divorced women with dependent children who disdain work as cleaners because of the 'bad image' it would project); wish to claim minimum welfare by persons whose access to employment cannot be contemplated without a 'lengthy detour' (university degrees in subjects with no openings, artists, political exiles, former convicts, etc).

14 For an account of the results of this experiment, see Stoleru (1974, pp. 160–181).

15 T-test higher than one.

16 In this and the following table, the reference categories ('ref.' in the tables) of education variable are systematically included since they are different in each table.

17 This level corresponds to the completion of secondary education (irrespective of whether they passed the baccalaureate or not). This was the highest level of education amongst the panel members. The other members achieved level V (final year of the *Certificat d'aptitudes professionnelles* or *Brevet d'études professionnelles* – the CAP or BEP vocational aptitude certificates, irrespective of whether or not they passed the diploma), level Vb (left school before the final year of the CAP or BEP) and level VI (left school during the first three years at secondary school).

18 The only variable with a significance level of 5 per cent.

References

Belorgey, J.-M. (Chair) 2000. *Minima sociaux, revenus d'activité, précarité*, Report du Commissariat Général du Plan (Paris, La documentation française).

Bernarrosh, Y. 2000. *RMIstes et chômeurs face à l'emploi précaire: interroger la notion de 'trappe d'inactivité'*, Paper presented at the symposium 'Working Poor' en France, 27 October (edited by Epee), Evry, Université d'Evry-Val d'Essonne.

Bourguignon, F. and Bureau, D. 1999. *L'architecture des prélèvements en France : état des lieux et voies de réforme*, Report du Conseil d'Analyse Economique (Paris, La documentation française).

Cahuc, P. and Zylberberg, A. 1996. *Economie du travail – La formation des salaires et les déterminants du chômage* (Brussels, De Boeck Université).

Gamel, C. (Coordinator) 2001. *L'avenir des minima sociaux: Partage révisé du risque de chômage ou intégration dans une allocation universelle? Approches théoriques et microéconométriques*, Final research report No. 22/1998 {in collaboration withD. Balsan, V. Di Paola, S. Forest, R. Kast, A. Lapied and J. Vero} (Paris, Commissariat Général du Plan).

Join-Lambert, M.-T. 1998. *Chômage: Mesures d'urgence et minima sociaux – problèmes soulevés par les mouvements de chômeurs en France fin 1997-début 1998* (Paris, La documentation française).

Rawls, J. 1971. *A theory of justice* (Cambridge, Mass., Harvard University Press).

Stoleru, L. 1974. *Vaincre la pauvreté dans les pays riches* (Paris, Flammarion).

van Parijs, P. 1995. *Real freedom for all – What (if anything) can justify capitalism?* (Oxford, Oxford University Press).

31

A FAILURE TO COMMUNICATE: THE LABOUR MARKET FINDINGS OF THE NEGATIVE INCOME TAX EXPERIMENTS AND THEIR EFFECTS ON POLICY AND PUBLIC OPINION

Karl Widerquist[1]

1. Introduction

Between 1968 and 1980, the United States Government conducted four negative income tax (NIT) experiments, and the Canadian government conducted one. They were designed to test the effects of a guaranteed income, which unconditionally assures all citizens some minimal level of income. The growing debate today about the basic income guarantee is greatly affected by the labour market findings of those experiments. Although the modern basic income guarantee movement tends to focus on the basic income variant of the proposal rather than on the negative income tax as tested in the experiments, the similarity between the two is so great that any conclusive findings from the experiments would be of great value for the current discussion. However, both basic income supporters and opponents quote the findings of these experiments with equal conviction.

At least 336 scholarly articles have been written on these experiments (see bibliography), but there is no clear consensus on what they implied for policy. The experimental results have been cited both by supporters and opponents of the redistribution of income as evidence for the workability or the unworkability of a negative income tax. For example, long after the results were in and the initial flurry of articles was over, Hum and Simpson (1993a) declared in the *Journal of Labour Economics*, 'Few adverse effects have been found to date. Those adverse effects found, such as work response, are smaller than would have been expected without experimentation.' But in the same issue or the same journal, Anderson and Block speculated about why social scientists continue to support the NIT 'in the face of an avalanche of negative results' provided by the experiments.

Political perceptions of the experiments have been equally confused. The experiments received attention in the popular press in a few brief periods in the 1970s, most particularly in 1977 when Congressional hearings examined the results as part of their investigation of President Jimmy Carter's ill-fated welfare reform proposal. The dozens of technical reports including large amounts of data were simplified down to two statements: NIT decreased work effort and increased divorce.

Dozens of editorials appeared in newspapers around the country criticizing the Government for spending millions of dollars simply to show that people work less when you pay people not to work. The meaning of the results has been disputed by scholars, but neither the results nor the disagreements about the results were understood by politicians or the media. Part of the reason for this misunderstanding is the natural difficulty of presenting complex technical results to a lay audience interested only in a bottom line. But part of the responsibility also rests with the scholars who presented bottom line results without clearly communicating just what these results did and did not show.

This paper examines the labour market results of the NIT experiments to determine what conclusions, if any, can be drawn from them conclusively, and how well these conclusions have been perceived by the media and the scholarly community. Section 2 summarizes the experiments. Section 3 discusses the ability of estimates of the work disincentive effect to determine the market equilibrium outcome of a national policy.

2. The Experiments

The US Government sponsored four guaranteed income experiments between 1968 and 1980 (see Table 1). The Canadian government conducted one experiment in the late 1970s. These experiments are known collectively as the income maintenance experiments, the guaranteed income experiments, or the NIT experiments. They began at a time when the elimination of poverty was the stated goal of the US administration, when there was a growing movement for economic rights, and when many social scientists and policymakers believed that social policy reform was heading in the direction of a guaranteed income. But by the time all the results were available the movement for eliminating poverty had dwindled and the idea of 'welfare reform' was beginning to be associated with dismantling rather than rationalizing the welfare system. To a large extent the NIT experiments simply outlived the movement that spawned them, but to a small extent the experiments contributed to the demise of progressive social reform.

The primary aim of the NIT experiments was to test the effects of a guaranteed income on the work effort of recipients, and thereby to get some indication of the costs and feasibility of such a programme. Their secondary aim was to test the effects of a guaranteed income on any other affected variable the experimenters could measure. These variables included health statistics, educational attainment and performance, the divorce rate, and many others. But a discussion of these effects is beyond the scope of this paper.

The NIT experiments came about at a time when the negative income tax was being promoted by social scientists of various political backgrounds as a scientific solution to poverty. They were the first large-scale social experiments to use the scientific method of randomly assigning human subjects into treatment and control groups, just as medical researchers do when testing drugs. Some social scientists have called the NIT experiments 'experiments in how to conduct experiments', and they have had a larger influence on the conduct of social experiments than in the examination of the policy they were designed to test.

Table 31.1 summarizes the basic facts of the five NIT experiments. The first, the New Jersey Graduated Work Incentive Experiment (which is sometimes referred to as the New Jersey Negative Income Tax Experiment or simply the New Jersey Experiment), was conducted from 1968 to 1972. The researchers originally planned to conduct the entire experiment in New Jersey, but they were unable to find enough poor whites in New Jersey and had to open a second location in Wilkes-Barre, Pennsylvania, in order to round out a racially representative sample. The treatment group originally consisted of 1,216 people and dwindled to 983 (due to dropouts) by the conclusion of the experiment. The sample size consisted of black, white and Latino two-parent families with a male head, that were not approaching retirement, and with incomes below 150 per cent of the poverty line. Treatment group recipients received a guaranteed income for three years.

The Rural Income Maintenance Experiment (RIME) was conducted in rural parts of Iowa and North Carolina from 1970 to 1972. It functioned largely as a supplement to the New Jersey experiment, which focused on an urban population. It began with 809 and finished with 729 experimental subjects. The treatment group received a guaranteed income for two years. Subjects met the same criteria as the New Jersey Experiment except that single parent, female-headed households were also included. Few, if any, Latinos were included in the sample. Both RIME and the New Jersey experiment began under the direction of the Office of Economic Opportunity (OEO) and were completed by the Department of Heath, Education, and Welfare when OEO was disbanded.

The largest NIT experiment was the Seattle/Denver Income Maintenance Experiment (SIME/DIME), which had an experimental group of about

Table 31.1 Summary of the negative income tax experiments in the United States and Canada

Name	Site(s)	Data collection	Sample size initial (final)	Sample characteristics	G*	t**
New Jersey graduated work incentive experiment	New Jersey and Pennsylvania	1968–1972	1216 (983)	Black, white, and Latino, two-parent families in urban areas with a male head aged 18–58 and income below 150% of poverty line.	0.5, 0.75, 1.0, 1.25	0.3. 0.5, 0.7
Rural income-maintenance experiment (RIME)	Iowa and North Carolina	1970–1972	809 (729)	Two-parent families and female-headed households in rural areas with income below 150% of poverty line.	0.5, 0.75, 1.00	0.3, 0.5, 0.7
Seattle/Denver income-maintenance experiments (SIME/DIME)	Seattle and Denver	1970–1976, (some to 1980)	4800	Black, white, and Latino families with at least one dependant and income below $11,000 for single parents, $13,000 for two-parent families.	0.75, 1.26, 1.48	0.5, 0.7, 0.7-0.025y, 0.8-0.025y
Gary, Indiana experiment	Gary, Indiana	1971–1974	1799 (967)	Black households, primarily female-headed, head 18–58, income below 240% of poverty line.	0.75, 1.0	0.4, 0.6
Manitoba basic annual income experiment (Mincome)	Winnipeg and Dauphin, Manitoba	1975–1978	1300	Families with, head younger than 58 and income below $13,000 for a family of four.	C$3,800, C$4,800, C$5,800	0.35, 0.5, 0.75

* G = Guarantee level(s). Guarantee levels for the US experiments are reported as a multiple of the poverty line; in Canada they are presented in Canadian dollars.

** t = marginal tax rate or 'take-back rate.'

Sources: Robins *et al.* (1980); Ferber and Hirsch (1978); Hum and Simpson (1993).

4,800 people in the Seattle and Denver metropolitan areas. The sample included black, white and Latino families with at least one dependant and incomes below $11,000 for single-parent families and below $13,000 for two-parent families. The experiment began in 1970 and was originally planned to be completed within six years. However, researchers were interested in how the long-term effects of a permanent guaranteed income might be different from the short-term effects of a temporary guaranteed income experiment, and so they obtained approval to extend the experiment for 20 years for a small group of subjects. This would have extended the project into the early 1990s, but it was eventually cancelled in 1980, so that a few subjects had guaranteed income for about nine years, during part of which time they were led to believe they would receive it for 20 years.

The Gary Income Maintenance Experiment (which is never abbreviated) was conducted between 1971 and 1974. Subjects were almost entirely black, single-parent families living in Gary, Indiana. The experimental group received a guaranteed income for three years. It began with a sample size of 1,799 families, which (due to a high drop-out rate) fell to 967 by the end of the experiment.

The Canadian government got into the business of conducting income maintenance experiments somewhat later. The Manitoba Basic Annual Income Experiment (Mincome) began in 1975 after most of the US experiments were winding down. The sample comprised 1,300 urban and rural families in Winnipeg and Dolphin, Manitoba with incomes below $13,000 per year. By the time the data collection was completed in 1978, interest in guaranteed income was on the wane and the Canadian government cancelled the project before the data was analysed. Fortunately, university-based researchers were eventually able to obtain and analyse the data, so that results are available today.

Two parameters are central to the design of any guaranteed income. The guarantee level or the minimum income level (G in Table 31.1) is the amount the recipient receives if she has no private income. The central goal of a guaranteed income programme is to ensure that no person's (or no family's) income falls below some given level for any reason. Theoretically, the guarantee level can be any number between zero and *per capita* GDP. A guarantee level that was too low would not significantly reduce poverty or increase income insecurity, but a guarantee level that was too high would have such strong work disincentive effects that the programme would not be affordable. The experiments intended to find out whether a guarantee level sufficient to reduce or even eliminate poverty was feasible. For that reason guarantee levels between 50 per cent and 150 per cent of the poverty line were tested.

The US experiments all defined the guarantee level relative to the poverty line. A guarantee level of 1.0 or higher would eliminate poverty as defined by official statistics. The smaller the guarantee level, the smaller the work disincentive and the smaller the cost of the programme, but the effect on the poverty rate would also be smaller. The larger the guarantee level, the larger the effect on the poverty rate, but the higher the cost and the greater the work disincentive. The five experiments tested nine different guarantee levels: 0.5 (50 per cent of the poverty level) was tested in the New Jersey and Rural Income Maintenance Experiments; 0.75 was tested in all four of the US experiments. 1.0 (just enough to eliminate official poverty) was tested in all of the US experiments except SIME/DIME; 1.25 was tested only in the New Jersey Experiment, and 1.26 and 1.48 were tested only in SIME/DIME. Mincome, which defined its guarantee level in Canadian dollars rather than relative to the poverty level, tested guarantee levels of $3,800, $4,800 and $5,800 per year.

The other central parameter of any guaranteed income system is the marginal tax rate (t in Table 31.1), also known as the 'take-back rate.' The practical working of the marginal tax rate is slightly different if the guaranteed income is administered as a basic income rather than a negative income tax, but because all five of the experiments tested the negative income tax version, this small distinction is not important here. The take-back rate is the rate at which benefits are reduced as the recipient makes private income. That is, it is the effective income tax rate per dollar of private income for recipients of the negative income tax; hence the term marginal tax rate. A higher marginal tax rate is associated with a lower overall tax-cost of the programme[2] but also with greater work disincentives, and a greater potential 'poverty trap'. A lower marginal tax rate is associated with a higher overall cost of the programme, but also with greater work incentives. A lower marginal tax rate is also associated with a greater redistribution of income towards people with incomes above the poverty line. Redistribution to this group might be desirable in terms of equity (as a reward for low-wage workers), but to do so would greatly increase the cost of a programme primarily conceived as an anti-poverty policy.[3] For these reasons, it is important to know what kinds of take-back rates are feasible and the work-disincentive effects of each. The experimenters also tested nine different take-back rates: 0.3 (a 30 per cent marginal tax rate) was tested in the New Jersey and Rural Experiments; 0.35 was tested only in Mincome: 0.4 was tested only in Gary; 0.5 was tested in all of the experiments except Gary; 0.6 was tested only in Gary; 0.7 was tested in the New Jersey Experiment, RIME, and SIME/DIME; 0.75 was tested in Mincome. SIME/DIME tested two non-linear income functions with marginal tax rates of 0.7 minus 0.025 times income and 0.8 minus 0.025 times income. The effect of these two non-linear functions was to impose higher marginal tax rates on lower levels of income and lower marginal tax rates on higher levels of income.

The use of so many different rates of G and t reduced the numbers of subjects receiving each type of treatment, and therefore reduced the statistical reliability of the results for each. Some of this trade-off is worthwhile to allow for testing of a greater variety of potential parameters, but the experiments might have benefited from more coordinated effort to test a uniform group of parameters. A larger sample subject to three or four broadly spaced parameters might have been more useful than smaller groups subject to nine different and unevenly spaced parameters.

The primary goal of the experiments was to test the effects of G and t on work effort. Most non-academic articles reported the simple summary statistics of how much less the treatment group worked than the control group, but these aggregated how the nine different levels of G and the nine different levels of t affected the work effort of men and women; primary, secondary, and tertiary household income earners; and whites, blacks, and Latinos in single-parent and two-parent families. From these results, researchers hoped to estimate the costs and effects of a national NIT programme and more generally to learn something about supply in the low-wage labour market. Table 31.1 summarizes the configuration of the experiments.

3. The Work Disincentive Results of the Experiments

Since 1966, the NIT experiments have been the subject of at least 336 scholarly articles, including working papers, journal articles, and book chapters (see bibliography B for a list). There is some overlap in this number because in certain cases the same or a very similar article was published in all three forms. Most were published in the late 1970s as the experiments reached completion, but a trickle of articles reassessing the experiments continues today. Figure 31.1 shows the number of articles published each year on the experiments. About half deal with theoretical, methodological and interpretational issues. Of those that report empirical findings, nearly half deal with the work disincentive effect.

Many of the researchers who conducted the experiments and others who examined the data, were strong backers of the programme and viewed the results as proving the feasibility of the NIT. But other researchers, as well as some politicians and media commentators, saw the results as proving the opposite: that a national guaranteed income could not or should not be adopted. The experimental results seem to be a scientific Rorschach test in which an observer can see whatever she wants to see. The most important reason for this disagreement is that the most general result of the experiment was what everyone expected before the experiment was conducted: the treatment group worked less than the control group, other things being equal. This agreed, the central question was how much less, for each demographic group

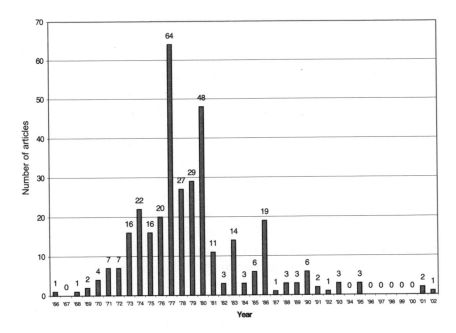

Figure 31.1 Academic articles published each year on the NIT experiments (working papers, journal articles and book chapters)

and for each level of G and t, and whether this work-disincentive effect fell into the acceptable range for a viable national NIT policy. However, the experiments alone could not answer these questions because they suffered two important limitations.

First, there is no clearly agreed objective criteria for how much effect on work effort is acceptable, allowing researchers with differing political views to draw opposite conclusions from the same results. Second, the experiments did not replicate the conditions of a national policy on a smaller scale, which allowed researchers to claim more meaning as to the effects of a national policy than the experiments warranted.

The work disincentive results met two criteria that were important to guaranteed income supporters. First, the fear that a negative income tax would cause some segment of the population to withdraw completely from the labour force was not confirmed by the experiments. None of the experiments found evidence of such behaviour; the lower work effort of the treatment group relative to the control group took the form of increased weeks of unemployment between jobs, or fewer hours worked per week, but not the wholesale labour market withdrawal critics feared. The distinction between these two different types of work disincentive effects has not been well understood and opponents of the basic income guarantee continue to voice this fear despite the lack of experimental evidence for it.

Second, the cost of the programme was not so great as to make the programme technically untenable. Critics of the guaranteed income have feared that work effort reductions would greatly increase the cost of the programme, requiring a large increase in taxes, which would further discourage work, and ultimately lead to the collapse of the programme. Whether this would happen depends on the level of the guarantee. It would inevitably happen if the minimum income was set near *per capita* national income, leaving a negligible work incentive; certainly it would not happen with a guarantee level of $1 a year which would have a negligible work disincentive. However, the results of the experiments implied that a guarantee level between 50 per cent and 150 per cent of the official poverty line would be financially tenable. Although the work disincentives of the programme would increase the cost of an NIT over what it would have been if it had no effect on hours worked, the impact was not so great as to make the programme unaffordable.

Inevitably, the same results gave ammunition to NIT opponents: there was a statistically significant work disincentive effect, and that work disincentive increased the cost of the programme over what it would have been if work hours were unaffected by the NIT. Although these results were completely expected, they were reported in the press (see Section 5) as if they were the critical findings of the experiments, and they largely shaped political and media perceptions that the experiments proved the failure of the guaranteed income.

Because the work disincentive effects of the NIT were greater than negligible but not so large as to make the programme unaffordable, the meaning of the figures depends on how large is large and how small is small. The work disincentive effect seems to have been just enough that supporters can claim it to be small and opponents can claim it to be large.

Researchers who look at the percentage decline in work effort can claim minimal effects. The basic findings were that male heads of households (men with wives and children) worked slightly fewer hours if at all (relative to the control group) – from 0 per cent to 9 per cent depending on the study and the data. The work effort of female heads of households (single mothers) declined slightly more. Hours worked by married women and teenagers living with parent(s) declined more substantially – in the neighbourhood of 20 per cent to 30 per cent. The decline in work effort among teenagers was not associated with increased hours of schooling, but it was associated with increased school performance in some studies. These figures are not terribly disturbing to guaranteed income supporters. Heads of households taking more time to look for work between jobs, but not dropping out of the labour force, is just the kind of result most supporters had hoped for. Parents spending more time with their children, and teenagers spending more time on their studies, are the kinds of benefits a guaranteed income would hope to give.

But as Keeley, Robins, Spiegelman and West (1978) and Burtless (1986) independently concluded, even these modest reductions in work effort can cause significant increases in the cost of the programme (relative to what the cost would be if there was no work effort response), because those whose earnings decline receive a larger share of the payments. Keeley, Robins, Spiegelman and West found that work disincentive effects increased the cost of the programme by more than 50 per cent, and Burtless found that in some cases a tax expenditure of $3 would be required to raise the incomes of recipients by $1 (the rest going to work-time reduction). Opponents of the guaranteed income have used these figures to claim that the project is a political non-starter.

But the meaning of these figures can be easily overblown. Imagine a minimum wage experiment in which the government picked out 1,000 low-wage workers and applied the minimum wage only to them. Such an experiment would no doubt find an enormous increase in unemployment in this group because they would be unable to compete with the lower cost of the millions of workers not receiving a minimum wage. But a minimum wage applied to all workers shows a small or even negligible relationship to the average unemployment rate, because the demand for labour responds differently to a change in supply in the market as a whole than it does to a change in supply of a small group in the market. To a lesser extent this problem affects the NIT experiments in the same way. The amount which the experiments cannot show is much greater than that which they can. Section 4 discusses the limitations to what the NIT experiments could reveal about the market effects of a guaranteed income.

4. What the Experiments Could not Measure

All these precise and technical estimates are small in comparison to what we simply do not know about the effects of a national guaranteed income programme, even if the responses of the experiment group are completely representative of the national response. At best, the experiments measured the short-run horizontal shift in labour supply caused by the experiments (the shift from A to B in Figure 31.2). But what we really want to know is the long-run market response to a permanent national negative income tax (the shift from point A to point C in Figure 31.3). Without knowing the market response it is impossible accurately to estimate the cost of a national programme or its effects on work hours and poverty. To determine the shift from A to C, researchers would need several important pieces of information that the NIT

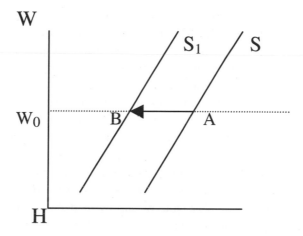

Figure 31.2 The work disincentive effect

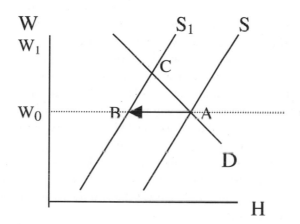

Figure 31.3 Workers receiving NIT

experiments could not measure. First, how does the long-run shift in supply caused by a permanent national programme differ from the short-run shift caused by a temporary experiment? Second, even if the experiments perfectly measured the long-run supply shift caused by a national programme, to determine the market outcome we would also need to know the long-run elasticities of both the supply of and the demand for labour (i.e. the shape of the supply and demand curves).

In Figures 31.2 and 31.3 the vertical axis shows the wage (W) and the horizontal axis shows the hours worked (H). The work disincentive effect causes the supply among the experimental group to shift from S to S_1. Because the experimental group is small in comparison to the size of the market the wage (W) is fixed and the shift from point A to point B shows only a decline in hours and no increase in the wage. The experiments give no information about the demand for labour or about the shape of the supply curve, only the size of the shift in supply (Figure 31.2).

If all workers received the NIT, the market would respond. The market outcome would go from A to C instead of A to B. This would reduce the drop in work hours, increase the income of recipients, and decrease the cost of the programme in terms of tax dollars and efficiency (Figure 31.3).

SIME/DIME made some attempt to measure the long-run shift in supply but as all the researchers involved knew, these experiments were unable to make any estimates of the elasticities of supply or demand. The rest of the section examines these issues in turn.

The difference between the long-run supply shift of a national policy and the shift measured in temporary experiments has been well discussed. This is a problem that is unique to social science experiments because they deal with human behaviour rather than human biology. If a thousand people in an experiment respond similarly to a vaccine, medical researchers can be reasonably sure that a million people will respond similarly in a national programme. But this may not be true in a social experiment. People behave differently in different circumstances. As Harold Watts described it, an experimental plan that recipients know will be in place for only a few years, is the equivalent of putting leisure time on sale. When laundry soap is on sale, people buy more of it, and we can expect a similar response from a temporary guaranteed income. People who might want to take a few weeks or months off work, sometime in the next 10 years, might as well take it while the experiment is going on. Therefore one would expect that the experiments overestimated the decline in work effort.

However, NIT opponents can make the opposite claim just as logically. Because the experiments are only temporary, and recipients know that they must return to the workforce eventually, they will be less likely to drop out for fear of losing work experience or losing their place in line for promotion. Further, some NIT opponents have argued that a national guaranteed income would create a 'culture of poverty', in which a subculture develops in which no one is ever expected to get a job. These claims are only speculation, but the NIT experiments were unable to shed any light on whether they are true or not. The only evidence provided by the experiments comes from the SIME/DIME recipients who received an NIT for nine years. These recipients did not behave very differently from other experimental recipients, but they were only led to believe that their income would be permanent for part of that time, it is uncertain whether they believed it, and clearly they would have been wise not to believe it. But even if the experiment had gone on for the full 20 years it could not have estimated whether a subculture of dropouts would develop if a national programme were put in place.

Therefore both those who want to believe that the long run supply shift will be larger than the experiments showed and those who want to believe it will be smaller have some theoretical justification for their claims. However, that does not mean that the two cancel out; one effect could be much larger than the other. It simply means that what we know about the labour market from these experiments is less than we would like to know. Those who assert that the long-run effect is certainly larger than the experimental effect (Burtless, 1986; Anderson and Block, 1993) are making unwarranted claims that are not supported by evidence.

The ability of the experiments to measure correctly the shift in supply is further complicated by the representativeness of the sample. Only families with low incomes were sampled. Most of the experiments sampled only families with incomes below 150 per cent of the poverty line, and only SIME/DIME sampled families with incomes as high as 240 per cent of the poverty line. The higher the income the less likely a person would be to reduce work effort in response to a programme giving them the possibility of a sub-poverty income without working. Because most of the population earns more than 150 per cent of the poverty line, the effects on the entire labour market would probably be much smaller than the effects measured in the experiments. However, arguably even a small decline in work effort among this group might be considered a serious problem. The experimenters were well aware that a 7 per cent eduction in work effort among recipients of an NIT would not mean that labour supply would decline by 7 per cent if an NIT programme was introduced: but if politicians and pundits understood this distinction they did not make it clear.

Further, very few if any single childless individuals were sampled. Aside from single parents, this is the group that would be most likely to drop out of the labour force in response to a guaranteed income. Single parents at the time were eligible for relatively generous (by current standards) Aid to Families with Dependent Children (AFDC) programmes, and so the relative effect of the NIT would be reduced. Single childless individuals are not eligible for any non-work-based benefits. Therefore, had they been sampled, one would have expected a larger response from this group, and researches may have found some of the wholesale withdrawals from the labour market that NIT opponents most fear.

These problems affect the accuracy with which the experiments measured the shift in the supply curve (the shift from A to B in Figure 31.1). But the shift in the supply curve does not give the market outcome, which is seriously affected by the elasticity of both supply and demand. The intuitive reason for this is that when supply decreases, demand responds by offering a higher price to elicit a return of the lost quantity supplied. How large this response is depends critically on the elasticities of both functions.

Examining the extreme cases can show the range of possible outcomes. As shown in Figure 31.4, if the demand for labour is perfectly elastic (if firms will hire any amount of labour at the going wage, but will not pay even a cent more for any amount of labour), the market equilibrium will be entirely determined by the horizontal shift in the supply of labour regardless of its elasticity. Figure 31.5 shows the effects of a perfectly inelastic demand for labour. If this is the case, firms need a fixed amount of workers and will pay anything to get it. If so, no amount of labour disincentive effect will cause any long-run decrease in work effort, and firms will pay workers whatever it takes to keep doing the same amount of work. If so, the result of the work disincentive effect would be solely to raise wages, and there would be no equilibrium decline in hours worked. Thus demand is completely inelastic; there is no equilibrium reduction in work hours (Figure 31.4). If demand is completely elastic (Figure 31.5), there is no change in the wage, and the full reduction in work hours in the experiments would occur in the market.

The more general results are that the equilibrium level of work effort will be somewhere between the initial equilibrium (point A) and the horizontal shift in supply (point B), and that the equilibrium wage will be as high or higher than the initial wage. In other words, the market equilibrium will be somewhere in the shaded area in Figure 31.6. Without information on elas-

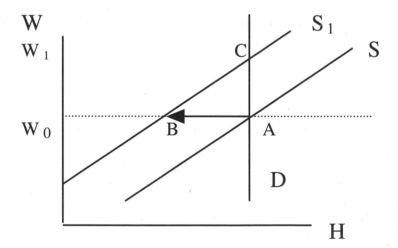

Figure 31.4 Completely inelastic demand

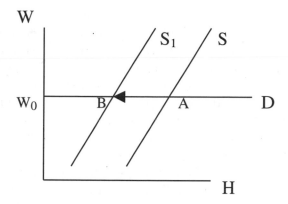

Figure 31.5 Completely elastic demand

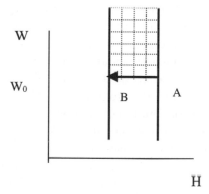

Figure 31.6 The range of possible market responses to a given horizontal shift in the supply of labour

ticities, it is impossible to say where in this region the equilibrium would be. Thus, instead of identifying the equilibrium outcome of a negative income tax, the experiments identified only the lower left-hand border of a region of possible outcomes.

It should be noted that it is theoretically possible for the equilibrium point to be in the region to the upper left of point B if the labour supply curve is backward bending. However, a backward-bending labour supply curve can be safely ignored in the case of a substantial guaranteed income because backward bending requires that workers' demand for goods is so inelastic that a decrease in wages will cause them to work more hours to maintain their level of consumption. That is quite reasonable for someone whose labour is the primary or only source of income. But if a guaranteed income was in place, the lower the wage, the smaller portion of the worker's income that comes from that wage; it becomes unreasonable to believe that workers will work more and more to maintain the level of such a small part of their income.

If a backward-bending labour supply curve is ruled out, the experiments found upper-bound estimates for the decline in hours worked, upper-bound estimates for the cost of the programme, and lower-bound estimates for the effect of the programme on the income of recipients.

All of the researchers who worked with the data from these experiments were aware of this shortcoming of the available results. It is extremely basic economics, and it was pointed out as early as 1971 (Browning). Yet, few of the researchers who wrote on the NIT experiments treated this issue with more than a passing mention. It seems to me that there are two reasonable ways to present results under these circumstances. One option is to obtain the best available estimates for the elasticities and simulate the outcome. The other is to present a range of possibilities. This would mean showing ranges like the one in Figure 31.5, and pointing out that, to the extent that the experiments were capable of correctly estimating the long-run shift in labour supply, they obtained only an upper-bound estimate of the effect on hours worked, a lower-bound estimate of the effect on the income of recipients, and an upper-bound estimate of the cost of the programme in terms of tax dollars. A few researchers took the first option; I know of none who took the other option.

The most common way of handling the results was to ignore or effectively to ignore the need to know the demand response. Some did not mention the need to know the demand response at all; others mentioned it only in passing as if it would have only a minor effect on the estimates, but nearly all presented their figures as if they were estimates of the equilibrium outcome rather than of the lower bound of possible outcomes. Whether a caveat was made or not, presenting estimates of boundaries of a range of possible outcomes as if they are point estimates of the actual values is clearly misleading. Certainly, economists understood this, but it is clear from looking at the Congressional testimony and from examining articles in the popular media that the policymakers and pundits did not understand these issues. The technical experts failed in their responsibility to make their lay audience understand the meaning of the results they were presented with.

5. Political and Media Perceptions of the Experiments

Sections 3 and 4 have tried to demonstrate that the findings of the NIT experiments are far more complex, subtle and ambiguous than one might be led to believe by figures citing an x per cent decline in hours worked. As this section shows, the complexity of the results was largely lost on the politicians and media to whom the findings were reported. Bibliography A contains a survey of about 50 articles from the popular media on the experiments.

The experiments gained significant attention in the press only twice: in 1970 and 1972, when Nixon's Family Assistance Plan (FAP) was under debate in Congress, and in 1977 and 1978 when Carter's Programme for Better Jobs and Income (PBJI) was under consideration. Both plans had elements of a negative income tax, but neither was a pure guaranteed income, although FAP was considerably closer to it than PBJI. In 1970, the first experiment had only been under way for two years and researchers believed that they were at least three years away from being able to produce meaningful results. But at the insistence of the administration and some members of Congress, the researchers released preliminary reports showing no evidence of any work disincentive effect. Some members of Congress (rightly) could not believe the result, and commissioned a review of the results from an independent auditor who concluded the results were 'premature' (as the researchers had initially warned).

The results of the fourth and largest experiment, SIME/DIME, were released while Congress was debating PBJI, and the existence of work disincentive effects caused quite a stir. Never mind that everyone going into the experiments agreed that there would be some work disincentive effect; when the results were publicized, members of Congress were appalled and columnists across the country responded with a chorus of negative editorials decrying the guaranteed income, and ridiculing the Government for spending millions of dollars to find out whether people work less if you pay them not to work.

United Press International (1977) simply got the facts wrong, saying that the SIME/DIME study showed that 'adults might abandon efforts to find work', when in fact no such evidence was found. UPI apparently did not understand the difference between a decline in work hours while continuing to work, and abandoning the labour market. The *Rocky Mountain News* claimed that the NIT 'saps the recipients' desire to work'. Jones (1978), writing for the *Seattle Times* presented a relatively well-rounded understanding of the results, but despite this simply concluded that the existence of a decline in work effort was enough to 'cast doubt' on the plan. Similarly Rich (*Washington Post*, November 18, 1978) implied that the evidence presented that the NIT 'might cause recipients to work less', is enough to disqualify the programme from consideration. Raspberry (1978) declared the experiments a failure simply because people worked less.

Senator Daniel Patrick Moynihan, who had written a book in support of the guaranteed income a few years earlier and who had been one of the architects of FAP, recanted his support for the guaranteed income as a result of the SIME/DIME findings. He was a sociologist and could have been expected to have a sophisticated understanding of statistical data, but he implied in a letter to William F. Buckley later published by the *National Review* (1978) that the mere existence of a work disincentive effect was an important factor in his recantation. He stated, 'But were we wrong about a guaranteed income! Seemingly it is calamitous. It increases family dissolution by some 70 per cent, decreases work, etc. Such is now the state of the science, and it seems to me we are honour bound to abide by it for the moment.' The Senator held Congressional hearings on the results in November 1977 to discuss the evidence, but media reports and politicians' comments did not display any real understanding of the results.

Headlines such as 'Income Plan Linked to Less Work' and 'Guaranteed Income Against Work Ethic' appeared in newspapers. The Knight News Service (1978) quoted Jodie Allen of the Labour Department commenting on Spiegelman's cost estimates saying, 'It could easily turn out that the Government might spend billions of dollars on benefit payments and have little effect on the families' incomes. Instead, most of the [Government] expenditures would offset reductions in earnings'. This statement was made apparently in complete ignorance of the possibility of a demand response and the affect it could have of increasing family earnings and reducing Government expenditures. Only a few exceptions such as Carl Rowan for the Washington Star (1978) considered that it might be acceptable for people working in bad jobs to work less. But he could not figure out why the Government would spend so much money to find out whether people work less when you pay them to stay at home.

Spiegelman, one of the directors of SIME/DIME, defended the experiments in the *Washington Star* (1978), saying that the experiments provided much-needed cost estimates that demonstrated the feasibility of the NIT. He said that the decline in work effort was not dramatic, but he did not offer an explanation for why so many commentators believed the results were dramatic and why they drew very different conclusions than he did. Demkovich (1978) is one of the few popular writers who considered the reduced work effort small, but the more common reaction was shown in the *Denver Post* (Brimberg, 1980). Citing only that a work disincentive effect existed, not its size, Brimberg quoted Senator Bill Armstrong of Colorado as saying the experiment was: 'An acknowledged failure. Let's admit it, learn from it, and move on.'

It may be an impossible task to communicate such complexities to an audience interested only in soundbites or the bottom line, but I cannot help thinking that social scientists have a responsibility to do a better job than we did in this instance. None of the articles in the popular media that I was able to find betrayed any understanding that the experiments measured only the horizontal shift in the labour supply function. None seemed to understand the elementary economic principle that a change in supply necessitates a demand response that will greatly affect the equilibrium outcome. The understandings of the NIT experiments displayed in the popular press were so superficial that it is reasonable to accuse social scientists of failing to communicate the meaning of their results.

6. Conclusions

Even if the public had been made to understand more of the complexities of the results, as long as there is a significant political block that believes any work disincentive is unacceptable, the NIT experiments were bound to give ammunition to NIT opponents. To that extent it was a mistake for any guaranteed income supporters to agree to the experiments in the first place. One writer asked what would have happened if the introduction of Social Security had been preceded by a retirement insurance experiment. It would certainly have shown that it caused people to save less for their retirement and to retire sooner than they otherwise would have, giving considerable ammunition to Social Security opponents. But to those who believe that low-wage workers need more power in the labour market, and that a basic income guarantee can give them that power, if it is affordable, the NIT experiments demonstrated the feasibility of a desirable programme. And, therefore, the NIT experiments, as long as they are discussed, will always mean different things to different people. But these differences are more philosophical than scientific. None of the facts of the findings are persuasive enough that they should cause either supporters or opponents to change their minds.

Why was the demand response to the NIT experiments so widely ignored? One reason is that scientists like to focus on the results, not the limits of their research. Another reason is that they probably assumed this fact was too obvious to be bothered with among social scientists and too difficult to be dealt with by a lay audience. Perhaps, opponents did not want to bring it up because it waters down their argument that the work disincentive is 'large' and the costs are 'high'. Perhaps, supporters didn't want to bring it up because it is much more difficult to make a case for NIT based on the desirable effect on wages that a work disincentive might have, than to make the case that the work disincentive is 'small'. Using the 'small' argument requires only an objective look at empirical evidence. But using the desirability argument requires not only empirical data that the experiments could not produce, but also a much more complex ethical argument. It affronts those who want to keep wages low to keep profits high and those who espouse the extreme version of the work ethic stating that everyone must at all times work. Although the basic income guarantee is not work-ethic friendly in that sense, it is worker friendly because it allows those who do work to command higher wages, and it gives those who might consider not working a positive incentive (rather than a punitive incentive) to work.

Is it worth it to allow some to drop out to increase the wages of those who do not? That answer depends on how big the increase in wages is and how big the decline in work effort is, whether it means fewer hours worked by many or the dropping out by some, and on other issues. If dropping out means leaving the labour force to become an unhappy idle soul who drains the resources of others, perhaps not. If dropping out means pursuing artistic, educational, spiritual, entrepreneurial, or care-giving activities that will ultimately benefit others, perhaps so. These issues, both positive and normative, are the ones that separate supporters from opponents of the idea. The NIT experiments were able to shed only a small amount of light on a few of these issues. The most important questions went unanswered. The NIT experiments were able to indicate only very tentatively that a basic income guarantee is financially feasible at the cost of certain side effects that people with differing political beliefs may take to be desirable or disastrous. To claim more would be to overstate the evidence.

Notes

1   University of Oxford, USA.
2   Theoretically, higher marginal tax rates could be associated with higher taxes costs if the supply of labour is highly elastic, but this was not expected and did not prove true in any of the experiments.
3   The basic income movement today puts less stress on the issue of poverty reduction and more stress on broader equity goals: to them this issue may be less important.

References A: A Sampling of Non-Academic Articles on the NIT Experiments

Andersen, M. 1978. 'Welfare reform on the same old rocks', *New York Times*, November 27.
Associated Press. 1978. 'Social experiment finds', *New Orleans Time-Picayune*, May 19.
Bartlett, C. 1978. 'A new hitch for welfare reform', *Washington Star*, November 20.
Brimberg, J. 1980. 'Income security project flounders; Halt sought: Guaranteed income programme fails', *Denver Post*, February 14.
Business Week 1976. 'Positive values of the negative income tax', *Business Week* November.
Cleberley, F. 1975. 'Manitoba's guaranteed income experiment', *Montreal Star*, August 30, pp. 76–77.
Cleverly, F. 1974. 'Manitoba tries guaranteed income', *Vancouver Sun*, March 1.
_____ 1976. 'Guaranteed income trail runs into difficulties', *Montreal Star*, March 6, p. 48.
Demkovich, L.E. 1978. 'Good news and bad news for welfare reform', *National Journal*, December 30.
_____ 1980. 'It may be a race against the clock for welfare reform package in 1980', *National Journal*, January 26.

Greene, L.M. 1979. 'Letter on income maintenance experiments: Too soon to jump to conclusions', *New York Times*, February 20.

Hum, D. and Simpson, W. 2001. 'A guaranteed annual income? From Mincome to the Millennium', *Policy Options/Options Politiques*, January–February.

Jones, M. 1970. '35 families join income plan; More to sign up next month', *Seattle Times*, November 28.

_____ 1978. '$60 million, 8-year social experiment: Test casts doubt on income plan', *Seattle Times*, May 18.

Kamien, A. 1977. 'HEW study links guaranteed income to family breakup', *Rocky Mountain News*, November 14.

Kershaw, D.N. 1972. 'A negative-income-tax experiment', *Scientific American*, 227(4), October, pp. 19–25.

Knight News Service 1978. 'Next welfare plan: Lower cost, benefits', *San Francisco Examiner*, November 16.

Lambro, D. 1979. 'Easy money at HEW', *Conservative Digest*, April. Reprinted from *Policy Review*.

Lenkowsky, L. 1979. 'Welfare reform and the liberals', *Commentary*, March.

Moffit, R.A. 1981. 'The negative income tax: Would it discourage work?', *Monthly Labour Review*, April.

Morris, M. 1970. '2,200 city families will get $5.1 million income aid', *Seattle Post Intelligencer*, June 16.

Moynihan, D.P. (Interview with) 1978. 'Some negative evidence about the negative income tax', in *Fortune Magazine*, December 4.

_____ 1978. 'Letter to William F. Buckley', *National Review*, September 29.

Nelson, D. 1970. 'Annual income experiment set', *Skagit Valley Herald*, March 9.

New York Times Editorial Board. 1979. 'Scare talk about welfare reform', *New York Times*, February 13.

New York Times News Service. 1977. 'Welfare "Sweetener" Blunts Criticism', *Washington Star*, Aug. 7.

New York Times. 1978. 'Moynihan says recent studies raise doubts about "negative Income tax" proposals', *New York Times*, November 16.

Newsweek, 1978. 'Welfare: A surprising test', *Newsweek*, November 27.

Ostrum, C. 1978. 'To each according to his need?', *Seattle Sun*, March 22

Pine, A. 1978. 'The negative side of negative tax', *Washington Post*, May 12.

Raspberry, W. 1978. 'A failed experiment in guaranteed income', *Washington Post*, November 20.

Reinhold, R. 1979. 'Test in Seattle challenges minimum-income plan', *New York Times*, February 5.

Rich, S. 1978. 'Welfare plan linked to family splits', *Washington Post*, May 2.

_____ 1978. 'Income plan linked to less work: Marriages break up, study also finds', *Washington Post*, November 16.

_____ 1978. 'Moynihan sees $6 billion increase in welfare cost under revision plans', *Washington Post*, November 18.

Rocky Mountain News Editorial Board. 1978. 'A valuable test', *Rocky Mountain News*, November 29.

Rowan, C.T. 1978. 'A little common sense in place of money', *Washington Star*, December 6.

Sacramento Bee Editorial Board 1978. 'Welfare and families', *Sacramento Bee*, March 18.

Samuelson, P.A. 1977. 'Welfare reform', in *Newsweek*, Aug. 29.

Schiller, B.R. 1978. 'When welfare families know their rights', *Wall Street Journal*, July 11.

Seattle Times 1971. '1,000 families to receive income aid', *Seattle Times*, February 3.

SocioEconomic Newsletter 1977. 'Califano relies on HEW tests to bolster welfare plan', *SocioEconomic Newsletter*, Vol. 2, No. 7, July.

_____ 1978. 'Flare-up on negative income tax', *SocioEconomic Newsletter*, January.

Spiegelman, R.G. 1978. 'Letter to the Editor', *Washington Star*, December 15.

_____ 1979. 'Letter to the Editor', *SocioEconomic Newsletter*, March.

Steiger, P.E. 1977. 'Divorce linked to income gains in welfare study', *Los Angeles Times*, November 4.

United Press International. 1977. 'Guaranteed income against work ethic', *Seattle Daily Journal Commerce*, November 16.

_____ 1978. 'Study raises questions on welfare reform', *Washington Star*, November 16.

United States News and World Report. 1977. 'ABC's of Carter welfare plan – and the changes it would bring', *US News and World Report*, August 22.

References B: Academic Articles on the NIT Experiments

Aaron, H. 1975. 'Cautionary notes on the experiment', in J. A. Pechman and M. P. Timpane, (eds.), *Work incentives and income guarantees: The New Jersey negative income tax experiment* (Washington DC., Brookings Institution), pp. 88–110.

_____ and Todd, J. 1978. *The use of income maintenance experiment findings in public policy, 1977–78*, Industrial Relations Research Association Series, Proceedings of the 31st annual meeting, pp. 46–56.

Adams, C. 1980. 'A reappraisal of the work incentive aspects of welfare reform', *Social Service Review*, Vol. 54, No. 4, pp. 521–536.

Anderson, G.M. and Block, W. 1993. 'Economic response to a guaranteed annual income: Experience from Canada and the United States: Comment', *Journal of Labour Economics*, Vol. 11, No. 1, S348–363.

Anderson, M. 1978. *Welfare: The political economy of welfare reform in the United States* (Stanford, Hoover Institution Press).

Ashenfelter, O. 1977. *The labour supply response of wage earners in the rural negative income tax experiment*, Working Paper No. 95 (Princeton University, Industrial Relations Sections).

_____ 1978. 'The labour supply response of wage earners', in J. L. Palmer and J. A. Pechman (eds.), *Welfare in rural areas: The north Carolina-Iowa income maintenance experiment* (Washington, DC., Brookings Institution).

_____ 1980. *Discrete choice in labour supply: The determinants of participation in the Seattle and Denver income maintenance experiments*, Working Paper No. 136 (Industrial Relations Section, Princeton University).

_____ 1983. 'Determining participation in income-tested social programmes', in *Journal of the American Statistical Association* 78, applications section, pp. 517–525.

_____ and Plant, W.M. 1990. 'Nonparametric estimates of the labour-supply effects of negative income tax programmes', *Journal of Labour Economics*, Vol. 8, No 1, Part 2, S396–S415 .

Atkinson, T., Cutt, J. and Stevenson, H.M. 1973. *Public policy research and the guaranteed annual income: A design for the experimental evaluation of income maintenance policies in Canada* (Toronto, York University).

AuClaire, P.A. 1977. 'Informing social policy: The limits of experimentation', *Sociological Practice*, Vol. 2, No. 1, pp. 24–37.

Avery, R. 1977. 'Effects of welfare "bias" on family earnings response', in H.W. Watts and A. Rees (eds.), *The New Jersey income-maintenance experiment volume III: The impact on expenditures, health, and social behaviour, and the quality of the evidence* (New York, Academic Press), pp. 303–322.

———— and Watts, H.W. 1977. 'The application of an error component model to experimental panel data' in H.W. Watts and A. Rees (eds.), *The New Jersey income-maintenance experiment volume II: Labour-supply responses* (New York, Academic Press), pp. 383–392.

Avrin, M.E. 1978. *The impact of income-maintenance on the utilization of subsidized housing*, Research Memorandum No. 54 (Center for the Study of Welfare Policy, Stanford Research Institute – SRI International).

———— 1980. 'Utilization of subsidized housing', in P. K. Robins *et al.* (eds.), *A guaranteed annual income: Evidence from a social experiment* (New York, Academic Press).

Barth, M.C., Orr, L.L. and Palmer, J.L. 1975. 'Policy implications: A positive view', in J. A. Pechman and P. M. Timpane (eds.), *Work incentives and income guarantees: The New Jersey negative income tax experiment* (Washington DC., Brookings institution).

Basilevsky, A. and Sproule, R. 1979. *The accuracy of income reporting in mincome Manitoba*, Technical Report No. 10, Mincome Manitoba.

———— Hum, D. and Sabourin, D. 1979. *Income reporting behavior in a negative income tax programme: A comparison of retrospective and prospective reporting methods in Mincome Manitoba*, Technical Report No. 9, Mincome Manitoba.

Bawden, D.L. 1970. 'Income maintenance and the rural poor: An experimental approach', *American Journal of Agricultural Economics*, Vol. 52, pp. 438–441 (August).

———— 1976. 'Implications of a negative income tax for rural people', *American Journal of Agricultural Economics*, pp. 754–760 (December).

———— 1977a. 'Income and work response of husbands', in D. L. Bawden and W. Harrar (eds.), *The rural income maintenance experiment: Final report* (Madison, Institute for Research on Poverty, University of Wisconsin).

———— 1977b. 'Income and work response of wives and dependents', in D. L. Bawden, and W. Harrar (eds.), *The rural income maintenance experiment: Final report* (Madison, Institute for Research on Poverty, University of Wisconsin).

———— 1977c. 'Purpose and design of the rural income maintenance experiment', *American Journal of Agricultural Economics*, Vol. 59, No. 5, pp. 855–858 (December).

Bawden, D.L. and Harrar, W.S. (eds.) 1977. *The rural income maintenance experiment: Final report* (Madison, Institute for Research on Poverty, University of Wisconsin).

———— 1978. 'Design and operation', in J. L. Palmer and J. A. Pechman (eds.), *Welfare in rural areas: The north Carolina-Iowa income maintenance experiment* (Washington, DC., Brookings Institution), pp. 23–54.

Benus, J., Halsey, H.I. and Spiegelman, R.G. 1979. *The Seattle and Denver income maintenance experiments' counselling programme and its utilization*, Research Memorandum No. 67 (Menlo Park, CA, Stanford Research Institute International).

Betson, D. and Greenberg, D. 1983. 'Uses of microsimulation in applied poverty research', in R. Goldstein and S. M. Sacks (eds.), *Applied policy research* (Totowa, NJ, Rowman and Allanheld).

Betson, D., Greenburg, D. and Kasten, R. 1980. 'A microsimulation model for analysing alternative welfare reform proposals: An application to the programme for better jobs and income', in R. Haveman and K. Hollenbeck (eds.), *Microeconomic simulation models for public policy analysis*: Vol. 1 (New York, Academic Press).

_____ 1980. 'Using Labour Supply Results to Simulate Welfare Reform Alternatives', in P. K. Robins *et al.* (eds.), *A guaranteed annual income: Evidence from a social experiment* (New York, Academic Press).

_____ 1981. 'A simulation analysis of the economic efficiency and distributional effects of alternative programme structures: The negative income tax versus the credit income tax', in I. Garfinkel (ed.), *Income-tested transfer programmes: A case for and against* (New York, Academic Press).

Billet, C., Komus, D., Basilevsky, A. and Sproule, R. 1979. *Issues in the administration of Mincome Manitoba: Three preliminary assessments*, Technical Report No. 11, Mincome Manitoba.

Bishop, J. 1980. 'Jobs, cash transfers, and martial instability: A review and synthesis of the evidence', *Journal of Human Resources*, Vol. 15, No. 3 (Summer).

Block, W. 1991. *Economic freedom: Toward a theory of measurement* (Vancouver, Fraser Institute).

Blum, B.B. 1986. 'Views of a policymaker and public administrator', in A. H. Munnell (ed.), *Lessons from the income maintenance experiments* (Boston, Federal Reserve Bank of Boston).

Boekmann, M. 1976. 'Policy implications of the New Jersey income maintenance experiment', *Policy Sciences*, 7, pp. 53–76 (March).

Boumol, W. 1974. 'An overview of the results on consumption, health, and social behaviour', *Journal of Human Resources*, Vol. 9, No. 2, pp. 253–264.

_____ 1977. 'An overview of the results', in H. W. Watts and R. Rees (eds.), *The New Jersey income-maintenance experiment volume III: The impact on expenditures, health, and social behaviour, and the quality of the evidence* (New York, Academic Press), pp. 1–14.

Bradbury, K. 1978. 'Income maintenance alternatives and family composition: An analysis of price effects', *Journal of Human Resources*, Vol. 13, No. 3, pp. 305–331 (Summer).

_____ 1986. 'Discussion of "non-labour supply responses to the income maintenance experiments" by Eric A. Hanushek,' in A. H. Munnea (ed.), *Lessons from the income maintenance experiments* (Boston, Federal Reserve Bank of Boston), pp. 122–125.

Brown, C.V. 1972. 'Negative income tax and the incentive to work', *New Society*, June, pp. 461–462.

Browning, E. 1975. *Redistribution and the welfare system* (Washington, DC., American Enterprise Institute for Public Policy Research).

_____ 1971. 'Incentive and disincentive experimentation for income maintenance policy purposes: Note', *American Economic Review*, 61, pp. 709–712.

_____ 1971. *Income redistribution and the negative income tax: A theoretical analysis*, Ph.D. dissertation (Princeton NJ, Princeton University).

Bryant, W.K. 1986. 'A portfolio analysis of poor rural wage-working families' assets and debts', in *American Journal of Agricultural Economics*, Vol. 68, No. 2, pp. 237–245 (May).

Burke, V.J. and Burke, V. 1979. *Nixon's good deed: Welfare reform* (New York, Columbia University Press).

Burtless, G. 1986. 'The work response to a guaranteed income. A survey of experimental evidence', in A. H. Munnell (ed.), *Lessons from the income maintenance experiments* (Boston, Federal Reserve Bank of Boston).

_____ 1989. 'The effect of welfare reform on employment, earnings, and income', in P. H. Cottingham and D. T. Ellwood (eds.), *Policy for the 1990s* (Cambridge, MA, Harvard University Press), pp. 103–140.

_____ 1990. 'The economist's lament: Public assistance in America', *Journal of Economic Perspectives*, Vol. 4, pp. 57–78.

_____ 1995. 'The case for randomized field trials in economic and policy research', *Journal of Economic Perspectives*, Vol. 9, pp. 63–84.

Burtless, G. and Greenberg, D. 1982. 'Inferences concerning labour supply behaviour based on limited duration experiments', in *American Economic Review*, Vol. 72, pp. 488–497 (June).

_____ 1978. *The limited duration of income maintenance experiments and its implications for estimating labour supply effects of transfer programmes*, Technical Analysis Paper No. 15 (Office of Income Security Policy, Department of Health Education and Welfare).

_____ and Hausman, J.A. 1978. 'The effect of taxation on labour supply: Evaluating the Gary negative income tax experiments', *The Journal of Political Economy*, Vol. 86, No. 6, pp. 1103–1130 (December).

Cain, G.C. 1977. 'Fertility behavior', in H. W. Watts and A. Rees (eds.), *The New Jersey income-maintenance experiment volume III: The impact on expenditures, health, and social behavior, and the quality of the evidence*. (New York, Academic Press), pp. 225–250.

_____ 1986. 'The income maintenance experiments and the issues of marital stability and family composition and the income maintenance experiments', in A. H. Munnell (ed.), *Lessons from the income maintenance experiments* (Boston, Federal Reserve Bank), pp. 60–93.

_____ and Watts, H. 1973. 'Towards a summary and synthesis of the evidence', in G. C. Cain and H. Watts (eds.) *Income maintenance and labour supply* (New York, Academic Press).

_____ (eds.) 1973. *Income maintenance and labour supply* (New York, Academic Press).

_____ and Wissoker, D. 1988. *Marital breakups in the Seattle-Denver income maintenance experiment: A different conclusion*, Discussion Paper No. 870–88 (Madison, Institute for Research on Poverty, University of Wisconsin).

_____ 1990. 'A reanalysis of marital stability in SIME/DIME', *American Journal of Sociology*,Vol. 95, No. 5. (March), pp. 1235–1269.

_____ 1990. 'Response to Hannan and Tuma', *American Journal of Sociology*, Vol. 95, No. 5, pp. 1299–1314 (March).

_____ and Watts, H. (eds.) 1974. 'The labour-supply response of married women, husbands present', *Journal of Human Resources*, Vol. 9, No. 2, pp. 201–223.

_____ 1977. 'Labour-supply response of wives', in H. W. Watts and A. Rees (eds.) *The New Jersey income-maintenance experiment volume II: Labour-supply responses* (New York, Academic Press), pp. 115–162.

Choudhry, S. 1989. *Income maintenance experiments and household transition dynamics: A temporal treatment of incremental effects*, Ph.D. thesis, University of Manitoba.

Christopherson, G. 1976. *The administration of the Seattle and Denver income maintenance experiments* (Princeton, NJ, Mathematica, Inc.).

_____ 1983a. *The final report of the Seattle-Denver income maintenance experiment, Vol. 2. Administration* (Princeton, NJ., Mathematica Policy Research).

_____ 1983b. 'Implementation', in *The final report of the Seattle-Denver income maintenance experiment, Vol. 1. Design and results* (Menlo Park, CA, Stanford Research Institute International), pp. 55–87.

Cogan, J.F. 1978. *Negative income taxation and labour supply: New evidence from the New Jersey-Pennsylvania experiment* (R-2155-HEW, Santa Monica, CA, The Rand Corporation).

_____ 1983. 'Labour supply and negative income taxation: New evidence from the New Jersey-Pennsylvania experiment', *Economic Inquiry*, Vol. 21, No. 4, pp. 465–84 (October).

Cohen, S.S. 1969. 'Administrative aspects of a negative income tax", *Pennsylvania University Law Review* 5, pp. 678–699.

Collard, D. 1980. 'Social dividend and negative income tax', in C. Sandford, C. Pond and R. Walker (eds.) *Taxation and social policy* (London, Heinemann), pp. 190–202.

Committee on Finance, United States Senate. *Welfare research experimentation*, Hearings of November 15–17, 1978 (Washington, D.C., US Government Printing Office).

Comptroller General of the United States 1981. *Income maintenance experiments: Need to summarize results and communicate the lessons learned*, Report to the Honorable Daniel P. Moynihan, the US Senate, US General Accounting Office.

Conlisk, J. and Watts, H. 1969. 'A model for optimizing experimental designs for estimating response surfaces', in *American Statistical Association Proceedings*, Social Statistics Section 64.

Conlisk, J. and Mordecai, K. 1972. *The assignment model of the Seattle and Denver income maintenance experiments*, Research Memorandum No. 15, July (Center for the Study of Welfare Policy, Menlo Park, CA, Stanford Research Institute).

Coyle, D. and Wildavsky, A. 1986. 'Social experimentation in the face of formidable fables', in A. H. Munnell (ed.), *Lessons from the income maintenance experiments* (Boston, Federal Reserve Bank of Boston).

Crest, D., Billet, C., Komus, D. and Quarry, A. 1979. *The administration of the payments system of Mincome Manitoba*, Technical Report No. 4, Mincome Manitoba.

Danzinger, S., Haveman, R. and Plotnick, R. 1981. 'How income transfer programmes affect work, savings and the income distribution: a critical review', *Journal of Economic Literature*, 19, pp. 975–1028.

Davis, V. and Waksberg, A. 1980. 'Data collection and processing', in P. K. Robins *et al.* (eds.), *A guaranteed annual income: Evidence from a social experiment* (New York, Academic Press).

De Vanzo, J. and Greenberg, D.H. 1973. *Suggestions for assessing economic and demographic effects of income maintenance programmes* (Santa Monica, CA, The Rand Corporation).

Dickenson, J. 1980. *The structure of labour supply response and the structure of preferences: Alternative estimates for SIME/DIME, Research memorandum*, Working Paper SRI-SD6 (Menlo Park, CA, Stanford Research Institute International).

Dickenson, K.P. and West, R.W. 1983. 'Impacts of counseling and education subsidy programmes', in *The final report of the Seattle-Denver income maintenance experiment, Vol. 1. Design and results* (Menlo Park, CA, Stanford Research Institute International), pp. 201–256.

Elesh, D. and Lefcowitz, M. J. 1977. 'The effects of health on the supply of and returns to labour', in H. W. Watts and A. Rees (eds.), *The New Jersey income-maintenance experiment volume II: Labour-supply responses* (New York, Academic Press), pp. 289–320.

_____ and MacCarthy, E. 1972. *Labour force participation among male heads of households in the New Jersey-Pennsylvania negative income tax experiments: Preliminary results*, Discussion Paper (Madison, Institute for Research on Poverty, University of Wisconsin).

_____, Ladinsky, J. and Lefcowitz, M.J. 1971. 'The New Jersey-Pensylvania experiment: A field study in negative taxation', in L. L. Orr, R. G. Hollister and M. J. Lefcowitz *Income maintenance: Interdisciplinary approaches to research* (Chicago, Marham), pp. 14–35.

Elmore, R.F. 1986. 'A political scientist's view of the income maintenance experiments', in A. H. Munnell (ed.), *Lessons from the income maintenance experiments* (Boston, Federal Reserve Bank of Boston).

Felder, H.E., Hall, A. and Weiss, Y. 1977. *The impact of income maintenance and manpower subsidies on the decision to invest in human capital: Interim results from the Seattle and Denver income maintenance experiments*, Research Memorandum No. 34 (Center for the Study of Welfare Policy, Menlo Park, CA, Stanford Research Institute International).

Ferber, R. and Hirsch, W. 1978. 'Social experimentation and economic policy: A survey', *Journal of Economic Literature*, 16, pp. 1379–1414.

Galligan, R.J. and Bahr, S.J. 1978. 'Economic well-being and marital stability: Implications for income maintenance programmes', *Journal of Marriage and the Family*, May, pp. 283–290.

Galloday, F.L. and Havemen, R.H. 1977. *The economic impacts of tax-transfer policy: Regional and distributional effects* (New York, Academic Press).

Garfinkel, I. 1973. 'On estimating the labour-supply effects of a negative income tax', in G. Cain and H. Watts (eds.), *Income maintenance and labour supply* (New York, Academic Press), pp. 205–264.

_____ 1974. 'Income transfer programmes and work effort: A review', in Joint Economic Committee, US Congress *How income supplements can affect work behavior*, Studies in Public Welfare, Paper No. 13 (Washington DC, US Government Printing Office).

_____ 1974. 'The effects of welfare programmes on experimental responses', *Journal of Human Resources*, Vol. 9, No. 4, pp. 530–555.

_____ 1974. 'The effects of welfare programmes on experimental responses', in H.W. Watts and A. Rees (eds.), *The New Jersey income-maintenance experiment volume III: The impact on expenditures, health, and social behavior, and the quality of the evidence* (New York, Academic Press), pp. 279–302.

_____ (ed.) 1982. *Income-tested transfer programmes: The case for and against* (New York, Academic Press).

Greenberg, D.H. 1983. 'Some labour market effects of labour supply responses to transfer programmes', *Journal of Social-Economic Planning Sciences*, Fall.

_____ and Halsey, H. 1983. 'Systematic misreporting and effects of income maintenance experiments on work effort: Evidence from the Seattle-Denver experiment', *Journal of Labour Economics*, Vol. 1, No. 4, pp. 380–407.

_____ and Hosek, J.R. 1976. *Regional labour supply response to negative income tax programmes* (Santa Monica, CA, The Rand Corporation).

_____ and Kosters, M. 1973. 'Income guarantees and the working poor: The effect of income maintenance programmes on the hours of work of male family heads', in G. Cain and H. Watts (eds.), *Income maintenance and labour supply* (New York, Academic Press), pp. 14–101.

_____ and Kosters, M. 1979. *Income guarantees and working poor: The effect of income maintenance programmes on the hours of work of male family heads* (Santa Monica, CA, The Rand Corporation).

_____, Linksz, D. and Mandell, M. 2002. *Social experimentation and policy making* (Washington, D.C., Urban Institute Press), Chapter 6 (on Income maintenance experiments).

_____, Moffit, R. and Friedmann, J. 1981 'Underreporting and experimental effects of work effort: Evidence from the Gary income maintenance experiment', in *Review of Economics and Statistics*, 63, pp. 581–589 (December).

Groenveld, L., Tuma, N. and Hannan, M. 1980a. 'The effects of negative income tax programmes on marital dissolution', in *Journal of Human Resources*, 15, pp. 654–674.

_____ 1980b. 'Marital dissolution and remarriage', in P. K. Robins *et al.* (eds.), *A guaranteed annual income: Evidence from a social experiment* (New York, Academic Press).

_____ 1980c. *Topics in the analysis of the effects of SIME/DIME on marital stability*, Technical Memo, SD 12 (Menlo Park, CA, Stanford Research Institute International).

_____ 1983. 'Marital stability', in *Final report of the Seattle-Denver income maintenance experiment, Vol. 1. Design and results* (Menlo Park, CA, Stanford Research Institute International), pp. 257–387.

Hall, A. R. 1980. 'Education and training', in P. K. Robins *et al.* (eds.), *A guaranteed annual income: Evidence from a social experiment* (New York, Academic Press).

_____ 1980. 'The counseling and training subsidy treatments', *Journal of Human Resources* 15, pp. 591–610.

Hall, R. 1973. 'Wage, income, and hours of work in the US labour force', in G. Cain and H. Watts (eds.), *Income maintenance and labour supply* (New York, Academic Press), pp. 102–162.

_____ 1975. 'Effects of the experimental negative income tax on labour supply', in J. A. Pechman and P. M. Timpane (eds.), *Work incentives and income guarantees: The New Jersey negative income tax experiment* (Washington, DC, Brookings Institution), pp. 115–147.

Halsey, H.I. 1978. *The effective federal income tax: Evidence from the Seattle and Denver income maintenance experiments*, Research Memorandum No. 55 (The Center for the Study of Welfare Policy, Menlo Park, CA, Stanford Research Institute International).

_____ 1980. 'Data validation', in P. K. Robins *et al.* (eds.), *A guaranteed annual income: Evidence from a social experiment* (New York, Academic Press).

_____, Kurz M. and Waksberg, A. 1977. *The reporting of income to welfare: A study in the accuracy of income reporting*, Research Memorandum No. 42 (The Center for the Study of Welfare Policy, Menlo Park, CA, Stanford Research Institute International-SRI).

Hannan, M. and Tuma, N. 1989. *A critique of Cain and Wissoker's reanalysis of the impact of income maintenance on marital stability in the Seattle-Denver experiment*, Technical Report 89–7 (Ithaca, New York, Cornell University, Department of Sociology).

_____ 1990. 'A reassessment of the effects of income maintenance on marital dissolution in the Seattle-Denver experiment', *American Journal of Sociology*, 95, pp. 1270–98.

_____, Beaver, S.E. and Tuma, N. 1974. *Income maintenance effects on the making and breaking of marriage: Preliminary analysis of the first eighteen months of the Denver income maintenance experiment*, Unpublished manuscript (Menlo Park, CA, Stanford Research Institute International).

_____, Tuma, N. and Groenveld, L. 1976. *The impact of income maintenance on the making and breaking of marital unions: Interim report*, Research Memorandum No. 28 (Menlo Park, CA, Center for the Study of Welfare Policy, Stanford Research Institute International).

_____ 1977. *A model of the effect of income maintenance on marital dissolutions: Evidence from the Seattle and Denver income maintenance experiments*, Research Memorandum No. 44 (Menlo Park, CA, Center for the Study of Welfare Policy, Stanford Research Institute International).

_____ 1977. *A summary discussion of the results on the effect of income maintenance on marital dissolutions: Evidence from the Seattle and Denver income maintenance experiments*, Research Memorandum No. 56 (Menlo Park, CA, Center for the Study of Welfare Policy, Stanford Research Institute International).

_____ 1977. 'Income and marital events: Evidence from an income-maintenance experiment', *American Journal of Sociology*, Vol. 82, No. 6, pp. 1186–1211.

_____ 1978. 'Income and independence effects on marital dissolution: Results from the Seattle and Denver income-maintenance experiments', in *American Journal of Sociology*, Vol. 84, No. 3, pp. 611–633.

_____ 1979. *Income an independence effects on marital dissolutions: Results from the first three years of SIME/DIME*, Research Memorandum No. 63 (Menlo Park, CA, Center for the Study of Welfare Policy, Stanford Research Institute International).

Hanusheck, E. 1986. 'Non-labour-supply response to the income maintenance experiments', in A. Munnell (ed.), *Lessons from the income maintenance experiments* (Boston, The Federal Reserve Bank of Boston), pp. 106–121.

Hausman, J. and Wise, D. 1976. 'The evaluation of results from truncated samples: The New Jersey income maintenance experiment', *Annals of Economic and Social Measurement*, 5 (Fall), pp. 421–475.

_____ 1979. 'Attrition bias in experimental and panel data: The Gary income mainte-nance experiment', in *Econometrica*, Vol. 47, No. 2, pp. 455–473.

_____ (eds.) 1985. *Social experimentation* (Chicago, University of Chicago Press).

Havenman, R.H. and Watts, H.W. 1976. 'Social experimentation as policy research: A review of negative income tax experiments, *Evaluation Studies*, 1, pp. 406–431.

Heckman, J. J. and Smith, J.A. 1995. 'Assessing the case for social experiments', in *Journal of Economic Perspectives*, Vol. 9, No. 2, pp. 85–110.

Hollister, R. 1974. 'The labour-supply response of the family', in *Journal of Human Resources*, Vol. 9, No. 2, pp. 223–252.

Hollister, R.G. and Metcalf, C.E. 1977. 'Family labour-supply response in the New Jersey experiment', in H. W. Watts and A. Rees (eds.), *The New Jersey income-maintenance experiment volume II: Labour-supply responses* (New York, Academic Press), pp. 185–220.

Hum, D. 1988. 'Integrating taxes and transfers', *Canadian Tax Journal*, 3, pp. 671–690.

_____ and Choudhry, S. 1992. 'Income, work and marital dissolution: Canadian exper-imental evidence', *Journal of Comparative Family Studies*.

Hum, D. and Simpson, W. 1991. *Income maintenance, work effort, and the Canadian experiment* (Ottawa, Economic Council of Canada).

_____ 1993a. 'Economic response to a guaranteed annual income: Experience from Canada and the United States', *Journal of Labour Economics*, Vol. 11, No. 1, Part 2, S263–S296.

_____ 1993b. 'Whatever happened to the guaranteed income idea?', in *Canadian Public Administration*, Vol. 36, No. 3, pp. 442–50.

_____ 1995. 'Reducing spending', in *Canadian Public Administration*, Vol. 38, No. 4, pp. 508–612.

_____ (ed.) 1979. *The sample design and assignment model of the Manitoba basic annual income experiment*, Technical Report No. 2, Winnipeg, Mincome Manitoba.

Hurd, M. 1976. *The estimation of nonlinear labour supply functions with taxes from a truncated sample*, Research Memorandum No. 36 (Menlo Park, CA, Socioeconomic Research Center, Stanford Research Institute International).

Husby, R. 1973. 'Impact of negative income tax on aggregate demand and supply', in *Western Economic Journal*, pp. 111–117.

_____ 1973. 'Work incentives and the cost effectiveness of income maintenance pro-grammes', in *Quarterly Review of Economics and Business*, pp. 7–13.

Johnson, T.R. and Pencavel, J.H. 1980a. 'Welfare payments and family composition', in P. K. Robins *et al.* (eds.) *A guaranteed annual income: Evidence from a social experiment* (New York, Academic Press).

_____ 1980b. *Utility-based hours of work functions for husbands, wives, and single females estimated from Seattle-Denver experimental data*, Research Memorandum No. 71 (Menlo Park, CA, Stanford Research Institute International).

_____ 1982. 'Forecasting the effects of a negative income tax programme', in *Industrial and Labour Relations Review*, 35 (January), pp. 221–234.

_____ 1984. 'Dynamic hours of work functions for husbands, wives, and single females', in *Econometrica*, 52 (March), pp. 363–389.

Johnson, W.R. 1980. 'The effect of a negative income tax on risk-taking in the labour market', in *Economic Inquiry*, Vol. 18, No. 3, pp. 395–407.

Joint Economic Committee, US Congress. 1974. *How income supplements can affect work behav-ior*, Studies in Public Welfare Paper No. 13 (Washington, D.C., US Government Printing Office).

Juster, T.F., 1974. 'Rethinking the allocation of resources in social research', in *Monthly Labour Review* (June), pp. 36–39.

Kaluzny, R.L. 'Changes in the consumption of housing services: The Gary experiment', in *Journal of Human Resources*, Vol. 14, No. 4 (Fall), pp. 496–506.

Keeley, M.C. 1977. *The impact of income maintenance on geographic mobility: Preliminary analysis and empirical results from the Seattle and Denver income maintenance Experiments*, Research Memorandum No. 47 (Center for the Study of Welfare Policy, Menlo Park, CA, Stanford Research Institute).

———— 1977. *Using post-experimental data to derive the effects of a permanent income maintenance programme*, Mimeograph (Menlo Park, CA, Stanford Research Institute-SRI).

———— 1978. 'The estimation of labour supply models using experimental data' *American Economic Review*, pp. 873–887(December).

———— 1978. *The impact of income maintenance on fertility: Preliminary findings from the Seattle and Denver income maintenance Experiments*, Research Memorandum No. 49 (Center for the Study of Welfare Policy, Menlo Park, CA, Stanford Research Institute).

———— 1979. *Taxes, transfers, and subsidies and demand for children: The impact of alternative negative income tax programmes*, Research Memorandum No. 65, (Center for the Study of Welfare Policy, Menlo Park, CA, Stanford Research Institute).

———— 1979. *The destination choices and earnings of migrants: The impact of alternative negative income tax programmes*, Research Memorandum No. 64, (Center for the Study of Welfare Policy, Menlo Park, CA, Stanford Research Institute).

———— 1980. 'Demand for children', in P.K. Robins *et al.* (eds.) *A guaranteed annual income: Evidence from a social experiment* (New York, Academic Press).

———— 1980. 'Migration', in P.K. Robins *et al.* (eds.) *A guaranteed annual income: Evidence from a social experiment* (New York, Academic Press).

———— 1980. 'The effects of negative income tax on migration', *Journal of Human Resources*, 15, pp. 695–706.

———— 1980. 'The effects of negative income tax programmes on fertility', *Journal of Human Resources*, 15, pp. 675–694.

———— 1981. *Labour supply and public policy: Critical review* (New York, Academic Press).

———— and Robins, P. 1980. 'Experimental design, the Conlisk-Watts assignment model, and the proper estimation of behavioral response', *Journal of Human Resources*, Vol. 15, No. 4, pp. 480–498.

———— 1980. 'The design of social experiments: A critique of the Conlisk-Watts assignment model', Originally (1978), Research Memorandum No. 57 (Center for the Study of Welfare Policy, Menlo Park, CA, Stanford Research Institute), in R. G. Ehrenberg (ed.), *Research in Labour Economics 3* (New York, JAI Press/Elsevier International).

————, Robbins, P.K. and Spiegelman, R.G. 1976. *The estimation of labour supply models using experimental data: Evidence from the Seattle and Denver income maintenance experiments*, Research Memorandum No. 29 (Center for the Study of Welfare Policy, Menlo Park, CA, Stanford Research Institute).

————, Spiegelman, R. and West, R. 1980. 'Design of the Seattle/Denver income-maintenance experiments and an overview of results', in P.K. Robins *et al.* (eds.), *A guaranteed annual income: Evidence from a social experiment* (New York, Academic Press).

————, Robins, P., Spiegelman, R. and West, R. 1976. *The estimation of labour supply models using experimental data: Evidence from the Seattle and Denver income maintenance experiments*, Research Memorandum No. 29, (Center for the Study of Welfare Policy, Menlo Park, CA, Stanford Research Institute).

_____ 1977a. *The labour supply effects and costs of alternative negative income tax programmes: Evidence from the Seattle and Denver income maintenance experiments, Part 1: The labour supply response function*, Research Memorandum No. 38, (Center for the Study of Welfare Policy, Menlo Park, CA, Stanford Research Institute).

_____ 1977b. *The labour supply effects and costs of alternative negative income tax programmes: Evidence from the Seattle and Denver income maintenance experiments, Part 2: National predictions using the labour supply response function*, Research Memorandum No. 39, (Center for the Study of Welfare Policy, Menlo Park, CA, Stanford Research Institute).

_____ 1977c. *An interim report on the work effort effects and costs of a negative income tax using results of the Seattle and Denver income maintenance experiments: National predictions: A summary*, Research Memorandum No. 39, (Center for the Study of Welfare Policy, Menlo Park, CA, Stanford Research Institute).

_____ 1978a. 'The labour supply effects and costs of alternative negative income tax programmes', *Journal of Human Resources*, 13 (Winter), pp. 3–36.

_____ 1978b.'The estimation of labour supply models using experimental data', *American Economic Review* 68 (December), pp.873–887.

Kehrer, B.H. and Wolin, C.M. 1979. 'Impact of income maintenance on low birthweight: Evidence from the Gary experiment', *Journal of Human Resources*, Vol. 14, No. 4, pp. 434–462.

Kehrer, K.C. 1977. *The Gary income-maintenance experiment: Summary of initial findings* (Princeton, NJ, Mathematica, Inc.)

_____ 1979. 'Introduction to the Journal of Human Resources special issue: The Gary income maintenance experiment', *Journal of Human Resources*, Vol. 14, No. 4, pp. 431–433.

_____ McDonald, J.F. and Moffitt, R.A. 1980. *Final report of the Gary income maintenance experiment: Labour supply* (Princeton, NJ, Mathematica Policy Research).

Kelly, T.F. and Singer, L. 1971. 'The Gary income maintenance experiment: Plans and progress', *American Economic Review*, 61 (May), pp. 30–42.

Kerachsky, S.H. 1977. 'Health and medical care utilization: A second approach', in H. W. Watts and A. Rees (eds.) *The New Jersey income-maintenance experiment volume III: The impact on expenditures, health, and social behavior, and the quality of the evidence* (New York, Academic Press), pp.129–50.

Kershaw, D. and Fair, J. 1976. *The New Jersey income-maintenance experiment volume I: Operations, surveys, and administration* (New York, Academic Press).

Kershaw, D.N. and Small, J.C. 1972. 'Date confidentiality and privacy: Lessons from the New Jersey negative income tax experiment', in *Public Policy*, Vol. 20, No. 2, pp. 257–280.

Kessleman, J. 1976. 'Tax effects on job search, training, and work effort', *Journal of Public Economics* 6, pp. 255–272.

_____ 1990. *Income security via the tax system: Canadian and American reforms*, Discussion Paper No. 90–31 (Vancouver, University of British Coumbia).

Killingsworth, M. 1975. *Must a negative income tax reduce labour supply: A study of the family's allocation of time*, Working Paper No. 78 (Industrial Relations Section, Princeton University).

_____ 1984. *Labour supply* (Cambridge, Cambridge University Press).

_____ and Heckman, J. 1986. 'Female labour supply: A survey', in O. Ashenfelter and R. Layard (eds.) *Handbook of Labour Economics*, Vol. 1, (Amsterdam, North Holland), pp. 103–204.

Knudsen, J.H., Scott, R.A. and Shore, A.R. 1977. 'Household consumption', in H.W. Watts and A. Rees (eds.), *The New Jersey income-maintenance experiment volume III: The impact on expenditures, health, and social behavior, and the quality of the evidence* (New York, Academic Press), pp. 251–276.

_____ *et al.* 1977. 'Information levels and labour response', in H. W. Watts and A. Rees (eds.), *The New Jersey income-maintenance experiment volume II: Labour-supply responses* (New York, Academic Press), pp. 347–368.

Kurz, M. and Spiegelman, R.G. 1971. 'The Seattle experiment: The combined effect of income maintenance and manpower investments', in *American Economic Review*, Vol. 61, No. 2, pp. 22–29.

_____ 1972. *The design of the Seattle and Denver income maintenance experiments*, Research Memorandum No. 18 (Center for the Study of Welfare Policy, Menlo Park, CA, Stanford Research Institute).

_____ 1973. *Social experimentation: A new tool in economic and policy research*, Research Memorandum No. 22, (Center for the Study of Welfare Policy, Menlo Park, CA, Stanford Research Institute).

_____ Robins, P.K. and Spiegelman, R.G. 1975. *A study of the demand for child care by working mothers*, Research Memorandum No. 27 (Center for the Study of Welfare Policy, Menlo Park, CA, Stanford Research Institute).

_____ Spiegelman, R.G. and Brewster, J.A. 1973. *The payment system for the Seattle and Denver income maintenance experiments*, Research Memorandum No. 19 (Center for the Study of Welfare Policy, Menlo Park, CA, Stanford Research Institute).

_____ Spiegelman, R.G. and West, R.W. 1973. *The experimental horizon and the rate of time preference for the Seattle and Denver income maintenance experiments: A preliminary analysis research*, Memorandum No. 21 (Center for the Study of Welfare Policy, Menlo Park, CA, Stanford Research Institute).

_____, Robins, P., Spiegelman, R., West, R. and Halsey, H. 1974. *A cross sectional estimation of labour supply for families in Denver 1970*, Research Memorandum No. 24 (Center for the Study of Welfare Policy, Menlo Park, CA, Stanford Research Institute).

Ladinsky, J. and Wells, A. 1977. 'Social integration, leisure activity, media exposure, and lifestyle enhancement', in H.W. Watts and A. Rees (eds.), *The New Jersey income-maintenance experiment volume III: The impact on expenditures, health, and social behavior, and the quality of the evidence* (New York, Academic Press), pp. 195–224.

Lampman, R. 1974. 'The decision to undertake the New Jersey experiment', in *Final report of the New Jersey experiment*, Vol. 4 (Madison, WI, Institute for Research on Poverty and Mathematica).

Lane, R. 1975. 'Social science research and public policy', in S.S. Nagel (ed.), *Policy studies and the social sciences* (Lexington, MA., Lexington Books D.C, Health and Company), pp. 287–291.

Lefcowitz, M. J. and Elesh, D. 1977. 'Health and medical care utilization', in H.W. Watts and A. Rees (eds.), *The New Jersey income-maintenance experiment volume III: The impact on expenditures, health, and social behavior, and the quality of the evidence* (New York, Academic Press), pp. 113–128.

Lernon, R.I. and Townsend, A.A. 1974. 'Conflicting objections in income maintenance programmes', *The American Economic Review*, Vol. 64, No. 2, pp. 205–211.

Levine, R.A. 1975. 'How and why the experiments came about', in J. Pechman and M. Timpane (eds.), *Work incentives and income guarantees: The New Jersey negative income tax experiment* (Washington, D.C., Brookings Institution).

MaCurdy, T.E. 1981. *An intertemporal anaysis of taxation and work disincentives: An analysis of the Denver income maintenance experiment*, Working Paper number 0624 (Cambridge, Mass., National Bureau of Economic Research).

Mahoney, B.S. and Mahoney, W.M. 1975. 'Policy implications: A skeptical view', in J.A. Pechman and P.M. Timpane (eds.), *Work incentives and income guarantees: The New Jersey negative income tax experiment.* (Washington, D.C., Brookings institution).

Mallar, C.D. 1977. 'The educational and labour-supply responses of young adults in experimental families', in H.W. Watts and A. Rees (eds.), *The New Jersey income-maintenance experiment volume II: Labour-supply responses* (New York, Academic Press), pp. 163–184.

Masters, S.H. 1978. 'Comments on Robert Michael: The consumption studies', in J.
Palmer and J. Pechman (eds.), *Welfare in rural areas: The north Carolina-Iowa income maintenance experiment* (Washington DC, Brookings Institution), pp. 171–173.

Masters, S. and Garfinkle, I. 1977. *Estimating the labour supply effects of income-maintenance alternatives* (New York, Academic Press).

Maxfield, M. 1977. *Estimating the impact of labour supply adjustments on transfer programme costs:
A microsimulation methodology* (Washington, D.C., Mathematica Policy Research Inc).

Maynard, R.A. 1977. 'The effects of the rural income maintenance experiment on the
school performance of children', *American Economic Review*, Vol. 67, No. 1, pp. 370–375.

Maynard, R. C. and Murnane, R. J. 1979. 'The effects of a negative income tax on school
performance: Results of an experiment', *Journal of Human Resources*, Vol. 14, No.4,
pp. 463–476.

McDonald, J.F. and Stephenson, S.P. Jr. 1979. 'The effect of income maintenance on the
school-enrolment and labour-supply decisions of teenagers', *Journal of Human Resources*,
Vol.14, No.4, pp. 488–495.

Metcalf, C. 1973. 'Making inferences from controlled income maintenance experiments',
American Economic Review 63, pp. 478–483.

_____ 1974. 'Predicting the effects of permanent programmes from a limited duration
experiment', in *Journal of Human Resources*, Vol. 9, No. 4, pp. 530–555.

_____ 1977. 'Consumption behavior: Implications for a permanent programme', in
H.W. Watts and A. Rees (eds.), *The New Jersey income-maintenance experiment volume III: The
impact on expenditures, health, and social behavior, and the quality of the evidence* (New York,
Academic Press), pp. 93–112.

_____ 1977. 'Predicting the effects of permanent programmes from a limited duration
experiment' in H.W. Watts and A. Rees (eds.), *The New Jersey income-maintenance experiment
volume III: The impact on expenditures, health, and social behavior, and the quality of the evidence*
(New York, Academic Press), pp. 375–399.

_____ 1977. 'Sample design and the use of experimental data', H.W. Watts and A. Rees
(eds.), *The New Jersey income-maintenance experiment volume III: The impact on expenditures,
health, and social behavior, and the quality of the evidence* (New York, Academic Press),
pp. 413–440.

Michael, R. 1978. 'The Consumption studies', in J. Palmer and J. Pechman (eds.) *Welfare in
rural areas: The north Carolina-Iowa income maintenance experiment* (Washington, D.C.,
Brookings Institution), pp. 149–171.

Middleton, R. and Allen, V.L. 1977. 'Social psychological effects', in H.W. Watts and
A. Rees (eds.) *The New Jersey income-maintenance experiment volume III: The impact on expenditures, health, and social behavior, and the quality of the evidence* (New York, Academic Press),
pp. 151–194.

Moffit, R. 1979. 'The labour supply response in the Gary experiment', *Journal of Human
Resources*, Vol. 14, No. 4, pp. 477–487.

_____ 1985. 'A problem with the negative income tax', *Economic Letters*, 17, pp. 261–265.

_____ and Kehrer. K. 1981. 'The effect of tax and transfer programmes on labour
supply: The evidence from the income maintenance experiments', *Research in Labour
Economics*, 4, pp. 103–150.

Morrill, W.A. 1974. 'Introduction to JHR symposium – The graduated work incentives
experiment', *Journal of Human Resources*, Vol. 9, No.2, pp. 156–157.

Moynihan, D. P. 1973. *The politics of a guaranteed income: The Nixon Administration and the family assistance plan* (New York, Random House).

Mroz, T. 1987. 'The sensitivity of an empirical model of married women's hours of work to economic and statistical assumptions', *Econometrica*, 55, pp. 765–799.

Munnell, A.H. (ed.) 1986. *Lessons from the income maintenance experiments* (Boston, Federal Reserve Bank of Boston).

Munson, C.E., Robins, P.K. and Stieger, G. 1980. *Labour supply and childcare arrangements of single mothers in the Seattle and Denver income maintenance experiments*, Research Memorandum No. 69 (Center for the Study of Welfare Policy, Menlo Park, CA, Stanford Research Institute International).

———— 1980. 'Labour supply and childcare arrangements of single mothers', in P.K. Robins (eds.), *A Guaranteed Annual Income: Evidence from a Social Experiment* (New York, Academic Press).

Murnane, R., Maynard, R. and Ohls, J. 1981. 'Home resources and children's achievement', in *Review of Economics and Statistics*, Vol. 63, pp. 369–377.

Murray, C. 1986. 'Discussion of the policy lessons', in A. H. Munnell (ed.), *Lessons from the income maintenance experiments* (Boston, Federal Reserve Bank of Boston).

Nathan, R.P. 1986. 'Lessons for future public policy and research', in A.H. Munnell (ed.), *Lessons from the income maintenance experiments* (Boston, Federal Reserve Bank of Boston).

National Council of Welfare (Canada) 1976. *Guide to the guaranteed income* (Ottawa, National Council of Welfare).

Neuberg, L.G. 1989. *Conceptual anomalies in economics and statistics: Lessons from the social experiment* (New York, Cambridge University Press).

Nicholson, W. 1977. 'Differences among the three sources of income data', in H. W. Watts and A. Rees (eds.), *The New Jersey income-maintenance experiment volume III: The impact on expenditures, health, and social behavior, and the quality of the evidence* (New York, Academic Press), pp. 353–374.

———— 1977. 'Expenditure patterns: A descriptive survey', in H. W. Watts and A. Rees (eds.), *The New Jersey income-maintenance experiment volume III: The impact on expenditures, health, and social behavior, and the quality of the evidence* (New York, Academic Press), pp. 15–44.

———— 1977. 'Relationship of female labour-supply characteristics of the experimental sample to those of other samples', in H. W. Watts and A. Rees (eds.), *The New Jersey income-maintenance experiment volume III: The impact on expenditures, health, and social behavior, and the quality of the evidence* (New York, Academic Press), pp. 323–340.

O'Connor, A. 2001. *Poverty knowledge: Social science, social policy, and the poor in twentieth century US history* (Princeton, NJ, Princeton University Press).

O'Connor, J.F. and Madden, J.P. 1979. 'The negative income tax and the quality of dietary intake', in *Journal of Human Resources*, Vol. 14, No. 4, pp. 507–517.

Office of Income Security Policy, US Department of Health and Human Services 1983. *Overview of the Seattle-Denver income maintenance experiment final report* (Washington, D.C., US Government Printing Office).

Ohls, J. 'The demand for housing under a negative income tax' in E. Stromsdorfer and G. Farkas, *Evaluation Studies Review Annual*, Vol. 5, p. 502.

Orcutt, G. and Orcutt, A. 1968. 'Incentive and disincentive experimentation for income maintenance policy purposes', in *American Economic Review*, 58, pp.754–72.

Orr, L.L., Hollister, R. and Lefcowitz, M. 1971. *Income maintenance: Interdisciplinary approaches to research* (Institute for Research on Poverty Monograph Series, Chicago, University of Wisconsin).

Palmer, J. and Pechman, J. (eds.) 1978. *Welfare in rural areas: The north Carolina-Iowa income maintenance experiment* (Washington DC, Brookings Institution).

Pechman, J.A. and Timpane, P.M. 1975. 'Introduction and summary', in J.A. Pechman and P.M. Timpane (eds.), *Work Incentives and Income Guarantees: the New Jersey negative income tax experiment* (Washington, D.C., Brookings Institution).

———— (eds.). 1975. *Work Incentives and Income Guarantees: the New Jersey negative income tax experiment* (Washington, D.C., Brookings Institution).

Pencavel, J. 1980. *Market work decisions and unemployment of husbands and wives in the Seattle and Denver income maintenance experiments*, Research Memorandum No. 68 (Center for the Study of Welfare Policy, Menlo Park, CA, Stanford Research Institute International).

———— 1986. 'Labour supply of men: A survey', in O. Ashenfelter and R. Layard (eds.), *Handbook of Labour Economics*, Vol. 1 (Amsterdam, North Holland), pp.103–204.

Poirier, D.J. 1977. 'Characteristics of attriters who took the attrition interview', in H.W. Watts and A. Rees (eds.), *The New Jersey income-maintenance experiment volume III: The impact on expenditures, health, and social behavior, and the quality of the evidence* (New York, Academic Press), pp. 399–412.

———— 1977. 'Spline functions and their applications in regression analysis', in H. W. Watts and A. Rees (eds.), *The New Jersey income-maintenance experiment volume II: Labour-supply responses* (New York, Academic Press), pp. 369–382.

———— 1977. 'The determinants of home buying', in H.W. Watts and A. Rees (eds.), *The New Jersey income-maintenance experiment volume III: The impact on expenditures, health, and social behavior, and the quality of the evidence* (New York, Academic Press).

Pozdena, R.J. and Johnson, T.R. 1980. 'Demand for assets', in P.K. Robins *et al.* (eds.), *A guaranteed annual income: Evidence from a social experiment* (New York, Academic Press).

Prescott, D., Swidinsky, R. and Wilton, D. 1986. 'Labour supply estimates for low-income female heads of households using Mincome data', in *Canadian Journal of Economics*, Vol. 19, No. 1, pp. 134–141.

President's Commission on Income Maintenance Programmes. 1970 (Washington, D.C., US Government Printing Office).

Rainwater, L. 1986. 'A sociologist's view of the income maintenance experiments', in A.H. Munnell (ed.), *Lessons from the income maintenance experiments* (Boston, Federal Reserve Bank of Boston).

Rea, S.A. 1977. 'Investment in human capital under a negative income tax', in *Canadian Journal of Economics*, Vol. 10, No. 4, pp. 607–620.

Rees, A. 1974. 'An overview of the labour-supply results', *Journal of Human Resources*, Vol. 9, No. 2, pp. 158–180.

———— 1977. 'Labour supply results of the experiment: a summary', in H.W. Watts and A. Rees (eds.), *The New Jersey income-maintenance experiment volume II: Labour-supply responses* (New York, Academic Press).

———— and Watts, H.W. 1975. 'An overview of the labour supply results', in J.A. Pechman and P.M. Timpane (eds.) *Work incentives and income guarantees: The New Jersey negative income tax experiment* (Washington, D.C., Brookings Institution).

Rivlin, A.M. 1974. 'How can experiments be more useful?', *American Economic Review*, Vol. 64, No. 2, pp. 346–354.

———— 1974. 'Social experiments: Their uses and limitations', *Monthly Labour Review* (June), pp. 28–35.

———— and Timpane, M.P. 1975. *Ethical and legal issues of social experimentation* (Washington DC, Brookings Institution).

Robins, P.K. 1977. *Job satisfaction and income maintenance: Evidence from the Seattle and Denver income maintenance experiments*, Research Memorandum No. 45 (Center for the Study of Welfare Policy, Palo Alto, CA, Stanford Research Institute).

_____ 1980. 'Job satisfaction', in P.K. Robins *et al.* (eds.), *A guaranteed annual income: Evidence from a social experiment* (New York, Academic Press).

_____ 1980. 'Labour supply response of family heads and implications for a national programme', in P.K. Robins *et al.* (eds.), *A guaranteed annual income: Evidence from a social experiment* (New York, Academic Press).

_____ 1984. 'The labour supply response of twenty-year families in the Denver income maintenance experiment', in *Review of Economics and Statistics*, 66, pp. 491–195.

_____ 1985. 'A comparison of the labour supply findings from the four negative income tax experiments', in *Journal of Human Resources*, Vol. 20, No. 4, pp. 567–582.

_____ and McNicoll, S. 1979. *The cross-experimental adjusted means project*, Memorandum (Menlo Park, CA, Stanford Research Institute International).

_____ and McNicoll, S. 1981. *Additional runs for the cross-experimental adjusted means project*, Memorandum (Menlo Park, CA, Stanford Research Institute International).

_____ and Tuma, N. 1977. *Changes in rates of entering and leaving employment under a negative income tax programme: Evidence from the Seattle and Denver income maintenance experiments*, Research Memorandum No. 48 (Center for the Study of Welfare Policy, Menlo Park, CA, Stanford Research Institute International).

_____ and West, R. 1978a. *Participation in the Seattle and Denver income maintenance experiments and its effects on labour supply*, Research Memorandum No. 53 (Center for the Study of Welfare Policy, Palo Alto, CA, Stanford Research Institute).

_____ 1978b. *A longitudinal analysis of the labour supply response to a negative income tax programme: Evidence from the Seattle and Denver income maintenance experiments*, Research Memorandum No. 59 (Center for the Study of Welfare Policy, Palo Alto, CA, Stanford Research Institute).

_____ and West, R. 1980a. 'Programme participation and labour-supply response', *Journal of Human Resources*, Vol. 15, No. 4, pp. 499–523.

_____ 1980b. 'Labour supply response of family heads over time', in P.K. Robins *et al.* (eds.), *A guaranteed annual income: Evidence from a social experiment* (New York, Academic Press).

_____ 1980c. 'Labour-supply response over time', *Journal of Human Resources*, Vol. 15, No. 4, pp. 524 –544.

_____ 1983. 'Labour supply response', in *Final report of the Seattle-Denver income maintenance experiment* (Washington DC, Government Printing Office).

_____ 1985. 'Programme participation and labour-supply response', *Journal of Human Resources*, Vol. 20, pp. 567–582.

_____ 1986. 'Sample attrition and labour supply response in experimental panel data', *Journal of Business and Economic Statistics*, 4, pp. 329-338.

_____, Brandon, N. and Yeager, K.E. 1980. 'Effects of SIME/DIME on changes in employment status', *Journal of Human Resources*, Vol. 15, No. 4, pp. 545–573.

_____ Tuma, N. and Yeager, K.E. 1977. *Effects of the Seattle and Denver income maintenance experiments on changes in employment status*, Research Memorandum No. 70 (Center for the Study of Welfare Policy, Palo Alto, CA, Stanford Research Institute).

_____ West, R.W. and Lohrer, M.G. 1980. *Labour supply response to a nationwide negative income tax: Evidence from the Seattle and Denver income maintenance experiments*, Research Memorandum draft, Socioeconomic Research Center, Menlo Park, CA, Stanford Research Institute International).

_____ West, R. and Stieger, G.L. 1980. *Breakeven status and the labour supply response to an NIT programme: Evidence from the Seattle and Denver income maintenance experiments*, Research Memorandum No. 73 (Center for the Study of Welfare Policy, Palo Alto, CA, Stanford Research Institute).

_____, Spiegelman, R., Weiner, S. and Bell, J.G. (eds.) 1980. *A guaranteed annual income: Evidence from a social experiment* (New York, Academic Press).

Ross, H. 1966. *A Proposal for a demonstration of new techniques in income maintenance* (Washington, D.C., United Planning Organization).

_____ 1974. 'Case study of testing eeperimentation: Income maintenance and social policy research', in J.G. Abert and M. Kamass (eds.), *Social experiments and social programme evaluation, Proceedings of the Washington Operations Research Council Symposium* (Cambridge, MA, Bollinger Press).

Rossi, P.H. 1975 'A critical review of the analysis of nonlabour force responses', in J.A. Pechman and P.M. Timpane (eds.), *Work incentives and income guarantees: The New Jersey negative income tax experiment* (Washington DC, Brookings institution).

_____ and Lyle, K.C. 1976. *Reforming Public Welfare: A Critique of the Negative Income Tax Experiments* (New York, Russell Sage Foundation).

Sabourin, D. 1985. *Participation in income-tested social programmes: Evidence from the Mincome experiment* (Institute for Social and Economic Research, Winnipeg, University of Manitoba).

Saupe, W.E. 1977. *The rural income maintenance expeimernt, welfare reform, and programmes for smaller farms* (Institute for Research on Poverty Discussion Papers, University of Wisconsin-Madison).

Sawhill, I.V. (ed.) 1975. *Income transfers and family structure*, Report 979-03 (Washington, D.C., Urban Institute).

Skidmore, F. 1974. 'Availability of data from the graduated work incentive experiment', *Journal of Human Resources*, Vol. 9, No. 2, pp. 265–278.

_____ 1975. 'Operational design of the experiment', in J.A. Pechman and P.M. Timpane (eds.) *Work incentives and income guarantees: The New Jersey negative income tax experiment* (Washington, D.C., Brookings Institution).

Solow, R.M. 1986. 'An economist's view of the income maintenance experiments', in A.H. Munnell (ed.), *Lessons from the Income Maintenance Experiments* (Boston, Federal Reserve Bank of Boston).

Spiegelman, R.G. 1983. 'History and design', in *Final report of the Seattle-Denver income maintenance experiment, voume. 1. Design and results* (Menlo Park, CA, Stanford Research Institute International-SRI), pp. 1–51.

_____ and West, R.W. 1976. 'Feasibility of a social experiment and issues in its design: Experiences from the Seattle and Denver income maintenance experiments', in *Proceedings of the American Statistical Association, Business and Economic Statistics Section*, pp. 168–176.

_____ and Yaeger, K.E. 1980. 'Overview of the special issue "The Seattle and Denver income maintenance experiments"', in *Journal of Human Resources*, Vol. 15, No. 4, pp. 463–479.

Spilerman, S. and Miller, R.E. 1977. 'The effect of negative income tax payments on job turnover and unemployment duration', in H.W. Watts and A. Rees (eds.), *The New Jersey income-maintenance experiment volume II: Labour-supply responses* (New York, Academic Press), pp. 221–252.

_____ 1977. 'The impact of the experiment on job selection', in H.W. Watts and A. Rees (eds.) *The New Jersey income-maintenance experiment volume II: Labour-supply responses* (New York, Academic Press), pp. 253–286.

Stafford, F.P. 1985. 'Income-maintenance policy and work effort: Learning from experiments and labour-market studies', in J. Hausman and D. Wise (eds.), *Social experimentation* (Chicago, University of Chicago Press), pp. 95–143.

Stanford Research Institute International (SRI). 1983. *Final report of the Seattle-Denver income experiment, volume I: Design and results* (Washington, D.C., US Government Printing Office).

Tella, A., Tella, D. and Green, C. 1971. *The hours of work and family income response to negative income tax plans: The impact on the working poor* (Kalamazoo, Michigan, W. E. Upjohn Institute for Employment Research).

Thoits, P. 1978. *Income maintenance, life changes, and psychological distress: Implications for the life events theory*, Research Memorandum No. 66 (Center for the Study of Welfare Policy, Menlo Park, CA, Stanford Research Institute International).

Thoits, P. and Hannan, M.T. 1978. *Income and psychological distress: Evidence from the Seattle and Denver income maintenance experiments*, Research Memorandum No. 50 (Center for the Study of Welfare Policy, Menlo Park, CA, Stanford Research Institute International)

———— 1980. 'Income and psychological distress', in P.K. Robins (ed.), *A guaranteed annual income: Evidence from a social experiment* (New York, Academic Press).

Tuma, N.B. 1986. 'Discussion', in A. Munnell (ed.) *Lessons from the Income maintenance experiments* (Boston, The Federal Reserve Bank of Boston), pp. 99–105.

———— and Hannan, M.T. 1979. 'Dynamic analysis of event histories', *American Journal of Sociology*, Vol. 84, No. 4, pp. 820–854.

———— and Robins, P.K. 1980. 'A dynamic model of employment behavior: An application to the Seattle and Denver income maintenance experiments', *Econometrica*, Vol. 48, No. 4, pp. 1031–52.

————, Groenveld, L. and Hannan, M. 1976. *First dissolutions and marriages: Impacts in 24 months of the Seattle and Denver income maintenance experiments*, Research Memorandum No. 35 (Center for the Study of Welfare Policy, Menlo Park, CA, Stanford Research Institute International).

———— 1977. *Variation over time in the impact of the Seattle and Denver income maintenance experiments on the making and breaking of marriages*, Research Memorandum No. 43 (Center for the Study of Welfare Policy, Menlo Park, CA, Stanford Research Institute International).

————, Hannan, M.T. and Groenveld, L. 1978. *Dynamic analysis of marital stability*, Research Memorandum No. 58 (Center for the Study of Welfare Policy, Menlo Park, CA, Stanford Research Institute International).

———— (ed.) 1974. *Measurement of unobservable variables describing families*, Research Memorandum No. 23 (Center for the Study of Welfare Policy, Palo Alto, CA, Stanford Research Institute).

United States Department of Health, Education, and Welfare 1973. *Summary report: New Jersey graduated work incentive experiment* (Washington, D.C., US Government Printing Office).

———— 1976. *Summary report: Rural income maintenance experiment* (Washington, D.C., US Government Printing Office).

———— 1983. *Overview of the Seattle-Denver income maintenance experiment final report* (Washington, D.C., US Government Printing Office).

United States General Accounting Office. 1981. *Income maintenance experiments: How to summarize results and communicate the lessons learned*, Report Number HRD 81–46 (Washington, D.C.,).

United States Senate 1978. *Welfare research and experimentation: Hearings before the Subcommittee on Public Assistance of the Committee on Finance, United States Senate* (Washington, D.C., US Government Printing Office).

Van Loon, R. 1979. 'Reforming welfare in Canada', in *Public Policy*, 27, p. 469.

Watts, H.W. 1970. *Adjusted and extended preliminary results from the urban graduated work incentive experiment* (Madison, Institute for Research on Poverty, University of Wisconsin).

_____ 1971.'The graduated work incentive experiments: Current progress', in *American Economic Review* 61, pp. 15–21.

_____ and Cain, G.C. 1973. 'Labour supply effects of the New Jersey-Pennsylvania graduated work incentives experiment', in *Final report of the graduated work incentives experiment* (Madison, Institute for Research on Poverty, University of Wisconsin).

_____ and David, H. 1977. 'Labour-supply response of husbands', in H.W. Watts and A. Rees (eds.), *The New Jersey income-maintenance experiment volume II: Labour-supply responses* (New York, Academic Press), pp. 57–114.

_____ and Mamer, J. 1977. 'Analysis of wage-rate differentials', in H.W. Watts and A. Rees (eds.) *The New Jersey income-maintenance experiment volume III: The impact on expenditures, health, and social behavior, and the quality of the evidence* (New York, Academic Press), pp. 341–352.

_____ and Poirier, D. 1977. 'The estimation of normal wage rates and normal income', in H.W. Watts and A. Rees (eds.), *The New Jersey income-maintenance experiment volume II: Labour-supply responses* (New York, Academic Press), pp. 393–414.

_____ and Rees, A. 1977. *The New Jersey income-maintenance experiment, volume II: Labour-supply responses* (New York, Academic Press).

_____ (eds.) 1977. *The New Jersey income-maintenance experiment volume III: The impact on expenditures, health, and social behavior, and the quality of the evidence* (New York, Academic Press).

_____ Peck, J.K. and Taussig, M. 1977. 'Site selection, representativeness of the sample, and possible attrition bias', in H.W. Watts and A. Rees (eds.), *The New Jersey income-maintenance experiment volume III: The impact on expenditures, health, and social behavior, and the quality of the evidence* (New York, Academic Press), pp. 441–466.

_____, Poirier, D.J. and Mallar, C. 1970. 'Sample, variables, and concepts used in the analysis', in *Adjusted and Extended Preliminary Results from the Urban Graduated Work Incentive Experiment* (Madison, Institute for Research on Poverty, University of Wisconsin), pp. 33–56.

_____ 1977. 'Sample, variables, and concepts used in the analysis', in H.W. Watts and A. Rees (eds.), *The New Jersey income-maintenance experiment volume II: Labour-supply responses* (New York, Academic Press), pp. 33 –56.

_____ and others. 1974. 'The labour-supply response of husbands', *Journal of Human Resources*, Vol. 9, No. 2, pp. 181–200.

Weiss, Y., Hall, A. and Dong, F. 1980. 'The effect of price and income on investment in schooling', *Journal of Human Resources*, Vol. 15, pp. 611–640.

West, R. 1978. *The rate of time preference of families in the Seattle and Denver income maintenance experiments*, Research Memorandum No. 51 (Center for the Study of Welfare Policy, Menlo Park, CA, Stanford Research Institute International).

_____ 1979a. *The effects of the Seattle and Denver income maintenance experiments on the labour supply of young nonheads*, Research Memorandum No. 60 (Center for the Study of Welfare Policy, Menlo Park, CA, Stanford Research Institute International).

_____ 1979b. *The impact of the Seattle and Denver income maintenance experiments on wage rates: An interim analysis*, Research Memorandum No. 61 (Center for the Study of Welfare Policy, Menlo Park, CA, Stanford Research Institute International).

_____ 1979c. *A preliminary analysis of the effects of the Seattle and Denver income maintenance experiments on the choice of occupation*, Research Memorandum No. 62 (Center for the Study of Welfare Policy, Menlo Park, CA, Stanford Research Institute International).

_____ 1980. 'Effects on wage rates: An interim analysis', in *Journal of Human Resources*, Vol. 15, pp. 641–653.

_____ 1980. 'Labour supply response of youth', in P.K. Robins *et al.* (eds.), *A guaranteed annual income: Evidence from a social experiment* (New York, Academic Press).

_____ 1980. 'The effects on the labour supply of young nonheads', *Journal of Human Resources*, Vol. 15, pp. 574–590.

_____ and Stieger, G. 1980. *The effects of the Seattle and Denver income maintenance experiments on alternative measures of labour supply*, Research Memorandum No. 72 (Center for the Study of Welfare Policy, Menlo Park, CA, Stanford Research Institute International).

Whiteford, P. 1981. *Work incentive experiments in the United States and Canada*, Research Paper No. 12. Research and Statistics Branch, Development Division, Department of Social Security, Australia.

Williams, W. 1972. *The struggle for a negative income tax* (Institute of Government Research, Seattle, University of Washington), pp. 2–11.

Wilson, J.O. 1974. 'Social experimentation and public-policy analysis', *Public Policy* 22, pp. 15–37.

Wooldridge, J. 1977. 'Housing consumption', in H.W. Watts and A. Rees (eds.), *The New Jersey income-maintenance experiment volume III: The impact on expenditures, health, and social behavior, and the quality of the evidence* (New York, Academic Press), pp. 45–72.

Wright, S. 1977. 'Social psychological characteristics and labour-force response of male heads', in H.W. Watts and A. Rees (eds.) *The New Jersey income-maintenance experiment volume II: Labour-supply responses* (New York, Academic Press), pp. 321–346.

Zellner, A. and Rossi, P.E. 1986. 'Evaluating the methodology of social experiments', in A.H. Munnell (ed.), *Lessons from the income maintenance experiments* (Boston, Federal Reserve Bank of Boston).

32

BASIC INCOME AND THE MEANS TO SELF-GOVERN

Simon Wigley[1]

1. Basic Income and the Right to Self-Government

One way of defending democratic rule is by appealing to the republican conception of liberty: namely, we are free to the extent that we are not vulnerable to the will of another.[2] Hence we are free in a political community to the extent that we have equal influence over the formulation of decisions to which we are then subject. The time-honoured challenge to the self-governmental credentials of democracy, however, is that the majority (or those who are able to influence it) always has the opportunity self-interestedly to rule the minority. Self-government may be thwarted by the fact that the less fortunate members of a democratic society may be the passive subjects of the laws and policies favoured by the more fortunate. The problem is not so much that the most rule the few, but rather that the 'haves' rule the 'have-nots'. For as Arend Lijphart has recently noted '... the inequality of representation and influence are not randomly distributed but systematically biased in favour of more privileged citizens – those with higher incomes, greater wealth, and better education – and against less advantaged citizens' (Lijphart, 1997, p. 1).[3]

Even a fairer distribution of voter turnout (engendered by, say, compulsory voting and proportional representation) will not avoid the problem of political inequality, because the more socially and economically fortunate are better placed to influence the outcome of election campaigns and the political agenda. Moreover, the separation of money from politics (at least to the extent that is practically possible) may not resolve the issue because, in order to ensure re-election, governments are reliant on the private sector to bring about economic success. As Robert Dahl puts it,

> ... in order to persuade investors and manufacturers in privately owned business firms to perform satisfactorily, a society must provide them with

strong inducements in the form of large financial rewards. But a structure of rewards substantial enough to persuade investors and managers to perform their social functions satisfactorily will create a highly inegalitarian distribution of wealth and income (Dahl, 1985, p. 102).

In other words, in those societies that associate well-being with the private accumulation of wealth and property, there is an implicit and pervasive decision-making bias towards the business community. Instituting a basic income, employment security and the like faces an uphill struggle.

Indeed, the bias towards the more fortunate coupled with the resulting lack of participation by the less fortunate, suggests that contemporary democracies have not moved much beyond the days when the right to vote was conditional upon the ownership of property (or, more accurately, a plural voting system where each citizen's voting power is indexed to their property and wealth). A basic income would mitigate that state of affairs insofar as the 'propertyless' would be guaranteed a basic means with which to choose and pursue their aims and ambitions. The classical republican defence of property ownership in a democracy was that it gave each person the means not to be dependent on the beck-and-call of others. In terms of political equality, the provision of a basic income would mean that those previously preoccupied with eking out a reasonable existence would now have more time to participate in the political process and therefore to protect themselves from partial and ill-conceived laws and policies (Ackerman and Alstott, 1999, pp. 184–185).

The problem is that while a basic income will enhance the opportunity to participate, it is consistent with substantial social and economic inequality and therefore inequality of political influence. While a basic income helps to ensure self-government in terms of one's private affairs, it still does not ensure self-government in terms of political decision-making. Hence, any justification of basic income on the grounds that it helps to protect the individual from the arbitrary whims of others, is undermined because the individual is left vulnerable to the wishes of those who are politically more influential. That being the case, the right to a basic income appears to be at best only partially derivable from the right to self-government. The less fortunate are only undominated insofar as the socio-economic disparity between them and the more fortunate is sufficiently narrow. In other words, deploying a basic income in order to provide the means to make each individual's formal freedom from interference effective may still leave each individual subject at the behest of the more fortunate. If I have the real opportunity to choose and pursue my ends, but others have the real opportunity to curtail or even revoke it (even though they might not), am I actually that free? In order to further clarify that conclusion it will be useful to consider John Rawls's analysis of the problem of political inequality.

2. The Fair Value of the Political Liberties

For Rawls the fair distribution of political influence in a democracy is crucial because it helps to establish a just procedure for determining how we are to be ruled. It provides a framework within which mutually justifiable rules of justice can be constructed (Rawls, 1993, pp. 339–340).[4] In addition, and in keeping with the classical republican tradition, the equal opportunity to affect the decision-making process provides a channel through which an active citizenry can protect themselves against possible encroachments upon their individual rights (Rawls, 1993, pp. 205–206). But Rawls also acknowledges that the constructivist and protective functions are inadequately provided for by the formal provision of political liberties (right to vote, assemble, free political speech etc.) as their usefulness varies according to the social and economic advantages at one's disposal (Rawls, 1971, pp. 204–205; 1993, pp. 325–326). This poses a significant problem for justice as fairness insofar as the difference principle permits inequalities in life prospects so long as the worst-off position is the least worst-off under all possible schemes (Rawls, 1993, p. 326; Rawls, 2001, pp. 59–60 and p. 149). Perhaps equal access to education required by fair equality of opportunity will enhance the ability of the less fortunate to ascertain and articulate their concerns, but after a certain point the disparities in social and economic advantage permitted by the difference principle will nullify that voice.[5] The disparity of political influence permitted by the difference principle compromises the fairness of the procedure and fails to protect the priority of the worst-off, let alone the basic liberties (Rawls, 1993, pp. 327–328 and pp. 330–331). For that reason Rawls acknowledges that we must ensure a fair distribution of the value of the political liberties (i.e. their effectiveness) rather than simply the formal possession of them (Rawls, 1971, pp. 224–225):

> ... this guarantee means that the worth of the political liberties to all citizens, whatever their social or economic position, must be approximately equal, or at least sufficiently equal, in the sense that everyone has a fair opportunity to hold public office and to influence the outcome of political decisions (Rawls, 1993, p. 327).

That requires that the fair distribution of the value cannot be trumped by arrangements designed to ensure fair equal opportunity or maximally level up the life expectations of the worst-off (Rawls, 2001, pp. 46–47).

However, Rawls does appear to allow that the worth of political liberties can vary according to motivation and talent (Rawls, 1971, p. 225; 1993, p. 358). I take it that by talent in this context Rawls means the ability to defend proposals based on substantive merit and to question the substantive merit of other proposals, and that the form of equal opportunity implied by fair value, coupled with fair equality of opportunity (e.g. access to education for all), provides the conditions under which those who possess it can shine through. For Rawls the distribution of realized ability can and should be used when it is to the benefit of all, and in particular, those who are less fortunate (Rawls, 1971, p. 30, pp. 101–102; 2001, pp. 75–77). Aside from their realized ability to reason publicly, however, citizens should have no other advantage in terms of influencing the outcome of elections and the passage of legislation. There is no guarantee that the more deliberatively able will deploy their greater powers of persuasion in a way that is beneficial to all, especially the worst-off, rather than to their own ends.[6] I take it that avoiding the possibility of the abuse of that advantage is contingent on whether its bearers are characterized by a plurality of competing points of view such that they are unlikely to comprise a self-serving faction (Rawls, 1993, xvi–xvii).

The relevance of the proposal for a basic income is that one of its supposed advantages is its consistency with the idea that departure from the default equal share of resources is justified insofar as the worst-off position is the least worst-off position possible. The underlying rationale here is that the opportunity of the more fortunate to be better off is only justified because it benefits the worst-off. Any other claim to be better off is illegitimate because the talents one is born with and socio-economic advantages one is born into are purely matters of brute luck (Rawls, 1971, pp. 100ff). Indeed, at one point Rawls suggests something close to a basic income by arguing that both components of his second principle of justice can be approximated if there is a social minimum, established via a negative income tax, in combination with the competitive market determination of wages (Rawls, 1971, pp. 276–277 and pp. 285–286).[7] The problem with permitting inequalities is that the better-off are then, through their greater political influence, in a position to dictate to the worst-off – perhaps to the extent that they may even be able to bring about the demise of the basic income itself. In contractarian terms, it would be reasonable for the less fortunate (e.g. the unskilled) to reject institutions of justice, such as a basic income, that leave them dependent on the ongoing benevolence of the more fortunate.

3. Redistributing the Worth of the Political Liberties

The standard response to the problem of unequal influence is to regulate the political process such that the worth of the political liberties of those who are better off is curbed. In other words, measures are taken to keep political parties, candidates and elected representatives independent from the background socio-economic inequalities, by limiting the ability to use private wealth in the political domain (e.g. limits on contributions and election expenses, and the disclosure of funding sources). Crucially, campaign finance limits do not restrict the points of view each citizen chooses to align with; rather they modify the ability to promote those points of view.[8] To the extent that such measures are successful, the relative worth of the political liberties of the less fortunate is raised. Hence, public discussion and decision-making are more likely to listen to the substantive merits of each and every proposal, rather than the particular interests of wealthy donors.

The problem with contribution limits is that candidates end up devoting more attention to canvassing for contributions, and those already in office, due to their higher public profile, find it easier to accumulate a sufficient amount of financial support than their challengers. Moreover it is difficult to detect hidden contributions and expenditures (e.g. former German Chancellor Helmut Kohl broke campaign financing laws put in place by his own Government when he accepted large and undisclosed contributions) and donors can employ alternative channels in order to finance a candidate or party (e.g. contributing to party-building rather than directly to a candidate, promoting a candidate independently, using contributed funds to promote an issue rather than an candidate or party *per se* etc.) (see e.g. Donnelly, 1997). The other standard way of equalizing the worth of each citizen's political liberties is the use of public funds to subsidize political activities. The difficulty then arises that if the public subsidy is combined with contribution or spending limits we are confronted with all the problems noted above, and if it is combined with no such limits then it fails to equalize the effective political liberty of each citizen.

One way around this problem, following a recent innovative proposal by Bruce Ackerman and Ian Ayres (Ackerman and Ayres, 2002), is to give each citizen a publicly funded voucher of the same value – stored on a citizen's credit card before each election – and leave them to choose which candidate they wish to support financially.[9] Hence, there is no need for a centralized bureaucratic agency to determine how public funds should be distributed as the amount a candidate receives tracks the level of support she accrues. The underlying idea here is to equalize the ability of each citizen to contribute and yet permit each candidate to acquire unequal amounts of financial support. The worth of the political liberties is equalized by levelling the playing field in terms of each citizen's 'purchasing power' as opposed to each candidate's 'purchasing power' (i.e. limits and subsidies). This amounts to something akin to a two-round election process: in the first round candidates compete for contributions (citizens influence each candidate's ability to persuade the electorate) and in the second round they use the contributions they have accrued to compete for votes (citizens influence the electoral outcome). Both in terms of opinion formation and the assessment of candidates, therefore, each citizen has equal influence. Clearly the effect of the voucher proposal would be to encourage candidates to treat all constituents equally, irrespective of socio-economic status, and thereby encourage the less well off to engage actively in the democratic process (and to begin to do so at an earlier juncture than the traditional 'one-round' electoral process).

Given that Ackerman and Ayres' proposal does not place any limits on contributions or spending, no bounds are placed on the total amount of money sloshing around in the system. Their argument is that the more resources available to candidates the greater the level of public debate that can take place. The real concern is establishing a fairer distribution of those resources. More money in the system will not enhance free discussion if those who have more of it are able to dominate proceedings to the point where ideas and concerns that do not fit their agenda are marginalized. In other words, we can defend the need for fair value on the grounds that it enhances freedom of expression; unless we are concerned about the free speech of candidates and contributors, as opposed to the free speech of citizens, fair value does not entail a conflict between equality and freedom of expression.[10]

To establish fairness in the distribution of effective political liberties, Ackerman and Ayres' contention is that if each citizen is eligible to donate $50 to a candidate of their choice, the influence of the big money of corporations and the wealthy will be substantially diluted.[11] Moreover, to get around the problem of individual candidates canvassing the wealthy for large contributions, Ackerman and Ayres propose that all contributions, whether private or voucher-based, must be anonymous (thus reversing the traditional disclosure approach and mirroring the idea of a secret ballot).[12] Ignorance of funding sources further encourages each candidate to treat each citizen and grouping equally. Moreover, donors and beneficiaries are not then in a position to appeal to the questionable argument that their personal freedom of expression has been infringed. In order to protect democracy, the voucher with anonymous contributions approach does not require interference by the State. Hence it neatly evades the following argument against contribution and spending limits: 'if the State limits free speech to protect democracy, in so doing it threatens democracy and therefore the idea should not even be contemplated' (Dworkin, 2000, p. 353).[13]

4. From Economic Citizenship to Democratic Citizenship

I have argued that Ackerman and Ayres' citizen voucher proposal provides the best means of realizing the fair opportunity to influence the decision-making process. Given the threat to the right to self-govern, and thereby to basic income itself, posed by social and economic inequality we can now go a step further and argue for an augmented and conditional component to the basic income. Given that many countries already subsidize political activities through public funds, expanding the basic income does not appear to be a controversial drain on government coffers; rather it denotes a fairer basis for apportioning those resources. However, as Ackerman and Ayres note, with the inception of anonymous contributions the level of private contributions will decline insofar as the donor cannot directly gain from the exchange. Hence the amount of public funding required for the voucher scheme will have to be increased in order to ensure a sufficient level of communication and debate.[14] It is at this juncture that a second strategy for ensuring the fair value of political liberties becomes relevant. In addition to insulating the election and legislative process from the background distribution of social and economic power, we can act to ensure that that power does not become concentrated (Rousseau, 1988, Book II, Chap. 11, pp. 115–116; Rawls, 1971, p. 225 and pp. 277–278; Rawls, 2001, p. 44; pp. 130–131 and pp. 160–161). Moreover, that may be necessary in order at least partially to counteract the bias of governments towards the business community (see Section 1). Thus, to finance the voucher scheme the State may tax (e.g. on inheritance and bequests) in order to ensure that social and economic power is sufficiently spread. The redistribution from concentrations of socio-economic power to citizen vouchers would thereby help to bring about fair value from two different angles.

That a proportion of an expanded basic income should comprise a payment in kind (i.e. a campaign finance voucher) can be defended on the following mildly paternalistic grounds: current voters may not be able to appreciate the impact on their future selves and future generations of an unequal distribution of the effective value of their political liberties.[15] That is to say, if citizens have discretion over the entire basic income they would be unlikely to use the expanded component in order democratically to protect themselves against the whims of the more fortunate.

Thus, the incorporation of a citizen voucher into the basic income would help to bring about democratic citizenship rather than just economic citizenship. In order to acquire a reasonable means to choose and pursue their own aims and ambitions over the span of their lives, citizens, and particularly the unskilled, would be rendered less dependent on the good grace of employers, spouses etc. and those who, through the assistance of sheer good fortune, are better positioned to influence the course of legislation.

Notes

1 Bilkent University, Ankara, Turkey.

2 Here I follow Philip Pettit's interpretation of republican freedom in terms of non-domination – a person is unfree to the extent that she is vulnerable to the arbitrary interference of others, even if they do not actually interfere (Pettit, 1997, Chap. 3).

3 However, compulsory voting reduces the class bias in terms of voting turnout (p. 3).

4 More generally see Lecture III; see also Cohen (1989).

5 It is worth pointing out, by way of indicating the urgency of the problem, that in the period since the publication of *A Theory of Justice* the worst-off group in US society has become worse off. 'The share of Americans living in poverty rose from 11.2% in 1974 to 15.1% in 1993, and the "poverty deficit" – or amount of money needed to lift all to the poverty line-doubled in real terms.' Moreover, 'income inequality has skyrocketed. In 1979, for example, on an hourly basis, the top decile of men earned four times what the bottom decile earned; by 1993 they were earning five times as much. This rise in inequality occurred in the context of general wage stagnation: the median male worker, for example, earns about 13 per cent less than the median male 15 years ago – despite his being older and having more education' (Freeman, 1996–97). Correspondingly, the political participation of the worst-off has declined over the same period (Schlozman *et al.*, 1997). Significantly, '...the proportion of Americans contributing to campaigns has nearly doubled over the past 20 years, rising from 13% to 23% of the population' and 'contributors at the top of the income ladder gave, on average, nearly 14 times as much as those at the bottom' *(Ibid.)*.

6 If only for that reason John Stuart Mill's proposal of granting greater voting power to those who are 'mentally superior' (roughly indicated, he contends, by occupational status) tilts the balance too far in favor of the more fortunate (Mill, 1861, latter half of Chapter VIII, pp. 335ff). Mill's objective is to augment the political influence of those who are more adept at identifying law and policy that will maximize overall happiness. In contrast to Rawls, it is not necessary that each and every individual benefit from the decisions that are reached. Mill's argument rides on the questionable presumption that the more able citizens are also less likely to participate for their own gain.

7 On the similarity between this and basic income, see van Parijs (1995, pp. 94–98) and van Parijs (forthcoming). Although both proposal requires the recipient to be employed, the negative income tax is graduated and therefore means-tested (van Parijs, 1995, pp. 35–37 and p. 57).

8 Hence it is misguided not to level down political financing on the grounds that it would limit freedom of expression (Rawls, 1993, pp. 357ff; Beitz, 1989, pp. 209–213; Dworkin, 2000).

9 David Adamany and George Agree proposed a similar approach (Adamany and Agree, 1976). However, they couple the voucher system with contribution limits (p. 199) and therefore render it vulnerable to the problems already noted.

10 Compare this conclusion with that of the United States Supreme Court in *Buckley v. Valeo* (1976): '... the concept that government may restrict the speech of some elements of our society in order to enhance the relative voice of others is wholly foreign to the First Amendment, which was designed "to secure the widest possible dissemination of information from diverse and antagonistic sources", and "to assure unfettered interchange of ideas for the bringing about of political and social changes desired by the people"'. Given that those with sufficient social and economic power can effectively delimit open discussion the court's argument appears tenuous even by its own criteria.

11 E.g. in the 2000 US elections $3 billion in campaign finance was contributed by special interests. $50 dollars for each of the 100 million voters would have generated $5 billion in new campaign finance.

12 To avoid the problem of donors 'tipping off' candidates, Ackerman and Ayres suggest that large donations be deposited into the candidate's account in installments and randomly.

13 The concern here is that in instituting fair value through finance limits we merely substitute domination by the more fortunate for domination by the State.

14 See footnote 10 above.

15 In other words, we are vulnerable to 'failures in intra-personal and intergenerational trusteeship' (Ackerman and Alstott, 1999, pp. 134–136; van Parijs, 1995, pp. 47–48). I have discussed this issue in a different context in Wigley (2000).

References

Ackerman, B. and Alstott, A. 1999. *The stakeholder society* (New Haven, Yale University Press).

_____ and Ayres, I. 2002. *Voting with dollars: A new paradigm for campaign finance* (New Haven, Yale University Press).

Adamany, D.W. and Agree, G.E. 1976. *Political money: A strategy for campaign financing in America* (Baltimore, John Hopkins University Press).

Beitz, C. 1989. *Political equality: An essay in democratic theory*, (Princeton, NJ, Princeton University Press), pp. 209–213.

Cohen, J. 1989. 'Democracy and democratic legitimacy', in A. Hamlin and P. Pettit (ed.), *The good polity: Normative analysis of the State* (Oxford, Blackwell).

Dahl, R.A. 1985. *A preface to economic democracy* (Berkeley, University of California Press).

Donnelly, D. Fine, J. and Miller, E. S. 1997. 'Going public', in *Boston Review*, April/ May, at http://bostonreview.mit.edu/BR22.2/donnelly.html.

Dworkin, R.M. 2000. 'Free speech, politics, and the dimensions of democracy' in *Sovereign virtue* (Cambridge, Mass., Harvard University Press), Chapter 10.

Freeman, R.B. 1996–97, 'Solving the new inequality', in *Boston Review*, December 1996 – January 1997, at http://bostonreview.mit.edu/BR21.6/freeman.html.

Lijphart, A. 1997. 'Unequal participation: Democracy's unresolved dilemma', in *The American Political Science Review*, Vol. 91, No. 1, pp. 1–14.

Mill, J.S., 1861. 'On representative Government', in J. Gray (ed.) (1991), *On liberty and other essays* (Oxford, Oxford University Press).

Pettit, P. 1997. *Republicanism: A theory of freedom and government* (Oxford, Oxford University Press).

Rawls, J. 1971. *A theory of justice* (Cambridge, Mass., Harvard University Press).

_____ 1993. *Political liberalism* (New York, Columbia University Press).

_____ 2001. *Justice as fairness: A restatement* (Cambridge, Mass., Harvard University Press).

Rousseau, J.J. 1988 (1762). 'On social contract', in *Rousseau's political writings*, translated by J. C. Bondanella (New York, W. W. Norton).

Schlozman, K.L. Brady, H.E. Verba, S. 1997. 'The Big Tilt', in *The American Prospect*, Vol. 8, No. 32, 1 May – 1 June at http://www.prospect.org/print/V8/32/schlozman-k.html.

van Parijs, P. 1995. *Real freedom for all: What (if anything) can justify capitalism?* (Oxford, Oxford University Press).

_____ Forthcoming. 'Difference Principles', in S. R. Freeman (ed.), *The Cambridge companion to John Rawls* (Cambridge, Cambridge University Press), Chapter 5.

Wigley, S. 2000. *Basic income and the problem of cumulative misfortune*, Paper presented at the 8th Congress of BIEN (Basic Income European Network), Berlin 6–7 October 2000, at http://www.etes.ucl.ac.be/BIEN/BerlinCongress/Berlin2000_papers/Wigley.doc

33

THE ALASKA PERMANENT FUND DIVIDEND: AN EXPERIMENT IN WEALTH DISTRIBUTION

Scott Goldsmith[1]

1. Introduction

For 20 years every Alaskan citizen has received an equal share of an annual dividend distribution from the Alaska Permanent Fund, capitalized by a portion of the revenues from publicly owned oil production. As the fund has grown in value, the size of the annual dividend has increased so that today about US$1 billion is distributed annually to 600,000 citizens – directly accounting for about 6 per cent of total household income.

This paper begins by reviewing the creation, history and structure of the fund and dividend. It then discusses the economic, social and political impacts of the dividend. Next it considers possible changes in the dividend and fund in response to changing economic conditions within the state. Finally it discusses the possible implications of the Alaska experience for other regions and for the concept of basic income.

2. The Alaska Permanent Fund

In 1977, oil production began from the largest oil field ever discovered in North America, Prudhoe Bay on the North Slope of the state of Alaska. Production, property and income tax revenues began to flow into the state treasury at an unprecedented rate. These revenues were augmented by royalty payments (an ownership payment) to the state because, as luck would have it, the field happened to be located on state lands, received from the federal government when Alaska had became the 49th state of the United States a few years earlier.

Shortly thereafter the Alaska Permanent Fund was established by a constitutional amendment to set aside a share of the revenues from oil production for future generations of Alaskans, in recognition of the inevitable depletion of the resource. This savings account was designed to convert a part of the depleting petroleum asset into a permanent and sustainable financial asset.

A secondary reason for establishing the fund was to keep some of the oil revenues away from politicians who, it was feared, would spend them on wasteful government operations and capital projects. The mistrust of politicians was grounded in the fact that an earlier $900 million payment to the state by the oil companies for the right to explore for oil, when left in the hands of the legislature, seemed to disappear overnight, leaving behind not a legacy of new assets, but rather one of bigger government without an enhanced ability to pay for it.

The constitutional amendment establishing the Permanent Fund required that at least 25 per cent of the royalties collected from the sale of all state-owned natural resources would be deposited into the fund, that the fund would invest only in income-producing assets, and that only fund earnings, but never fund principal, could be spent. In practice, the deposit rule has meant that about 10 per cent of the total revenues from oil production have been deposited into the fund, along with insignificant amounts from other mineral production.

The fund balance grew slowly in its first two years, reaching $137 million by the end of fiscal year 1979. Shortly thereafter the price of oil took a dramatic leap upward and by 1988 the fund balance, including sub-accounts, passed the $10 billion mark. Growth has continued, albeit at a slower pace, and at the end of fiscal year 2002 it stood at $23.6 billion. This is about $3 billion below its peak of $26.5 billion in 2000, due to the stock market decline.

In addition to the deposits of royalties required by the constitution, the size of the fund has been augmented by legislative appropriation. Each year a deposit is made to offset the effect of inflation on the real value of the fund (based on the purchase price, rather than the current market value, of assets). In addition, in some years a deposit has also been made from revenues deemed unnecessary for current operations.

During its early years the fund attracted little attention beyond a debate to establish its investment policy. The notion of using the fund as a savings account won over the competing idea of using it as a source of investment capital for Alaskan regional economic development projects. Consequently the fund is invested in a diversified portfolio of stocks and bonds, and its annual earnings are not correlated with the performance of the Alaskan economy. Furthermore, financial markets provide a clear rate-of-return benchmark for fund performance.

The Alaska Permanent Fund has been a successful device for converting a portion, but not all, of Alaska's depleting oil resource into a renewable financial resource. We cannot say whether conversion to a financial asset is necessarily in the best economic interests of the state compared to investment in physical infrastructure, human capital, or some other resource. However, cash is fungible and thus the fund preserves the option of conversion to a different form of wealth in the future.

Some of the reasons for the success of the fund are clear:

- First, it grew out of the desire not to repeat the perceived waste of the original $900 million windfall associated with the Prudhoe Bay lease sale.
- Second, it had its formative years, and years of most rapid growth, at a time when the state treasury was bursting with oil revenues and the diversion of a small share of those revenues into the fund was hardly noticed.
- Third, its ultimate purpose was not clearly defined. Its general purpose as a savings account to prevent all oil revenues from being spent when received was agreed upon. However, there was little discussion and no agreement as to what the savings would eventually be spent on, since that was a decision that could be postponed. This allowed the fund to gain support across a broad political spectrum, from those in favour of limited public spending to those concerned about the ability of the state to support a large variety of public programmes.
- Fourth, the investment policy became insulated from the political arena when the decision was made to invest the portfolio in stocks and bonds rather than in Alaskan loan programmes or infrastructure building.
- Fifth, the management of the fund was vested in an independent corporation headed by a board of directors with the narrow and focused goal of maximizing the financial earnings of the fund. The corporation operates independently of the state treasury and has not become involved in any discussions regarding the best use of fund earnings, a decision left in the hands of the legislature.
- Sixth, the fund acquired a powerful constituency with the establishment of the Alaska Permanent Fund Dividend programme, an annual cash distribution to all residents from earnings.

3. The Alaska Permanent Fund Dividend Programme

Two years after the Alaska Permanent Fund was established, the world oil price jumped and Alaska state revenues, primarily from oil, quadrupled. The state responded by simultaneously expanding its budget and eliminating broad-based taxes. Operating programmes, the capital budget, transfers to individuals, as well as loan programmes for businesses, students, and homeowners all benefited from the availability of higher oil revenues. Because the availability of revenues was not a real constraint on spending, the criteria for budget appropriations was to make certain that all groups were receiving a fair share of the revenues from oil flowing through the state treasury. This included all types of households and businesses as well as every special interest group from senior citizens to construction workers to government bureaucrats.

There were ample revenues to pay for this expansion of government without recourse to the earnings of the Alaska Permanent Fund, which were then insignificant. However, as time passed, attention began to focus on the question of what to do with the earnings of the Alaska Permanent Fund, which were not restricted by the constitution and could be put to any purpose.

The Alaska governor at the time, Jay Hammond, proposed a distribution of the annual earnings of the fund under a programme called 'Alaska Inc.'. Every citizen would receive an annual payment from the earnings of the fund, with the size of the payment based on length of residence in the state up to a maximum of 25 years. A one-year resident would be entitled to one share; a two-year resident would receive two shares, etc.

There were several attractive features of this proposal:

• First, it would provide a vehicle for sharing some of the revenues from the publicly owned natural resource to all citizens regardless of their status as a member of a special interest group.
• Second the distribution would be in cash, so that individuals could use it for any purpose, thus creating the maximum economic benefit.
• Third, since the size of the individual payment depended upon how long a person had lived in the state, it was both an incentive for people to stay in the state and a reward for long-term residents.

The incentive to remain addressed the problem of high population turnover and the reward gave a larger share of the wealth to older Alaskans. The reward was a way to deal with the thorny question of the appropriate intergenerational distribution of the public wealth. 'Alaska Inc.' would give a larger share to older citizens who would not have as many years to participate in the distribution as their children and grandchildren.

The notion of a cash distribution from the earnings of the fund was popular, but did not have unanimous support. It passed into law, but the 'Alaska Inc.' idea quickly ran up against the equal treatment clause of the United States Constitution. The court ruled that a distribution contingent on the number of years of residency in the state was not equal treatment for all, and the 'Alaska Inc.' plan died.

In response, the legislature quickly passed a simpler plan; an equal annual cash distribution to every resident taken from half the earnings of the Alaska Permanent Fund. To get the programme rolling, in the initial year the Alaska

Permanent Fund Dividend (PFD) was $1,000 and was paid out of general revenues rather than fund earnings.

The following year the PFD fell to $386 based on the formula that has been in use ever since. The amount available for payout is half of the five-year average realized earnings of the Alaska Permanent Fund. The dividend formula is designed to provide some stability to the annual payout as well as insulate long-term management of the Permanent Fund from the political pressure to maximize the dividend in the short term. The size of the individual PFD depends upon the number of people who apply for and are eligible for a share of the available payout.

As the fund and its earnings have grown, the PFD has also increased in size. It had grown back to $1,000 by 1995 ($990). The largest PFD, $1,963, was paid in 2000. Falling earnings have subsequently reduced the size of the dividend. In 2002, the twenty-first year of the dividend distribution, it was projected to be about $1,550. The cumulative value of all 21 dividends, if invested for a 3 per cent real rate of return, would today be $31,000.

The dividend is paid to every resident who indicates an intention to remain in the state, regardless of age. Parents receive the dividends in trust for their children. About 600,000 dividend checks are distributed shortly before the Christmas shopping season begins to about 95 per cent of the people living in the state, directly increasing total personal income in Alaska by about $1.1 billion, or 6 per cent, in 2002.

The PFD has some interesting features:

- First, it is absolutely democratic. Every citizen who is eligible receives the same amount regardless of circumstances. The only eligibility test is whether a person has been and intends to remain a resident. (This of course does result in some interesting arguments and debates.)
- Second, although the dividend is taxable income, the federal tax burden is small because a sizable share goes to residents with no other taxable income. (There is no state personal income tax.) The after-tax dividend distribution consequently favours lower-income individuals and families with large numbers of children.
- Third, because some income support programmes are contingent on monthly cash income, the state has instituted a 'hold harmless' programme to offset the temporary loss of benefits that some households would otherwise suffer in the month that the dividend is distributed.

The PFD programme was not initially popular among politicians, many of whom thought there were better uses for the money, particularly if invested in infrastructure for economic development. A study of the initial dividend payout was done to determine the extent to which Alaskans were 'wasting' it. But there was no evidence of a widespread increase in spending on 'wine, women and song' as some had feared.

As the dividend has grown in size and become a regularly anticipated part of the budget of Alaska households, support for it among politicians has solidified. Most now consider it political suicide to suggest any policy change that could possibly have any adverse impact today, or in the future, on the size of the PFD. It has been extremely successful in creating a political constituency for the Permanent Fund that did not previously exist. Since the establishment of the PFD, there have been virtually no suggestions that the Alaska Permanent Fund be dissolved, with one recent exception.

There is a strong feeling among a portion of the population that the state-owned oil resource belongs to them as individuals rather than to all citizens collectively. This has strengthened the notion that the dividend is entitlement rather than government expenditure. This line of reasoning has led some to the conclusion that the Permanent Fund itself should be cashed out, with the proceeds distributed equitably to all residents in one big dividend of about $40,000. However, a formal proposal of this nature was recently rejected because it included the condition that subsequent oil revenues would be used to fund government expenditures rather than a continuing, but smaller, dividend programme.

At the time that the PFD was created there were other ideas proposed for directly sharing the income from oil with Alaskans. An intriguing alternative was to link a series of dividend payments to different oil fields as they were discovered. Residents at the time each field was discovered would be eligible for the royalties from production from that field. As new fields were discovered there would be new dividends paid to subsequent groups of eligible residents. This would have eliminated the problem of people being attracted to the state by the PFD.

4. Economic Effects of the Permanent Fund Dividend

Most interest within Alaska has centred on the macroeconomic effect of the PFD, and in particular the number of jobs and the amount of personal income generated within the regional economy by the consumer spending associated with the dividend. This stems from the fact that in part the perceived value of public expenditures in Alaska depends upon the number of jobs they produce in the private economy.

The size of this impact depends on a number of factors including:

- The share of dividends paid to residents;
- The extent to which the PFD is viewed as permanent rather than transitory income (will continue to be paid out in future years);

- The average of the marginal income tax rates of all dividend recipients;
- The average of the marginal propensities to consume of all dividend recipients;
- The extent to which parents allow their children to decide how their dividends will be spent;
- The extent to which consumers are constrained in their normal purchases by liquidity constraints (the ability to borrow to purchase investment goods).

Unfortunately (at least for economists), in spite of the size of the PFD programme, which is the largest appropriation of state government (exceeding even primary and secondary education), there has never been an audit to determine how the funds have been used – including what parents are doing with their children's PFDs. We do not know what share parents spend, what share the child spends, and what share is invested for the future education or other needs of the child.

This reluctance to study what people do with their dividends comes from two sources. First, many people view the PFD as a distribution of income from assets owned by individual citizens rather than as an appropriation of government. Thus how the income is spent is a private matter. Second, there is reluctance among politicians to give the appearance, by studying the effects of the dividend, that they might be considering some change in the programme.

However, we can make a reasonable estimate of the macroeconomic impact of the programme since it has been in existence for 20 years, and goes in equal amounts to rich and poor Alaskans in a single annual payment. Most economists feel that a large share of the annual distribution is spent when received and goes towards the purchase of consumer durable goods (those with an extended life), producing jobs and income in the trade and service sectors of the economy. Anecdotal evidence supports this notion, with auto dealers, furniture and appliance stores, and other durable goods retailers stepping up their advertising and marketing campaigns in the weeks prior to the annual distribution. However, travel agents and financial advisors are also especially busy during this time of the year. Of course, for higher income households the dividend is more likely to be simply treated like other income in the way it is spent, although a share is saved either for retirement or for a bequest.

Informal attempts to determine how expenditure patterns have been influenced by the PFD have used the method of asking people what they did with their dividend checks. A common response is that the money was used to buy winter coats for the children. Given the harsh climate in Alaska, it is unlikely that most families would have forgone winter coats for their children in the absence of the dividend, but this perception and response underscores the importance and value people place on the PFD. Of course, the impact of spending of the dividend checks depends upon how the total annual allocation of household income has changed as a result of the dividend, and observing where the money goes does not give the answer to that question.

Initially there was some interest in the effect of the dividend on the supply of labour, but there have been no studies of this effect, which from casual observation appears to be small. This may partly be the result of the method of distribution. Because it comes in a single payment at the beginning of the Christmas shopping season, consumers may be predisposed to view the PFD as a 'gift' rather than as part of their regular income. Consequently, decisions about work effort might be largely insulated from the income represented by the dividend. However, this effect might well be different among different age cohorts or ethnic groups. In the aggregate, however, there is no evidence of a large impact on current labour force participation, although the effect might be to reduce future labour force participation through earlier retirements.

A complicating factor for determining the effects of the dividend, particularly on the supply of labour, is the open border between Alaska and the rest of the United States, allowing the free movement of population in response to wage and income differentials between regions. The PFD may be inducing migration into the state, particularly among large lower-income families. There is some anecdotal evidence that this might be happening, but the effect is moderated by the one-year residency requirement. This migration effect of course works in both directions, and it may be reducing the rate of out-migration that would otherwise be taking place among young adults and retirees. Consequently we cannot say whether the labour supply has decreased or increased as a result of the dividend.

Even without a PFD-induced increase in the labour supply, the PFD could be exerting downward pressure on the wage differential between Alaska and other, lower-cost regions of the United States. If employers could lower the Alaskan wage rate because of the dividend, then determining the impact of the dividend on the distribution of income would be more complicated than simply observing the addition to incomes directly attributable to the dividend. Of course, the dividend could also be driving up the wage rate if, in the absence of in-migration, the labour force participation rate fell.

The average real wage in Alaska has fallen by about 10 per cent in the last decade, but it is unclear the extent to which that is due to other factors such as a change in the mix of jobs and a fall in the relative cost of living. But it does raise the possibility that the apparent higher incomes from the dividend are being partially offset by lower real wage rates. As a result, some of the intended benefit of the dividend is being dissipated. But since a large share of the dividends goes to Alaskans who are not in the labour market, a total dissipation of income would not occur.

In spite of the potential effect on the average wage rate, it is safe to say that the dividend has had a dramatic effect in making the distribution of income in Alaska among the most equitable in the entire United States. This is suggested by data reported by the Economic Policy Institute showing that in the last 10 years the income of the poorest fifth of Alaskan families increased by 28 per cent compared to a 7 per cent increase for the richest fifth. In contrast, for the US as a whole over the same period the increase for the poorest fifth was 12 per cent compared to 26 per cent for the richest fifth.[2] Other forces have, however, contributed to this levelling. During the 1990s Alaska's economic growth was slow, with most of the new jobs coming in sectors that provided employment opportunities at the lower end of the income distribution. (This effect has not attracted attention within Alaska because the dividend has not been viewed as a policy tool for the purpose of influencing the income distribution.)

The dividend should help to empower low-income Alaskans in various ways. One might expect to see such things as an increase in volunteer work, an increase in wage rates in unattractive work situations, or a reduction in instances of spousal abuse. Since most people, however, will not be impacted in any of these ways, in the aggregate the effects cannot be discerned.

An important economic effect of the PFD is to stabilize the flow of cash to rural Alaska where *per capita* money incomes are among the lowest in the US and non-government sources of income are variable and uncertain. In some areas, the PFD now directly accounts for more than 10 per cent of cash income. This safety net against unexpected reductions in household income or unanticipated expenditures is an important feature of the dividend. This is particularly true where cash income is most dependent on the production of fish and other natural resources that are subject to dramatic fluctuations in harvest and price.

In addition, the dividend has served as an important 'automatic stabilizer' for the economy of the state, reducing the regional business cycles associated with swings in energy prices and production.

5. Social and Political Effects of the Permanent Fund Dividend

Although Alaskans have enjoyed the PFD for 20 years, no one has formally studied its social impacts. One of its obvious consequences is that an entire generation of Alaskans has grown up in an environment where government distributes cheques to citizens instead of citizens sending cheques to government; Alaska has neither a personal income tax nor a broad-based sales tax. One can speculate on the effect of this on public understanding of fiscal issues and participation in public dialogues on the allocation of public resources.

Some feel that the only interest many Alaskans display regarding public issues is the size of their annual dividend cheque, and their only interaction with the government comes when they cash that cheque. The dividend may also be fostering an environment preoccupied with consumption that may be detrimental to investment and the longer-term needs of society.

Young Alaskans, who have been receiving an annual cheque since birth, have very little understanding of the source and rationale for the dividend. When asked, a class of middle-school children felt that the dividend either was compensation for the high cost of living in the state, the hardships associated with life on the 'last frontier' as it is sometimes called, or for the high taxes paid by their parents.

The immense popularity of the PFD now means that politicians are virtually falling over one another to demonstrate to the public their efforts to defend the programme. Any politician who even suggests considering a policy that might adversely impact the size of the annual distribution had best look for another career. This obsession with the PFD threatens normal discourse over the state budget since every issue is viewed through the lens of what its potential impact will be on the PFD. This is a problem because now oil revenues have fallen to the point where earnings from the Permanent Fund might logically be used as a replacement source of revenue.

6. The Future of the Permanent Fund Dividend

Alaska has relied almost exclusively on oil revenues to fund state government for a generation, but they have been declining for a decade and budget cuts alone have not been sufficient to offset this revenue loss. Some combination of using the earnings of the Permanent Fund, including reduction of the size of the PFD, and re-instituting the personal income tax is the most obvious solution.

Those who would prefer a reduction of the PFD to a personal income tax point to the disincentive to work and investment created by an income tax, the unfairness of putting the burden for paying for government entirely on workers, and the apparent illogicality of government collecting an income tax with one hand while simultaneously distributing a dividend with the other.

Opponents of using a portion of the PFD to pay some of the costs of government present a number of arguments, suggesting that an income tax would be preferable. First, paying for government out of the dividend would result in a bloated public sector, since this method would not require government to ask citizens to contribute through taxation. Second, the impact would fall almost entirely on Alaskans, in contrast to an income tax that would be partially paid by non-resident workers. Third, the state personal income tax is deductible from the federal income tax, effectively reducing the cost to Alaskans of funding government by this method compared to a dividend reduction. Fourth, re-instituting the income tax would re-establish the link between the public costs of economic development and the revenues to pay for them.

Finally, the argument is made that reducing the dividend would put the burden of paying for government on those least able to pay – the poor. It is interesting that the argument is being made that reduction of the dividend would be the most regressive method of tax, since this was never an argument in support of the dividend or of any suggestion to increase the size of the dividend.

Some of the features that have made the Permanent Fund a success are now proving to be an impediment to finding a solution to Alaska's fiscal problems. At the time of its creation, many people envisaged that the earnings of the fund would be part of the solution. But because this was not clearly enunciated, and because many newer residents do not share the historical perspective of these longer-term residents, there is no consensus today on what role fund earnings should play in dealing with the current and expected future state budget shortfalls. A significant minority of the population feels that under no circumstances should the earnings of the fund be used to help pay for state government.

The separation of the management and accounting of the fund from the rest of state government has exacerbated this problem. For most of the past decade the state general fund has operated at a substantial deficit. At the same time, the Permanent Fund has generated large surpluses after payment of the dividend, and taken together the consolidated account of the general and Permanent Funds has usually shown a surplus. The public has become confused and suspicious when they get the inconsistent message that the general fund is in deficit but the consolidated account of the state is in surplus.

7. What Can the Basic Income Movement Learn from the Alaska Permanent Fund Dividend?

7.1 People View the Alaska Permanent Fund Dividend as an Entitlement that all Alaskans Share Rather than as a Public Expenditure

The Alaska Permanent Fund Dividend has reduced poverty and inequality of income- distribution in a political climate that is in many respects opposed to the notion of using public resources to increase the purchasing power of the least well-off Alaskans. For example, during the last legislative session, it became clear that Alaskans prefer a sales tax to an income tax as a method for raising revenue, in spite of the evidence that a sales tax is regressive compared to an income tax. In fact, a significant share of the population felt that a progressive income tax would unfairly punish workers – the productive

---

members of society – by requiring that they be the ones to support government spending. In contrast, it was argued that a sales tax would fall fairly on everyone because all Alaskans are consumers.

The apparent inconsistency between the simultaneous support for the dividend and regressive taxes can be resolved if the Alaska Permanent Fund Dividend is viewed, not as a government appropriation, but rather as a distribution of earnings from an asset owned by each Alaskan. Since each resident owns a share of the Permanent Fund, each resident is entitled to an equal share of its earnings. The dividend programme is not viewed as a government programme for helping the neediest Alaskans through cash grants.

The reality, however, is different from the perception. Individual residents are not owners of a share of the Permanent Fund. No one can use their share as collateral for a loan at their local bank. The Permanent Fund is a public asset, and residents can share in decisions about its disposition only as long as they remain in the state. When they die or move outside the state, they lose their interest.

7.2 How People Use Their Dividends Depends Partially on Public Perceptions of How the Dividends Should be Used

Although there is no direct evidence to verify differences among ethnic groups and age cohorts in how the dividend is perceived, there is some anecdotal evidence that some Alaskans treat the dividend income differently than other income because of the advertising campaigns and general level of 'hype' that accompanies its distribution each fall. There is considerable interest and attention leading up to both the annual announcement of the size of the dividend and the date on which the dividends will be deposited in recipients' bank accounts. (A large share of the dividends is distributed on a single day.) Perhaps in the absence of the media barrage, a smaller share of dividends would be spent on consumer durables or Christmas presents. The dividend has been in existence for 21 years and is likely to continue so it should not be viewed as a windfall, but it does continue to have the aura of being special income.

7.3 The Form of the Distribution is Important in Determining How It Will Be Spent

The dividend distribution occurs as a lump sum in the fall of the year. For a family of four of modest means, $6,000 in the form of four dividend cheques might represent the equivalent of two or three months' worth of regular income. This lump sum gives the family the opportunity to purchase expensive consumer durables that they might not otherwise be able to, either because of an inability to save the required amount or to obtain the necessary credit. If, on the other hand, the distribution were made in 12 equal payments spread over the course of the year, consumption would more likely be directed towards non-durable goods.

7.4 The Macroeconomic Impacts of the Dividend May Include 'Unintended Consequences'

In particular, there has been some concern in recent years that the dividend may be acting as a 'population magnet', either attracting people to the state who are not in the labour market, or creating an incentive for people to stay – such as students or retirees. However, another possible effect of the dividend that has been completely ignored might be a reduction in the Alaskan wage rate by the amount of the dividend. If the labour market worked in this way, Alaskan workers would be sharing the benefits of the dividend with business owners, non-workers, and non-residents.

7.5 The Dividend Distribution Has Changed the Relationship Between the Individual and Government

Since the dividend came into existence 21 years ago, an entire generation of residents has grown up in an environment where the government sends each resident a check each year rather than a tax bill. This has fostered a feeling that the government exists to distribute cash to its citizens, but that individuals do not need to contribute to public life. These young people have not been schooled in the responsibilities that come with living in a representative democracy. They do not understand where the money comes from to support public expenditures, they have little interest in how public funds are allocated among programmes since they are not required to pay for them, and they feel little responsibility for the general welfare.

A public education programme would help to offset this trend. But in the absence of concrete measures to create a sense of responsibility, the dividend will continue to foster a distorted sense of the function of the public sector. People feel that the dividend should be protected regardless of any resulting deterioration in other public programmes. It is easy for people to rationalize that their dividends are spent on personal necessities like winter clothes for their children, whereas politicians would waste the money on ridiculous and useless projects.

7.6 For Many Households the Dividend Makes Only a Marginal Difference in Income

As one moves up the income distribution the impacts of the dividend decline, both because the federal income tax drains off a larger share and because the dividend represents a smaller share of total household income. The potential effects of interest, such as changes in labour force participation rates and enhanced personal opportunities, are concentrated among a small portion of the population at the lower end of the income distribution. This can make these effects more difficult to detect and monitor simply because they are not a concern for most people. It also means that, from a narrow financial perspective, the programme is not targeted if its primary objective is to assist people of modest means.

Notes

1   University of Alaska, USA.
2   Economic Policy Institute, *State Income Equality Continued to Grow in Most States in the 1990s, Despite Economic Growth and Tight Labour Markets*, news release of January 18, 2000, accessed at http://www.cbpp.org/1-18-00-sfp.htm.

34

SOCIAL CITIZENSHIP AND WORKFARE IN THE UNITED STATES AND WESTERN EUROPE: FROM STATUS TO CONTRACT

Joel Handler[1]

'We have ended welfare as we know it.' President Bill Clinton

'No one has a right to be lazy.' Chancellor Gerhard Schröder

'Men fought for the right to live from their labour, not to be supported by the welfare state. Thus, progress demands reinventing the idea of the right to work, rather than shaping a right to income.' Pierre Rosanvallon

'Insertion contracts are a load of rubbish, they don't guarantee anything.' French RMI recipient

1. Introduction

This paper deals with 'welfare' in the United States, the programme primarily for poor single mothers and their families, and 'workfare' – or, the preferred term, 'activation' in western Europe, the 'active labour market policies (ALMP) that deal primarily with the long-term unemployed, unemployed youth, lone parents, immigrants, and other vulnerable groups, usually lumped together as the 'socially excluded.' I explore the ideologies that have led to these changes, comparing different views of social citizenship. The western Europeans argue that their reforms, although they resemble those of the United States in some respects, are significantly different both in ideology and in practice. I raise questions about those claims.

The move towards active labour market policies in western Europe represents a fundamental change in both the meaning of social citizenship and the administration of social welfare. Social benefits are rights that are attached to status – the status of citizenship. Under the new regime, benefits become conditional. Rights only attach if *obligations* are fulfilled. In this sense, social citizenship changes from status to contract. What brought this about? There have been significant changes in the labour market: an increasing demand for higher levels of skills and education; new service jobs for the low skilled; an increase in part-time and flexible work. While these developments have increased opportunities, they have also created barriers for the low-skilled and under-educated in the form of low wages and employment insecurity, especially for women and youth (European Union, 2001, pp. 14–15). There has been a big increase in female labour market participation. Most significantly, for more than two decades, most Western European countries have been struggling with sluggish economies and persistent long-term unemployment – a condition named 'Eurosclerosis' by Huber and Stephens (2001). In some countries, growth and employment have resumed, but in several, long-term unemployment remains high. There is deep concern about 'worklessness,' and the socially excluded. Welfare states are under great stress – from the unemployed, an ageing population, rising health care costs – but government budgets are constrained by Europe's monetary union.

The economic establishment and most political leaders think that a major part of the problem is due to the costs and inflexibility of the labour market, caused, in part, by an overly generous welfare state which discourages work and feeds a dependency culture. In order to increase employment, labour must become more flexible and the welfare state must be changed 'from passive to active.' An 'active' welfare state will not only encourage job growth, it will also help bring the socially excluded back into the paid labour market and thereby restore true citizenship. It is a programme of *inclusion*.[2]

Thus, in both the United States and western Europe, the proponents of workfare believe that the surest, most stable path to inclusion is via the paid labour market. Lawrence Mead (1986) says that the employable poor want to work, but that the permissiveness of the United States welfare system has led them astray. The poor need authority, the imposition of obligations. Mead claims to be interested in helping, not punishing the poor.[3] Pierre Rosanvallon, in his book, *The New Social Question: Rethinking the Welfare State*, believes that workfare contracts between the government and the client *empower* the client. It is through the welfare contract that the capacities of the socially excluded are developed, so that they are reintegrated back into society and citizenship.

The thesis of this paper is that inclusion through workfare obligations is contradictory. Positive acts of inclusion necessarily result in *exclusion* – of those who cannot negotiate the barriers. Some barriers are structural, many of them beyond the control of welfare departments. Others are individual. The significance of the shortcomings in individual capacities is obvious. Therefore the point that I want to emphasize is administrative capacity – an issue of critical importance which is often ignored. Active programmes make significant new demands on field-level administration. Workfare is administered at local offices. Field-level workers are required to make individualized discretionary decisions as to whether the obligations have been fulfilled, what classes as an excuse, and what sanctions, if any, to impose. Selectivity rules are invariably complex. In addition to the usual forms of bureaucratic disentitlement – delays, frustrations, unfriendly relationships, errors, and so forth – behavioural tests require officials to interpret, apply and monitor regulations, benefits and sanctions (Standing, 1999). Organizations are responsive to their political and social environments for support and cooperation and to avoid hostility. To manage these competing demands, officials stereotype claimants by processing those more likely to respond and deferring or sanctioning those judged to be difficult. There is inevitably exclusion of those who cannot, for whatever reason, comply with the rules.

In this paper, I will first introduce the concept of social citizenship. Today, the concept of citizenship is much debated. It is argued, for example, that citizenship should be transnational or global rather than bound by the nation, that it is a process rather than a status (Bosniak, 2000; Nussbaum, 1996; Turner and Hamilton, 1994; Falk, 2000). Here, I will take the more traditional definition of social citizenship as developed in western Europe after the Second World War. I contrast this definition with the concept of citizenship in the United States, which is based on contract rather than status. I then introduce the European 'Third Way' which also redefines social citizenship as contractual in an effort to cope with the current strains on the welfare state. A brief description of the experience of the recent United States welfare-state reforms highlights the questions that I raise concerning western Europe. I discuss the changes in western Europe – in ideology and in welfare state policies. Thus far, there is not a great deal of empirical data coming out of Europe, but there are indications of significant similarities in administration (FAFO Institute, 2001). I conclude with an argument for a Basic Income Guarantee to provide, among other things, an exit option for welfare recipients when 'contracting' with government.

2. Social Citizenship

Citizenship commonly refers to a legal/political status within a nation state. The status has certain entitlements: the right to permanent residence within the State; to hold property; to use the legal system; and (with some qualifications) to vote and to hold office. Social citizenship refers to entitlement to welfare state provisions – the supports that are designed to reduce the risks of sickness or disability, old age, unemployment or lack of income. States vary as to whether non-citizens can receive such benefits. Citizenship, then, describes concrete, positive, legal entitlements. Citizenship is, however, also used in an ideological or symbolic sense – to distinguish people from others within a set of borders or from those who are outside the borders. It is often used as a term of exclusion, of moral superiority, a construction of the other.

Social citizenship rights are commonly analysed in economic terms – for example, decommodifying labour is seen to protect against risks to earning capacity and to reduce poverty. The core, though, of social citizenship rights, as with all citizenship rights, is fundamentally moral. Redistribution is an act of solidarity, of *inclusion*. The moral issues are multi-dimensional. They are captured in the Anglo-American concept of the 'undeserving poor'. Although ostensibly about work effort, these moral judgments involve race, ethnicity, gender, family responsibilities, sexuality, and various forms of deviant behaviour (Smith, 1997; Forbath, 2000). Western Europe is experiencing increasing strains in solidarity resulting from the numbers of the socially excluded and the huge volume of cross-border migration from all over the world (Bhabha, 1998; Tamas, 2000).

As stated, this paper will be restricted to the traditional concept of social citizenship developed in Western Europe in the decades following the Second World War, now referred to as the 'Golden Age'. The initial formulation of social citizenship is attributed to the British economist, T.H. Marshall. In Marshall's formulation, *civil rights*, developed in the eighteenth century, included free speech, access to the legal system, rights to a fair trial, and rights of contract and property. *Political rights* – the extension of the franchise, the secret ballot, the right to hold office – were products of the nineteenth century (for men). *Social rights* belong to the twentieth century – entitlements to social security when faced with unemployment, sickness, old age, and other kinds of hardship – that is, protections from the rigours of capitalist labour markets (Marshall, 1950).

Marshall was concerned with the contradiction between formal political equality and individual freedom, on the one hand, and significant social and economic inequality on the other. The social entitlements of the welfare state would reconcile, or at least lessen the conflicts between capitalism and civil and political citizenship (Hemerijck, 1999). Social rights would enable people to exercise civil and political rights. Social rights would give individuals a sense of security, which, in turn, would foster a sense of a collective identity between the state and its citizens. He coined the term 'social citizenship.'

Marshall was writing at a time when the economies of western Europe were enjoying strong growth and very low unemployment rates. It was during this period that the exemplary welfare states were created. Although the various countries took different paths, the starting point was the granting of rights with 'the legal and practical status of property rights' (Esping-Andersen, 1990).

Because these rights are based on 'citizenship rather than performance, they will entail a decommodification of the status of individuals *vis-à-vis* the market (p. 3)'. Decommodification is a matter of degree. The extent to which an individual is liberated from the market depends on the nature of the social benefit – both the conditions of aid and its adequacy. When benefits are low and based on need, the market is actually strengthened. Even when benefits are generous and based on fairly strong insurance-like entitlements, there still will not be much decommodification, if contributions are based on employment (p. 22). It was only in the late 1960s and 1970s that some States approached decommodification; with minimum proof of medical impairment, one could receive sickness insurance benefits equal to his or her normal wage for as long as deemed necessary. The same would be true for unemployment benefits, pensions, maternity leave and childcare.

Looking at various social welfare states in terms of social rights and social stratification, Esping-Andersen constructed his three clusters of regime-types:

- The 'liberal' state (the United States, Canada, Australia) is characterized by mainly means-tested, low benefits designed to reinforce labour-market participation; here, decommodification is at a minimum.
- In the historic corporatist-statist model (Austria, France, Germany, Italy), status differences are upgraded to take account of new class structures. There is only modest redistribution. There is also considerable emphasis on the traditional family; family benefits encourage motherhood and discourage mothers in the paid labour force (e.g., minimal day care benefits).
- In the 'social democratic' regime-types (Scandinavia), universalism and decommodification have been extended into the new middle classes to promote equality between workers and the middle class. While benefits reflect earnings, there is no private social insurance market. Family costs are socialized to allow women to choose the labour market. The viability of this high-cost welfare state depends on most people working and the fewest number being dependent on transfers.[4]

2.1 Social Citizenship in the United States

Fraser and Gordon (1994) note that, in the United States, while there is a rich discourse on civil citizenship – civil rights, individual liberties, freedom of speech – there is almost a total disregard of the concept of 'social citizenship'. The reason is that 'social citizenship' implies entitlements:

People who are 'social citizens' get 'social rights', not 'handouts'. In the United States, welfare is usually considered grounds of disrespect, a threat to, rather than a realization of citizenship. The connotations of citizenship are so positive, powerful and proud, while those of 'welfare' are so negative, weak, and degraded, that 'social citizenship' here sounds almost oxymoronic. (Fraser and Gordon, 1994, p. 92)

In the United States, welfare was always coupled with obligations, a contract. It is not a formal, legal contract, but a contract based on the moral obligations of citizenship. There is always the concern that severing the link between work and income will erode the work ethic.

With the War on Poverty and the legal rights movements in the 1960s, welfare became an 'entitlement.' Conservatives then attacked the liberal welfare regime on two fronts. Charles Murray, in *Losing Ground* (1984) argued that the Great Society programmes of the 1960s, by rewarding the 'undeserving poor,' were responsible for the rise in unemployment, crime, single-parent households, and out-of-wedlock births among African-Americans. Lawrence Mead, in *Beyond Entitlement: The Social Obligations of Citizenship* (1986), argued that by not insisting on behavioural changes – primarily work – these policies resulted in an erosion of the work ethic. The poor want to work, want to be responsible citizens, but 'it is something they would like to do, but not something they feel they must do at any cost. It is an aspiration but not an obligation' (p. 162). Mead said that workfare is not coercive; rather it is an exercise in authority (p. 166). As will be discussed, in the 1980s, the liberals also endorsed the obligation to work (Ellwood, 1988; Garfinkel and McLanahan, 1986). This is now the current United States welfare policy. Entitlements have been abolished. Welfare recipients have obligations, not rights. 'Contract' remains the moral definition of social citizenship.

2.2 The European 'Third Way' Position

As noted, conservatives or neoliberals look at the United States and now the United Kingdom and argue that labour has to become more 'flexible' – more part-time jobs, less protection against lay-offs, lower employment-related benefits, lower payroll taxes – and that the welfare state has to be changed from 'passive' to 'active' to provide incentives for the socially excluded to enter the labour market. The opposition says that, in the United States, there is unprecedented inequality and growing poverty. In most western European countries, the conservatives have been rejected. Social democrats were returned to office with the pledge of finding a path to economic recovery that would, at the same time, preserve the welfare state. There have been some changes in the welfare states, but so far the basic programmes – pensions, disability and health care – have remained intact, and with changes in labour and demography, are now very costly. In most countries, unemployment remains unacceptably high, especially for the most vulnerable, the conflicts between the haves and have-nots have not diminished, and tensions over immigrants are increasing. However, the demands for welfare state preservation, if not expansion, conflict with the budgetary austerity requirements of the European Union. There now seems to be a swing back to the conservatives.

In an attempt to move out of this impasse, the social democrats adopted the 'Third Way', which seeks to steer a middle course between the traditional defenders of the existing welfare state and the neoliberals who want to dismantle it. I take as one example of the Third Way, Pierre Rosanvallon, an intellectual figure within the 'second left' in France.[5] Agreeing with the neoliberals, Rosanvallon thinks that, with long-term unemployment and social exclusion, the passive welfare state becomes 'pernicious.' It destroys solidarity by increasing the indirect costs of labour, which eventually further reduces employment. Is there a way out? Rosanvallon argues that the 'logic of solidarity' will now have to be built on a system of direct redistribution, which will rely on citizenship that in turn, depends on 'a sort of moral covenant' (2000, p. 57). Here, Rosanvallon develops his ideas of contract. He argues that there are individual differences which may account for social exclusion. Certain differences should be dealt with through anti-discrimination policies, others, such as disability, through social and political means. But the central problem revolves around 'behavioural' variables – the disparities that arise from 'voluntary actions' that have both a moral and a psychological character. The welfare state has to deal with these individual differences. There has to be a new form of reintegration with 'an expanded re-understanding of social rights.' This means changing 'payment for idleness to payment for work.' This arrangement is called the 'right to work', and has to be applied to specific individuals. Rosanvallon recognizes that there is a history of requiring work, which shows the risks of the state attempting to control behaviour. However, he argues that these negative effects can be avoided through a new conception of the social management of employment. This would build on the concept of inclusion. The reforms in France (the *revenu minimum d'insertion*) and the United States are good examples of this middle way. They are based on a mutual commitment between the individual and the collective. The excluded have a right to a minimum income to allow them to re-enter society, but also a contract – the beneficiary's 'commitment to inclusion.' The commitments are diverse: training; public works; personal efforts at readjustment (e.g., detoxification). These are individually determined – the 'individualized right.' The *revenu minimum d'insertion* does supervise behaviour; thus, it is not a right in the strictly legal sense, but it also not 'legal charity.' Rosanvallon claims that RMI signals a 'third type of society' – one that gives neither traditional social aid nor classic social protection that is mechanically distributed to beneficiaries. The same thinking lies behind the current American form of welfare, which will soon become familiar in Europe. 'Neither the market nor the state can "solve" the problem. In both cases, social rights are reinterpreted as a contract articulating rights and obligations' (Rosanvallon, 2000, pp. 84–87). Democratic inclusion has to be based on equality through contract.

According to Rosanvallon, the relationship of contract will be empowering. Individuals become full members of society. They not only have the right to live, 'but the right to live in society.' The obligation is also a 'positive constraint' on society. Society is to take rights 'seriously'. This is the 'path of mutual involvement'; 'The subject is considered an autonomous, responsible person capable of making commitments and honouring them' (p. 88). Thus, the RMI contract 'is not a restriction of freedom but an instance of constructing society, a radical reconsideration of the organizing principles of individualistic society' (p. 88). He calls this 'contractual individualism' (p. 92).

While there are many negative attitudes and stereotypes implicit in the recent welfare changes, this is not true of Rosanvallon, the 'Third Way', and many of the United States liberals who now favour obligations. Rather, they believe that re-integration into the paid labour market is the one sure way of re-establishing social citizenship. Nevertheless, there are many objections to this re-definition of social citizenship. Clients are to become integrated through contract, a contract of obligation. In theory, contract assumes independent, knowledgeable, voluntary individuals. It is here that the concern arises. The assumption of equality of contracting parties is far from reality. Welfare recipients are dependent people; they are in no position to bargain. We will return to this issue more fully after we review the experience in the United States and western Europe.

3. The American Welfare Reform

Under the 1996 American reform, welfare is no longer an 'entitlement'. Temporary Assistance to Needy Families (TANF) has replaced Aid to Families with Dependent Children (AFDC).[6] What is new is the significant ideological and policy commitment to work, enforced by time limits. Previously, welfare would last as long as the youngest child was under 18. Now, recipients cannot receive welfare for more than two continuous years and there is a cumulative five-year limit on federal cash assistance (with exceptions for no more than 20 per cent of the caseload). States are required to move an increasing percentage of welfare recipients into the work force increasing to 50 per cent by 2002, and to reduce grant amounts for recipients who refuse to participate in 'work or work activities'.[7]

The basis of the reform is the 'work first' strategy. The assumptions behind this position are:

- there are plenty of jobs for those who want to work;
- by taking and persisting with a job, even an entry-level job, a person will move up the employment ladder;
- the problem with welfare recipients is that they do not have the motivation or the incentives to leave welfare and enter the paid labour market;
- the state programmes have shown that recipients can be moved from welfare to work. The idea is to move not only current recipients but also applicants – before they get on welfare into the labour market as quickly as possible rather than place them in longer-term training or education programmes.

Despite the publicity, the results of earlier State demonstration projects have been very modest. There was very little difference in employment between the control groups and the experimentals. Earnings increased by only about $500 per year and often failed to account for the costs of working, while most leavers remained in poverty. Welfare payments were however reduced, thus resulting in welfare savings for the Government (Michalopoulos, Schwartz and Adams-Ciardullo, 2000, pp. 4,7–8).[8] The reason for these modest results is that the assumptions behind welfare-to-work programmes totally misconceive the characteristics of the low-wage labour market and the identity of welfare recipients.

The 'success story' of the United States economy is well known. Since 1990, over 20 million new jobs have been created, with low unemployment and inflation. On the other hand, there has been stagnation in the real wages of the less skilled, less educated workers (Freeman, 2000, pp. 27–37). For a while, the inequality in women's wages narrowed, primarily because of an increase in the hours worked and the decline in male earnings (Mishel, Bernstein and Schmitt, 1999). Jobs are increasingly contingent or short-term, and without benefits. Hours per week vary a great deal causing conflicts with family arrangements, other jobs, and transportation (Lambert, Waxman and Haley-Lock, 2001, pp. 134–135). Turnover rates among new hires are high (p. 19). Thus, employment instability and low wages continue to be a major problem for the less-skilled and disadvantaged workers – young workers, minorities, single-parent families, and those who lack a high-school diploma (Burtless, 1999). Low-wage workers are not moving up the economic ladder (Mishel et al., 1999; Katz and Allen, 1999; Wright and Dyer, 2000). Strict time limits on welfare fail to take into account the instability of lower-wage work (Lambert et al., 2001, p. 19). Given the characteristics of the low-wage labour market, it is no surprise that there are still millions living in poverty or close to it. In 2000, 11.3 per cent of the population (31 million people) were living below the official poverty line of $17,603 for a family of four (United States Census Bureau, 2001). Moreover, 13.8 million had incomes of less than one-half of the poverty line (United States Census Bureau, 1998; Heclo, 1994, p. 420). Thus, although more Americans are working harder, inequality and poverty remain severe among the working poor.

3.1 The Work Experience of Welfare Recipients

Contrary to the stereotype, most welfare recipients are adults with small families (1.9 children, on average) and are on welfare for relatively short periods – between two and four years. Long-term dependency (five years or more) is rare – pehaps as low as 15 per cent. The largest proportion of welfare recipients are connected to the paid labour market, and the most common route off welfare is via a job. However, those who leave welfare often have to return. In the low-skilled labour market, workers go back and forth between work and welfare (Handler and Hasenfeld, 1997). They have to use welfare because in most states, they do not qualify for unemployment insurance.[9]

Welfare recipients do not fare particularly well in the competition for these low-skilled jobs. Employers of low-skilled workers are looking for high school diplomas, work experience, and social skills ('soft skills'). They often hire through networks, and, in general, prefer workers with similar ethnic backgrounds. African-Americans are at the end of the queue. Nevertheless, between half and two-thirds of those leaving welfare find jobs shortly afterwards (Loprest, 1999). Most of the jobs are in sales, food preparation, clerical support, and other service jobs. There are substantial periods of unemployment. The pay is between $5.67 and $8.42 per hour. Average reported annual earnings range from $8,000 to $15,144, thus leaving many families in poverty. Most do not receive employer-provided health insurance, paid sick or vacation leave Strawn et al., 2001, pp. 6–7). It would be hard to exaggerate the difficulties of child care for poor working mothers; yet most do not receive child care subsidies (Pavetti, 1999, p. 16). Under the new law, welfare recipients no longer automatically qualify for Medicaid and Food Stamps and there has been a serious drop in enrolments (Greenberg and Larcy, 2000, p. 12).

Those still remaining on the rolls face the most serious barriers to employment. Nearly 50 per cent of recipients have not completed high school (Pavetti, 1999). Three-quarters of the adults on welfare have at least one potential barrier to employment, including poor mental or physical health, limited education, minimal or no work experience, and family responsibilities (Danziger et al., 2000, p. 34).

3.2 The Decline in the Welfare Rolls

If employment is so uncertain, then what accounts for the dramatic decline in the welfare rolls, which have fallen from 12.2 million people in 1996 to

5.3 million (Pear, 2002)? Politicians, of course, claim that welfare reform is 'working' – despite the fact that rolls were declining significantly before many of the work requirements were enacted (DeParle, 1997; Brito, 1999).[10] Most economists agree that the macro economy is responsible for a decline in the welfare rolls, but differ as to the relative importance of the economy versus welfare reform; estimates as to the effect of welfare reform range from 'trivial' to 30 to 40 per cent (Figlio and Ziliak, 1999; Meyer and Rosenbaum, 1999; Ellwood, 1999; Council of Economic Advisors, 1999).

A major difficulty involves the meaning of 'welfare reform'. There are a number of possibilities: the welfare-to-work programmes; the time limits; the sanctions, or combinations of all three. Another complication arises from the use of discretion in administering these reforms. Not only states, but also individual offices, vary greatly in how they interpret and apply these rules.[11] Then, there has been a significant increase in benefits to working families that provide strong incentives to work but are not considered part of 'welfare reform'. Since the late 1980s, benefits have increased from about $5 billion (1997 dollars) in federal aid to more than $50 billion in 1997. About half of this growth is accounted by the Earned Income Tax Credit – a refundable tax credit of up to 40 per cent of earnings for low-income families (Ellwood, 1999, p. 3; Figlio and Ziliak, 1999; Meyer and Rosenbaum, 1999). Some scholars consider the Earned Income Tax Credit the single most important influence on the decline in welfare rolls (Meyer and Rosenbaum, 1999). Other factors could include the increase in the minimum wage in 1997 (Stapleton *et al.*, 2001).

3.3 Administrative Capacity

Since the 1960s, the federal and the state Governments have imposed strict quality control measures on local offices to try to reduce eligibility and payment errors. Extensive documentation is required including birth certificates and Social Security numbers as well as details on all changes in income and assets, and other eligibility and income data. The 1996 welfare reform required offices to shift from checking eligibility to individual, intensive casework to guide clients into the labour market. However, this has not happened. At the street level, the focus is still on reducing errors, eliminating fraud and completing the work in a timely manner (Gais *et al.*, 2001, pp. 13–16). The TANF requirements were simply added to this culture of compliance, greatly increasing administrative burdens. Many more client contacts are necessary both to guide and to check on workfare progress and compliance, yet information systems are inadequate and officials are often unable to obtain even basic information on individual recipients. In some states, caseworkers could not even tell clients how much time they had left (Gais *et al.*, 2001, pp. 33–34).

3.4 Implementing Sanctions

Most states have chosen to implement strict sanctions. Thirty-seven states have full-family sanctions for violations of work and other personal responsibility requirements.[12] At least 31 states have implemented some form of diversion programme (Diller, 2000). A widespread practice is to require applicants to conduct a job search while the application is pending. Requirements range from two to six weeks and from two to 40 employer contacts before benefits can start. The responsibility is on the individual rather than the programme. Again, there is considerable caseworker discretion as to who is required, who is excused, and what constitutes an excuse.

There are also difficulties in communicating the most basic information about sanctions and time limits (Pavetti and Bloom, 2001, pp. 8–9). Despite repeated explanations, there is evidence that recipients tend not to understand them and large numbers of recipients were not aware that they had been sanctioned, what was expected of them, what benefits they would lose and for how long (Hasenfeld et al., 2001).[13] Virtually all states have some form of grievance procedure whereby clients can appeal.[14] In the past, the right of appeal in welfare cases was already largely ineffectual (Handler, 1986). Under the present regime, there is even more confusion and lack of awareness.

It is now clear that states make widespread use of sanctions (Haskins and Blank, 2001, p. 24). A General Accounting Office study in the US (1998) found that an average of 135,800 families each month (4.5 per cent of the national caseload) received a full or partial sanction; an average of 16,000 families were cut off completely (Hasenfeld et al., 2001, p. 11). Seven states reported that sanctions accounted for one-fifth or more of their case closures in 1999 (Hasenfeld et al., 2001, pp. 11–15; Pavetti and Bloom, 2001, pp. 19–21). Sanctioned recipients face a number of employment barriers. Most sanctions are imposed because of missed appointments and deadlines; clients are seldom aware of 'good cause' exemptions and often think that the sanctions for non-participation are more severe than in reality. These results indicate the difficulty that welfare offices have in adequately communicating welfare requirements and sanctions to clients. The combination of cognitive barriers and poor communication plays a major part in the decision to impose sanctions (Hasenfeld et al., 2001, pp. 11–12). Many agency staff firmly believe that sanctions communicate the seriousness of the requirements (Kaplan, 1999, p. 6).[15] Other studies show that neither the threat of sanctions nor the imposition of sanctions changes behaviour. The available data suggests that most people do not comply with programme requirements even after a sanction is imposed (Pavetti and Bloom, 2001, pp. 15–16).

3.5 Some Lessons from the American Experience that Might be Applicable to Western Europe

Here, I highlight some important, general characteristics of the American welfare experience and ask to what extent are these relevant to Europeans.

Welfare Office Strategies: Moral Typification; Myth and Ceremony

Previous work programmes were never really enforced. Most recipients were deflected (put on administrative 'hold') and few found jobs. The reason for the general failure of implementation was the lack of administrative capacity. I have described how offices came to emphasize strict monitoring controls. The staff became eligibility clerks and technicians who are under-trained, under-paid, and overworked. Yet, policymakers make the political, symbolic gestures of reform and do not worry about administration. This is especially true with the welfare-to-work programmes. The path that welfare has taken is thus con-tradictory. The emphasis on controlling 'waste, fraud, and abuse' has resulted in bureaucratization, computerized rule enforcement, and the proletarianiza-tion of the workforce. In short, it has produced an organization that is admin-istratively incapable of carrying out work programmes, which, at least in theory, are supposed to require individualized consultation and assessment, planning, contracts, supervision, and follow-up. The delegation of authority further complicates implementation. Federal and state work requirements are in the form of mandates addressed to the local offices. There are over 3,000 counties in the United States and in the larger counties there are several local offices. Thus, there are thousands of local variations in the day-to-day admin-istration of the work programmes. These local offices, in turn, often have to rely on other local service providers (e.g., for employment and training) who have missions other than serving welfare recipients.

Recipients must accept suitable offers of employment or participate in pre-employment activities. If, without cause, they fail to do so, they are subject to sanction. Within these seemingly simple requirements lie volumes of rules, regulations, standards, and interpretations. There is an enormous amount of paperwork; everything has to be documented and computer systems are often faulty. But despite the quantity of rules, a great many of the most crucial deci-sions require discretion on the part of the field-level workers. The work pro-gramme is an add-on to the welfare office. The welfare office is directed to run an employment programme, but it is not an employment service and it does not want to be an employment service. It has neither the expertise nor the resources. All organizations, welfare agencies, community colleges and adult education programmes seek legitimacy and support from their environments.

They try to present themselves as efficient, capable institutions that are fulfilling their mission. Thus, welfare agencies will select clients who fit the rules, who follow the rules, and who do not cause problems.

Selecting, processing, and changing people involves moral judgments. Yeheskel Hasenfeld (1983) has described the process as moral typification. Workers classify clients according to preconceptions. The welfare agency will attempt to select those clients who fit organizational needs. They screen in confirming information and ignore conflicting information. Client responses become self-fulfilling prophecies. Programmes select and train the most promising and reject those who may need the services the most. Agencies punish those who fail to comply. Caseworkers apply rules strictly, impose sanctions, minimize errors, and try to get through the day as quickly and painlessly as possible. Changes consume scarce administrative time and run the risk of error. Clients with problems become problems. Whatever the programme demands, the staff response will be survival, and not necessarily service to clients. Because individual field-level decisions are shrouded in factual assessments, supervision is difficult, even if there is the will to do so.

The idea of the 'contract' in this setting is an exercise in myth and ceremonies. In her study of Job Opportunities and Basic Skills Training (JOBS) in Chicago (2002), Evelyn Brodkin and her colleagues (2002) showed how the caseworkers fit led the clients into available slots and ignored information about service needs they could not respond to. Caseworkers would send clients on job searches even though they did not meet the required level of education or literacy proficiency. 'Favoured' clients received education or vocational training. In discussing the impact of 'performance-based contracts,' Brodkin says,

> [Such] contracts were almost perfectly designed to reward [service contractors] for placing clients in lower-wage jobs with the least to offer, jobs, not surprisingly, which are in relatively constant demand, due to their volatility. Even the state's minimal 'retention' measure (150 non-consecutive days of work) can be satisfied by churning individuals through a sequence of low-wage, dead-end jobs (pp. 23–24).

The welfare recipients had little recourse in trying to get the welfare department to meet its part of the contract.

These findings are not surprising and are replicated in many other instances. Yet, it is disturbing that welfare reformers seem to learn so little from history. As Alvin Schorr (1987) reminds us, social contracts were the social work strategy of the 1950s and 1960s. They did not work then, primarily as a result of the same administrative constraints that Brodkin describes over 40 years later. In the past, the workers would deflect the more troublesome cases. Now, they are sanctioned.

If the above is the general story of the welfare-to-work programmes, what accounts for their continued re-enactments? Here, we are in the realm of symbolic politics, of myth and ceremony. The current myth is the 'work first' strategy. The country was determined to 'end welfare as we know it.' The 'work first' strategy was clear, it was effectively communicated and it did not matter that of those who worked, almost all remained in poverty. The companion myth, which is prevalent in the western European 'Third Way', is contract. The welfare recipient and the socially excluded will enter into a contract of inclusion with the welfare department; both sides will mutually agree on an individualized decision; and through participation, the excluded will re-enter society.

4. Workfare in Western Europe

There have been a variety of policy responses to Eurosclerosis. Here, we are concerned with workfare, or the preferred term, *active labour market policies* (ALMP), now common throughout Europe. In return for benefits, recipients must seek work or participate in work-related activities, including, if appropriate, education and training (Lødemel and Trickey, 2001). The 'job first' principle has spread throughout Europe (Ferrera and Rhodes, 2000, p. 4; Supiot, 1999, p. 34). While most countries are pursuing reforms according to their own so-called 'path dependent' traditions and institutions (Kitschelt *et al.*, 1999), 'benefit conditionality [has] moved to centre-stage' (Clasen, 2000, p. 89). Moreover, the ideology behind activation is not just a response to Eurosclerosis. Compulsory activation is increasing in Denmark, despite its low unemployment, according to the principle that 'everyone with at least some work capacity to work should work' (FAFO, 2001, p. 46). Norway, with no welfare crisis, has adopted workfare (Lødemel, 2001, p. 133). Both right- and left-wing parties agreed that extensive rights to generous benefits threatened the ability to become self-sufficient, and that individual responsibilities and obligations were more important than individual rights. Means-testing would be more positively viewed as 'targeting' rather than as an unfortunate remnant of the past. This change was not the result of a conservative backlash against the welfare state. Rather, according to Lødemel, the Norwegian Labour Party was following in the path of contemporary social democrats in other countries that have endorsed changes in the welfare state.[16]

There are three basic components of workfare:

- existing policies of encouraging the disabled and older workers from leaving the labour force should be reversed;

- those who are on the 'margins' of the labour force should be placed in jobs or training; and
- work requirements for the unemployed should be tightened.

What is new are activation measures applied to *social assistance* recipients. The goal is to prevent the 'deserving' from becoming 'undeserving' and to reintegrate the 'undeserving' (Standing, 1999, p. 314).

While changes are occurring in all western European countries, I can only very briefly summarize some of the workfare experiences in the United Kingdom, Sweden, Norway, the Netherlands, Denmark, France and Germany. The United Kingdom initiated the change from a passive to an active welfare state and, at this point, is probably the furthest down the road. Sweden and Norway are at the other end of the spectrum – the most universal, decommodified welfare states that are still intact. Denmark and the Netherlands are the most frequently cited examples of countries that have successfully met the challenge of persistent long-term unemployment. In France and Germany, Social Democratic governments have publicly rejected the US-UK model of low-wage jobs and increasing income inequality, but have not yet found a way to reduce persistent long-term unemployment as well as other high costs of the welfare state.

The record thus far on active labour market policies is mixed. Most of the goals cannot be accomplished quickly and, with few exceptions, the empirical evidence at the field level is uneven. A recent report evaluating workfare in France, Germany, the Netherlands, Norway, Denmark and the United Kingdom concluded that most of the studies were not sufficiently well designed to answer the basic question of whether the participants benefited from the programmes or were worse off; the results are 'suggestive rather than conclusive' (FAFO, 2001, pp. 73–74). As I am concerned with the risks to the most vulnerable, I will be emphasizing negative findings more than positive ones. It is easier for governments and other proponents of the reforms to emphasize the positive and ignore or downplay those who drop through the cracks; this is what mainstream society wants to hear.

In the United Kingdom, New Labour has extended the policies of mandatory activity to 'workless' groups. In the New Deal for Young People, after six months of benefits, there is a 'gateway' period consisting of an intensive job search, followed by options including training, education, subsidized employment, or work in voluntary or environmental jobs, and self-employment. If there is still no unsubsidized employment, there is a 'follow-through' period for further intensive support. During the gateway period (which can last up to four months), the participant is supposed to be available for an option and actively seeking work. Each participant is assigned a 'personal advisor' who draws up an 'action plan' which is supposed to set 'realistic achievable job goals'. A new generation of front line Employment Service personal advisers has been given more flexibility to identify and deal with barriers and assist claimants with job search. The purpose is to 'forge an entirely new culture' by promoting a work orientation for all claimants (Finn and Blackmore, 1997, pp. 8–9). There can be sanctions for 'wilfully and persistently' refusing to participate. Once the gateway is over, the options are compulsory. Sanctions can be two to four weeks, depending on whether there has been a previous sanction (Trickey and Walker, 2001, pp. 199–202). The New Deal for the Over 25s is for the long-term unemployed. This group faces more barriers than the young and the programme is less successful.

Finn and Blackmore (1997) report on surveys and focus groups in four areas of high long-term unemployment.[17] An individual action plan (The Job Seekers Agreement or JSAg) is settled at the start of benefits. All the focus group participants were scornful of the JSAg – it was a ten-minute interview with a person 'who knows nothing about you'. 'The claimants sign to get the benefits'. The terms of the participation contracts seem to be largely determined by the officers rather than the recipients. A survey of clients found that less than 30 per cent reported that their fortnightly job search review lasted longer than six minutes, and 30 per cent had interviews that lasted for two minutes or less; 43 per cent reported that there was actually no discussion about job search, rising to over 90 per cent in some offices. Overall, there is broad agreement that too many JSAgs are drawn up mechanically and too many people are forced into meaningless activities. Most respondents had a very critical view of the Employment Service in terms of its ability to help them find work or improve their employability. They felt that the Employment Service offered the least attractive jobs, was inefficient in updating vacancies and the staff did not have enough time or experience to deal with them as individuals. The primary goal of the Employment Service staff was to remove them from the unemployment rolls rather than offer genuine help. They doubted the value of training when, having completed the courses, they were still unable to find jobs. They resented compulsory job-search courses as a waste of time, especially when they were repeated. They attended only to prevent loss of benefits.

The Employment Service staff pointed to a shortage of job opportunities and emphasized that clients often had significant personal barriers to employment. They complained of a lack of time and resources to perform all the tasks, especially the fortnightly interviews for persons out of work for over six months, which were supposed to take only seven minutes per person. They felt that the performance targets were counterproductive and 'interfere with listening to jobseekers'. Their problems were exacerbated because jobseekers resisted taking low-quality jobs. Only a third believed that sanctions and penalties were effective at enforcing compliance. The greatest challenge was the 'revolving door' – participants took jobs but then a large number were likely subsequently to become unemployed. A common feeling among both claimants and Employment Service staff was one of frustration – claimants because of not being able to find suitable work, staff because of high caseloads and performance targets.

In Sweden, by 1993, unemployment had risen to 8.2 per cent and there was a large increase in the Government deficit. All political parties favoured reducing entitlements (Huber and Stephens, 2001, pp. 245–249). There was a modest increase in work incentives and a large investment in research, development, training, and education. The economy recovered. There has been a significant growth in public employment, largely female, and very expensive. There has also been a huge expansion in temporary work, but part-time employment is not differentiated from regular employment. In short, Sweden has rebounded with an intact welfare state (Andrews, 1999). Nevertheless, Sweden has tightened unemployment benefit conditions. It also has workfare (Torfing, 1999, p. 13).[18] Sweden provides support for education and training of the unemployed, offering people between 20 and 24 years of age a place in a municipal work programme or a competence-development scheme for up to 12 months (Kuhnle, 2000, p. 214). They have to accept any offer or risk losing benefits. The wages are at the same level as assistance and there are no unemployment, sick relief, or pension benefits (Kildal, 2000). Thus far, it is unclear what effects the changes have had on employment. Many of the participants found work but it was usually temporary (Roche, 2000, pp. 36–37).

In Norway, workfare is for social assistance recipients only, and is supposed to be a last resort. The local authorities have wide discretion and can apply workfare to a range of recipients such as refugees, asylum-seekers and single parents. Work is restricted to local authority services, and can either be newly created or existing work performed by regular employees. Training to accompany along with work is also discretionary (Lødemel, 2001, pp. 145–146). Some local authorities have used workfare to fill regular city jobs, at about one-third of the regular wage; others have used it to discourage claimants. The result, according to Lødemel, was that Norway has created a 'social division of activation'. Most who are in active labour market schemes enjoy regular wages, regular working hours, and have time for training. Those who are left – the 'residuals' – are considered the least deserving and are subject to social assistance workfare. Thus, at least according to Lødemel, the Norwegian system resembles the United States rather than the other European countries (Lødemel, 2001, pp. 153–156).

The Netherlands stands out because of its transformation from a nation with falling productivity, high unemployment and an expensive, dysfunctional welfare state to a competitive economy, low unemployment, and a leaner, more active welfare state; from the 'Dutch Disease' to the 'Dutch Miracle'. Most people think that wage moderation in return for a reduction in working hours, lower taxes and social security contributions was the key. Unemployment was significantly reduced (to 5.8 per cent in 1997) by the creation of part-time jobs, mostly taken by women, which accounted for two-thirds of the net new jobs (Teague, 1999, pp. 124–125).[19] Despite a series of measures designed to reduce the large numbers of working-age people on sickness and disability benefits or in early retirement, there still remains a great deal of 'hidden unemployment' as well as gender discrimination (Huber and Stephens, 2001, pp. 285–286).

By the late 1980s and early 1990s, '*work, work, work*' became the major political slogan, with widespread popular support (Spies and van Berkel, 2001, p. 113). Social assistance recipients are now expected to accept a job, and the unemployed must actively seek work (Becker, 2000, p. 226). The various activation programmes have been consolidated under the Jobseeker's Employment Act. There are three principal programmes: subsidized regular employment, subsidized municipal employment and training or 'social activation,' which can be combined with subsidized employment. Working conditions are covered by sectoral collective agreements. The wages, usually for a 32-hour week, are a little above the minimum but are combined with welfare. Subsidized municipal employment is supposed to lead to a regular job but, in practice, has become an 'end station'. Training and activation is mainly for people who are ready for employment but have a specific barrier. Those in training and activation, which is compulsory for the young, remain on welfare. The income is below the minimum wage; for the young, it is very low (Spies and van Berkel, 2001, pp. 119–121). The young in subsidized municipal work have different conditions than regular workers. The work is considered 'second-rate' but is the only option if they want any income (Spies and van Berkel (2001), pp. 121–22). Thus far, cooperation between social services and employment offices has 'not been optimal', especially with respect to the 'hard core'. The employment offices generally 'cream off the best', and there is a serious dropout problem. In 1996, 54 per cent of leavers found regular employment; 8 per cent went back to school; 25 per cent dropped out and lost benefits; and 13 per cent left for other reasons. The dropouts, who generally have more problems than the other participants, are entirely on their own and are considered at serious risk of 'severe marginalization' (Spies and van Berkel, 2001, pp. 124 –27).

Research on the Jobseeker's Employment Act (JEA) is not yet available. Under the Guaranteed Youth Employment Act (GYA), which in 1998 became part of JEA, municipalities were required to offer a contract even if placement opportunities were not available. In 1996, about 20 per cent of the vulnerable groups (low-education, immigrants, no work experience) were on 'empty contracts', that is, no placements were available. The participation percentages only included the young unemployed who had registered at the employment agencies and were thus outside the official systems – e.g., drifters, young migrant women workers who are not allowed to do paid work, etc. A study of Rotterdam showed that the young outside the system had very problematic backgrounds, and benefited least from the programme (Roche, 2000, pp. 37–38).

In the mid and late 1990s, Dutch policy was changed to require lone mothers on social assistance with children over five years of age to seek work (Knijn and van Wel, 2001, pp. 235–251). The composition had changed from predominantly widows to divorced and unmarried women. There was an increase in poverty. Activation policies were introduced, but childcare was not developed and remained of poor quality. These mothers therefore tended to reject work because they felt that child-care arrangements were inadequate. Municipal-level caseworkers, who were after all trained only as payment officers, also resisted the policy. Placing lone mothers in various activation categories would significantly increase their tasks, and they were ambivalent as to how to deal with this class of social assistance clients. The caseworkers were reluctant to add to their own administrative responsibilities by forcing the lone mothers to work full-time for no improvement in income. As a result, a majority were exempted (Knijn and van Wel, 2001, pp. 242–249).

According to Uwe Becker, non-employment is still high (Becker, 2000, p. 227). Work has been redistributed to part-timers and younger and healthier workers (p. 224–35). Muslim males from Turkey and Morocco show six times the unemployment rate of Dutch males; males from Surinam and the Dutch Antilles four times, and other cultural minorities five times. The overall unemployment rate of immigrants is three times the Dutch indigenous rate. In France and Germany, the immigrant employment rate is 60–70 per cent higher than for Dutch immigrants (pp. 235–236).

In Denmark, unemployment reached 12.2 per cent in 1993. Activation focused on improving skills and work experience, emphasizing training and education, and empowerment. But social assistance could be denied to those who rejected a fair offer of activation (Torfing, 1999, p. 17). In 1998, about 74,000 participated in active labour market policies. The largest number was in subsidized employment in the private sector. Within a year, a little over half (51 per cent) of the short-term unemployed found regular employment as compared to less than 20 per cent of the long-term unemployed. Job placements in the private sector were the most successful in producing regular employment, which, according to Roche, may have been the result of putting the most promising people in these placements (Roche, 2000, p. 40).

By 1999, unemployment was 6 per cent. However, there were large numbers on unemployment benefits, social assistance, early retirement and sickness benefits (Rosdahl and Weise, 2001, p. 159). Youth unemployment remained high and there was an increase in social assistance. Soon, part-time work and workfare were supported by all political parties (except the extreme Right, *Ibid.*, pp. 177–78). Successive governments have established an 'Active Line' for the 'workless' based on two principles: both the State and the private sector have an obligation to provide opportunities for inclusion; long-term strategy to reduce unemployment and remove social barriers is required for the 'highly marginalized'. There is a division of responsibility between the Ministries of Labour and Social Affairs and local authorities. The municipalities fund half the costs of social assistance (*Ibid.*, p. 170). Workfare is to be 'offensive' rather than 'defensive' – improving skills, self-sufficiency, training and education rather than work-for-benefits; empowerment rather than control and punishment; and more inclusive than just targeting the unemployed. Beneficiaries must take 'responsibility for the offers that are being made' (Torfing, 1999, p. 17; see also Cox, 1998, pp. 397–414). Social services have been separated from income transfers and employment. All recipients under 30 years of age are required to be activated within 13 weeks. The activation period is either six or 18 months. On completion of the activation period, the client has the right to a new activation offer within another 13 weeks. There is no specified length of activation period for those over 30.

As employment increased and the pool of recipients became less skilled and less suited for job training, the trend was more towards a greater use of workfare for social assistance. Unemployment began to be considered 'voluntary' and local authorities started to use workfare as a work test (Rosdahl and Weise, 2001, pp. 175–76). By 1997, nearly two-thirds of all activated recipients were in workfare (pp. 173 174). With low unemployment, those who remain on social assistance have more significant barriers. At the same time, activation to address broader social problems has proven difficult to implement. Questions are being raised as to whether the goals for this group should be labour market participation (pp. 178–179).

In the meantime, activation policy has been tightened for all social assistance recipients, and, as of 1998, became obligatory.[20] Applicants for social assistance have to demonstrate that they do not have a 'suitable work offer', which is decided by the local authority. The prior wage is not relevant. Recipients must also accept a 'reasonable' activation offer. Families on social assistance receive 80 per cent of the maximum unemployment insurance benefit. The young receive 40 per cent if they are living alone, and 20 per cent if they are living with their parents. Generally, there is no time limit for benefits.[21] The quality of the plans and the offers are uneven. The well-qualified unemployed are creamed off into long-term education plans. There are difficulties in activating weak and marginal groups. At the local level, about one-third of social assistance claimants have difficulty with activation measures because of serious social problems (Torfing, 1999, p. 21) and there remains a large group of marginalized unemployed. According to a recent study, only half of those in activation measures were actually looking for work. Many claim that they have been put in low-pay, low-quality work (Torfing, 1999, p. 23). In the meantime, fears that immigrants are exploiting the welfare system has fuelled a dramatic rise in anti-immigration politics. The Liberal Party leader 'pledged to crack down on foreigners trying to cheat the system'.[22]

In France, a guaranteed minimum allowance was established in 1988 through RMI (*revenu minimum d'insertion*), which replaced a variety of local and targeted social assistance programmes. RMI, which is means-tested, provides the right to a minimum income and a right to 'insertion' into the labour market (Enjolras *et al.*, 2000, p. 49). It applies to all citizens and long-term residents over the age of 25. While job placement is one of the objectives, there is no job search requirement. The RMI pays about half the minimum wage; there are supplements for a couple (50 per cent) and per child (30 per cent). The insertion contract is between the individual and the 'Commission for Insertion'. In theory, all recipients are entitled to an insertion contract, but work-based placements are limited. In 1994, only 70 per cent of RMI recipients signed contracts. One-third concerned 'social autonomy' (health, daily living, etc.); one-third related to jobs in the public and voluntary sectors; and one-third concerned looking for work. The degree of obligation is ambiguous with varying interpretations at the local level. Sanctions for refusing to take a job are few. Many RMI recipients are hard-to-employ (Levy, 1999, p. 9–12).

In 2000, the social partners who manage the unemployment system introduced 'PARE' (*plan d'aide au retour à l'emploi*) which is similar to the United Kingdom Jobseeker's Agreement. This 'activation' of unemployment insurance proved to be very controversial, and at first was rejected by both the Government and certain unions. After some changes and considerable public debate, the system was enacted in 2001.[23]

The insertion programmes increasingly target the young who are more likely to work outside the regular labour market in return for benefits. In France, this is considered 'workfare'. (Enjolras *et al.*, 2001, p. 59). There are additional programmes for the young – vocational training, subsidized private-sector jobs apprenticeships, and jobs outside the private market (typically in caretaking and upkeep of community areas). About 250,000 full-time jobs have been created, two-thirds of which are apprentice contracts and assisted employment in the non-market sector. The training courses and the subsidized jobs have countered unemployment, at least in the short-term, for several hundred thousand young people. Insertion, however, is problematic because of the growing lack of secure working conditions (Roche, 2000, pp. 61–67). In theory, the French social protection and insertion policy is conditioned on reciprocal obligations. In practice, RMI has turned out to be a very loose form of constraint. There is a 'right' to insertion, but, as stated, only about seven in ten participate. The policies are ambiguous in terms of objectives and implementation. Sanctions are rare both for adults and the young (Enjolras et al., 2001, pp. 66–67). Employers are substituting subsidized placements rather than creating new jobs. Clients tend to move from placement to placement within the subsidized sector. The programmes enhance traditional labour market selectivity – the more skilled enter better programmes and secure better jobs. Lødemel and his colleagues believe that the programmes nevertheless continue because they act as a substitute for the absence of social programmes for the young. Since social assistance is not available, the social activation programmes prevent youth from falling into poverty (Enjolras et al., 2000, pp. 60, 65). Immigrants, especially from North Africa and the Middle East, including children who were born in France, suffer discrimination that further diminishes their chances for labour market success. A great many are confined to squalid housing estates and are greatly disadvantaged in the competitive education system.[24] In the meantime, there continues to be public confrontation over unemployment funds, health reform, and pension reform.[25] There are higher levels of unemployment, inequality and social exclusion. Public expenditures are now at an all-time high, but with the economy seemingly beginning a recovery and with predictions of stronger growth, proposed austerity measures are resented more than ever.

In Germany, reunification brought on a severe recession; by 1996, the unemployment rate was 10.3 per cent (Huber and Stephens, 2001, p. 265). The first response was to encourage retirement, which proved to be very costly, and is slowly being restricted (Manow and Seils, 2000, pp. 142–150). In the meantime, unions continue to defend real wages, costs continue to rise and unemployment remains high (Supiot, 1999, p. 44). Social assistance, financed and administered by the local authorities, is intended to cover basic needs. The amount varies with family size and it is considered to be a safety net of last resort. There are two parts. One, 'Assistance in Special Situations', is for the ill and disabled. The other, 'Cost-of-Living Assistance' (COLA), is for people who lack sufficient income (Voges et al., 2001, p. 75).[26] This programme contains a high proportion of single mothers and the long-term unemployed. There have been significant changes in the social assistance rolls with the growth of unemployment and the decline in skilled work. Among the unemployed, the social assistance recipients are the most poorly qualified. Social assistance has also increased with the growth in refugees and asylum-seekers (Voges et al., 2001, p. 78).

Changes have been introduced to make social assistance more 'active.' There have been several reductions in benefits although they have increased for lone mothers who are acknowledged as reproductive workers (Kahl, 2002, p. 22; Kahl, 2001). There have been a series of increases in workfare schemes. In part, this is due to the rising costs of social assistance for the local authorities and, in part, to provide greater 'work-testing' of the unemployed (Voges et al., 2001, p. 88). The public favours work in return for benefits. Germany, at least at the Federal level, is now committed to active labour market policies. All employable recipients are in principle required to participate. Activation focuses on direct job placement in the low-wage sector: recipients are required to accept any job that is offered either through the unemployment office or the local authority social assistance office; benefits are cut if the recipient refuses to accept any job (Kahl, 2002, p. 24). There are exceptions if the work is 'overtaxing,' or endangers the future pursuit of a previous occupation, or endangers child rearing (Voges et al., 2001, pp. 76–77).

In the meantime, local authorities have become increasingly reluctant to continue supporting social security claimants, especially the long-term unemployed (Clasen, 2000, p. 95). They introduced a range of 'activation' policies called Help Towards Work (HTW) (Ibid., p. 103). HTW creates two forms of work requirement. One is work under an employment contract, which carries standard wages and is incorporated into the social insurance system. The other is more casual work that is not subject to an employment contract. In addition, local authorities may provide vocational training (Voges et al., 2001, p. 81). For the most employable, there are subsidized regular jobs with standard working conditions. These positions are limited to one year. However, if the worker is not hired permanently, he or she is eligible for unemployment benefits, and thus is not a charge for the local authority. There are community jobs with reduced wages for those with more barriers to employment. In 2000, a law was passed to merge social assistance and unemployment, with one uniform activation system for both programmes and with an emphasis on direct, quick job placement or a work programme. There is pending legislation that provides for agreement on an individual re-integration plan at the beginning of unemployment. Recipients have to meet their obligations or face a complete severance of benefits for at least 12 weeks (Kahl, 2002, p. 46).

The few existing studies report that there is considerable 'creaming'. It is easier to place the more employable in contract jobs, which are then covered by social insurance in case of unemployment instead of by the local authority social assistance budget (Voges et al., 2001, p. 72). Until 1993, local authorities used their discretion not to impose sanctions; they are now required by Federal law to impose sanction after a warning by a social worker. It is reported that social workers sometimes refuse to issue a warning to avoid having to impose a sanction and a majority of local authorities still do not sanction (*Ibid.*, pp. 88–87; Clasen, 2000, p. 95). Most of the long-term unemployed are more than 50 years old and have long work histories. It is easier to encourage exit than activation.[27] On the other hand, it seems that sanctions for social assistance recipients will increase. It is claimed that local authorities are not necessarily unwilling to sanction, but are unable to offer sufficient work and training opportunities. There is a strong commitment to activation at the Federal level, and the Federal Government is increasing its monitoring and tightening national guidelines (Kahl, 2002, p. 34).

In sum, there are mixed results. According to the FAFO Institute (2001), in France, those with insertion contracts tend to be younger and better educated, and only about 25 per cent of recipients leave RMI for work. In the Norwegian compulsory programmes, there were no positive effects on either employment or earnings. In France, Denmark, the Netherlands, and the United Kingdom, those who were younger, better educated, and with fewer social problems, tended to benefit. Thus, concludes the FAFO Institute, they would have been more likely to find jobs on their own. Norway, on the other hand, did help people with less work experience and more problems. In the Netherlands, the most disadvantaged seemed to be worse off as a result of the programmes. While overall satisfaction was generally high, a significant portion said that the programmes were a waste of time (FAFO, 2001, pp. 71–73).

Others report similar findings. While most target groups are positive about social inclusion programmes, there remain many difficulties. The employment service offices have difficulty in sustaining a client-centred approach rather than an employment placement-centred approach (Roche, 2000, p. 77). Creaming seems to be widespread. Most programmes to help the long-term unemployed have had modest effects on re-employment while offering employers windfalls. Positive outcomes sometimes contribute to new exclusions (Silver, 1998, p. 20). The most motivated and skilled workers disproportionately reap the benefits of subsidy and training programmes. The European Union White Paper expressed concern that, of the 10 million new jobs created during the 1980s, only three million were taken by those on unemployment registries. New labour force entrants rather than the socially excluded took the vast majority (Silver, 1998, p. 12). Workers who most need income protection – part-timers, domestics, home workers, flexi-workers, black or shadow economy workers, etc. are usually not affected by regulatory labour laws (Standing, 1999, pp. 293–298; Supiot, 1999, p. 35). In all countries, the take-up rate for social assistance is well below 100 per cent. Moreover, of those who do receive benefits, many still remain in poverty because of lack of coverage, low benefits, and low take-up rates (Behrendt, 2000).

Gender discrimination remains a serious issue throughout Western Europe. Pay differentials remain large.[28] Women continue to face discrimination in terms of the benefits and conditions in the standard labour contract. More women than men work part-time (32 per cent versus 5 per cent), but, with the exception of the Netherlands and Scandinavia, a high proportion of these women indicated that they would prefer to work full-time. The hourly wage rate for part-time is lower than for full-time work and has not led to a redistribution of family responsibilities.[29] A significant amount of occupational segregation persists (Supiot, 1999, p. 131).

Immigration is a major issue in all countries – a preoccupation that will continue to grow in importance. Immigrant workers, both skilled and unskilled, are needed because of declining birth rates (European Union, DATE, p. 20); yet most countries are facing increasing anti-immigration sentiments – increasing ghettoization, xenophobia, race riots and even race murders (even in Norway) (Cowell, 2002). In some countries, there has been a rise in anti-immigration political parties – most recently in Denmark.[30] Unemployment among ethnic minorities is considerably higher in all countries. Even the Nordic countries, which are most successful in dealing with social exclusion, have problems integrating immigrants into the labour market (EXSPRO, 2001, p. 19).

Several observers believe that the differences in implementation in the European programmes are related to the stereotyping of the target groups. Heather Trickey says that because the programmes follow the selectivity of the regular labour market, there is not only creaming, but also 'exclusion trajectories' or 'sink options' where clients are recycled. Thus, those who fail may face even more social exclusion (Trickey, 2001, pp. 287–88). Employment service workers are under pressure to meet targets. In the Netherlands, compulsion has led to an increase in social exclusion (Spies and van Berkel, 2001, pp. 124–27; Trickey, 2001, pp. 289–90). Alongside this, there are no new anti-exclusion policies (Roche, 2000, p. 43). The EXSPRO report comes to the same conclusion: the socially excluded are not likely to benefit from either a more flexible labour market or activation. Rather, activation is most successful for those around the poverty level, not those far below (EXSPRO, 2001, pp. 3, 20). Targeting mandatory programmes on the most disadvantaged may further stigmatize those already excluded and thus hinder re-integration (Silver, 1998, p. 17).

Thus far, the response of social democrats has been defensive. They have tried to resist the decline in the legitimacy of the welfare state by advocating tougher conditionality (Standing, 1999, pp. 289–90). To receive benefits, the socially excluded now have obligations. This is the new contract.

5. Contracts in Bureaucratic Relationships

In theory, both sides in a contract benefit from it. This assumes independent, knowledgeable individuals as contracting parties. However, with the workfare contract, the client is dependent and relatively powerless. Rosanvallon minimizes the imbalance by saying that the State has an obligation to respond to the beneficiary. Thus, the process of contract – as envisaged by Rosanvallon – *empowers* the beneficiary. The client is listened to, his or her views are considered, and he or she is treated as a subject rather than an object (EXSPRO, 2001, p. 14).

Empowerment is the ability to control one's environment. Here, the environment is the citizen-bureaucratic or regulatory relationship. In most human service relationships, the agency is in the dominant position. Empowerment involves not only challenge but also consciousness-raising. We have seen that there is a large amount of dissatisfaction on the part of clients who nevertheless feel that they have to accept the terms of the contract to obtain the benefits. On the other hand, most clients seem satisfied. How is satisfaction to be interpreted? Are these clients empowered? Acquiescence becomes problematic when power relationships are unequal. Steven Lukes, in *Power: A Radical View* (1974), describes three dimensions of power. The one-dimensional approach is where A induces B to do something he otherwise would not have done, assuming that grievances and conflicts are recognized and acted upon and that decision-making arenas are more or less open. Quiescence lies in the characteristics of the victims, such as apathy or alienation, and is not constrained by power. In the two-dimensional view, power operates to exclude participants and issues altogether (Bachrach and Baratz, 1962, 1970; Bachrach and Botwinick, 1992). Some issues never reach the political agenda. Apparent inaction is not related to the lack of grievances. The third dimension focuses on how power may affect even the *conception* of grievances. The absence of grievances may be due to a manipulated consensus. Furthermore, the dominant group may be so secure that it is oblivious to anyone challenging its position – 'the most effective and insidious use of power is to prevent . . . conflict from arising in the first place' (Lukes, 1974, p. 23). A exercises power over B by 'influencing, shaping and or determining his every wants'. The third dimension combines the hegemonic social and historical patterns identified by Gramsci (1971) and the subjective effects of power identified by Edelman (1971).[31] Third-dimensional mechanisms of power include the control of information and socialization processes, but also self-deprecation, apathy, and the internalization of dominant values and beliefs – the psychological adaptations of the oppressed to escape the subjective sense of powerlessness. Moreover, a culture of silence may lend legitimation to the dominant order (Freire, 1985; Gaventa, 1980, pp. 15–16). Lukes' three faces of power have been criticized by the post-structuralists who argue that power is never that complete; there is always some resistance (Honneth, 1991; Clegg, 1989; Gilliom, 2001). But, for the most part, welfare client resistance is relatively minor. Workfare clients can sometimes hide additional income or fudge a missed appointment, but they cannot seize a job.

Concepts of empowerment mirror the multiple meanings of power. Empowerment involves a sense of perceived control, of competence, and activities that, in fact, exert control (Zimmerman and Rappaport, 1988; Zimmerman, 1993). It is often a long-term process of learning and development (Keiffer, 1984). Keiffer emphasizes the importance of the connections between the experiences of daily life and perceptions of personal efficacy. The process must be specific; generalized feelings of injustice or consciousness-raising are not sufficient. Zimmerman and Rappaport (1988) report that empowerment is a combination of personal beliefs about control, involvement in activities to exert control, and a critical awareness of one's environment. They, too, emphasize behaviours designed to exercise control as well as consciousness-raising.

The faces of power and empowerment become relevant when considering workfare. The worker/client relationship depends on the power that each person has over his or her own interests. Agencies, which have a monopoly of services, exercise considerable power over clients. On the other hand, clients can exercise considerable power if they possess desirable characteristics. With vulnerable groups, relationships tend to be involuntary. The agency is not dependent on the client for its resources and most agencies are in monopoly positions. The clients usually have no alternatives. The more powerful the agency, the more it will use its advantages to maintain its position. To maintain a superior practice, it will select the more desirable clients. Poor clients tend to receive poor services. This results not only in an inequality of practice but, Hasenfeld argues, the practice of inequality (Hasenfeld, 1983).

Hasenfeld's description of power in human service agencies tracks the three dimensions of power. A dependent person applies for welfare; a condition of aid is a work assignment, which the person feels obliged to accept as the price of receiving assistance. Assume that the agency is acting illegally. The client knows of the illegality but needs the aid, and lacks the resources to challenge the agency. Suppose, however, that the agency is acting according to a legislatively determined rule. The client is now precluded from voicing her grievance, certainly in this forum. This would be a case of the second dimension of power. There is a grievance but she has been effectively precluded from contesting the decision.

There are variations on the third dimension of power where the absence of conflict is due to the manipulation of consensus, A shaping and determining the wants of B. Even if the client thinks she is entitled to welfare, and would like to remain at home, there are competing norms. The obligation to work may be deeply ingrained; as discussed, there is very little support for the idea that one is entitled to a minimum level of support without any corresponding obligations Hartmann, 1987). To the extent that the client has internalized these values, the dominant group has prevented even the conception of the grievance.

The social and historical patterns and the subjective effects are, of course, much more deeply rooted and pervasive than even the complex example of the work obligation. Both the powerful and the powerless take into the relationship their respective characters and self-conceptions – their root values, nurtured through immediate as well as past social relationships. Who they are and where they come from – class, race, childhood, education, employment, inter-personal relations, social standing – crucially affect their languages, social myths, beliefs, attitudes and behaviour.[32] It is no surprise that the vast majority of clients fail to pursue their grievances or to even conceptualize a grievance. In human service organizations that deal with the poor and minorities, official power is, for all intents and purposes, almost total. To be sure, there is resistance but it is often quite feeble and at the margins (Handler, 1992; Gilliom, 2001).

6. Those Who Remain

What can be done? A variety of policies are necessary; they build on one another rather than being mutually exclusive. A full-employment economy, with flexible jobs that are *good* jobs and that allow for the demands of family life is essential. The same applies to education and training. There is plenty of evidence, both in the United States and Europe, that many of the 'workless' would prefer a decent job to social assistance. However, as pointed out, neither jobs alone nor activation will affect substantial numbers of the socially excluded.

At the European Union level, there is some transnational protective labour legislation (e.g., freedom of movement). But, it is generally agreed that such legislation will have to be repeated at the national level (see, e.g., Kitschelt *et al.*, 1999). At the national level, there is a variety of legislation dealing with labour protection, anti-discrimination, flexible working conditions, and so forth. Although fixed statutory rights can lead to respect for the law and social movement activity (Handler, 1978; McCann, 1994), command-and-control regulation is usually viewed with disfavour across the EU. The member states have agreed to establish an Open Method of Coordination, which commits them to work together to promote sustainable economic growth, increase employment and combat poverty and social exclusion.[33] All member states agreed to complete National Action Plans addressing social inclusion and setting out their priorities and best practices in a format of benchmarking. The idea was that benchmarking would encourage the dissemination and adoption of these practices in the various states. Thus far, all 15-member states have filed the first round of National Action Plans. At this point, as expected, the reports vary and the practices that are discussed are not evaluated (European Council, 2001, pp. 8–9). A key problem is the lack of agreed relevant indicators, thus limiting comparability, but efforts are being made to improve the plans (pp. 90–91). The Open Method of Coordination does hold promise because it encourages governments to change, and can lend support to social movement groups and organizations of the socially excluded. It and benchmarking allow for experimentation and flexibility. On the other hand, the procedure also allows governments and firms to obscure information. Flexibility is not necessarily a one-way process.

In the end, there will be a substantial number of socially excluded who are unable to benefit from flexible labour markets. Here, the issue is administrative capacity and accountability. Accountability has to be developed at the local level. There are a number of steps that can be taken to create conditions which facilitate and provide incentives for agency workers to treat the client as a subject. The service/employment offices must be separated from the benefits office and this has already taken place in some countries. The accountability demands on the payments office are speed and accuracy. The service office should make professional, individualized judgments. Sufficient suitable jobs in the general economy will reduce the pressures on the agencies by reinforcing the normal incentives to enter the labour market. The offices provide information and support services for those ready to work. For those who need more assistance, attention has to be paid to education and training. But these programmes have to be specifically geared to the socially excluded rather than the usual adult education.

There should not only be a separation of the two offices, but no sanctions either.[34] Many claim that sanctions are necessary to impress upon clients the seriousness of the workfare requirements. But there is considerable evidence that sanctions do not change behaviour. And there is much evidence (at least in the United States) that sanctions are much abused. It is too easy for the busy caseworker who has little sympathy for the client to impose sanctions readily rather than try and solve problems. We have found in our research in the United States that government agencies cannot combine patient professionalism with sanctions, and that the latter tend to drive out the former. Sanctions are symbolic politics. They reassure majoritarian society that 'those bums are not going to get something for nothing.' But they do cause harm. It must be acknowledged, that no matter how good the workfare programme, there will be a certain number of people unable to succeed in the paid labour market. Those who do not succeed should not be held hostage under the commonly held, but mistaken, idea that this is necessary to deter others who might want to choose welfare over work. We tried that during the Poorhouse days.[35]

Without sanctions, agency staff have to work harder with more difficult clients. Here, incentives have to be restructured. Workers have to be rewarded for progress, placements and follow-up. But there have to be safeguards against creaming. The goal of restructuring is to redefine the professional task so that fulfilment is more readily accomplished when there is an active, participating and knowledgeable client. When the worker reconceives her professional task, the client becomes part of the solution, a subject rather than an object (Handler, 1997). A variety of things can be done to induce case-workers to be more professional and caring but, in the final analysis, they will continue to hold most of the cards. There is always the danger that traditional bureaucratic practices will creep back.[36] Programmes have to be constantly monitored and renewed.

Are there ways to make clients less dependent? There are many situations where organizations bargain rather than rely strictly on commands. Contracts can also be made with dependent clients. There are situations analogous to the creaming example – where agency workers realize that, for them to suc-ceed, the clients have to succeed. But a reconceptualization of the officer's goals to include the client is not enough. The client has to respond, change behaviour and work to fulfil these goals. Thus, the client has to know what is expected of him or her as well as trusting that the officer has his or her best interests at heart. Trust has to be reciprocal. The officer has to believe that the client understands what is expected, is willing to perform and will reliably report back. In other words, the clients become subjects rather than objects (Handler, 1990). However, even communication and good intentions are not enough. There has to be what I call *reciprocal concrete incentives*: the client enters a job or accomplishes some other project and the caseworker is rewarded for the client's success. There are examples of this in healthcare, long-term care, special education, worker safety and public housing tenancy (Handler, 1986, 1990). There are also examples where this occurs in workfare – where agency officers listen to clients, work with them, and share the rewards for success.

The question then becomes: what mechanisms are there to foster contracts between dependent clients and those administering workfare? A Basic Income Guarantee (BIG) would facilitate this process. It would not only provide a basic means of subsistence, alleviate poverty and restore social citizenship as a status, but it would also give the client an *exit* option. Thus, the client would no longer be forced to accept the offer of the social service agency worker. Instead, the office would have to make the offer sufficiently attractive for the client to accept willingly.

The Basic Income Guarantee is 'an income unconditionally paid to all on an individual basis, without means test or work requirements' (van Parijs (ed.), 1992). In part, the arguments for a Basic Income Guarantee are based on lack of credible alternatives – either Keynesian reflation or the unattractiveness of the United States low-wage labour market.[37] But the more important reasons are to restore social citizenship, alleviate poverty and provide 'real freedom' for people in terms of work, human capital development, and non-paid work. In this perspective a BIG would be:

> a *right* to a basic income for every individual, regardless of work status, marital status, age or other income. It would be given as an *individual* right. It would not require any past or present labour performance, not would it be made conditional on any labour commitment. The thrust of the idea is to give income security that is not based on past or present labouring status but on *citizenship*. It would give income security based not on judgmental decisions about 'deserving' and 'undeserving' behaviour or status, merely on the need for, and right to, basic security. However, it would be a modest security, so as to give incentives to work and for *sustainable risk-taking* (Standing, 1999, p. 355).

As Standing and other proponents have emphasized, a basic income is not a panacea. Rather, it is part of the package that includes labour market and welfare reform. At the same time, it 'should allow for adequate incentives to work, save and invest' (Standing, 1999, pp. 354 –357).[38]

The BIG (as distinguished from the Negative Income Tax) is paid to everyone and all earned income is taxed. Most other redistribution programmes (e.g., welfare, family allowances, unemployment insurance) are no longer necessary and are eliminated since the basic income is supposed to provide a decent minimum. Thus, there should be significant savings in administrative costs, although there would be some special needs (e.g., persons with disabilities). It is also argued that there would be no need for a minimum wage, since workers would have the option of refusing jobs that do not offer decent wages and working conditions. Thus, according to Erik Wright (2000), BIG should increase wages and improve working conditions. Since BIG is universal, poverty is reduced without the stigma of means-tested programmes. There are no poverty traps. Earnings are taxed progressively. It would reduce generational inequalities in opportunities, especially for poor children. It would reduce the inequalities of wealth and income that tend to undermine democracy and the community. BIG provides support for uncompensated care-giving as well as voluntary activities. It avoids the need to make distinctions between what is socially useful participation and what is not, which inevitably will be arbitrary (Standing, 1999, p. 366).

Thus, BIG sharply reduces, if not eliminates, the major concern of this paper. By providing an *exit* option, BIG changes the terms of the social contract. Recipients are no longer subject to the whims of an overtaxed welfare system trying to decide whether recipients have fulfilled the necessary conditions of aid. Social services, education, training and employment opportunities will still be offered by the State. But the workers will have to listen to the clients, assess their individual needs, and make offers attractive enough to encourage a client who is now free to decide whether to participate.

On the other hand, as Wright says, most people must still work in the paid labour force to generate the production and taxes needed to support BIG. The basic grant has to be high enough to reduce poverty significantly, but low enough to encourage people to seek paid labour.[39] Rosanvallon, too, worries about disincentives. He argues that a basic income, in practice as well as theory, will subsidize a permanent *excluded* group – those who are not self-sufficient. As pointed out, the fears of disincentives may be exaggerated. There is strong evidence in both the United States and western Europe that most welfare recipients go to great lengths to leave welfare even when they become worse off by doing so (Standing, 1999, p. 365). Rosanvallon argues that the excluded group would be stigmatized because they would not be working. But if the programme were universal, the lines between work and non-work would be blurred (Wright, 2000), and this would encourage people to seek work in addition to having the Basic Income Guarantee. BIG is not put forward as an alternative to the above-mentioned proposals to reform the low-wage labour market. With genuine full employment and good jobs, the jobless would most likely be people with multiple handicaps or with special childcare or family care problems. From past experience, we know that many of these people would welcome rehabilitation and other supportive opportunities provided by effective social services, part-time or sheltered work, or participation in community-based child and family care. These people would not be stigmatized by receiving a basic income guarantee.

There will be some who will not participate. There may be depression, other forms of mental illness or substance abuse. There will be others – a group currently demonized by society – who take advantage of the system. For over 600 years, Anglo-Saxon welfare policy has been under the shadow of the 'sturdy beggar'.[40] And ever since, Anglo-Saxon welfare policy has had a sorry record in trying to separate the 'deserving' from the 'undeserving poor'. This shadow now hangs over western Europe. It is the spectre of this group – and the fear that decent, hard-working poor people might slide into this group – that leads to bureaucracy and sanctions in social welfare systems. How many people would really turn down a job with decent working conditions to join the socially excluded? The disincentives to work are more a function of the available labour market conditions than welfare benefits. Western Europeans should not follow the Anglo-Saxon example in the vain hope that they are 'different'. The benefits of a basic income should not be sacrificed to the spectre of the few who choose to remain among the socially excluded.

Ralf Dahrendorf (1994) warns that once rights lose their unconditional quality, the door is open not just for the market but for rules that tell people what to do. Obligations of citizenship must remain general and public; they must be strictly circumscribed. He agrees that a fundamental challenge comes from the socially excluded. The presence of an underclass is the most tangible evidence of the loss of social citizenship entitlements (pp. 10–19). While it is economically and politically feasible to tolerate the underclass, ignoring the underclass means suspending the basic values of citizenship for one category of people and thus weakening the intrinsic universality of citizenship claims. Doubts will then spread to the validity of other claims. 'The majority will pay a high price for turning away from those who consistently fail to make it, and the fact that the price is intrinsically moral rather than economic should not deceive anyone about its seriousness' (Dahrendorf, 1994, p. 16ff).

Notes

1 University of California at Los Angeles, USA.
2 Huber and Stephens (2001) argue that persistent unemployment is the primary cause of the changes in western Europe. However, as will be discussed, Norway, with its oil surpluses and strong economy, adopted workfare, illustrating the importance of Third Way ideology.
3 Mead proposes extensive amounts of supporting services – considerably more than is currently spent on welfare per person.
4 While Esping-Andersen argues that most welfare states do cluster within the three types in terms of the quality of social rights, social stratification, and the relationship between State, market, and family, he emphasizes that none are pure; all incorporate elements of the others – for example, the United States social security system is redistributive and compulsory.
5 The 'second left' distinguishes itself from the traditional, Jacobin left by its rejection of centralized, statist methods. Similarly to the conservatives, the 'second left' criticizes state solutions and bureaucracy. Instead, it seeks strong associations – grassroots organizations, bottom-up politics, collective bargaining and civil society – as the key to creating a progressive social and economic order. Rejecting neo-liberalism, the 'second left's' agenda used to be a non-statist road to socialism; now it is a non-statist road to social democracy (Jonah Levy, e-mail communication, June 27, 2001).
6 Personal Responsibility and Work Opportunity Reconciliation Act of 1996.
7 In addition to the work requirements, there are a variety of provisions dealing with 'family values'. For example, the Act prohibits the use of federal funds for parents under 18 years of age who are not in school or other specified educational activities or living in an adult-supervised setting. States are required to reduce a family's grant by 25 per cent if it fails to cooperate (without good cause) with efforts to establish paternity. States may eliminate cash assistance to families altogether, or provide any mix of cash or in-kind benefits they choose. They can deny aid to all teenage parents or other

selected groups; deny aid to children born to parents receiving aid; deny aid to legal immigrants (since modified); or establish their own or lower time limits for receipt of aid. States can provide new residents with benefits equal to the amount offered in their former states for up to one year (since ruled unconstitutional). States may choose to deny cash assistance for life to persons convicted of a drug-related felony (which in many states can consist of possession of a small amount of marijuana).

8   The analysis excluded the Earned Income Tax Credit as well as work-related expenses such as payroll and income taxes, child care costs and transportation costs.

9   Some do not satisfy the minimum hours and earnings requirements. Most fail to satisfy the 'non-monetary' eligibility conditions, which exclude work separations for misconduct or a voluntary quit, and require the worker to seek and be willing to accept available work. In many states, 'available work' means full-time work regardless of how many weekly hours the applicant worked in the last job. Women, especially married women, are much more likely than men to have 'involuntary' reasons for leaving a job – i.e., quitting a job because of child care and other family responsibilities and transportation difficulties. In other words, for these women, welfare is the equivalent of unemployment compensation.

10 For example, rolls had declined 26 per cent in Maryland, 24 per cent in Wisconsin, 21 per cent in Indiana, 18 per cent in Oklahoma, 15 per cent in Louisana, and 14 per cent in Michigan (Pear, 1996).

11 This has convinced some economists that they cannot look at data since 1996 (Figlio and Ziliak, 1999).

12 In 15 of these states, the full-family sanction is imposed immediately; in the remaining 22, the grant is initially reduced as a warning signal. In seven states, continued or repeated non-compliance may result in a lifetime ban. Only six states use the lesser sanction – eliminating the non-compliant adult only and continuing the grant for the children. The remaining eight states have increased the amount of the sanctions but do not completely eliminate the family grant. Some of these states only provide assistance in the form of vendor payments (Pavetti and Bloom, 2001).

13 Lawrence Mead found that work programmes that sanctioned many cases tended to perform poorly in terms of job placements and other performance measures. Offices that performed well-made work expectations clear in more effective and informal ways. They threatened sanctions but rarely needed to impose them (Pavetti and Bloom, 2001, p.9).

14 Utah requires an individual 'case staffing' to develop a plan to avoid the sanction. In Tennessee, a required review prior to termination reduced the number of cases sanctioned incorrectly by over 30 per cent (Pavetti and Bloom, 2001, pp.10–11).

15 Rector and Yousef (2000) find that states with an immediate full-family sanction had an average caseload decline of 41.8 per cent (between January 1997 and June 1998) which was 24 per cent higher than states which only deducted the adult's portion of the grant.

16 As an example of how far right the Left has gone, The New York Times (Cowell and Andrews, 2001) reported the reaction of several European countries to the apparent adoption of Keynesian policies in the United States to cope with the downturn in the economy. France and Germany, as well as European Union officials rejected the US approach as inflationary. Former Prime Minister Jospin said: '[I]t turns out the Americans . . . seem to forget the universal laws of the market.' Chancellor Schröder thus far has rejected the advice of five economic research institutes that Germany 'should relax its adherence to the stability pact by accelerating tax cuts and certain

spending programmes'. When *The Economist* endorses the re-election of Tony Blair, you know how far the Left has shifted!

17 The reports are based on large surveys (1,800 clients and nearly 1,500 frontline Employment Service staff), plus focus groups of just under 80 long-term unemployed and detailed interviews with over 50 street-level key workers.

18 Those under 25 years of age, without an education, were given the right and the obligation to 18 months of education if unemployed for six of the last nine months. There were a certain number of public-service-improvement 'quota-jobs' for the unemployed – e.g., nature preservation, environmental protection, and day care. Later the 26 weeks period was raised to 52 weeks.

19 For example, workers on call have to be paid for at least three hours, the contract with the temp agency is now considered an employment contract and after 26 weeks legal rules for a sequence of temporary employment contracts apply (e.g., entitled to a tenured position after three temporary contracts with the same employer. Collective bargaining rules can set additional rules (Hemerijck, 1999, p.17).

20 There are exceptions for sickness (verified by a physician), pregnancy or custody of a child under six years old, where adequate child care is available; people in these groups can participate if they want to.

21 There are minimum rules sets by the national Government, e.g., there are various time limits for different groups after which there must be activation.

22 'Denmark shifts right in election centering on immigration', *New York Times*, November 21, 2001, p. A6.

23 Communication from Alain Supiot, April 21, 2002.

24 'According to opinion polls, almost two-thirds of French adults believe that there are too many Arabs (and therefore Muslims) in France.'

25 Even a 'whiff of prosperity' may be something of a 'mixed blessing'. In 1999, 30 billion francs more were collected than expected, and in 2000, 50 billion. There have been fierce public battles to spend this windfall – tax cuts, subsidizing low-wage workers, more money for teachers and hospital workers – even though France continues to have a large budget deficit (Levy, 2000, pp. 22–26).

26 In addition, there are income-support programmes for specific groups considered to merit compensatory payments such as victims of war, crime or publicly supported vaccinations. These benefits are usually not based on need. There are also grant programmes for education, vocational training, housing, and children's allowances, which are means-tested.

27 'Germany's poor East: More cash, please', *The Economist* May 12, 2001, p. 55.

28 Female hourly wages average only 83 per cent of male hourly wages (Social Exclusion and Social Protection (EXSPRO), 2001, p. 7).

29 E.g., 85 per cent Sweden, 71 per cent France, 60 per cent United Kingdom (Supiot, 1999, p. 134).

30 See 'France, race and immigration. Who gains?', *The Economist*, March 2, 2002, pp. 49–50.

31 'Political actions chiefly arouse or satisfy people not by granting or withholding their stable, substantive demands but rather by changing their demands and expectations' (Edelman, 1971, p. 13).

32 There is a vast theoretical and empirical literature dealing with the problems of lack of rights consciousness.

33 This was agreed upon and affirmed at the European Councils of Lisbon (March 2000), Nice (December 2000), and Stockholm (June 2001) (European Council, 2001, p. 6).

34 This is more fully discussed in Handler and Hasenfeld (1997).
35 The hostage theory of welfare policy comes from Katz (1986).
36 See author's discussion of the Madison (Wisconsin) special education programme in Handler (1986).
37 As an example of basic income, Block and Manza (1997) reopen the case for a negative income tax. Their proposed schedule of guarantees would bring all citizens to within 90 per cent of the poverty line (pp.473–510).
38 This is a distinction from Atkinson's version of a BIG which would require some form of participation (Atkinson, 1998).
39 As Esping-Andersen points out, the degree of decommodification depends on the level of basic benefits (Esping-Andersen, 1990).
40 The Statute of Labourers (1348), the first welfare statute, prohibited the giving of alms to sturdy beggars.

References

Andrews, E. 1999. 'Sweden, the welfare State, basks in a new prosperity', *New York Times*, 8 Oct.

Atkinson, A. 1998. *Poverty in Europe* (Oxford, Blackwell Publishers).

Bachrach, P. and Baratz, M. 1962. 'Two faces of power', *American Political Science Review*, Vol. 56, pp. 947–52.

———— 1970. *Power and poverty: Theory and practice* (Oxford, Oxford University Press).

Bachrach, P. and Botwinick, A. 1992. *Power and empowerment: A radical theory of participatory democracy* (Philadelphia, Temple University Press).

Becker, U. 2000. 'Welfare state development and employment in the Netherlands in comparative perspective', *Journal of European Social Policy*, Vol.10 (3), p. 226.

Behrendt, C. 2000. 'Do means-tested benefits alleviate poverty? Evidence on Germany, Sweden and the United Kingdom from the Luxembourg Income Study', *Journal of European Social Policy*, Vol. 10(1), pp. 30–36.

Beneria, L. and Stimpson, C. (eds.) 1987. *Women, households and the economy* (News Brunswick, New Jersey and London; Rutgers University Press).

Bhabha, J. 1998. '"Get back to where you once belonged": Identity, citizenship, and exclusion in Europe', *Human Rights Quarterly*, Vol. 20, pp. 592–627.

Block, F. and Manza, J. 1997. 'Could we afford to end poverty? The case for the progressive negative income tax', *Politics and Society*, 25, pp. 473–510.

Bosniak, L. 2000. 'Universal citizenship and the problem of alienage', *Northwestern Law Review*, Vol. 94, No. 3, pp. 963–982.

Brito, T. 2000. 'The welfarization of family law', *48 Kansas Law Review 229*.

Brodkin, E; Fuqua, C. and Thoren, K. 2002. *Contracting welfare reform: Uncertainties of capacity building within disjointed Federalism*, Working paper of the project on the public economy of work, University of Chicago, pp. 23–24.

Bumiller, K. 1988. *The civil rights society: The social construction of victims* (Baltimore, Johns Hopkins University Press).

Burtless, G. 1999. Growing American Inequality: Sources and Remedies', *Brookings Review* (Winter), pp. 31–35.

Clasen, J. 2000. 'Motives, means and opportunities: Reforming unemployment compensation in the 1990s', in M. Ferrera and M. Rhodes (eds.), *Recasting European Welfare States* (London, Frank Cass), pp. 89–112.

Clegg, S. 1989. *Frameworks of power* (London, Sage).

Council of Economic Advisors 1999. *Technical report: The effects of welfare policy and the economic expansion on welfare caseloads: An update* (Washington D.C, The White House).

Cowell, A. 2002. 'After black teenager is slain, Norway peers into a mirror', *New York Times*, January 3, p.1.

_____ and Edmund, A. 2001. 'European converts to laissez faire see the rush to intervene as heresy', *New York Times*, October 25, C1.

Cox, R. 1998. 'From safety net to trampoline: Labour market activation in the Netherlands and Denmark', *Governance*, Vol.11, No. 4, pp. 397–414.

Dahrendorf, R. 1994. 'The changing quality of citizenship', in B. van Steenbergen (ed.), *The condition of citizenship* (London, Sage)

Danziger, S., Sandefur, G. and Weinberg, D. (eds.). 1994. *Confronting poverty: Prescriptions for change* (Cambridge, Massachusetts; London, England; University Press).

_____, Corcoran, M., Danziger, S. and Heflin, C. 2000. 'Work, income and material hardship after welfare reform', *Journal of Consumer Affairs*, Vol. 34, No. 1, pp. 6–30.

DeParle, J. 1997. 'Lessons learned: Welfare reform's first months – a special report: Success, frustration as welfare rules change', *New York Times*, December 30.

Diller, M. 2000. 'The revolution in welfare administration: Rules, discretion and entrepreneurial Government', *New York University Law Review*, 75, pp. 1121 –1220.

Edelman, M. 1971. *Politics as symbolic Action: Mass arousal and quiesence* (Chicago, Markham Publishing).

Ellwood, D. 1988. *Poor support: Poverty in the American family* (New York, Basic Books).

_____ 1999. *The impact of the earned income tax credit and social policy reforms on work, marriage, and living arrangements* (Harvard University, Kennedy School of Government).

Enjolras, B., Laville, J.L., Fraisse, L. and Trickey, H. 2000. 'Between subsidiarity and social assistance – the French Republican route to activation', in I. Lødemel and H. Trickey *An offer you can't refuse – Workfare in international perspective* (Bristol, The Policy Press).

Esping-Andersen, G. 1990. *The three worlds of welfare capitalism* (Princeton, New Jersey, Princeton University Press).

European Union (EU) 2001. Joint report on social inclusion. Part I – The European Union executive summary (Brussels), pp.14–15.

Fafo Institute for Applied Social Science 2001. *Workfare in six European nations: Findings and evaluations and recommendations for future development* (Olso, Norwegian Ministry of Health and Social Affairs; Fafo Institute for Applied Social Science).

Falk, R. 2000. 'The decline of citizenship in an era of globalization', *Citizenship Studies*, Vol. 4, No.1, pp. 5–17.

Felstiner, W., Abel, R. and Sarat, A. 1980–81. 'The emergence and transformation of disputes: Naming, blaming, claiming', *Law and Society Review*, Vol. 15, No. 3–4, pp. 631–54.

Ferrera, M. and Rhodes, M. (eds.). 2000. 'Recasting European welfare states: An introduction', *West European Politics*, Vol. 23, No. 2, pp. 1–10.

Figlio, D. and Ziliak, J. 1999. *Welfare reform, the business cycle, and the decline in AFDC caseloads*, JCPR working paper No. 77 (Northwestern University/University of Chicago Joint Center for Poverty Research).

Finn, D. and Blackmore, M. 2001. 'Activation: The point of view of clients and "front line staff"', in *Labour Market Policies and the Public Employment Service* (Paris, OECD), pp. 293–306.

Forbath, W. 2002. 'When Jews, Italians, Greeks, and Slavs belonged to races different from "We, the people": Race, class, and national identity', in *Immigration Law and Policy*,

1882–1924, Paper presented at the New York Uiversity Legal History Workshop, 6 March and at the Columbia Law School Faculty Colloqium, 11 April.

Fraser, N. and Gordon, L. 1994. 'Civil citizenship against social citizenship? On the ideology of contract-versus-charity', in B. van Steenbergen (ed.) *The condition of citizenship* (London, Sage).

Freeman, R. 2000. 'The rising tide lifts . . .?', *Focus*, Vol. 21, No. 2, pp. 27–37.

Freire, P. 1985. *The politics of education: Culture, power, and liberation* (New York, Bergin and Garvey).

Gais, T., Nathan, R., Lurie, I. and Kaplan, T. 2001. 'The implementation of the Personal Responsibility Act of 1996: Commonalities, variations, and the challenge of complexity', in R. Blank and R. Haskins (eds.), *The new world of welfare* (Washington, D.C., Brookings Institution), pp. 35–64.

Garfinkel, I. and McLanahan, S. 1986. *Single mothers and their children: A new American dilemma* (Washington, D.C., Urban Institute Press).

Gaventa, J. 1980. *Power and powerlessness: Quiescence and rebellion in an Appalachian Valley* (Urbana, University of Chicago Press).

Gilliom, J. 2001. *Overseers of the poor: Surveillance, resistance, and the limits of privacy* (Chicago, University of Chicago Press).

Gramsci, A. 1971. *Selections from the prison notebooks* (London, Lawrence and Wishart).

Greenberg, M. and Larcy, M. 2000. *Welfare reform: Next steps offer new opportunities* (Washington, D.C., Neighbor Funders Group), p. 12.

Handler, J. 1978. *Social movements and the legal system: A theory of law reform and social change* (San Diego, Academic Press).

_____ 1986. *The conditions of discretion: Autonomy, community, bureaucracy* (New York, Russell Sage Foundation).

_____ 1990. *Law and the search for community* (Philadelphia, University of Pennsylvania Press).

_____ 1992. 'Postmodernism, protest, and the new social movements', in *Law and Society Review*, Vol. 26, No. 4, pp. 697–732.

_____ 1997. *Down from bureaucracy: The ambiguity of privatization and empowerment* (Princeton, New Jersey, Princeton University Press).

_____ and Hasenfeld, Y. 1997. *We the poor people: Work, poverty, and welfare* (New Haven, Yale University Press).

Hartmann, H. 1987. 'Changes in women's economic and family roles', in L. Beneria and C. Stimpson (eds.) *Women, households and the economy* (New Brunswick, New Jersey and London; Rutgers University Press).

Hasenfeld, Y. 1983. *Human service organizations* (Englewood Cliffs, NJ, Prentice Hall).

_____ Ghose, T.J. and Hillesland-Larson, K. 2001. *Characteristics of Sanctioned and Non-Sanctioned Single-Parent CalWORKS Recipients; Preliminary Findings from the First Wave Survey in Four Counties: Alameda, Freson, Kern, and San Diego* (UCLA School of Public Policy and Social Research, The Lewis Center for Regional Policy Studies).

Haskins, R. and Blank, R. (eds). 2001. *The new world of welfare* (The Brookings Institution).

Heclo, H. 1994. 'Poverty politics', in S. Danziger, G. Sandefur and D. Weinberg (eds.), *Confronting poverty: Prescriptions for change* (Cambridge, Harvard University Press).

Hemerijck, A. 1999. *Prospects for inclusive social citizenship in an age of structural inactivity*, Working paper 99/1 (Cologne, Max Planck Institute for the Study of Societies).

Honneth, A. 1991. *Critique of power: Reflective stages in a critical social theory* (Cambridge, Massachusetts, Massachusetts Institute of Technology Press).

Huber, E. and Stephens, J. 2001. *Development and crisis of the welfare state: Parties and policies in global markets* (Chicago, University of Chicago Press).

Jordan, B. 1996. *A theory of poverty and social exclusion* (Cambridge, Polity Press).

Purdy, D. 1994. 'Citizenship, basic income and the State', *New Left Review*, Vol. 208, pp. 30–48.

Kahl, S. 2002. *Beyond workfare: Strategies towards the hard to serve on social assistance in the U.S., the UK, Australia, the Netherlands, Norway, Sweden, Finland, Switzerland and Germany*, Paper presented at the Law and Society Association Meeting, Vancouver, Canada, 30 May – 1 June.

Kaplan, J. 1999. 'The use of sanctions under TANF', *Welfare Information Network, Issue Notes*, Vol. 3, No. 3.

Katz, M. 1986. *In the shadow of the poor house* (New York, Basic Books).

Keiffer, C. 1984. 'Citizen empowerment: A developmental perspective, Prevention', *Human Services*, Vol. 3, pp. 9–36.

Kildal, N. 2000. *Workfare tendencies in Scandinavian welfare policies*, Paper presented at a European Research Seminar on The Activation Welfare State: New Ways of Fighting Poverty and Social Exclusion in Europe, Lund University, 27–28 October.

Kitschelt, H., Lange, P., Marks, G. and Stephens, J.D. (eds). 1999. *Continuity and change in contemporary capitalism* (Cambridge, Cambridge University Press).

Knijn, T. and van Wel, F. 2001. 'Careful or lenient? Welfare reform for lone mothers in the Netherlands', *Journal of European Social Policy*, Vol. 11, pp. 235–51.

Kuhnle, S. 2000. 'The Scandinavian welfare state in the 1990s: Challenged but viable', in M. Ferrera and M. Rhodes (eds.) 2000. 'Recasting European welfare states: An introduction', *West European Politics*, Vol. 23, No. 2, pp. 1–10.

Lambert, S., Waxman, E. and Haley-Lock, A. 2001. *Against the odds: A study of instability in lower-skilled jobs* (School of Social Service Administration, U. of Chicago).

Levy, J. 2000. 'French social policy in an age of high unemployment', in P. Hall, J. Hayward and H. Machin (eds.), *Developments in French politics 2*, (New York, Macmillan, forthcoming).

————— 2001. 'Partisan politics and welfare adjustment: The case of France', *Journal of European Public Policy*, Vol. 8, No. 2, pp. 265–285.

Lødemel, I. 2001. 'National Objectives and Local Implementation of Workfare in Norway', in I. Lødemel and H. Trickey (eds.), *An offer you can't refuse. Workfare in international perspective* (Bristol, Polity Press).

Loprest, P. 1999. *Families who left welfare: Who are they and how are they doing?*, Discussion paper No. 10 (Washington, D.C., The Urban Institute).

Lukes, S. 1974. *Power: A radical view* (London, Macmillan).

Manow, P. and Seils, E. 2000. 'The employment crisis of the German welfare state', in M. Ferrera and M. Rhodes (eds.), 'Recasting European welfare states: An introduction', *West European Politics*, Vol. 23, No. 2, pp. 1–10.

Marshall, T. 1950. *Citizenship and social class* (Cambridge, University Press).

McCann, M. 1994. *Rights at work* (Chicago, University of Chicago Press).

Mead, L. 1986. *Beyond entitlement: The social obligations of citizenship* (New York, Free Press).

Meyer, B. and Rosenbaum, D. 1999. *Welfare, the earned income tax credit, and the labour supply of single mothers*, NBER Working Paper Series No. 7363 (Cambridge, Massachusetts, National Bureau of Economic Research).

Michalopoulos, C., Schwartz, C and Adams-Ciardullo, D. 2000. *National evaluation of welfare-to-work strategies. What works best for whom: Impacts of 20 welfare-to-work programmes by subgroup. Executive summary* (New York, Manpower Demonstration Research Corporation, August), pp. 4, 7–8.

Mishel, L., Bernstein, J. and Schmitt, J. 1999. *The state of working America 1998–99* (Washington, D.C., Economic Policy Institute).

Molotch, H. and Boden, D. 1985. 'Talking social structure: Discourse, domination, and the Watergate hearings', *American Sociological Review*, Vol. 50, No. 3, pp. 273–288.

Murray, C. 1984. *Losing ground* (New York, Basic Books).

Nussbaum, M. 1996. *For love of country: Debating the limits of patriotism* (Boston, Beacon Press).

Pavetti, L. 1999. 'How much more can welfare mothers work?', *Focus*, Vol. 20, No. 2, p. 16, Spring.

———— and Bloom, D. 2001. *Sanctions and time limits: State policies, their implementation, and outcomes for families* (Brookings Conference: The New World of Welfare: Shaping a Post-TANF Agenda for Policy, sponsored by the Gerald Ford School of Public Policy, University of Michigan, 1–2 Feb., Washington, D.C.).

Pear, R. 1996. 'Most states find goals on welfare within easy reach', *New York Times*, 23 Sept., 1996, A1.

———— 2002. 'House Democrats propose making the '96 welfare law an antipoverty weapon', *New York Times*, 24 January, A, 24.

Rosanvallon, P. 2000. *The new social question: Rethinking the welfare state* (New Jersey, Princeton University Press).

Rector, R. and Yousef, S. 2000. *The impact of welfare reform: The trend in state caseloads, 1985–1998* (Wahington D.C., Heritage Foundation).

Roche, M. (coordinator) 2000. *Comparative social inclusion policies and citizenship in Europe: Towards a new European social model* (Sheffield University, United Kingdom, Social Exclusion and the Development of European Citizenship Network, final report).

Rosdahl, A. and Weise, H. 2001. 'When all must be active – Workfare in Denmark', in I. Lødemel and H. Trickey (eds.), *An offer you can't refuse. Workfare in international perspective* (Bristol, Polity Press).

Schorr, A. 1997. 'Welfare reform, once (or twice) again', *Tikkun*, November–December.

Silver, H. 1998. *Modernizing and improving social protection in the European Union* (Brussels, Belgium, COM 102 Final).

Social Exclusion and Social Protection (EXSPRO). 2001. *Social exclusion and social protection in the European Union: Policy issues and proposals for the future role of the European Union* (London, South Bank University, European Institute).

Smith, R. 1997. *Civic ideals: Conflicting visions of citizenship in United States history* (New Haven, Yale University Press);

Spies, H. and van Berkel, R. 2001. 'Workfare in the Netherlands – young unemployed people and the Jobseeker's Employment Act', in I. Lødemel and H. Trickey (eds.), *An offer you can't refuse. Workfare in international perspective* (Bristol, Polity Press).

Standing, G. 1992. 'The need for a new social consensus', in P. van Parijs (ed.), *Arguing for basic income. Ethical foundations for a radical reform* (London and New York, Verso).

———— 1999. *Global labour flexibility: Seeking distributive justice* (New York, St. Martin's Press).

Stapleton, D. and the Lewin Group. 2001. *How well have rural and small metropolitan labor marketts absorbed welfare recipients?* (Fairfax, VA, The Lewin Group).

Strawn, J., Greenberg, M. and Savner, S. 2001. *Improving employment outcomes under TANF* (Washington, D.C., Center for Law and Social Policy – CLASP).

Supiot, A. 1999. *The transformation of labour and the future of labour law in Europe: Final report for the Commission* (Paris, Flammarion).

Tamas, G.M. 2000. 'On post-fascism: How citizenship is becoming an exclusive privilege', *Boston Review*, Summer, pp. 42–46.

Teague, P. 1999. *Economic citizenship in the European Union: Employment relations in the new Europe* (New York, NY, Routledge).

The Economist 2001. *The melting-pot that isn't*, July 28, pp. 50–51.

Torfing, J. 1999. 'Workfare with welfare: Recent reforms of the Danish welfare state', *Journal of European Social Policy*, Vol. 9, No.1, p. 13.

Trickey, H. 2001. 'Comparing welfare programmes – Features and implications', in I. Lødemel and H. Trickey (eds.), *An offer you can't refuse. Workfare in international perspective* (Bristol, Polity Press).

―――― and Walker, R. 2001. 'Steps to compulsion within British labour Market programmes', in I. Lødemel and H. Trickey (eds.), *An offer you can't refuse. Workfare in international perspective* (Bristol, Polity Press).

Turner, B. 1992. 'Outline of a theory of citizenship,' in C. Mouffe (ed.) *Dimensions of radical democracy* (London, Verso).

Turner, B. and Hamilton, P. (eds.) 1994. *Citizenship: Critical concepts, Vol. 11* (London, Routledge).

United States Bureau of the Census 1998. *Poverty in the United States. March 1998 supplement to the current population survey (CPS)* (Washington, D.C).

―――― 2001. *Poverty in the United States. March 2001 supplement to the current population survey (CPS)* (Washington, D.C.).

van Parijs, P. 1992. *Arguing for basic income. Ethical foundations for a radical reform* (London and New York, Verso).

―――― 1995. *Real freedom for all. What (if anything) can justify capitalism?* (Oxford, Oxford University Press).

Van Steenbergen, B. (ed.), 1994. *The condition of citizenship* (London, Sage).

voges, W., Jacobs, H. and Trickey, H. 2000. 'Uneven development – Local authorities and workfare in Germany', in I. Lødemel and H. Trickey (eds.), *An offer you can't refuse. Workfare in international perspective* (Bristol, Polity Press).

Wright, E. 2000. 'Reducing income and wealth inequality: Real utopian proposals', *Contemporary Sociology*, pp. 143–156.

Wright, E. and Dwyer, R. 2000. 'The American jobs machine: Is the new economy creating good jobs?', *The Boston Review*, Vol. 25, No. 6, pp. 21–26.

Zimmerman, M. 1993. 'Empowerment theory: Psychological, organizational and community levels of analysis', in J. Rappaport and E. Seidman (eds.), *Handbook of Community Psychology* (New York, Plenum).

―――― and Rappaport, J. 1988. 'Citizen participation, perceived control, and psychological empowerment', *American Journal of Community Psychology*, Vol. 16, pp. 725–50.

Promoting Income Security as a Right: Europe and North America